# From Mud to Music

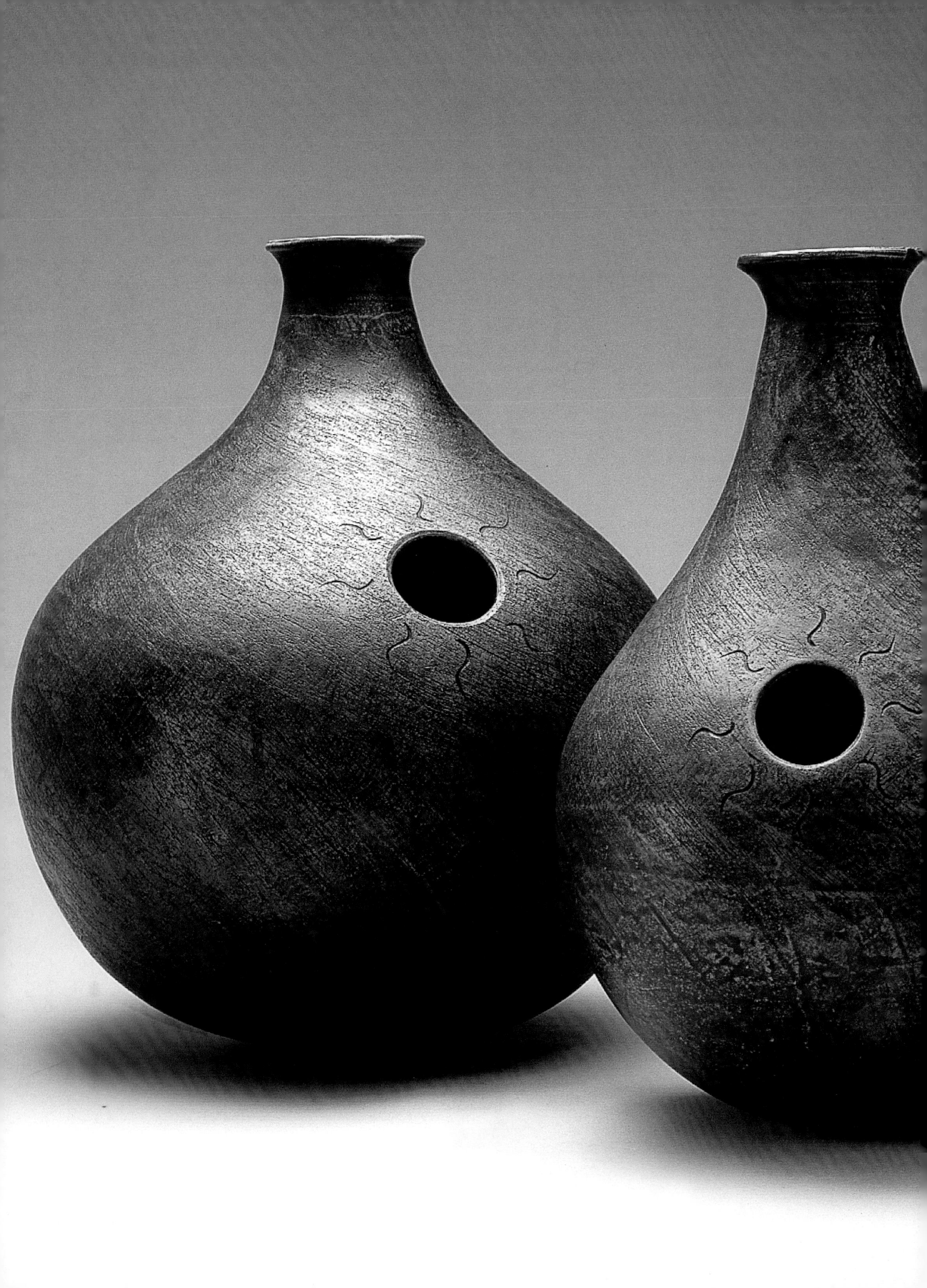

# From Mud to Music

making and enjoying ceramic musical instruments

by Barry Hall

*Published by*

The American Ceramic Society
735 Ceramic Place, Suite 100
Westerville, Ohio 43081

The American Ceramic Society
735 Ceramic Place, Suite 100
Westerville, Ohio 43081



10 09 08 07 06 5 4 3 2 1

ISBN: 1-57498-139-0

# Dedication

To my parents, Percy and Nancy Hall, who rooted and nurtured my love of music and encouraged my fascination with musical instruments.

# Acknowledgements

Hundreds of people around the globe contributed to this project, to whom I am extremely grateful. First and foremost, my thanks to Daryl Baird, my partner throughout this five-year project, whose ideas and assistance were essential to bringing this project to fruition. In addition to all of the contributors whose photos and sounds appear in this book and CD, I express special thanks to Ward Hartenstein, Brian Ransom, and Fred Sweet for manuscript review; Bart Hopkin for research support, manuscript review, and writing the foreword; Richard and Sandi Schmidt for inspiration, encouragement, manuscript review and the idea for the book's name; Jason Allen for field research in South America, Africa, Asia and the Middle East including photos, recordings, instrument acquisitions, translations and cultural insights; Rosa Pereira for translations and support in Brazil; Sibila Savage for photography; Dr. Toby Mountain for CD mastering; Richard Smith, Geoff Brown and Alan Tower for musical inspiration and support; Dr. Stephen Nash at the Field Museum and Leslie Freund at the Phoebe Hearst Museum; the online communities Ocarinaclub, Oddmusic, Ceramicmusicalinstruments and the Mills College Didjeridu list; Gisela Barrett, Roberto Velazquez Cabrera, Dr. Arturo Chamorro, Didier Ferment, Robin Goodfellow, Dr. Guy Grant, Lars Grue, Christoph Haas, Thomas Hastay, Ganesh Kumar, Jim Santi Owen, John Pascuzzi, Spencer Register, Randy Raine Reusch, Alex Schmidt, Andree Thompson, Mario Cortes Vergara and Uli Wahl; all the great folks in the Walnut Creek Clay Arts Guild; Barry (Baz) Jennings who did much to promote the ocarina worldwide, and sadly passed away during the writing of this book; Sherman Hall, Rich Guerrin, Bill Jones, Mary Cassells and everyone at ACerS for believing in this project and helping to make it a reality; and finally to my wife Beth and daughter Avery for their love and patience during the long and arduous task of preparing this book.

I also express deep gratitude and respect to the many ancient cultures that have advanced the art of ceramic musical instruments for thousands of years. It is upon your shoulders that we stand today. Thank you all.

— Barry Hall

# Contents

**Foreword** ........ ix

**Chapter 1:** Introduction ........ 1

The Early Days ........ 2

What's in This Book? ........ 5

A Classification System for Musical Instruments ........ 6

**Chapter 2:** Idiophones

*Sonorous Objects* ........ 9

Shaken Idiophones ........ 9

Struck Idiophones ........ 15

- Vessels ........ 16
- Bowls and Bells ........ 17
- Bars ........ 18
- Gongs and Plates ........ 20
- Tongue Drums ........ 21

Concussion Idiophones ........ 23

Plucked Idiophones ........ 25

Scraped Idiophones ........ 26

**Chapter 3:** Membranophones

*Skinned Drums* ........ 27

General Comments ........ 27

About Drumheads ........ 28

Vessel Drums ........ 29

Goblet Drums ........ 32

Hourglass Drums ........ 35

Frame Drums ........ 36

Tubular Drums ........ 42

Other Drum Styles ........ 42

**Chapter 4:** Aerophones

*Wind Instruments* ........ 45

How Aerophones Work ........ 45

Flutes (Edgetone Aerophones) ........ 47

- Side-Blown Flutes ........ 49
- End-Blown Flutes ........ 50
- Airduct Flutes ........ 55
- Chamberduct Flutes ........ 83

Horns (Lip-Reed Aerophones) ........ 85

- Trumpets ........ 87
- Cornetti ........ 92
- Didjeridus ........ 96
- Globular Horns ........ 99

Reeds ........ 104

Free Aerophones ........ 105

Plosive Aerophones ........ 105

- Tubular Plosive Aerophones ........ 105
- Globular Plosive Aerophones ........ 107

Resonators ........ 117

**Chapter 5:** Chordophones

*Stringed Instruments* ........ 119

Musical Bows ........ 120

Zithers ........ 121

Harps and Lyres ........ 121

Lutes . . . . . . . . . . 122
Other Chordophones . . . . . . . . . . 128

**Chapter 6:** Hybrids . . . . . . . . . . 129

**Chapter 7:** Technology Issues . . . . 135
Selecting Clay . . . . . . . . . . 136
To Glaze or Not to Glaze? . . . . . . . . . . 143
Tuning and Shrinkage . . . . . . . . . . 148
Repair . . . . . . . . . . 153

**Chapter 8:** Gallery . . . . . . . . . . 155

**Chapter 9:** Profiles . . . . . . . . . . 171
Frank Giorgini . . . . . . . . . . 172
Ward Hartenstein . . . . . . . . . . 174
Brian Ransom . . . . . . . . . . 177
Robin Hodgkinson . . . . . . . . . . 180
Geert Jacobs . . . . . . . . . . 182
Ragnar Naess . . . . . . . . . . 184
Winnie Owens-Hart . . . . . . . . . . 186
Susan Rawcliffe . . . . . . . . . . 188
Richard and Sandi Schmidt . . . . . . . . . . 190
Aguinaldo da Silva . . . . . . . . . . 192
Sharon Rowell . . . . . . . . . . 194
Dag Sørensen . . . . . . . . . . 197
Stephen Wright . . . . . . . . . . 200

**Chapter 10:** Demonstrations . . . . 203
Side-Hole Pot Drum . . . . . . . . . . 204
Ocarina . . . . . . . . . . 208
Goblet Drum . . . . . . . . . . 213
Side-Blown Flute . . . . . . . . . . 218
Whistle Flute . . . . . . . . . . 222

**Appendix:** A Clay Music Sampler
*Notes on the CD* . . . . . . . . . . 225

**Glossary** . . . . . . . . . . 238

**Bibliography** . . . . . . . . . . 245
Books . . . . . . . . . . 245
Articles . . . . . . . . . . 246
Videos . . . . . . . . . . 247
Recordings . . . . . . . . . . 247

**Resources and Materials** . . . . . . . 249

**Contributors** . . . . . . . . . . 251

**Photo Credits** . . . . . . . . . . 254

**Index** . . . . . . . . . . 255

# Foreword

In the world of musical instruments, those shaped from clay have a special place. It may not seem like a very prominent place—after all, none of the widely used instruments of Western music are made from ceramics. Yet you will discover, as you explore this book, that it is a unique place, a place of wide-open possibility, and a place of exceptional beauty. Clay has limitations that make it less than ideal for reproducing some of the instruments normally made from wood or metal. But the nature of the medium, with its infinite "shapability," gives rise to a world of other sound-making forms with a musical nature all their own, and a very inviting world it is.

*From Mud to Music,* with its magnificent photographs and tantalizing audio CD, offers a delightful introduction to the world of ceramic instruments. Here you'll find pieces by many of today's leading makers, presented alongside historical instruments going back to ancient times. Author Barry Hall provides full descriptions and background information, while the photos and CD complete the picture. Hall also gives practical information for your own hands-on work. He provides broadly applicable information on fabrication techniques and the acoustics of ceramic instruments, as well as specific instructions for the construction of several instruments. The book is unique—you won't find this information under one cover anywhere else, and to have it presented so clearly, knowledgeably and tastefully is a real pleasure.

One of the wonderful facets of this collection is the way it brings out a sense of continuity between ancient and contemporary artisans, and between makers working in different parts of the world. The surviving wind instruments of pre-Columbian Central America have exerted a particularly liberating influence in the present: Their strangely stirring shapes and sounds have inspired ceramists of today not only to try to capture the spirit of the early instruments in reproductions, but to craft ever more exotic forms—forms that otherwise might never have been imagined. In this book, you'll see this in the work of Susan Rawcliffe, Brian Ransom and others. Certain African percussion traditions have had a similar effect. Udu drums (side-hole pot drums from Nigeria) produce a distinctive and particularly deep, satisfying tone, which has inspired non-African makers not only to study the traditional instruments and their fabrication techniques, but to experiment with a diversity of beguiling new forms. The work of Frank Giorgini, Winnie Owens-Hart and Stephen Wright provides just a few examples—a similar open-ended dynamic plays out in the work of countless other artisans represented here.

Notice that these developments could only have happened in clay, based as they are in the subtleties of shape that arise from direct hand-forming, and the kind of spatial conceptualizing that goes with it. This kind of thinking will serve you well, too, as you look through this book and listen to the accompanying CD. Rather than seeing musical instruments in specific standardized types, you'll be seeing the infinite variability of clay taking shape in hundreds of one-of-a-kind forms. Rather than hearing standardized scales and musical styles, you'll be hearing sounds that are unique to each individual instrument. It is in the nature of the medium that this should be so.

So open the book, put on the CD, and take in the sight, sound and feel of clay. I know you'll enjoy it.

Bart Hopkin

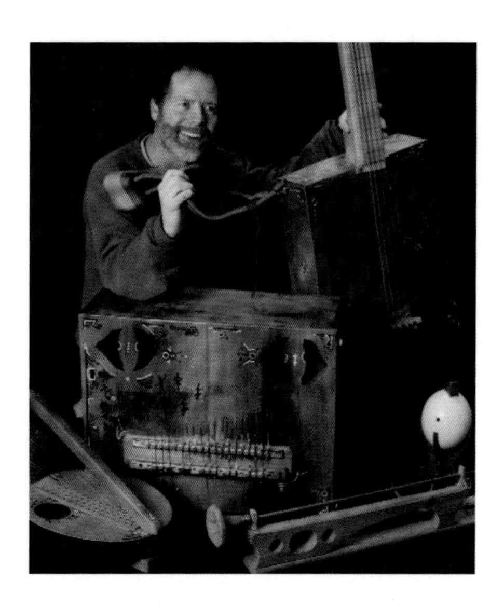

*Bart Hopkin is an accomplished author, educator and maker of acoustic musical instruments. He is the founder and director of Experimental Musical Instruments, an organization devoted to all manner of interesting and unusual musical instruments. In addition to editing the highly acclaimed quarterly journal* Experimental Musical Instruments *for 15 years, Bart has written a number of books on instruments and their construction, and produced several CDs featuring the work of innovative instrument makers worldwide.*

## chapter one

# Introduction

*The spirit of an ancient musician is captured in a prized instrument. Though thousands of years have passed, the mark of the maker's hands is preserved in the clay, and the breath of the instrument's first player still lingers in its chambers. Countless musicians have come and gone, but the instrument remains. Today the instrument still speaks the same tones that the ancients played, and perhaps will continue to for thousands of years. The masterful musical creations of our distant ancestors inspire us to build upon their inventiveness, pressing onward and outward while adding a bit of ourselves. We share our own creations with today's world and place them, as an offering, in the hands of the future.*

This book is about ceramic musical instruments. It is about a truly remarkable transformation: how the simplest of materials—clay or mud—can be used to make tools for producing one of the most complex human expressions—music.

Musical instruments are the focus of this work, but these objects don't make music by themselves. Music is the result of a player's energy and artistry channeled through an instrument. The instrument is a tool that transforms energy—blowing, tapping or strumming—into sound, and the player's artistry is what organizes that sound into music that speaks to others.

Since making music is an art, it is sometimes difficult to quantify or describe. However, the technology of how musical instruments work is based on the rather inflexible laws of physics and acoustics. Instruments must be designed and built according to certain technical rules and limitations, or they just won't work. Despite these requirements, building instruments is also very much an art, as you'll see from the remarkable creations and variations shown in the pages of this book. You'll also discover that the visual aspects of musical instruments have an impact on their sound and the way we perceive it.

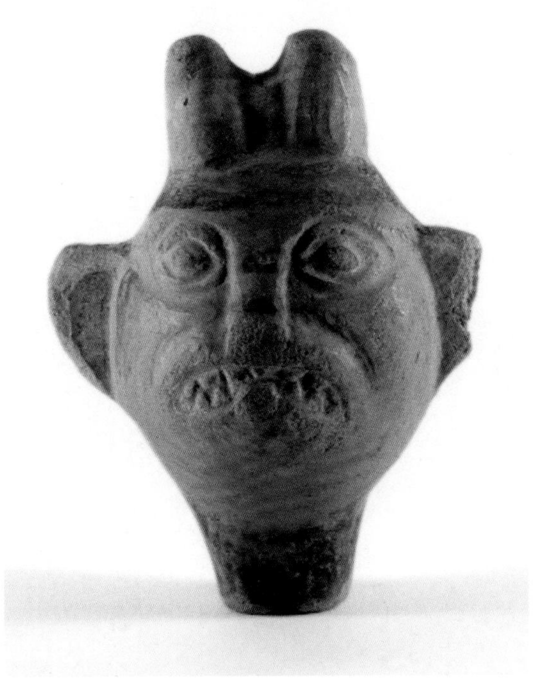

Fig. 1.1
**Pre-Columbian Rattle**
Ceramic rattle in the form of a head. 3 inches in height, from the Suchiman site, Santa Valley, Peru. Field Museum collection.

Is all sound music? Are all sound-producing devices musical instruments? Attempting to answer those questions could fill a book—another book, not this one—so you'll have to decide for yourself. This book's definition of music is broad, as you'll

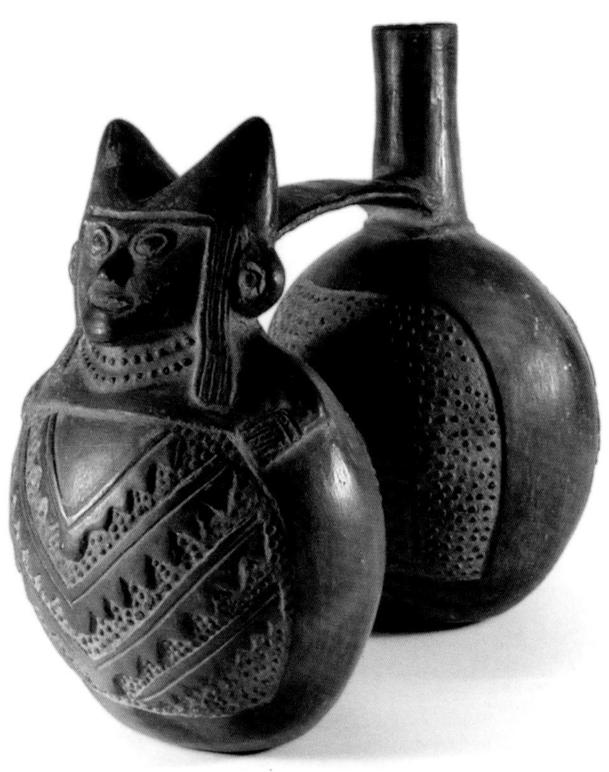

Fig. 1.2
**Chimu Whistling Vessel**
8 inches in height, Chimu culture, Peru, 1000-1470 A.D.
Field Museum collection.

discover when you listen to the wide variety of selections on the accompanying recording—from the refined melodic strains of Vivaldi and Tchaikovsky to the earthy, primal wailings of bizarre pre-Columbian wind instruments. Despite their stylistic diversity, all of the sounds on the CD are united by their common source in clay.

*From Mud to Music* is also about the art of combined forces. Clay instruments have been made in all parts of the world for thousands of years, and will likely continue to be made for countless years to come. This book will help you explore and experience clay instruments from all over the globe, from the past to the present. As you'll see, modern builders of ceramic musical instruments continue a tradition that reaches back to ancient times, and is still vibrant today.

## The Early Days

The origins of musical instruments are enshrouded in the mists of prehistory. It is likely that instruments have been around since the dawn of humankind's existence, but little is known about the earliest people or what role music and instruments played in their lives. Most musicologists, anthropologists and archaeologists agree that the earliest musical instruments were probably fashioned from natural objects, such as bamboo, gourds, fruit skins, nut shells, hollow logs, stones, bones and animal horns. Many of these materials can be played as percussion or wind instruments in their naturally found state, or with simple modifications such as blow holes or finger holes. However, very few examples of these instruments survive from prehistoric times, because most of these materials easily decompose when exposed to the elements. Additionally, items that have survived in well-protected sites such as graves and tombs can be subject to a variety of interpretations as to their possible musical use. Was a bone or a gourd with holes in it played as a flute, or did it serve some other purpose?

To early people, the concept of a musical instrument may have been radically different from what it is to most of us today. The modern world considers an instrument to be an inanimate object, a tool for making music. Most, if not all, indigenous cultures hold animistic beliefs. Animists possess an understanding that everything in the universe has a spirit and life force. Believing in the interconnectedness of all things, these societies might think of an instrument's voice as the spiritual union of all the entities and forces—clay, fire, air, wood, animal hides, tools and humans—that communed to create it. If an instrument was formed in the image of a deity, these combined forces might make it a potent entity and a respected force in the domain of a shaman or spiritual leader.

Some ancient cultures used musical instruments symbolically. For example, in sacrificial rituals honoring the Aztec divinity Tezcatlepoca, a young man was prepared for sacrifice by being instructed in how to play a clay flute. For a brief time he lived a life of luxury, traveling among his people with a royal retinue. He would often be stopped in the streets to play a melody on his flute as the crowd bowed before him and treated him as a representative of their deity. When the time came for him to be sacrificed, he performed a symbolic ritual, breaking a clay flute on each of the steps of the temple as he ascended to his ultimate death.

For many people today, music is little more than a commodity that provides entertainment, but in earlier times it played a more significant role in daily life. Work was often wedded to song, in order to synchronize communal labors such as pounding grain, weaving fabric, towing ropes and pulling oars. Music's carrying power was used for signaling and communicating. Huge African slit drums transmitted coded messages over long distances from village to village. The powerful roar of drums, trumpets, cymbals and pipes played an important role in military battles. Immense ancient Indian kettledrums measuring five feet in diameter and weighing 450 pounds were transported into battle on the backs of elephants, their raucous din emboldening warriors and striking fear into the hearts of enemies.

Beyond its practical uses, music was also an element in sacred ceremonies such as marriages, funerals and adulthood initiations. A 17,000-year-old cave painting in France depicts a dancing shaman wearing an animal skin and playing what appears to be a musical instrument. For thousands upon thousands of generations, music has been used as a tool to heal the sick, appease the gods, communicate with ancestors and divine the future.

Even today music transcends the ordinary and seems magical in its power. Though we are not always consciously aware of its effect, music is a powerful stimulant to the senses. Sounds merely vibrate our eardrums, but music penetrates much deeper, speaking to our minds and our hearts. A simple melody has the ability to transport us to another time or remind us of a special moment. Music is often the preferred method of communicating with the gods. Singing and chanting are spiritual practices used to focus on the divine in many religious traditions such as Buddhism, Hinduism and Native American spirituality. Music is one of the best aphrodisiacs, creating an atmosphere for intimacy and connection. Whether or not one believes in the inherent magical influence of an instrument or the sounds it produces, the raw power of music remains a tangible and undeniable truth. Music has changed people's lives and their perceptions of the world, and has altered the course of history countless times.

Clay seems magical in its transcendence as well. In firing, it changes from something extremely frag-

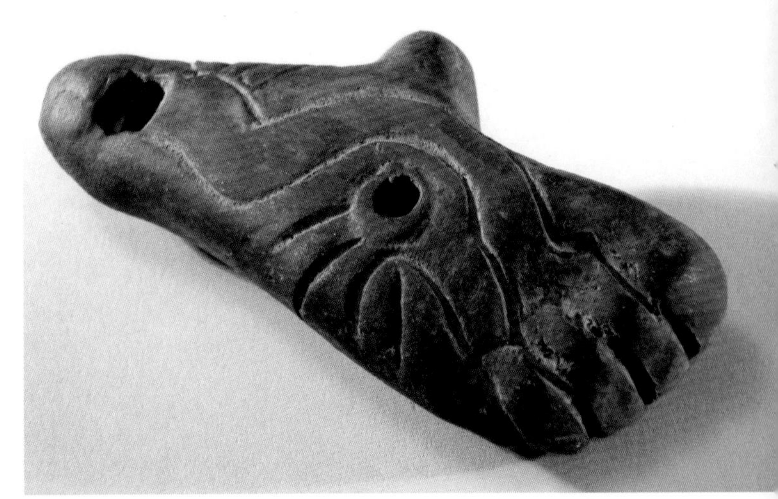

Fig. 1.3
**Foot Whistle**
5 inches in length, replica (Mexico, 20th century) of a whistle from the Tlatilco culture, Mexico, pre-classic period approx 1000-300 B.C. Collection of Barry Hall.

ile—dried mud—to a material strong enough to survive for millennia. Clay's remarkable plasticity allows it to be shaped into an incredible variety of forms for musical instruments, yet when fired it is one of the most durable natural materials on our planet. Fired clay's inherent permanence is one reason that so many ancient examples of ceramic musical instruments have endured for thousands of years, allowing us to explore and appreciate them today.

Unlike the earliest instruments, which were made from sticks, gourds, bones or shells, clay instruments are made "from scratch." That is, they aren't built by modifying an existing object, but created from a moldable substance: the material of the Earth itself. This infinite "shapability" provides ceramics artists with an unparalleled flexibility to express themselves—their ideas, beliefs, hopes, fears and fantasies. In a way, it enables ceramics artists to pour themselves into the vessels they create. Evidence of this very personal process abounds throughout the pages of this book.

In addition to clay's durability, the preservation of so many early ceramic instruments results from their special treatment as objects of reverence and special significance. A number of ancient cultures, from Egyptians to Mayans to Vikings, buried musical instruments with their dead, perhaps intending them for use in the afterlife. As a result of the protection provided by tombs and graves, some ancient clay instruments are so well preserved they can still make music today.

We learn about early cultures from the objects they leave behind. We can "see" into the past through paintings, textiles, sculpture and ceramics that depict people performing both ordinary and special activities. Ancient musical instruments let us "hear" into the past through the sounds and music they produce. This avenue of communication with our ancestors is extremely powerful because it is so intensely direct. Music is truly a universal language. Its vocabulary is primal and timeless, and speaks to all people regardless of their culture, geography, or the time in which they live. A musical instrument can be a thread of communication between people who have never met, never lived in the same time or place, and never even seen or experienced the same things. Alfonso Arrivillaga Cortés, a musicologist and researcher from Madrid, illustrates this connection to the past in the following description of his experience playing ancient Central American instruments in the dusty cellar of a Guatemalan museum:

> *It thrilled me to think that some of these pieces had not been played for centuries, that where my lips now rested, ages before had rested the lips of an ancient musician, priest or simple farmer in Central American Guatemala.*

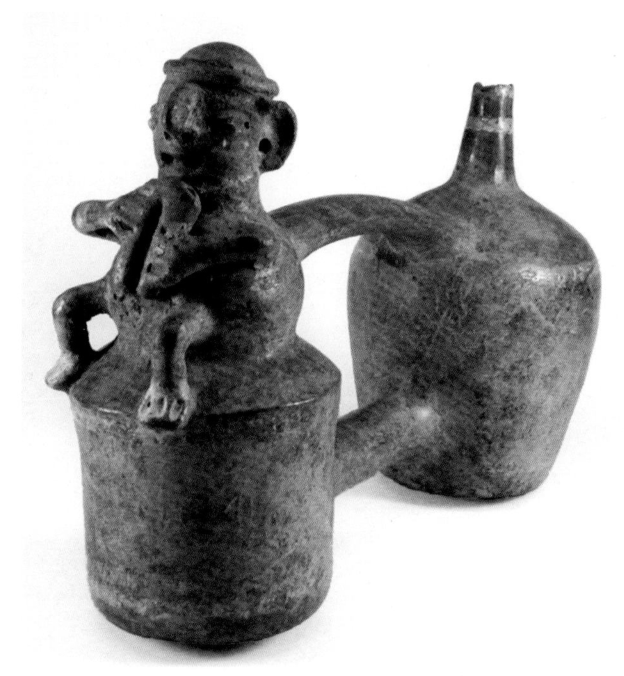

Fig. 1.4
**Peruvian Whistling Vessel**
7 inches in height, from the Vicus culture, Peru, 400 B.C.-700 A.D. In this double-chambered vessel, the whistle assembly depicts a person playing a double flute. The instrument's sound emanates from holes where the figure holds the flute to his mouth. Phoebe Apperson Hearst Museum collection.

*This sensation was amplified by the situation of my study quarters, made up of one table among the cellars of the Popol Vuh Museum, filled with an infinity of beautiful censers, stone axes, polychrome drinking vessels, sublimely decorated plates, stonework, obsidian and who knows how many more objects or vestiges left to posterity by these wise peoples.*

*As I prepared to sound an instrument, I anticipated that, with the first note, I would see in the thousand and one ancient artistic representations that surrounded me a jubilant display of smiling and crying, as the figurines felt for the first time in centuries the caress of the enchanting, powerful sounds bouncing around them.*

*I couldn't know what music the ancients played, nor did I want to. It was enough for me to know that I reproduced the real sounds, the very same musical scales that at one time were used in ceremonies to pacify the gods, in the inauguration of leaders, in the king's court, in times of war, in the hunting of animals or simply in the songs of a corn farmer who worked to support his family.*

This book is about that connection with the past and with the earth—music and art, spanning the globe and reaching through time. It is about the breath and rhythm of countless people, blowing and pulsing from the beginning of our time on this planet, through the present and into the future. Clay is the remarkable substance that makes this possible. You are about to embark on an incredible journey—the journey from mud to music.

## What's in This Book?

At first glance, the topic of "ceramic musical instruments" may appear narrow in scope. However, as you flip through this book, you will be delighted to see the abundance of extraordinary ceramic musical applications. In this book a ceramic musical instrument is defined as any object made primarily from clay, which is designed to produce sound. As you'll soon see, there are scores of instruments from many cultures that fit this definition. Rather than include an exhaustive itemization of the world's ceramic instruments, the intent of this book is to identify and describe representatives from each family of instruments, with a focus on today's designers and contemporary building techniques.

Our journey will have several stages, starting with a look at numerous instruments, from both the past and the present. By systematically exploring each family—drums, wind instruments, strings, and others—we'll examine the variations of ceramic instruments that have been created through the years. We'll see how ancient instrument designs have inspired modern artists to recreate and evolve them, and in some cases virtually reinvent them. Next is a discussion of some of the technical properties of clay and glazes. We'll learn how instrument makers use the technology of ceramics to their best advantage in making instruments. We'll meet a number of today's

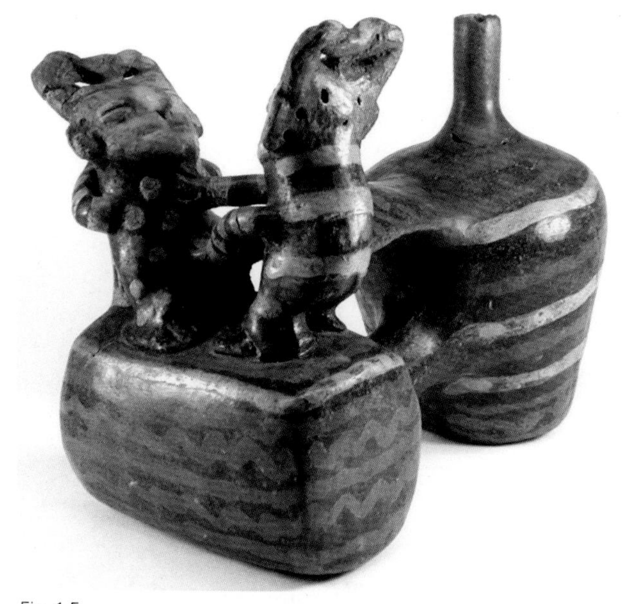

Fig. 1.5
**Peruvian Whistling Vessel**
7 inches in height, from the Vicus culture, Peru, 400 B.C.-700 A.D. This lusciously decorated ancient instrument depicts two animated figures engaging in some unknown act. Notice the whistle's sound exit holes on the rear of the figure's head. Phoebe Apperson Hearst Museum collection.

leading ceramic instrument builders, and hear about their inspirations and insights. The book closes with step-by-step demonstrations of how to build several clay instruments.

*From Mud to Music* will help you learn about many different instruments and the ceramic, musical, and acoustical principles behind them. But hopefully it will also help you enjoy these instruments by seeing and hearing them. Spread throughout these pages are hundreds of photographs of ceramic musical instruments made by people from all over the world. The accompanying CD is packed with examples of music played on clay instruments. As you listen, remember that every sound on the CD is made by a ceramic instrument, demonstrating the remarkably wide range of musical colors and sounds that clay can produce.

## A Classification System for Musical Instruments

There are many different types of musical instruments. In order to proceed methodically through a wide variety of instruments, organization of this book requires a classification system to categorize instruments into families. Fortunately there are a number of systems from which to choose.

The earliest documented system of instrument classification was created in China during the Zhou Dynasty, around 3,000 years ago. Instruments were grouped into eight categories based on the material used in their construction—metal, stone, clay, skin, silk, wood, gourd and bamboo. While it is an interesting and intriguing system, it is not useful for our purposes since all of the instruments we're concerned with fall in the same category—clay.

Fast-forward a few thousand years to 1914, when the "Sachs-Hornbostel" classification system was published by Erich von Hornbostel and Curt Sachs. This system is now widely accepted by musicologists, acousticians, and organologists (people who study musical instruments), and will fit our needs for this book. It groups instruments according to the way in which their sound is produced—that is, what makes the primary driving vibration. The main categories are:

- **Idiophones** (sonorous objects) – instruments whose bodies vibrate to produce sound
- **Membranophones** (skinned drums) – instruments with vibrating stretched membranes
- **Aerophones** (wind instruments) – instruments that enclose a vibrating body of air
- **Chordophones** (string instruments) – instruments that produce sound through the vibrations of strings.

There are significant benefits to using this classification approach. First, because an instrument can be on only one "branch," the system provides a unique, unambiguous and easily-describable category for each type of instrument (most of the time). This makes the system like a library card catalogue—it's a good way to clearly organize and find instruments.

This type of approach also bases the classification on observable attributes of the physical instrument, rather than details of how it is made or used or what role it plays in art and society. This avoids cultural biases and other confusing factors, lessening the likelihood of disagreement about classification.

However, as we'll discover, this system isn't flawless. It requires that an instrument be included in only one category, while in actuality some instruments aren't easy to pigeonhole because they have components from multiple categories. A simple example is a side-hole clay pot drum (often called an udu drum). This instrument's sound is produced by air vibrating inside a vessel, which makes it an aerophone. But striking the vessel's clay shell also produces sounds, which makes it an idiophone.

So how should a side-hole clay pot drum be classified? Is it an aerophone or idiophone? Well, if one of the sound-producing systems in an instrument dominates the others, then it's common to use that classification. For example, the traditional playing style of side-hole pot drums uses the air sounds almost exclusively, and as a result the udu is commonly classified as a "plosive aerophone" (an aerophone whose air is excited by striking an opening in a chamber or tube).

It is not as clear-cut with contemporary udu-like instruments because a significant component of their sound is idiophonic (produced by tapping the clay body itself). So the category in which to classify these instruments is subject to interpretation. This book includes udus in the aerophones section for historical reasons, and also because the most striking and dominant component of their sound is usually aerophonic. But their cousin, the ghatam clay pot drum from India, is classified here as an idiophone. Like its Nigerian relative, it also has both shell sounds and air sounds; however, the ghatam's traditional playing style places more emphasis on the shell-striking sounds.

Since there are ceramic instruments in each of the Sachs-Hornbostel categories, a chapter is devoted to each family of instruments—idiophones, membranophones, aerophones, and chordophones. An additional chapter showcases "hybrid" instruments, in which two or more different sound-producing systems are combined in ways that interact with each other.

Admittedly, some of the ceramic instruments in this book have non-clay components; for example, drum heads made from animal skin, and strings made from gut or steel. However, every instrument in these pages uses clay as its primary construction material.

While this classification system isn't ideal, it does provide a common framework to examine instruments and identify and discuss the ways that they produce sound. Remembering the basic categories of this system will help you appreciate the way this book is organized. If nothing else, you can impress people at a party by discussing the Sachs-Hornbostel system of instrument taxonomy and its relevance to organology!

## Traditional Instrument Names From Around the World

Instruments from many traditional cultures are represented in these pages. Some instruments that are widely used are called by a variety of names. For example, in different places and cultures, a goblet drum might be called a doumbek, darrabukka, darbukka, darabouka, darambuka derbouka, darbaka, derbanka, derbekki, derbocka, dobouk, donbak, tombak, gedombak, tarambuka, dumbeg, dumbelek, deblek, deblet, debuldek, delbek, dirimbekki, tabl, tabla, tablak, toubeleki, tumbaknari—and many other names as well. Additionally, each of these names may have a variety of common spellings, for example, doumbek, dumbec, or dümbek. This book is not intended to be an exhaustive encyclopedia of all the different names for traditional ceramic instruments. So in most cases, a single name has been chosen and used throughout the book.

## chapter two

*In the beginning was noise. And noise begat rhythm. And rhythm begat everything else. This is the kind of cosmology a drummer can live with.*

—Mickey Hart

# Idiophones
## *Sonorous Objects*

Idiophones are members of the percussion instrument family. Their name means "self-sounders" because they are instruments whose bodies vibrate to produce sound. In other words, their sound is produced by the vibration of the sonorous materials from which they are made. Idiophones are sounded in a variety of ways; they can be shaken, struck, hit together, plucked or scraped.

There are many types of ceramic idiophones. From the crisp articulation of clay rattles to the gentle tinkling of rain sticks, from the crystalline tones of bells and xylophones to the exotic "thonk" of tongue drums, a broad spectrum of idiophonic sounds can be coaxed from objects made from fired clay. The ceramic idiophones discussed in this chapter are organized into the following subcategories:

- Shaken Idiophones
- Struck Idiophones
  - Vessels
  - Bowls and Bells
  - Bars
  - Gongs and Plates
  - Tongue Drums
- Concussion Idiophones
- Plucked Idiophones
- Scraped Idiophones

### Shaken Idiophones

Shaken idiophones produce their sound when shaken. The most common examples are vessel rattles (also called shakers), which consist of a vessel filled with loose pellets. Early rattles were made from a wide variety of materials, such as dried gourds, fruit, seaweed, seed pods, tortoise shells, leather and just about anything else that would serve as a container. The materials inside could be pebbles, sand, seeds or grains. Examples of ancient clay rattles have been found all over the world. Two 5000-year-old rattles from Mesopotamia are shown in figure 2.1. Pear-shaped rattles from around 800 B.C. were found in Central Europe. Clay rattles were also very popular in pre-Columbian America (figure 1.1). The sounds of pre-Columbian rattles from Guatemala can be heard on track 7 of the accompanying CD. *Maracas* are a very popular type of non-clay shakers used in

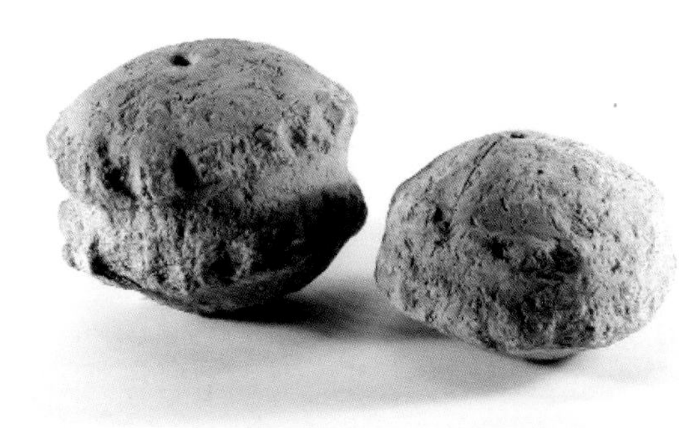

Fig. 2.1
**Sumerian Rattles**
Two rattles, hollow with pellets inside, to 3 inches in height, from the Mesopotamian city-state of Kish, in present day Iraq. Early Dynastic period, approximately 3000 B.C. Field Museum Collection.

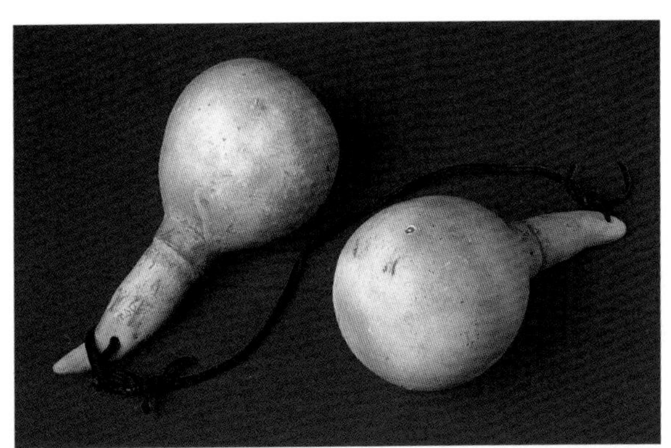

Fig. 2.2
**Sonajas**
Aguinaldo da Silva, Olinda, Pernambuco, Brazil. Clay maracas with clay pellets inside. Earthenware.

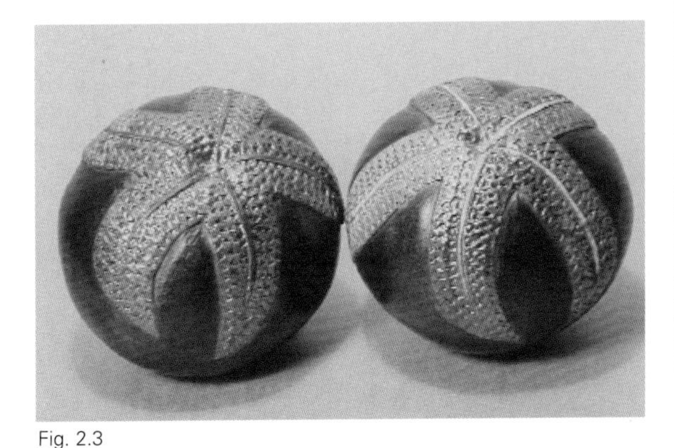

Fig. 2.3
**Starfish Shakers**
Jan Lovewell, Powell River, British Columbia, Canada. Living near the sea inspired Jan's design for these shakers. She forms each of her shakers individually paying careful attention to the way they feel in the hand. As Jan puts it, "I want them to feel smooth and pleasant to touch and secure in the hand for exuberant shaking." Made from grogged stoneware coated with terra sigillata, burnished and raku fired. 2 and 3 inches in diameter.

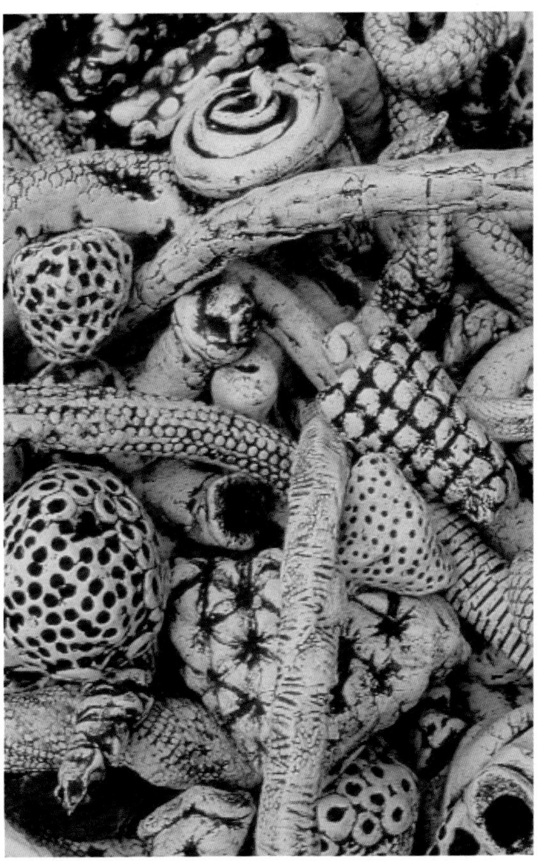

Fig. 2.4
**Rattle Collection**
Kelly Jean Ohl, Lanesboro, Minnesota, USA. Kelly Jean works with slabs of clay that are rolled under doilies, crocheted pot holders or any unique fabric with interesting texture that she can find. The slab is shaped into a closed vessel but before it is sealed shut, clay balls are poured in. They don't stick together because Kelly Jean bisque fires them first. After the rattles are bisque fired they are rubbed with oxides to accentuate the patterns, then fired again to cone 10. To 6 inches in length.

Latin American music, and are usually made of wood or gourds with seeds inside. A pair of clay maracas or *sonajas* made by Aguinaldo da Silva are shown in figure 2.2. Modern clay rattles can be heard on tracks 11, 12, 15, and 35 of the accompanying CD.

As ancient people discovered, clay makes an excellent material for rattles. Any vessel form with pellets inside can be rattled, so clay rattles are quite easy to make, and can have an almost infinite variety of shapes, sizes and designs. The sound of a clay shaker or rattle is influenced by the size and shape of the chamber, the thickness of the walls, the type of clay and firing temperature, and the size of, amount of, and material used for the pellets. Some common and effective shapes for shakers are eggs and cylinders, though almost any shape will work well. Different surfaces or wall thicknesses will allow

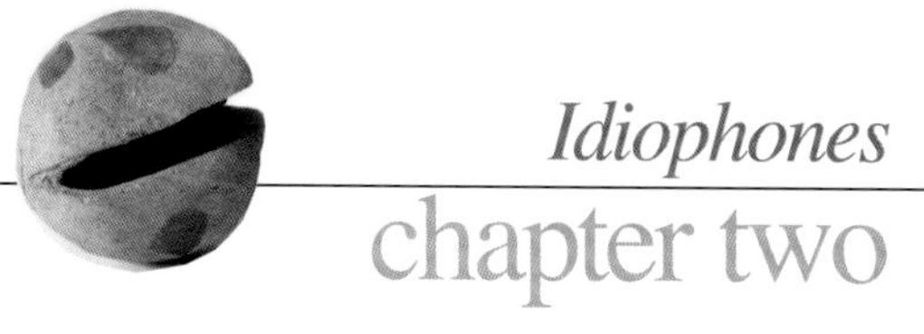

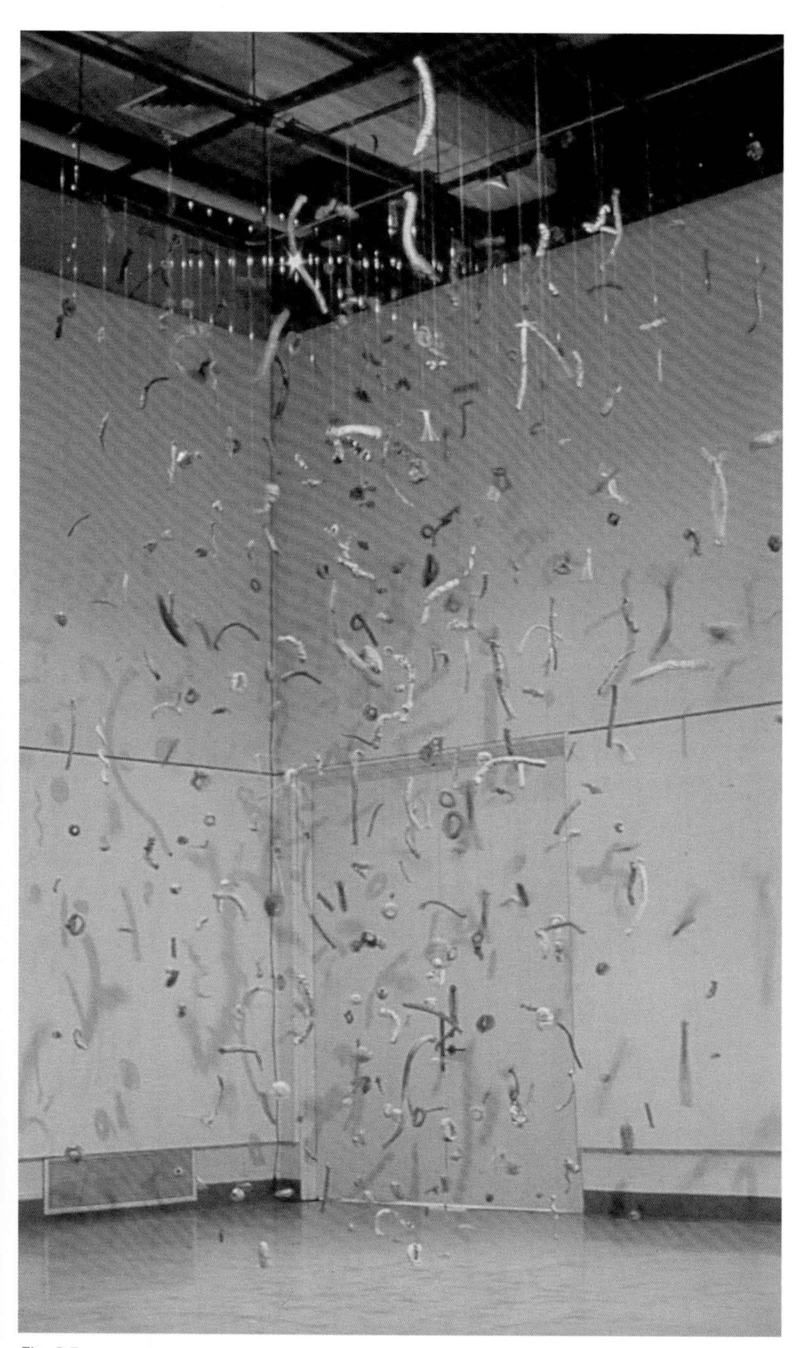

Fig. 2.5
**Hanging Rattles**
Kelly Jean Ohl, Lanesboro, Minnesota, USA. For this performance piece, Kelly Jean made 500 rattles and suspended them. To encourage viewers to play with the rattles she provided bowls full of more rattles like those hanging from the ceiling. The visitors picked up a loose rattle as they entered the space, then started to sample the unique sounds of the hanging rattles.

a single instrument to produce a variety of sounds depending on how it is shaken. Thinner walls usually produce a brighter and louder sound, as do instruments that are fired to bisque rather than higher temperatures.

The "purest" form of clay rattle uses bits of clay for the pellets inside, but many other materials also can be used, such as seeds, pebbles, sand or ball bearings. If you use non-clay materials, it is advisable to add them after you fire the clay body of the rattle, since they may burn or melt if fired inside the rattle. To make clay pellets you can use a variety of methods such as rolling small balls of clay between your fingers, extruding long strings of clay and slicing them into bits, shaving leather hard clay with a rasp, or pulverizing dry clay scraps or fired shards. Clay cat litter produces a nice, light sound when fired inside the rattle. If you decide to use cat litter, be sure to find a brand of litter that is pure clay, and test it at your desired firing temperature to ensure that it fires properly.

Usually, a more consistent shaker sound is achieved by using pellets of similar size and shape. If you have large quantities of shavings or crumbs, you can quickly sort them into various size categories by sifting them through screens, grates or strainers with different sized openings. Use a screen with the smallest openings to sift out the dust, and discard it. Run your remaining bits through a larger screen, and what falls through will be the bits larger than the first screen but smaller than the second. Repeat this process with progressively larger screens or strainers to get other sizes of pellets.

Another idea is to make a clay rattle with one or more membranes (figure 6.7). The

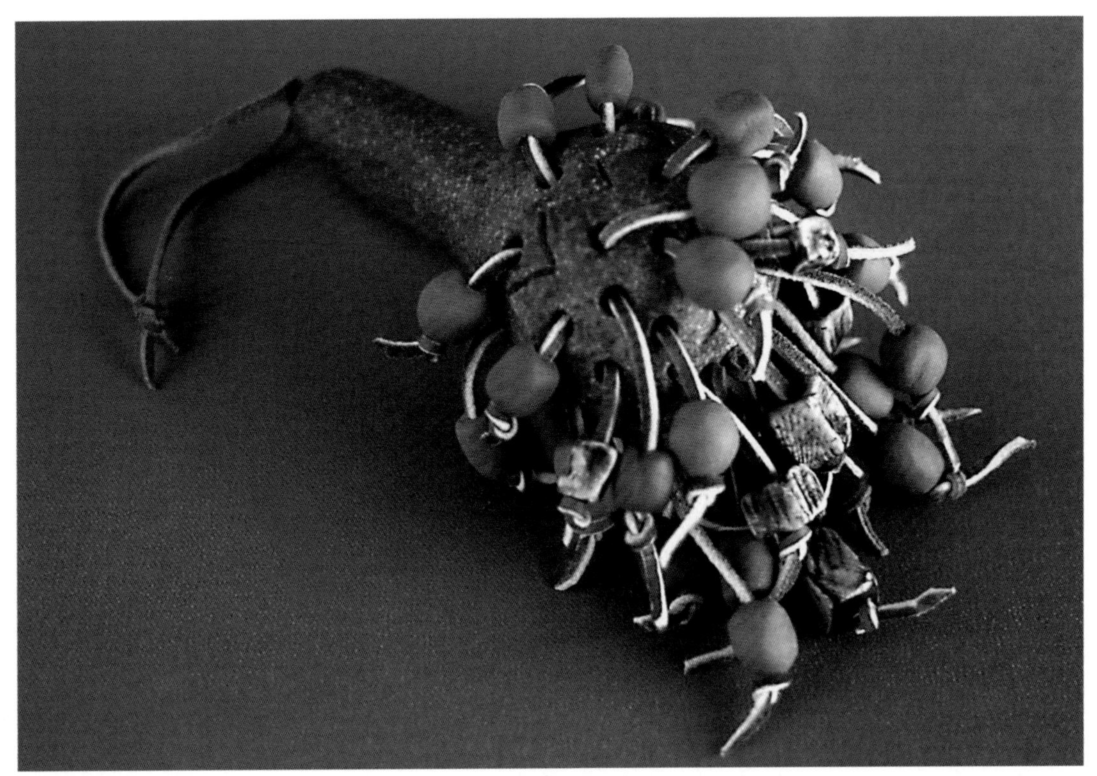

Fig. 2.6
**Shaker (2001)**
Janie Tubbs, Lindsborg, Kansas, USA. The body of this external shaker is in two parts. This allowed easier access for stringing the beads. Leather was knotted on the outside top and pulled through the bottom and knotted to keep the two pieces together. High-fired stoneware and pigment, red earthenware and glaze, leather. 4.5 inches in height.

membranes, like small drum heads made of animal skin, add a different sound to the rattle. A rattle of this type made by Stephen Wright (figure 6.7) can be heard on track 11 of the CD. A clay membrane rattle combined with an ocarina is shown in figure 6.9 and discussed in Chapter 6.

Pellet bells are another type of vessel rattle. Sleigh bells are an example of pellet bells—a small, usually round, chamber that rings when shaken due to a loose pellet inside. Though pellet bells are often made of metal, ancient clay examples have been found on several continents. Two large Chinese pellet bells from the Sung dynasty are shown in figure 2.7.

A more enigmatic relative of the pellet bell is the tripod rattle bowl, an ancient Mayan item which appears to be a functional ceramic bowl or vase, but has rattles incorporated into its three legs (figure 2.8).

Other pre-Columbian functional ceramic vessels also included rattling components. For example, some cups, bowls and incense burners had hollow bases filled with pellets. We can only guess the purpose for such vessels—but it seems likely that they had special or magical significance. Often they are richly decorated, which implies that they were not intended for everyday use. One particularly striking example of a rattling vessel from Lake

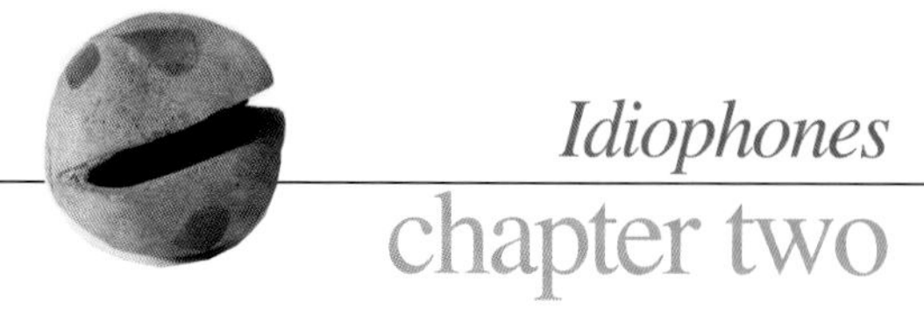

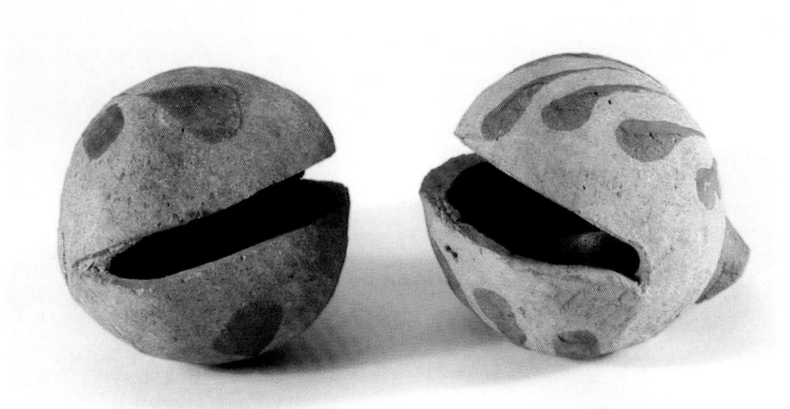

Fig. 2.7
**Chinese Pellet Bells**
Two ceramic pellet bells from the Sung Dynasty (960-1279 A.D.) A single large ceramic pellet is inside each vessel. The rear of each pellet bell has a clay loop so it can be attached to a cord.
3 inches. Field Museum Collection.

Titicaca is a goblet-shaped cup with a hollow base filled with pellets. The exterior of the cup has a painting of a rattlesnake, most obviously related to the sound the cup makes when shaken. In the animistic pre-Columbian societies, imbuing such an object with its own voice would presumably enhance its power.

Another cousin of rattles is known as a tubular needle rattle, often called a *rain stick*. This instrument is common today in Latin America, though some believe it originated in Africa and was brought to America via the slave trade. The Latin American version is usually made from the skeleton of a cactus stalk, or sometimes from a bamboo stalk. When the rain stick is tipped, it emits a long sustained tinkling sound which is reminiscent of falling rain; hence its common name. To make such an instrument, a cactus' thorns are pulled off and pushed back through the soft cactus flesh. Then the stalk is left to dry, with the thorns on the inside. When dry, the hollow cactus is filled with small pebbles and the ends are sealed. The sound is produced by the pebbles bouncing off each other and the internal walls of the cactus as they traverse a convoluted path through the twisted maze created by the needles barricading the inside of the stalk.

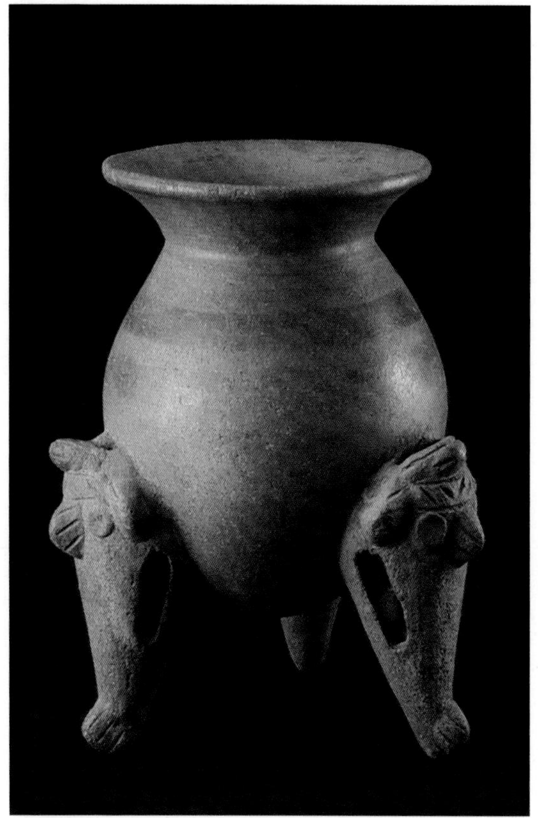

Fig. 2.8
**Tripod Rattle Bowl**
Pre-Columbian earthenware vessel with three sculpted legs of zoomorphic design, each containing a loose clay pellet which rattles when the vessel is shaken. 7 inches in height.
Collection of Barry Hall.

Rain sticks are also made from a stalk of bamboo pierced with wooden spikes at regular intervals. In Mexico, a rain stick called a *chicauaztli* is connected with fertility and rain gods and used as an implement to make holes in the earth for sowing seeds.

A rain-stick-like instrument can be created from clay, with a delightful sound resulting (figures 2.9 and 8.2). The plasticity of clay also allows a clay rain stick to take a variety of shapes rather than a straight tube, including a circular "doughnut" form which can be sounded constantly by continual turning—unlike the traditional form, which must be repeatedly turned over when all the internal pieces have settled in one end.

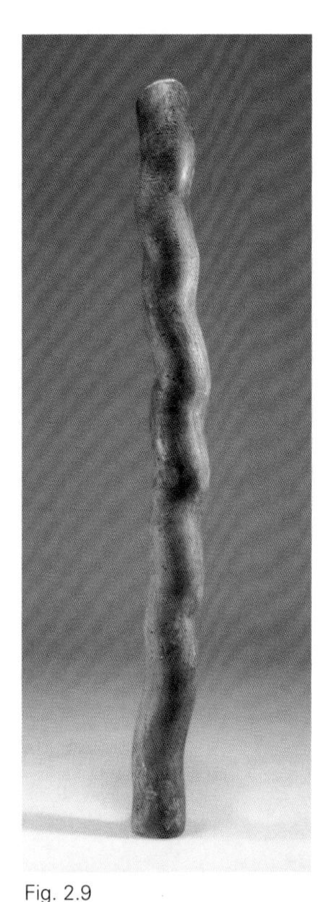

Fig. 2.9
**Rain Stick**
Barry Hall, Westborough, Massachusetts, USA. Inspired by a South American instrument made from a cactus stalk, this extruded ceramic rain stick contains a complex internal network of clay needles and pellets. When it is tipped, it emits a sustained tinkling sound, reminiscent of falling rain. Bisqued stoneware. 48 inches in length.

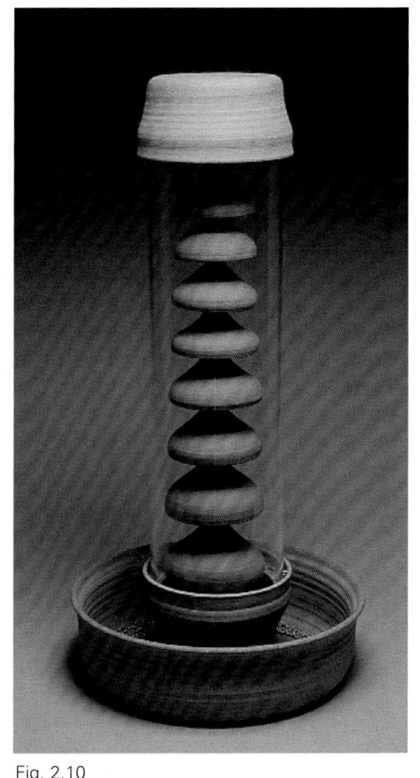

Fig. 2.10
**Fountain Chime**
Ward Hartenstein, Rochester, New York, USA. A column of stoneware bell shapes suspended within an acrylic tube mounted on a clay base. The player drops a handful of BBs through holes in the top. They cascade down over the suspended bells to produce a chiming, rain-stick-like sound. The BBs collect in the base and can be scooped up and dropped again. This is an extremely addictive instrument that requires no performance skills. 25 inches in height. Hear this instrument on CD track 3.

Ward Hartenstein created an instrument related to a rain stick, called a *fountain chime* (figure 2.10). Interestingly, he designed and built his fountain chime without knowing about rain sticks. In the fountain chime, a column of stoneware funnel-shaped bells are suspended within an acrylic tube mounted on a clay base. The player drops one, two or a handful of BBs (small metal ball bearings) through holes in the top. They cascade down over the suspended bells to produce a chiming, rain-like sound (listen to CD track 3). The BBs collect in the base, where they can be scooped up and dropped again.

Ward has built larger versions using ball bearings, and has also experimented with bell shapes with upturned rims and internal holes for the BBs to drop through. One of his interesting design challenges is to try to control the movement of the BBs so that they bounce around as much as possible on their way down, extending the time it takes them to reach the bottom.

The *gravity chime* is another instrument Ward created, which may be most closely related to pellet bells, though it is a unique instrument unto itself (figure 2.11). Marbles are dropped so that they traverse through a sound-producing array of stoneware chambers, producing random bell-like sounds as they descend through the instrument (listen to track 41 on the CD). This hanging sculpture is composed of a variety of acoustically designed ceramic forms, which are suspended so that they can vibrate freely. Some are bell- or bowl-shaped, and others are hollow tubes. Some of the tubes have tongue-shaped slits carved into them, which alter the course of the pellet and produce unique sounds in the process.

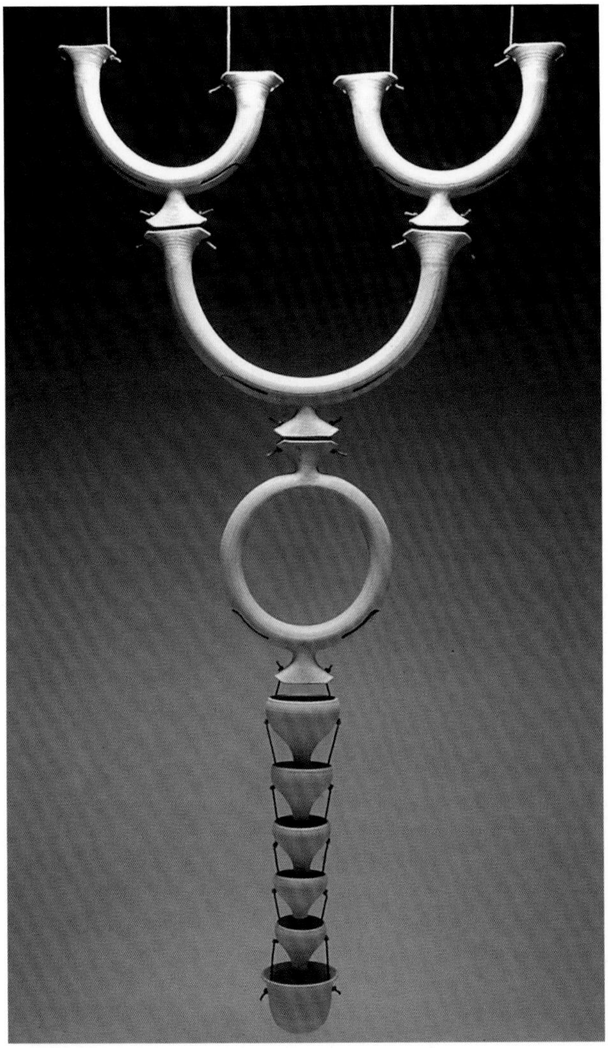

Ward reports that some people are irresistibly drawn to the gravity chime. It is easy to play and produces an immediate reward, yet you can control the sound by varying the number and frequency of the marbles dropped. The variations of shape and arrangement of curved tubes and bowls make for endless possibilities of design, limited only by the weight that can be supported by the walls or ceiling from which the gravity chime is suspended.

It also has a fascinating visual quality: watching a marble bounce and roll, waiting for it to emerge at the bottom. Ward has designed some gravity chimes with one entry point at the top and branching pathways leading to multiple exit chambers. Where will the marble come out? What sounds do the different pathways make?

Fig. 2.11
**Gravity Chime**
Ward Hartenstein, Rochester, New York, USA. An array of individually shaped hanging stoneware chambers through which a marble falls to produce random bell-like sounds. The tubular forms are constructed from hollow, wheel-thrown rings into which tongue-shaped slits have been carved. 60 inches in height. Hear this instrument on CD track 41.

## Struck Idiophones

Struck idiophones are the largest category of idiophones. These instruments are made to sound by striking them with your hand, or a stick or beater. Struck idiophones can be classified into the following families, based on their form:

- Vessels
- Bowls and Bells
- Bars
- Gongs and Plates
- Tongue Drums

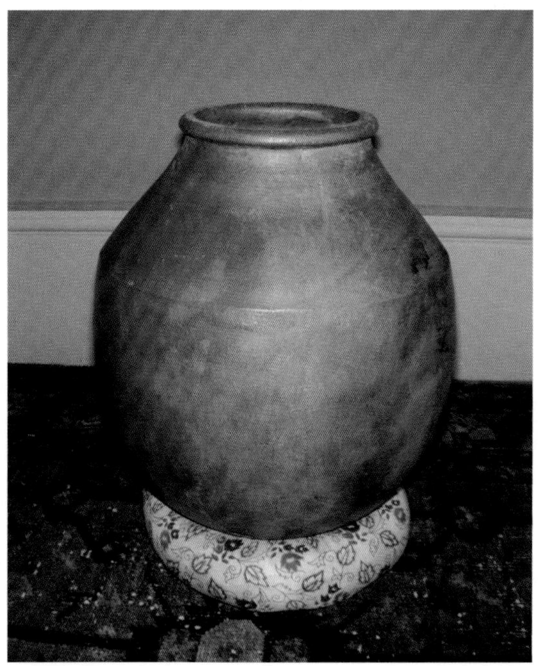

Fig. 2.12
**Ghatam**
Kesavan, Manamadurai, India. A traditional, thick-walled instrument from a respected ghatam-building family in South India. Earthenware. 16 inches in height. Collection of T. H. Subash Chandran. Hear this instrument on CD track 42.

### *Vessels*

A clay pot is one of the simplest ceramic instruments. Unlike most other drums, the clay pot "drum" has no membrane or skin head—the sounds are produced solely by the pot's ringing clay shell and the air resonating inside the vessel. This is one of the essential "sounds of clay," and it's quite a powerful sound as well.

Clay pot drums are ceramic vessels that are played percussively, usually using only the player's hands to produce sounds by tapping, striking or rubbing. These instruments can take a wide variety of forms. Even vessels originally made as pots for domestic purposes often make excellent sounding instruments. But the simple ceramic cooking vessel or storage pot has risen to a much higher purpose in some societies.

A *ghatam* is a clay pot drum found in southern India. It is an ancient drum used to accompany the voice and melodic instruments in Carnatic classical music, and is the second principal instrument in South Indian percussion ensembles. (In the north it's called a *ghata* and is used for accompanying folk music.) In the classical concert setting, the ghatam player is first and foremost an accompanist to both the lead melodic instrument and the double-headed *mrindangam* drum (see the "Membranophones" chapter). At different points during a performance, the ghatam player may mimic the *taal* (rhythmic cycle) established by the mrindangam player or imitate the melodic pattern of the lead melodic instrument. The ghatam player uses high-pitched finger tones to cut through the ensemble at specific times in the music when space is left open by the mrindangam.

The ghatam is a roughly spherical clay pot with a somewhat narrow mouth opening. It is made from clay that is mixed with brass filings before the pot is fired. This gives the ghatam its distinctive sound. Each ghatam shell resonates at a specific musical pitch. A ghatam player will often have a collection of pots covering many different pitches, so he can match the instrument to the key of the music he wishes to accompany. In the more traditional ghatams the clay walls are quite thick—as much as one inch—though others have much thinner walls. The thicker-walled ghatams are considered by some to have a superior sound, though they are more difficult to play.

Although the ghatam is simple in design, there are a wide variety of complex playing techniques. A ghatam player uses both hands, wrists, all ten fingers, knuckles and fingernails to strike the pot on its neck, center and bottom surfaces. In addition to the sounds produced by the clay shell, deep tones are also produced by the air in the vessel's resonant cavity. Their pitch can be raised or lowered by opening and closing the mouth hole against the skin of the player's stomach. In general, the butt of the left hand is used to produce low pitches while the fingers and nails of the right hand create higher pitches. At the climax of a performance, some players throw the instrument into the air and catch it in time with the music. As a spectacular finale, the pot may be smashed on the ground to accent the final beat of a piece! However, this is not a common practice today since professional-quality instruments can be expensive, and pots of certain pitches are difficult to obtain.

The ghatam shown in figure 2.12 was made by a potter named Kesavan from Manamadurai, a village in South India with a long tradition of ghatam builders. The art and trade of ghatam-making has been passed down from father to son in Kesavan's family for many generations, and he is now teaching his sons to become master builders. They make instruments of the traditional, thick-walled style. The family's clay recipe includes, among other things, brass filings and ground egg shells, though the exact formula is a carefully guarded secret. Track 42 of the CD is a ghatam solo by T. H. Subash Chandran, a South Indian percussionist, performed on this ghatam made by Kesavan. Many master players, including Subash, consider ghatams made by Kesavan's family to be the finest available in the world.

A number of Western makers have created instruments influenced by the ghatam. Ceramist Stephen Freedman made porcelain ghatam-like instruments for the percussion group "The Antenna Repairmen." These, along with many of Stephen's other ceramic instruments, are featured on the Antenna Repairmen's CD titled *Ghatam* (see the discography in the Appendix). Steven Wright also makes ghatam-family instruments, shown in figure 7.9 and played on track 20 of the accompanying CD.

Other ceramic musical pots—most notably the Nigerian udu drums—are included in the "Aerophones" chapter of this book. Though they are closely related to the ghatam in many ways, their primary sound is produced by the air in the pot's cavity, rather than the sounds from striking the shell. Although the ghatam also has these "air tones," in most playing styles they are secondary to its shell tones.

### Bowls and Bells

Given their pleasant sound, it's not surprising that many types of clay bells have been made. Small porcelain and china bells can be found in many cultures, both modern and ancient.

In fact, most ceramic bowls, whether designed as instruments or not, produce beautiful bell-like tones when struck near the rim. Many factors influence the pitch and tone of a clay bowl or bell, including the type of clay and firing temperature, as well as the size, shape and thickness of the various sections of the bowl. You can carefully control the resulting pitch of a ceramic bowl by adding or removing material at the rim or the base. Adding material at the rim lowers the pitch; more material at the base raises the pitch. However, a bowl will not sound a tone until after it's fired. This makes it difficult to fine-tune a bowl to produce a specific pitch, because once it has been fired the only way to modify it is by grinding away the fired clay body—a process that can be delicate, time-consuming, and hazardous to the lungs. With water-tight bowls, another option exists for lowering pitch: adding water.

The *jaltarang* is a traditional set of musical bowls from India, which are graduated in size to produce the pitches of a scale over two or three octaves. Jaltarang (which translates to "water waves") bowls are precisely tuned by adding water

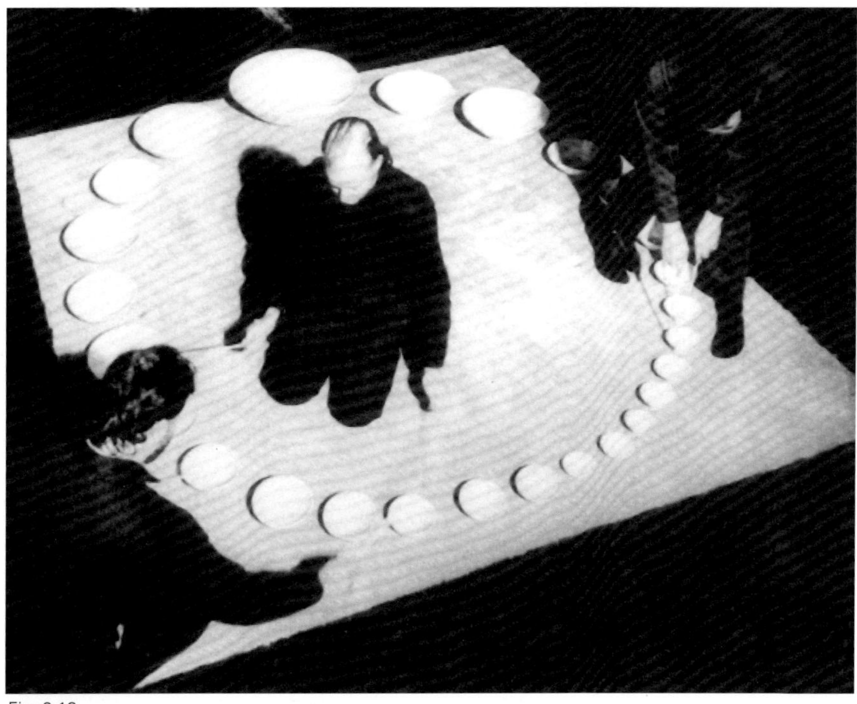

Fig. 2.13
**Jaltarang**
Stephen Freedman, Kurtistown, Hawaii, USA. An instrument of 26 porcelain bowls played with sticks. This photo shows The Antenna Repairmen performing their piece titled "Jaltarong," which can be heard on track 14 of the CD.

to the bowls, which lowers the pitch. They are struck on their rims with thin bamboo or wooden sticks. Delicate nuances of sound are possible by dipping the sticks into the water while the bowl is vibrating. An extended jaltarang of twenty-six bowls built by Stephen Freedman can be seen in figure 2.13, and heard on track 14 of the CD.

Terra cotta flowerpots usually have a very nice tone. To use them as a musical instrument, they can be arrayed on the floor, suspended from a knotted rope, or mounted to a post or other type of stand. The *flowerpotophones* shown in figure 2.15 are collections of regular gardening flowerpots mounted on a wooden frame. These pots were carefully selected and arranged so their pitches complement each other, but even a random collection of pots can produce wonderful-sounding melodies. Flowerpots can be struck with a variety of implements, including mallets with rubber, cork and yarn tips, as well as chopsticks and brushes. Mallets with superball tips produce especially good tones on medium to large flowerpots. (See "About Mallets" page 24.)

Ceramic bowls or bells also can be bowed, i.e., stroked with a horsehair bow like those used on bowed string instruments such as the violin or double bass. This technique works best with larger clay objects that are relatively thin and resonate well, such as clay bowls, plates and other flat objects. Pulling the bow across the edge of the object with gentle but continuous pressure produces a sustained sound. To hear this sound for yourself, listen to Ward Hartenstein's bow bowls (figure 2.17) on track 3 of the accompanying CD.

### *Bars*

Bar idiophones are instruments consisting of a set of individual, or "free," bars that are tuned to differing pitches and usually struck with mallets. Common instruments in this category are *xylophones, marimbas,* and African *balafons.* Clay instruments in this family are rare; however, Ward Hartenstein has spent years developing a family of ceramic free bar instruments. His clay marimbas

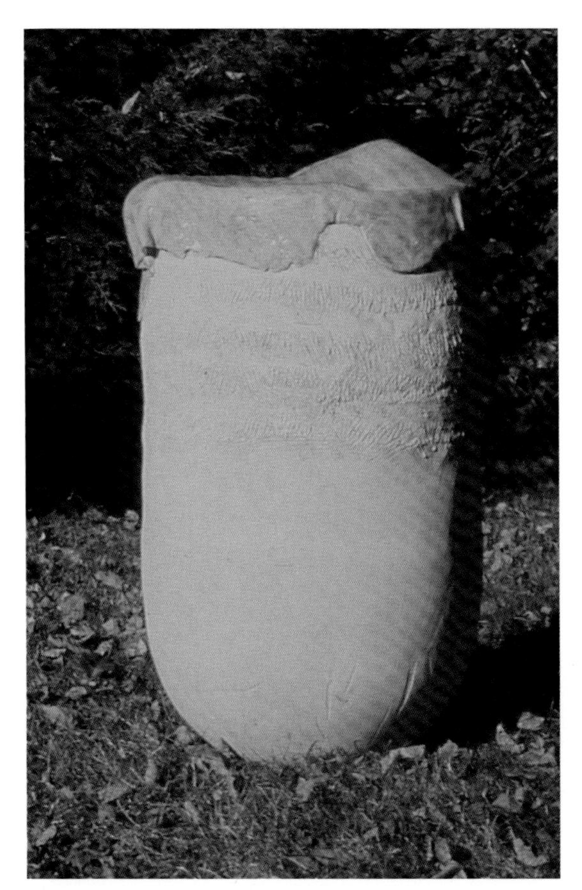

Fig. 2.14
**Waiting**
Diane Baxter, Douglas, Alaska, USA. A sculptural ceramic vessel Diane created as part of her series titled "Waiting" which was displayed in 2001. She recorded the process of making the sculptures and played the recordings as a sound environment for the gallery display. Hear this instrument on CD track 22.

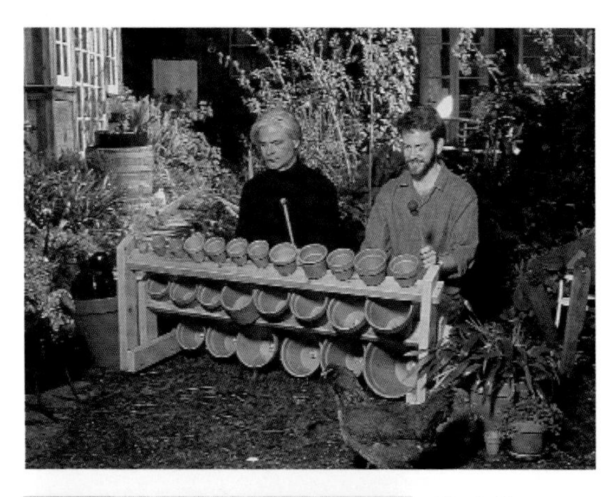

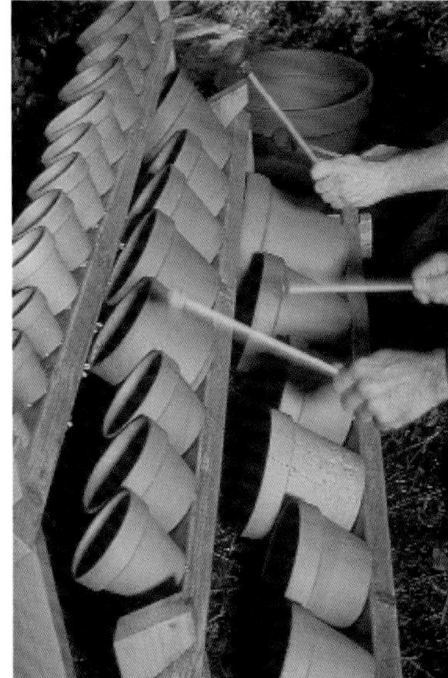

Fig. 2.15
**Flowerpotophones**
Barry Hall, Westborough, Massachusetts, USA. These instruments are made from commercial Italian terra cotta flowerpots, played with mallets, brushes or hands. The pots are mounted on wooden frames using metal and rubber hardware. The round pots produce clear bell-like tones, while the rectangular and oval pots have a complex sound rich with nonharmonic overtones. These large, outdoor instruments are especially fun for multiple players.

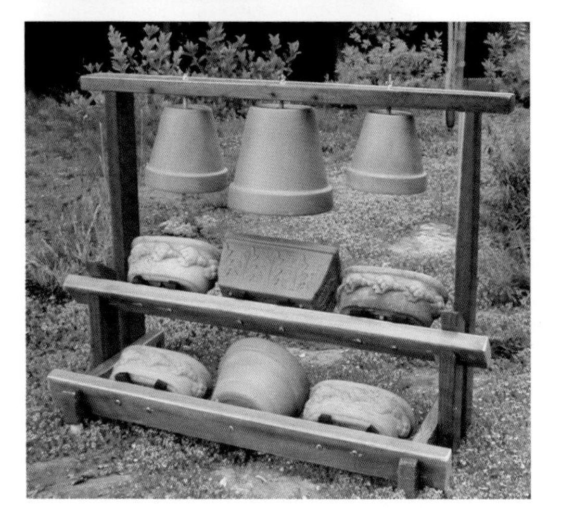

(figures 2.19, 7.4, 7.26 and 8.20) are made of unglazed porcelain or stoneware clay, which are very hard and dense when fired.

Although this instrument isn't unbreakable, it can withstand repeated striking, moderate changes in temperature and humidity, and the passage of time with very little effect on its pitch or tone quality. The bars are shaped by hand so that they are thinner in the middle and thicker at the ends. After firing, Ward tunes them by grinding with a diamond

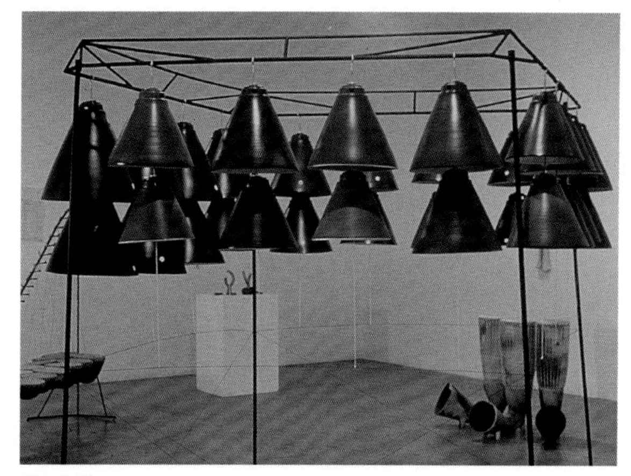

Fig. 2.16
**Quarter Tone Bells**
Brian Ransom, St. Petersburg, Florida, USA. Slip-cast earthenware, steel, wire. 7.5' x 10' x 9'.

Fig. 2.17
**Bow Bowls**
Ward Hartenstein, Rochester, New York, USA. Three nested stoneware bowls attached to a wooden base. The edges of the bowls are bowed with a bamboo and horsehair bow. The sound is similar to the rubbing of a wine glass with moistened fingers. The larger the bowl, the lower the pitch, although upper harmonics also can be produced. 7 inches in height. Hear this instrument on CD track 3.

lapidary wheel. Just as with wooden bars, removing material from the ends raises the fundamental pitch, and removing material from the middle lowers the fundamental pitch. The overtones of the bars are also manipulated, using similar techniques.

The bodies of Ward's clay marimbas consist of large ceramic vessels made on a potter's wheel with the addition of handbuilt segments. The air chambers underneath the bars serve as resonators that reinforce and amplify the tone of the bars. The bars are attached with rubber bands to cords tied across from end to end of the resonating vessel base. Some of his instruments have bars arranged in two layers, with the ends of the larger bars protruding from beneath the smaller bars.

Mallets for Ward's clay marimbas range from 13 to 15 inches in length and have a clay bead at their core, wrapped with yarn. (See "About Mallets" on page 24.) They are much lighter in weight than orchestral marimba mallets, so as not to break the clay bars. The clay marimba has a bright and glassy sound with a sharp attack in the upper register. In the lower register, the sound is fuller and more resonant with a clear sense of pitch and a decay time of three to four seconds.

### *Gongs and Plates*

Flat plates or shallow bowls of clay can make a variety of sounds. An easily made instrument of this type is a set of wind chimes with suspended plates of different sizes and shapes, which will produce a variety of pitches and tones. The various pieces can be cut from a flat piece of clay.

Ragnar Naess created a number of sets of clay gongs for his *EarthSounds* ceramic orchestra. For more on EarthSounds see the "Profiles" chapter and listen to track 21 on the CD. Some of his gongs were built from clay slabs and others were wheel thrown. These were arranged in multiple sets organized in gamelan-like systems. An objective of Ragnar and his collaborators was to achieve a wide variety of sounds. He discovered that different slab thicknesses produced different *timbres*. Playing technique also has a large impact on the sound. For example, one set of giant crescent-shaped gongs, called *moons*, sounds entirely different when struck on their edges rather than on their broad, flat surfaces.

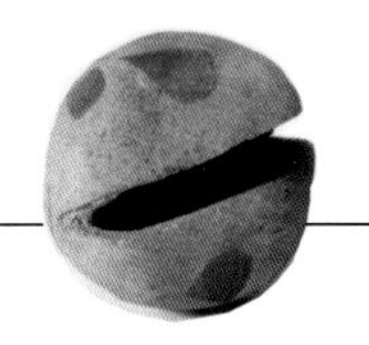

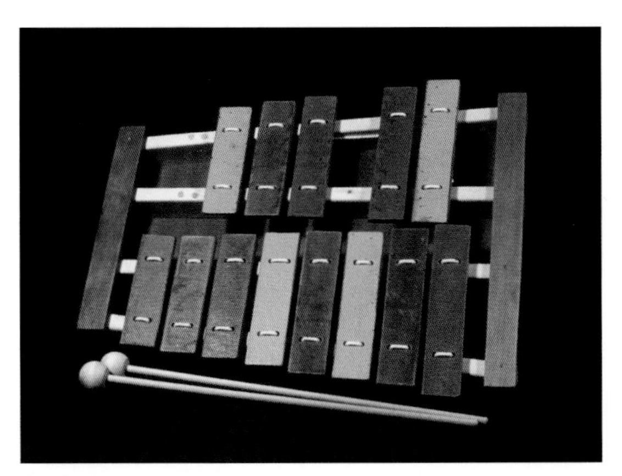

Fig. 2.18
**Ceramic Xylophone**
Chester Winowiecki, Fremont, Michigan, USA. Glazed stoneware bars, reduction fired, mounted on a resonator box made from pine, cherry and masonite. 20 inches in length.

Another example of plate-shaped idiophones is Stephen Wright's "Claypans" (figure 2.22). When a percussionist showed him a wooden salad bowl that made a great sound, Stephen set out to create a clay version. After experimentation, he ended up with a thin clay plate, 1.5 inches deep, that is designed to be played as a frame drum. You can hear Stephen's Claypans on track 11 of the CD, played by N. Scott Robinson, the owner of the original wooden salad bowl.

### *Tongue Drums*

Tongue drums or slit drums are a type of idiophone that is almost always made from wood, but sometimes metal. They are often made from a length of

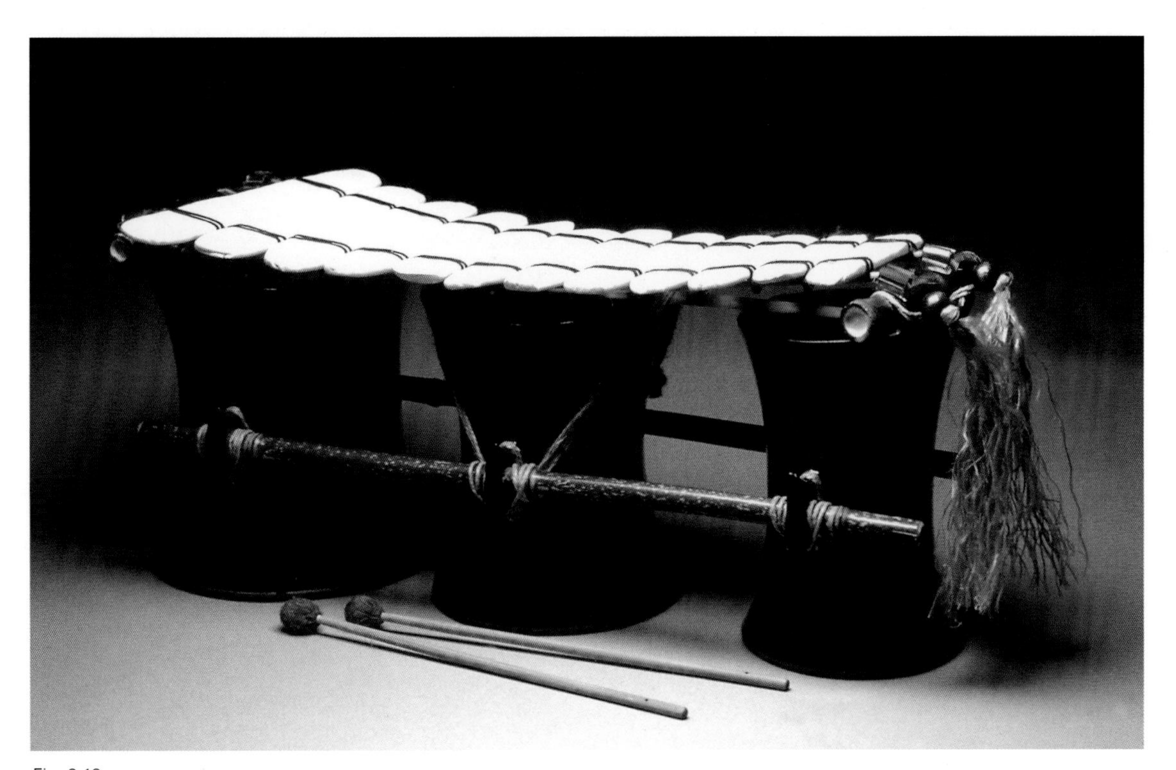

Fig. 2.19
**Clay Marimba**
Ward Hartenstein, Rochester, New York, USA. Porcelain bars suspended over glazed stoneware resonating chambers bound together with bamboo and fiber. The bars are made roughly to size, and then fine-tuned after firing by grinding on a diamond lapidary wheel. Grinding at the ends raises the pitch; grinding at the middle lowers the pitch. The range of pitches is from C4 (middle C) to C7. Mallets are made of bamboo with a clay bead wrapped in wool yarn. 11 inches in height. Hear this instrument on CD track 3.

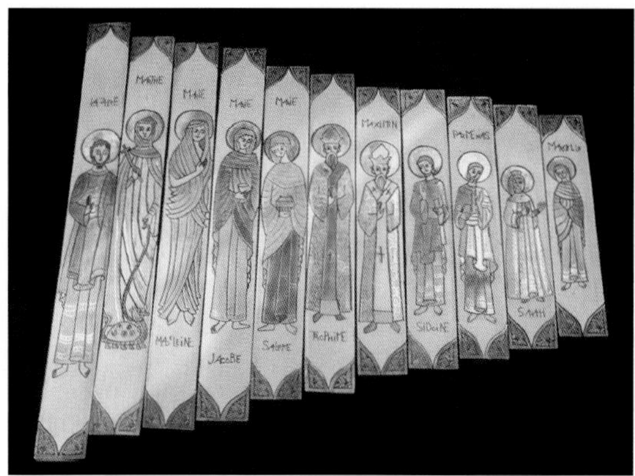

Fig. 2.20
**Marimba Bars**
Marie Picard, Marguerittes, France. Ornately decorated tone bars from a ceramic marimba.

wood or bamboo hollowed out through a slit. More modern versions are made from wooden boxes. Various shaped "tongues" or tabs of wood are cut or carved into the hollow log or box. When these tongues are struck, they produce a sound that is reinforced by the resonant cavity inside the log or box.

As with bar idiophones, Ward Hartenstein is an innovator in ceramic tongue drums. His handbuilt stoneware petal drum (figure 2.23) is unique in design, sound and appearance. The petal shapes are struck with soft mallets to produce rich, resonant tones of unpredictable pitch. The drum is supported on a stand that permits it to vibrate as freely as possible by having only a few soft support points.

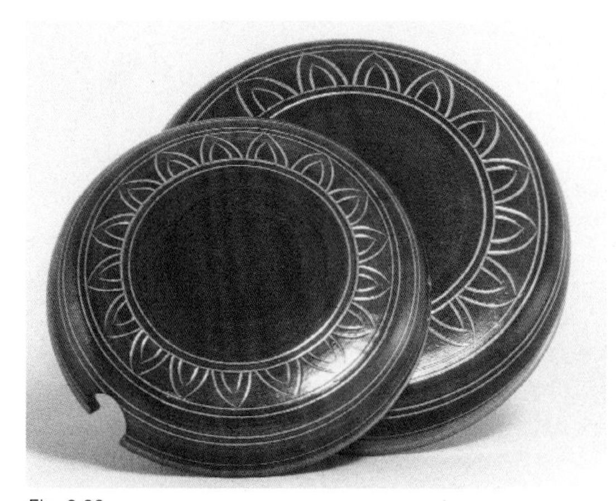

Fig. 2.22
**Claypans**
Stephen Wright, Hagerstown, Maryland, USA. Played like a frame drum, the variations in thickness of these all-clay instruments produce a variety of high and low sounds. To 11.5 inches in diameter. Hear these instruments on CD track 11.

Ward's design for these instruments is to build them in a modular fashion, mimicking the natural growth patterns of a sunflower seed cluster or a sea anemone. This provides some wonderful opportunities to develop a visual style with patterning and construction details. However, he laments, there is a strong likelihood of structural failure due to the number and complexity of joints and seams. Ward says, "It is kind of like trying to build a bubble out of snowflakes."

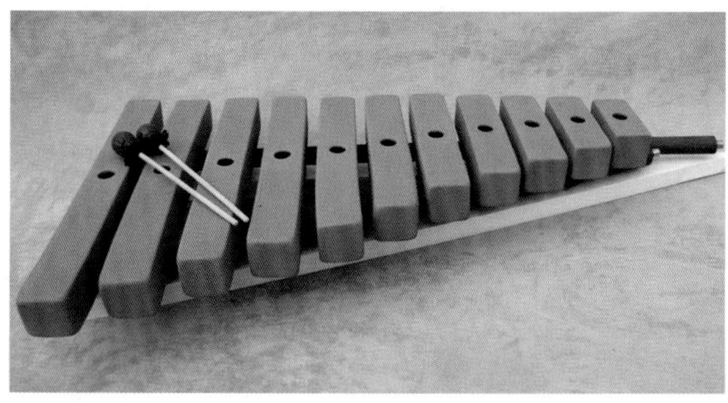

Fig. 2.21
**Xylophone**
Rod Kendall, Tenino, Washington, USA. Each tube in this large xylophone measures 2.5 inches square. Cone 6 stoneware body, 48 inches long.

Ward fires his petal drums upside down in the kiln, supported by a bisqued form. On the occasions when a petal drum survives the firing process and emerges with an array of clear and resonant tones, he feels that he's achieved a kind of ceramic magic. He says, "Getting the clay to hold and sustain the energy of vibration is an intriguing and rewarding goal, yet one that is often elusive."

Another of Ward's tongue drums, the "Serpent Drum", is shown in figure 6.3. A special challenge with tongue drums is that, since the clay tongues

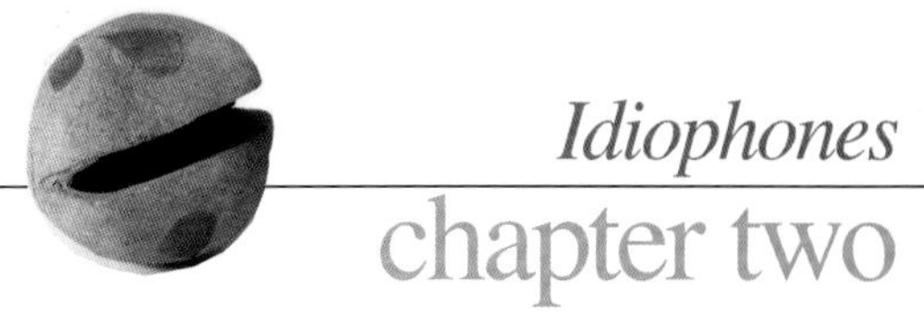



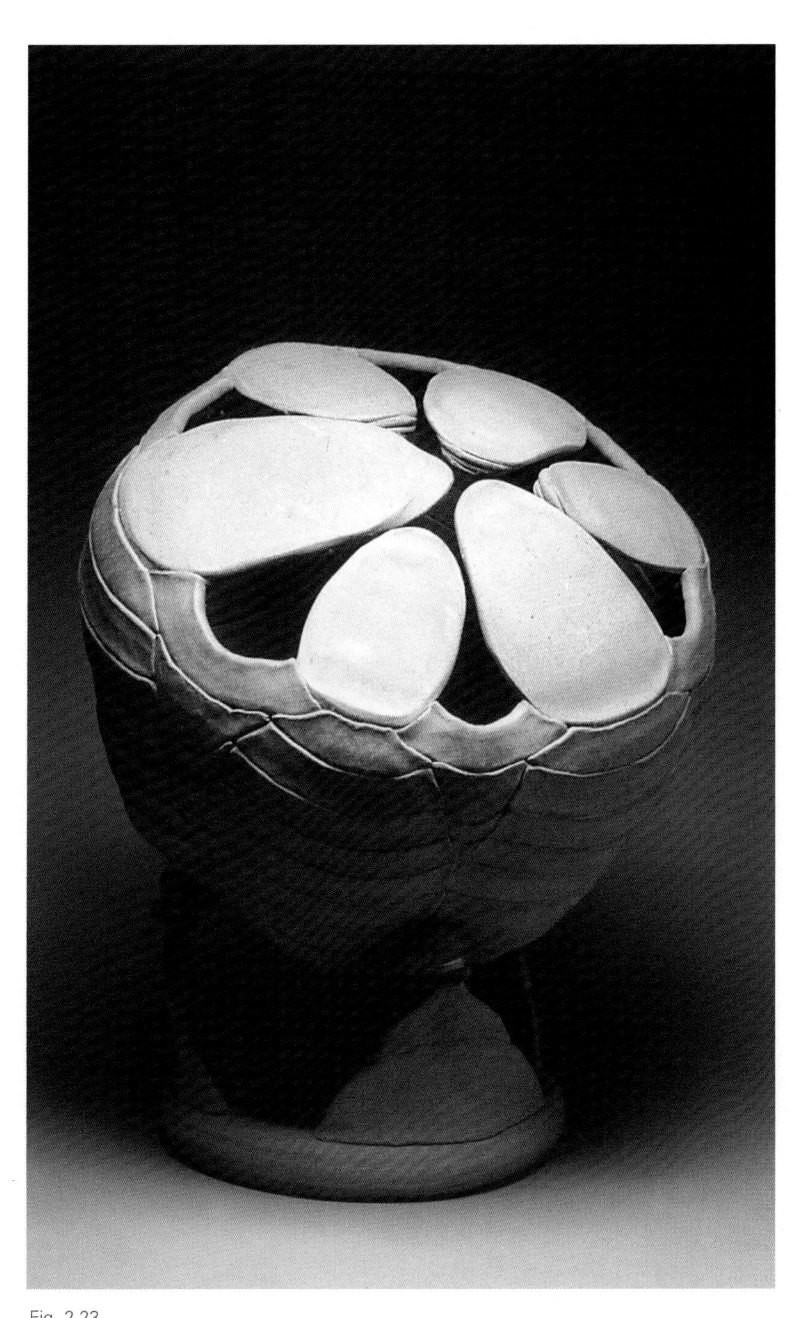

Fig. 2.23
**Petal Drum**
Ward Hartenstein, Rochester, New York, USA. Handbuilt of stoneware, the petal shapes are struck with soft mallets to produce rich, resonant tones of unpredictable pitch. The drum was constructed and fired upside down on a bisque crank (support form.) The stand isolates the vibrating structure with soft support points. 22 inches in height. Hear this instrument on CD track 3.

are attached only at one end, they can break if struck too hard or with too sudden an impact. Ward has dealt with this challenge by designing special mallets and developing special techniques for striking the clay. (See "About Mallets" page 24.)

Many of Ward Hartenstein's ceramic idiophones described in this chapter can be heard in his composition "Moon Watcher" on track 3 of the accompanying CD.

*Temple blocks* are another type of slit drum usually made from wood, shaped like round or square vessels that have been hollowed out through a small slit that goes halfway around their circumference. They are used in the ritual music of China, Japan and Korea. Temple blocks are struck on one of their intact halves with a mallet, and give a pleasant pitched "chunk" sound. They are often played in sets of several different sizes, which produce a variety of pitches. See the ceramic "head blocks" in figure 8.8.

### Concussion Idiophones

Concussion idiophones produce their sound when two or more similar parts hit together. An example are *wind chimes,* made from suspended clay pieces that are set into motion by the wind or a person, and produce their sound by striking each other. Ceramic wind chimes can take an endless variety of forms. Some successful ceramic wind chimes are hollow tubes of different lengths, and flat plates of different shapes and sizes. A massive ceramic wind chime can be heard on track 16 of the CD. Terra cotta flowerpots also make a nice concussion instrument when suspended from a rope. A set of pots can be attached to a sin-

## About Mallets

Although some struck idiophones, such as the ghatam, are played with the hands, many can be played with sticks or mallets. Choosing the right type of mallet is important to the sound, and may also be critical for the survival of your instrument, since clay is more fragile than most other materials used for struck idiophones. Clay will break if struck too forcefully, or if struck with a mallet that is too hard.

Ward Hartenstein, creator of clay marimbas, tongue drums and other ceramic idiophones, designs mallets specifically weighted and layered with rubber and yarn to impart a cushioned impact to the clay which sets it into vibration without overtaxing it. One of his designs uses a clay bead as a core, for weight and hardness, surrounded by a rubber or plastic layer (such as latex or tool grip compound), then wrapped with layers of wool yarn.

Other materials that work well for mallet tips are rubber "superballs," discs cut from discarded tire rubber, Styrofoam, and cork. These can be left as is, or wrapped with other materials such as felt, yarn, leather, rubber bands or strips cut from inner tubes.

The tone produced by a mallet depends on several factors, including the hardness of the mallet's surface material, the size and weight of the mallet, the springiness of the shaft, and its balance. While dense, hard materials such as wood, metal or clay are usually not appropriate for directly striking clay instruments because they may break them, they are good materials to use as a core for a mallet head, when covered with other, softer materials. The denser, harder material at the core of the mallet gives weight and balance, which increases the tone.

For mallet shafts, wooden dowels are an excellent material, as are narrow pieces of bamboo, or strips cut from larger diameter pieces of bamboo. Some professionally made percussion mallets use carbon fiber or other strong, flexible plastic as shafts. These materials may be difficult to obtain for homemade mallets, but often you can find other materials to re-use.

Other materials that produce great sounds as beaters, while still safe for ceramics, are brushes (such as broom corn and other plastic or wire drum brushes), strips or paddles cut from soft foam rubber (such as computer mouse pads) and drum sticks made from foam pipe insulation.

Ward Hartenstein says, "My ear provides a pretty good indicator for how hard to hit the clay. A strike that is too hard will sound harsh and clinky. A mallet that is too heavy will sound dull and lack attack. Striking too hard with a mallet that is too heavy may break the clay. As with any percussion instrument, one must develop a playing technique that brings out the best qualities of the instrument. In the case of ceramic idiophones, this seems to be a quick bouncy stroke with a light to medium weight mallet. The amount of force used is less than for a wooden xylophone or marimba, and as a result, the amplitude of the tones produced is also less. But the clay has a clarity of pitch (if tuned properly) and a sharpness of attack (in the upper register) that allows it to hold its own against the other orchestral percussion instruments. I have performed many times with percussion ensembles and have found a timbral niche for the clay marimba that is unique from the other mallet instruments."

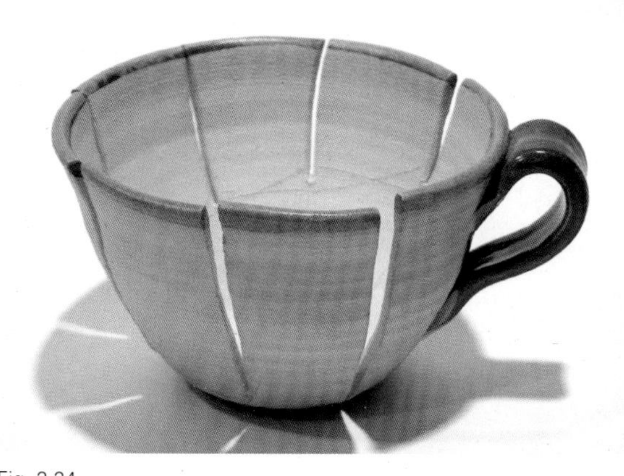

Fig. 2.24
**Teacup Chimes**
Jonathan Walsh, Aylett, Virginia, USA. The inspiration for this instrument is the wonderful tinkling sound of a cup of tea being stirred. When struck with a stick, the pentatonically tuned tongues of the Teacup Chimes ring with a sound somewhere between a glockenspiel and a tongue drum. An interesting effect can be achieved by "stirring" the inside of the cup. Stoneware fired to cone 6 with glaze accents on the rim and handle. 7" x 3.5" x 5.5".

gle rope, with decreasing sizes going down the rope so that each pot is hung partially nested inside the larger one above it. In this way, each pot acts as a bell clapper for the one above when the rope is shaken from the bottom.

*Castanets,* often associated with flamenco dancing, are a type of hand-held concussion idiophone. Although these are usually made from wood, a ceramic set of castanets can be seen in figure 8.8.

### Plucked Idiophones

Plucked idiophones are sounded by plucking something, usually a tine or rod, which transmits its vibration to a soundboard or resonator. A *thumb piano* is a common plucked idiophone. Native to Africa, the instrument has spread around the world. It has many traditional names; among the more

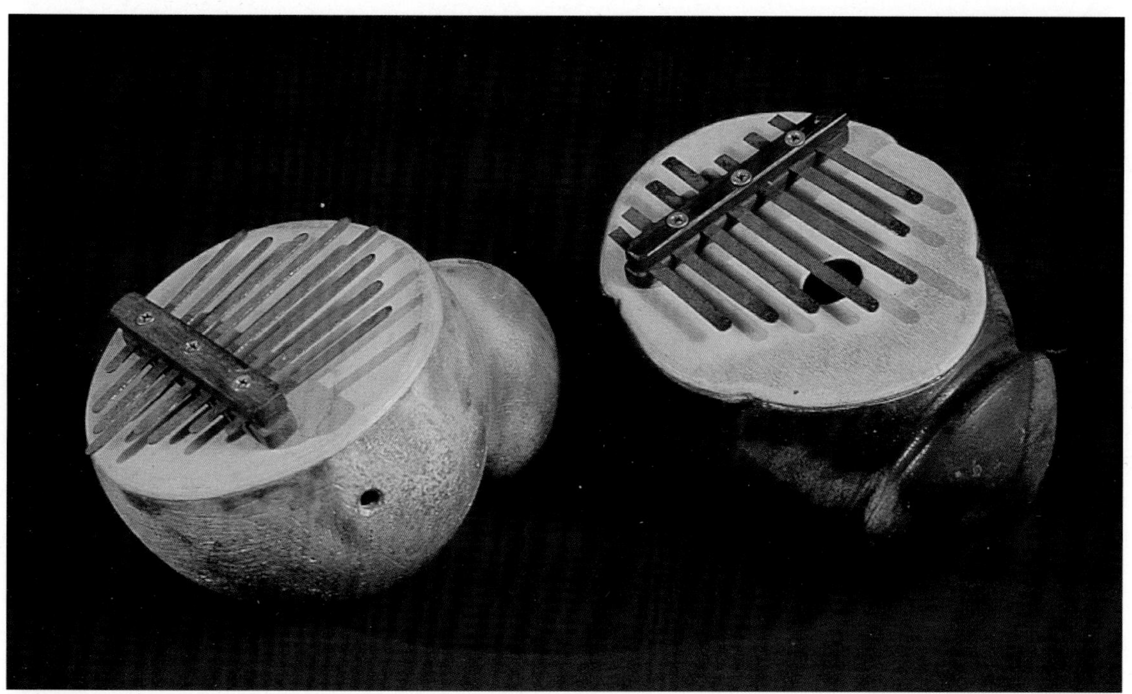

Fig. 2.25
**Kalimbas**
Brian Ransom, St. Petersburg, Florida, USA. Clay body, spruce soundboard, steel tines and hardware.
6" x 20" x 9" (group). Hear these instruments on CD track 36.

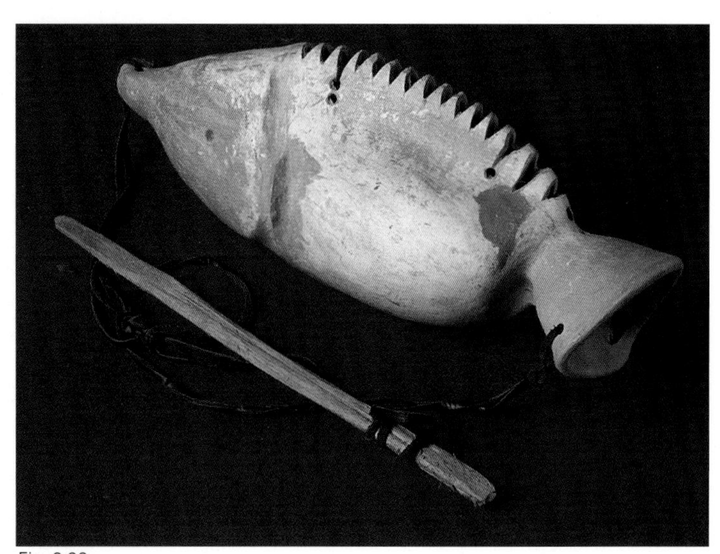

Fig. 2.26
**Reco Reco**
Aguinaldo da Silva, Olinda, Pernambuco, Brazil. A scraped idiophone in the shape of a fish. Earthenware, wood and cord.

common are *kalimba, mbira* and *sansa.* A more technical name is *lamellaphone* because it consists of a number of metal or split-bamboo tongues, or *lamellae,* attached to a wooden base or box for plucking with the thumbs. Sometimes a gourd is attached below the wooden soundboard as a resonant cavity.

Brian Ransom has created ceramic plucked kalimbas (figure 2.25). You can hear their "plucky and boingy" sound on track 36 of the CD.

## Scraped Idiophones

Scraped idiophones have a notched or ridged surface that produces sound when scraped. A well-known example is the *guiro* (popular in Latin music) which is often made from wood, gourds or metal springs. This instrument can be replicated in clay by making a closed vessel or open tube with lateral ridges or grooves on the exterior, which are scraped with a wooden stick or other implement. Figure 2.26 shows a ceramic *reco-reco,* a Brazilian scraped idiophone made by Aguinaldo da Silva.

The hollow body of this type of scraped idiophone acts as a resonant chamber that reinforces and colors the scraping sound. In fact, if you add finger holes to the vessel and cover and uncover them while scraping, you can play a tune on such an instrument. The same thing also can be done with a scraped tube, open at one or both ends.

Since fired, unglazed clay has a naturally rough surface texture, a scraped idiophone can be created by rubbing almost any two pieces of clay together. Some people find this to be a hair-raising sound, like fingernails scraping on a chalkboard, but it can be quite musically effective when played slowly and sustained, or faster and rhythmically.

A *cabasa* or *afuche* is a scraped and shaken idiophone used in Latin American dance music. Often made from a gourd encased in a net strung with beads or shells, it is played using a combination of striking with the hands, shaking, and rubbing the net across the surface of the vessel to create rhythmic patterns. A ceramic cabasa can be seen in figure 8.8.

## chapter three

*Clay drums have a unique and memorable resonance that lingers after they are struck.*

—Brian Ransom

# Membranophones

## *Skinned Drums*

A membranophone is a drum with a skin head, or "membrane." This membrane is the initial sounding element of the instrument. The drum's body provides a rigid frame over which to stretch the skin. Both the skin and the ceramic body or "shell" contribute to a drum's sound. From the deep, thundering bass tones of giant ceramic djembe drums, to the melodic "pip-pop" of graduated sets of extruded tubular drums, membranophones are a versatile and powerful member the ceramic instrument family.

A membranophone can be classified into one of the following subcategories based on the shape of its body:

• Vessel drum – a membrane stretched over the opening of a pot or bowl.

• Goblet drum – a single membrane atop a narrow-waisted, open-bottomed goblet-shaped body.

• Hourglass drum – a waisted drum with two membranes and a mechanism for changing pitch while playing

• Frame drum – one or two membranes stretched over a shell that is wider than it is deep.

• Tubular drum – a cylindrical tube with a drumhead on one end.

• Other drum styles – barrel shaped, u-shaped and friction drums

For completeness' sake, mirlitons (such as the kazoo) are a small group of membrane instruments that are not considered drums.

Each of the preceding drum styles are examined in this chapter. In the "Demonstrations" section of this book you will find a detailed demonstration showing how to build a ceramic goblet drum and attach a goat skin drumhead.

### General Comments

Drumheads are most commonly made from stretched animal skin, though sometimes an animal bladder or a synthetic material is used. When struck, a drumhead's vibration produces a sound. However, clay membranophones also have a ceramic body that provides a resonant cavity to deepen and amplify the sound of the vibrating drumhead. The simplest form of drum body is a frame drum, which is little more than a hoop over which the membrane is stretched. As a drum's body size is increased from a simple frame, it encloses more air to resonate and influence the drum's sound. In many cases, a ceramic body's size and shape determine a specific perceived musical pitch that the drum produces. For example, a long tubular drum will sound a pitch based on its length. Other drum body shapes will produce pitches based on different factors, which will be explored in the following pages.

Clay is a good material for membranophones for several reasons. Due to its outstanding plasticity, a wide variety of drum body shapes can be created. Fired clay is very strong and rigid, providing a sturdy frame for the skin. It is impervious to water, which is a benefit for drums that either contain water or are frequently dampened in order to tune the skin (wooden drums, in contrast, may swell, crack or rot with constant exposure to moisture). Additionally, clay drums often have a bright, clear ringing tone that cannot be duplicated with other materials.

The challenges of using clay for membranophones include fragility (as with all clay instruments) and a more limited set of options for attaching and tensioning the head. Many non-ceramic drums use mechanical tuning systems, with metal bolts that can be adjusted to fine-tune the head. Unfortunately these mechanisms are impractical on most ceramic drums. The most common methods for attaching a skin head to a clay drum are lacing and gluing. Lacing uses cord or sinew (strips of intestine or skin) to lash the membrane to the drum. A simple but effective method for gluing a skin head to a clay drum is detailed in the "Demonstrations" section of this book.

## About Drumheads

Drum membranes, or heads, can be made from many different materials, but traditionally they are made from animal skins or hides. The most popular hides used are goat and calf, but many other skins are used, such as elk, mule, antelope, buffalo, fish, snake, lizard, squirrel—even bat wings and elephant ears! In fact, almost any animal may find its skin continuing to sing after the rest of its body has departed this life.

It is important to understand that the animal skins used for drumheads are almost always rawhide. Though drum skins are sometimes referred to as "leather," they are very different from the soft, tanned leather that is made into luggage and clothing. The natural properties of rawhide skin that make it an excellent material for drumheads are its exceptional strength and flexibility (which is important because it is repeatedly struck), the fact that it stretches when wet and tightens when dry (important for tuning and building), and the naturally sticky compounds it contains—like hide glue—that help it adhere to the rim of a drum (important for tuning and longevity of the head).

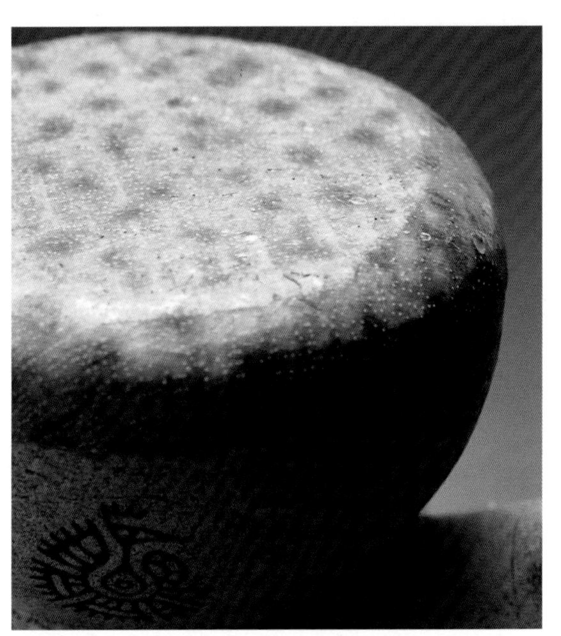

Fig. 3.1
A fish skin head on a drum made by Barry Hall.

In modern times, synthetic materials are also used for drumheads. These are most commonly very thin, strong plastics. One of their advantages over natural skin heads is that their tension doesn't fluctuate with changes in humidity. Although synthetic drumheads work well on wooden and metal drum shells that have mechanical tensioning hardware, they are not well suited for ceramic drums, where the skins are usually glued or laced to the drum shell. As you'll see later in this chapter, lacing and gluing methods rely on the natural shrinking of the skin as it dries. This phenomenon doesn't apply to synthetic materials.

There are other materials that can be used for ceramic drumheads, including rubber, thin plywood, vinyl, Formica and even paper soaked in hide glue. However, most of these materials will not produce a drum sound as loud as that produced by a rawhide skin.

The greatest blessing of a rawhide drumhead is also its biggest curse—the fact that its tension fluctuates, often radically, with changes in humidity. This fluctuation can make it challenging to get a consistent tone from a drum in varying environments (indoor vs. outdoor) and throughout the year (winter vs. summer). However, this natural stretching is an essential feature that permits the skin to be attached to the drum in the first place.

Rawhide's natural stretching property also can be exploited to adjust a drum's tuning. Moisture makes a rawhide skin stretch more easily, which loosens a drumhead's tension, lowers its pitch, and gives it a "boomier" sound. Conversely, dryness causes a skin to shrink, which tightens a drumhead's tension and raises the pitch. These characteristics can be used, within reason, to control the tension and sound of a drum. You can loosen a drum's head by lightly spraying it with water or moistening it with a damp cloth, and you can tighten it by rapidly rubbing the skin with your hand to create friction heat, or putting the drum in sunlight or near a heat source such as a light bulb, heating pad or hair dryer. For the long-term health of a drumhead, heating and drying should be done sparingly, because over time this practice will cause the membrane to lose its natural flexibility and it will become progressively more difficult to tension.

### Vessel Drums

A vessel membranophone is a vessel, such as a bowl or pot, with a drumhead stretched over the opening. A simple example of a ceramic vessel drum, from Nigeria, is shown in figure 3.2. A more elaborate example, from the Ashanti people of Ghana, is shown in figure 3.3.

*Naqqara* are a type of vessel drums used in the Islamic world since the Middle Ages. The drums are bowls made of clay, wood, or metal, that have skin heads laced over their opening. Naqqara are beaten with sticks. They are widely used in military music, as well as religious and folk music. Naqqara are almost always played in pairs of two drums of different pitches, and are often played on horseback or on camels, especially when used for military or court music.

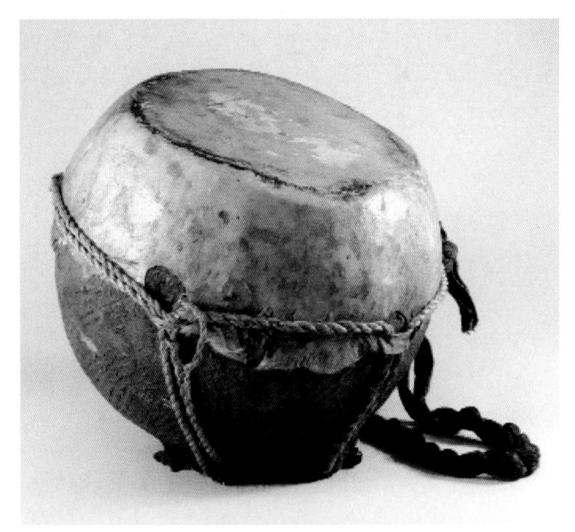

Fig. 3.2
**Nigerian Vessel Drum**
Hausa people, Nigeria. African drum with earthenware body, animal skin head and rope. 12 inches in height. Field Museum collection.

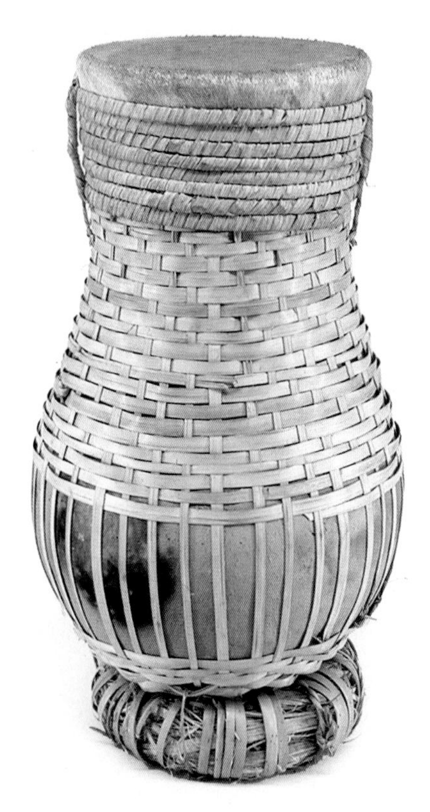

Fig. 3.3
**Ashanti Vessel Drum**
Ashanti people, Ghana. African drum with earthenware body, animal skin head and reed basketry. 30 inches in height. Field Museum collection.

It is very common and effective to use a ceramic vessel for the body of a drum. Ceramic kettledrums similar to naqqara are found in most parts of the world, including India, Africa, America and Asia. A water pot or cooking bowl can easily be made into a vessel drum by stretching a membrane over the opening. If the vessel has a groove just below the top lip, then a tightly wrapped cord can be used to hold the skin in place.

Since there is usually no opening in their body to allow air to escape, vessel drums are sometimes not as loud as other types of drums. Modern kettle drums have a small hole to improve their tone, as do some older styles of similar drums. With or without such a hole, when beaten with sticks vessel drums can still raise quite a racket. Imagine the formidable sound of military drummers perched atop their war-horses or elephants, pounding gigantic kettle drums to strike terror into the hearts of their enemies!

Naqqara are considered the ancestors of modern European kettle drums and orchestral tympani (now made of metal), as well as the smaller metal or ceramic *nakers* popular in Europe during the Middle Ages. These nakers were usually played in pairs, suspended from the player's belt or shoulder. Often one or both drums had snares. In modern days, clay naqqara are popular in Iran and Morocco. The Moroccan variety is usually two drums of different sizes laced together with sinew, as shown in figure 3.4, and are often played with fingers rather than sticks.

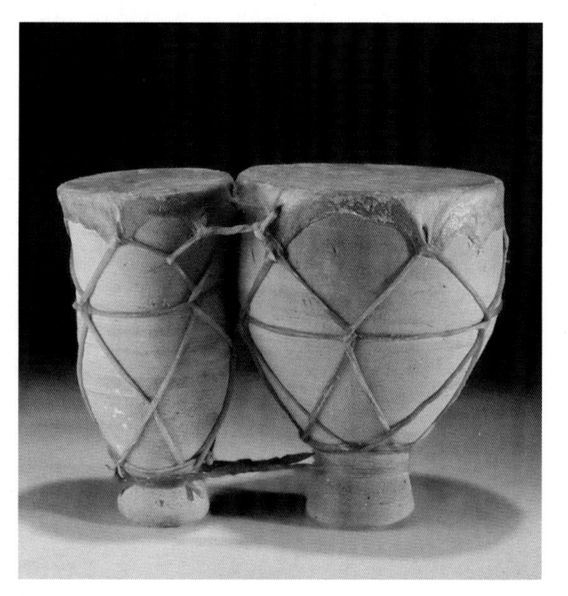

Fig. 3.4
**Naqqara**
Morocco. Set of earthenware drums with laced skin heads. The two drums are lashed together with sinew. 8 inches in height. Collection of Barry Hall

Another popular type of vessel drum is the *tabla,* a pair of drums used in North Indian classical music (figure 3.6). The popularity of the tabla has spread around the world in the 20th century and as a result they are heard in all types of music. The lower pitched drum of the pair, called the *baya,* is made of clay or metal, and the higher drum, called the tabla, is made of wood or clay. One interesting feature of the tabla is that the skin heads are weighted in the center with a dot of black paste made from iron filings mixed with boiled rice. This enhances and deepens the fundamental tone of the drum. The tabla are played with the hands and fingers, and extremely complex rhythms are learned by players through a highly-developed school of rigorous study and practice.

A number of other drums, both from India and other countries, are tuned with paste applied to the center or the side of the head. One African drum from the Sahara region is tuned with a paste concocted of goat's brains and soot from cooking pots!

Ceramic vessel drums are also popular in many Native American cultures. A somewhat unique feature of North American vessel drums is that they are often partially filled with water before being played. These *water drums* usually have a small hole in the side to enable filling and draining the water. The drum is shaken before playing to wet the head. Though not loud at close range, it is said that the special sound-conducting qualities of water enable these drums to carry well over long distances and therefore they are useful for signaling. Some Native American water drums use tanned buckskin instead of rawhide for the drum's membrane. Other materials such as canvas or heavy linen can serve as an effective membrane on

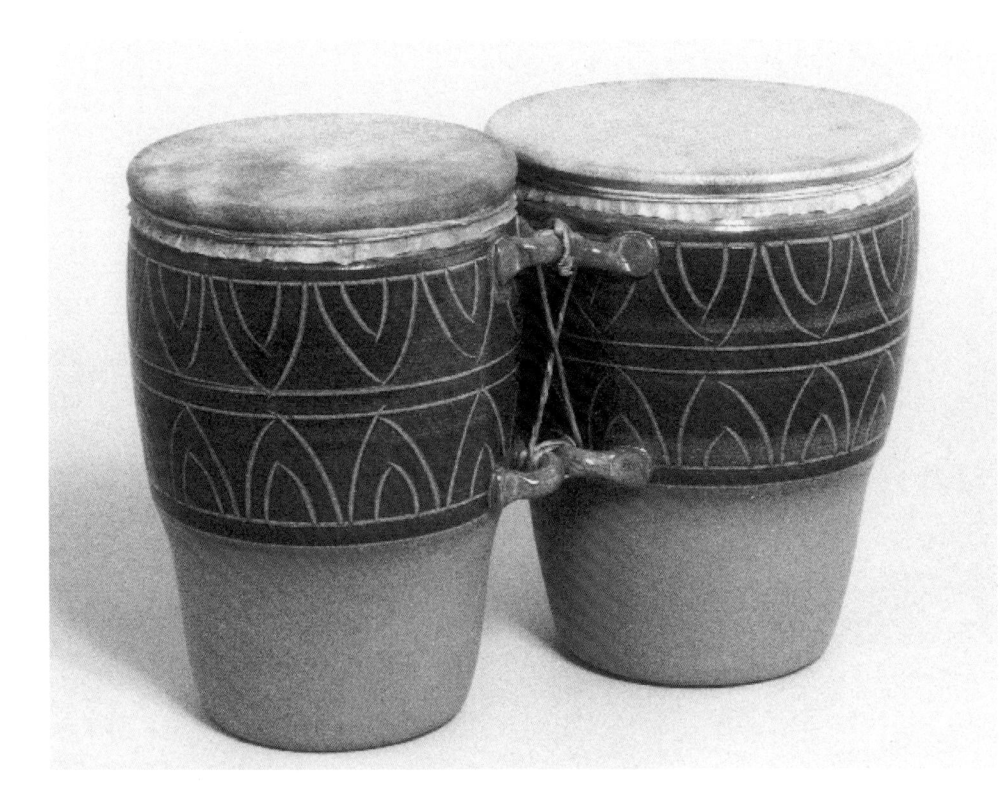

Fig. 3.5
**Bongos**
Stephen Wright, Hagerstown, Maryland, USA. Stephen's design for this instrument is inspired by classic Moroccan clay bongos. Each drum is decorated with slip then carved. Head sizes are 5 inches in diameter and 8 inches in diameter.

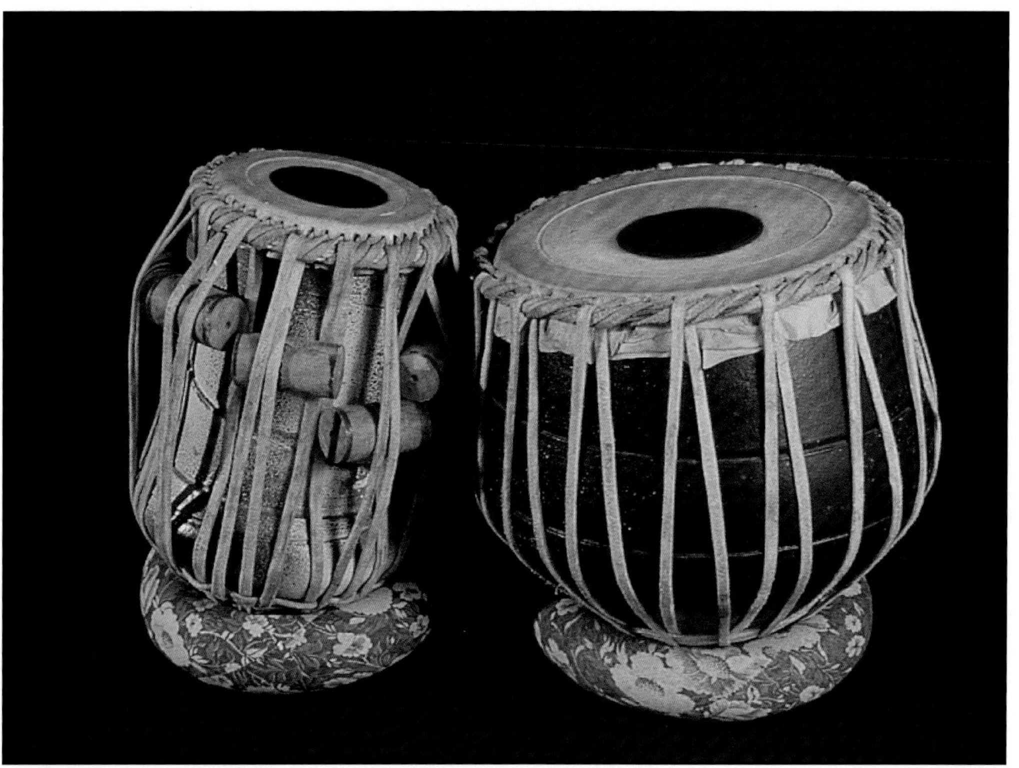

Fig. 3.6
**Tabla**
Brian Ransom, St. Petersburg, Florida, USA. North Indian tabla are traditionally made from wood, clay and/or metal. In this set, both drums are made from clay. Vapor-fired ceramic, goat skin, wood and steel. 11" x 25" x 12" (set).

a water drum. Unlike rawhide, these materials shrink when wet, which helps maintain tension on the drumhead.

## Goblet Drums

Goblet membranophones have a more complex body shape than vessel drums, and are probably the most popular type of ceramic drum in use today. Goblet drums get their name from their goblet-like shape. They have a chamber at the top, with a narrow or constricted "waist" that opens into a conical bell. Unlike vessel drums, which have a completely enclosed air chamber, goblet drums are open at the bottom. This acoustical shape enables them to produce booming low tones, as well as crisp high tones. The range of sounds from a single drum is quite extraordinary. Goblet drums are most commonly played with hands rather than sticks, and there are a variety of different sounds that can be produced from a single drum. Strokes in the center of the drumhead (called "doum") usually produce deep tones, while strokes on the rim (called "tek") produce high-pitched tones. Skilled players use different hand, finger and muting techniques to coax a variety of sounds from the drum. Listen to tracks 12 and 19 on the CD for some examples of goblet drum playing techniques.

The goblet drum's roots are quite ancient. Two large clay goblet drums dating from 2000 B.C. were found in Bohemia. An interesting feature of these drums is the method in which the skin head was attached. Many small knobs of clay protrude around the rim of the drum, and the animal skin head would have been looped, hooked or lashed over these knobs to hold it in place. A similar technique is used today on some wooden drums in Africa and elsewhere.

Today, ceramic goblet drums are very popular in the Middle East and North Africa. They have many different names in different countries and languages, but some of the more common are *doumbek, darrabukka,* and *tabla* (not to be confused with the North Indian vessel drum also called a *tabla* mentioned earlier). In some Middle Eastern cultures they are the main drums for classical and theatrical music, and are also extensively used in popular music. People in the West often associate them with belly dancing. In addition to the Middle East, goblet drums are found in many other cultures, although they are often made of wood or metal rather than clay.

Goblet drums usually range from 12 to 18 inches from end to end, with a drumhead from 8 to 14 inches in diameter. The drumhead is usually either laced or glued to the clay shell, or both.

There are several factors in the construction of a ceramic goblet drum that allow it to produce such a wide range of sounds. First of all, there are two different components that impact the pitch of a tone played on the drum – the tension of the drumhead, and the shape and size of the drum cavity. The pitch, tone and volume of the low "doum" sound are primarily controlled by the air enclosed in the drum. The cavity, with its narrow constricted opening, naturally resonates at a strong, low pitch. The exact pitch is determined by the size of the chamber (larger chamber = lower pitch) and the size of the opening or waist of the drum (narrower opening = lower pitch). However, a drummer can manipulate this basic pitch in real time

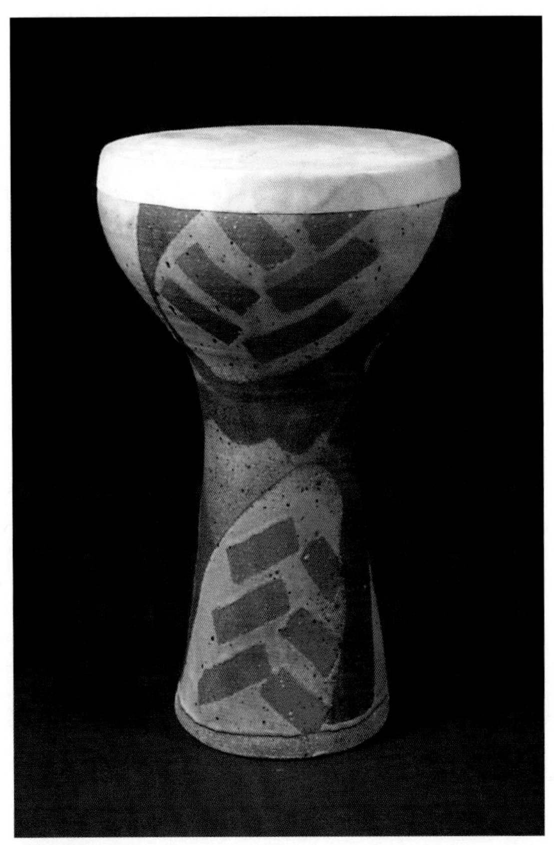

Fig. 3.7
**Doumbek**
Chester Winowiecki, Fremont, Michigan, USA. A traditionally shaped doumbek that was fashioned from stoneware clay, glazed, and reduction fired. 15 inches in height.

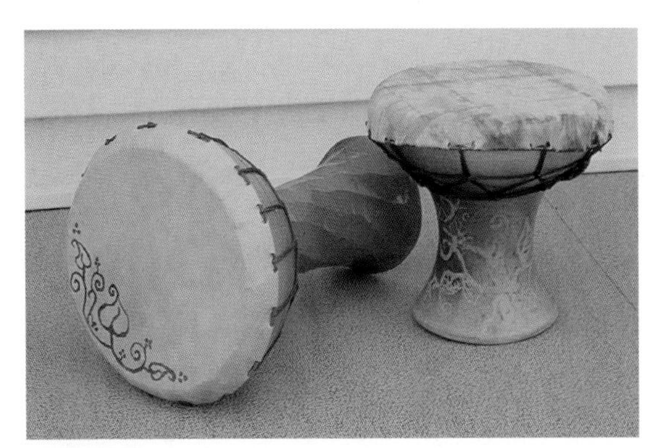

Fig. 3.8
**Goblet Drums**
Keith Lehman, Gibsons, British Columbia, Canada. Keith used low- and high-fire clays for these goblet drums. The goat skin heads are decorated with henna (left) and tie-dye (right). To 16 inches in height.

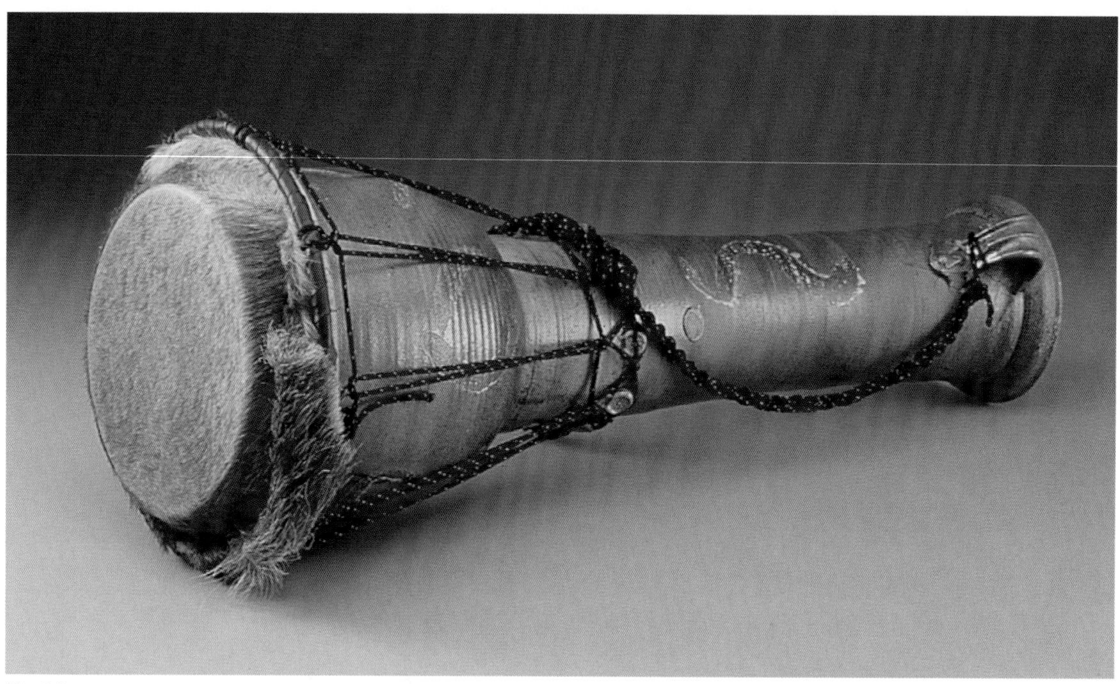

Fig. 3.9
**Tall Drum**
Jason Gaddy, Rochester, Washington, USA. This goblet drum's design is inspired by the Klong Yaw drum from the Buddhist temples of Thailand. Its sound is similar to that of a conga drum. Note the clay "tabs" on the body of the drum that help anchor the rope lacing. Shino glazed and wood fired. 28" x 11" x 11".

while playing, by inserting one hand in the open bottom of the drum, effectively changing the size of the opening. (See "Helmholtz resonators" in Chapter 4 for more details on the principles of this type of resonating chamber.)

The high pitched "tek" sounds, which are produced by sharply striking the head right at the point where it meets the clay lip of the drum, are the result of the design of the rim and lip of the clay drum shell, which is gradually rounded over and extends an inch or more inward from its outermost edge. The tek sounds its best when there is a very clean contact point between the head and the lip of the rim, when the clay is reasonably thin at that point, and when the head is extremely tight. Unlike other membranophones, on which the drumhead is tightened or loosened to obtain

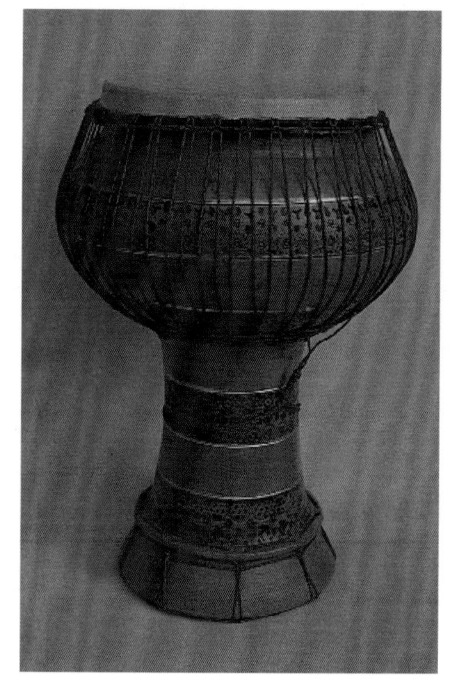

Fig. 3.10
**Greek Doumbek**
Anastasia Mamali, Athens, Greece. Anastasia makes doumbeks with this particular shape, which she explains is a hallmark of traditional Greek goblet drums. Made from Greek earthenware, fired in an electric kiln. 18 inches in height.

an optimal tension, with doumbeks, the general rule is "the tighter the better." Professional players in performance often keep their instruments with natural skin heads resting on an electric heating pad, which gently warms the head and keeps it at its maximum tension, ready for playing.

### Hourglass Drums

Hourglass drums are so named because their shape is similar to an hourglass—wide at the ends and narrow in the middle. They have two heads, one at each end, that are laced together in such a way that the pitch of the drum can be changed while playing. The laces that tension the two drumheads run from one end of the drum to the other. The drum is held under the arm, and by squeezing the laces the drummer increases the tension of the drumheads and raises the drum's pitch.

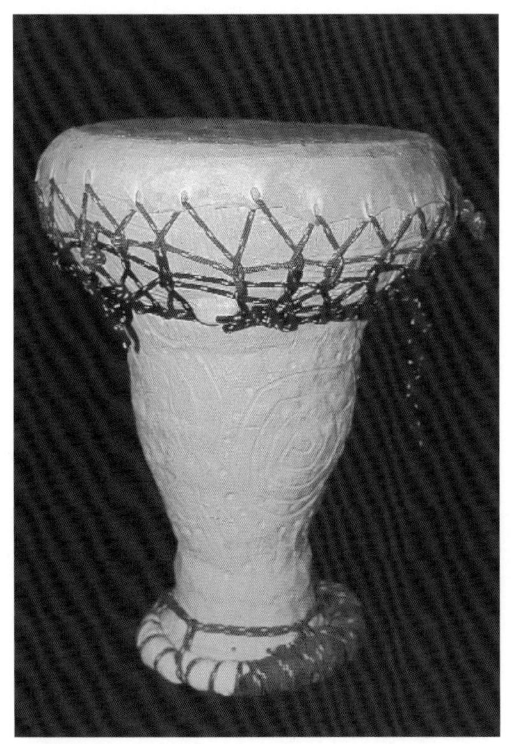

Fig. 3.11
**Drum**
Hide Ebina, Vancouver, British Columbia, Canada.
Hide handbuilds her drum bodies using what she calls a "no water" throwing method. This one is earthenware decorated with engobes and fired to Cone 6, oxidation. The goat skin head is tensioned with rope.

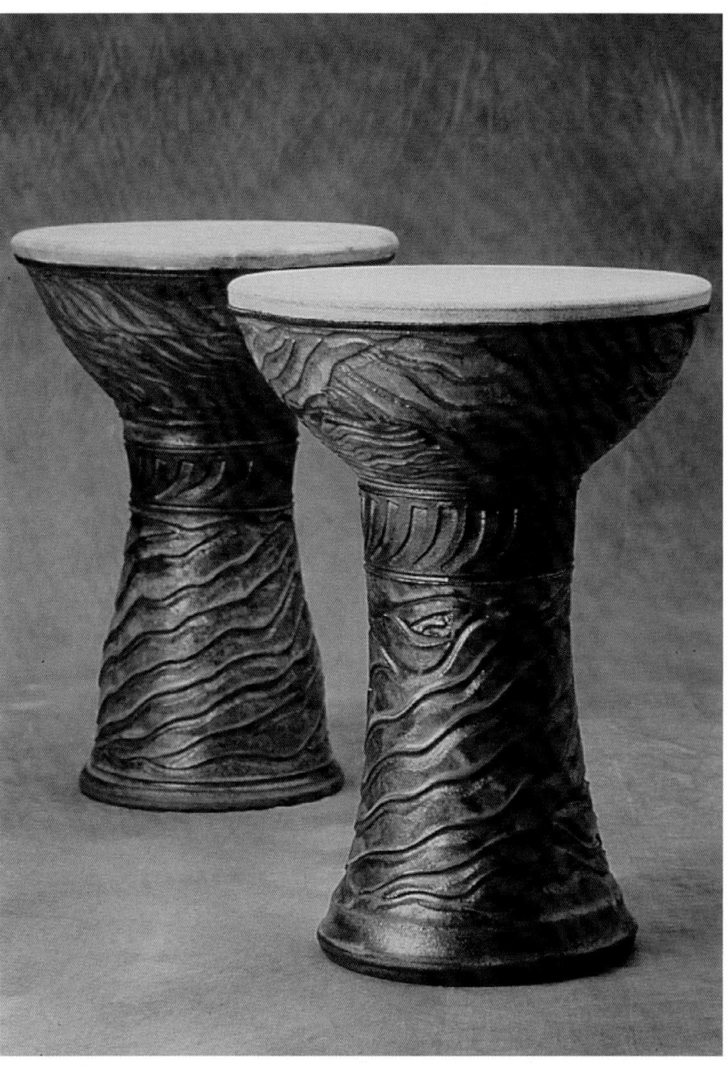

Fig. 3.12
**Doumbeks**
Tim McMullen, Palm Desert, California, USA. Two drums with a rich carved texture, finished with red iron oxide.

The *kalangu* is a wooden hourglass drum from Nigeria, also known as a *talking drum* because it is

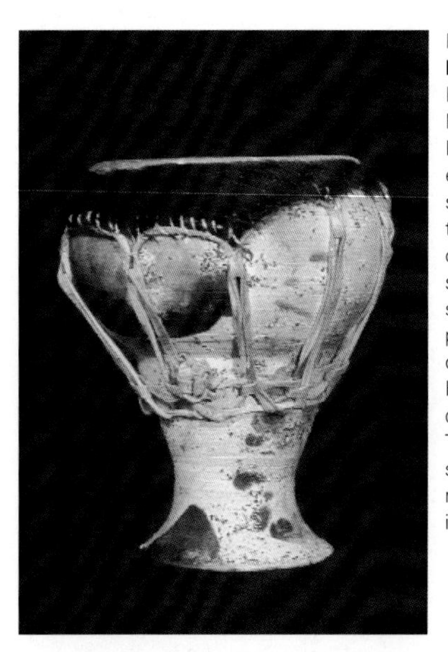

Fig. 3.13
**Darbukka**
Heather McQueen, Hereford, England. Made from a mix of earthenware and stoneware clays, this drum was decorated with white slip after metal shavings were pressed into the clay while still wet. Heather pit-fired the drum and used a Tunisian method to skin the drum with rawhide laces. 11 inches in height.

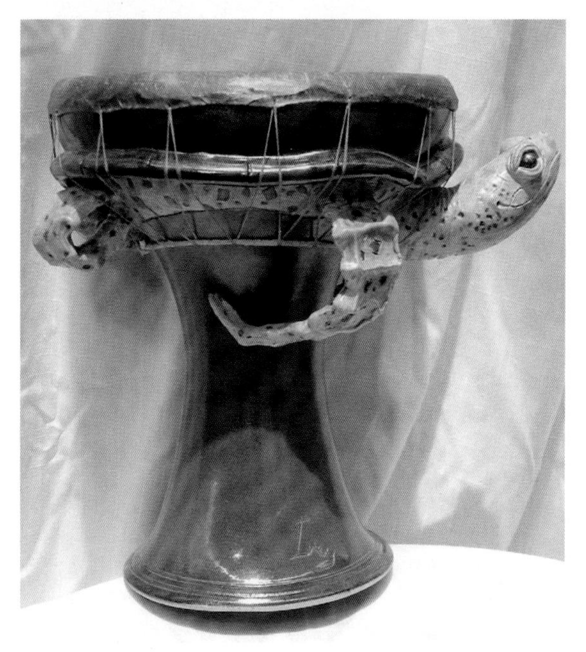

Fig. 3.14
**Turtle Drum**
Don Ivey, Los Gatos, California, USA. Don used a wheel to form the body of the drum and hand sculpted the turtle. The tenmoku, navy blue and barium turquoise matt glazes were brushed and sprayed. Don chose a sturgeon skin for the head to complement the spirit of the fantasy sea turtle.

used to imitate the rhythms and intonations of the human voice, and thus it "speaks." However, calling this specific drum "the" talking drum is a bit of a misnomer, since many drums in Africa are made to speak. The kalangu is one of the most expressive of the talking drums because of its ability to create inflections over the range of an octave. It is played with the hand or a curved stick. The kalangu is used in drum ensembles and popular music, as well as in the courts of Yoruba chiefs to announce a royal visitor or a royal occasion, or to warn the populace of danger to the community.

Most hourglass drums, such as the Nigerian kalangu and the Japanese *tsuzumi* are made from wood. However, in Bengal there is a traditional hourglass drum, called the *dugdugi,* which is made from clay. Also the *utukkai* and *udukku* of southern India are hourglass drums sometimes made from clay. These Indian drums are played with the fingers and have a snare made from two crossed wires or hairs underneath the skin head.

Lori Twardowski-Raper and her husband Troy Raper make ceramic hourglass drums (figure 3.19). Lori believes that clay talking drums sound better than wooden ones. She advises that symmetry and proper proportions are key to getting the best sound from a talking drum. The waist, or narrowest part of the body, should be at the middle and the rim over which the skin is stretched should be even all the way around. Lori learned early on that some of her free-form body shapes, while artistically pleasing, didn't make the best-sounding drums.

## Frame Drums

Frame drums are very popular around the world, though there are few ceramic examples. A frame drum is usually a simple hoop of wood or other material over which a skin head is stretched. Clay is often not a good choice for this style of drum because the shape of such a drum shell is not very

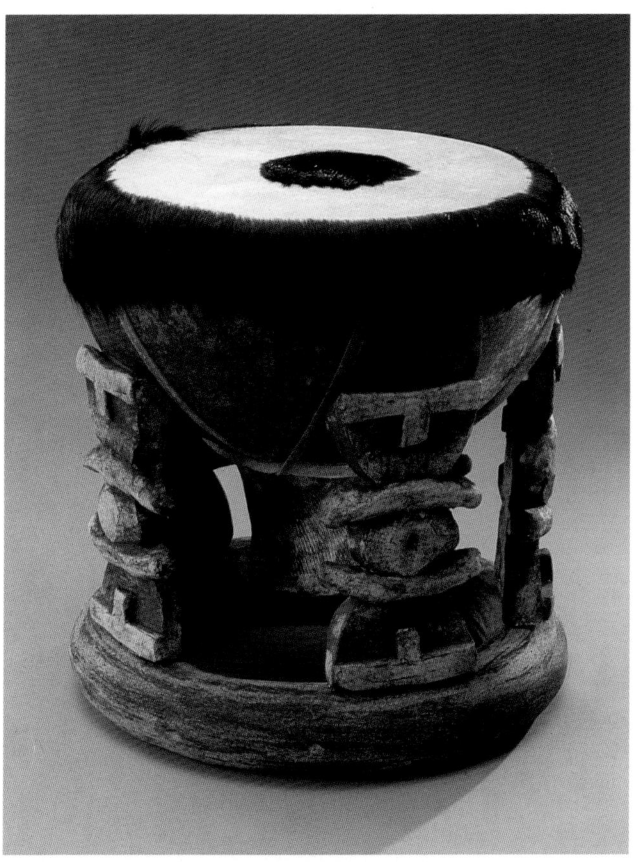

Fig. 3.15
**Ceremonial Drum**
Barry Hall, Westborough, Massachusetts, USA. A large goblet-style drum. Selectively shaving the goat skin to leave hair around the rim and in the center gives this drum a dark, round sound similar to a very deep conga drum. Stoneware with oxides, goat skin and calf hide lacing. 15 inches in height.

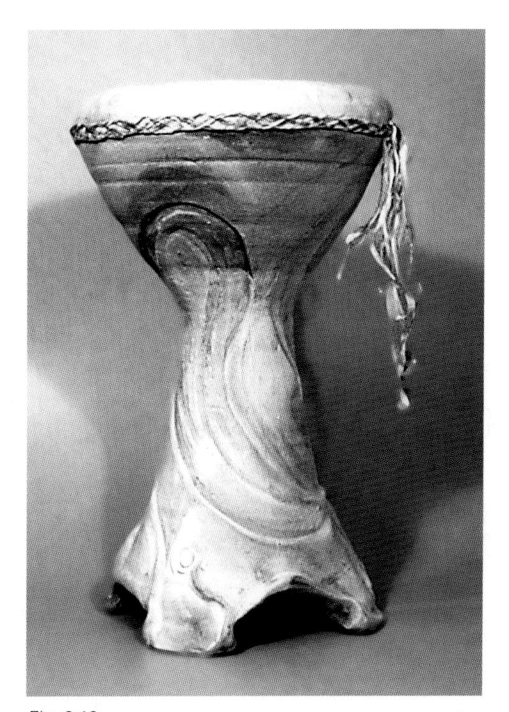

Fig. 3.16
**Katunga Drum**
John Hansen, Louisville, Colorado, USA. John's flowing design for this large, floor-standing goblet drum terminates in a set of legs integrated into the drum's body. This raises the base, permitting the sound to radiate while the drum sits on the floor. Low-fire sodium vapor. 22 inches in height.

strong or sturdy when made from clay. However, there are a few solutions to this challenge.

The *sakara,* made by the Yoruba people of Nigeria, is a frame drum with an earthenware shell (figure 3.20). The skin head is secured to the ceramic shell with a cord and many short pieces of stick or cane, inserted through the head and against the shell in the pattern of a pinwheel. The sakara is played with a thin stick, usually in combination with other styles of drums. The combination of the ceramic frame and the thin stick gives the sakara a bright, ringing sound that complements the other drums in the ensemble.

An original ceramic frame drum designed and built by Ørgen Karlsen of Silsand, Norway, is shown in figures 3.21 and 3.22. Ørgen's inspiration was a traditional style of frame drum used by the indigenous Saami people of northern Scandinavia, where he lives. The traditional Saami version of this drum has a wooden frame, and its head is covered with painted images and symbols that are used by a shaman (called a *Noaid*) to contact the spirit world and divine future events. A metal ring or pointer is suspended on the drumhead, and as the drum is struck with a hammer the ring dances among the symbols painted on the drumhead, for interpretation by the Noaid.

Like the Saami drums, Ørgen's has a reindeer-skin head, with an image of the Saami sun-symbol applied to the center of the drumhead with red paint made from alder bark and reindeer blood. However, Ørgen's drum is not made from wood, but from a shallow and wide, carved and pierced clay bowl. This makes it a cross between a vessel drum and a frame drum. Ørgen digs and prepares clay local to his home in Norway, and forms the drum using a slump mold and coiling techniques. The carving on the drum is inspired by patterns and ornaments from Saami handicraft, mostly wood carving. The drum is kiln-fired and then smoked to obtain its wood-like coloring. The drumhead, from a reindeer calf, is sewn to the

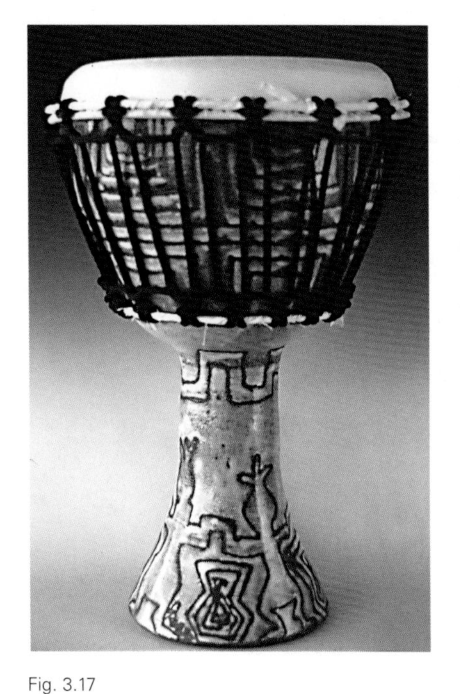

Fig. 3.17
**Djimbek**
Lori Twardowski-Raper and Troy Raper, Grand Junction, Colorado, USA. The Rapers call this drum a "djimbek" because it's a blend of a doumbek and a djimbe. The size is that of a large doumbek with a broad sound range and deep bass like a djimbe. Thrown in two parts from Cone 5 black clay, then assembled, fired and fitted with a goat hide drumhead. 22 inches in height.

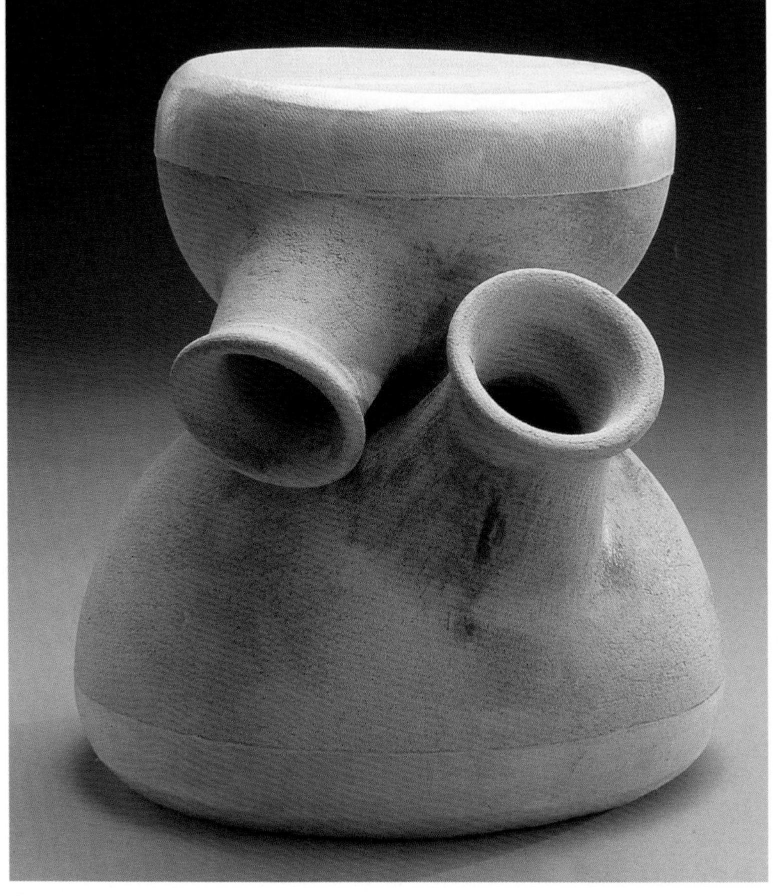

Fig. 3.18
**Double Doumbek**
Barry Hall, Westborough, Massachusetts, USA. Two doumbek-type drums with acoustically separate chambers integrated into a single drum body. The drums are pitched a fifth apart and can be played individually or together. Stoneware with light glaze, goat skin. 10 inches in height.

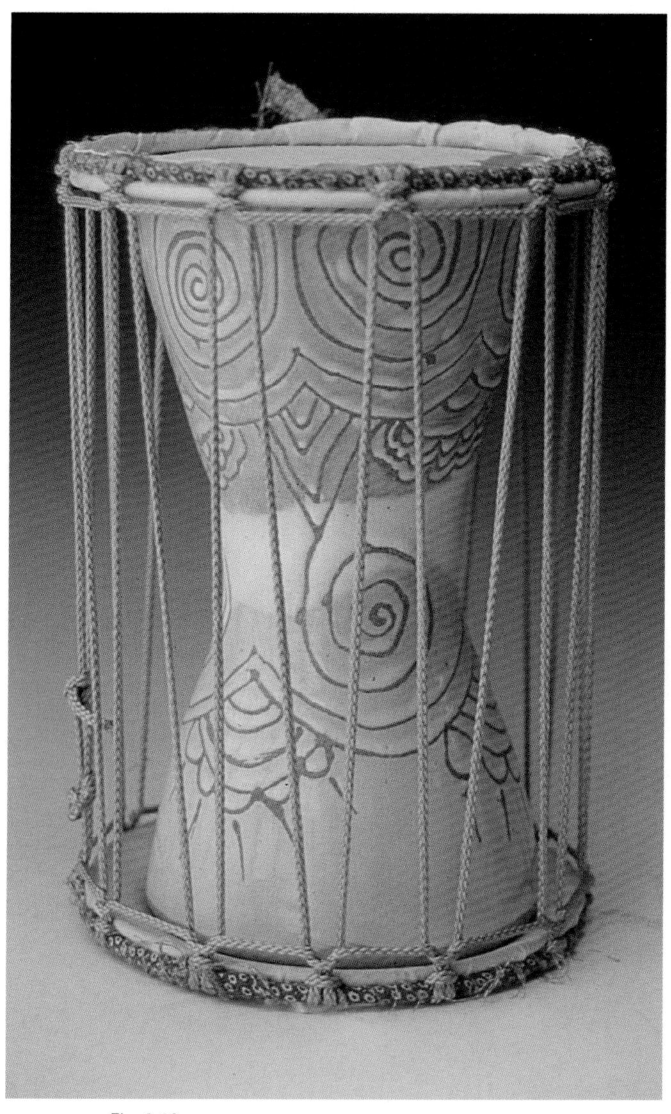

Fig. 3.19
**Talking Drum**
Lori Twardowski-Raper and Troy Raper, Grand Junction, Colorado, USA. Lori and Troy collaborate on the design of many instruments such as this hourglass-shaped talking drum. Wheel thrown from Cone 5 red clay. Fitted with goat skin heads. 10 inches in height.

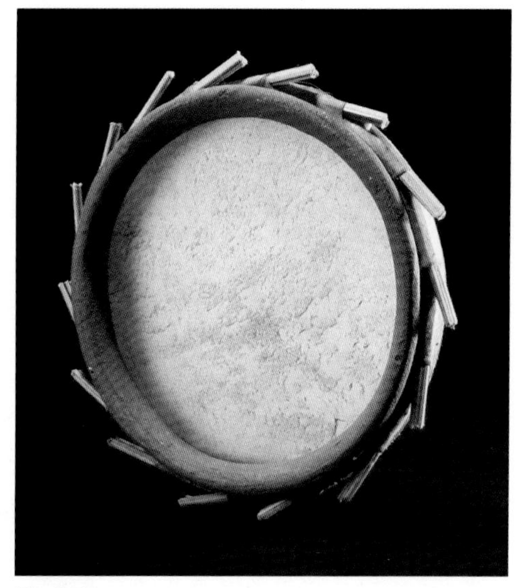

Fig. 3.20
**Sakara**
Nigerian ceramic frame drum, played with a thin stick. Earthenware, with an animal hide head tensioned with pieces of reed. 9 inches in diameter. Collection of Barry Hall.

drum, using a series of holes in the clay body around the rim. Ørgen's hammer for playing the drum has a wooden shaft and a ceramic head. The drum is held in one hand by the handle in the center of its back while the other hand strikes the drumhead with the hammer.

Stephen Wright's *gunta* drum (figure 3.23) shares some features with Ørgen's drum, since it's a pseudo-frame drum with a vessel body. However, the gunta's acoustics are very different, due to its "neck" on the side, from which the sound exits. The drum's sealed body chamber (except for this opening) provides a strong resonance for producing sounds like a doumbek, but since the drum's head is much broader in proportion to body size than a typical doumbek, the drum can also produce many "head sounds" more typical of a frame drum. Another ceramic frame drum is the *didji-bodhrán* (figure 6.12), on which a hollow extruded

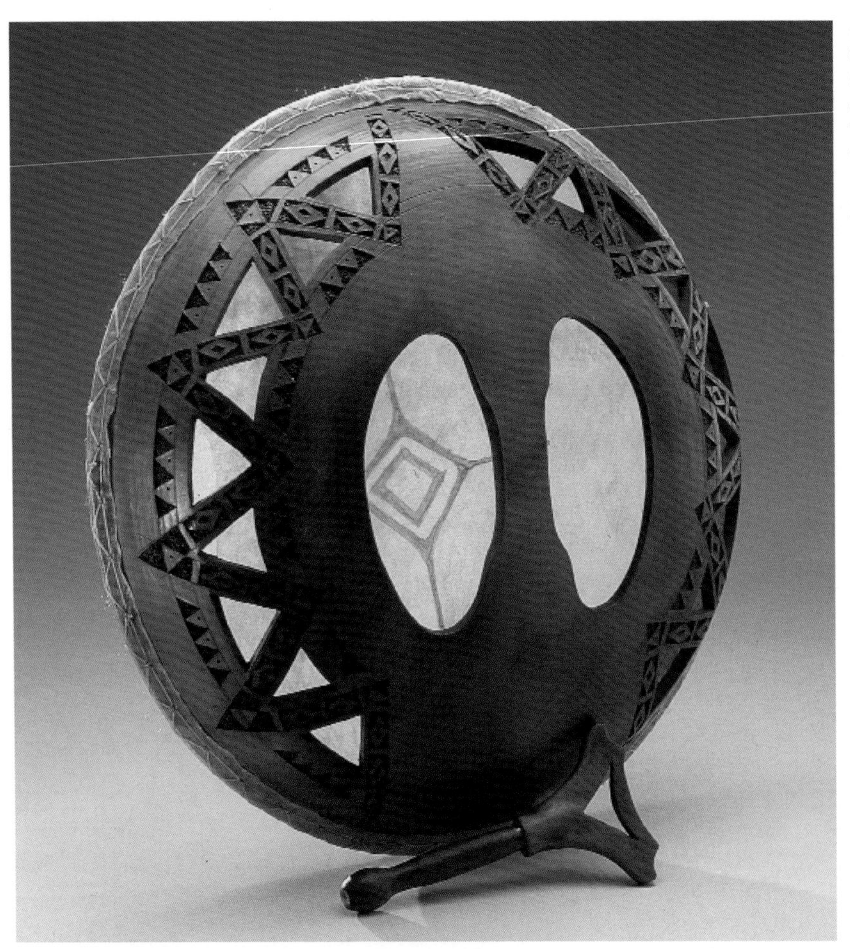

Fig. 3.21
**Saami Drum**
Ørgen Karlsen, Silsand, Norway. An original drum inspired by those used by the Saami people of northern Scandinavia. Earthenware clay, fired and smoked, with reindeer skin head. The drum's beater has a clay head and wooden shaft. The Saami sun symbol is painted on the head with a paint made from tree bark and reindeer blood. 18 inches in diameter.

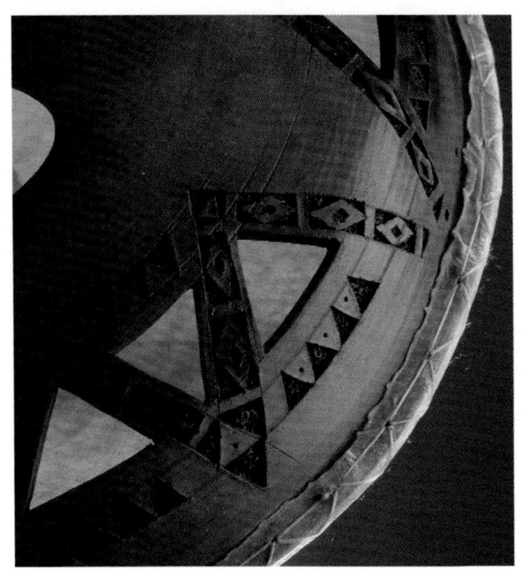

Fig. 3.22
**Detail of Saami Drum**
Ørgen Karlsen, Silsand, Norway. Detail of Ørgen's drum showing drumhead attachment, clay carving and pierced sound holes.

clay tube serves as the drum's frame and also functions as a didjeridu (a type of horn, described in detail in Chapter 4). The didjibodhrán, which is a combination aerophone and membranophone, is described in more detail in Chapter 6.

Ceramic frame drums are not very common. As stated earlier, the traditional wooden frame for a frame drum does not adapt well to a ceramic version because of its inherently fragile shape and structure when made of clay rather than wood. The examples of ceramic frame drums in this section have dealt with this design challenge in different ways. The Nigerian *sakara* uses a

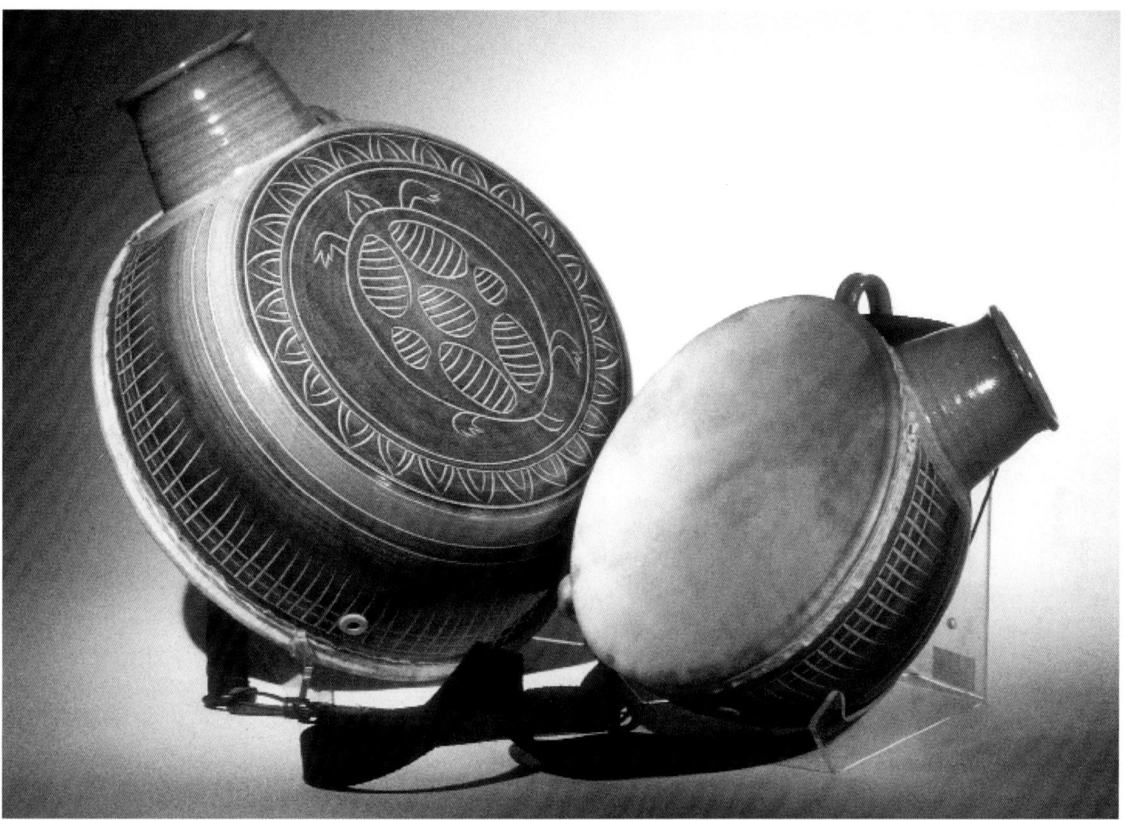

Fig. 3.23
**Gunta**
Stephen Wright, Hagerstown, Maryland, USA. This drum of Stephen's own design is a cross between a frame drum and a doumbek. It has a shallow solid bottom and a side sound hole. The bottom and side hole are individually thrown on the wheel then assembled. After sgraffito decoration and firing, the drum is fitted with a fixed goat skin head. The design allows for the addition of an internal microphone and a shoulder strap. Sizes range from 10-14 inches in diameter.

solid ring of clay, with articulations designed to hold the skin in place. Ørgen's drum uses a structurally strong bowl-shaped form, which is then pierced and cut away to approach the form and function of a frame drum. Stephen's gunta also uses a rigid vessel shape instead of an open frame, and the didjibodhrán uses another sturdy form, a hollow ceramic tube, as a frame.

Much of the sound of a frame drum comes from the membrane itself, rather than the frame. So you may ask, "If clay is not the best choice for a frame drum, and it doesn't greatly influence the sound, then why bother building a frame drum from clay?" First of all, if instrument builders thought so practically all the time, we might not have many of the ceramic instruments shown in this book! Also, while the tones of a frame drum that come from striking the drum in the center of the head are not significantly colored by the sound of the frame, the edge tones or rim strokes of a ceramic drum most certainly do reflect the sound of the ceramic shell. And it's a sound unlike that of any other frame drum.

For another take on clay frame drums, see Stephen Wright's *Claypans* (figure 2.22). These instruments aren't membranophones, but they share some characteristics and inspiration with

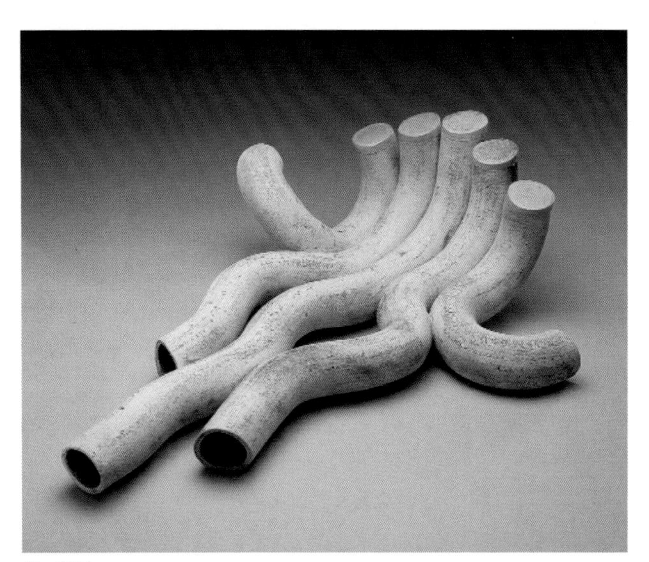

Fig. 3.24
**ConunDrums**
Barry Hall, Westborough, Massachusetts, USA. A set of tuned tubular drums, each with a goat skin head. The length of each tube determines its pitch. Stoneware clay treated with stains. 27 inches in length. Hear this instrument on CD track 15.

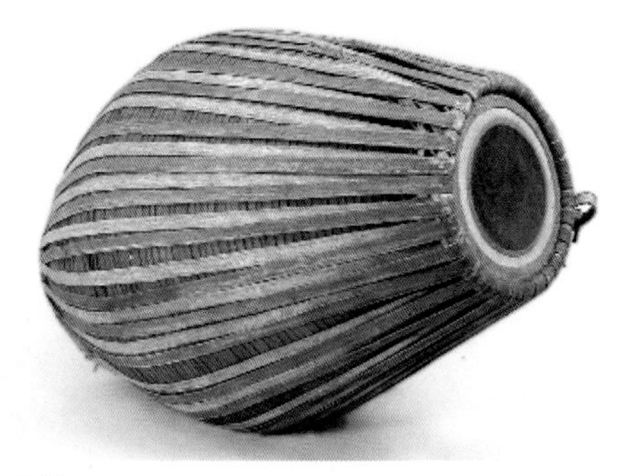

Fig. 3.25
**Khol**
A ceramic folk drum from Bengal, India. The barrel-shaped clay body has a skin head at each end. The black dots on the drumheads are made from a paste containing iron filings, which enhances the fundamental tone of the drum. Clay and animal hide. 36 inches in length. Field Museum collection.

frame drums. However, instead of a skin membrane, they have a vibrating "drumhead" made from thin clay.

## Tubular Drums

Tubular membranophones are drums that have cylindrical bodies. The drum body can be short and wide, or long and narrow. If the drum tubes are long relative to their diameter then they produce strong fundamental pitches when their heads are struck. Long narrow tubular drums like these can be combined in sets of different lengths to produce a fixed set of pitches, somewhat like a xylophone (figure 3.24).

A similar type of tubular drums is made without membrane heads. Instead, the tubes are open at both ends, and the player slaps the open end of the tube with a hand or a paddle. Since these are plosive aerophones rather than membranophones, they are described more fully in Chapter 4 (figures 4.116 and 4.117).

Short and wide tubular ceramic drum shells are not common, probably because they are not a very strong ceramic form. Adding a bottom to the ceramic cylinder makes it much stronger, but then it's no longer a tubular drum—instead it becomes a vessel drum. Other ways to strengthen the design of a clay cylinder are to add a bulge in the center (to create a barrel-shaped drum like the *khol* described in the next section) or narrow the waist to make a goblet-shaped drum.

## Other Drum Styles

A few drum shapes (vessel, goblet, frame, tubular) have been presented in detail because there are a significant number of examples of clay drums in those forms. However, there are more drum shapes not yet discussed—barrel, conical, and others—and most of these shapes have fewer ceramic examples. To finish our discussion, this section will describe a

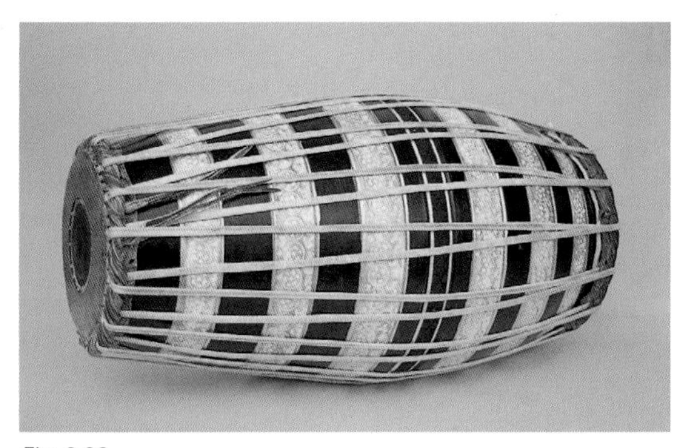

Fig. 3.26
**Mrdangam**
Anastasia Mamali, Athens, Greece. A double-headed South Indian ceramic folk drum. Like the tabla and khol, the heads have dots made from iron paste. 25 inches long.

few other ceramic membranophones that don't fit into the categories already presented.

The *khol* is a ceramic drum from northeast India with a large, bulging, barrel-shaped body and heads of different sizes on each end (figure 3.25). The heads are held in place by leather thongs with zigzag lacing that cover the drum's entire body. The khol's heads, like the tabla's (see "Vessel Drums"), have paste dots on them to influence the tone. The right-side head is much smaller than the left side, and is 2 or 3 inches in diameter. It produces a high-pitched metallic sound, while the left-side head produces a deep bass sound. The khol is the most widely used percussion instrument of Bengal and is used to accompany devotional music, as well as in rural folk music.

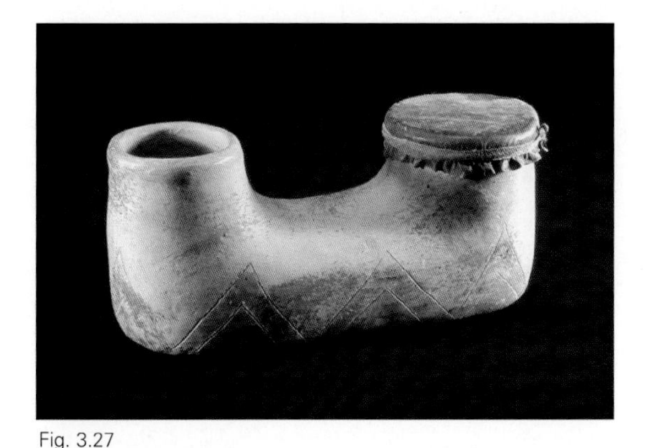

Fig. 3.27
**Mayan U-Shaped Drum**
Mexico. Reproduction of a drum depicted in ancient Mayan drawings. One side of the u-shaped body has a skin membrane; the other is open. Water may be put inside the drum while playing. 12 inches in length. Collection of Barry Hall.

The khol (whose name translates to "clay-ey") is very similar to the *mrdangam* (figure 3.26), a drum used in South Indian classical music. The mrdangam was also historically made from clay ("mrd" means "clay" in Sanskrit) but is now commonly made from wood. The mrdangam and the clay pot *ghatam* (figure 2.12) are two important percussion instruments in South Indian classical music.

An unusually shaped drum, which is pictured in an ancient Mexican codex, can be seen in figure 3.27. The drum's ceramic body is in the shape of a "U," with two openings, both pointing upward. A skin head is stretched over one opening and the other is left open. A player can easily manipulate

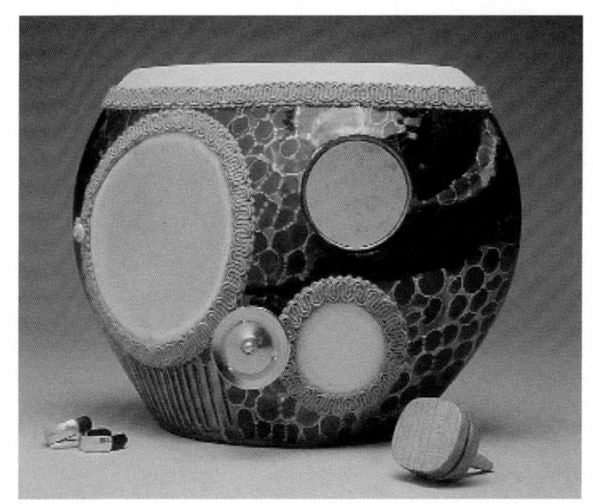

Fig. 3.28
**Lapdrum**
Ken Lovelett, Mt. Tremper, New York, USA. A drum designed to be held in the player's lap, with three calfskin heads that offer a variety of playing techniques and tonal effects. The "portal" is an opening used to modify the pitch of the drum. A small socket holds an interchangeable tambourine jingle, finger cymbal or miniature wood block. This drum also has a series of slotted indentations in the clay surface that can be scraped like a guiro with aluminum thumb rings. The drum is equipped with a port on the bottom to accommodate a small internal microphone. Hear this instrument on CD track 10.

the drum's pitch by covering and uncovering the open side of the drum with one hand while striking the head with the other hand.

A *friction drum* is a drum or pot where the membrane head is made to vibrate, not by striking it, but by rubbing a stick, a cord of gut or horsehair that is attached to the center of the head. The stick or cord is treated with wax or rosin to create friction when rubbed by the player's fingers. One of the most common friction drums today is the Brazilian *cuica*. Friction drums are also popular in Africa, Asia and throughout Europe, where they are often associated with Christmas carols. The *rommelpot* is a Dutch or Flemish friction drum, made from a ceramic pitcher or pot, sometimes filled with water, with a pig's bladder used as the membrane. Some smaller varieties of friction drums are whirled in the air by a string.

The sound of a friction drum can be very expressive and sometimes comical, ranging from rhythmic squeaking and grunting, to imitations of a roaring lion, chicken, frog or crickets. Accomplished players can control the pitch well enough to play simple melodies.

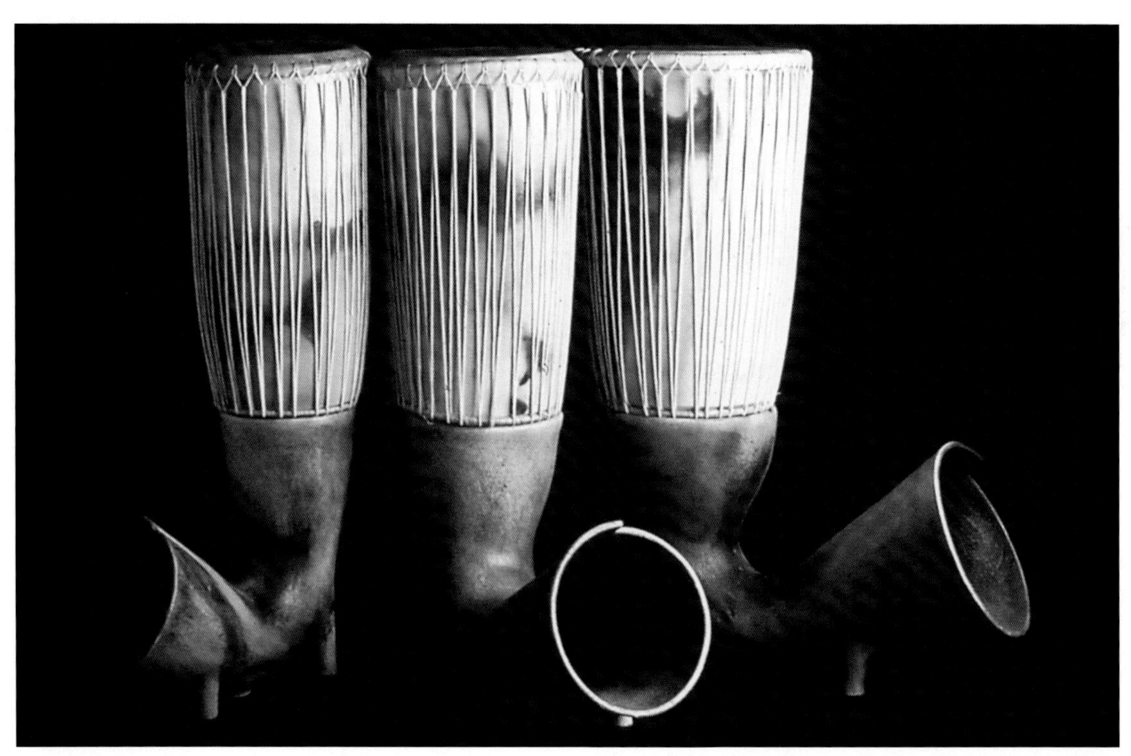

Fig. 3.29
**Directional Congas**
Brian Ransom, St. Petersburg, Florida, USA. Vapor-fired ceramic, animal hide, steel rings, raffia and cotton cord. 42"x 33"x 25".

## chapter four

*I am your flute. Reveal to me your will. Breathe into me your breath like into a flute, as you have done to my predecessors on the throne.*

—Inaugural prayer of an Aztec king

# Aerophones
## *Wind Instruments*

Aerophones, or wind instruments, are instruments in which sound is produced by the vibration of air. They can have a variety of forms—trumpets, flutes, and even jugs and pots—but they all share one characteristic: An internal volume of air vibrates to produce their sound.

Clay aerophones have a long history, spanning thousands of years. Ancient examples have been found in China, India and throughout the Americas. The pre-Columbian inhabitants of America created some of the most complex and acoustically advanced ceramic aerophones known to this day. In fact, modern acousticians are amazed and sometimes baffled by some of the pre Columbian designs. In some cases, X rays have revealed sophisticated internal designs with multiple hidden chambers. Unfortunately, much of the ancient flute-makers' knowledge has been lost.

Even today, aerophones are the most popular and diverse family of ceramic instruments. This predominance is due in part to clay's excellent suitability for making the vessels and tubular shapes required for aerophones. Clay's plasticity also permits—in fact, almost encourages—an extensive variety of shapes and forms, from experimental to whimsical. Clay is a forgiving medium, so finger holes can easily be changed in size and relocated at the whim of the builder. In contrast, when using materials such as wood or bamboo it is not easy to move holes or reduce their size.

### How Aerophones Work

This short technical explanation will help differentiate the subcategories of aerophones described in this chapter.

There are three components of an aerophone or wind instrument that combine to make its sound:

> *The initial vibration.* For flutes, an air stream directed over an edge creates a vibration called an edgetone (described in more detail below). Reed instruments use a vibrating flexible mechanism, usually called a "reed" and often made from a plant stem. For the horn family, it's the player's buzzed lips, called a lip reed. With pots

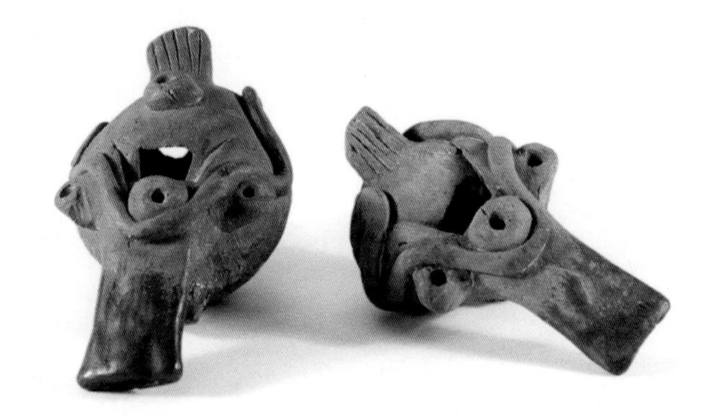

Fig. 4.1
**Pre-Columbian Aztec clay flutes**

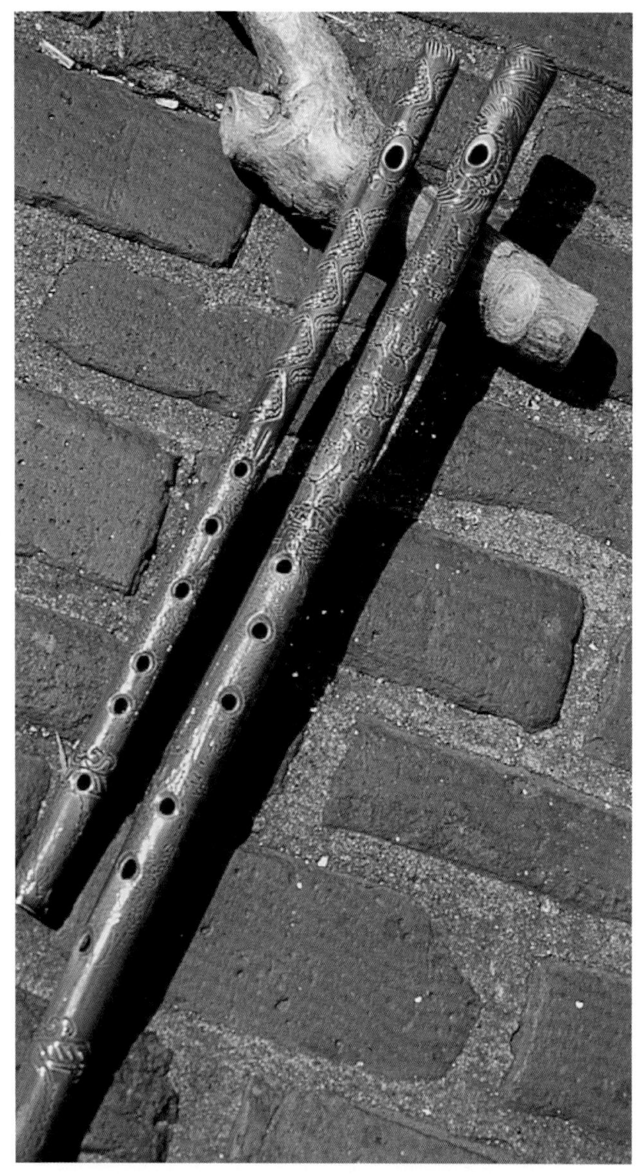

Fig. 4.2
**Transverse Flutes**
Richard and Sandi Schmidt, Seattle, Washington, USA Extruded and altered. Porcelain with semi-transparent cobalt glaze, fired to cone 5. 24 inches in length.

and tubes, called plosive aerophones, it's a hand or paddle striking an opening on the instrument.

*An instrument "body" that contains the air that resonates.* This air cavity helps to focus and resonate the sound of the initial vibration. Aerophone bodies are either tubular or globular—the differences are described in the sidebar "Tubular vs. Globular Aerophones." (Free aerophones are one exception described later in this chapter. They have no resonating body.)

*Something that allows the player to change the pitch.* This is usually either finger holes (in the case of the flute family) or mechanical valves (for brass instruments).

Throughout this chapter, you'll see how these three components combine in different ways to make a variety of wind instruments, as presented in the following subcategories:

Flutes (edgetone aerophones)
- Side-blown flutes
- End-blown flutes
  - –Tubular flutes
  - –Globular flutes
  - –Polyglobular flutes
- Airduct flutes
  - –Tubular flutes
  - –Globular flutes
  - –Pitch-jump flutes
  - –Nose flutes
  - –Water flutes
- Chamberduct flutes

Horns (lip reed aerophones)
- Trumpets
- Cornetti
- Didjeridus
- Globular horns

Reeds

Free aerophones

Plosive aerophones (struck aerophones)
- Tubular plosive aerophones
- Globular plosive aerophones
  (Clay pot drums)

Resonators

## Flutes (Edgetone Aerophones)

The sound of every flute starts with an edgetone—an air stream directed over an edge or blade that divides the stream of air and creates a vibration. The body of the flute, shaped like a tube or a chamber, has a specific resonance that controls and enriches the edgetone. The air crossing the edge creates turbulence, and the instrument's cavity imposes its frequencies on that air turbulence. The result is a tone of specific pitch.

Virtually all flutes work this way; transverse flutes such as the modern silver flute, fipple or airduct flutes such as recorders, whistles and ocarinas, and end-blown flutes such as panpipes or shakuhachi. Even jugs and bottles operate on the same principle when blown across their rim.

The edge that creates the edgetone can have one of four basic forms:

1. An open hole (or *blowhole*) in the side of a tubular instrument. These are side-blown flutes.
2. A sharp or distinct edge at the end of a tube or the mouth of a vessel. These are end-blown flutes.
3. An *airduct assembly,* in which a narrow air channel directs the air stream across the edge. These are airduct or fipple flutes.
4. A *chamberduct assembly,* in which air blown through a small chamber creates an edgetone. These are chamberduct flutes.

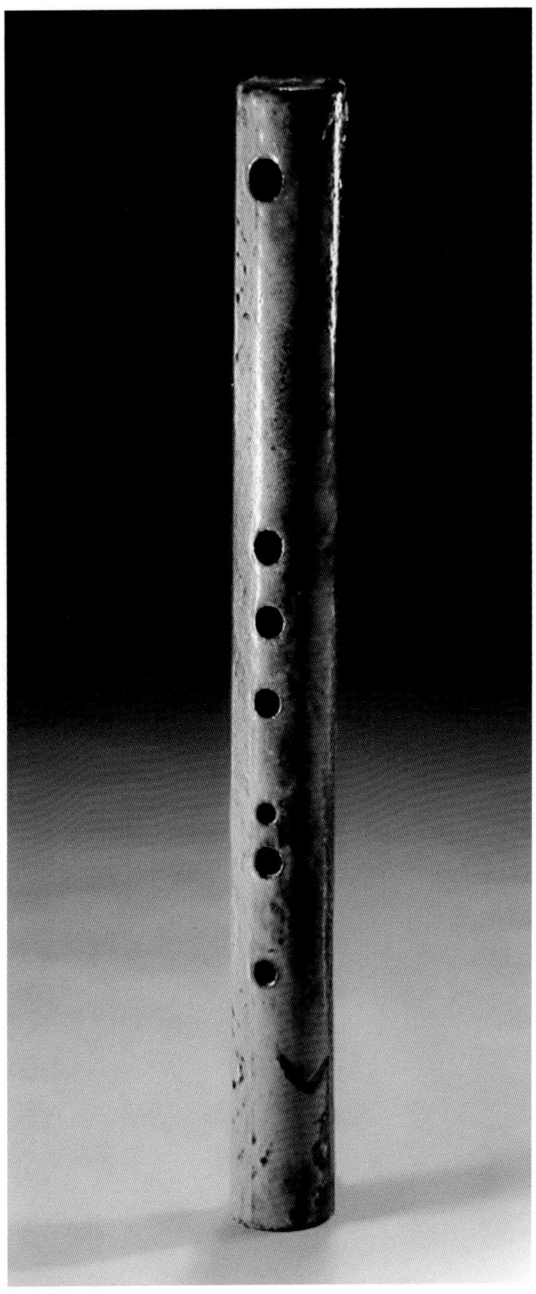

Fig. 4.3
**Transverse Flute**
Barry Hall, Westborough, Massachusetts, USA. Glazed stoneware, reduction fired. 14 inches in length.

## Tubular vs. Globular Aerophones

Most aerophones fall into two categories, based on the shape of their vibrating mass of air: tubular or globular. With tubular aerophones, such as a flute or trumpet, the sound is produced by a vibrating column of air inside a tube-shaped container. Globular aerophones, such as an ocarina or udu, use an entirely different vibrating system, where the sound is produced by air vibrating in a chamber or vessel, rather than a tube.

Although their resulting sounds may be similar, the physics of sound production are significantly different between tubular and globular instruments. In a tubular instrument, where a vibrating column of air produces the sound, the length of the air column is the primary factor determining the pitch. The pitch can be modified by uncovering tone holes along the body of the instrument, which effectively shorten the length of the air column and raise the pitch. In contrast, with globular instruments, in which the air vibrates in a chamber or vessel, the shape of the vessel and the position of the finger holes are generally irrelevant to the pitch. The pitch is determined by the total volume of air contained in the vessel and the size of all the openings including the blow hole and finger holes.

The vibrating system of a globular instrument is commonly called a *Helmholtz resonator,* because it was described in detail by the German acoustician Hermann Helmholz in the mid-1800s. A Helmholtz resonator is a globular chamber of air open to the atmosphere through a single small opening. Its resonance is dominated by a single, very strong pitch. That pitch is controlled by three variables:

1. The size of the chamber: the larger the chamber, the lower the pitch.
2. The size of the opening: the larger the opening, the higher the pitch.
3. The depth of the opening: the deeper the opening, or the longer the "neck," the lower the pitch.

A number of instruments in this book are based on Helmholtz resonators, and as a result are influenced by these three basic principles. These instruments include ocarinas, udus and ghatams (clay pot drums), doumbeks, and globular horns.

Another difference between tubular and globular systems is that tubular instruments can produce overtones but globular instruments can not. A bugle, for example, has no tone holes but can still produce a whole set of pitches, determined roughly by the harmonic series of overtones above the instrument's fundamental pitch. This is the same principle that allows you to play multiple octaves on flutes and whistles. By narrowing the space between your lips and increasing the speed of the airstream (called overblowing), you can cause a tubular flute's pitch to jump to the next octave. However, it's not possible to play overtones on globular instruments. Because of this, their pitch range is usually much more limited than their tubular cousins. For example, most ocarinas have a range of little more than one octave, while tubular flutes, through overblowing, can have a range of two or three octaves.

The table below summarizes the primary differences between globular and tubular instruments.

However, all is not black and white in the world of musical instruments. Some instruments are both globular and tubular, or contain elements of both systems. Polyglobular flutes and horns, and globu-tubular horns are examples of such instruments with hybrid acoustical systems. Both are discussed later in this chapter.

| | **Tubular Instruments** | **Globular Instruments** |
|---|---|---|
| Instrument shape | Tube | Chamber |
| Vibrating air shape | Air column | Air cavity |
| Overtones/overblowing | Yes | No |
| How tone holes impact pitch | Size and position | Size only |

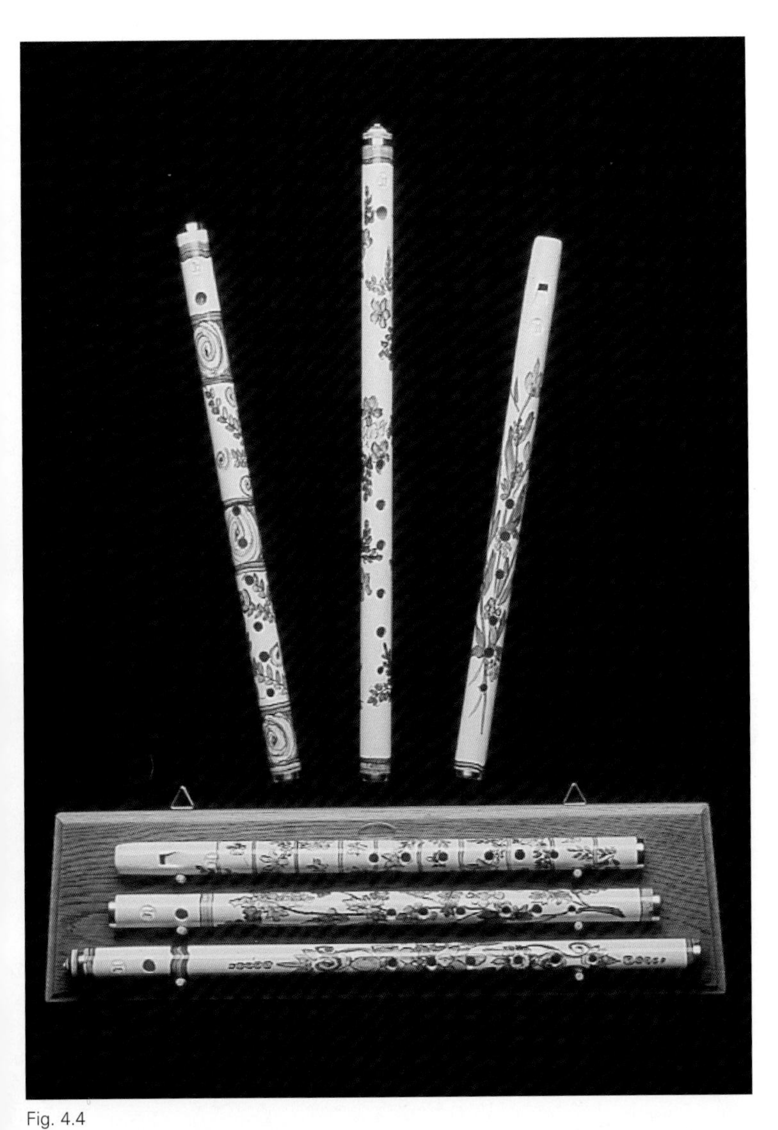

Fig. 4.4
**G Flute, D Flute and Recorder**
Geert Jacobs, Milsbeek, Netherlands. Geert fashions his flutes from a porcelain clay mix including talc and kaolin with grog. The tube of the flute is formed with an extruder and dies that Geert custom made. His G, F and D flutes are made using a die that produces a tube with a 16.5 millimeter bore.

each of these four types are described in the next sections.

The body of an aerophone can have one of two basic forms: tubular or globular. These are described in the sidebar "Tubular vs. Globular Aerophones" on page 48.

### *Side-Blown Flutes*

A side-blown flute is also called a *transverse* flute, because the airstream is blown across the axis of its length, rather than along it. Most ceramic side-blown flutes are "simple flutes," which means that they have open finger holes, rather than the mechanical keys that are used on most modern metal and wooden flutes.

A ceramic simple flute is a tube of clay. One end is stopped, and the other end is open. The end can be stopped with clay before firing, or the tube can be fired with both ends open, and stopped with a cork afterward. Near the stopped end is a mouth hole. Finger holes, or tone holes, are cut into the body of the flute and are stopped with the player's fingers to produce different tones or pitches. Most simple flutes have between four and six tone holes.

The inside cavity of the flute's tubular body is called the *bore*. The bore can have either a cylindrical shape (where the bore is the same diameter for the entire length of the flute) or conical (where the bore tapers slightly, being widest at the stopped end). A conical bore is common in traditional Irish wooden flutes and gives a warmer and softer tone, whereas a cylindrical bore generally gives a brighter sound. Since a conical bore is more difficult to create, most ceramic flutes (and non-ceramic flutes) that you'll find have cylindrical bores. Modern concert flutes are tapered at the top end near the mouthhole, and then even out to a cylindrical bore for the rest of their length. Concert flutes

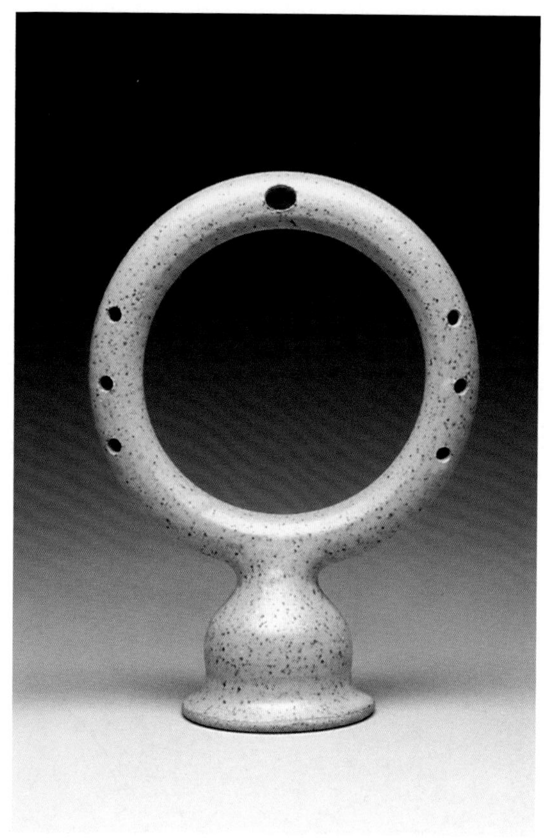

Fig. 4.5
**Circle Flute**
Ward Hartenstein, Rochester, New York, USA. A wheel-thrown form with an attached bell, it has a standard flute embouchure with three finger holes on each side. Ward says that the tuning is somewhat inexact, but has a vaguely Middle Eastern sound. 8 inches in height. Hear this instrument on CD track 3.

are very carefully crafted with great precision, and their designs are the result of many years of experimentation and refinement. However, this level of precision is not required to make a great sounding flute out of clay or other natural materials.

Chapter 10 demonstrates how to make a ceramic side-blown flute. Listen to track 30 on the CD to hear a solo ceramic side-blown flute. Tracks 2, 9 and 21 also feature side-blown flutes, played with other ceramic instruments.

Ancient ceramic side-blown flutes are relatively uncommon. In pre-Columbian cultures, (the pre-eminent clay flute makers of all time), airduct and end-blown flutes were much more prevalent than side-blown flutes.

### *End-Blown Flutes*

End-blown flutes have an open end that is blown across to create their sound. **Tubular end-blown flutes** include the *ney, shakuhachi* and *quena.* All of these traditional instruments are most commonly made from cane, a naturally hollow material well-suited for flute making. They are open at the top and bottom, and have finger holes. The player blows across the edge of the open top end of the flute (in the same way you would blow across the top of a bottle to make a tone). Some types, such as the *quena,* have a U- or V-shaped notch cut in the top edge against which the player blows to create the edgetone. For this reason, they are also referred to as *notch flutes.*

Ceramic quenas were made by the Chancay people (1300-1438 A.D.) on the coast of Peru. These were made in the *blackware* style, an ancient pottery firing technique which produced rich black-colored ware. A modern ceramic quena can be seen in figure 4.7.

*Panpipes* are tuned sets of pipes stopped at the bottom and held together in a row, like a raft. The pipes are sounded by blowing across the tops of the pipes, with each tube giving a single pitch, based on its length. The pipes in a typical set range from three to twelve inches long, and there may be from three to forty pipes in a single set. A set of panpipes is also known as a *syrinx.*

Panpipes are traditional to many cultures around the world. They are most commonly made from cane or wood, and the individual pipes are lashed together with cord or leather. In certain

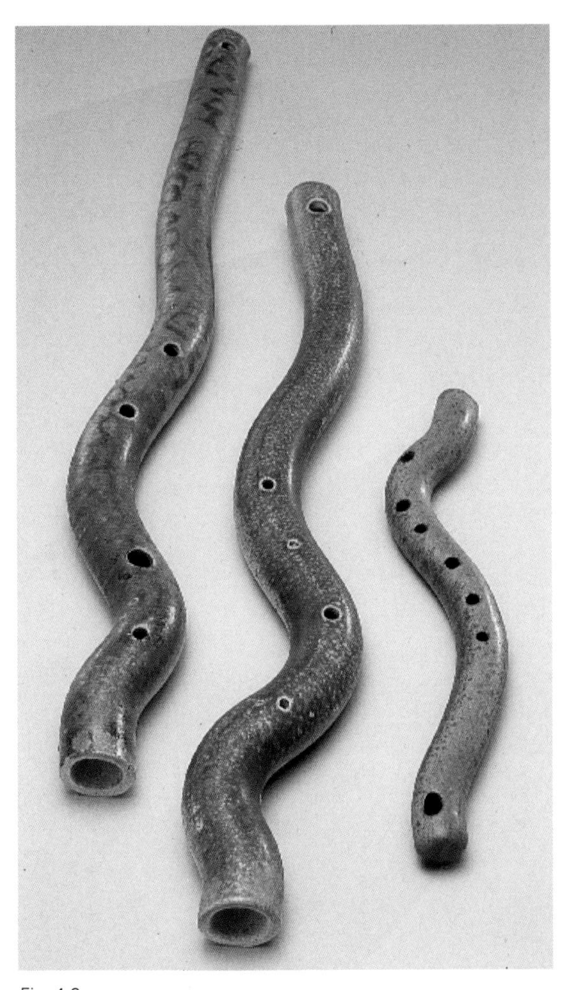

Fig. 4.6
**Curved Flutes**
Barry Hall, Westborough, Massachusetts, USA. Three curved flutes made from glazed stoneware. The two on the left produce four-hole pentatonic scales; the one on the right produces a six-hole diatonic scale. The flute bodies are curved to mirror the shape and position of the player's hands. 25, 23 and 14 inches long.

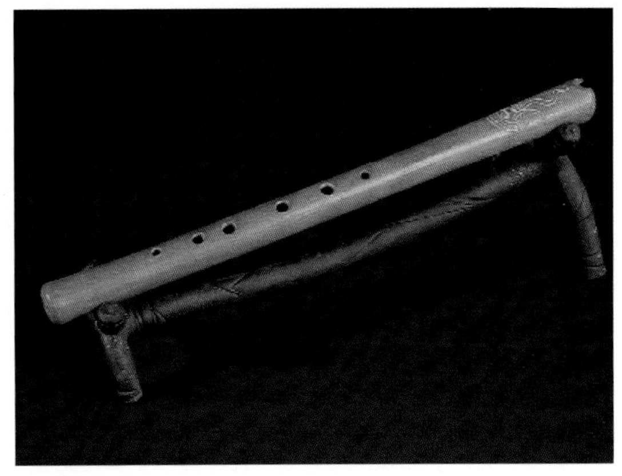

Fig. 4.7
**Notch Flute**
Brian Ransom, St. Petersburg, Florida, USA. Vapor-fired ceramic. 24 inches in length.

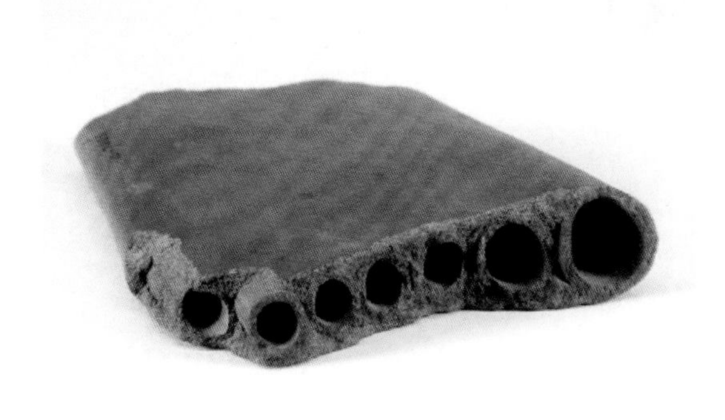

Fig. 4.8
**Pre-Columbian Ceramic Panpipe Fragment**
From Peru, near Supe. Note the precise construction and graduated pipe diameters. 5 inches in length. Collection of the Phoebe Apperson Hearst Museum

parts of South America they were also made from clay, most notably by the Nazca culture of Peru (200 B.C. – 600 A.D.). Figure 4.8 shows a fragment of pre-Columbian ceramic panpipes. Modern clay panpipes made by Dag Sørensen and Brian Ransom are shown in figures 4.9 and 7.3 and can be heard on track 36 of the CD.

**Globular end-blown flutes,** unlike their tubular cousins, are most commonly made from clay. An example is the traditional Chinese *xun* (or *hsün* or *hsuan*), a small egg-shaped ceramic vessel with several finger holes (figure 4.10). With origins reaching back at least 6,000 years in China, the xun is used for Confucian rituals as well as everyday

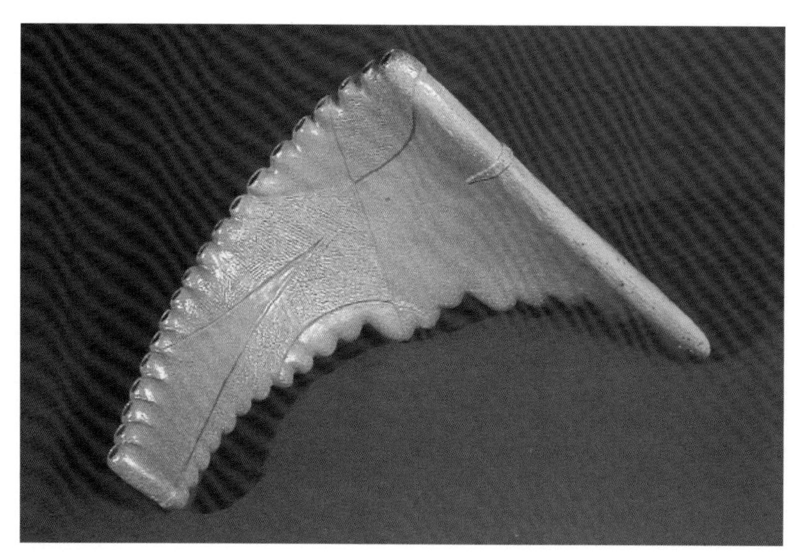

Fig. 4.9
**Pan-Flute**
Brian Ransom, St. Petersburg, Florida, USA. Vapor-fired ceramic. 18 inches in length.
Hear this instrument on CD track 36.

music-making. Similar instruments are traditional to Korea, Vietnam and Japan.

The xun is played by blowing across the open hole at the top or apex of its egg-shaped body. Finger holes on the instrument can be opened or closed to change the pitch. The earliest xuns had two or three finger holes, but "modern" instruments (made in the last 1000 years) have from six to eight holes for the fingers and thumbs of each hand. The range of these instruments is usually an octave or less. In 1961, Pen-Li Chuang set out to improve the design and capability of the traditional xun. He developed and built a porcelain model with sixteen holes, capable of producing all the chromatic scale tones over the range of an octave plus a third. With this instrument, each finger covers two holes, which can be opened individually or simultaneously to obtain different pitches.

Some xuns are elaborately decorated, often having a multicolored dragon or phoenix painted on or incised into the clay. Others are very simple, with a plain black traditional finish as shown in figure 4.10.

Xuns are related to ocarinas (described in the next section) but are more primitive because they lack the ocarina's airduct assembly. However, this "limitation" does have a benefit: It allows a player more freedom to alter the pitch or sound of the instrument by changing the shape and position of their lips. For example, an additional tone below the lowest pitch can often be produced by turning the lips down and blowing lightly.

Another globular end-blown flute is the ceramic jug, a large vessel with a small, narrow neck. Blown across the top to produce a low, pulsing bass tone, this instrument is popular in some types of American folk music, such as the "jug band" popularized by black musicians in the southern United States in the 1920s and '30s. Jugs are also played in this manner for bass accompaniment in certain types of folk music in many other countries.

Instruments played by the wind, rather than human breath, are called *aeolian* instruments. A ceramic aeolian aerophone from China's Han dynasty (206 B.C.–220 A.D.) took the form of a whistling roof ornament that depicted an animal sitting on a pole. Wind blowing over the rooftop sounded the instrument by blowing across the vessel's open mouth.

A clever pre-Columbian aeolian double globular flute from around 500 A.D. depicts two female figures seated on a swing. Each figure has a whistle mouthpiece incorporated into her back. When the swing is set into motion, the resulting airflow causes the whistles to sound.

A more complex aeolian aerophone is the Portugese singing windmill. Portugal, a country exposed to strong winds from the Atlantic Ocean, has long used wind power, as has much of Europe for approximately 1000 years. However, some Portugese windmills have the unique feature of ceramic vessels. These earthenware jugs are positioned in such a way that when the bars or blades of the windmill turn, air currents across the mouths of the jars cause them to emit a chorus of flutelike sounds, which vary according to the wind speed and weather conditions.

According to Dr. Jorge Miranda, the president of the Portuguese section of the International Molinological Society (*molinology* is the study of mills powered by wind, water or animals), the

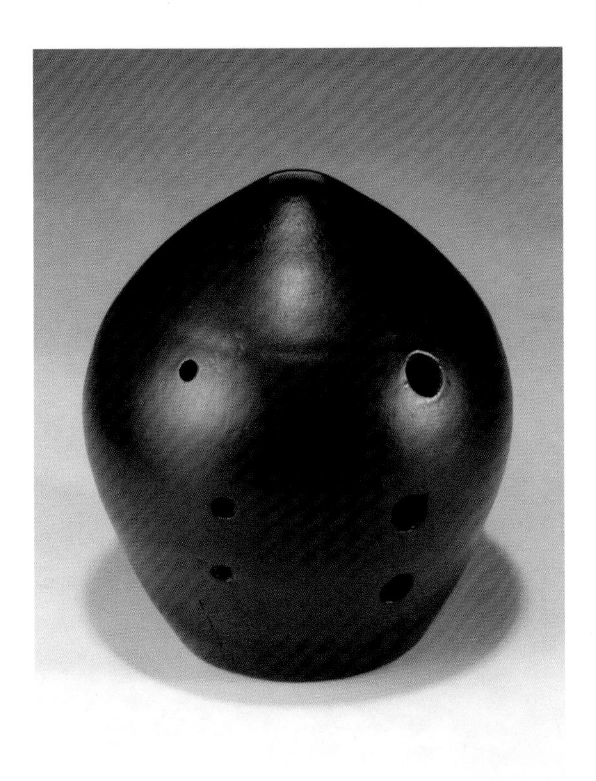

Fig. 4.10
**Xun**
China, 20th Century. A modern style xun, with eight finger holes (six in the front, two in the rear). 4 inches in height. Collection of Barry Hall.

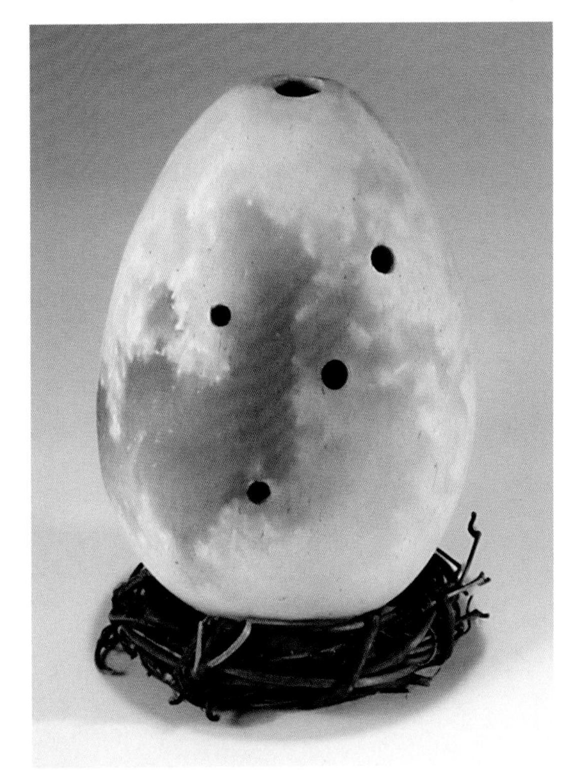

Fig. 4.11
**Xun**
Barry Hall, Westborough, Massachusetts, USA. Stoneware, saggar fired. 5 inches in height. Hear this instrument on CD track 34.

millers in Portugal developed these sounding jars for both practical and aesthetic reasons. The windmills were complex devices designed to grind the farmers' grain, and the sound of the ceramic vessels provided an audible monitoring device for the mill. Each mill would have its own sound if it were operating correctly. If the mill became damaged or out of alignment, the miller would immediately hear a change in the sound, even if he were far away, and know that he had to adjust the mechanics of his mill. Also, since the sound changed with increasing wind speed and relative humidity variations in the air, an abnormal sound was an early warning before a storm or bad weather.

Aesthetically, the mills were also intended to sound pleasing. The miller took great care with the tones and harmonies produced by the particular clay jars he selected. Where there were several mills standing in close proximity, the whole ensemble had to be perfectly matched in order not to offend the ear.

Today, the jars are produced by local potters in a variety of sizes and tones (figures 4.12-4.13). Several different basic forms are used. The smallest are called *jarras* (vases) and have the form of a vase with a flat foot. They have a wide flaring lip, below which is an indentation or waist on the jar which permits it to be securely lashed with rope to the windmill's bars, or to ropes that connect the bars. Larger forms, called *búzios* (hummers) are narrow-mouthed vases with a bulbous body and a constricted waist at their middle. The búzios may be as large

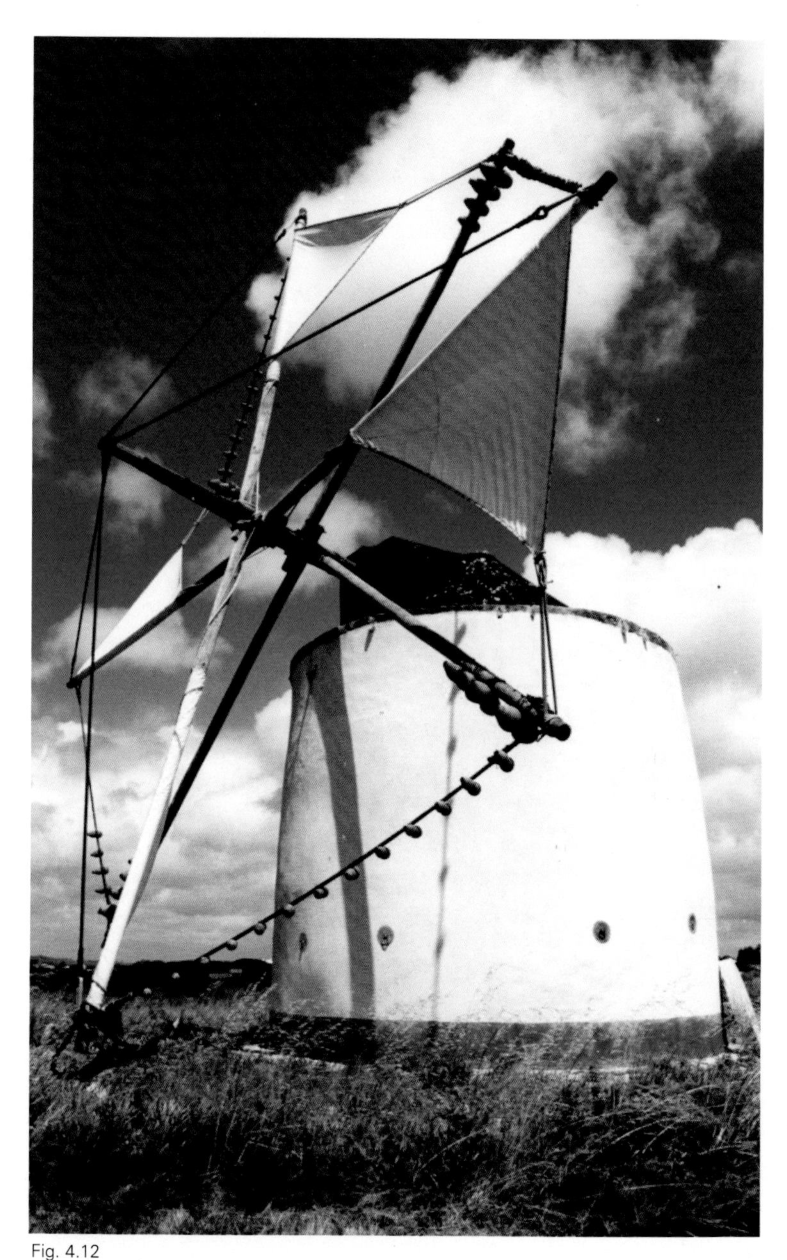

Fig. 4.12
**Portugese Singing Windmill**
The singing earthenware jars attached to this windmill in Portugal range in size from several inches to several feet in length.

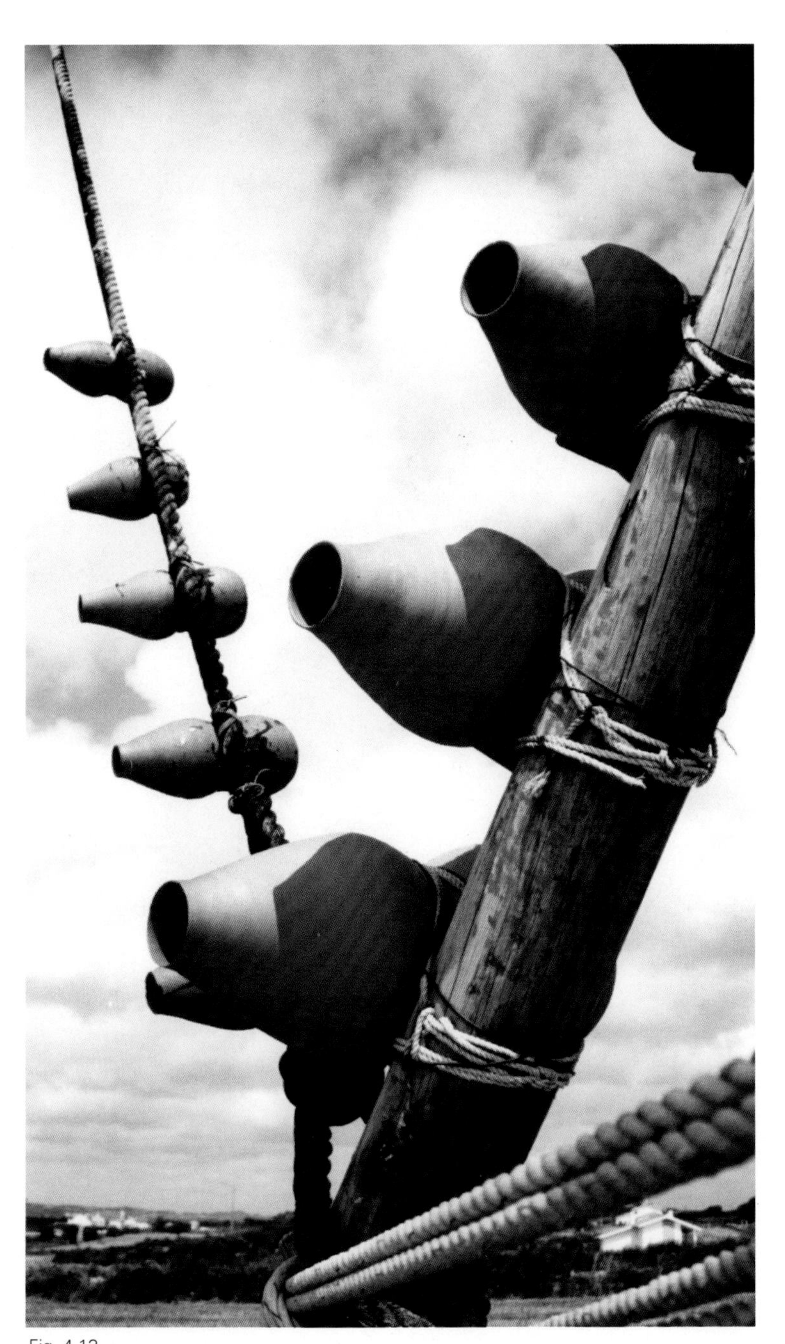

Fig. 4.13
**Portugese Singing Windmill**
Detail of earthenware jars attached to windmill blades.

as two feet across, with a capacity of five gallons. Similar to the constricted neck of the jarras, the búzios' narrow waist permits them to be attached to the windmill's bars or ropes. The búzios may have an opening at one end, or at both ends. Those with an opening at one end are technically *polyglobular flutes*—edge-blown aerophones with multiple interconnected chambers.

A smaller type of end-blown **polyglobular flute,** also known as a ball-and-tube flute, consists of a series of small spherical chambers interconnected by tubular sections. These very unusual ceramic flutes were made uniquely by pre-Columbian peoples in America. They usually have two or three linearly-connected chambers, and are blown through an open mouthpiece at one end, with a lip rest that extends upward from the blowhole. Ball-and-tube flutes sometimes have several finger holes, but since they are neither tubular nor globular instruments, the pitches resulting from opening successive finger holes are often unpredictable. Susan Rawcliffe has studied many pre-Columbian ball-and-tube flutes, and has created some of her own design, which can be heard on track 26 of the accompanying CD.

### *Airduct Flutes*

Airduct flutes (or ducted flutes) come in many shapes and sizes, but their common characteristic is an airduct assembly, also called a *fipple*. (Since the term "fipple" has been used through the years in different, contradictory ways, this book will follow the recommended practice of today's acousticians and use the less-ambiguous term "airduct" or "airduct assembly" instead of fipple.)

The airduct flute family includes many popular instruments such as the ocarina, whistle and recorder. An airduct assembly makes it easier for a novice to play a flute, since it removes the requirement that a player carefully position their mouth and lips in the precise way necessary to get a proper tone. However, as a trade-off, it limits the subtle variations in tone and pitch that a skilled player can coax from an edge-blown instrument.

An airduct assembly is complicated to build, but easy to play. The basic components of an airduct assembly are identified in figures 4.15-4.16. The aperture functions the same as the blowhole of a side-blown flute. The windway is a narrow channel that performs the same function as a player's lips with a side-blown or end-blown flute—it focuses the air stream and directs it across the edge of the blowhole. The edge is a sharpened blade of clay that sits across the aperture from the windway, precisely aligned so that it splits the stream of air coming from the windway.

There are many variations of airduct assemblies. The aperture can be square, rectangular, round or oval. The edge can be short and thick, or thin and very sharp. The windway can also have many variations in shape. Some pre-Columbian airduct instruments have additional unusual features such as walls that frame the aperture and hoods that partially cover the aperture. These features impact the flute's pitch and tone and have the added benefit of partially protecting the aperture from unwanted wind when playing outdoors.

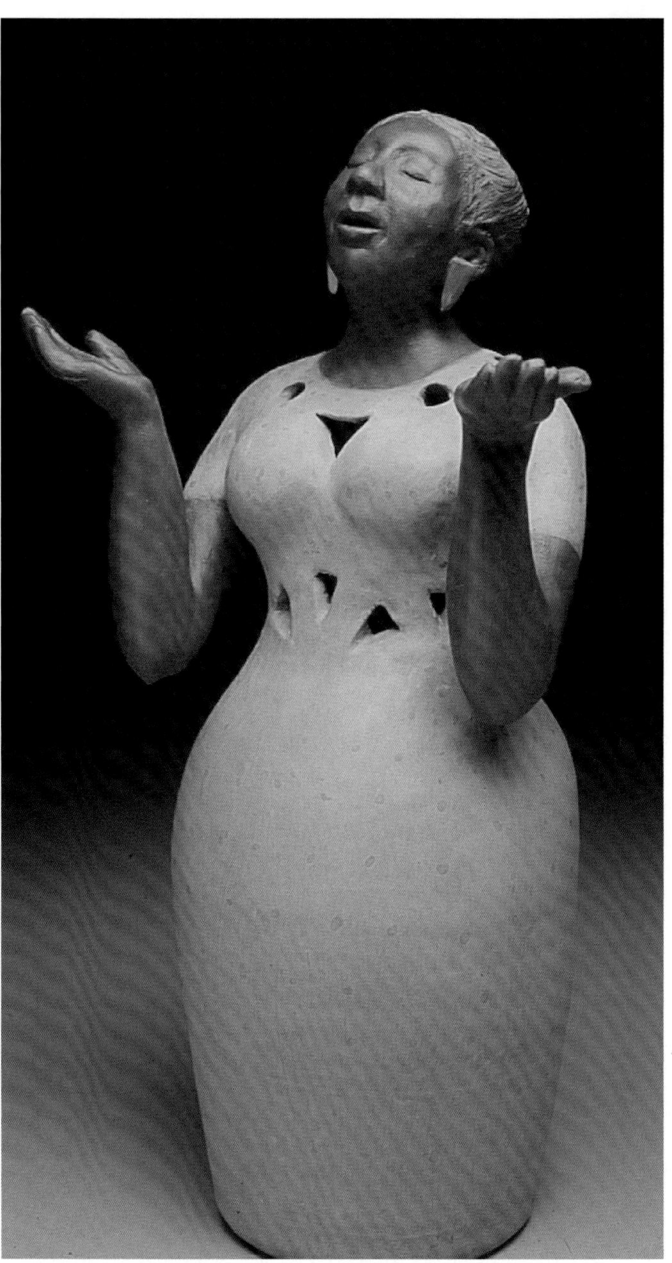

Fig. 4.14
**Praying Woman Whistle**
Janet Moniot, Petal, Mississippi, USA. The whistling mechanism is a South American ball & tube assembly design hidden inside the upper body of the figure. The perforations are decorative but essential for the whistle's sound to escape. Composed of wheel formed, extruded and handbuilt components. 4.5 inches in height.

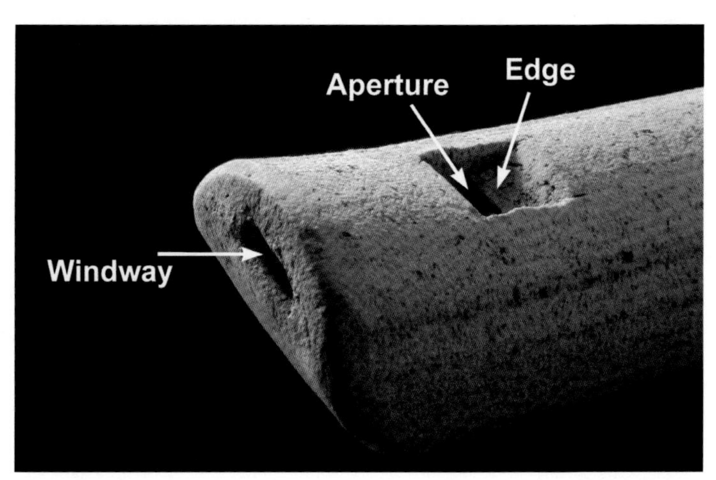


Fig. 4.15
**Components of an airduct assembly**

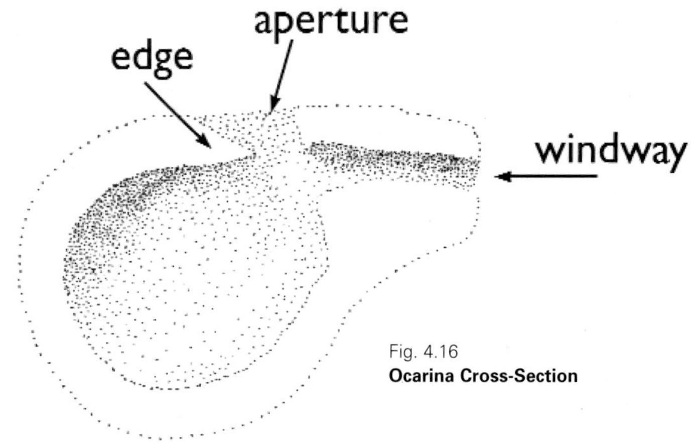


Fig. 4.16
**Ocarina Cross-Section**

The reedy, raspy sounds of a hooded flute built by Susan Rawcliffe can be heard on track 24 of the accompanying CD. For detailed information on how airduct design factors affect a flute's tone quality, see the sidebar "Factors in Airduct Assembly Design."

Making airduct assemblies for clay instruments is a combination of science and art. Although it's not too difficult to make a working model, many artists have spent years perfecting the subtle variations, and learning from trial and error what designs sound the best to their ears.

A unique benefit of airduct assemblies is that they permit the creation of *multiple flutes*, which are two or more flutes that are joined and played as one instrument that produces simultaneous pitches and harmonies. Multiple flutes can be made with tubular or globular bodies. The flutes can be attached together or separate, but each operates as an independent instrument controlled by the breath of a single player. Several types of multiple flutes are described later in this section.

*Tubular Airduct Flutes*

Tubular airduct flutes, sometimes simply called *pipes*, are tube-shaped flutes with an airduct assembly at one end. Common examples are the recorder and pennywhistle. They can be designed as either end-blown or side-blown, though end-blown instruments are much more common. They can have any number of finger holes, or none at all.

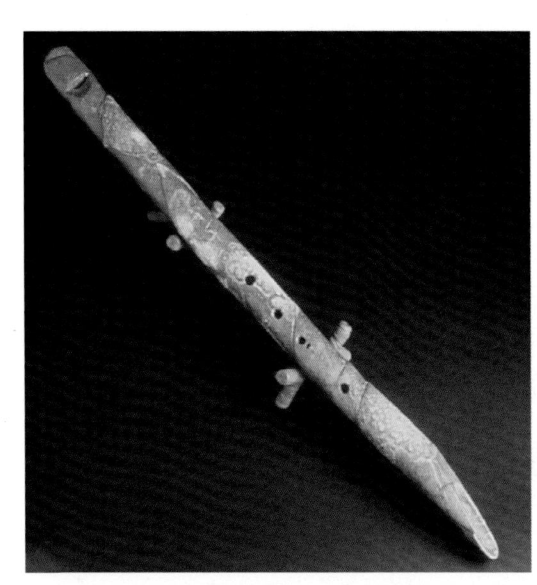

A flute with no finger holes is called a harmonic flute or overtone flute because it produces only the pitches of the natural harmonic or overtone series. The player controls the pitches by varying air pressure. Blowing a faster air stream forces the pitch up to the next overtone in the harmonic series. Additional pitches are achieved by stopping the distal end of the flute with the player's finger. Even though the flute has no finger holes, if it is long enough it will enable a musician to play

Fig. 4.17
**Flute**
Brian Ransom, St. Petersburg, Florida, USA. An end-blown flute with a recorder style (airduct assembly) mouthpiece. Salt-fired earthenware. 20 inches in length.

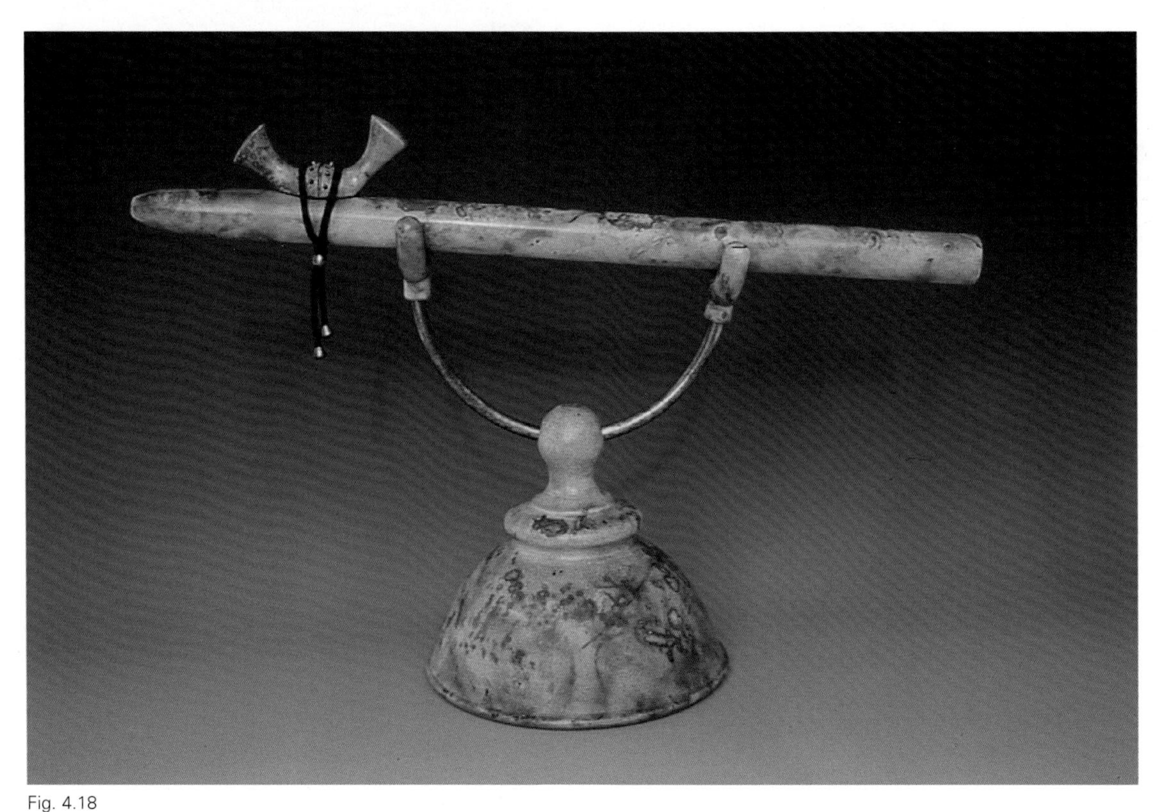

Fig. 4.18
**Native American-Style Flute**
Rod Kendall, Tenino, Washington, USA. This flute in the key of F was made from white, Cone 6 stoneware clay using an extruder and a potter's wheel. The sound block or "bird" atop the flute is hand sculpted. It was finished with a sprayed coat of yellow iron oxide then saggar fired. Hear this instrument on CD track 43.

## Factors in Airduct Assembly Design

The following factors affect tone quality in airduct flutes:

**Aperture size:** The larger the opening between the windway and the edge, the higher the instrument's overall pitch. Larger apertures also require larger tone holes on the flute body to achieve the same pitch relationships.

**Aperture shape:** Short, wide openings (short distance from windway to edge; wide edge) produce a clear, focused tone. With all edgetones, pitch tends to rise as the speed of the air stream increases, but the pitch-bending effect is less pronounced with short, wide apertures. Instead, such flutes tend to overblow to the second octave easily. Recorders exemplify this approach, with apertures that are typically over three times as wide as they are long.

Long, narrow apertures produce a breathier tone and require more blowing pressure. The pitch bends broadly in response to variations in wind pressure, but the octave doesn't overblow as readily. Some pre-Columbian flutes were made this way, with apertures a little over twice as long as they are wide.

**Windway size and shape:** The windway must focus the air stream as much as possible, so windways are made very thin—often less than a sixteenth of an inch high, even for moderately large flutes. Their width should be the same as that of the edge opposite. Some are made with parallel upper and lower walls, while some become narrower toward the exit as a way to increase the air stream's focus. Less focused windways make for breathier tone. The passageway must be smooth; roughness or irregularities inhibit the sounding of high pitches.

**Angle of incidence:** The windway should be oriented in such a way that it directs the air stream head-on to the edge, centered so that the edge cuts the air stream roughly in half. For most airduct flutes, this means that the windway should be parallel to the tube walls, not heading down from above.

**Acuteness of the edge:** Recorders generally use a sharp, narrow edge, at about 20 or 25 degrees. Many ocarinas and clay flutes use thicker edges at about 45 degrees, and you can get decent tone with still coarser edges, such as the rounded edges of bottles and jugs.

**Frames and hoods:** Some of the early Mesoamerican flutes have walls built up around the non-edge sides of the aperture, or hoods formed over the top. Frames lower the pitch and make the sound more directional. Hoods alter the overtone content in highly variable ways, creating a reedier tone and making it possible to dramatically shift timbre through changes in wind pressure.

If you wish to delve further into this subject, turn to the literature on organ pipes, in which edgetone mechanics and related topics are studied extensively.

*Source:* Musical Instrument Design *by Bart Hopkin. Used with permission.*

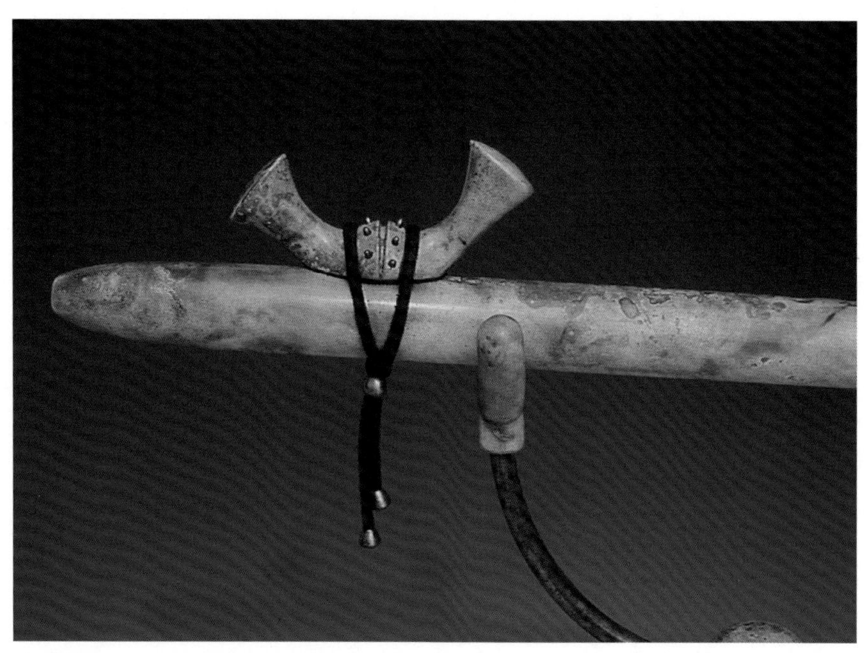

Fig. 4.19
**Detail of Native American-Style Flute**
Rod Kendall, Tenino, Washington, USA. Flute showing the bird adorned with copper studs. The tie is made of black deer hide leather with handmade copper beads.

melodies using only its overtone pitches. Since long, narrow air columns tend to break up into overtones more readily than short and fat air columns, they are a better choice for overtone flutes. A ceramic overtone flute can be heard on track 12 of the accompanying CD.

Adding finger holes enables the flute to produce additional pitches. A flute with six or seven holes can usually produce all the tones in a diatonic scale (such as the white keys on a piano) and will also often permit chromatic pitches (the black keys) using techniques called cross fingering and half holing (see the "Glossary" for details).

A 2,000 year old clay airduct flute was found in India, and most other cultures around the world have developed some form of tubular airduct flute. Naturally-hollow tubes such as cane and certain bones are ready-made materials for tubular flutes, so they are the materials of choice for many cultures. However, the pre-Columbian cultures of the Americas also developed a large variety of ceramic flutes, many of which have survived to this day.

A clever and unique pre-Columbian flute from Mexico has a clay pellet inside a long, straight tubular flute without finger holes. As the flute is tipped, the pellet rolls back and forth inside the tube, shortening and lengthening the vibrating air column and producing a continuously varying pitch like that of a slide whistle. Flutes of this type were often ornately decorated.

The Native American flute is a traditional design from North and Central America that uses a unique style of airduct assembly. The windway is on the outside of the flute and is covered on its top side by a movable block, also called a *fetish* because it is often shaped like a bird or other animal associated with magical or spiritual powers. These flutes are traditionally made from wood, but Seattle potter

Rod Kendall makes them from clay (see figures 4.18-4.19, and listen to track 43 of the CD). Rod explains, "I started making ceramic Native American flutes as a project for my daughter's birthday party, from instructions I found in a book. It was the haunting quality of the sound that sparked my interest in making the flutes—they seem to reach a deeper place in my soul." Rod makes each flute unique by inlaying materials such as copper, fossilized ivory and abalone.

He continues, "There is a real reverence to the process of creating these flutes. From the family outing to gather the seaweed for the saggar firing, to being in the right frame of mind to create the instruments, to giving the piece over to the firing process that ultimately provides the visual satisfaction. Each is unique and different and I never know what to expect when opening the kiln."

The sound quality of Rod's ceramic flutes is similar to their wooden counterparts. One of the advantages of using clay instead of wood is clay's superior porosity, which prevents condensed water from the player's breath from blocking the narrow windway.

*Multiple tubular flutes* are two or more flutes that are played as one instrument. Usually a player

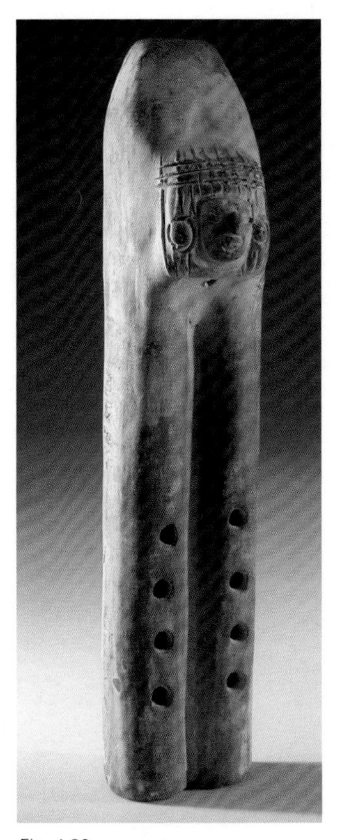

Fig. 4.20
**Double Flute**
Replica (Mexico, 20th century) of a pre-Columbian double flute. Earthenware. 11 inches in length. Collection of Barry Hall.

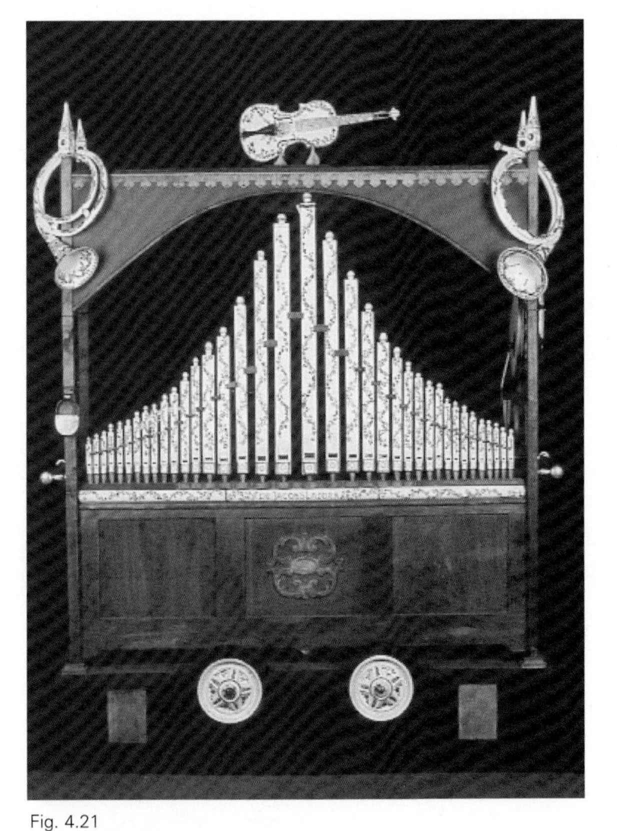

Fig. 4.21
**"Jacob's Ladder" Barrel Organ**
Geert Jacobs, Milsbeek, Netherlands. Geert's large mechanical organ makes its music via a vast array of hand-made porcelain pipes. A hand crank operates a bellows, which produces air that powers the pipes. A series of holes carefully cut in cardboard sheets control the production of each note by directing the air to specific pipes for specific durations. Hear this instrument on CD track 32.

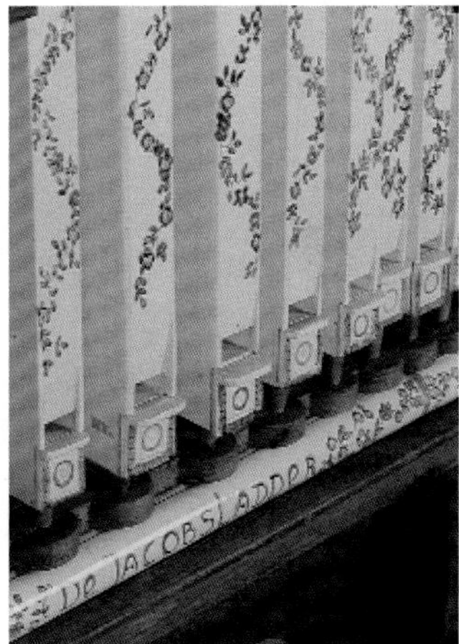

Fig. 4.22
Detail of the porcelain organ pipes in Geert Jacobs' barrel organ.

blows into a single windway, which then branches out to feed two or more separate flutes, each with their own aperture and edge. Sometimes one of the flutes has finger holes for playing melodies, while the other flute has no holes and is used as a drone to accompany the melody. Sometimes each flute has its own holes, differently spaced to permit a variety of melodies, drones and chords. Some of the earliest known double flutes are ceramic models found in Mexico. Triple and quadruple clay flutes were made by the Teotihuacán culture in Mexico as early as 500 A.D. On track 13 of the accompanying CD, Susan Rawcliffe plays a triple flute that she built based on a pre-Columbian-inspired design (figures 4.20 and 9.31).

Many organ pipes are, in fact, tubular airduct flutes. *A barrel organ* is a mechanical instrument in which a wooden cylinder, or barrel, is slowly turned by a hand crank, and in doing so selectively controls the airflow that sounds a set of tubular airduct pipes blown by a bellows. The pipes are commonly made from metal or wood. However, Geert Jacobs in Holland made a very unusual barrel organ with ceramic pipes. The mechanism is somewhat similar to a player piano—each note is controlled by a small hole that is handcut in a long strip of folded cardboard, which is slowly cranked through the organ. Geert's ceramic barrel organ is shown in figures 4.21-4.22 and 9.22 and can be heard on track 32 of the accompanying CD.

*Globular Airduct Flutes (Ocarinas)*

Globular flutes with airduct assemblies are commonly called ocarinas, though sometimes such instruments without finger holes are called whistles. An ocarina or globular whistle has a vessel body that can be almost any shape, and an airduct assembly that causes the vessel to sound. If the instrument has finger holes they can be placed just about anywhere on its body, since it is their size,

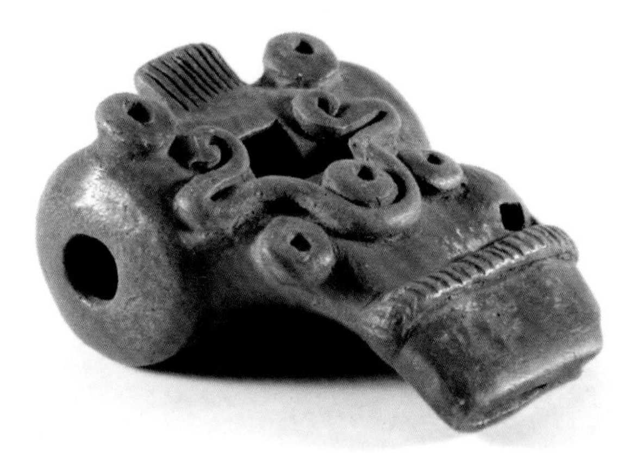

Fig. 4.23
**Aztec Double Whistle**
A pre-Columbian double whistle from Mexico. The mouthpiece is at the right. The main chamber has a single tone hole at the end. The second, much smaller, chamber and aperture can be seen above the rightmost edge of the mouthpiece. By varying the opening of the large chamber, the player can create a variety of pitch combinations with the smaller, fixed-pitch chamber, including beats. 3". Field Museum Collection.

not position, that determines the pitch they produce. (See the sidebar "Tubular vs. Globular Aerophones" earlier in this chapter for more details on how air cavity size and finger holes impact the sound of an ocarina.)

Whistles and ocarinas are quite possibly the most widely-known and popular ceramic instrument of all time, with traditions in virtually all parts of the world. They have been made since prehistoric times, from a variety of materials. Ancient clay whistles have been found throughout Europe, and in India, Egypt and China, among other places. Although the name "ocarina" was coined in 19th-century Italy, the instrument itself has a much longer history.

Early inhabitants of Mesoamerica and South America were prolific whistle and ocarina builders and designers for a period of several thousand years. The variety and creativity of their globular flutes is remarkable and unparalleled. These cultures ingeniously extended the design of the basic

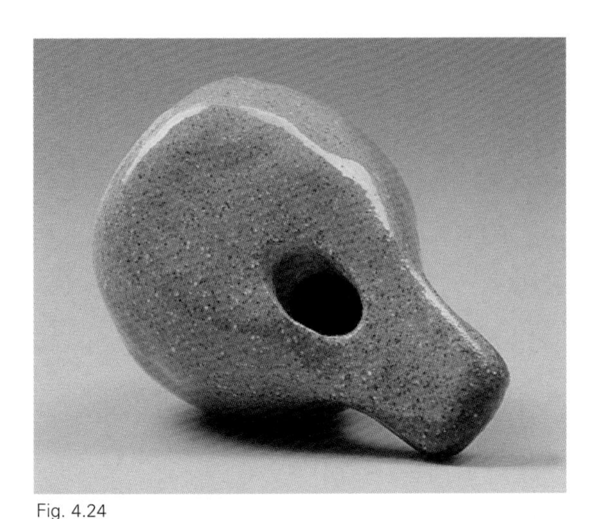

Fig. 4.24
**One-Note Whistle**
Daryl Baird, Sagle, Idaho, USA. This simple whistle, made from stoneware and fired with a clear glaze, is the result of Daryl's first attempt at a making a whistle. It was made by carefully following the instructions provided in Janet Moniot's book, *Clay Whistles: The Voice Clay.*

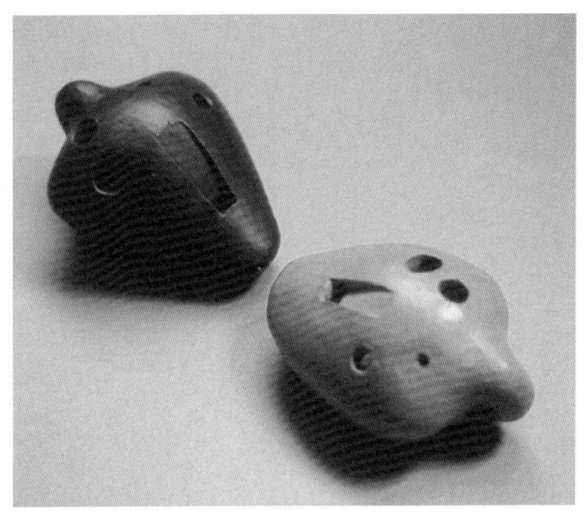

Fig. 4.25
**Two Ocarinas in G**
Barry Jennings, London, England. Terra cotta clay, burnished and wood fired.

airduct assembly by adding frames and hoods, developing incredible multiple flutes that produced mind-bending combination tones, and creating intriguing water-powered whistles. Many of their developments and refinements have since been lost in the dust of time, to be only recently rediscovered via the examination of ancient artifacts.

Ocarinas in pre-Columbian America were usually highly decorated, and they often depicted human figures and animals. In addition to their instruments, many pre-Columbian sculpted effigies incorporated one or more whistles or rattles in their internal cavities. As with rattling bowls and cups (see the "Idiophones" chapter), whistles were also integrated into utilitarian vessels and other objects. Jose-Luis Franco, a researcher in ceramic instruments, relates the following about the people of Veracruz, Mexico, during the Classic Period (100-900 A.D.), "It is interesting to consider the amount of thought and work spent by the people

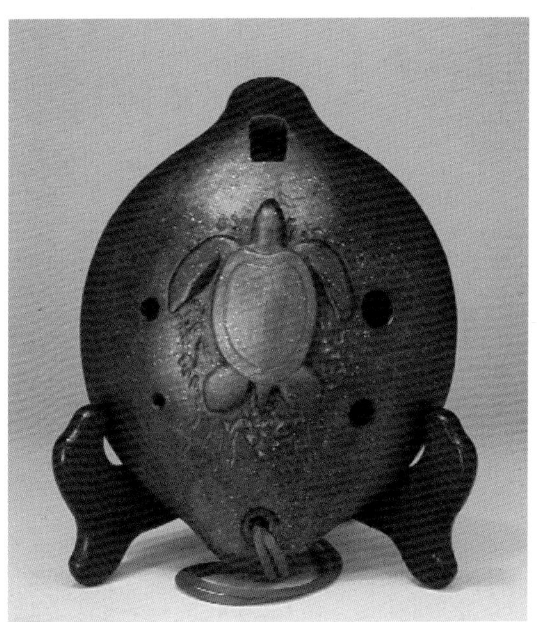

Fig. 4.26
**Turtle**
Ron Robb, Powell River, British Columbia, Canada.

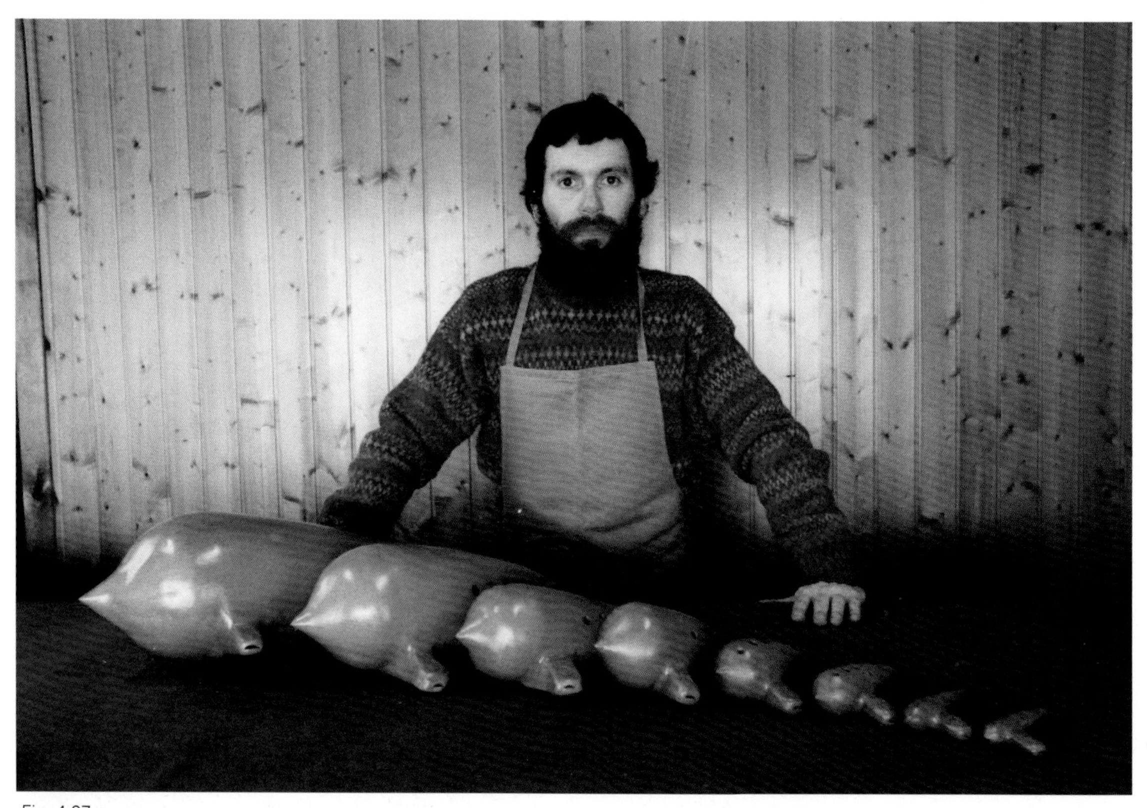

Fig. 4.27
**Budrio Ocarinas**
Fabio Menaglio, Bologna, Italy. Fabio with his full range of Budrio ocarinas from piccolo to contrabass. Hear these instruments on CD track 33.

of Classic Veracruz in the suppression of silence in their daily lives. The most unexpected objects have a built-in musical or sound producing element. All figurines of a maneuverable size have a whistle somewhere or contain rattling pellets, and in some cases combine both features. A musical instrument may have another miniature instrument attached to produce an extra sound."

A related uniquely pre-Columbian instrument is the whistling water vessel, described later in this chapter (see "Water Flutes").

The sounds that some pre-Columbian whistles produce are considered bizarre by today's standards. Whistles with two or more chambers (figure 4.23) are tuned so that multiple pitches combine to

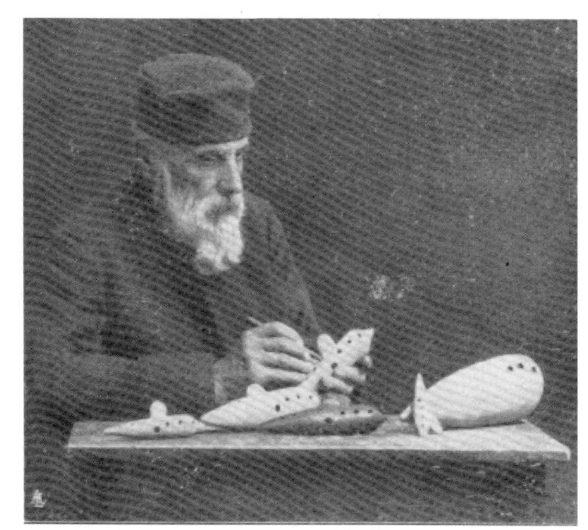

Fig. 4.28
Giuseppe Donati, considered the "father" of the modern ocarina, making ocarinas in the late 1800s.

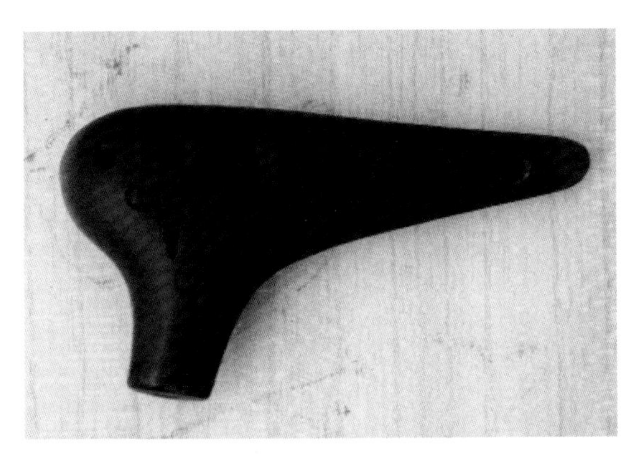

Fig. 4.29
**Cantare Ocarina**
Takao Hiramoto, Kasama, Japan. Takao and his sons manufacture the precisely tuned Cantare ocarinas in seven sizes, from piccolo in C to great bass in F. He says, "the ocarina takes you back to the past and also brings the past into the present."

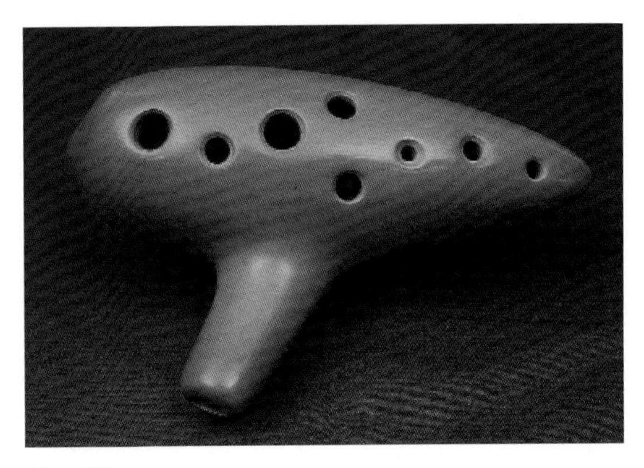

Fig. 4.30
**Ocarina**
Sergio Garcia and Marco Donoso, Quilpue', Chile. Sergio and Marco's ocarinas are made using plaster molds with clay local to their rural town. After drying, each ocarina is tuned then burnished with a stone. The instruments are fired in a wood-fueled kiln. Sergio and Marco draw their inspiration and some of their building techniques from the pre-Columbian cultures from their area of Chile. 6.5 inches in length.

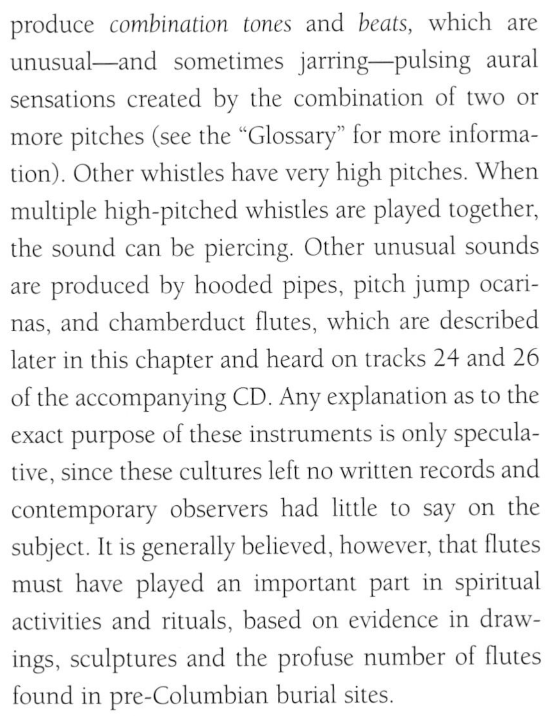

produce *combination tones* and *beats,* which are unusual—and sometimes jarring—pulsing aural sensations created by the combination of two or more pitches (see the "Glossary" for more information). Other whistles have very high pitches. When multiple high-pitched whistles are played together, the sound can be piercing. Other unusual sounds are produced by hooded pipes, pitch jump ocarinas, and chamberduct flutes, which are described later in this chapter and heard on tracks 24 and 26 of the accompanying CD. Any explanation as to the exact purpose of these instruments is only speculative, since these cultures left no written records and contemporary observers had little to say on the subject. It is generally believed, however, that flutes must have played an important part in spiritual activities and rituals, based on evidence in drawings, sculptures and the profuse number of flutes found in pre-Columbian burial sites.

Most pre-Columbian ocarinas had four or fewer finger holes and could produce a range of a sixth or less, though instruments with a range of over an octave were sometimes created. (The greater the desired range of an ocarina, the more precise the construction of the airduct assembly and body must be.) Ocarina-making skills were passed down through the centuries and from culture to culture, and over time developed to a high level of sophistication. Eventually, skills and knowledge dwindled, and as a

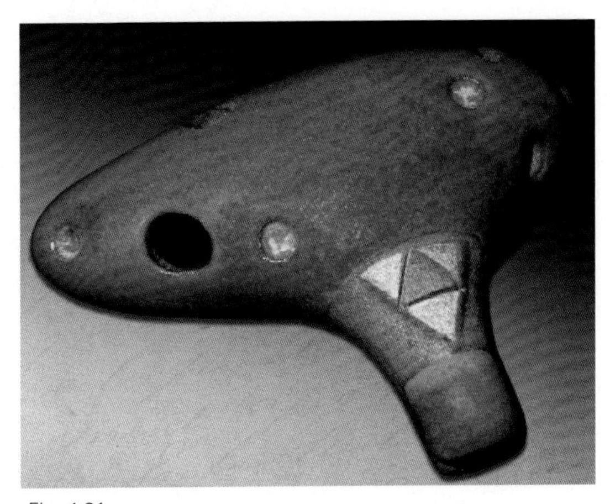

Fig. 4.31
**"Zelda" Ocarina**
Richard and Sandi Schmidt, Seattle, Washington, USA.
An ocarina inspired by the popular video game. Cone 5 stoneware slip cast body, with hand-cut airduct assembly and finger holes. Double glazed. 4 inches in length.

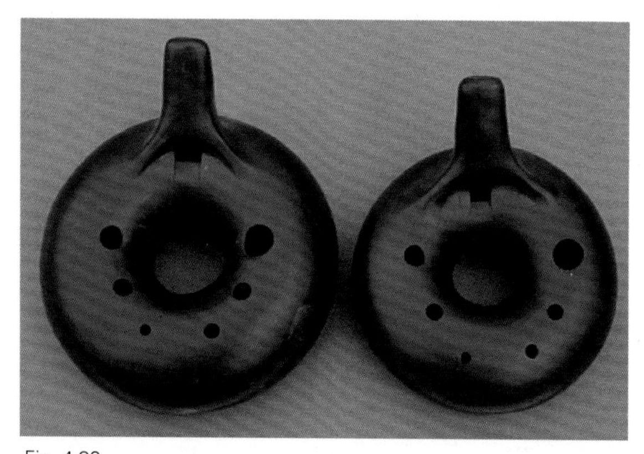

Fig. 4.32
**Torus Shaped Ocarinas**
John Taylor, Wiltshire, England. John developed this design in 1998. Each of the ocarinas has eight holes including two thumb holes, which provides a chromatic range of an octave and a fourth. Reduction fired earthenware. 5 inches and 6 inches in diameter.

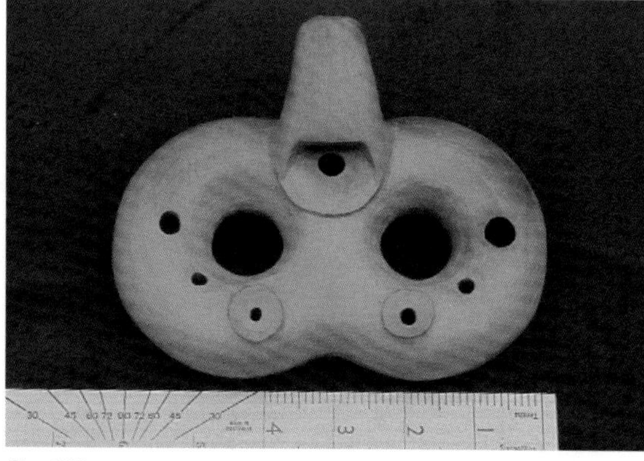

Fig. 4.33
**Figure Eight (Double Torus) Ocarina**
John Taylor, Wiltshire, England. John developed this interesting design during the winter of 2001. It has eight holes including two thumb holes and a range of an octave and a fourth. According to John it has a strong tone and good tuning properties. Earthenware, semi-reduction fired. 6 inches in length.

result some later instruments are crude compared to earlier ones. If musical instruments were an important part of sacred pre-Columbian rituals, then it is not surprising that their manufacture declined rapidly following the Conquest, when many traditional activities were suppressed by the European invaders.

As the art of ocarina making began to decline in the New World, it gained popularity in Europe. It is speculated that this surge in interest may have been sparked by a visiting party of Aztec dancers and musicians, reputedly brought to Spain by Cortez to demonstrate their native culture for the emperor Charles V. At that time, European ocarinas were crude in comparison to their sophisticated American counterparts, and most commonly made by bakers in their ovens as toys or novelties. That is, until Giuseppe Donati, a baker from Budrio, Italy, took the next step in the ocarina's evolution.

In 1853, Donati designed and created a type of globular flute which he named the *ocarina*. "Ocarina" means "little goose" in Italian, and is reflective of the instrument's shape (not its sound!). Donati's serious and meticulous approach elevated the instrument from the common perception that it was a children's toy, to a serious musical instrument on which a capable musician could perform a variety of music. He is credited with developing the first ocarinas that were precisely tuned for playing in ensemble and had a range of over one octave. Donati eventually designed ocarinas in a wide range of sizes and musical keys—from piccolo to bass—that could be played together by musical ensembles. The Gruppo Ocarinistico Budriese (Budrio Ocarina Ensemble) was soon formed to perform Italian folk music, classical, and opera music on Donati's instruments, and the group is still active today. They can be heard on track 33 of the accompanying CD performing "La Primavera" from Vivaldi's *Four Seasons*, using a consort of seven ocarinas.

In the latter half of the 19th century Donati continued to expand his designs. One of his later catalogs includes, among other things, double ocarinas with a two-octave range, and triple voice ocarinas. His apprentices carried on the craft, and made incremental improvements to the design, quality and methods of production. They developed tunable ocarinas with moving metal plungers, and molds and presses to increase production. More ocarina ensembles were formed, and through their tours and public concerts, public awareness and interest was raised. This created more demand for the instruments, which were soon produced throughout Europe. The ocarina was affordable and easy to play, and as a result many people owned them. Serious solo players and ocarina ensembles continued to raise its respectability in the concert hall as well. A few orchestral composers of the day even wrote parts for ocarinas in their scores.

In the early 20th century, the Japanese sculptor Aketa began to make ocarinas, and stimulated a robust Japanese fascination with the instrument that continues to this day. In America, the Italian design was called a "sweet potato" because of its shape. Materials such as plastic and metal were used to mass-produce ocarinas and make them even more an "instrument of the people." Soldiers carried them into World Wars I and II. Schoolchildren were taught music on ocarinas (as they still are today in Japan). However, in the latter 20th century, mass production and the cheapening of materials precipitated the ocarina's general decline back to the realm of toys and novelties.

In the 1960s and 1970s there was a rebirth of interest in the ocarina, especially in its traditional ceramic form. John Taylor, a British mathematician and instrument builder, developed an ocarina tuning system that produced an almost entire chromatic scale over one octave, but required only four finger holes. Up to this time, most ocarinas with that range had eight to ten finger holes. (Notable exceptions are some pre-Columbian instruments with four finger holes that had a range of over an octave.) Taylor's four-hole system, commonly called the "English" system, made it simpler to build tuned ocarinas, and also allowed the creation of much smaller instruments since only four fingers were necessary to play instead of eight or ten. One of John's contemporaries, Barry Jennings, modified his design by adding two thumb holes to extend its upper range. He also incorporated a pre-Columbian innovation, a lip hole, to enable a player to drop the instrument's lowest pitch by an additional semitone. A lip hole is a tone hole near the airduct assembly that can be covered and uncovered by a player's lip.

At the end of the 20th century, an immensely popular Nintendo™ video game called "Legend of Zelda: Ocarina of Time"™ exposed a whole new generation to this ancient instrument, and created new interest and demand for ocarinas.

Today, Fabio Menaglio carries on Donati's tradition in Budrio, Italy, making Budrio Ocarinas (figure 4.27). These are regarded as some of the finest ocarinas made today, and can be heard on track 33 of the CD. The modern Japanese school of ocarina makers, including Cantare, Aketa and Ogawa, have

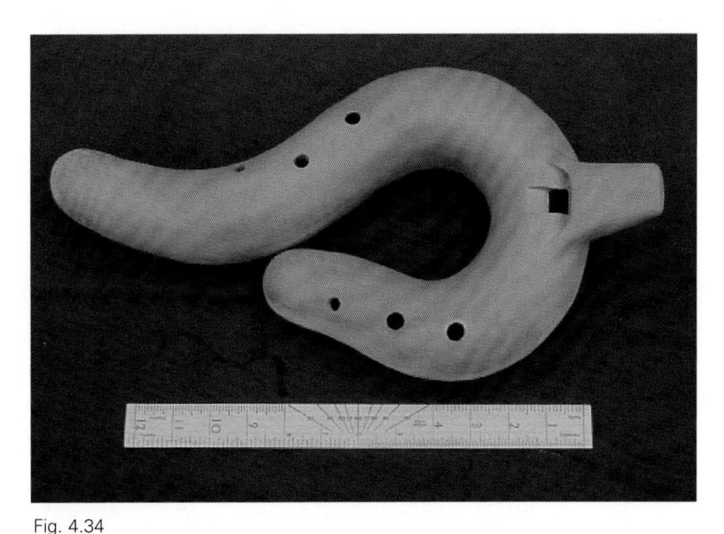

Fig. 4.34
**Ocarina**
John Taylor, Wiltshire, England. This large earthenware ocarina-type instrument in the key of F below middle C is unusual in that it overblows a higher register. Eight holes, including two for the thumbs, produce a range of an octave and a fifth. The body was formed on two plaster molds for the interior. 15 inches in length.

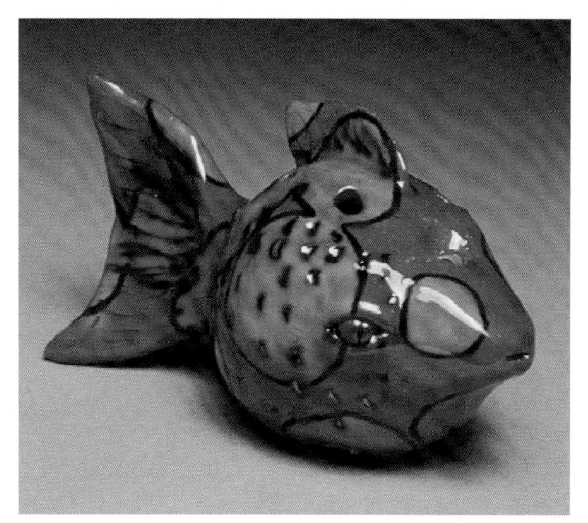

Fig. 4.35
**Tropical Fish Ocarina**
David Chrzan, Roswell, GA, USA.

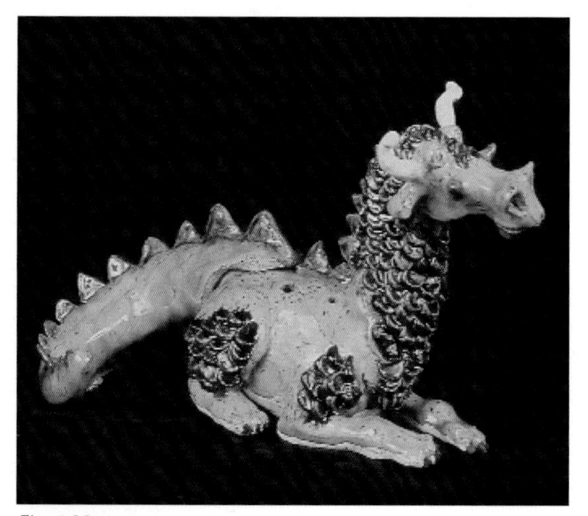

Fig. 4.36
**Dragon Ocarina**
Kathleen Moore, Lewisburg, Ohio, USA.

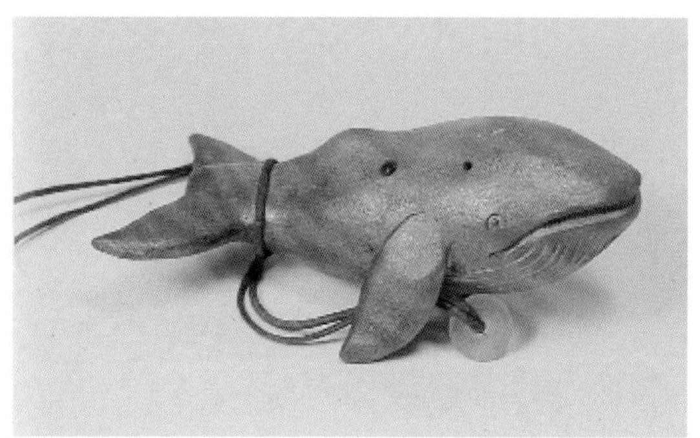

Fig. 4.37
**Baby Whale Ocarina**
Ron Robb, Powell River, British Columbia, Canada.

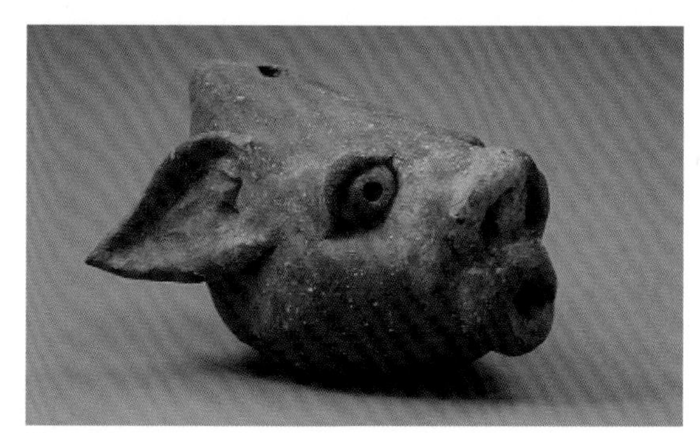

Fig. 4.38
**Gargoyle Whistle**
Kelly Averill Savino, Toledo, Ohio, USA.

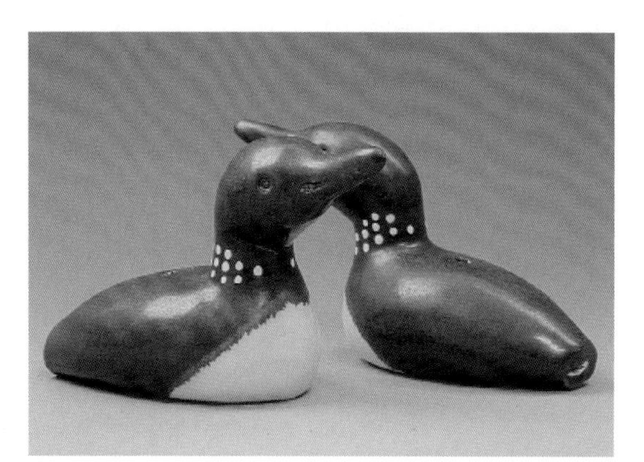

Fig. 4.39
**Loon Whistles**
Reed Weir, Robinsons, Newfoundland, Canada.

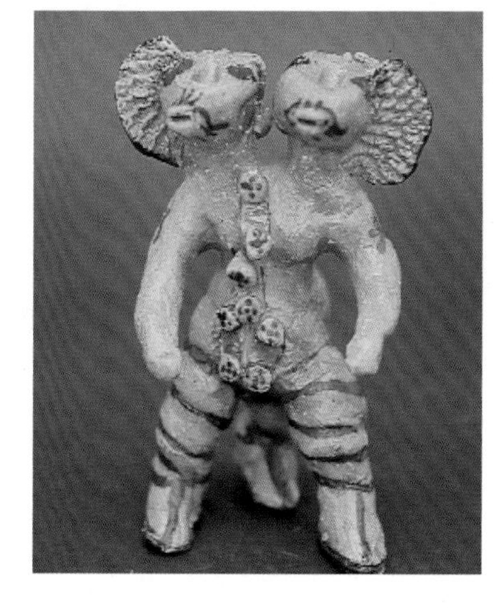

Fig. 4.40
**Alien Heavenly Twins Whistle**
Carla Lombardi, Glen Mills, Pennsylvania, USA.

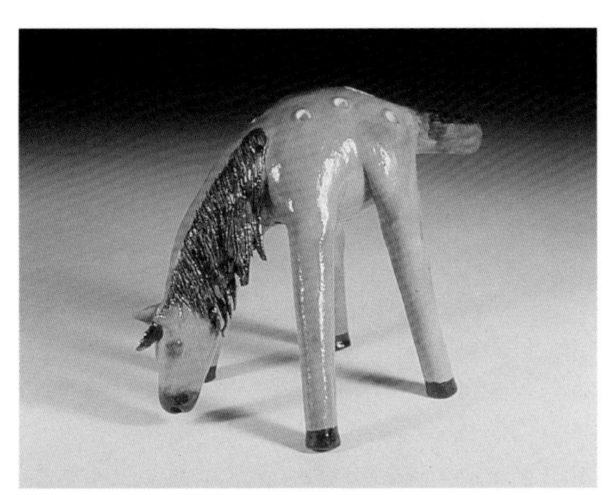

Fig. 4.41
**Buckskin Colt Ocarina**
Robert Santerre, Zionsville, Indiana, USA.

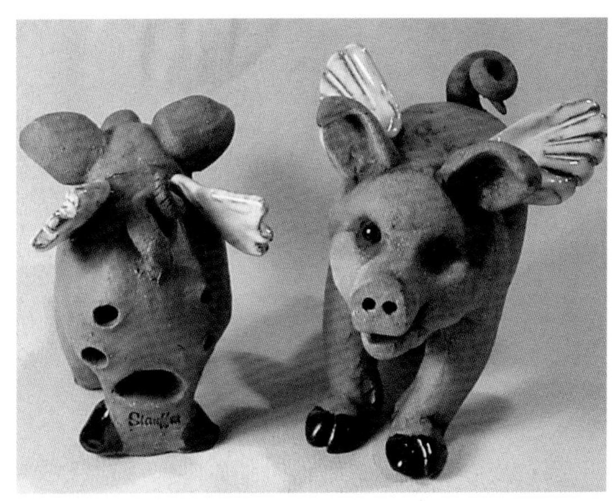


Fig. 4.42
**Flying Pig Ocarinas**
Linda Stauffer, Quakertown, Pennsylvania, USA.

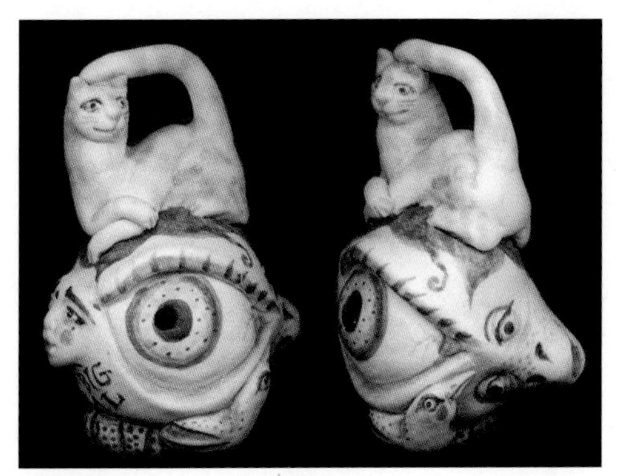

Fig. 4.43
**Cat on Eyeball Ocarina**
Theresa Bayer, Austin, Texas, USA.

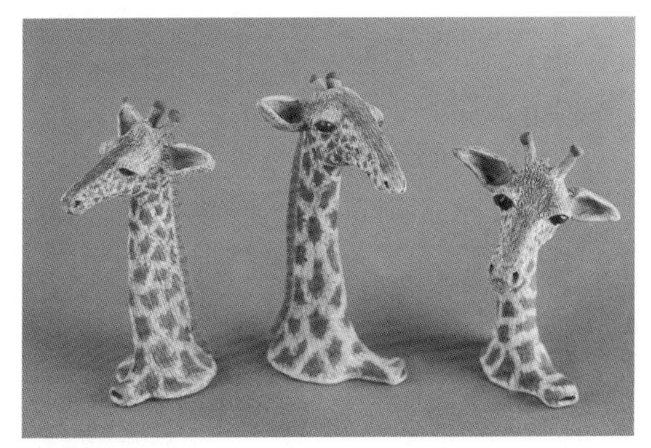

Fig. 4.44
**Giraffe Whistles**
Janie Tubbs, Lindsborg, Kansas, USA.

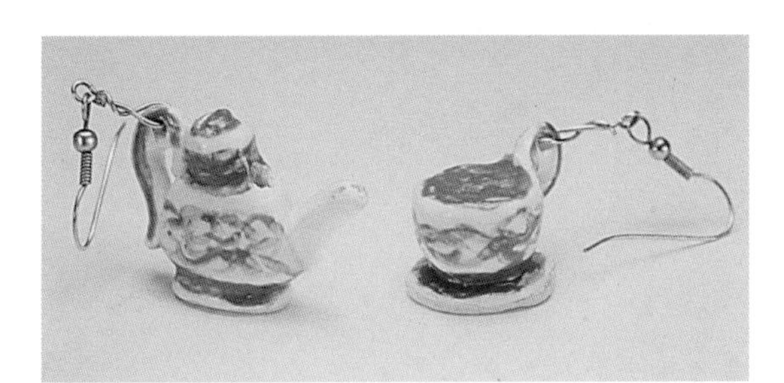

Fig. 4.45
**Teapot and Cup Whistling Earrings**
Bryna Brashier, Pittsburgh, Pennsylvania, USA.

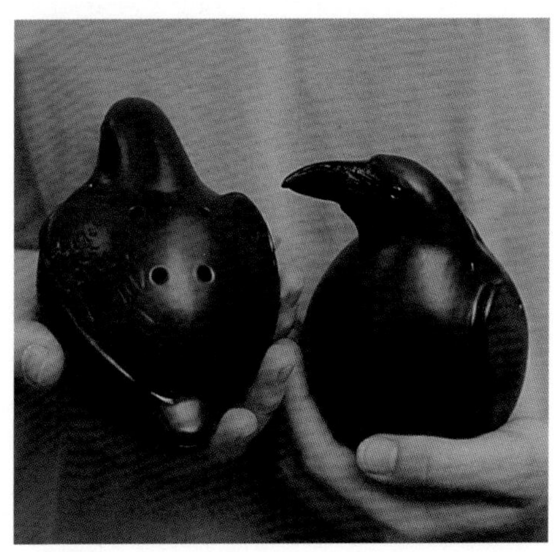

Fig. 4.46
**Raven Flutes**
Beatrice Landolt, Hopewell, New Jersey, USA.

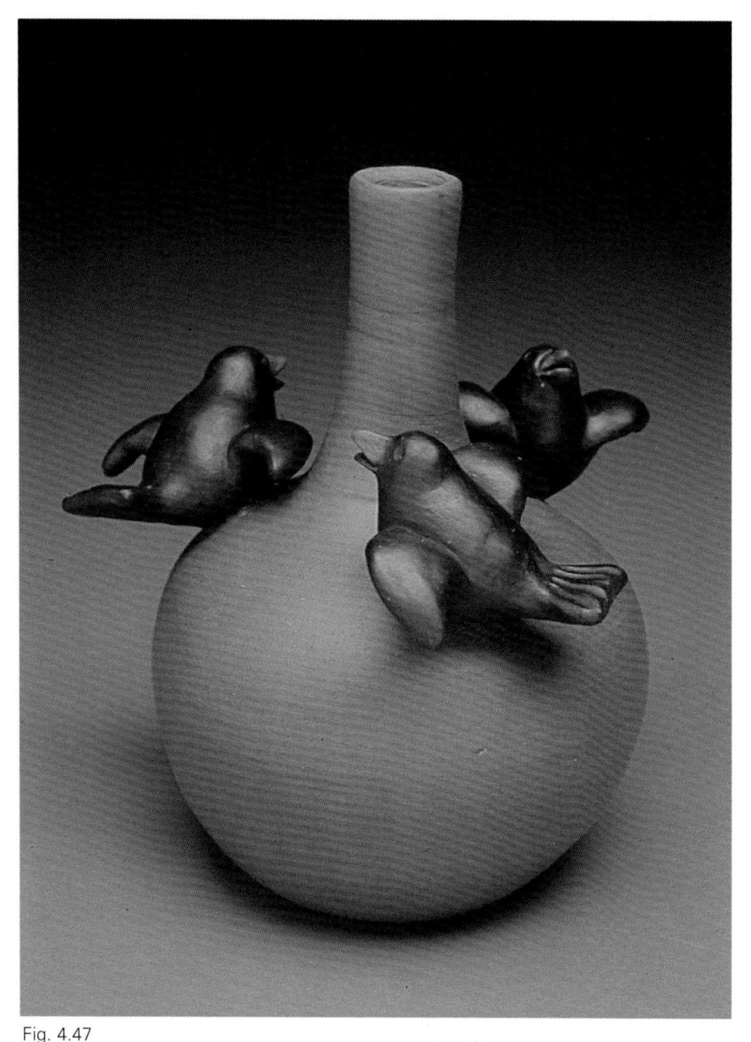

Fig. 4.47
**Three Bird Bottle Whistle**
Janet Moniot, Petal, Mississippi, USA. A three-parrot whistle Janet saw at the American Museum of Natural History in 1995 inspired this beautiful piece. It is made from terra cotta. The bottle was formed on the wheel. The birds are hollow and each has a small hole in its belly. The bottle is pierced with a small hole where each bird is attached. When you blow in the spout the air passes through all three birds at once and out the holes in their bellies. 5.5 inches in height.

expanded Donati's ten-hole design to twelve or thirteen holes which permits a wider range and additional chromatic pitches. There are many more fine makers around the world, and instruments from some of them are represented in this book.

The ocarina's deceptively simple design also compels many craftspeople to make ocarinas as a hobby or a profession. Making a good ocarina requires skill and patience, but many people find it to be very satisfying. Richard and Sandi Schmidt of Clayzness Whistleworks in Seattle, Washington have made more than 150,000 ocarinas over the last twenty-five years. They also founded the Ocarina Club, a popular internet community of ocarina builders and enthusiasts that has several hundred members, a testimony to the instrument's popularity. (Read more about Richard and Sandi in the "Profiles" chapter. Instructions for joining the Ocarina Club are in the "Resources and Materials" section.)

It appears that the physics of the basic ocarina design limit its musical range to about an octave and a half, although contemporary ocarina makers continue to push at the boundaries. A few creative design and playing techniques allow players to coax a wider range of pitches from some instruments. By "shading" or partially blocking the aperture with a finger or lip, the pitch of some ocarinas can be dropped a few semitones. Varying breath pressure also extends the range, as do *harmonic overtones,* which are overblown partials that can be obtained on some smaller instruments. Higher pitches also can be obtained using a complex technique in which a player cups his or her hand around the outside of

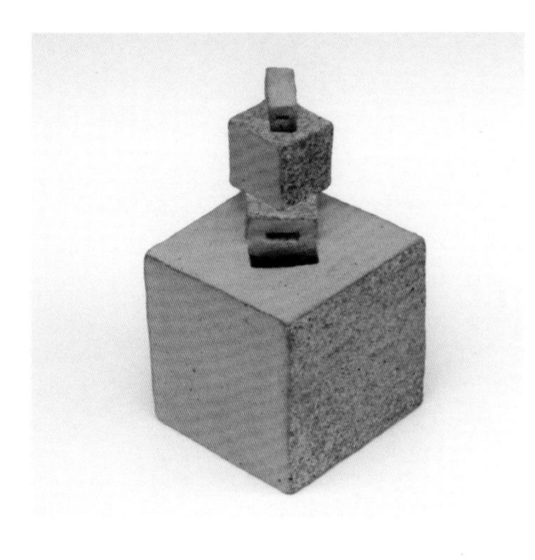

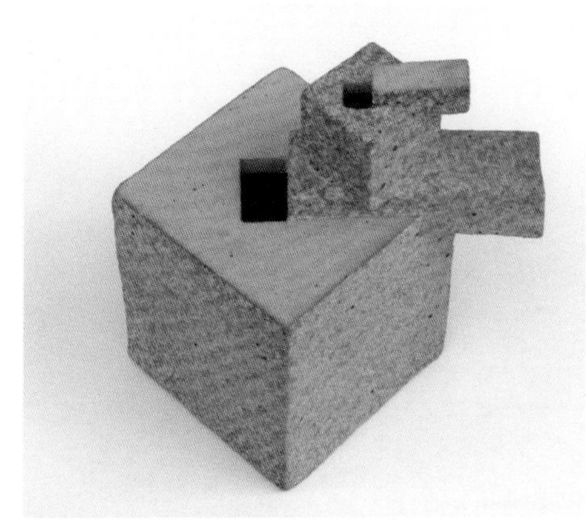

Fig. 4.48
**Double Whistle**
Hester Heuff, Dublin, Ireland. This cube-shaped instrument was slab-built from white clay and sprayed with dry white base and stains using a masking tape resist. Fired in electric kiln to cone 8. 7 inches in height.

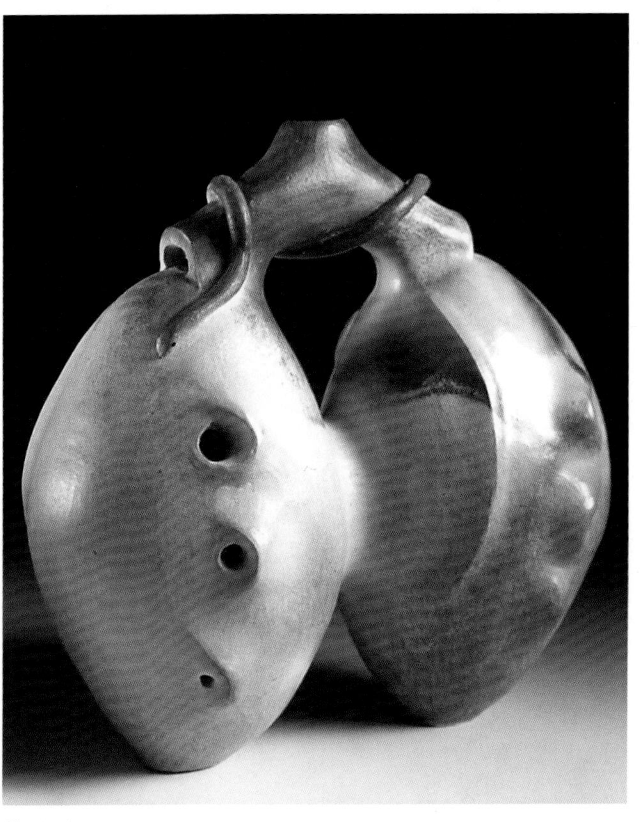

Fig. 4.49
**Double Ocarina**
Janie Rezner, Mendocino, California, USA. Janie has developed her own variations of the multiple-chambered ocarina. She plays one of her instruments on track 23 on the CD.

the aperture, creating a second, smaller chamber which reacts in a way similar to pre-Columbian pitch-jump flutes. (Pitch-jump flutes are described later in this section.)

Figures 4.53, 7.25 and 9.41 show remarkable multiple-chamber ocarinas, called *huacas,* created by Sharon Rowell. Meticulously crafted and precisely tuned, Sharon's huacas have from two to five chambers, with three being the most common. Usually, two of the chambers are for playing melodies and have a four-hole, one octave tuning, but with the four holes in line so that each chamber can be played with one hand. The two melody chambers are often tuned to play the same pitches—but they are carefully "de-tuned" from each other by a tiny amount to create a subtle "beating" effect in the player's ears when the two are played in unison. This meticulous adjustment has a profound effect—it produces a rich, full sound and a unique aural experience for the player. The third

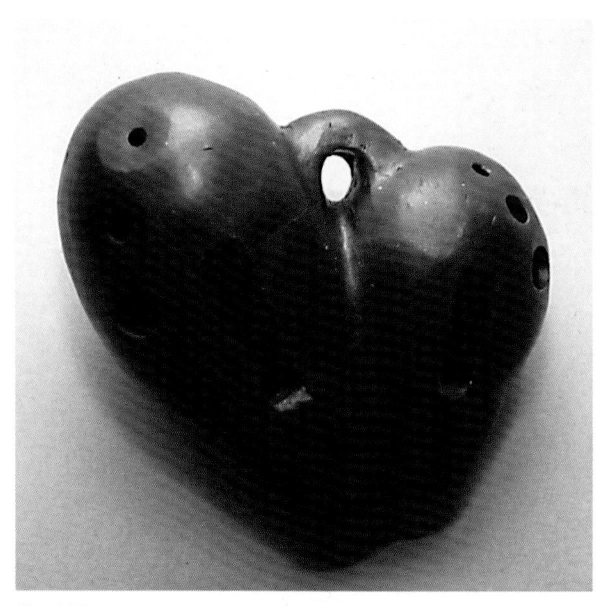

Fig. 4.50
**Double Ocarina Tuned to B Flat and F**
Barry Jennings, London, England. Terra cotta clay, burnished and wood fired using a special steel saggar.

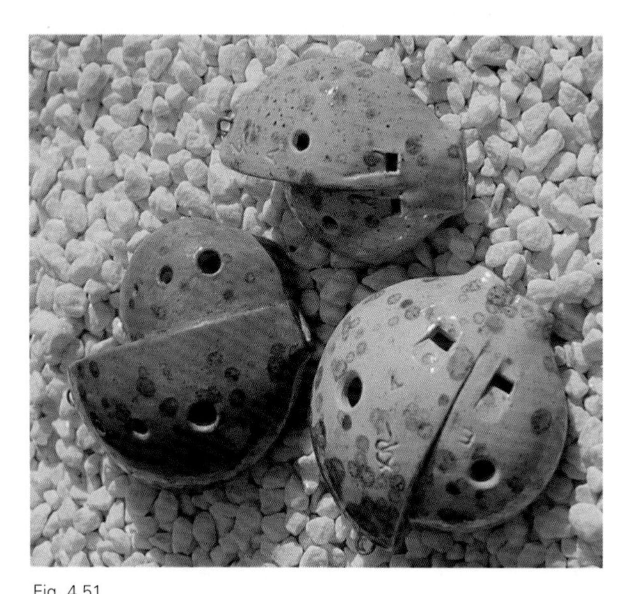

Fig. 4.51
**Twin-Chambered Ocarinas**
Terry Riley, Leicestershire, England. Three double ocarinas with chambers of differing sizes.

chamber of Sharon's instruments is usually designed as a drone, playing a single pitch to accompany the two melody chambers. However, Sharon's drone chambers often have one or two pitch holes that can be closed by the heels of the player's hands to alter the drone's pitch. The windways from the three (or more) chambers join each other in a single mouthpiece, and sometimes the drone windway is channeled separately. This allows the player to selectively engage and disengage the drone chamber, by blocking that part of the mouthpiece with their lower lip.

Alan Tower, a virtuoso performer who uses Sharon's instruments, has encouraged Sharon to create a variety of unusual huacas, further expanding the range of her instruments. These include instruments with melody chambers tuned to two different keys to enable more complex harmonies to be played, and melody chambers with five or even six holes for each hand, which permit a wider pitch range and additional chromatic pitches. Alan has composed many pieces for Sharon's instruments; two of them are included on the accompanying CD (tracks 6 and 15).

You can learn more about Sharon Rowell and her huacas in the "Profiles" section of this book. Sharon has taught many others the craft of making huacas, and some of their work is featured in this book and on the CD (see figure 4.49 and the appendix and listen to tracks 1 and 23).

Aguinaldo da Silva, a Brazilian potter, has developed his own unique designs for multiple ocarinas. As you can see from figures 4.54, 4.55 and 9.36, Aguinaldo's instruments have a fantastically organic appearance. His ocarinas have from two to nine chambers, and some are quite large. The windways from each individual chamber converge at the top of the instrument in a single row, allowing a player to blow into one at a time to perform a simple melody, or two or more simultaneously to produce

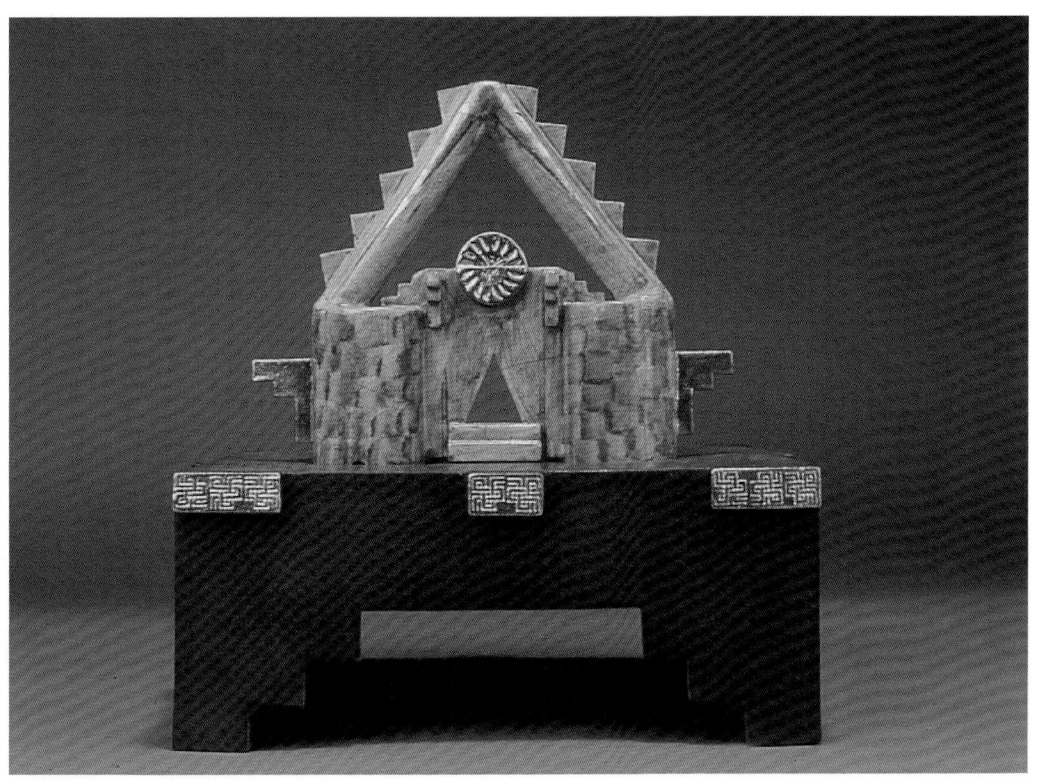

Fig. 4.52
**Temple of Sound (1998)**
Robin L. Hodgkinson, Haydenville, Massachusetts, USA. This double vessel flute with platform is made of white earthenware. Robin used slabbed, extruded and thrown components in its construction and fired it multiple times, raku style, to Cone 07. It has accents of acrylic paint, gold leaf and copper foil. The right chamber is tuned to play a chromatic octave, and the left plays the 1st, 3rd, 5th and 6th tones of the same scale. 15" x 14" x 12".

harmonies. Some of the chambers produce a single pitch, and others have finger holes. Since each instrument is actually an amalgamated collection of several ocarinas of different sizes, its overall pitch range can be very broad—as much as three octaves on his larger instruments.

*Pitch-Jump Flutes*

Pitch-jump flutes are highly unusual instruments unique to pre-Columbian America. Though there are several different designs, their name comes from a common characteristic—when a player blows harder, the flute's pitch jumps discretely from a lower to a higher tone.

In these airduct flutes, two or three chambers share a single windway and aperture. One type of pitch-jump flute has a small whistling chamber inside a larger, partially open chamber. A second type has a chamber around the aperture of a whistle or ocarina. Susan Rawcliffe developed a pitch-jump flute based on this design, that she calls a *whiffle ocarina.* In this instrument, one chamber is enclosed and has finger holes, while the second chamber is open like a cup. To play it, one hand operates the finger holes on the first chamber, and the other hand slides over the large open end of the second chamber, closing and opening it. The chambers interact with each other depending on the player's breath pressure, permitting a range of vocal sounds and bird and animal calls. Susan's whiffle ocarina can be seen in figure 4.58 and heard on track 24 of the CD.

A third type of pitch-jump flute has three chambers; one chamber with an airduct leading to its aperture, another with its aperture positioned directly opposite, and a third open chamber that surrounds the other two.

*Nose Flutes*

With nose flutes, sound is created by air blown through a player's nose. Some people believe that the breath from the nose contains the spirit, and this imparts a different and more meaningful quality to the music. A number of cultures have traditional nose flutes, in a variety of forms. Some have airducts and some are end-blown or side-blown.

One style of ducted nose flute uses the player's mouth as a globular resonating cavity. Air from the nose is blown through a windway and across an aperture positioned over the player's mouth. Pitch is changed using the throat, tongue and cheeks to manipulate the mouth cavity. On this instrument it's easy to play tones that slide from pitch to pitch, imitate bird calls, and make other musical sound effects. Listen to track 17 on the accompanying CD for examples.

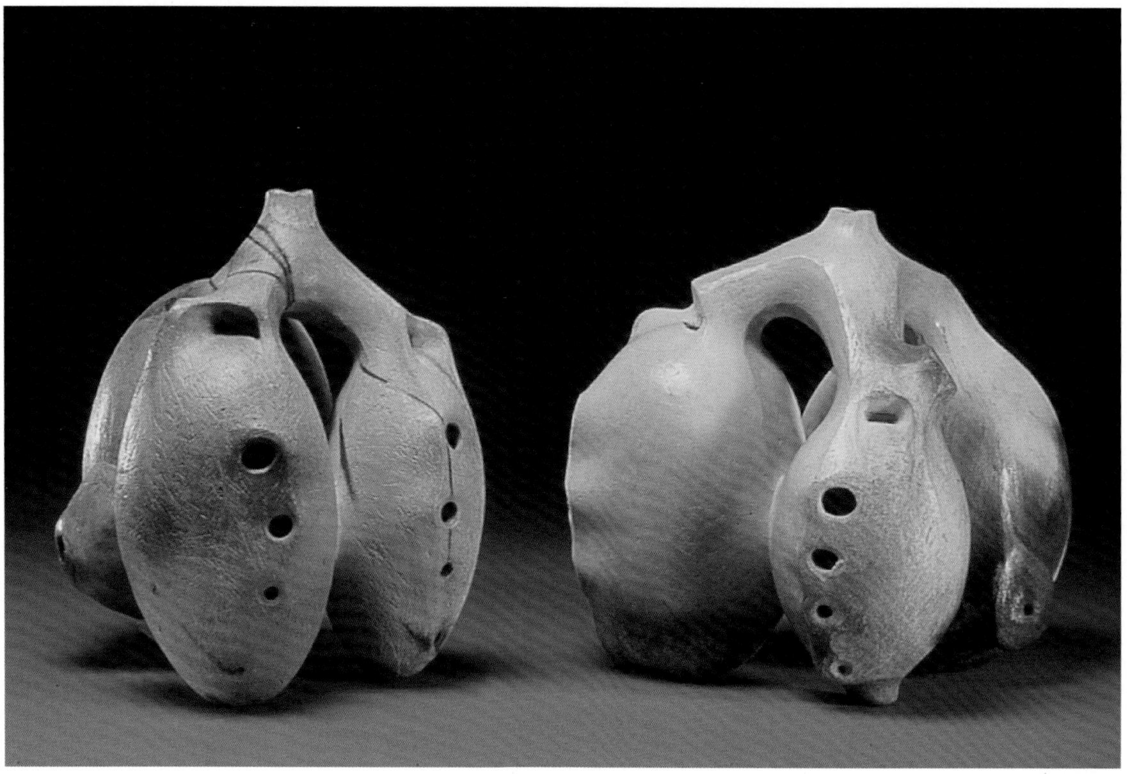

Fig. 4.53
**Huacas**
Sharon Rowell, Stinson Beach, California, USA. Triple-chambered ocarinas with two melody chambers and one drone chamber. These two instruments, designed in collaboration with Alan Tower, are unique among Sharon's creations in that each of the three chambers is tuned to a different key. Stoneware, saggar fired. 8 inches in height. Hear this instrument on CD track 15.

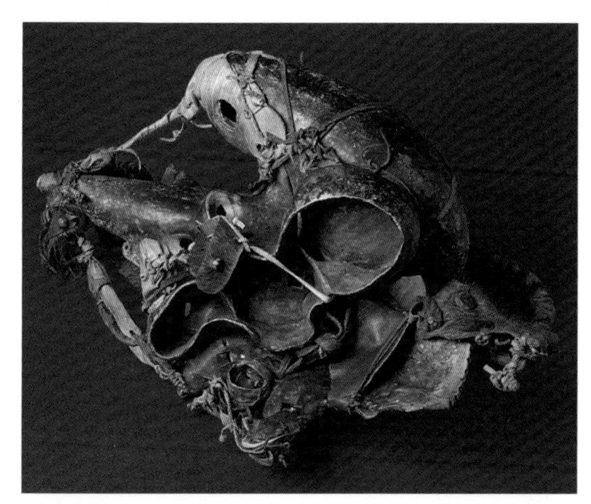

Fig. 4.54
**Multiple-Chambered Ocarina**
Aguinaldo da Silva, Olinda, Pernambuco, Brazil. An ocarina with seven chambers. Each chamber has its own windway, and they all converge in a row of blow holes that can be seen in the lower right of the photo. Some of the chambers have finger holes, others are drones. Earthenware and leather.

An extension of this design channels all of the sound from the aperture through a long hollow tube (figure 4.57). This tubular resonator forces the instrument's pitches to conform to the harmonic series dictated by the length of the tube. What goes into the tube as a continuously varying pitch comes out as a series of discrete intervals. Listen to track 37 on the accompanying CD to hear this effect.

*Water Flutes*

Some airduct flutes rely on water inside to alter the pitch, tone or airflow of the instrument. A simple example is a small bird whistle, popularly known in many cultures as a *nightingale* or *cuckoo*. Water is held in a small pot with a whistle attached to its spout. The instrument makes chirping, birdlike sounds when air blown through the whistle exits through the water.

Susan Rawcliffe's water flutes (figure 4.59) have a mouthpiece (either airduct or end-blown) that connects to a long perpendicular tube with ball-shaped chambers on each end. The flute is rocked back and forth while the player blows into the mouthpiece. This causes the water inside the tube to move and vary the flute's pitch by changing the effective length of its air chamber. A finger hole in each of the balls provides the player some control over the motion of the water, by holding or releasing the vacuum created by the water's motion. Susan indicates that the water impacts the instrument's tone in ways that can't be fully controlled. Her water flute can be heard on track 8 of the CD.

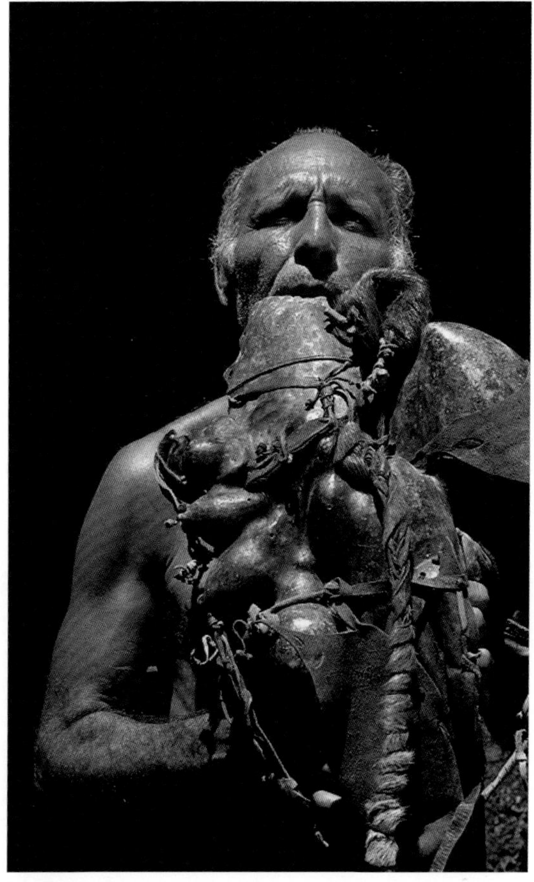

Fig. 4.55
Aguinaldo da Silva playing his multiple-chambered ocarina.

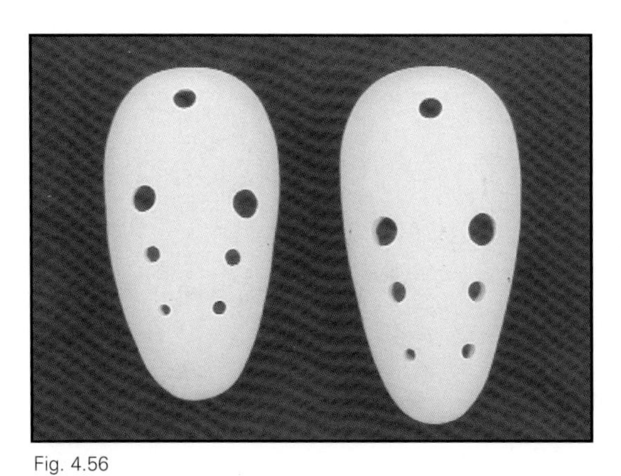

Fig. 4.56
**Nose Ocarinas**
John Taylor, Wiltshire, England. These instruments are played with the nose, blowing across the open blowhole. Their range is an octave and a fourth. John notes that they are easy to play and provide good tone control. They were formed on a pair of wooden interior molds. Earthenware. 5 inches in length.

Pre-Columbian whistling water vessels are a unique and intriguing form of ceramic instrument. They were produced by a variety of cultures over a period of several thousand years, in a wide geographical area stretching from Peru to Mexico. However, following the Conquest their production ceased, and although their mechanics are understood by modern scholars and musicians, their use remains a mystery.

The outward appearance of whistling water vessels varies widely. Most have two chambers, but there are many with a single chamber, and some have been found with as many as six chambers. The two chambers in the double-chambered versions are connected at the bottom by a hollow tube

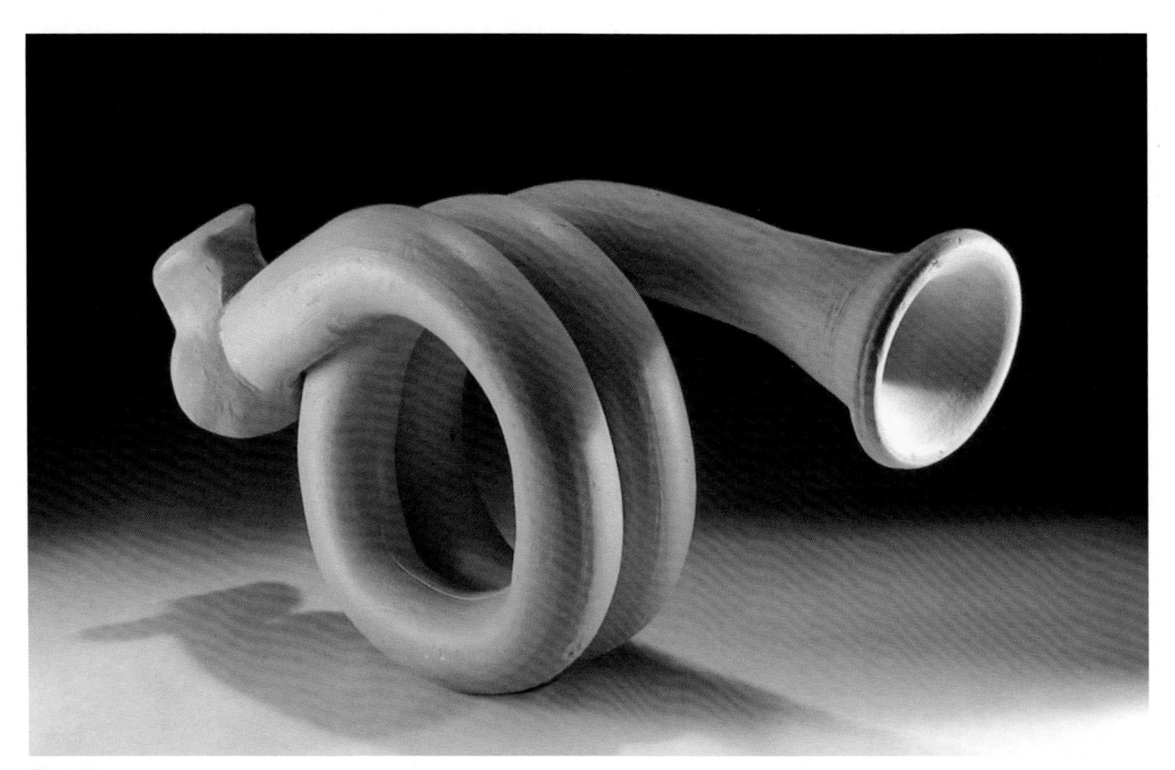

Fig. 4.57
**Nose Flute with Tubular Resonator**
Barry Hall, Westborough, Massachusetts, USA. This ducted nose flute uses the player's mouth as a globular resonating cavity. Air from the nose is blown through a windway and across an aperture positioned over the player's mouth. Pitch is changed using the throat, tongue and cheeks to manipulate the mouth cavity. The sound from the aperture is channeled through a long hollow tube that forces the instrument's pitches to conform to the harmonic series dictated by the length of the tube. What goes into the tube as a continuously varying pitch comes out in a series of discrete intervals. Listen to track 37 on the accompanying CD to hear this effect. 11 inches in length.

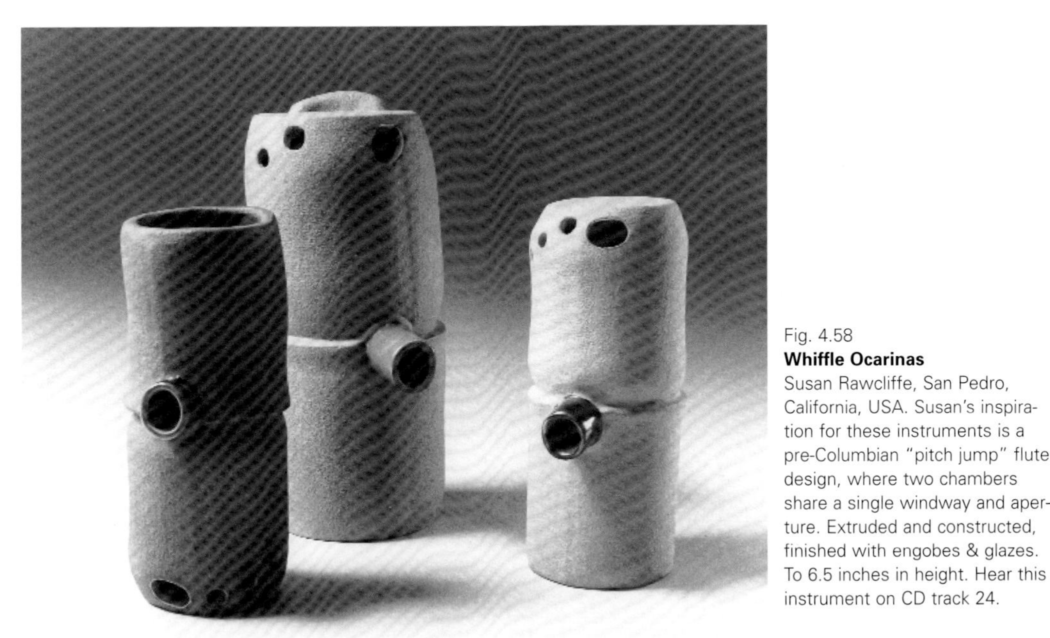

Fig. 4.58
**Whiffle Ocarinas**
Susan Rawcliffe, San Pedro, California, USA. Susan's inspiration for these instruments is a pre-Columbian "pitch jump" flute design, where two chambers share a single windway and aperture. Extruded and constructed, finished with engobes & glazes. To 6.5 inches in height. Hear this instrument on CD track 24.

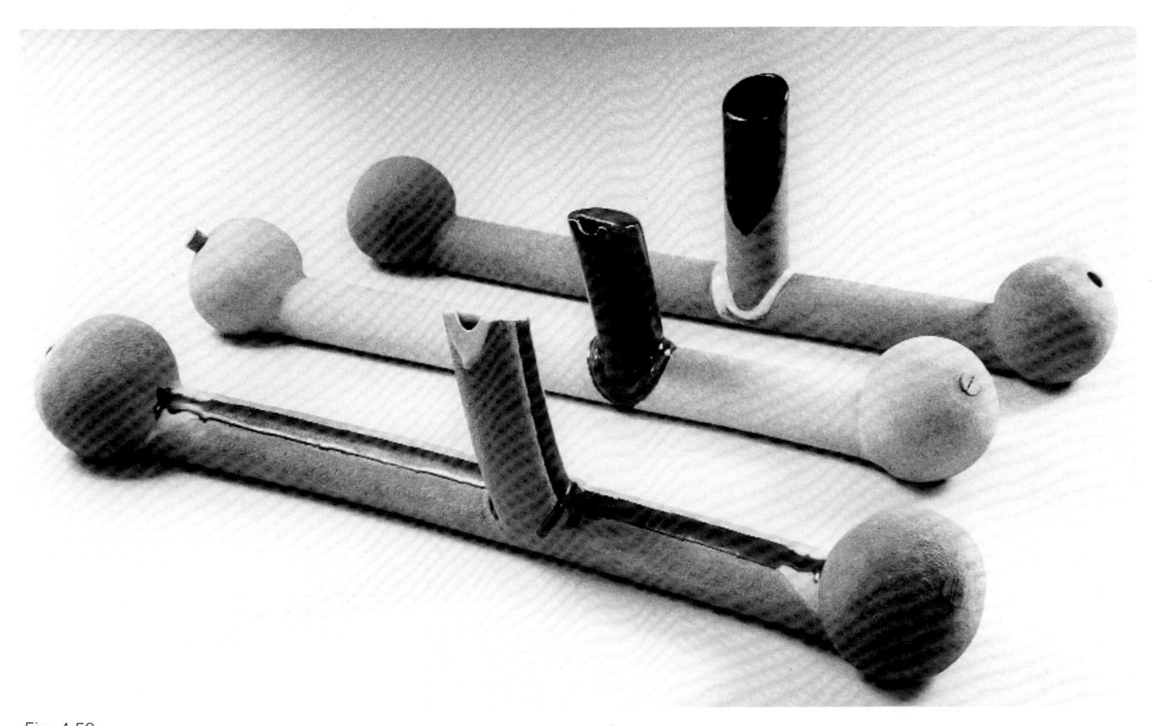

Fig. 4.59
**Water Flutes**
Susan Rawcliffe, San Pedro, California, USA. Water inside the ball and tube structure flows back and forth as the flute is rocked while being blown, creating a variety of pitch change effects. Extruded, pinched and constructed, finished with engobes & glazes. Approximately 22 inches in length. Hear this instrument on CD track 8.

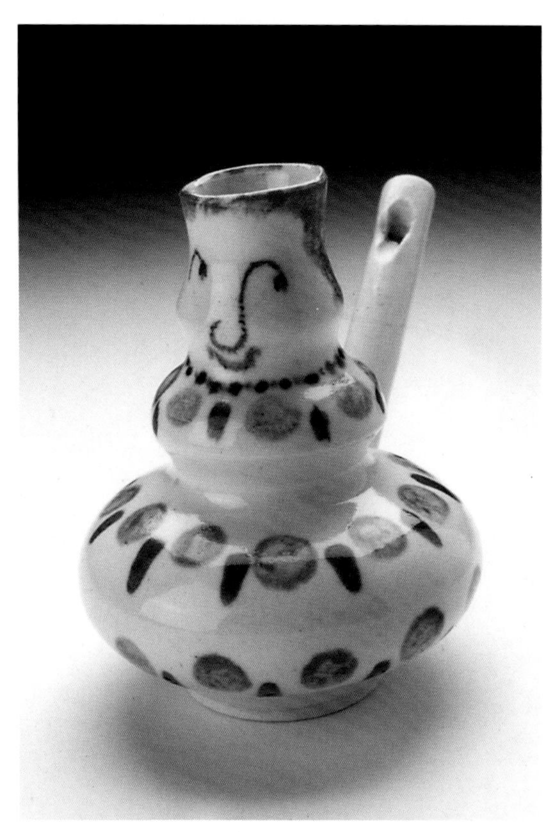

Fig. 4.60
**Water Whistle**
Constance Sherman, Garrison, New York, USA. This porcelain whistle, blown through its stem, produces a warbling, birdlike sound when water is inside the vessel. Connie says, "the challenging thing about a water whistle is that you can't really test it until it has been bisque fired, and by then it's too late to correct mistakes."

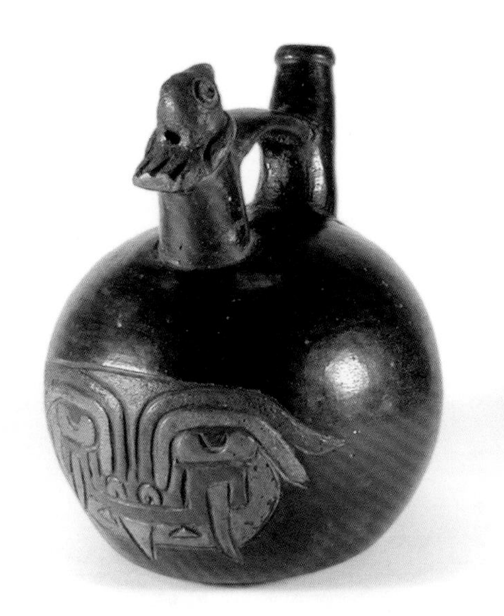

Fig. 4.61
**Whistling Pot**
From the Ica Valley, Peru. 8 inches in height. Field Museum collection.

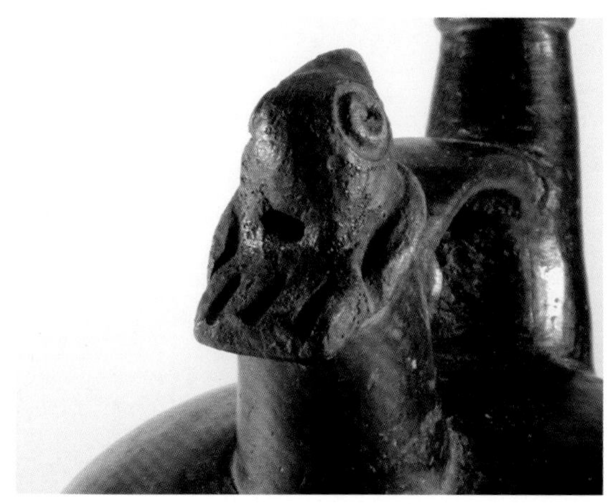

Fig. 4.62
Detail showing the sound hole.

and bridged at the top by a handle. One chamber has a vertical spout and the other often has a sculpted figure, which may depict an animal, multiple animals, humans or deities. A small globular airduct whistle is embedded inside the figure or on the handle. The windway leads from the interior of the chamber to the whistle.

Modern investigators have determined that whistling water vessels can be played several ways. The simplest is to blow into the spout, which forces air through the chambers and out through the whistle assembly. Those with two or more chambers can be played without blowing, by filling the vessel half-full of water and rocking it back and forth. As the vessel is tipped, water runs from one chamber to the other through a small tube. The air

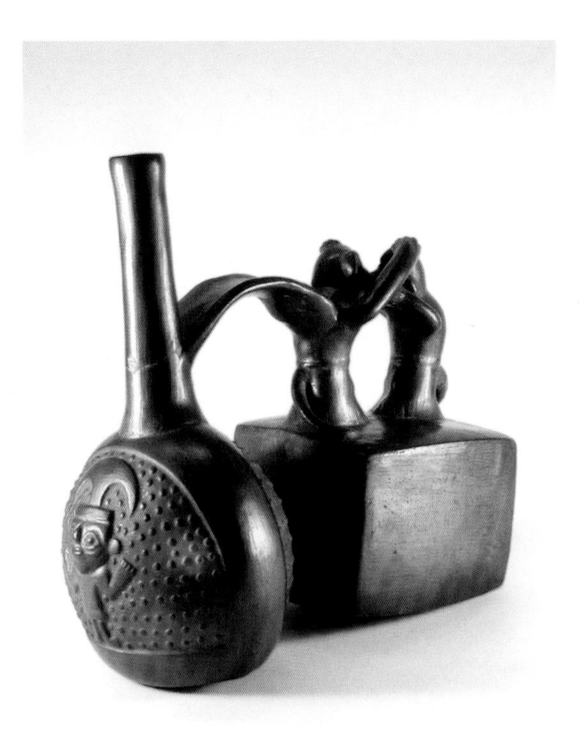
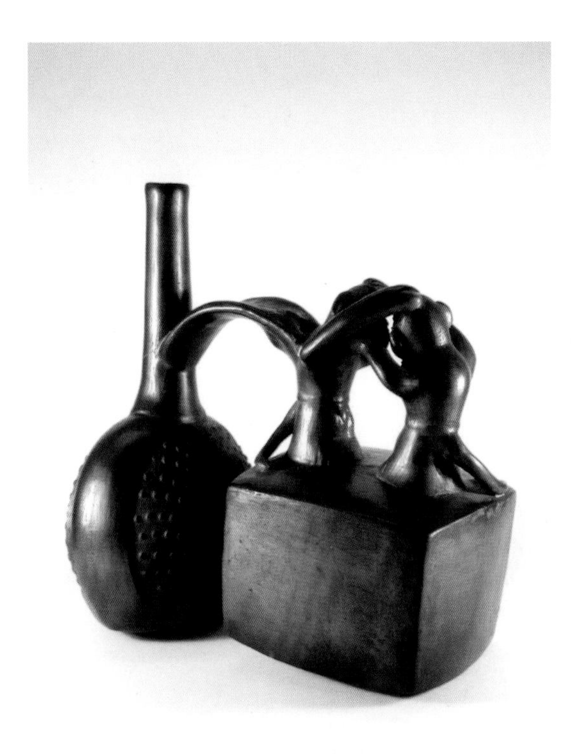

Fig. 4.63 - 4.64
**Whistling Monkey Vessel**
Two monkeys appear to wrestle or play atop one chamber of this double-chambered whistling vessel from the Moche Valley, north coast of Peru. Approx. 1000 A.D. 9 inches in height. Field Museum collection. Hear instruments like this on CD track 25.

displaced in the second chamber is pushed out through the whistling assembly, causing it to sound, as illustrated in figure 4.65. Since the whistle assembly constricts the exiting air to a narrow passage, if the vessel is tipped quickly, some of the water will bubble back through the tube into the first vessel, which causes a bubbling sound in the chambers and a warbling sound in the whistle. See figure 4.66 for a visual representation of this playing technique.

A third way to play the vessels is to blow into them while they are partially filled with water, which produces a variety of burbling and chirping sounds. Track 25 on the accompanying CD demonstrates some of the effects that can be produced with the breath and with water.

The whistling assemblies are more acoustically complex than they may at first appear, and this is part of the reason that these instruments can produce such a wide variety of interesting sounds. Many of the whistling assemblies are covered or enshrouded in a semi-closed cap, which may take different forms, depending on the sculpted figure in which the whistle is contained. By restricting the flow of air that escapes from the whistle, the cap over the whistling mechanism creates a "breaking tone" or pitch jump. This is similar to the design of pitch-jump flutes described earlier in this chapter. The air volume inside the cap and the size of the opening impact the pitch, volume and timbre of the breaking tone. These factors were manipulated with extreme precision by the ancient builders of

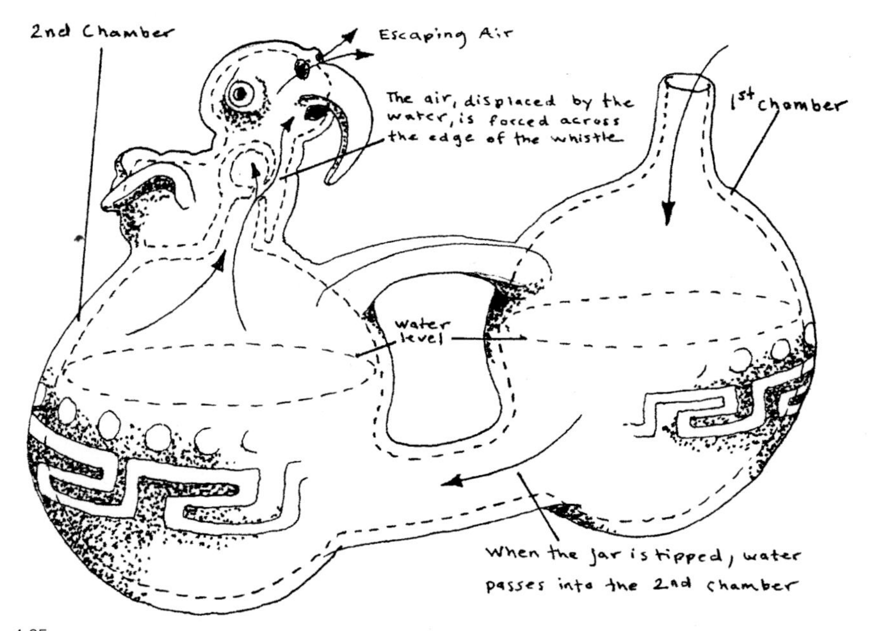


Fig. 4.65
**Mechanics of Whistling Water Vessels**
Diagram showing how water operates the whistling mechanism on a vessel from the Vicus culture. Illustrated by Brian Ransom.

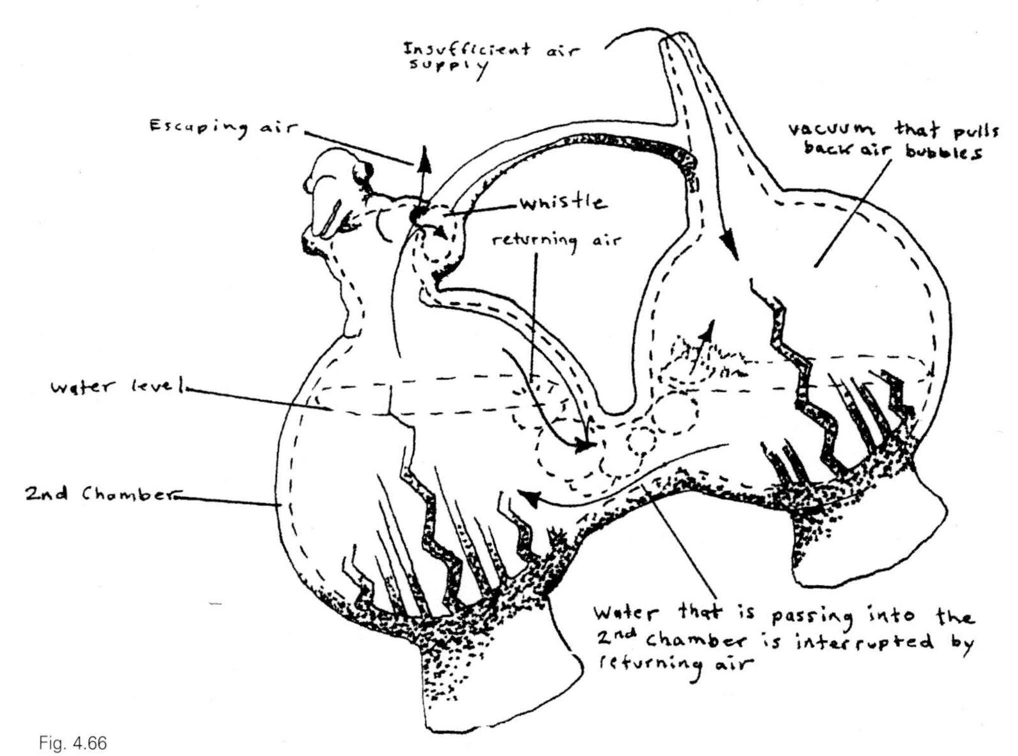


Fig. 4.66
**Mechanics of Whistling Water Vessels**
Diagram illustrating how a warbling sound is created in a vessel from the Chancay culture. Hear this effect on CD track 25.

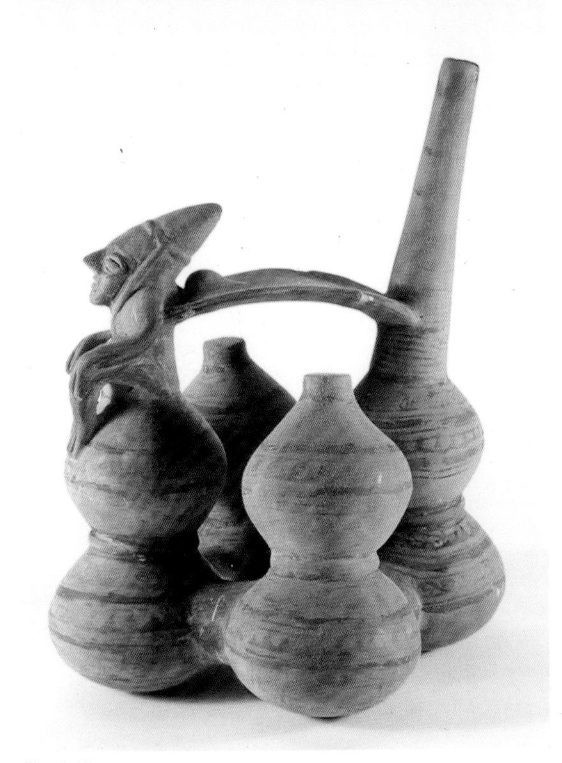

Fig. 4.67
**Four-Chambered Whistling Vessel**
An unusual example with four chambers. Moche Valley, north coast of Peru. Approx. 1000 A.D. 10 inches in height. Field Museum collection.

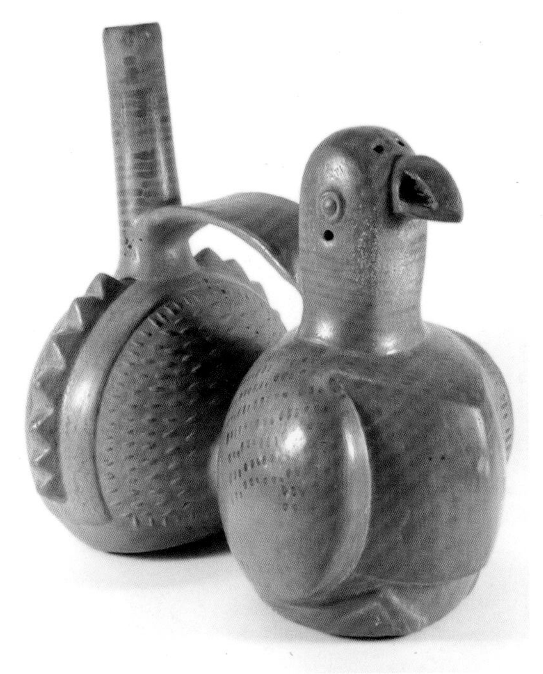

Fig. 4.68
**Double-Chambered Whistling Vessel**
Moche Valley, north coast of Peru. Approx. 1000 A.D. 8 inches in height. Field Museum collection.

these instruments to create a wide variety of sounds from the vessels.

Virtually all whistling vessels depict some sort of figure. Many are birds, but there are also other animals, humans and deities. Some experts have postulated that the sound of a particular vessel is intended to imitate the figure depicted on it. Brian Ransom, who examined, measured and recorded hundreds of these instruments in Peruvian museums and collections as part of a research fellowship, strongly agrees. He concluded that there is a noticeable correlation between the sound produced by the vessel and the figure it depicts. Although many of the vessels expertly imitate bird sounds, some of the more unusual examples Brian examined included a vessel depicting a sea lion figure, which produced a howling sound like a sea creature, and a vessel in the image of a swimming person, which produced bubbling water sounds.

Brian believes the sounds are most likely the "spiritual voices" of the figures depicted by the vessels. The societies that made these instruments were animistic, which means that they believed that every natural object had its own soul or spirit. Brian suggests that the whistling vessels were "objects of power" in cultures where the impact of musical instruments resided in their voice more than their form. He speculates, "If the images

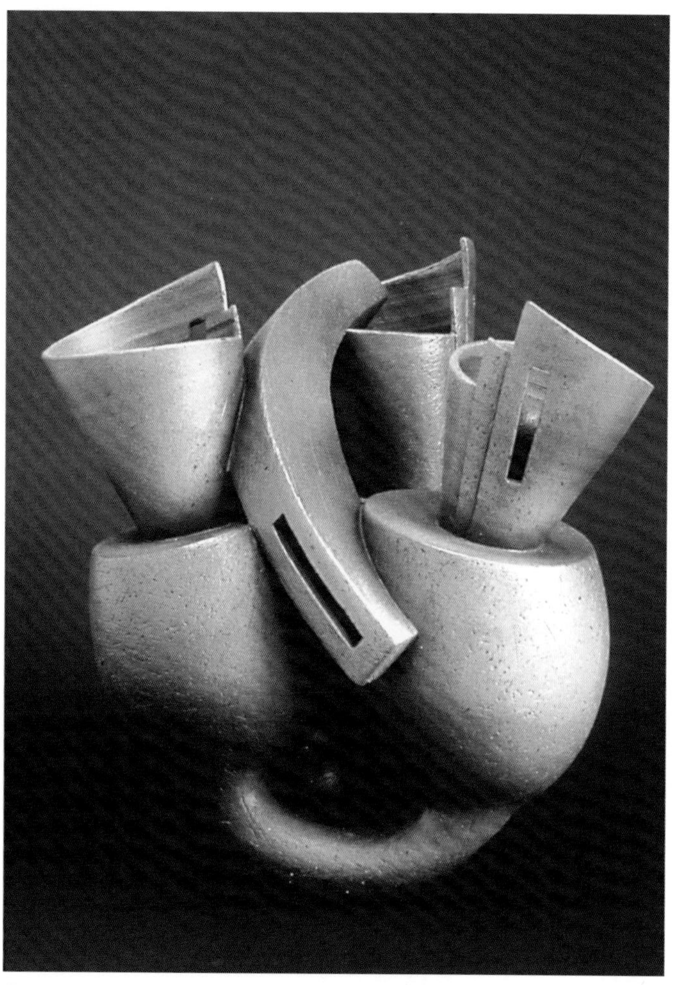

Fig. 4.69
**Triformation VI**
Brian Ransom, St. Petersburg, Florida, USA. Triple-chambered earthenware whistling water vessel that sounds when tipped, like its pre-Columbian ancestors. 8 inches in height.

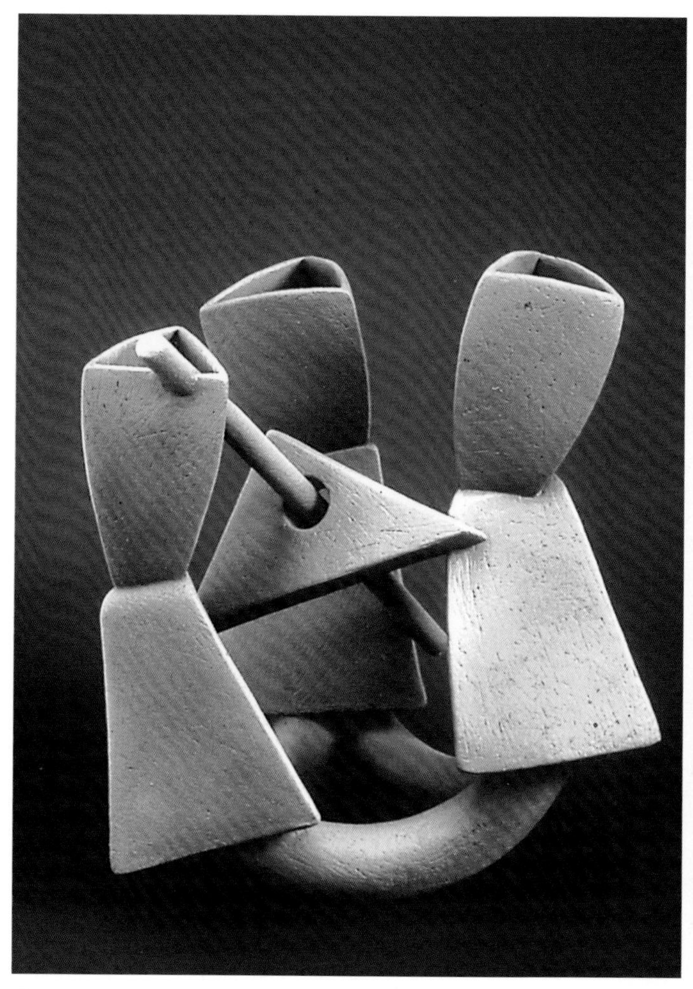

Fig. 4.70
**Triformation VIII**
Brian Ransom, St. Petersburg, Florida, USA. Earthenware whistling water vessel. 10 inches in height.

depicted in the ceramics of these pre-Columbian cultures were thought to have the ability to exert power through contact with the deity they represented, then how natural it must have been to give that deity a voice through which to speak in the form of a whistling vessel."

Daniel Statnekov's life was radically changed by a pre-Columbian ceramic whistling vessel, which he bought on a whim at an auction. He discovered that blowing into the vessel produced a profound personal spiritual awakening, which induced him to refocus his life in order to devote all his energy to studying these vessels. Daniel researched other examples in museums, explored their sounds, visited sites in Peru where they were used, and even become a ceramist and learned to reproduce them. Based on his experiences and research, he postulates that ancient Peruvian civilizations used the

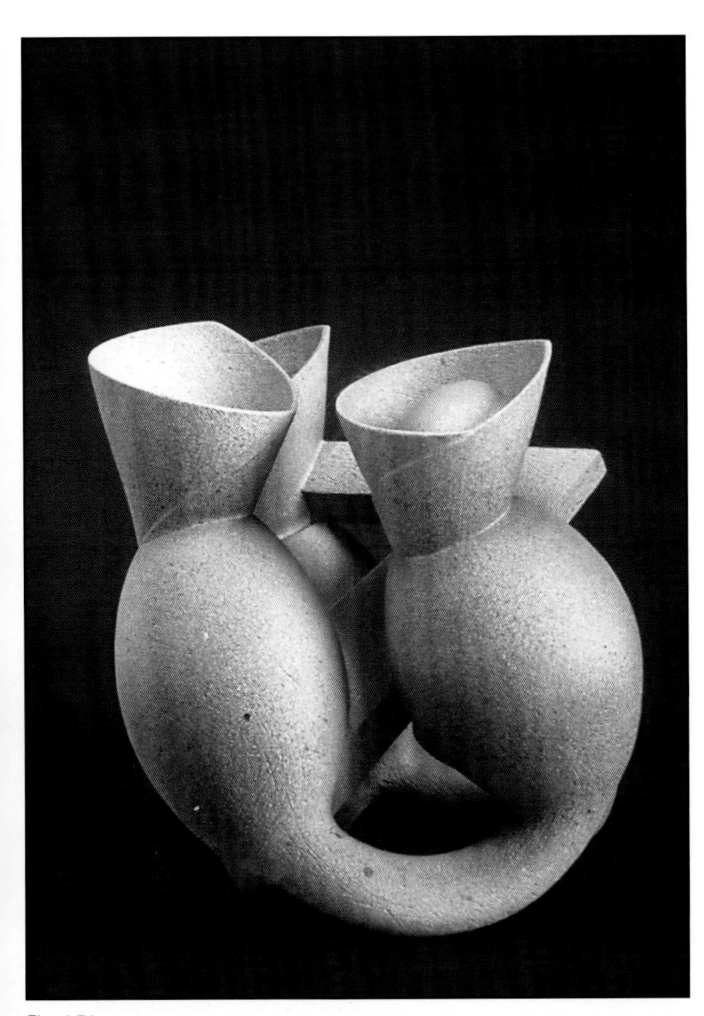

Fig. 4.71
**Triformation III**
Brian Ransom, St. Petersburg, Florida, USA. Earthenware whistling water vessel. 7.5 inches in height.

sound of these instruments to effect psycho-physiological reactions. He wrote about his experiences in a book titled *Animated Earth* (see the "Bibliography"). Others, including Daniel's apprentice Don Wright, build and play these vessels today for this purpose. They believe that carefully tuned whistles, when blown by a group of people, can produce vibrations in the players that induce an expanded state of consciousness, "opening the portal to the shamanic realm."

Although the design and craftsmanship of these ancient vessels was highly evolved, their purpose remains a mystery to us, and may be lost for all time. Painted or sculpted scenes on pre-Columbian pottery depict many other musical instruments and most aspects of life, but strangely there are no known depictions of whistling water vessels or how they were used. This seems to support the assertion that they had a sacred or ritualistic use.

In the realm of ceramic instruments, whistling water vessels are unique and enchanting. Listen to their sound on track 25 of the accompanying CD and see if you agree.

### *Chamberduct Flutes*

A *chamberduct* is another mechanism for creating an edgetone. It is different from an airduct assembly or an open blow hole, but serves the same purpose. A chamberduct assembly has a small chamber with two holes opposite each other. When air is blown through the chamber, it creates an edgetone. This is similar to the workings of the whistle on a modern teapot. Another resonating chamber can be constructed around the hole on the far side of the chamberduct, and finger holes can be added to the chamberduct itself to make an instrument capable of producing multiple pitches.

The use of a chamberduct assembly on a musical instrument is unique to the pre-Columbian world, where they were used as early as 800 B.C. by the Olmec culture. Susan Rawcliffe, who devised the term "chamberduct" to describe this sound-producing mechanism, has studied and reconstructed a variety of pre-Columbian chamberduct instruments with multiple chambers. She indicates that the multiple chambers interact as a complex, acoustically-coupled unit and must have properly-proportioned volumes in order to produce sound. Susan concludes that "The demanding construction of these acoustically very complex

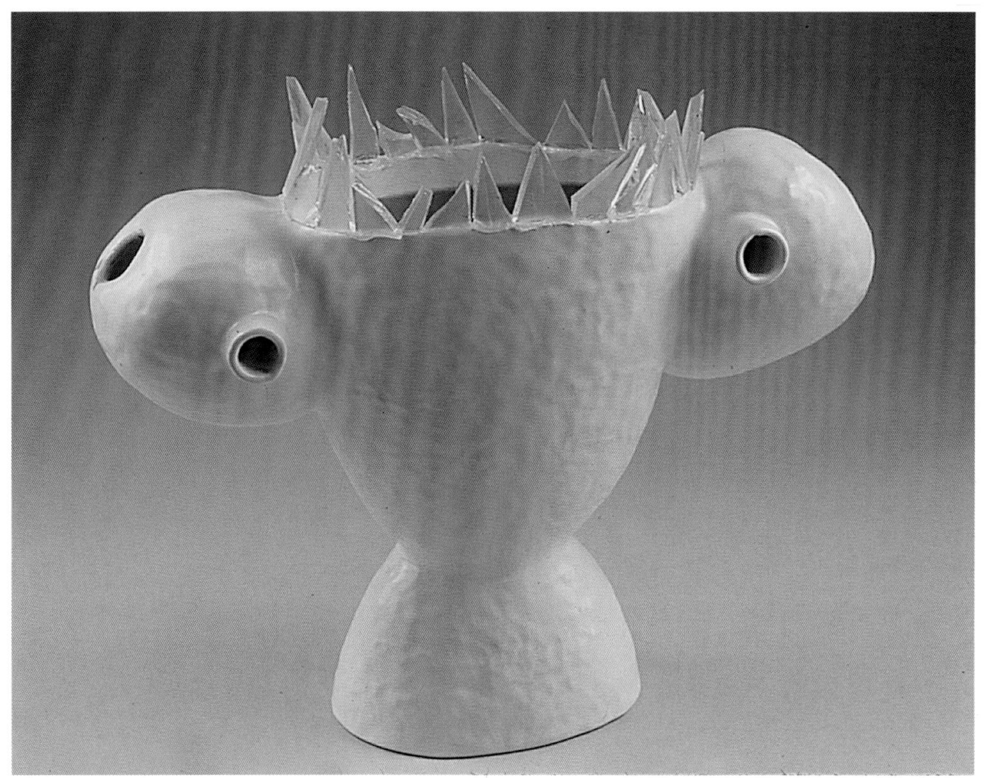

Fig. 4.72
**After the Ball: Double Chamberduct Flute**
Susan Rawcliffe, San Pedro, California, USA. This unusual chamberduct flute, a mixture of ancient and modern aesthetics, is designed for two players at once. Coiled & constructed white talc clay with white glaze; glass, silicone and colored water. 13 inches in height.

instruments must be the product of centuries of evolution."

The sound of a chamberduct flute is often reedy, and the instrument is capable of many variations in timbre that range from raspy gurglings to wrenching cries. Susan Rawcliffe demonstrates some of these sounds on track 26 of the accompanying CD.

A remarkable double chamberduct flute from the Bahia culture has a shared blowing chamber that connects two four-chambered flutes, each with two finger holes. A related instrument is the Mayan

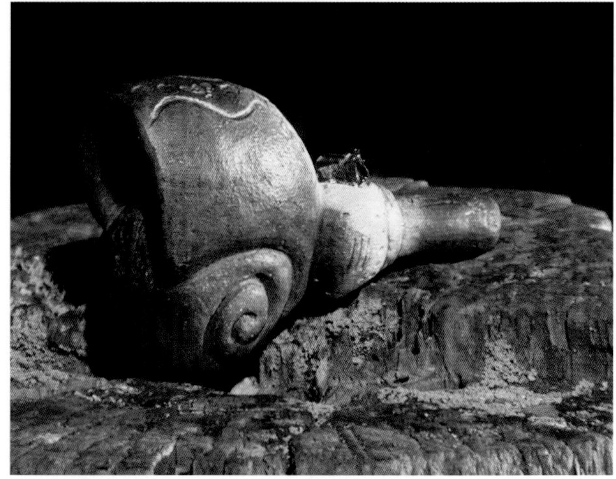

Fig. 4.73
**Ehecatl**
Rafael Bejarano, Guadalajara, Mexico, an ancient Mexican chamberduct flute design, in a shape reminiscent of a seashell. Stoneware, pit fired, gold paint. 4 inches in length. Hear this instrument on CD track 1.

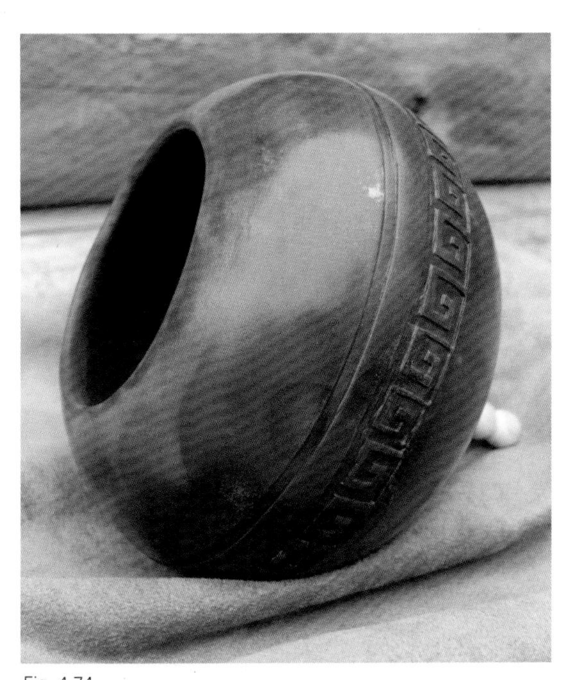

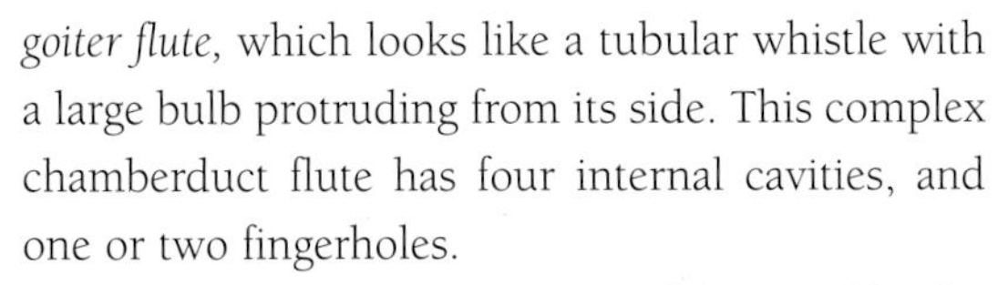

Fig. 4.74
**Wind Whistle**
Rod Kendall, Tenino, Washington, USA. Similar to the ehecatl, this instrument does not produce a specific musical pitch. Rod describes its sound as, "a soft wind sound rising into a hollow haunting howl, reminiscent of the wind howling through the trees." Saggar fired, red Cone 6 stoneware body with turned fossil walrus ivory mouthpiece, 4 inches in diameter.

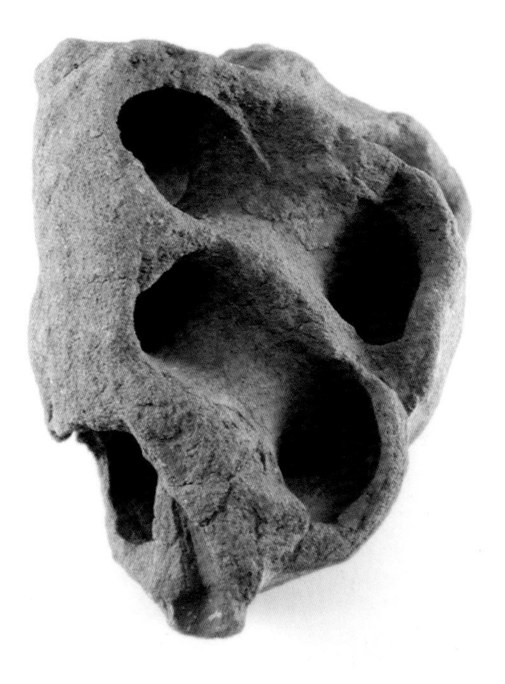

Fig. 4.75
**Ceramic Conch Trumpet**
Moche culture, Peru, circa 100-800 A.D. A fragment of a ceramic trumpet imitating the form of a conch shell. This cross-section shows the intricately shaped spiral interior of the horn. 5 inches in height. Collection of the Phoebe Apperson Hearst Museum.

*goiter flute,* which looks like a tubular whistle with a large bulb protruding from its side. This complex chamberduct flute has four internal cavities, and one or two fingerholes.

Another ancient chamberduct flute, used by the Mexicas or Aztecs, is commonly called an *ehecatl.* In Mexica mythology, Ehecatl is the god of the wind. The instrument's long blowing tube focuses an airstream into a chamberduct-type assembly. Figure 4.73 shows an ehecatl made by Rafael Bejarano, in the shape of a seashell. The ehecatl produces an unusual raspy sound, sometimes similar to a howling wind. The voice of this instrument can be heard on track 1 of the accompanying CD. Historically, these instruments were often formed in the shape of a human skull, and are sometimes referred to as "the whistle of death." However, Rafael believes that a macabre interpretation of this instrument is misleading. Instead, he says, it represents the death of the ego and the freedom of the spirit, "for the wind represents the Spirit, and this instrument creates the sound of the wind, with its softness, gentleness and strength."

## Horns (Lip-Reed Aerophones)

Members of the horn family are more accurately called lip-reed aerophones. These are wind instruments whose sound is activated by the player's buzzed lips making a "raspberry" sound into a mouthpiece. The mouthpiece is usually, but not always, a small cup or bowl shape. Well-known examples of lip-reed instruments include the modern brass family such as the trumpet, trombone, French horn and tuba. Although these instruments are commonly made from metal, it's possible to make many types of horns from clay.

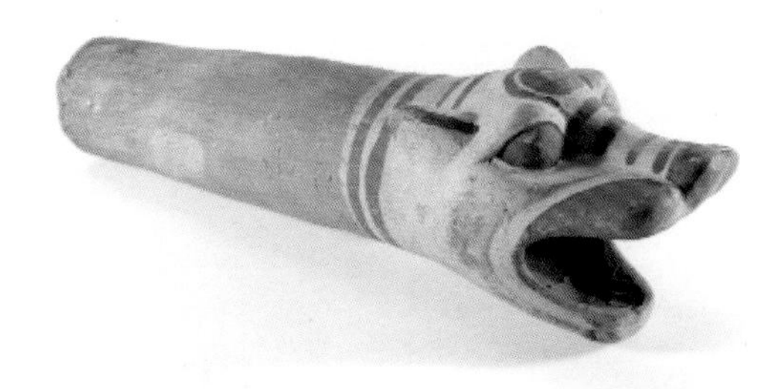

Fig. 4.78
**Jaguar Trumpet**
Chimbote site, Peru. The bell from a pre-Columbian ceramic trumpet, in the shape of a jaguar's head. The sound of the trumpet emanated from the jaguar's mouth. 12 inches in length. Field Museum collection.

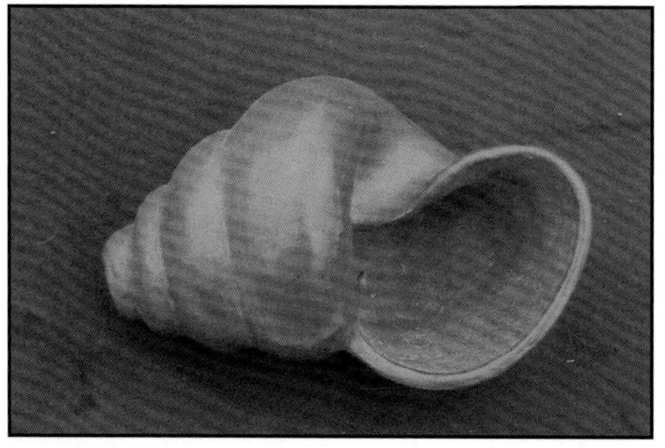

Fig. 4.76
**Conch Trumpet**
John Taylor, Wiltshire, England. This modern version of an ancient conch horn has a left hand spiral and is in the key of G. It was made by adding small sections around a spiral shaped cone. Earthenware, 6 inches in length.

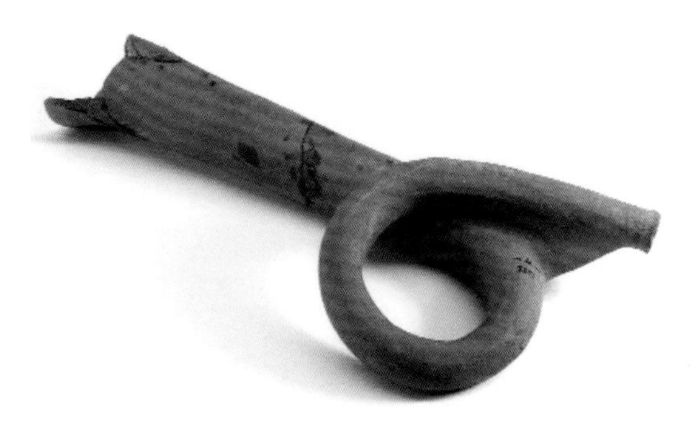

Fig. 4.77
**Ceramic Trumpet**
Moche culture, Peru, circa 100-800 A.D. An almost complete ceramic trumpet, except for the mouthpiece (missing from the right side of the instrument in the photo) and a fragment of the bell (on the left end). 14 inches in length. Collection of the Phoebe Apperson Hearst Museum.

A horn's sound is produced by a vibrating column or chamber of air, which is put into motion and reinforced at a certain frequency by the vibration of a player's lips. Clay is a good material for constructing lip-reed aerophones because it's a dense, rigid material that supports a stable vibration and provides a clear tone. Additionally, most horns have the advantage that they can be sounded and tuned before firing, while the clay is still in its leather-hard state.

One challenge of using clay is that some horn family instruments require narrow tubular sections that are four to eight feet long, or even longer. If these tubes were straight they would not fit into an average kiln, and once fired the instruments would be very fragile due to their unwieldy size. To mitigate these concerns it's usually necessary either to develop a design where the tube is convoluted or twisted around in a way that significantly reduces the overall dimensions of the instrument, or to fire the instrument in multiple sections that are joined after they are fired.

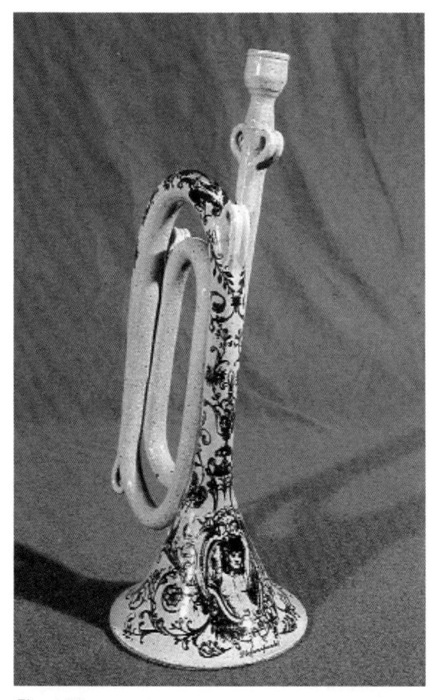

Fig. 4.79
**Trumpet**
Richard Schneider, Stevens Point, Wisconsin, USA. Constructed from extruded tubes and wheel-thrown pieces. Glaze was poured inside the horn for a smooth surface. The exterior was spray-glazed, fired to cone 9. 17 inches in height.

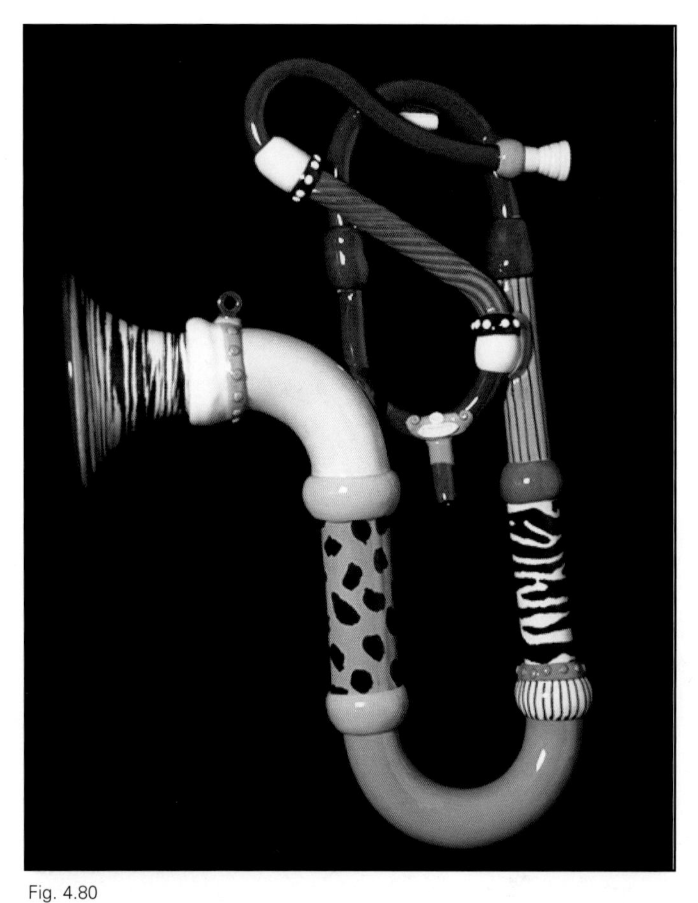

Fig. 4.80
**Sax-Bugle**
Steve Smeed, Eugene, Oregon, USA. The Sax-Bugle is a bugle designed with a saxophone-like shape. Seen here with a standard sized bell, it also can be made to stand on its own large bell. Porcelain clay colored with stains, clear glaze, high-fired. 21 inches in height.

The lip-reed ceramic instruments presented in the following sections are organized into the following families:

- **Trumpets** - basic horns.
- **Cornetti** – shorter trumpet-like instruments with open tone holes.
- **Didjeridus** – a specific style of drone horn with an open mouthpiece.
- **Globular horns** – sound-producing vessels or chambers (rather than tubes).

### *Trumpets*

Although the name *trumpet* often refers to a specific modern brass instrument, this book will use the term in a broader sense to refer to the family of lip-reed tubular horns. The horns themselves are composed of a long tube which is either the same diameter throughout or gradually increases in size from the mouthpiece to the distal end, which often terminates in some sort of flare or "bell."

The earliest trumpets were probably made from animal horns, hollow bones, bamboo, or sea shells

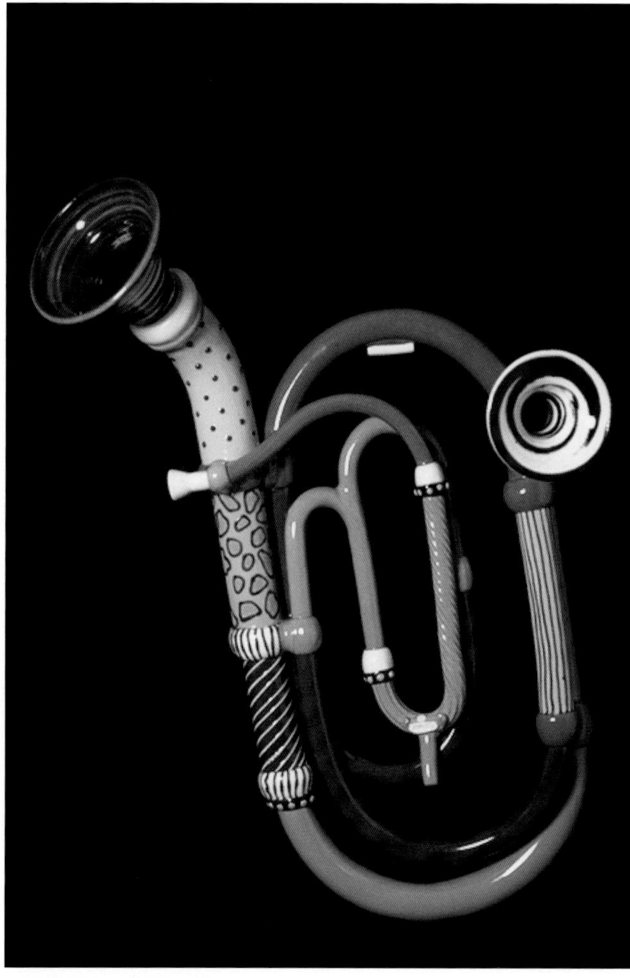

Fig. 4.81
**Double-Belled Euphonium**
Steve Smeed, Eugene, Oregon, USA. Since he was a teenager Steve has had a fascination with this instrument, which inspired him to join his junior high school band. Now he has made one from clay. 28 inches in height.

with a spiral bore, such as the conch. All of these materials, with the addition of a mouth hole, can be played in trumpet fashion. In fact, some early ceramic trumpets surviving from pre-Columbian America are imitative replicas of sea shells and animal horns. The interior of a ceramic seashell-style trumpet from Peru is shown in figure 4.75. Notice the elegantly spiraling bore of the instrument, and

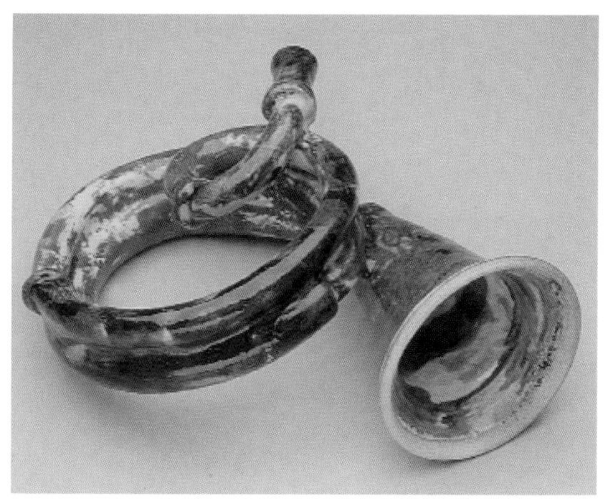

Fig. 4.82
**Wood-Fired Spiral Horn**
Jason Gaddy, Rochester, Washington, USA. This horn is played like a bugle. Several octaves are achievable and rich varied tones are available to a skilled horn player. 15 inches in length.

imagine the building techniques necessary to create such an object.

Another common pre-Columbian ceramic trumpet design is a gradually tapering tube with a single loop and a bell. Figure 4.77 shows the basic form of many of these trumpets, though the bells were often highly decorated with human figures or the heads of animals, such as the jaguar trumpet bell shown in figure 4.78.

Ceramic trumpets also have roots in other cultures. Small earthenware horns have been found in Egyptian burial sites. In medieval Europe, clay horns were probably used for signaling since they were found beneath castles rather than in grave sites. At carnival time, small curled pottery trumpets were sold as novelties at fairs in Southern Europe.

A number of modern makers have created ceramic trumpets and horns. It is interesting to consider that, although most of these modern horns are imitative of their brass cousins, ceramic trumpets may have a history dating back at least as far as metal trumpets.

**_Making a Spiral Ceramic Horn with Dag Sørensen_**

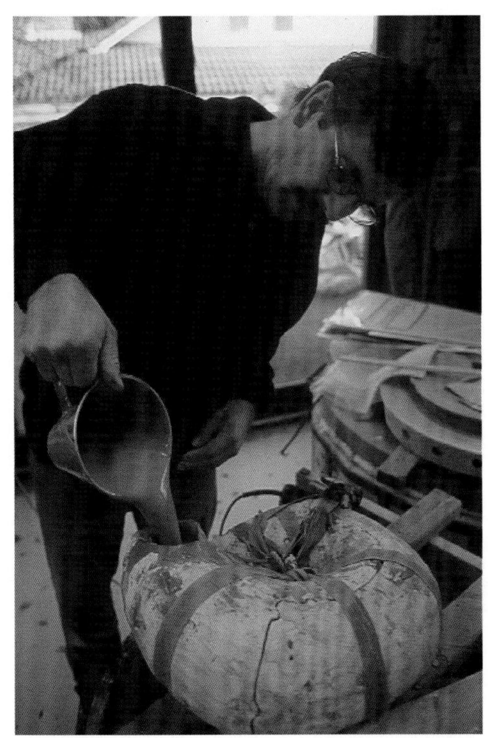

Fig. 4.83
Pouring slip into the plaster mold.

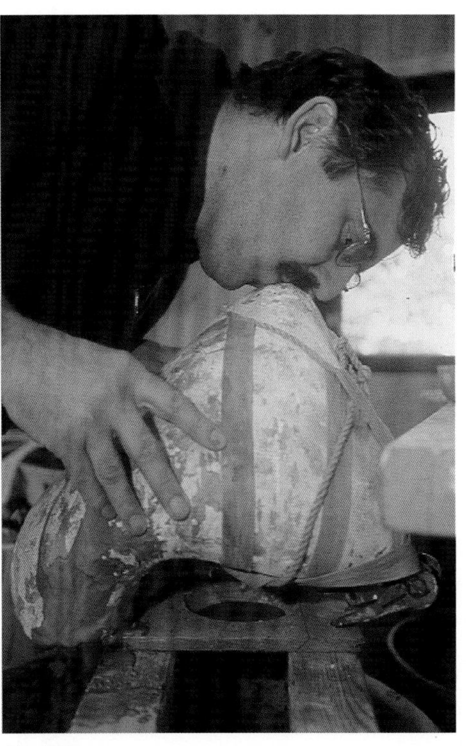

Fig. 4.84
Blowing to check for an open air channel.

Steve Smeed makes a variety of unusual and sometimes whimsical bugles from porcelain and stoneware (figures 4.80 and 4.81). His instruments are a combination of extruded, slab-built, wheel-thrown and slip-cast sections, assembled and fired as one piece. Steve used a basic bugle design as a starting point for his explorations, which have evolved into a variety of instruments with tubes, chambers, multiple bells and even multiple mouthpieces. They also include a device that's standard equipment on modern brass instruments: a *spit valve,* which is a small opening that helps a player drain the collected moisture from inside the crooks of the horn.

Dag Sørensen in Norway has produced several unique ceramic instruments in the trumpet family. Some are spiral horns, with carefully crafted gradually increasing conical bores and elegantly flaring bells. Figures 4.83 through 4.90 illustrate Dag's process of building a spiral horn, an instrument that sounds like a French horn and looks like a cross between a hunting horn and a seashell. Dag creates this instrument by slip-casting the body using a plaster mold and attaching a wheel-thrown bell and mouthpiece.

Another very long ceramic trumpet, imitative of a Swiss alphorn, was also built by Dag Sørensen.

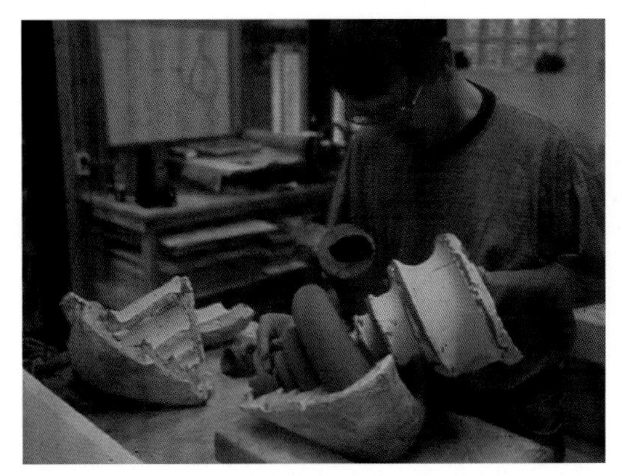

Fig. 4.85
Removing the horn from the mold after drying for two days

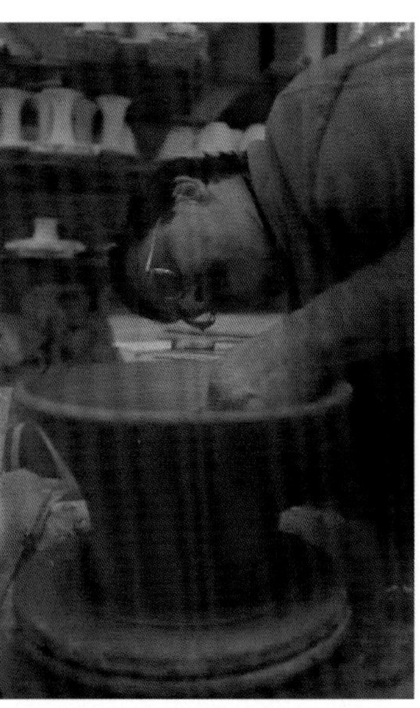

Fig. 4.86
Throwing the bell section

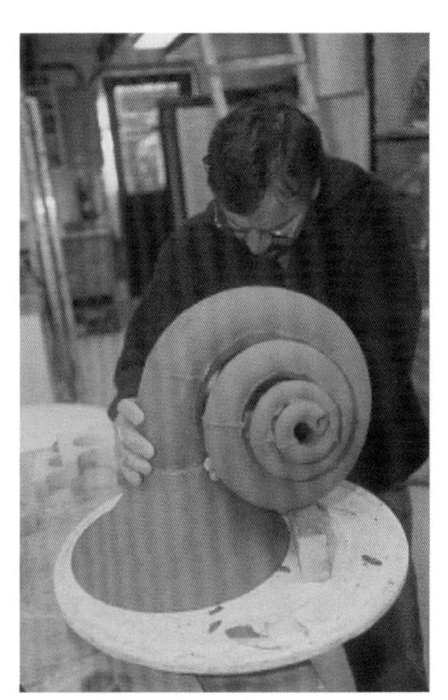

Fig. 4.87
Attaching the bell

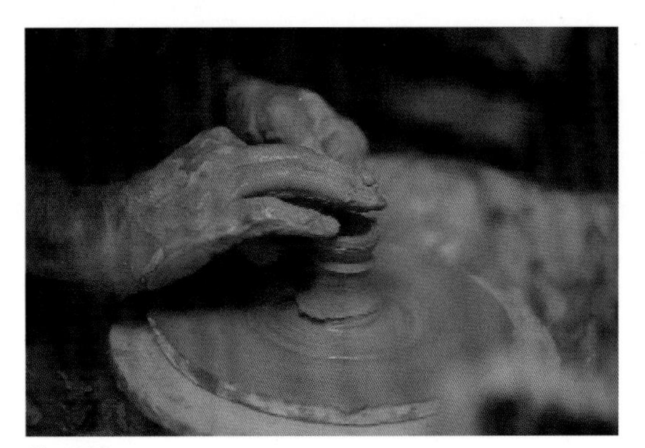

Fig. 4.88
Throwing the mouthpiece

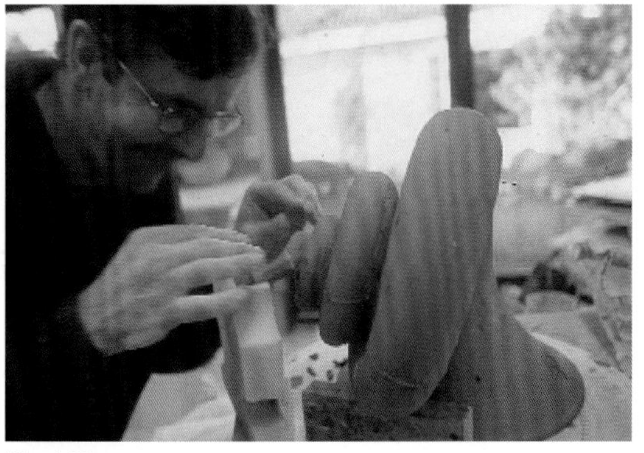

Fig. 4.89
Attaching the mouthpiece

Alphorns, or alpenhorns, are a family of ancient signaling instruments made by herdsmen in the mountainous regions of Europe. Traditional alphorns may be six to ten feet long, with some as long as 17 feet. They are made from staves of wood bound tightly with tree bark to make the horn airtight. As with other "natural" horns such as the bugle or hunting horn, the alphorn player produces different pitches by overblowing. This is a technique of narrowing the aperture between the lips and blowing a faster airstream to produce higher tones in the harmonic series related to the basic, lowest pitch of the horn (which is determined by its length and bore shape). Dag's ceramic alphorn is thirteen feet long; perhaps one of the largest ceramic horns ever built (figure 9.43).

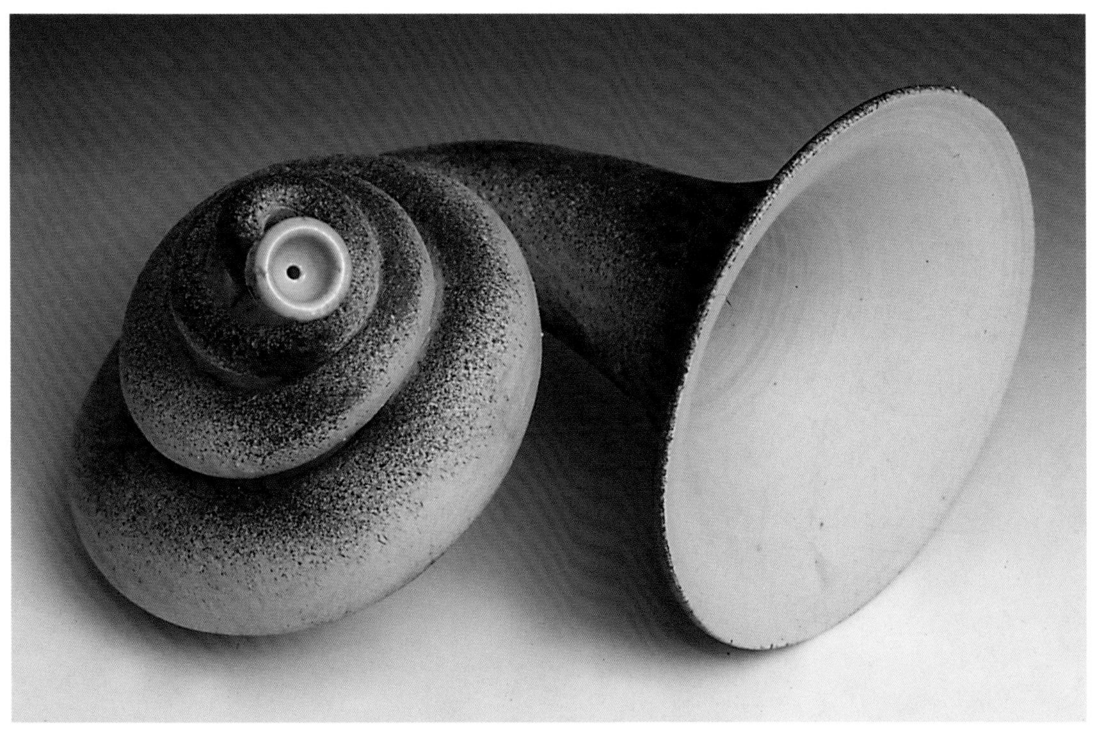

Fig. 4.90
**Spiral Horn**
Dag Sørensen, Sandnes, Norway. Thrown and molded. Stoneware with manganese dioxide, fired to cone 10. 13 inches in height.

Adding to the complexity and creativity of his instrument is a convoluted "knot" in the middle of the horn, through which the air passes. Dag built his ceramic alphorn from twenty-one pieces, which were joined when leather hard, to become five sections. These sections were fired separately and then joined into a single horn using silicone-based flexible glue. Most of the individual parts were wheel thrown, except the first section which was slab rolled, and the "knot" section which was built from two thrown and four molded pieces.

The trumpets described above are known as "natural" trumpets because they don't have finger holes or valves that allow a player to change the length of the horn and therefore produce a wider variety of pitches. Modern instruments in the trumpet family have mechanical rotary or piston valves to accomplish this. It is infeasible to create valves from clay due to the precision required for them to move smoothly and remain airtight. However, Brian Ransom has cleverly taken the best of both worlds and created a ceramic flugelhorn from earthenware tubes and brass trumpet parts (figure 9.12). The flugelhorn is a relative of the modern trumpet, with a wider, flaring bore and a more mellow tone.

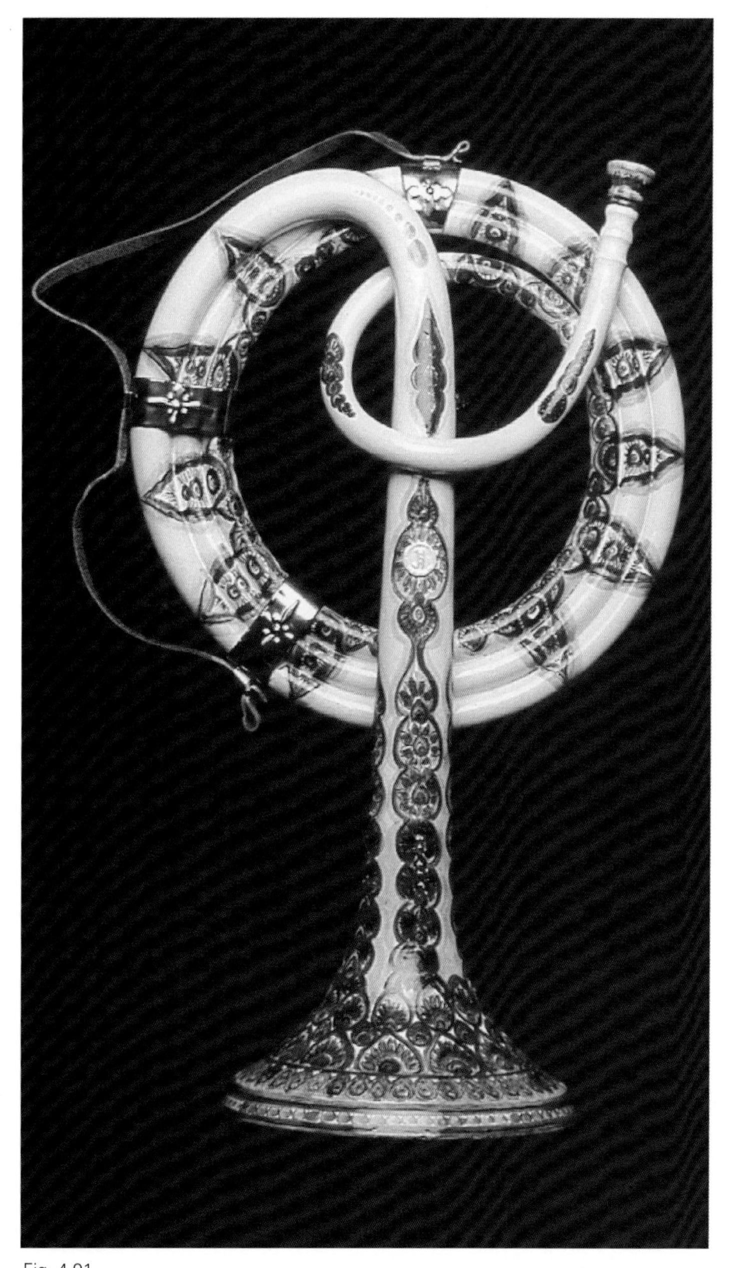

Fig. 4.91
**C Bass Horn**
Geert Jacobs, Milsbeek, Holland. The individual components for each of Geert's horns—the bell, neck, pipe and mouthpiece—are thrown on the wheel and then assembled. See Chapter 9 for construction details. 27.5 inches in height.

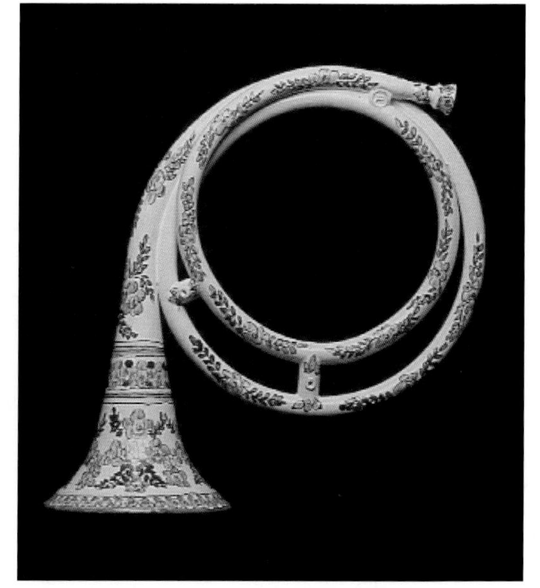

Fig. 4.92
**G Horn**
Geert Jacobs, Milsbeek, Holland. 16.5 inches in height.

## Cornetti

Many cultures have created musical or signaling horns from animal horns, and some of these instruments have finger holes designed to manipulate the sound. An example of such an instrument is the Scandinavian kohorn or cow horn. This instrument, used for signaling and cow herding, is made from a cow horn and usually has three finger holes. The range of the kohorn is about a fifth. This type of instrument lends itself to ceramic construction because of its relatively small size and simple shape.

From these simple animal horns developed one of the great virtuoso instruments of the European Renaissance: the *cornetto.* The cornetto is the soprano member of a family of similar instruments with a variety of names, but the entire family is generally referred to in plural as *cornetti.* Usually they were made

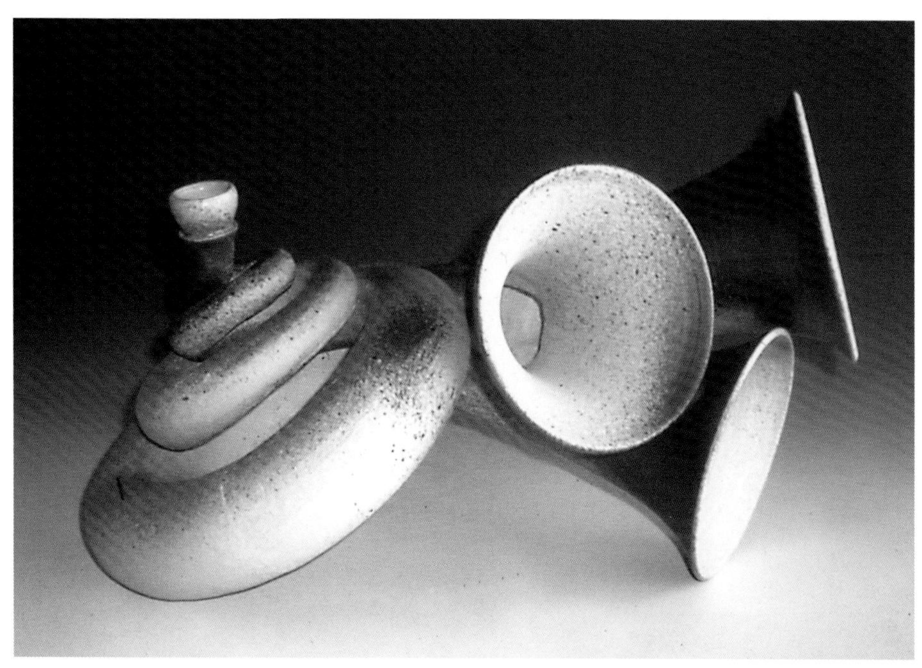

Fig. 4.93
**Triple Spiral Horn**
Dag Sørensen, Sandnes, Norway. Thrown and molded. Stoneware with manganese dioxide, cone 10. 16 inches in height.

of wood and often covered with leather, though some modern reproductions are cast from resin. Like their animal horn ancestors, cornetti have a conical internal bore and are much shorter in length than most other tubular horns, ranging from less than a foot in length for the highest instrument (the *cornettino*) to several feet long for the convoluted tube of the bass instrument (the *serpent*). This short length relative to other horns, combined with their open tone holes or finger holes, gives cornetti their distinctive sound, which is often compared to the human voice. Indeed, cornetti were often used to accompany vocal music in the Renaissance period when they were most popular.

This family of instruments has some unique features that make them good candidates for ceramic construction. First, they are shorter in length than other tubular horns, which helps

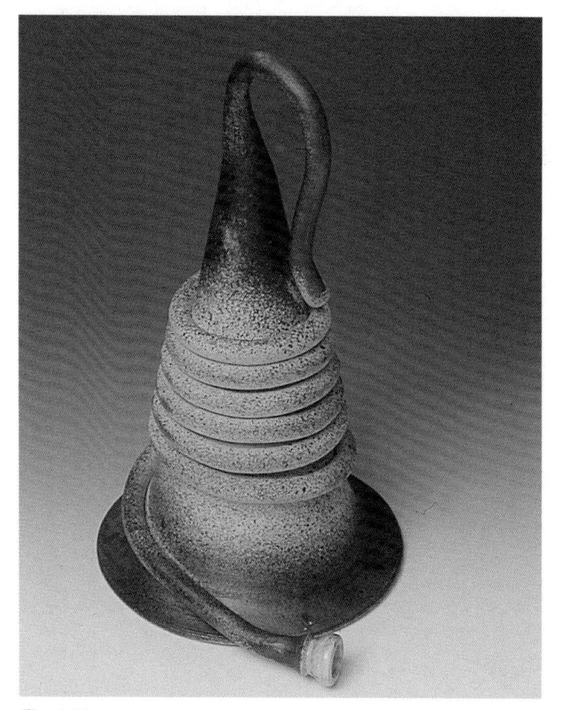

Fig. 4.94
**Witch Horn**
Dag Sørensen, Sandnes, Norway. Thrown and extruded. Stoneware with manganese dioxide, cone 10. 16 inches in height.

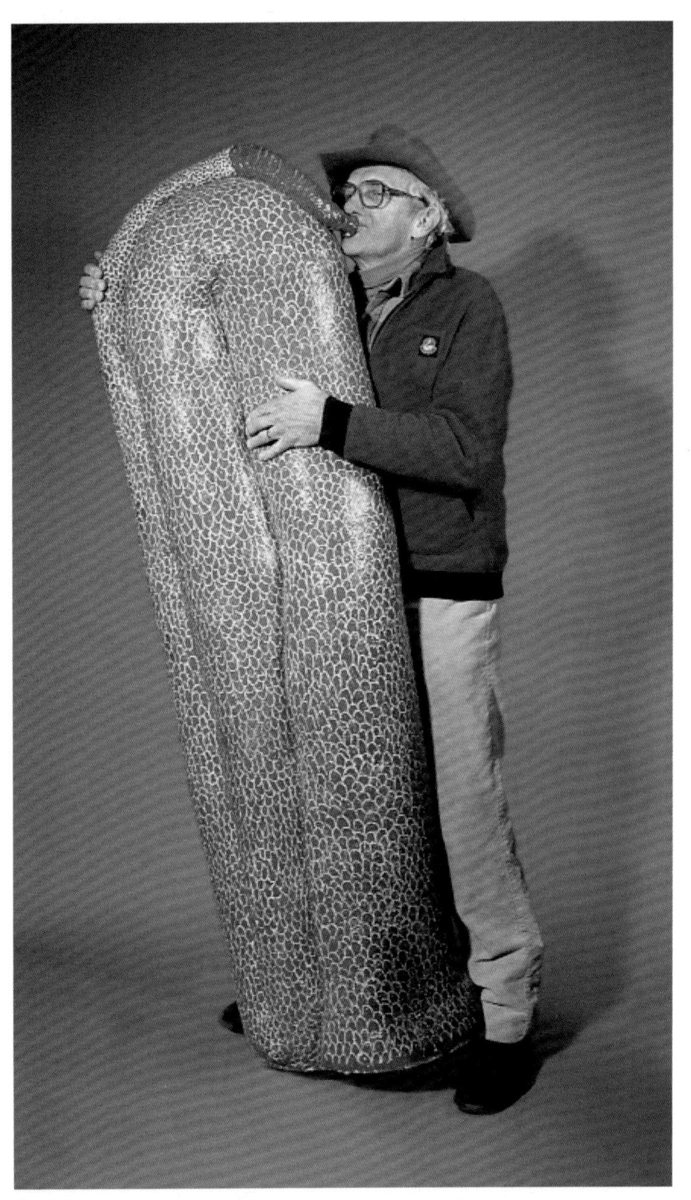

Fig. 4.95
**Snakes Are Nice Too (1989)**
Don Bendel, Flagstaff, Arizona, USA. Don says, "The snake horn is a mutation of the typical poisonous snake. They are rarely dangerous and when a human does approach them they immediately assume the friendly position for the inevitable toot." Stoneware covered with earthenware slip, sgraffito decoration and clear glaze. Fired to 1940°F in the Bendel kiln. 67 inches in height.

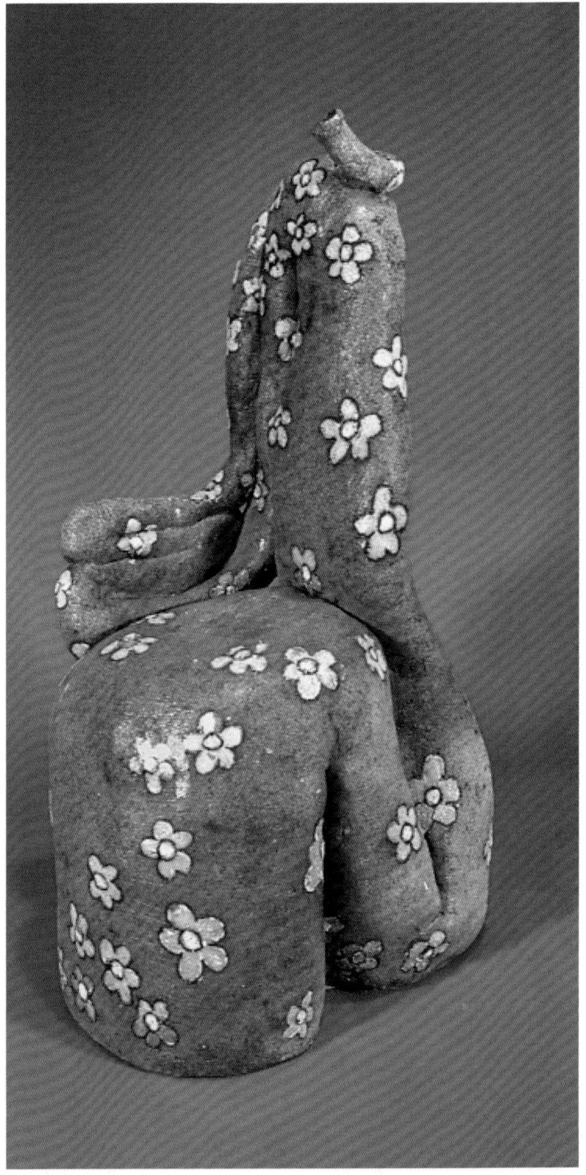

Fig. 4.96
**Chair Horn (1990)**
Don Bendel, Flagstaff, Arizona, USA. Don explains, "The chair horn was a cousin of the lowly worm. Although common at one time, they were overused and are now believed to be extinct." Stoneware clay inlaid with blue engobe, painted with white and yellow engobe. Single-fired in an Anagama kiln. Constructing a piece of this complexity requires a considerable amount of planning. Don says "I make lots of sketches, which give me not so much a picture of the outcome, but a concept of the procedure I need to follow. From there, I go where the clay leads me." 36 inches in height.

mitigate the challenges of size, fragility and fitting inside a kiln. Additionally, their construction and tuning is relatively straightforward and similar to a transverse flute or recorder. Finally, they have a very unique sound.

The disadvantages of cornetti are that their conical body is not the easiest shape to make from clay (it can be done by coiling or starting with a slab) and the instruments are difficult to tune in the second octave. Additionally, they can be difficult to play due to their very small mouthpieces, and the open finger holes make playing in tune a challenge.

Two ceramic cornetti are shown in figure 4.97. The horn's basic design is a conical body with a small mouthpiece cup no larger on the inside than the tip of a small finger. The edge of the mouthpiece is narrow and much sharper than the edge of a modern trumpet mouthpiece. This is a key factor in achieving the cornetto's characteristic tone. The finger holes are cut after the mouthpiece is formed when the instrument is leather hard, and are made, like a flute, starting from the bottom (distal end) and working up toward the mouthpiece. Higher pitches in the second octave can be played by overblowing. Tuning an instrument for the second octave can be difficult, since it is highly influenced by the shape of the interior bore. If you wish to explore the complexities of this issue, scale drawings and plans are available online and in various books (for example, *The Amateur Wind Instrument Maker* by Trevor Robinson). However, a nice sounding, more primitive, one-octave instrument is relatively easy to make without any detailed planning.

A ceramic cornetto can be heard on track 28 of the accompanying CD. A similar open-holed ceramic horn can be heard on track 2.

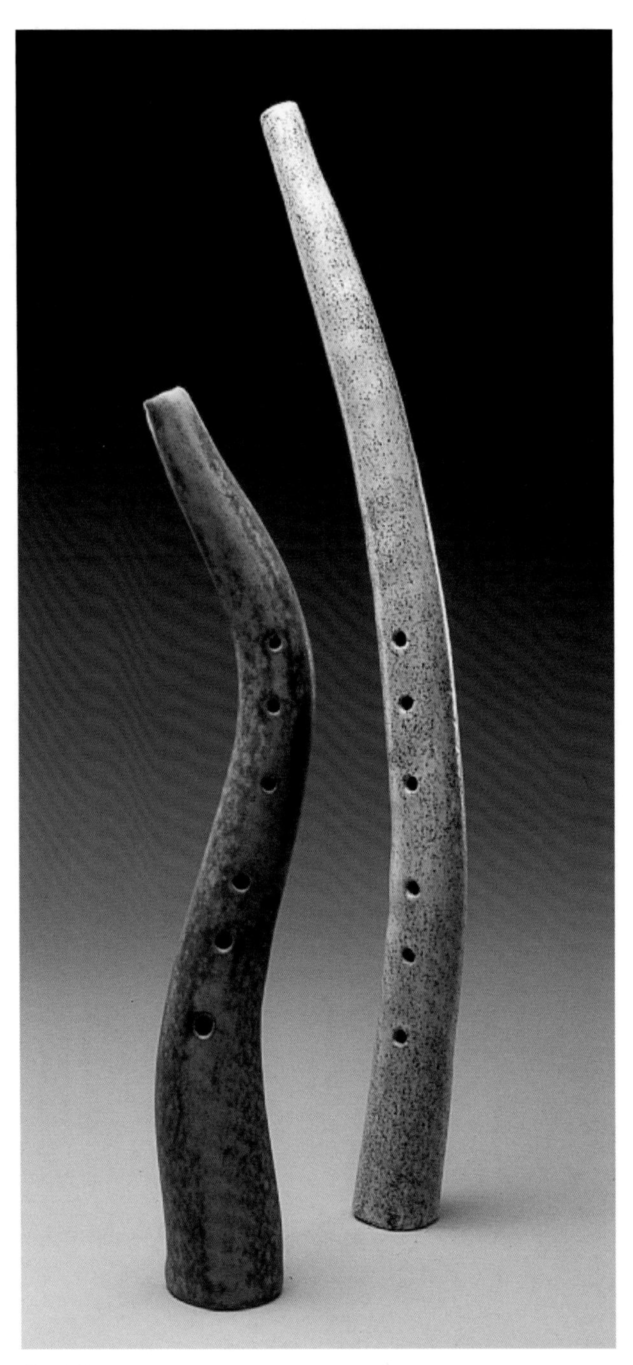

Fig. 4.97
**Cornetti**
Barry Hall, Westborough, Massachusetts, USA. Ceramic interpretations of a European Renaissance wind instrument from the trumpet family. Stoneware, manganese slip and glaze, cone 10. To 22 inches in length. Hear this instrument on CD track 28.

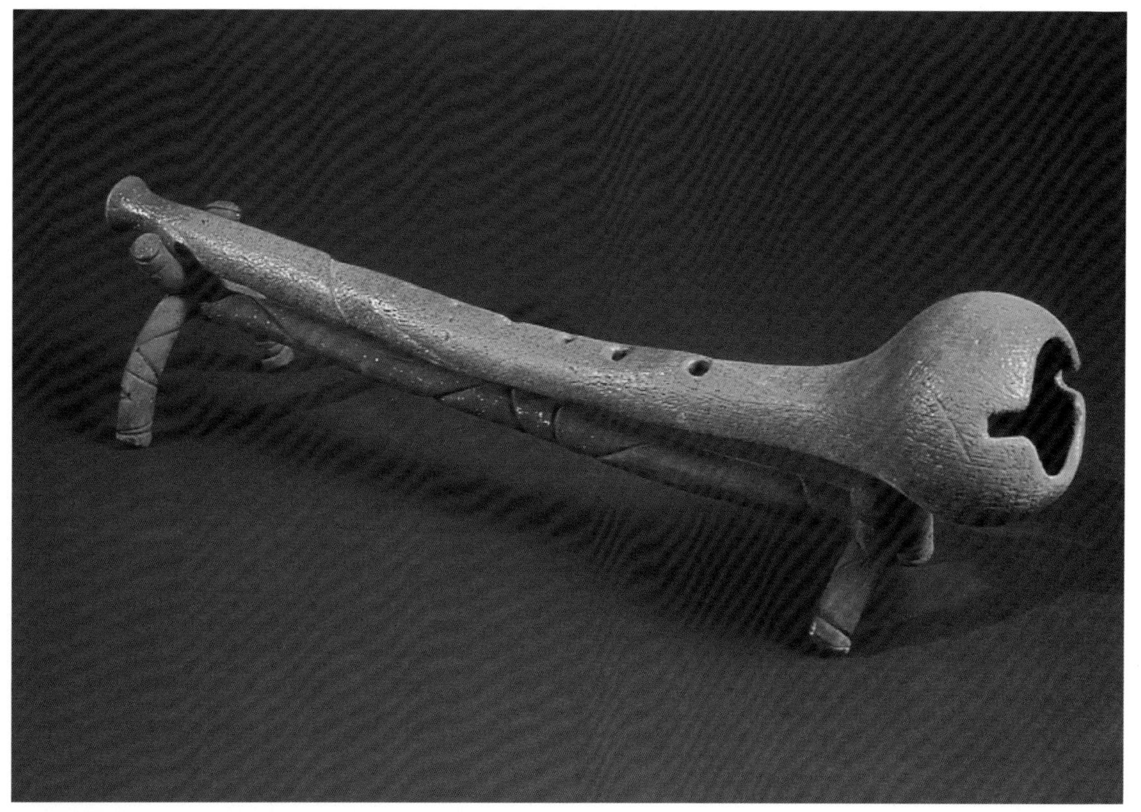

Fig. 4.98
**Straight Horn**
Brian Ransom, St. Petersburg, Florida, USA. An open-hole straight horn. Vapor-fired ceramic. 32 inches in length. Hear this instrument on CD track 2.

## Didjeridus

The *didjeridu* is an instrument originating from Australia. Didjeridu (or *didgeridoo*) is a name intended to imitate some of the instrument's sounds. This name was coined by Colonists who were some of the first Westerners to encounter this unique instrument and its traditional playing styles in the tropics of the Northern Territory in a region known as Arnhem Land. The didjeridu is part of a family of similar instruments that have a number of traditional names such as *mako, bambu,* and *yirdaki.* This book uses the common term "didjeridu" to refer to all instruments in the didjeridu family, as well as their non-traditional relatives.

The didjeridu is traditionally used as an accompaniment to song and dance as a part of ceremonial functions. It also can be used in the same manner for casual entertainment. Colorful designs with spiritual significance are sometimes painted on the outside of didjeridus that are used for ceremonial purposes. This instrument is a sacred sound tool for a deeply spiritual culture with roots and traditions reaching back to the dawn of humankind.

Bamboo was originally used for the manufacture of didjeridus in western Arnhem Land prior to the introduction of metal tools, about 400-600 years ago, by the Makassans from Indonesia. However, today most traditional didjeridus are constructed from a tree trunk, four to five feet long and two or more inches in internal diameter, which has been naturally hollowed out by termites (also called white ants). Beeswax is sometimes added to the end of the hollow stick in order to make a comfortable mouthpiece. Remarkably, that's all there is to a didjeridu—it's just a hollow tube. But despite this instrument's simple design, its sound and playing techniques can be quite complex.

What differentiates a didjeridu from other lip-reed instruments? First, its mouthpiece is an open hole at the end of a tube, rather than a cup that narrows into a throat before joining the rest of the instrument, as in most other lip-reed instruments. This configuration permits a player to employ some of the techniques unique to the didjeridu. Second, the instrument is usually played using a technique called *circular breathing*. This allows a player to blow a continuous stream of sound for several minutes, or even longer, replenishing the air supply in the lungs by breathing in through the nose while continuously exhaling from the mouth. Most importantly, the playing techniques of the didjeridu are unlike any other wind instrument. This is due to its use of a single drone pitch to make complex music. (Some styles of playing utilize *overtones* or *partials*, which are higher pitches that can be played by more advanced players, but the essence of didjeridu playing is working from a single drone pitch.) Even more unusual are the multitude of techniques that players use to manipulate the tone of the drone pitch and add rhythms

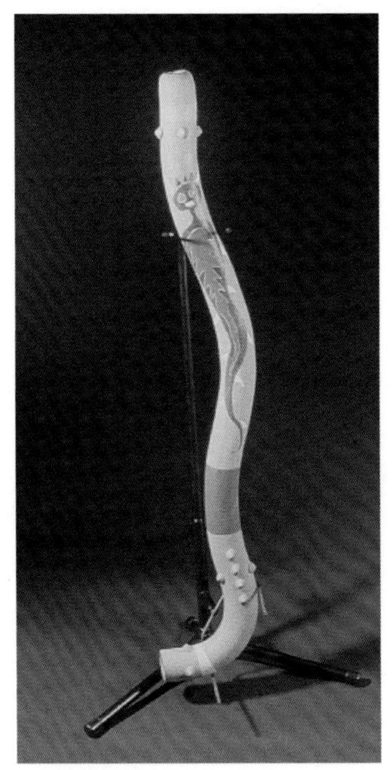

Fig. 4.99
**Didjeridoo**
Chester Winowiecki, Fremont, Michigan, USA. Stoneware decorated with colored slips and engobes. 40 inches in length.

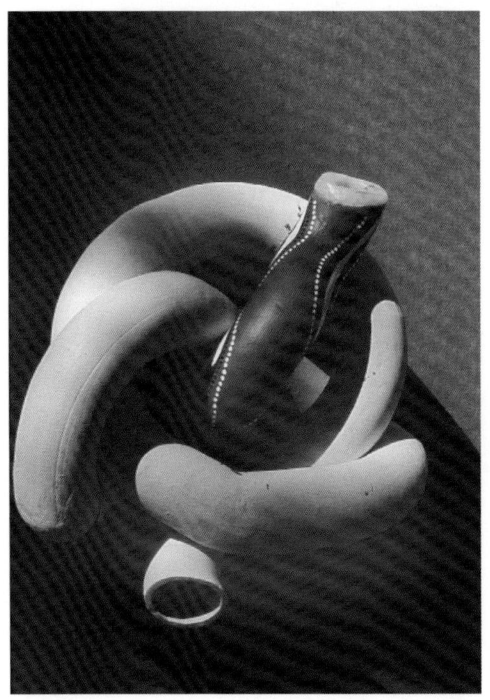

Fig. 4.100
**Didgeridoo**
Kevin Sebastian Costante, Oberlin, Ohio, USA. Stoneware fired to Cone 6 in oxidation. Acrylic paint and beeswax mouthpiece. If straightened out, the tube would be 80 inches in length. 6″ x 13″ x 12″.

and other effects to the sound. These techniques include using the cheeks, tongue, and even pumping the diaphragm to produce rhythms, creating tonal variations by manipulating the mouth cavity, and humming, singing and screaming into the instrument while still blowing the drone pitch. Most people, upon first hearing the sound of a didjeridu, are astonished by the variety of sounds that this simply constructed pipe can produce in the hands of a skilled player.

Continued interest in the didjeridu by many cultures outside of Australia has led, in recent years, to craftspeople constructing didjeridus from a variety of non-traditional materials, including clay, metal, plastic, cardboard, leather, papier mache, glass, and plant stalks such as agave and yucca.

A significant challenge when making a large clay didjeridu is figuring how to fit it in a kiln. Most kilns will not accommodate a tube four to five feet long, so some convolution is necessary. Curves and twists in the tubing will not significantly impact the sound of the instrument as long as the curves are not too sharp and the internal diameter of the tube does not vary throughout the turns. A ceramic didjeridu tube can be created using slabs, coiling, or extruding. A flare or bell at the end of the tube creates a louder instrument and often brightens the tone by emphasizing higher frequencies.

Susan Rawcliffe's *clay-doos* (figure 9.29) are "folded" ceramic didjeridus with one or two fingerholes that allow a player to change their pitch. Susan says that two clay-doos playing together can sound "like mastodons calling in the swamp

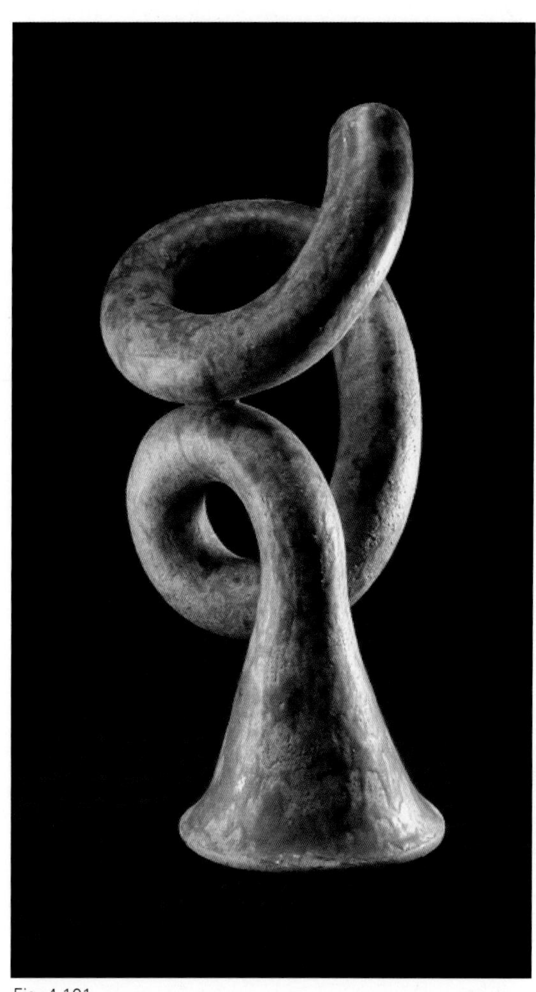

Fig. 4.101
**Pretzel Didjeridu**
Barry Hall, Westborough, Massachusetts, USA. This glazed stoneware didjeridu was built by extruding component pieces of clay tubing, allowing them to firm to a near-leatherhard state, and then assembling them, incorporating a wheel-thrown bell. 20 inches in height. Hear this instrument on CD track 4.

### *Globular Horns*

All of the lip-reed aerophones discussed so far are tubular instruments—that is, their sound is produced by a vibrating column of air inside a tube-shaped instrument. An entirely different vibrating system exists, where the sound is produced by air vibrating in a chamber rather than a tube. These are called *globular horns* or *vessel horns*. Globular horns are related to tubular horns in the same way that ocarinas and other globular flutes are related to tubular flutes. (Refer to the sidebar "Globular vs. Tubular Aerophones" page 48) Although the extension from globular flutes to horns seems logical and natural, globular horns are very uncommon.

#### *Basic Globular Horns*

Clay is an excellent, and perhaps ideal, material for globular horn construction. Another material is hard-shelled gourds, and some traditional African gourd trumpets may be considered globular horns.

A basic globular horn (figure 4.102) can look much like a side-hole clay pot drum, such as the udu described in the "Plosive Aerophones" section of this chapter. This is, in its simplest form, a Helmholz resonator. (In fact, most udus with a side hole can be played as a globular horn.) These instruments, when blown through the side hole with buzzed lips like a brass

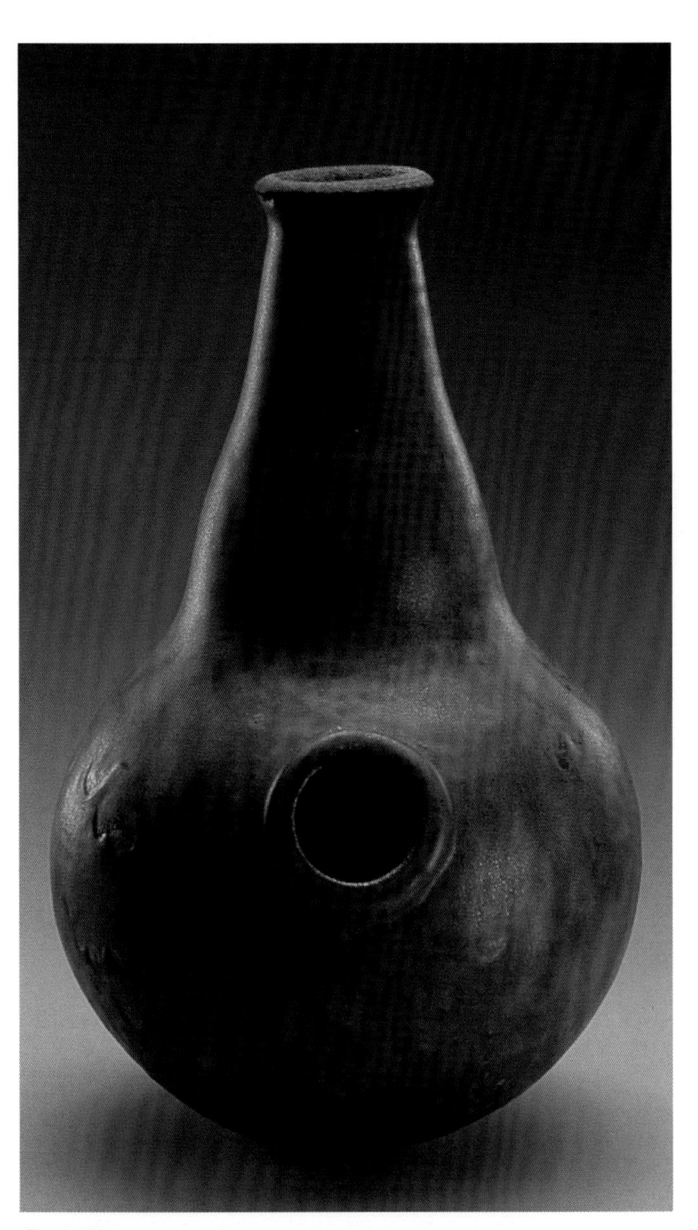

Fig. 4.102
**Globular Horn**
Barry Hall, Westborough, Massachusetts, USA. The basic form of a globular horn, based on a "Helmholtz resonator." Glazed stoneware, Cone 10. 14 inches in height.

instrument or didjeridu, are very resonant at a single pitch. They have a hollow, ringing tone, which a player can augment with higher partials to produce an edgier sound by manipulating the air cavity within their mouth.

However, a basic globular horn of this type produces only one basic pitch. The pitch range of this instrument can be expanded in several ways: by "lipping," by "shading the bell" and by adding finger holes.

Lipping is a process of modifying the shape or tension of your lips to change the pitch of the horn. Generally, lipping will produce pitch changes of only one semitone, but on some horns larger intervals are possible. Also, some horns permit advanced players to create subharmonics, which are extremely low pitches resulting from much slower lip vibrations.

Shading the bell is a technique that involves partially covering the instrument's air exit. This can

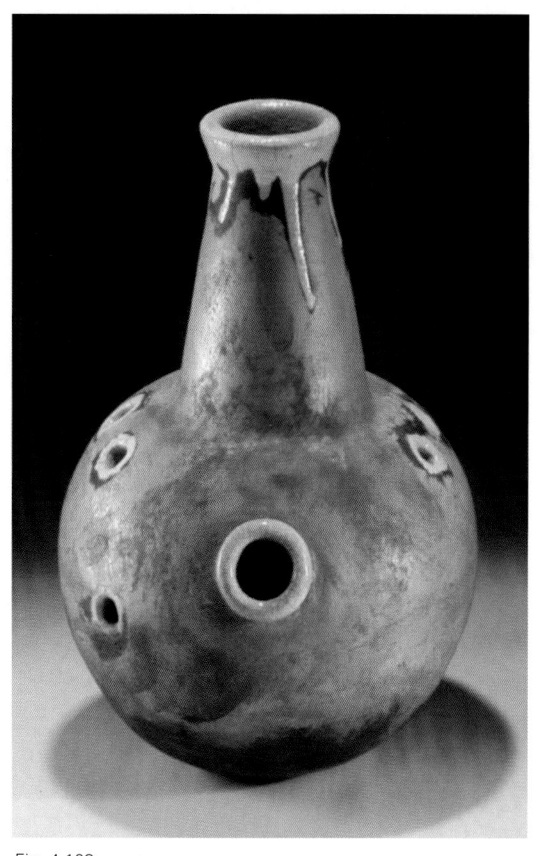

Fig. 4.103
**Chromatic Globular Horn**
Barry Hall, Westborough, Massachusetts, USA. Adding tone holes to a globular horn enables it to produce multiple pitches. This instrument has a one-octave range. Raku fired.
12 inches in height.

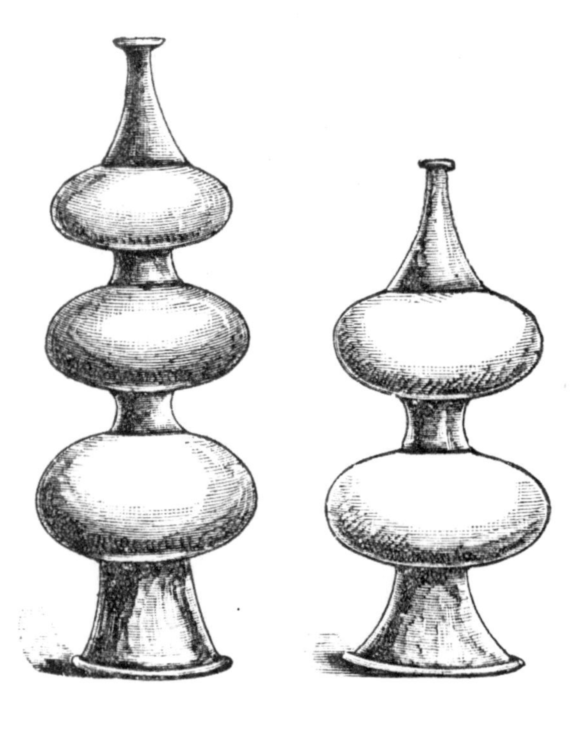

Fig. 4.104
**Botuto (Polyglobular Horn)**
Drawing by the 18th century Spanish priest, Jose Gumilla, depicting a pair of ceramic trumpets with multiple chambers, played by the Saliva Indians in the Orinoco region of Colombia and Venezuela.

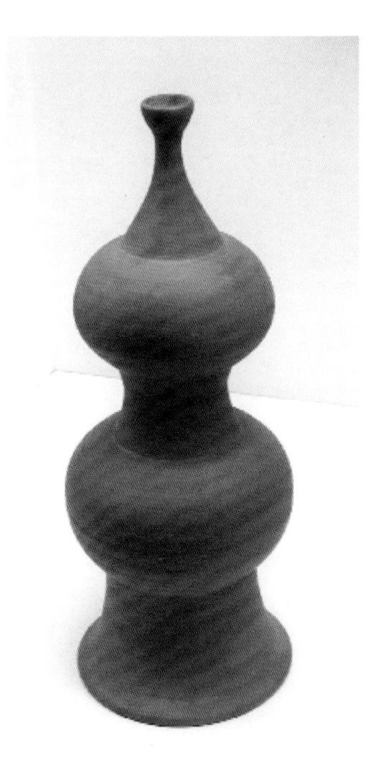

Fig. 4.105
**Botuto Horn**
Richard Baxter, Leigh-On-Sea, Essex, England. An instrument inspired by South American polyglobular horns. Unglazed terra cotta clay, wheel thrown in five pieces.
18 inches in height.

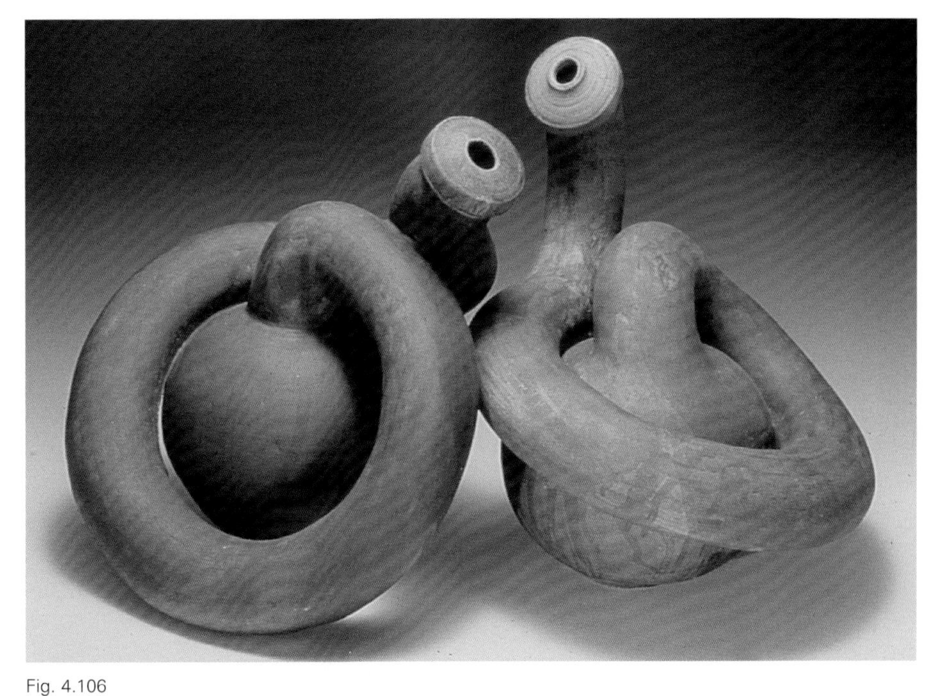

Fig. 4.106
**Cowguts**
Ragnar Naess, Brooklyn, New York, USA. These trumpet-family members of Ragnar's EarthSounds ceramic orchestra have a tubular body terminating in a vessel resonating chamber. Hear this instrument on CD track 21.

be done by covering the neck opening of the resonator with your palm, or by inserting one or more fingers into the neck opening. The more you constrict the air flow, the lower the pitch. With some practice, you can play different distinct pitches by quickly changing hand positions, as well as sliding from pitch to pitch (*glissando*) by gradually moving your hand.

Finger holes can be added in any part of the horn's body. Figure 4.103 shows a globular horn with six tone holes that allow it to produce pitches over the range of one octave. However, finger holes in globular horns may be only marginally successful, since they weaken the strong resonance present in the fundamental pitch of the instrument. There's an expression about the cornetto family (see the section earlier in this chapter), which says that "opening a tone hole doesn't make a pitch happen, it just makes it somewhat more likely to happen." This is doubly true for globular horns, partially due to the small size of the tone holes relative to the size of the resonant air cavity. Globular horns also can be made with palm-sized tone holes. These large tone holes are easier to control, but still compromise the instrument's tone somewhat.

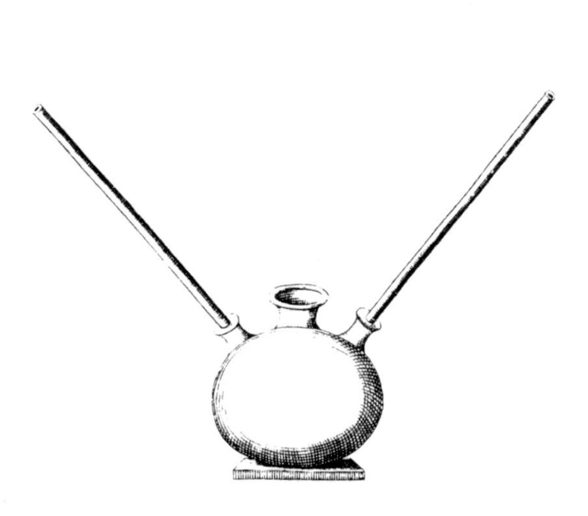

Fig. 4.107
**Jaguar Pot Trumpet**
Drawing by the 18th century Spanish priest, Jose Gumilla, depicting a cane trumpet terminating in a pottery jar that acts as a resonator or bell. Gumilla wrote "No words can describe the awful darkness and dismal moaning that the breath draws from these canes."

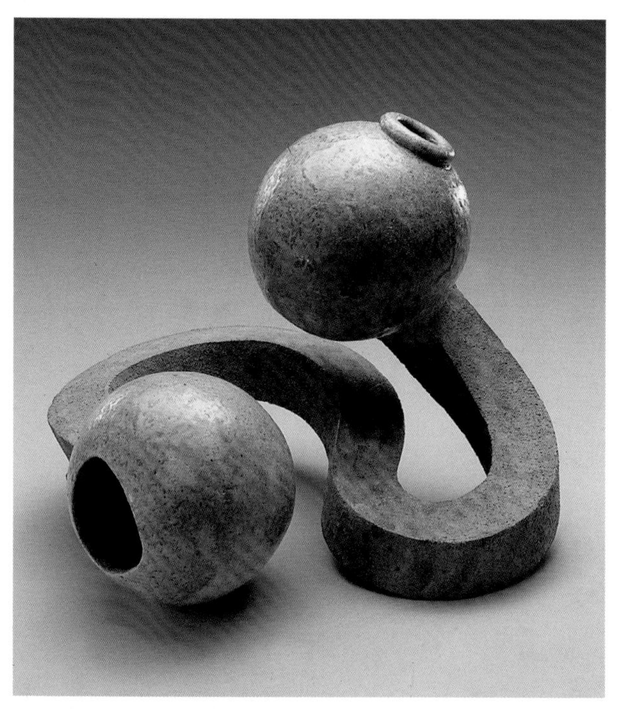

Fig. 4.108
**Double Ball Globutubular Horn**
Barry Hall, Westborough, Massachusetts, USA. A horn consisting of a tubular mid-section with a globular chamber at each end. The mouthpiece chamber lowers the horn's pitch dramatically and the distal chamber impacts the instrument's tone. Glazed stoneware reduction fired to cone 10. 15 inches in height. Hear this instrument on CD track 35.

Globular horns are generally more successful in larger sizes, since smaller sized chambers require a player to use a very tight lip position. As a result, large globular horns necessitate large mouth openings. An open (as opposed to cupped) mouthpiece design lends these instruments to a playing style similar to a didjeridu (described earlier in this chapter). Also, since many globular horns are capable of producing only one pitch, they are good candidates for the many varieties of articulation, harmonics, vocalizations and other creative techniques commonly used by didjeridu players to enhance the basic drone.

*Polyglobular Horns*

As they were with flutes, ancient Native Americans were also innovative in the design of globular horns. In the 18th century, Pater Gumilla, a Jesuit priest, documented a pair of unique polyglobular ceramic trumpets, used in funeral ceremonies by the South American Saliva Indians (figure 4.104). These trumpets were end-blown and straight, with a bell and several globular swellings along their length. They were played in pairs, one of which had two bellies and the other had three. They were generally from three to four feet long, but some were enormous. Gumilla described their tone as "dark and deep." These instruments were also documented in the early 20th century in Guiana.

Richard Baxter's "Botuto Horn" (figure 4.105) uses a design inspired by these instruments. Susan Rawcliffe, who has done much experimentation with polyglobular flutes, has also made ceramic polyglobular horns inspired by this design (figure 9.30). Trumpets of this type have a very primeval and intense sound, which may explain why they were traditionally used in funeral rites.

*Globu-Tubular Horns*

Combining globular and tubular sections into a single hybrid *globu-tubular* horn is surprisingly effective. A relatively small globular section at the beginning of a tube produces a pitch much lower than a tube of the same length. This allows for the creation of very low-pitched instruments that are surprisingly compact. Moving the globular section toward the exit end of the tube decreases its pitch-lowering effect. A globular section at the very end of the tube doesn't lower the pitch at all, but acts as sort of a "reverse bell" or resonator. A traditional flaring bell (like on a brass trumpet) makes the instrument brighter sounding and louder. A bell that curves back in on itself to form a chamber does the opposite—decreases volume and makes a hollow, constricted tone. An example of this instrument is Ragnar Naess' creation, called "Cowguts", shown in figure 4.106 and heard on track 21 of the CD. Another example, shown in figure 4.108, is a tubular horn with chambers at both ends.

This principle of a hollow chamber at the end of a trumpet is also used by some South American cultures. Figure 4.107 shows a

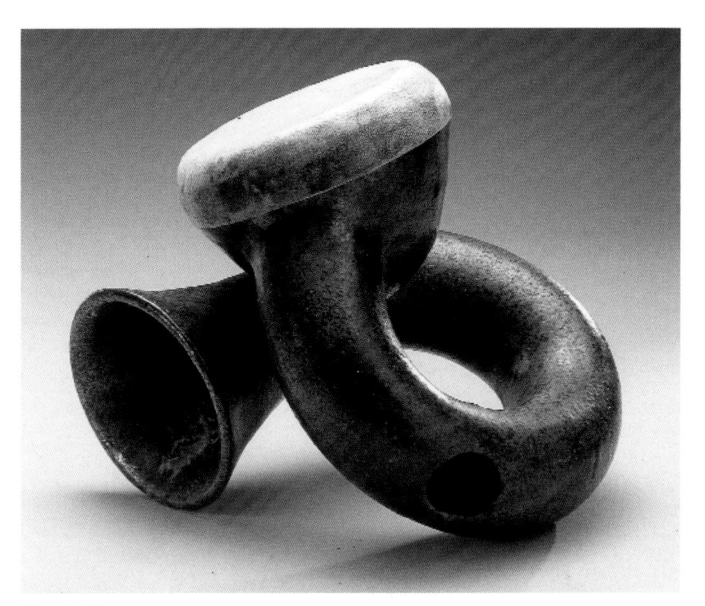

Fig. 4.109
**Globutubular Horn with Resonator**
Barry Hall, Westborough, Massachusetts, USA. This instrument has a goat skin membrane affixed to the globular chamber which enhances the horn's volume and tone. The mouthpiece is located part way along the horn's tubular section. Mouthpiece position on a globutubular horn can be significantly varied with little or no resulting impact on the instrument's pitch or sound. Glazed stoneware reduction fired to cone 10. 10 inches in height. Hear this instrument on CD tracks 12 & 29.

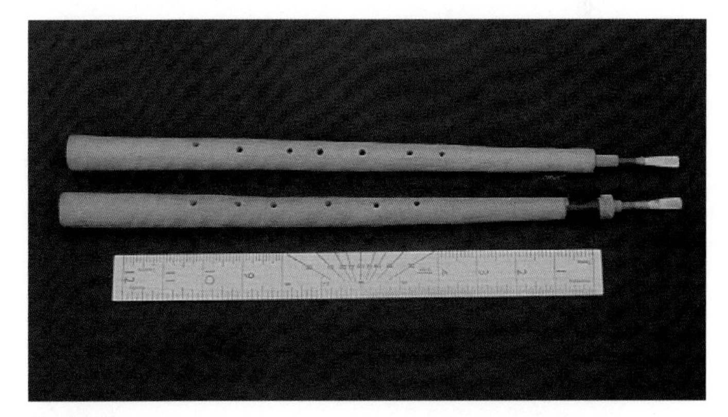

Fig. 4.110
**Oboes**
John Taylor, Wiltshire, England. A tapered dowel was used to mold these conical-shaped double reed instruments. Earthenware, with standard oboe reeds. 15.5 inches in length.

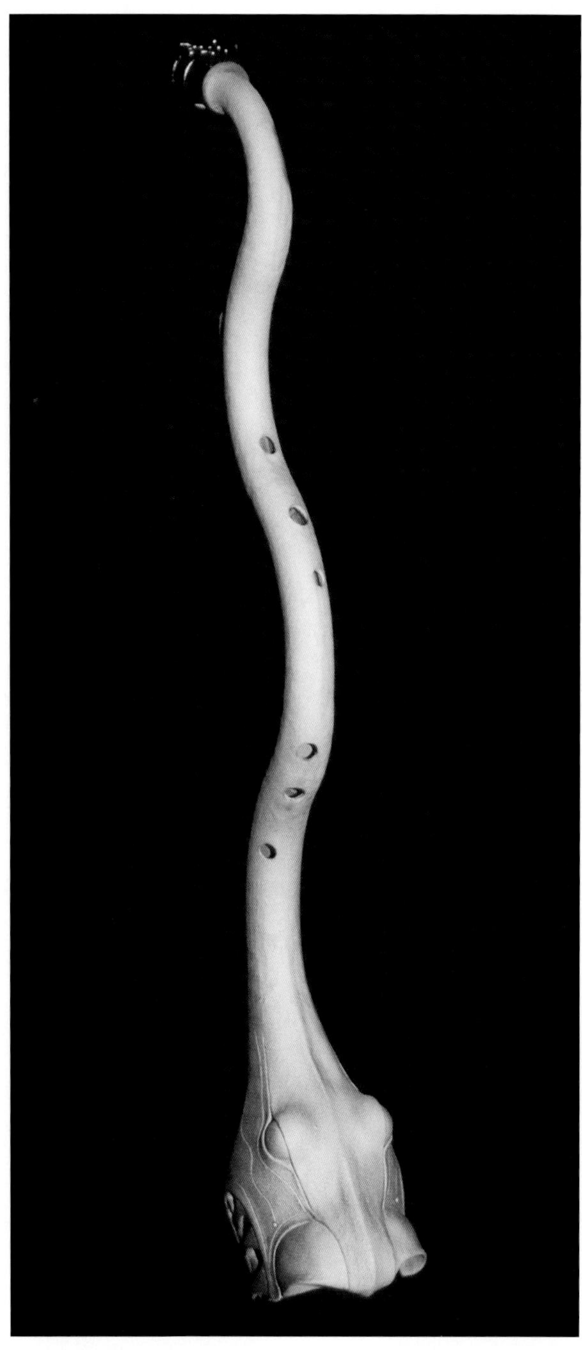

Fig. 4.111
**Sax-O-Snake**
Brian Ransom, St. Petersburg, Florida, USA. Vapor-fired ceramic with tenor saxophone mouthpiece. 37 inches in length.

trumpet made of bamboo, which was then inserted into a specially-made clay jar to act as a resonator and change the sound coming out of the trumpet before it reached the listener's ear. In some cases, special pots were constructed with two or three narrow neck openings, to permit multiple trumpets to be inserted into a single clay resonating vessel. Apparently the sound resembled a jaguar, and this instrument was used to imitate the jaguar demon for mask dances, and even to lure jaguars. Other versions of the instrument had smaller ceramic or gourd resonators directly attached to a cane trumpet.

### Reeds

Reed aerophones have a flexible reed in their mouthpiece, which is excited into motion when a player blows through it. Its rapid vibrating creates a buzzing sound, whose pitch and tone is focused and modified by the instrument's body cavity. The reed may be made of cane (as in a saxophone, clarinet or bagpipe), metal (as in a harmonica), or even plastic.

Reed instruments such as the clarinet, oboe and saxophone follow the same general rules and construction techniques as other tubular aerophones. Although modern versions of these instruments have mechanical keys, their ancestors, and many contemporary folk reed instruments, are made with open finger holes. These instruments offer broad expressive capabilities when compared to modern versions due to the flexibility (and perhaps instability) of their intonation.

Ceramic reed instruments are less common than most other types of ceramic aerophones. Some inspirational examples are shown in figures 4.110-4.114.

## Free Aerophones

Free aerophones produce sound by freely using air as the primary vibrating means. Sometimes also called "outer air instruments," they have no air chambers but instead simply excite the air in the open atmosphere.

An example is the *bullroarer* (figure 4.115), an instrument known by many names and prevalent throughout many cultures across the world. It consists of a blade with a string attached at one end which the player whirls in a circle by holding the string at the other end. The blade rotates rapidly as it swings through the air, producing a buzz that varies in pitch as the speed of rotation changes. In many societies the bullroarer has been used since prehistoric times, and may be considered a fertility symbol, the voice of ancestral spirits, and a tool for initiation rites.

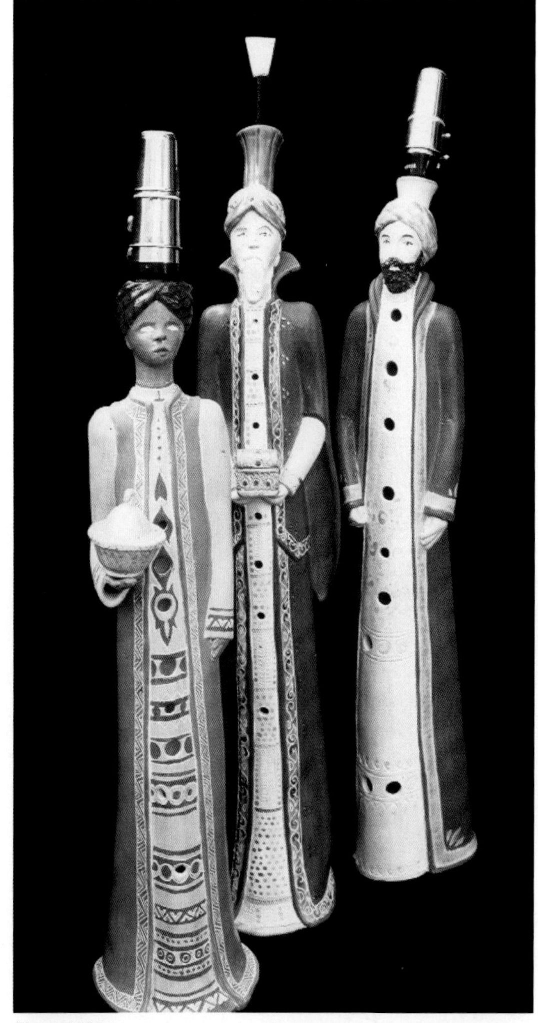

Fig. 4.112
**Clarinet, Oboe and Sax**
Marie Picard, Marguerittes, France. Single- and double-reed ceramic instruments: a clarinet, oboe and soprano saxophone, in the form of "Roi Mage" or magician kings bearing gifts. Smoked, enameled and gilded.

## Plosive Aerophones (struck aerophones)

Plosive aerophones are instruments in which the air inside a tube or vessel is set into vibration by a strike of a player's hand or other implement. The resulting sound is usually percussive, with a strong attack and a quick decay. However, with the proper resonating cavity—either tubular or globular—a strong and clear pitch can be obtained, permitting bass lines and melodies to be played.

### *Tubular Plosive Aerophones*

Unlike tubular drums with membrane heads, tubular plosive aerophones are simply hollow tubes open at both ends. Striking the end or the side of the tube causes the air inside to resonate.

The *bassoon drum* is such an instrument created by Dag Sørensen . It can be seen in figure 4.116 and heard on track 27 of the CD played by Eddie Andresen. The idea came from a 20-foot length of road pipe. Eddie was fascinated by the sound and encouraged Dag to create a similar sound using clay. For practical and sculptural reasons, the instrument's shape is folded back on itself. The first instrument Dag built looked like a bassoon, and the name stuck. Eddie describes its sound as "a mixture of Gregorian chant and roaring dinosaurs."

Stephen Freedman's ceramic tubular drums, seen in figure 4.117, are arrays of ceramic tubes

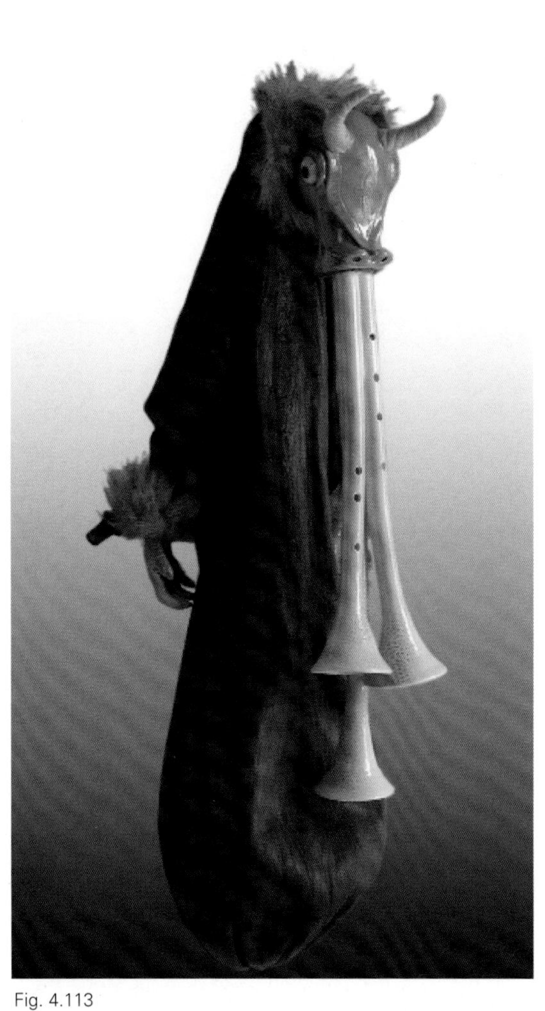

Fig. 4.113
**Dragon Bagpipe**
Marie Picard, Marguerittes, France. This polyphonic bagpipe has two chanters to play melodies and harmonies and a third pipe which drones a single pitch. 26 inches (bag) x 15 inches (pipes). Hear this instrument on CD track 40.

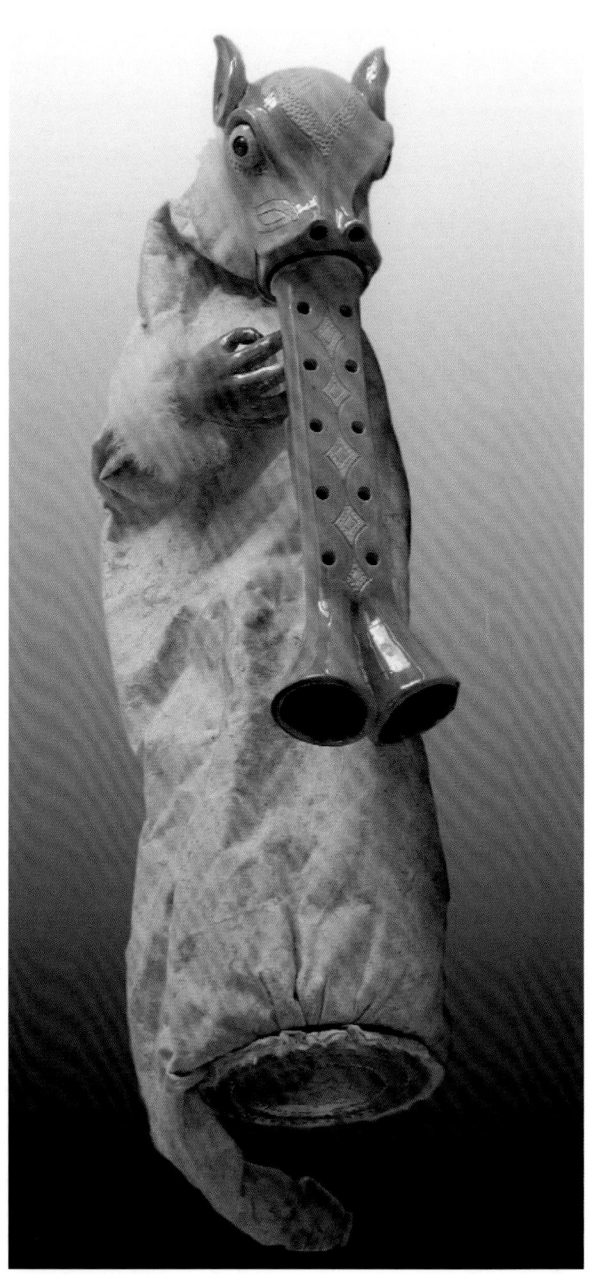

Fig. 4.114
**Tunisian Bagpipe**
Marie Picard, Marguerittes, France. This Tunisian-style bagpipe has a double chanter to play melodies and harmonies. 20 inches (bag) x 7 inches (pipes).

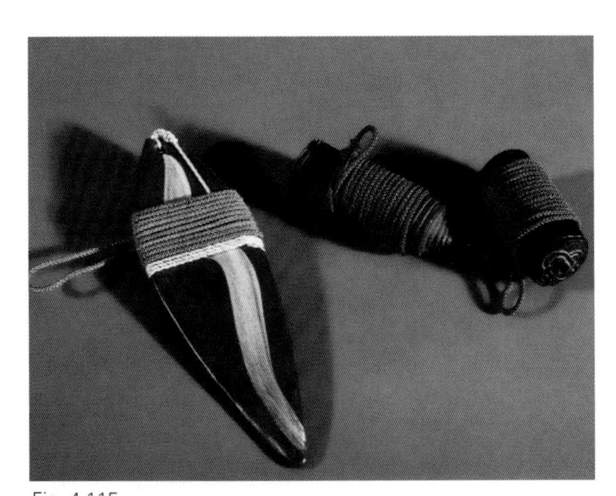

Fig. 4.115
**Thrumming and Whistling Bullroarers**
Brian Ransom, St. Petersburg, Florida, USA. Two types of ceramic instruments intended to be spun through the air on a cord. The flat type on the left is a free aerophone that creates a "thrumming" sound by rotating as it is swung in a circle. The whistling type on the right develops a flutelike edge tone sound as a result of its spinning.

mounted in wooden frames. These unglazed stoneware tubes are approximately two inches in diameter, but flare out at their top end so they can be slid into a wooden stand and held in place by friction. The percussion ensemble, The Antenna Repairmen, perform on these sets of tubular drums, striking the open ends with foam sandals, which produce a full tone. They also strike the ends and sides of the tubes with a variety of other implements, including wooden sticks that have been split with a saw, to combine wooden "clacking" sounds with the chime-like tones of the ceramic tubes.

### *Globular Plosive Aerophones*

Plosive aerophones with globular-shaped bodies are used all over the world. A simple example is a jar, jug or narrow-necked vase. Striking the neck opening with your hand or a soft paddle excites the vessel's resonant cavity and produces a tone—a high plopping sound from a small jar, or a low booming bass tone from a large jar.

No culture has developed the making and use of these instruments more than the people of Nigeria, with their clay percussion pot commonly called an *udu*. This simple instrument has ancient traditions and is still today an important instrument in many types of music. Furthermore, in recent years the udu has obtained international prominence due to its production by American and European instrument builders and its use by professional percussionists in many performances and recordings. The udu's mysterious, bubbling, liquid sounds can be heard in movie and television soundtracks, commercials, and all types of recorded popular music.

Outside Africa, udu is probably the most popular name for a Nigerian clay pot drum, but it is only one of a number of traditional names given to various forms of this instrument. A few other Nigerian names for clay pot drums are *abang mbre* (which means "pot for playing"), *idudu egu, kuku* and *kimkim*. For simplicity, this book uses the term "udu" or "clay pot drum" to refer to any and all of the many variations of this instrument.

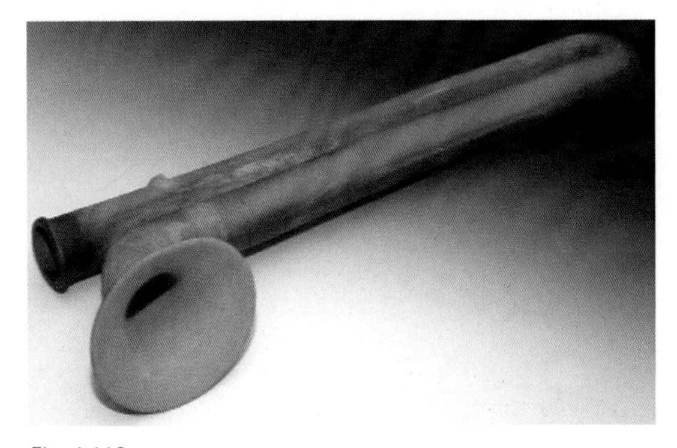

Fig. 4.116
**Bassoon Drum**
Dag Sørensen, Sandnes, Norway. This stoneware thrown and molded tubular plosive aerophone was inspired by a length of road pipe. Eddie Andresen, co-inventor with Dag, describes its sound as "a mixture of Gregorian chant and roaring dinosaurs." Hear it for yourself on track 27 of the CD. 43 inches in length.

There are a variety of different forms in which clay pot drums are made. The most common shape is a spherical pot with a short narrow neck (figure 4.118). There is usually one hole on the side of the spherical body, but some versions of the instrument, especially larger ones, do not have a side hole. Another common form is a dumbbell shape—two spheres connected by a narrow neck, with open holes at each end (figure 4.120).

There are no standard sizes, but the spherical body of an udu is generally between six and sixteen inches in diameter. The neck is usually between two and six inches in length, and from one to three inches in diameter. The side hole is usually between one and two inches in diameter. A side hole larger than two inches may be difficult to seal with your palm when playing. A hole smaller than one inch may not produce a significant pitch change, except on very small pots.

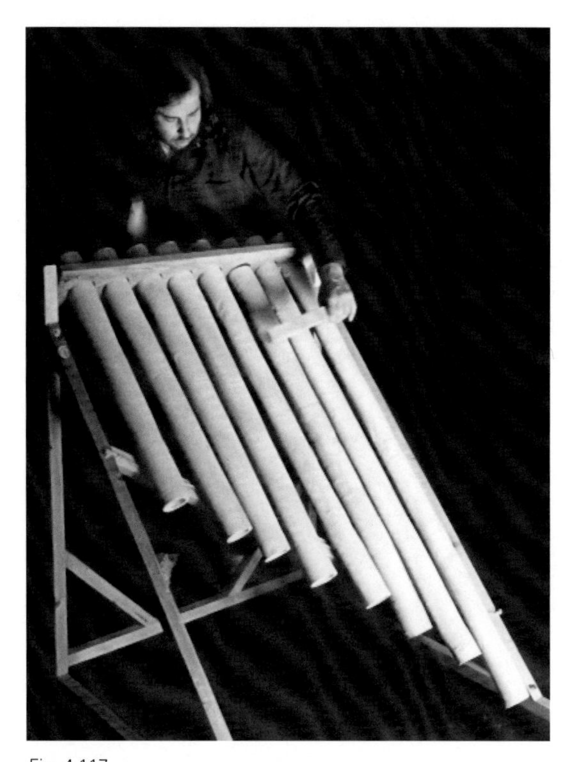

Fig. 4.117
**Tubular Drums**
Stephen Freedman, Kurtistown, Hawaii, USA. Robert Fernandez of the performance group The Antenna Repairmen plays tubular clay drums built by Stephen Freedman. Open at both ends, the tubes are struck on the end with foam sandals to produce aerophonic pitches based on the tube's length, and struck with other implements along their length for idiophonic sounds. (The Antenna Repairmen perform on other instruments built by Stephen Freedman on track 14 of the CD.)

The pot-shaped udu is held in the player's lap or placed on the ground and struck on the side hole and the neck hole with both hands. It may also be played by swatting its neck opening with a palm frond or leather-covered paddle. The dumbbell-shaped instrument is grasped around its waist with one hand, and alternatively slapped on its top hole with the other hand and brought down upon the player's leg to open and close the bottom hole.

Udus are traditionally built and played by a number of peoples in Nigeria, including the Ibo, Ibibio, Kalabari, Kagoro, Attakar and Morwa. They are traditionally women's instruments—most often made by women potters and played by women, though in some societies men play them as well.

In Africa, udus are used in a wide variety of musical situations. Solo or in combination with other instruments, they accompany popular music for singing and dancing, and they also accompany hymns in church. Udus are often played in groups of two or more. They are a key instrument used by secret women's societies for ritual performances, and also for public celebrations such as the "festival of the girls," an engagement ceremony.

There are two types of sounds that can be produced with a clay pot drum: air sounds and shell sounds.

Air sounds—which range from deep, resonant bass tones to plopping and whooping sounds—are created by the movement of air in the interior resonant cavity of the drum. Air vibrates to produce these tones when it is excited into motion by slapping the side and neck holes on the instrument with the flat palm of the hand. The shape and size

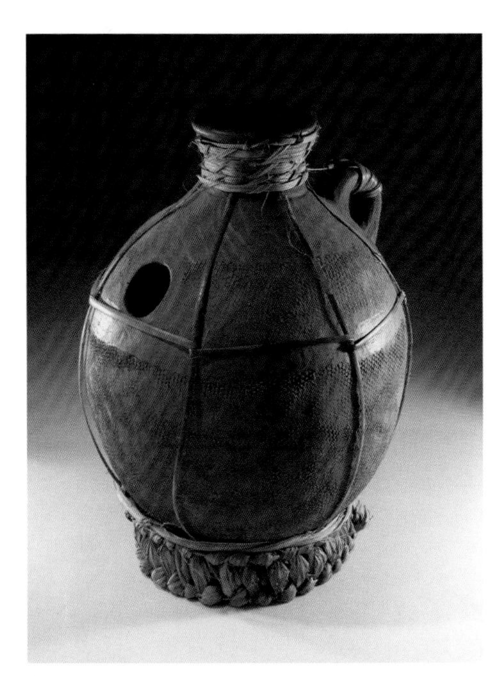

Fig. 4.118
**Nigerian Clay Pot Drum**
Unknown maker, Nigeria. A traditional Nigerian clay pot drum. Earthenware, pit fired. 18 inches in height. Collection of Barry Hall.

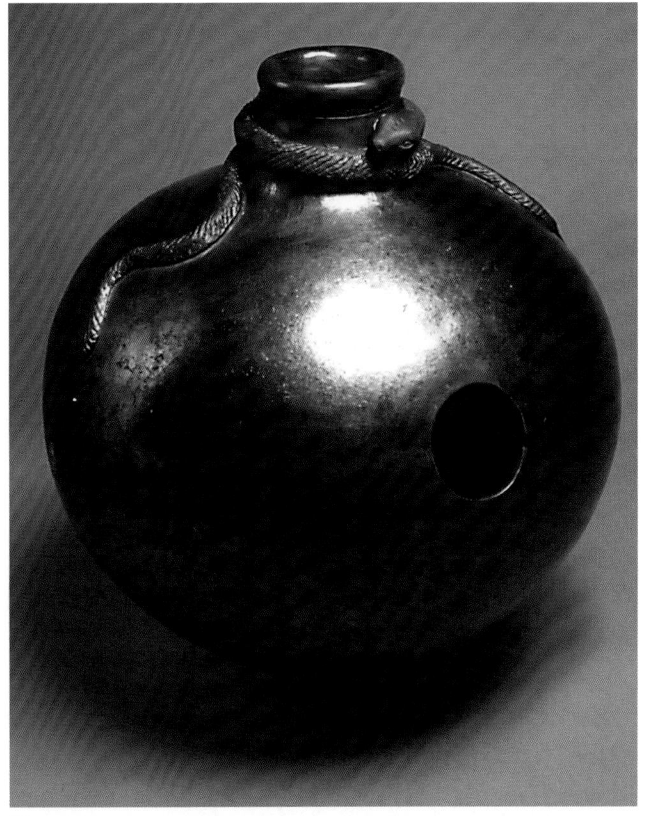

Fig. 4.119
**Snake Drum**
Frank Giorgini, Freehold, NY, USA. Coiled earthenware, coated with terra sigillata, burnished, and smoke fired. 14 inches in height.

of the interior cavity and its openings determines a specific resonant pitch for the drum. The way these dimensions interact to determine a particular instrument's pitch is as follows:

• The larger the spherical body, the lower the pitch

• The longer the neck, the lower the pitch

• The wider the neck, the higher the pitch

• The larger the side hole, the higher the pitch (when the side hole is open)

Shell sounds are produced by striking the clay body of the instrument, creating pinging, ringing, slapping, tapping, rubbing and scrubbing sounds. The main factors that impact the shell sound are the type of clay, the thickness and shape of the shell, and the firing temperature.

An udu is built up gradually from the bottom using a process called *coiling*. Coils of clay are added to the body gradually, building up the shape an inch at a time. The coils are allowed to stiffen in between in order to support the growing structure.

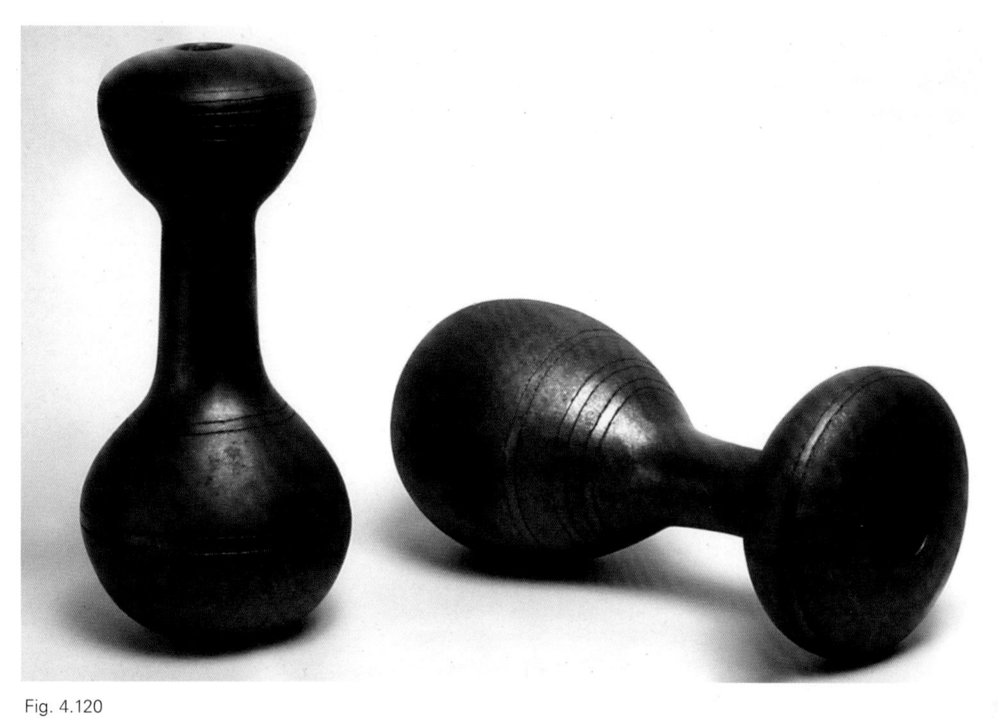

Fig. 4.120
**Kim Kims**
Frank Giorgini, Freehold, NY, USA. Instruments based on traditional Nigerian dumbbell-shaped drums. Low-fire with terra sigillata, burnished, and smoke fired. 16 inches in height.

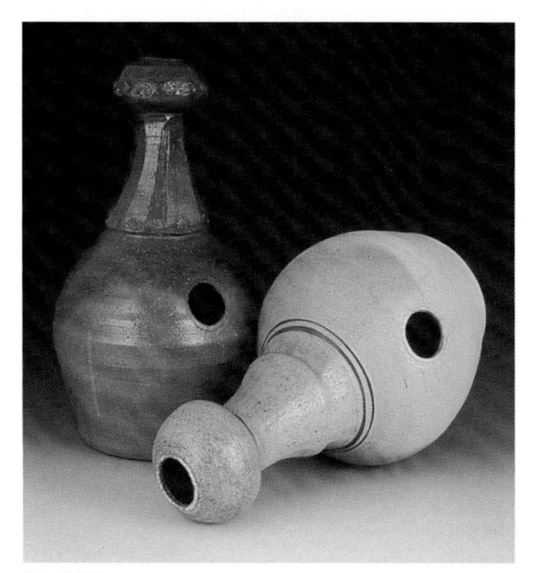

Fig. 4.121
**Udu-Style Pot Drums**
Daniel Gorno, Bellaire, Michigan, USA. Daniel Gorno is a musician/percussionist and a potter. He throws his drum shapes on a potter's wheel using soft stoneware clay. The pots are decorated with brushed-on colored slips and fired in a wood kiln. 18 inches in height.

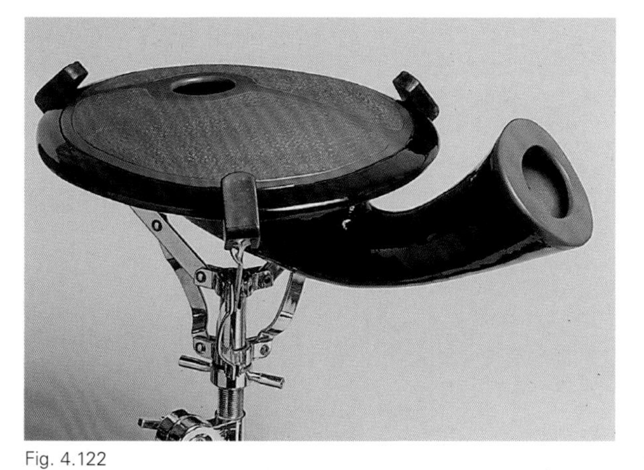

Fig. 4.122
**Tambuta**
Frank Giorgini, Freehold, NY, USA. An inverted, flattened udu designed to be played on a stand. The textured clay surface can be rubbed to create additional sound effects. Slipcast with black glaze.

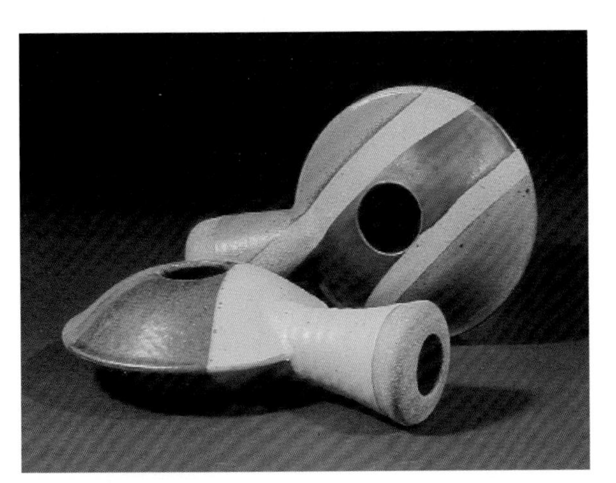

Fig. 4.123
**Plosive Aerophones**
Chester Winowiecki, Fremont, Michigan, USA. Chester assembled these drums from separately thrown pieces. He used stoneware clay that was bisque fired then glazed and fired in a gas kiln. 12 inches in length.

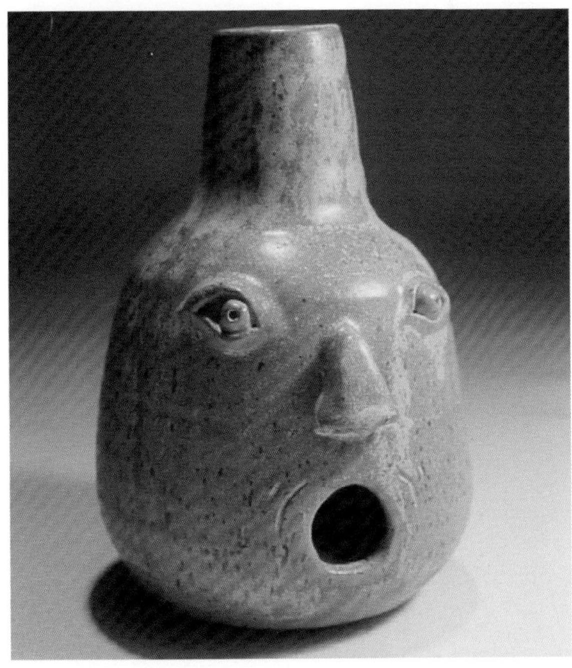

Fig. 4.124
**Pot Drum**
Donna Anderson, Cloverly, Maryland, USA. Donna throws her pot drums in two pieces. Care is taken to ensure that both pieces have the same wall thickness. Decorated with a bronze green matt glaze and fired to Cone 6.

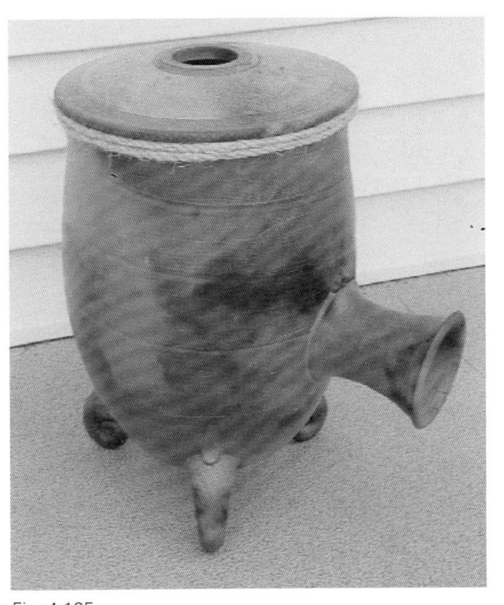

Fig. 4.125
**Flat Top Podrum With Squiggly Legs**
Keith Lehman, Gibsons, British Columbia, Canada. Keith's designs are inspired by Nigerian water jug drums and clay cooking pots. He also collaborates closely with professional percussionists. According to Keith, the podrum's sounds are reminiscent of an Indian tabla. He uses a kickwheel to throw the individual pieces for his drums, and describes his clay as "specially formulated and ever evolving." Smoke-fired, 15 inches in height.

One advantage of coiling is that it permits control of the vessel's thickness at all points. Whereas wheel-thrown pots are generally thicker near their base, udus produce the best sound when they are a consistent thickness throughout the entire drum. This produces consistent sounds from all areas of the vessel and allows it to vibrate and resonate more freely.

Ibibio potters build the body of these drums from coils on a pottery turntable in a single day. After the body has dried overnight, the neck is added using more coils and the side hole is cut with a sharp stick. Some potters add a coil of clay to create a small lip around the side hole. A variety of decorations are employed on traditional udu drums, from geometric patterns to representations of lizards and other animals. These are carved with sticks or palm leaves, and sometimes additional clay is used to add relief figures or handles to the pots. Some pots are treated before firing with a red slip containing hematite, in order to enhance their appearance.

After drying for a week, the pots are fired in small bonfires. The Ibibio use fuel consisting of palm leaves, sticks and grasses, which burn quickly—making the entire firing as brief as 15 minutes. The Attakar fire their pots in a slow-burning fire of dried cow dung, grass and broken pots. The pots are usually taken to market later the same day.

The dumbbell-shaped kimkim is usually not fired. It is made from clay mixed with extremely fine sand, and after drying and burnishing with a smooth stone, the pot is ready for playing.

In recent years, Abbas M. Ahuwan of Zaria, Nigeria has expanded the udu's popularity to the rest of the world by teaching potters in America the traditional methods for making Nigerian clay pot drums. Probably his most prolific student is Frank Giorgini, who learned udu-making from Abbas in the 1970s and went on to

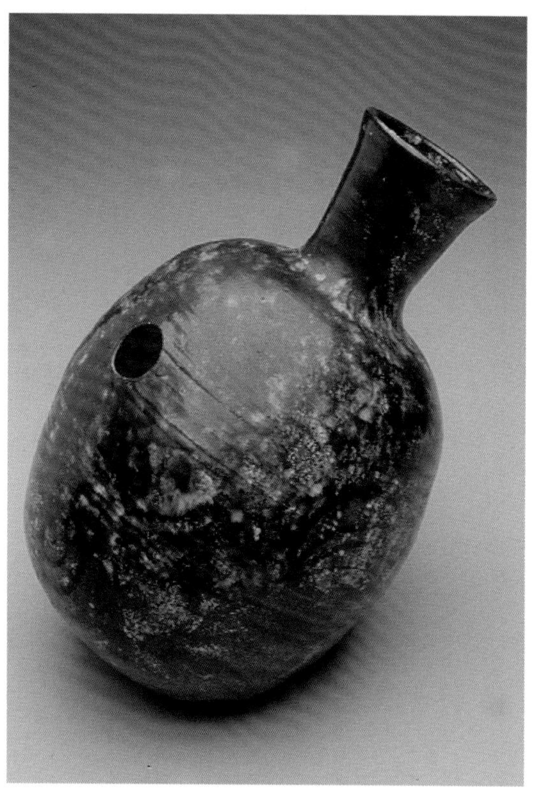

Fig. 4.126
**Sun Spot Udu**
Jason Gaddy, Rochester, Washington, USA. This drum was fired in a low-temperature reduction in a wood burning kiln. 16 inches in height.

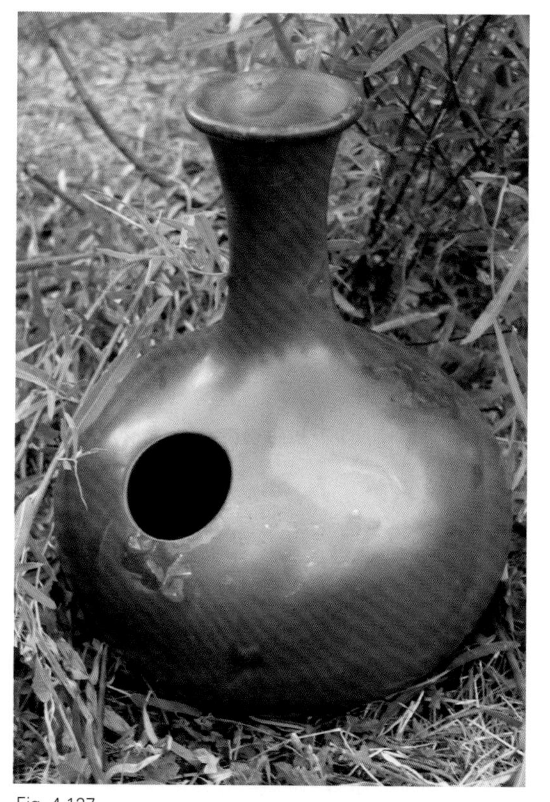

Fig. 4.127
**Udu**
Rod Kendall, Tenino, Washington, USA. Saggar fired, red cone 6 stoneware body. Hand polished with diamond sanding pads prior to firing, and finished with microcrystalline wax polish. 13 inches in height.

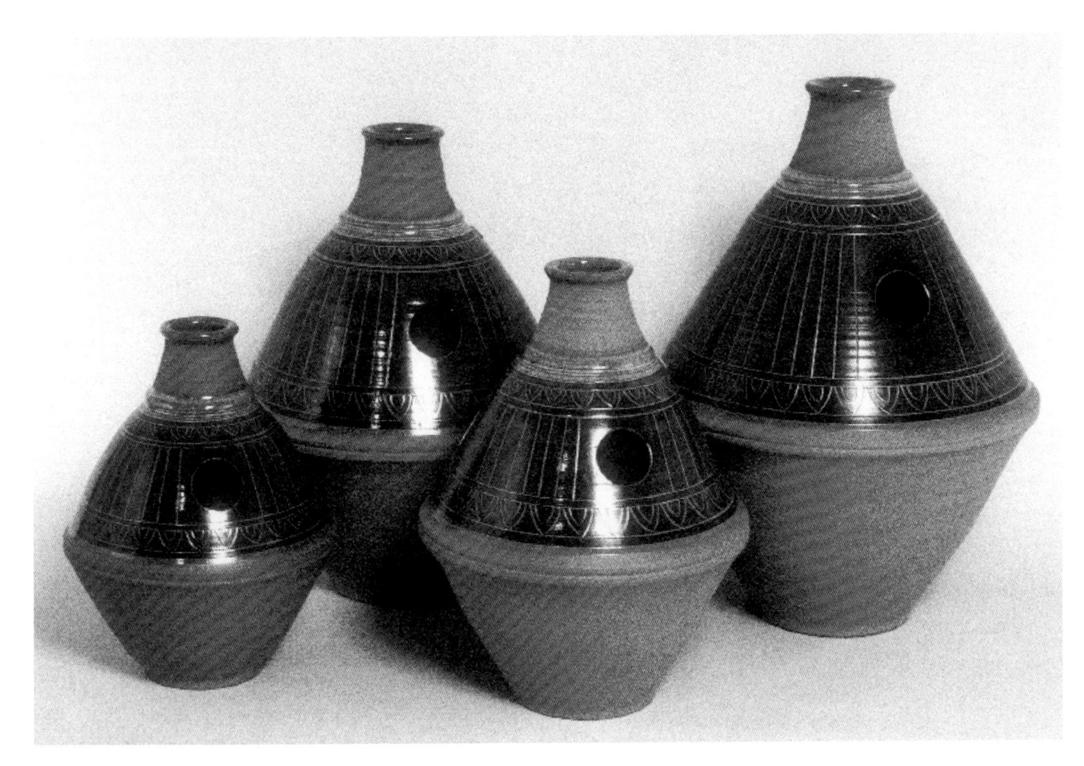

Fig. 4.128
**Ubangs**
Stephen Wright, Hagerstown, Maryland, USA. Set of four drums tuned to the keys of A, E, D and low C. Each drum has an opening to permit an internal microphone. Hand carved designs, colored slip and glaze. To 18 inches in height.

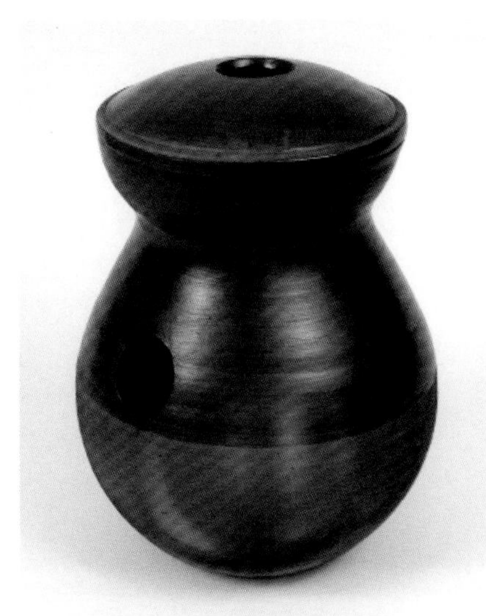

Fig. 4.129
**Udu Drum**
Frank Kara, Southbury, Connecticut, USA. Frank threw the base and neck of this drum in two pieces, then joined them and added the hand-formed domed top in the leatherhard stage. The top section is decorated with a burnished terra sigillata, and the drum is raku fired. 13 inches in height.

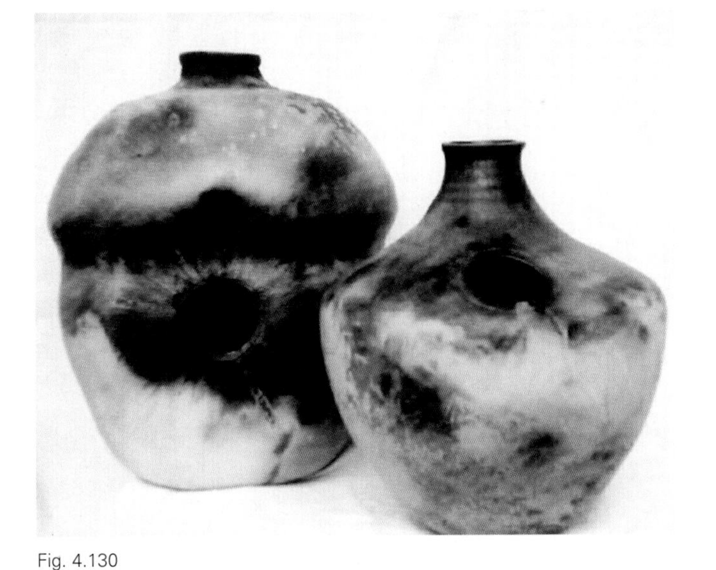

Fig. 4.130
**Udu Drums**
Cedar S. Sorensen, Victoria, British Columbia, Canada. These drums were coil-built, scraped, paddled and burnished. The clay, a mixture of red and white stoneware was bisque fired to cone 05, then smoke fired. Copper tape and wire were applied to the larger piece before firing, and various organic materials (including banana peels, seed husks and straw) were used in the fire to create surface markings. To 16 inches in height.

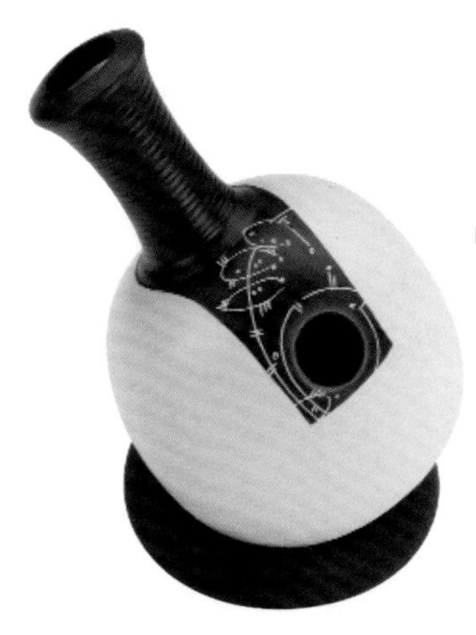

Fig. 4.131
**Neck Udu**
Kai Koesling, Schlagwerk Percussion, Gingen/Fils, Germany. Kai's drums are made from stoneware clay on a potter's wheel. Tapping or scraping the extra-long ribbed neck provides sound capabilities in addition to the basic udu sounds. The neck area is painted with a black slip, and sgraffito designs are drawn through the dark slip, while still wet, to reveal the white clay beneath. 14 inches in height.

popularize and develop udu-style drums for a Western audience.

Starting with the traditional Nigerian design, Frank has developed many variations of the instrument, approaching it from a visual and sculptural approach and considering the ergonomics of hand percussion. The result of his approach has yielded a sonic variety of visually appealing instruments that are also comfortable to play. In addition to exploring a multitude of shapes, Frank has added textures to the clay surface that can be used to produce rubbing sounds, and developed methods for using internal microphones for amplification and recording. Some of his self-named designs include the Tambuta (figure 4.12), the Udongo and Mbwata (figure 9.4) and the Hadgini (figure 9.3) which he developed jointly with percussionist Jamey Haddad. (Learn more about Frank in the "Profiles" chapter.)

Other contemporary makers have embraced the udu and its variations. Winnie Owens-Hart was first exposed to the art of udu making from Abbas Ahuwan and went on to several apprenticeships in a Nigerian women's pottery village where she studied traditional ceramic techniques. (Learn more about Winnie in the "Profiles" chapter.)

A number of makers build clay pot drums using less traditional methods, such as wheel-throwing. Stephen Wright builds clay pot drums that he calls *ubangs*—a combination of two traditional

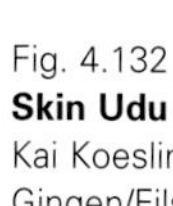

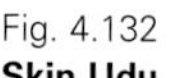

Fig. 4.132
**Skin Udu**
Kai Koesling, Schlagwerk Percussion, Gingen/Fils, Germany. This instrument has a neck and side hole, like a traditional udu, but also has an additional opening covered with a thin natural skin. Areas of varying clay thickness permit the drum's shell to produce two different body sounds, and a ribbed section of the exterior can be played by scraping. Stoneware with slips. 17 inches in height.

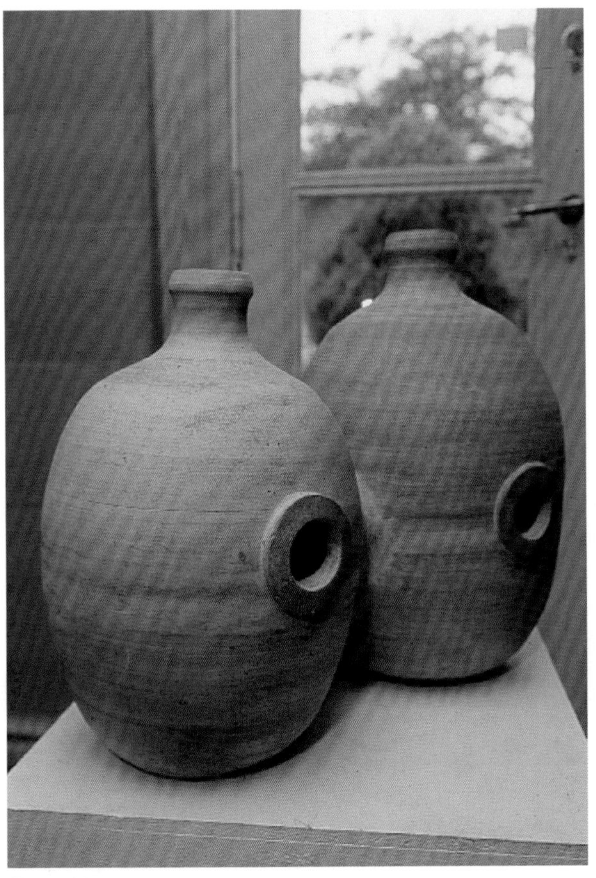

Fig. 4.133
**Doubledrum**
Dag Sørensen, Sandnes, Norway. Two pot drums attached at the waist. Stoneware colored with manganese dioxide, fired to cone 10. 21 inches in height.

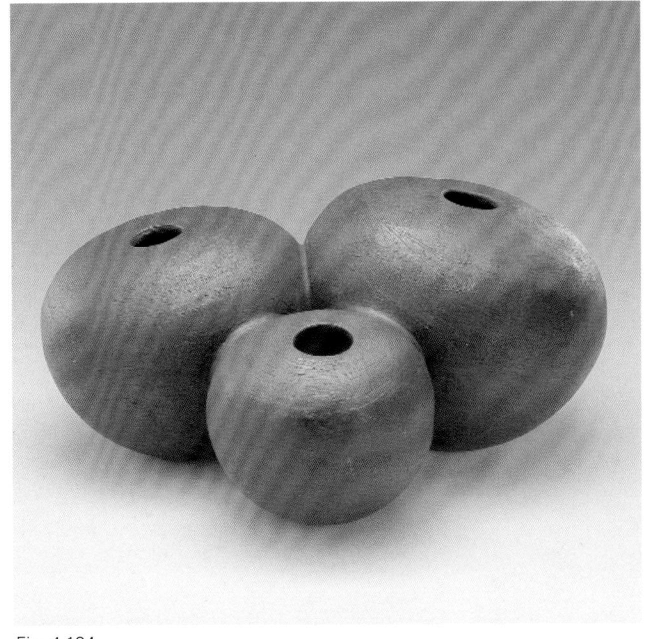

Fig. 4.134
**Triple Clay Pot Drum**
Barry Hall, Westborough, Massachusetts, USA. Three interconnected chambers produce a variety of pitches. Coil-built stoneware. 17 inches in width.

names, *udu* and *abang*. Stephen's drums are assembled from wheel-thrown components and glazed (figure 4.128). Udus from a number of other makers are shown in this chapter. The popularity of the clay pot drum among ceramists attests to its simple but powerful design.

Clay pot drums similar to the Nigerian variety are found in other parts of Africa. The *zinli* or *canarí*, is a percussion pot of the Fan of Dahomey. This clay pot is struck with a flat, round beater formed to fit its open mouth. It is used in funeral ceremonies, and was also introduced to Brazil and Cuba by Dahomey slaves.

In Spain and Portugal a ceramic pitcher called a *cantaró* provides rhythmic accompaniment to folk dances. A player flaps a basketry fan against the mouth of the pitcher, which gives a thumping bass sound like a large drum. This instrument, also used in the Americas, may be partially filled with water to raise its pitch.

A *moringa* is a side-hole clay pot drum popular in Brazil and other parts of South America.

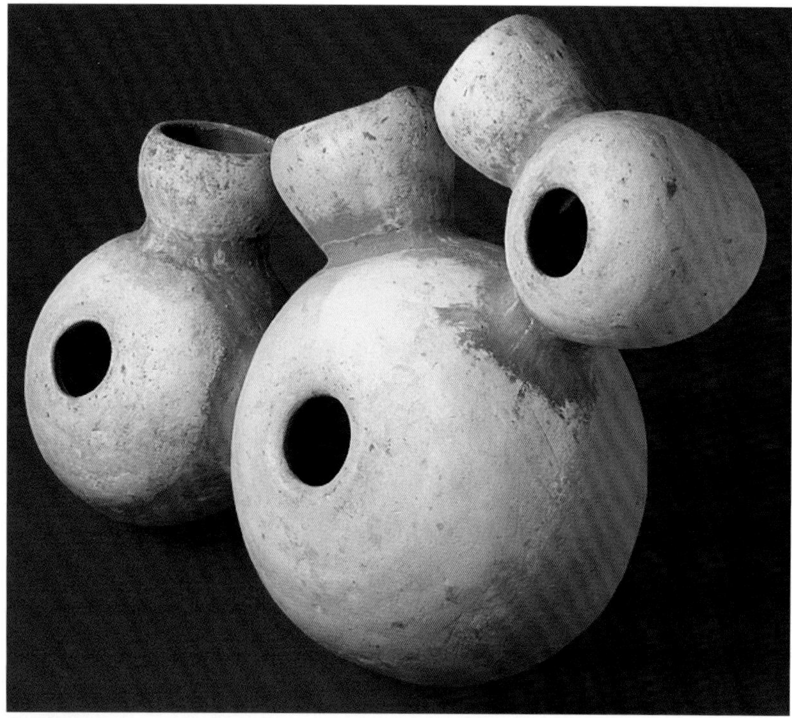

Fig. 4.135
**Bum d'Agua**
Aguinaldo da Silva, Olinda, Pernambuco, Brazil. A bum d'agua ("water boom") triple clay pot drum made from earthenware. Aguinaldo builds these multiple instruments with as many as seven chambers.

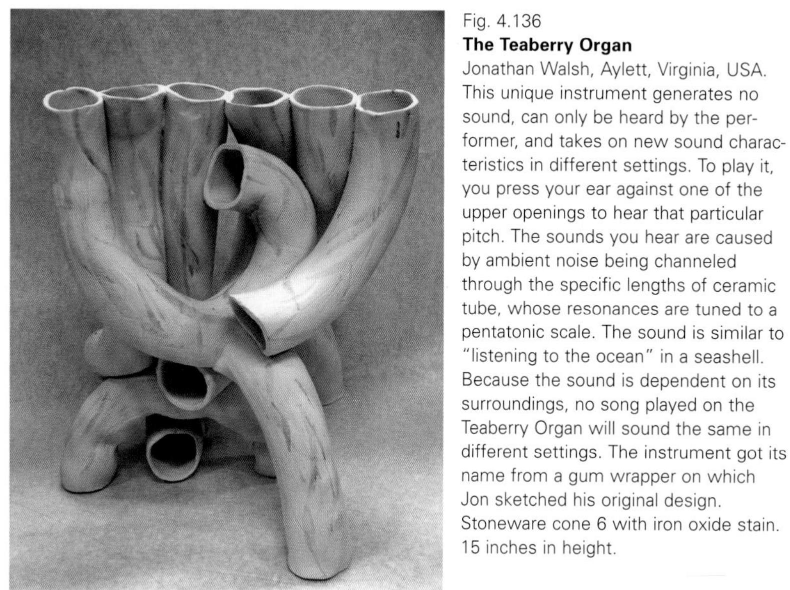

Fig. 4.136
**The Teaberry Organ**
Jonathan Walsh, Aylett, Virginia, USA. This unique instrument generates no sound, can only be heard by the performer, and takes on new sound characteristics in different settings. To play it, you press your ear against one of the upper openings to hear that particular pitch. The sounds you hear are caused by ambient noise being channeled through the specific lengths of ceramic tube, whose resonances are tuned to a pentatonic scale. The sound is similar to "listening to the ocean" in a seashell. Because the sound is dependent on its surroundings, no song played on the Teaberry Organ will sound the same in different settings. The instrument got its name from a gum wrapper on which Jon sketched his original design. Stoneware cone 6 with iron oxide stain. 15 inches in height.

Moringa is Portugese for "clay jar". These instruments, while used in Brazilian traditional music, may be based on African instruments imported via the slave trade, since another common name for them is *pote Africano* (African pot). However, unlike their African counterparts, many of the instruments found in Brazilian markets are manufactured from utilitarian ceramic oil or water jars, with a side hole cut later. Brazilian potters also make the moringa in a style similar to its African cousin.

Not all Brazilian clay pot drums are linked to Africa. Aguinaldo da Silva of Pernambuco developed an udu-like instrument, having never before seen a side-hole pot drum (figure 4.135). He named his instrument *bum d'agua* ("water boom") because of its water-like sound. He has expanded his original design to include multiple—as many as seven—chambers in a single instrument.

Ragnar Naess created *resonating jars* as part of his EarthSounds ensemble (see more on Ragnar and EarthSounds in the "Profiles" chapter). In search of a good shape and combination of resonating air chamber, neck and striking surface, Ragnar made a number of vases of various proportions. After much experimentation, he returned to a form he'd made for many years as a production vase—a long trumpet neck on an almost spherical resonator (figure 9.24). Though it was not designed as a musical instrument, it served that purpose well. Soft foam rubber paddles are used to strike the opening of the jar.

As many potters have discovered, large clay vessels make fantastic aerophonic sounds when struck while the raw, unfired clay is at the stage in the drying process called leather hard (stage at which the clay has stiffened but is still damp). Diane Baxter explored these sounds, as well as the idiophonic sounds of the same vessels after firing, in her piece "Genesis" on the accompanying CD (figure 2.14 and CD track 22).

## Resonators

Any basic pot, but especially one with a mouth that is narrower than its waist, can serve as a resonator. This means that it will accentuate certain sound frequencies that are spoken or played into its interior. Try speaking or singing into a pot, jar or vase. If you sing different pitches, you may find one or two pitches that resonate well while others do not. You'll also notice that, even when speaking into the pot, the sound character of your voice is changed by the particular acoustic resonances of the vessel. Since fired clay has a relatively hard surface that reflects sound efficiently, ceramic pots work well as resonators.

The *musical pot* or German *Sprechtopf* (speech pot) is just what its name implies—a clay vessel into which a performer sings or speaks. The resonant chamber modifies the sound of the voice, which may make it appear like a spirit or an animal. In a more practical vein, clay resonator vessels were used in the Roman theater and early churches to accentuate certain pitches of a speaker's voice.

Some musical instruments also use clay vessels as resonators, to enhance or color the sound of a vibration produced by other means. There are many examples elsewhere in this book, including the berimbau (a musical bow in the "Chordophones" chapter), the clay marimba (in the "Idiophones" chapter) and the jaguar pot trumpet described earlier in this chapter. The clay drum shells of most membranophones also serve a similar function.

A final example of clay resonators comes from the world of high-end audio loudspeakers (figure 4.138). While speakers are not considered musical instruments in the strictest sense, it is relevant that clay was selected as the material for these esoteric audiophile speaker enclosures due to its acoustical properties and its impact on sound quality.

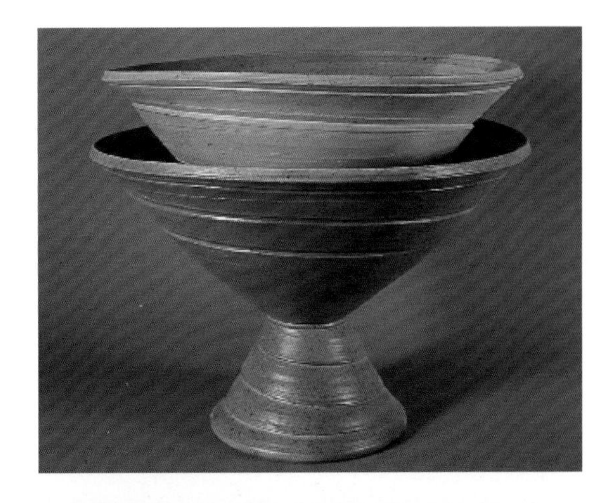

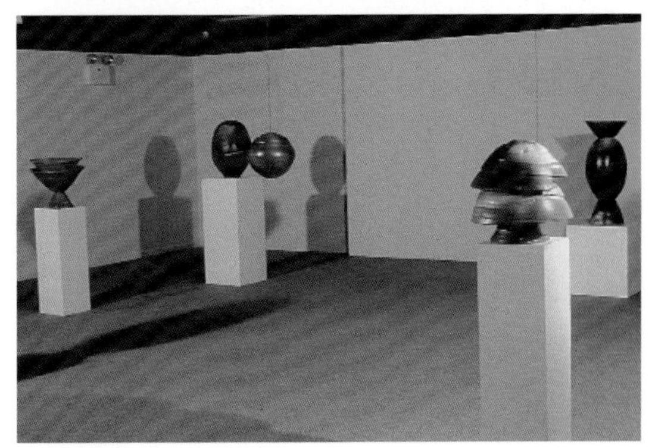

Fig. 4.137
**Ceramic Resonator Vessels**
Brian Ransom, St. Petersburg, Florida, USA. Components of a sonic installation consisting of a set of earthenware resonating vessels powered by electronic tone generators which activate a standing wave or resonant pitch in the vessel's chamber. Visitors to this installation experience pressure where sonic waves peak creating louder sounds and decompression in the valleys of the waves creating softer sounds. The gallery space is tuned through the careful alignment of the tones of nine ceramic resonators. Sonic waves overlap to cause a strobe-effect where waves move in and out of phase with one another. As the visitor walks through the installation, the physical waves of sound are perceived as an interactive sonic environment. In this way, each visitor composes a personal piece of music by choosing a route through the gallery.

Fig. 4.138
**nOrh Ceramic Loudspeaker**
Michael Barnes, Bangkok, Thailand. These high-end loudspeakers, designed for clean sound reproduction, have been ranked among the best in the world by audiophile magazines. Michael uses ceramic shells because fired clay has a very good ability to reflect rather than absorb sound. The speaker enclosure's unorthodox shape is inspired by the acoustical properties of a traditional Thai drum. 15 inches in length.

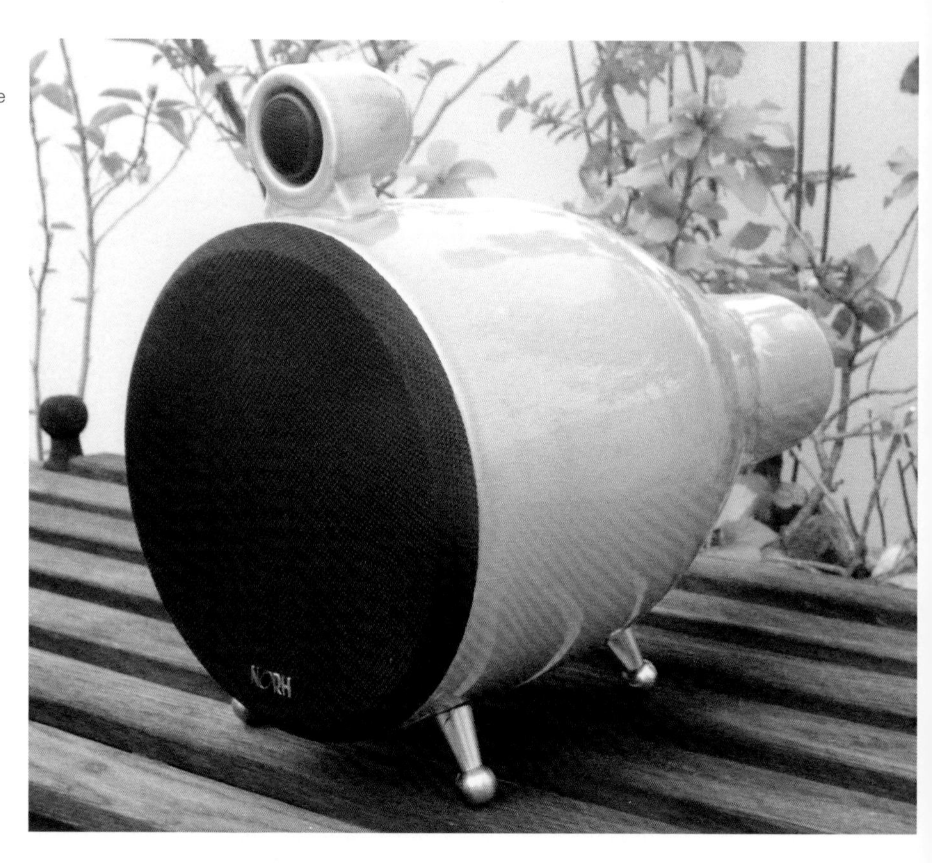


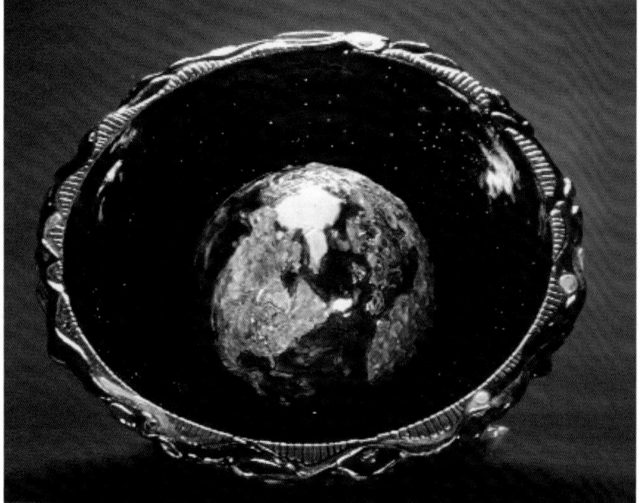

Fig. 4.139
**Planet Speaker**
John Hansen, Louisville, Colorado, USA. This "ceramic reflexive sound lens" loudspeaker was created by John Hansen in collaboration with sound designer Bruce Odland for a public art installation in Linz, Austria. The design, inspired by Austrian astronomer Johannes Kepler's model of the solar system, consists of two nested ceramic spheres, with a speaker driver mounted inside the smaller in order to reflect a focused, directional beam of sound. Stoneware, cone 6. 18 inches in diameter.

## chapter five

*A few can touch the magic string, and noisy fame is proud to win them; alas for those that never sing, but die with all their music in them!*

—Oliver Wendell Holmes

# Chordophones
## *Stringed Instruments*

Chordophones are instruments in which the sound is made by vibrating strings. The strings can be made from a variety of materials—metal, gut, silk, nylon and even horse hair—and are set into motion by plucking, striking or bowing. This chapter explores the following types of chordophones:

- Musical bows
- Zithers
- Harps and lyres
- Lutes
- Other chordophones

Stringed instruments are probably the most difficult instruments to make from clay. As a result, there are fewer clay instruments in the chordophone family than in the other families explored in this book. This is due to several inherent attributes of clay that present challenges when making chordophones.

The first is clay's inherent inflexibility, which makes it poorly suited for creating a *soundboard,* the device that radiates the sound of most string instruments. When a string vibrates, it produces very little sound on its own. Therefore, most string instruments rely on other materials to amplify their sound. A common arrangement is the one used in a guitar or violin. In this setup, a string is stretched over a wooden bridge, which transmits the string's vibrations to a thin, flat, flexible wooden soundboard (such as the face of the guitar), which amplifies the bridge's vibration and radiates the sound. A resonant chamber (the guitar's body or soundbox) enclosed below the soundboard further amplifies the instrument and enhances its tone quality. Certain types of wood (and other flexible materials) make good bridges and soundboards due to their flexibility and "springiness," which gives them a warm, mellow tone. Clay usually doesn't fare as well for these purposes, because it tends to be more rigid, which results in a bright, edgy tone.

The second challenge of clay chordophones relates to their pegs or other tuning devices. Tuning

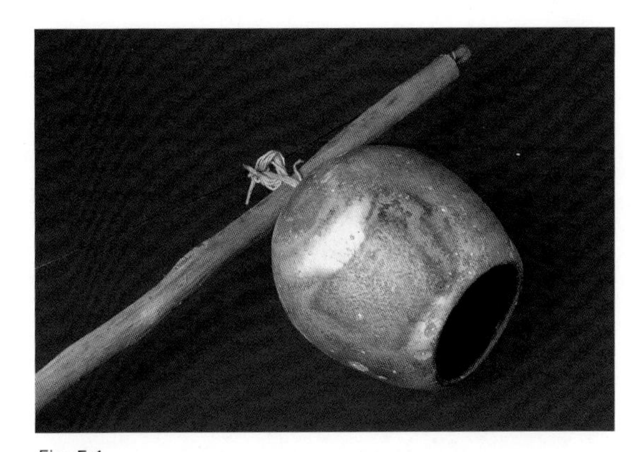

Fig. 5.1
**Berimbau**
Aguinaldo da Silva, Olinda, Pernambuco, Brazil. The berimbau is a musical bow from Brazil, with African origins. This berimbau uses a clay vessel as a resonator, in place of a gourd which is traditionally used for that purpose.

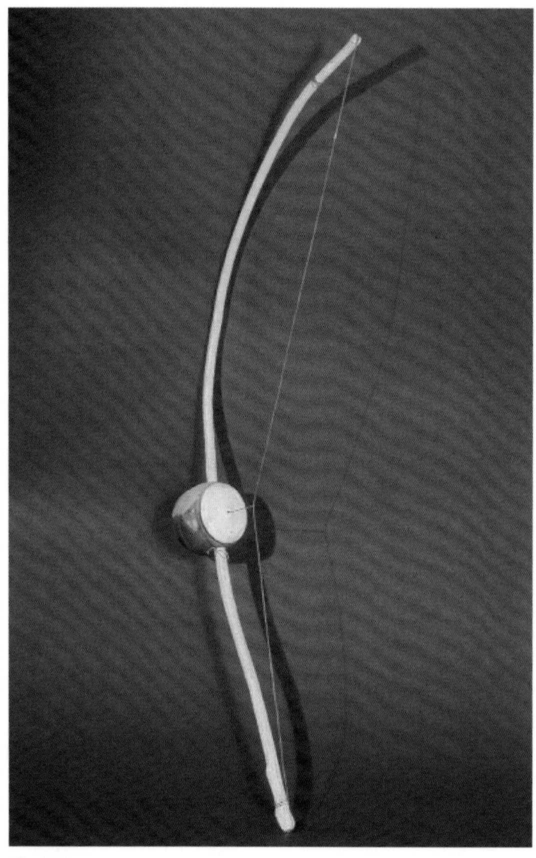

Fig. 5.2
**Berimbau**
Brian Ransom, St. Petersburg, Florida, USA. Saggar-fired ceramic, steel, wood. 60" x 6" x 4".

a string instrument requires a mechanism that enables precise string tensioning. This is especially important if the instrument has more than one string, because the pitch relationship between the strings must be precisely controlled. A common approach on traditional violins and many other stringed instruments is a wooden peg carefully friction-fitted into a hole—not too tight and not too loose—which provides the proper amount of control to enable precise tuning. Clay is not well suited for making pegs or the holes in which they fit for several reasons. It is brittle and fragile, so the pegs can break from the tension or friction of tuning. Clay usually has a gritty rather than smooth surface, which grinds away at a wooden peg and makes it difficult for a peg to turn smoothly. In addition, clay doesn't have the flexible or springy properties of wood that are necessary to ensure a secure friction grip between the peg and its hole.

Despite these limitations, ceramic artists have created a variety of very successful clay chordophones. Some incorporate non-ceramic materials for the soundboard, bridge and tuners, while others are more courageously absolute in their use of clay, even using delicate ceramic soundboards. As you'll see from the examples in this chapter, clay can be used for almost every component of a stringed instrument—except the strings!

## Musical Bows

The musical bow is the oldest and simplest stringed instrument, and variations of it are used around the world. It consists of a flexible wooden stick held under tension by a string stretched between its two ends. The bow is played by striking, plucking or rubbing the string, and sometimes by rubbing the stick. Often a resonator is attached to the bow, which amplifies the sound. The most common resonator material is an open gourd. However, some bows use a clay pot as a resonator, either attached to the bow or held against it.

The *berimbau* is a well-known Brazilian musical bow of African origin. A player strikes its steel string with a stick while changing the tone of the string with a coin or small stone. The berimbau is the principal accompanying instrument for the Brazilian martial art called *capoiera*. Its resonator is usually made from a gourd; however, figures 5.1 and 5.2 show berimbaus with ceramic resonators.

The *villadivadyam* from southern India is a complex musical bow, played by two or more performers as an accompaniment to their own singing. It consists of a long bow, seven or eight feet in length, which is held against the neck of a ceramic pot. Several bronze bells are attached to the bow. One singer holds the bow against the pot and beats the open neck of the pot with a fan, and the side of the pot with a coin. The other singer beats the bow's string with sticks that have jingles attached. The villadivadyam is played for popular entertainment at temple festivals, in an ensemble with several other instruments, including the *ghatam* (see the "Idiophones" chapter).

### Zithers

Zithers are instruments with strings stretched across a body. The body may be a stick, box or bowl shape.

A clay zither-like instrument from northeast Thailand called the *phin hai* consists of a graduated set of clay pots. A wide rubber band is stretched across the neck of each pot, and the player plucks these bands to produce low bass tones. The size of each pot and the tension of its rubber band determine the pitch it will produce. As part of a traditional Thai *ponglang* ensemble performance, it is customary for a young woman to dance and simulate playing the phin hai.

### Harps and Lyres

Harps and lyres are instruments with multiple strings. With harps, the strings run at an angle from a soundbox and attach to the instrument's neck. With lyres, the strings run over a bridge on the soundbox, and are attached to a crossbar held by two beams. Both types of instruments are played in a similar fashion, usually plucked with fingers and thumbs.

Brian Ransom's "Ceramic Harp" (technically a lyre) uses an animal skin membrane for a soundboard, in the style of many African harps and lyres

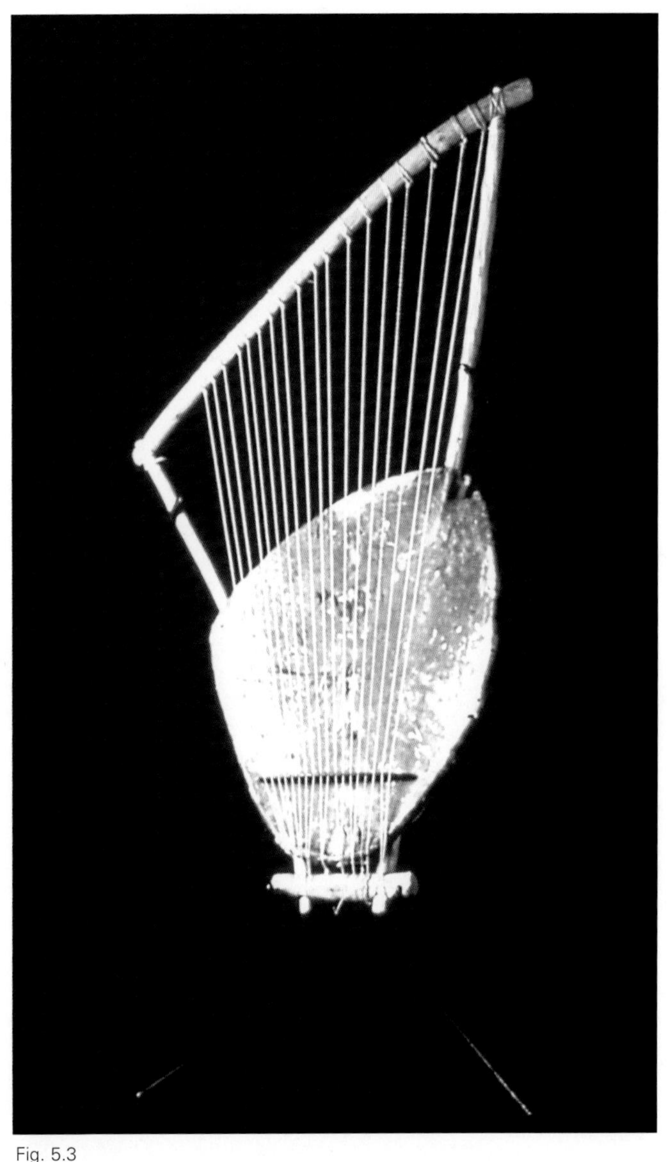

Fig. 5.3
**Ceramic Harp**
Brian Ransom, St. Petersburg, Florida, USA. This 18-string lyre has a ceramic body with a skin membrane for a soundboard. 42 inches in height. Hear this instrument on CD tracks 2, 9 and 36.

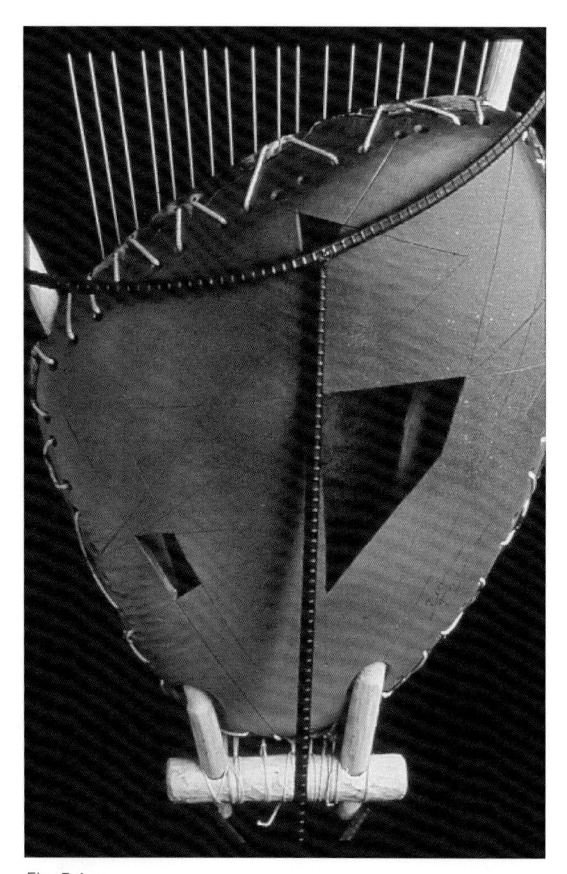

Fig. 5.4
**Ceramic Harp detail**
Brian Ransom, St. Petersburg, Florida, USA.

(figure 5.3). The skin is laced to a ceramic vessel that forms the soundbox. Brian's clay harp can be heard on several tracks of the accompanying CD.

Ward Hartenstein's harp drum (figure 6.1) uses a hollow ceramic form as a soundbox. This chambered tube structure has a goat skin head attached so it also can be played as a drum. The steel strings produce a soft sound from the rigid ceramic soundbox. The strings are tensioned by wooden pegs, about which Ward says, "The tuning pegs, being friction-fitted, suffer somewhat from abrasion by the clay surface, but I have found that burnishing the ceramic peg sockets with a tapered wood tool while the clay is leather hard helps to push in the grog particles and create a smoother surface." Another technique for setting clay pegs is to make the hole in the clay body slightly larger than the peg, and then inset a small piece of wood into the hole to serve as the peg's receptacle. This technique is used for the snare tensioning pegs on the drums in figures 6.12 and 8.16.

Rob Mangum's *Five Stringer* (figure 5.5) might be classified as a *triple lyre-harp*. Whatever it is technically, it's certainly very interesting to look at. The three stoneware soundboxes have bridges integrated into their form—a very clever way to take advantage of clay's plasticity to avoid using the separate bridges required with wooden instruments.

## Lutes

Lutes are chordophones that have a soundbox and a neck, with strings running parallel to them. There are two types of lutes—those that are played by plucking the strings (such as a guitar or banjo) and those whose strings are bowed (such as a violin or cello).

As part of his EarthSounds ensemble, Ragnar Naess created both plucked and bowed ceramic lutes, and named them, appropriately, *pluckers* and *bowers* (figures 5.7-5.8). These instruments are made from stoneware clay. The bridges, strings and pegs are borrowed from traditional string instruments, but the bodies, necks and soundboards are made from clay. Ragnar found that clay soundboards produce the best tone when they are very thin—between 1/16 and 3/32 of an inch. He relates that a big challenge is keeping the thin soundboard intact while the instrument dries.

Both the pluckers and bowers have steel strings. The crook in the neck of the bower is inspired by the *erhu,* a traditional Chinese fiddle. The round body and short neck of the plucker is reminiscent of a Chinese "moon guitar." Their sound is soft, but

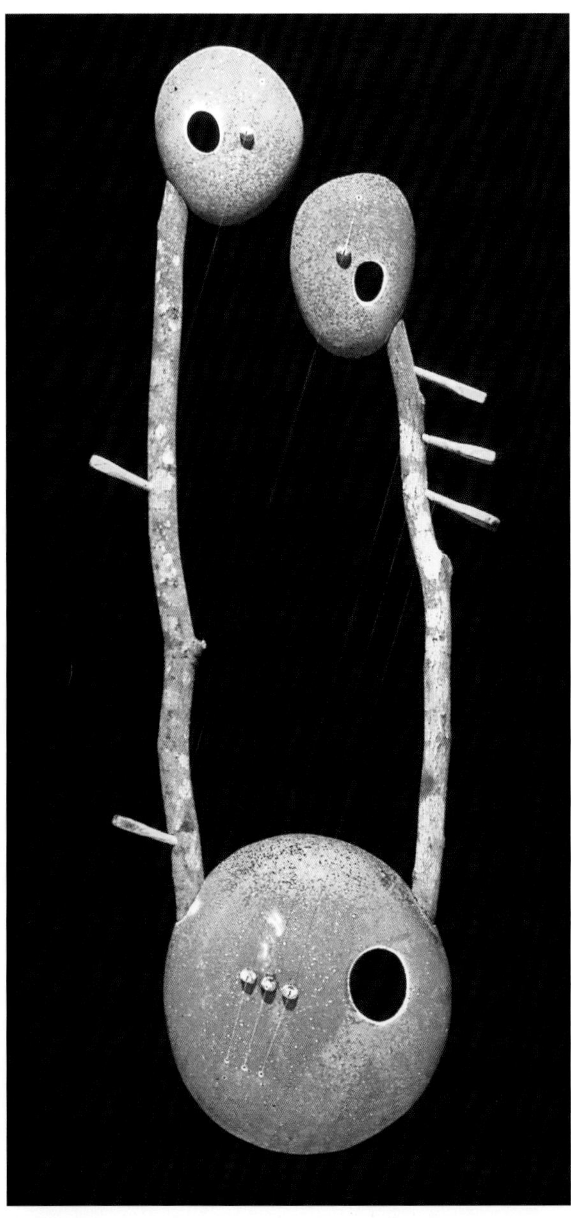

Fig. 5.5
**Five Stringer**
Rob Mangum, Weaverville, North Carolina, USA. The ceramic components were finished with a barium glaze and fired to cone 06 in reduction. The neck is fashioned from a poplar branch with cedar pegs. 46 inches in length.

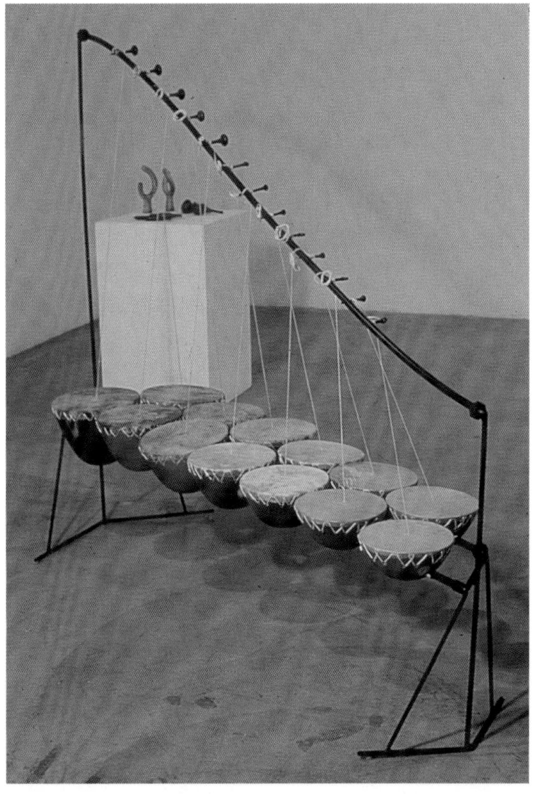

Fig. 5.6
**Bass Harp**
Brian Ransom, St. Petersburg, Florida, USA. Each silk string in this large-scale lyre is attached to the center of an animal hide resonator, which is laced to an earthenware bowl. The bowls have openings in the bottom and are carefully tuned to resonate at the pitch of the string they support. Approx. 6 x 6 feet.

the ceramic soundboards and steel strings combine to give them a bright, crystalline tone. In performance their bodies are also struck with mallets, which produce a rich "clonking" sound.

Ragnar's pluckers and bowers can be heard on track 21 of the accompanying CD. The bower is featured in a solo near the end of the selection. To learn more about the EarthSounds instruments, see Ragnar's profile in the "Profiles" section.)

At the bottom end of the plucked lute spectrum are the clay bass instruments made by Brian Ransom and Rob Mangum shown in figures 5.11 and 5.12.

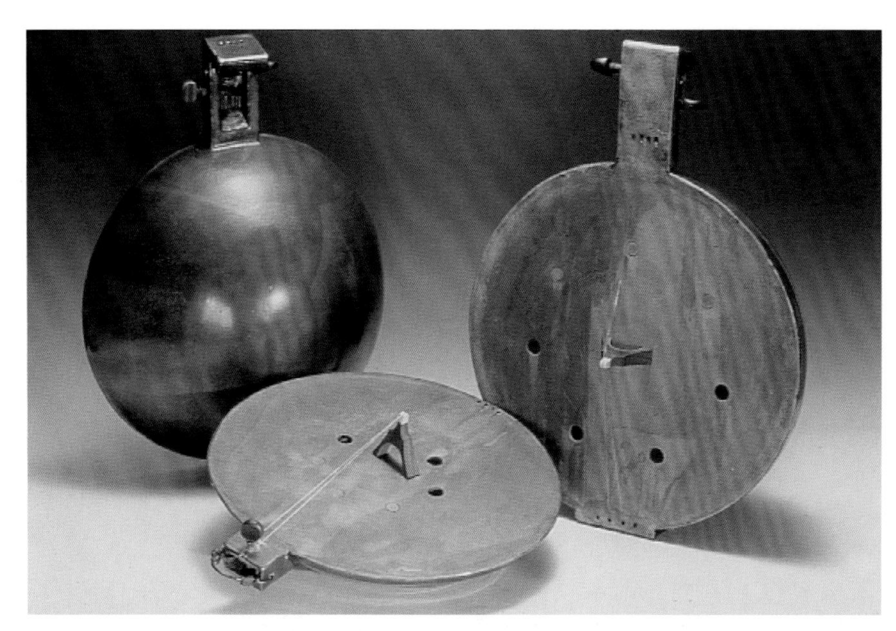

Fig. 5.7
**EarthSounds Pluckers**
Ragnar Naess, Brooklyn, New York, USA. Examples of string instruments from the EarthSounds ceramic orchestra created by Ragnar Naess in collaboration with celebrated Chinese composer and performer Tan Dun. See the profile of Ragnar Naess in chapter 9 for more details about the EarthSound instruments. Hear these instruments on CD track 21.

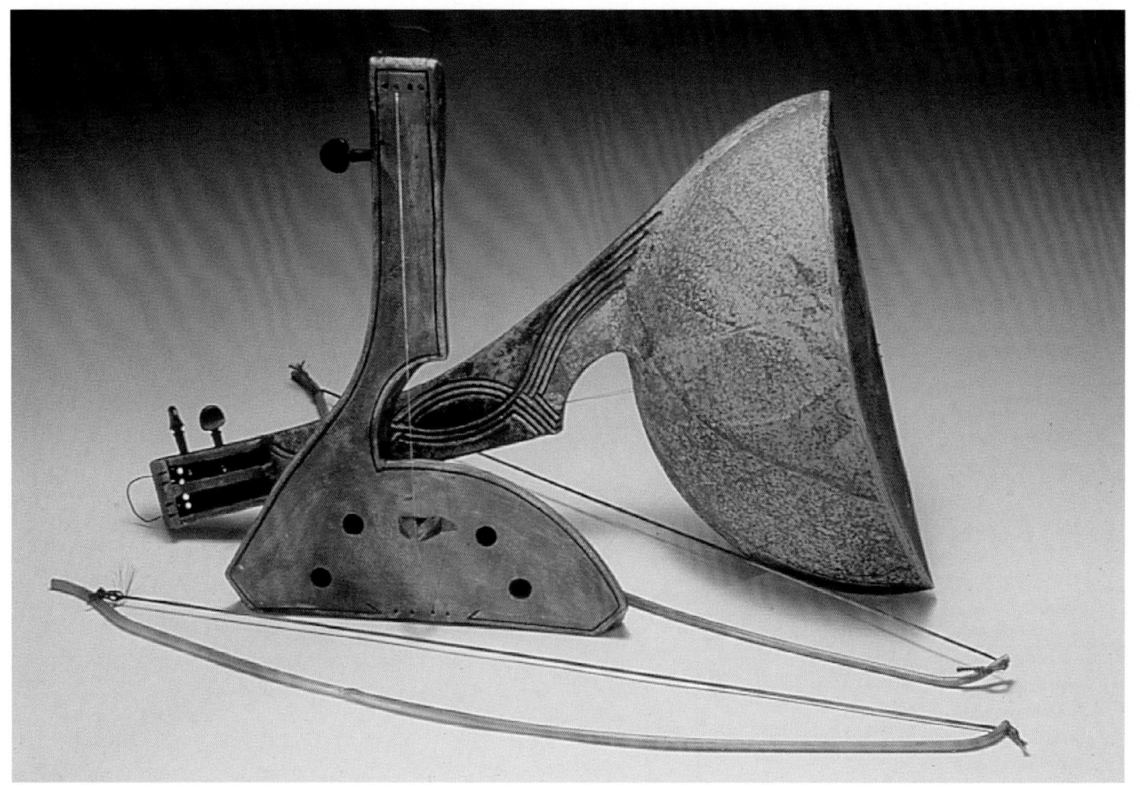

Fig. 5.8
**EarthSounds Bowers**
Ragnar Naess, Brooklyn, New York, USA.

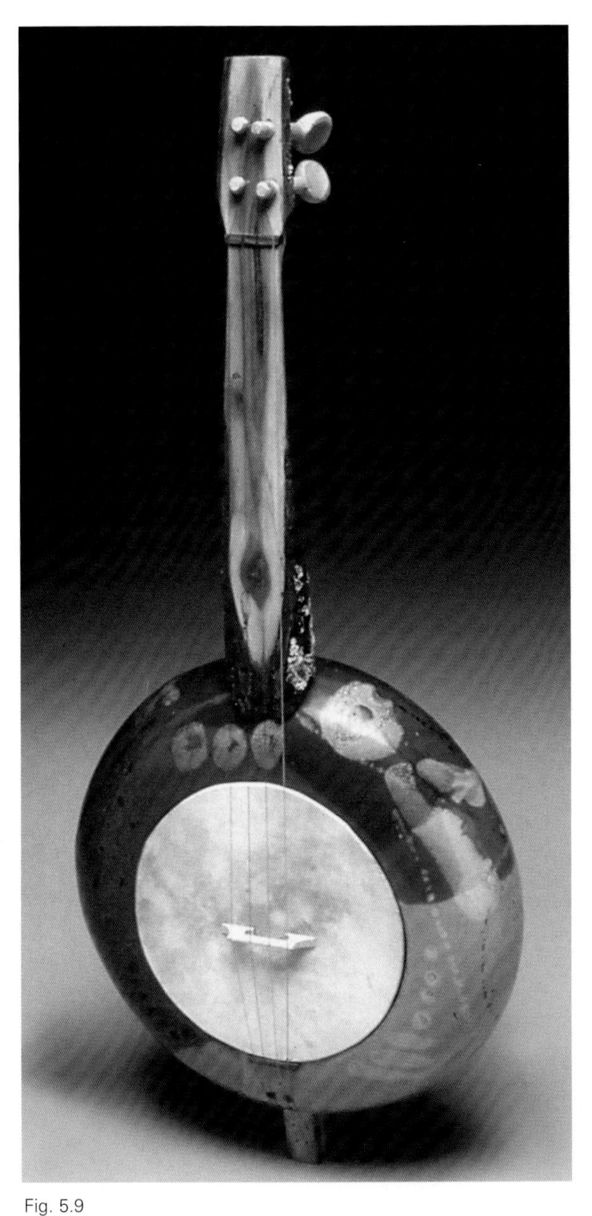

Fig. 5.9
**Tenor Banjo**
Rob Mangum, Weaverville, North Carolina, USA. Rob very cleverly combines selected woods with ceramic vessels to create instruments with distinctive looks and playing characteristics. Stoneware fired to Cone 9 in oxidation, walnut branch, maple pegs and goat skin face.

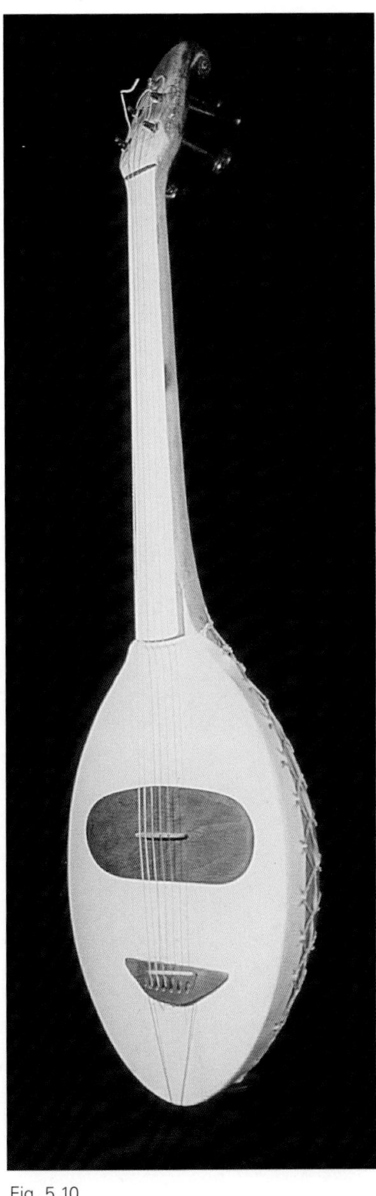

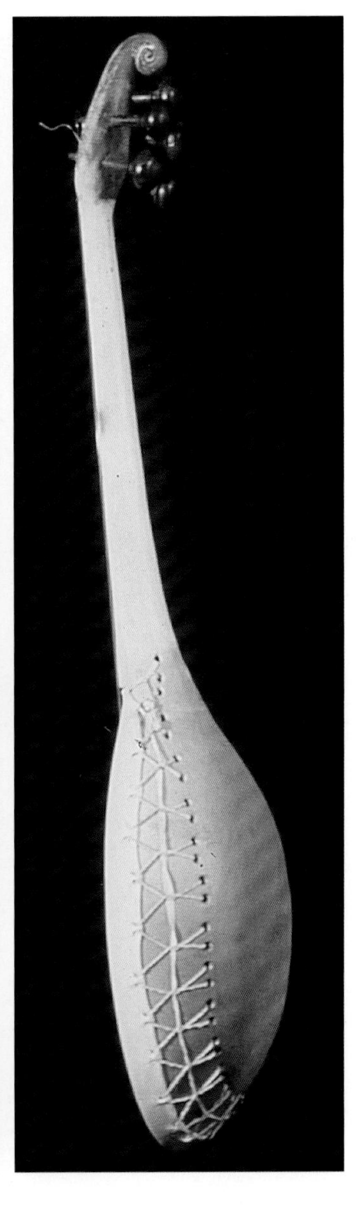

Fig. 5.10
**Ceramic Quinto Guitar**
Brian Ransom, St. Petersburg, Florida, USA. The body, neck and pegbox of this large fretless guitar are vapor-fired ceramic. The soundboard is deer hide, laced through a series of holes pierced through the rear of the soundbox. The pegs are ebony and the bridge, nut and tailpiece are pecan wood. 44 inches in height. Hear this instrument on CD track 38.

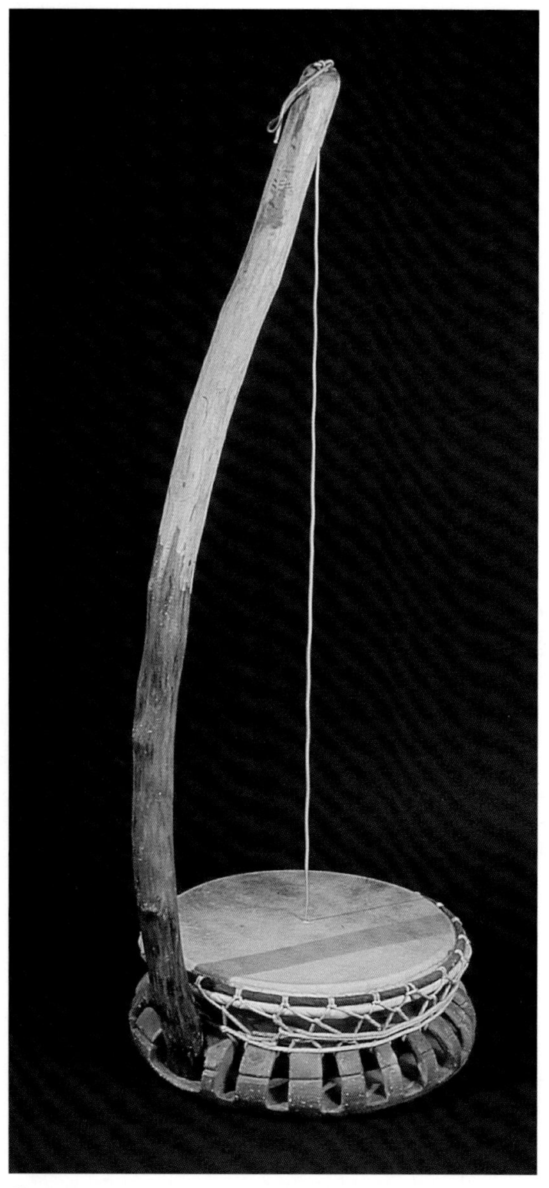

Fig. 5.11
**Gut Bass**
Brian Ransom, St. Petersburg, Florida, USA. This instrument is played similar to a washtub bass or "gut bucket" bass. Although there is only one string and no fingerboard, different pitches can be played by tilting the upright pole, which alters the string's tension and thus varies the instrument's pitch. 60 inches in height.

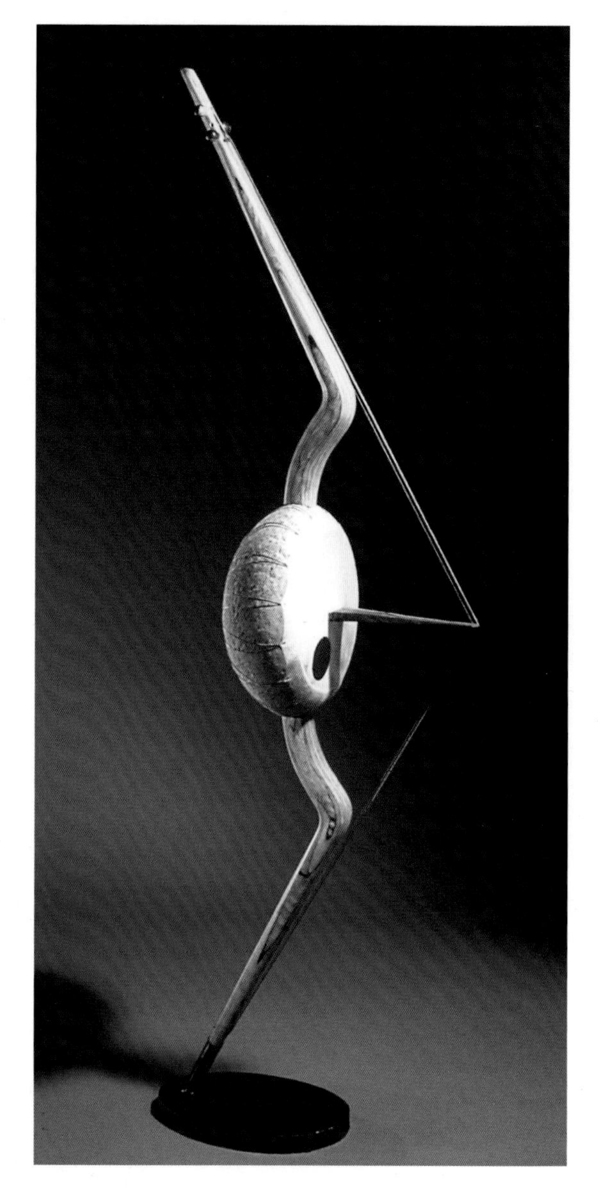

Fig. 5.12
**Double Bass**
Rob Mangum, Weaverville, North Carolina, USA. This "double bass" uses a ceramic body with goat skin soundboard and wooden bridge and neck made from laminated pine and walnut. Finished with a barium glaze and fired to cone 06 in oxidation. 86 inches in height.

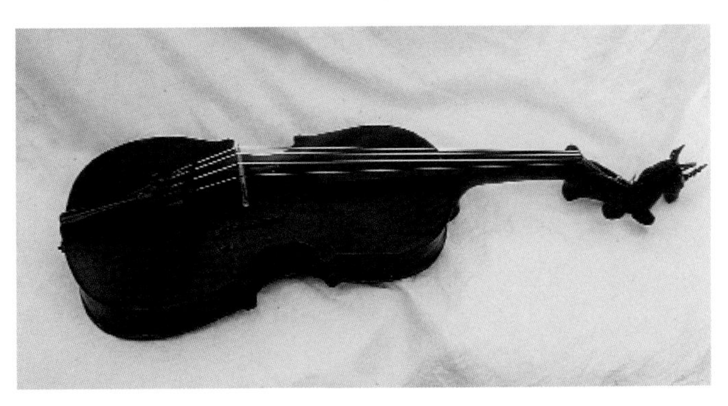

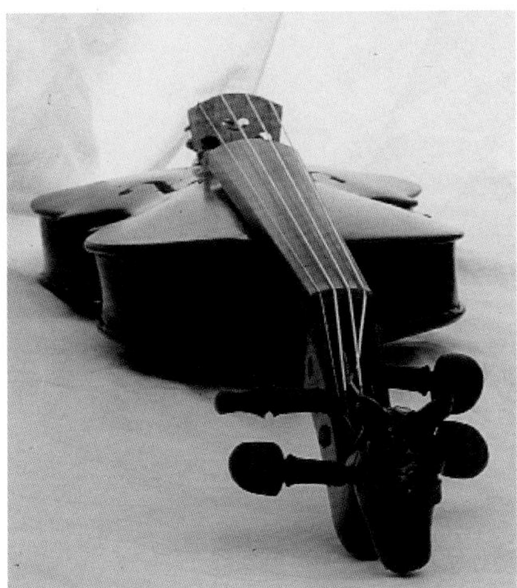

Fig. 5.14
**Ceramic Violin**
John Stevens, Deal, Kent, England.
Ceramic violin body with wooden pegs, bridge and tailpiece. After building this model of a violin, John Stevens couldn't help but wonder how it would sound. Hear it for yourself on track 39 of the CD.

The fiddle built by Rob Mangum (figure 5.13) looks much like a traditional violin; however, the body is made from clay and has a beautiful crackle raku finish. A similar ceramic violin was built by John Stevens of Kent, England (figure 5.14). He built his violin as a sculpture, never intending it to be played. However, after it was fired he noticed that the violin's hollow ceramic body had a nice tone when he drummed on it, so he had it fitted with a wooden fingerboard and tailpiece and strung it up. To John's amazement, his instrument was playable, and produced an earthy, haunting sound. He presented it to Joe O'Donnell, a well-known Irish fiddler, to hear what could be done in the hands of an accomplished player. Joe immediately took a liking to the unusual fiddle, and began using it in concerts and on recordings. Since it is not very loud acoustically due to its ceramic soundboard, Joe had the violin fitted with an internal pickup that allowed him to amplify the instrument to any volume. A solo

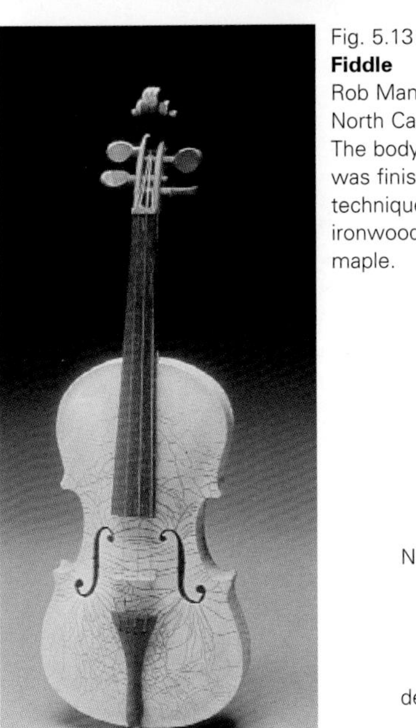

Fig. 5.13
**Fiddle**
Rob Mangum, Weaverville, North Carolina, USA.
The body of this instrument was finished using a raku technique. Its neck is African ironwood and the pegs are maple.

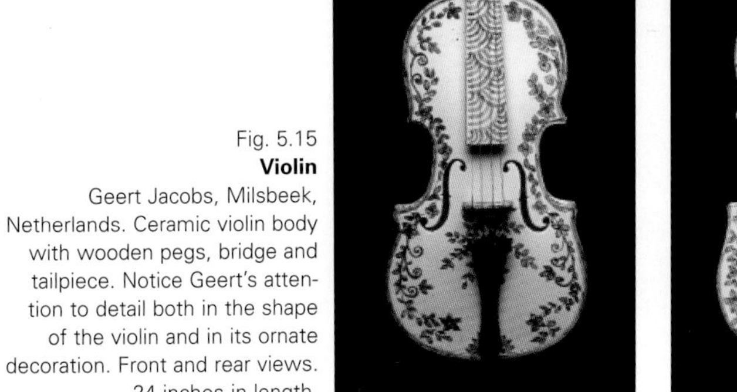

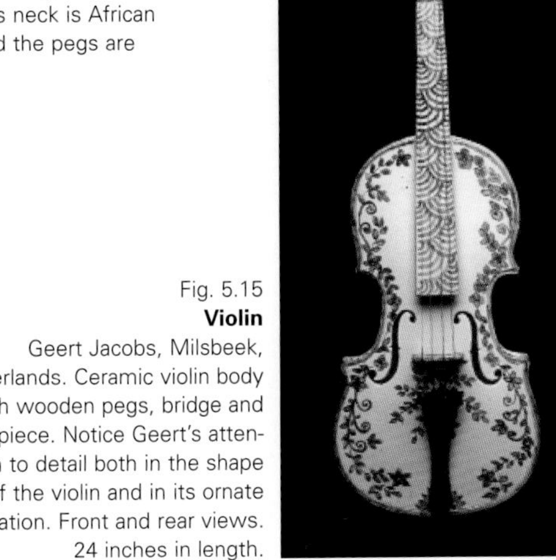

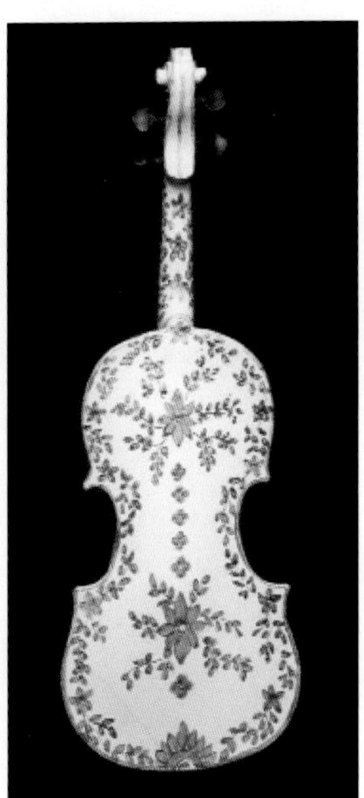

Fig. 5.15
**Violin**
Geert Jacobs, Milsbeek, Netherlands. Ceramic violin body with wooden pegs, bridge and tailpiece. Notice Geert's attention to detail both in the shape of the violin and in its ornate decoration. Front and rear views. 24 inches in length.

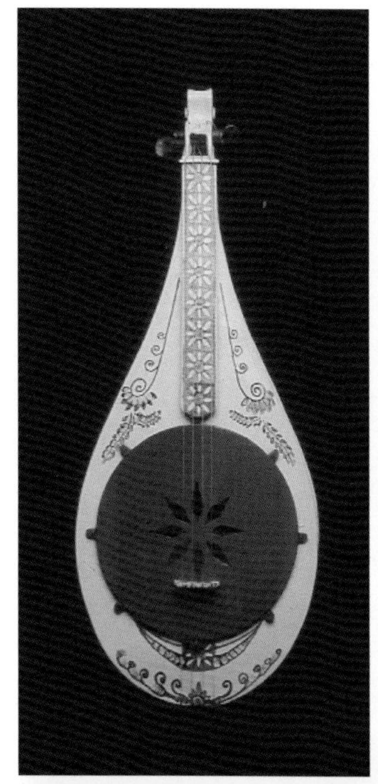

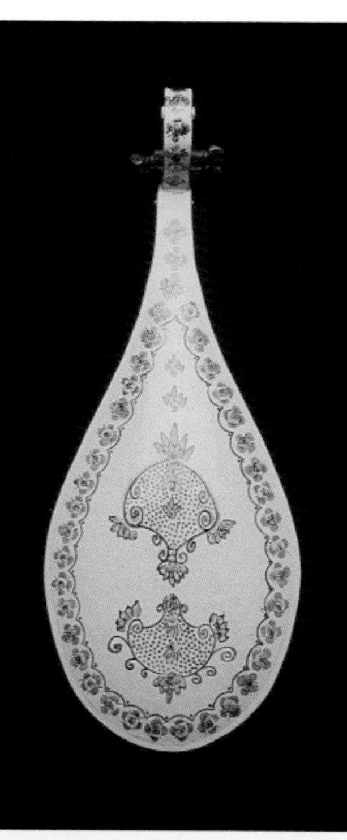

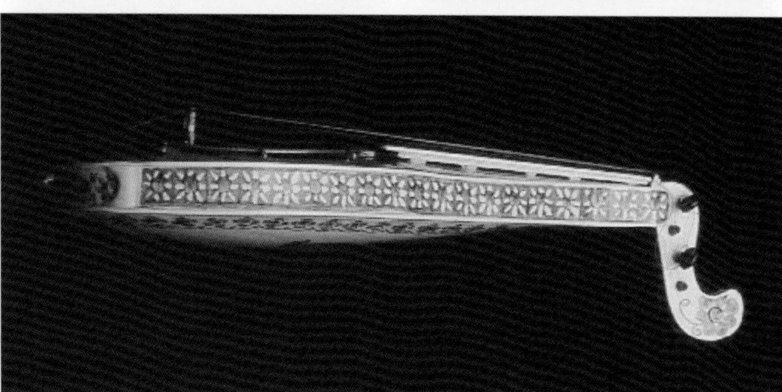

Fig. 5.16
**Renaissance Rebeck**
Geert Jacobs, Milsbeek, Netherlands. A rebeck or rebec is a Medieval ancestor of the violin, most probably derived from bowed lutes of Arabic North African cultures. Like the violin, they were traditionally made from wood. Geert's model has a ceramic body with wooden pegs, bridge and inset soundboard. Front, rear and side views. 24 inches in length.

performance on this fiddle is included on track 39 of the accompanying CD.

## Other Chordophones

This chapter closes with a description of two traditional Indian ceramic chordophones which don't fit into the other categories.

The *pulluvan kudam* is a single-stringed clay instrument played by the Pulluvan, who are astrologers, healers and priests of a serpent-worshipping religious order on the Malabar coast of South India. A round, narrow-necked clay pot has a cow or iguana skin stretched over an opening in its bottom. A gut string attached to the center of this membrane is attached to a half gourd, which is attached to a plank. Holding this plank under his foot and the pot under his arm while seated, the player plucks or strikes the string. By pressing on the pot with his arm the player can manipulate the string's pitch.

The *tantipanai* is a related chordophone from southern India. The narrow mouth of a spherical clay pot is covered with a skin membrane. A gut or wire string is anchored to the center of the skin with a small wooden or metal button. Seven metal jingles are threaded on the string as it passes through the pot, and out the bottom through a small hole, where it is fastened to the outside of the pot with a wooden tensioning peg. The player taps the skin and the button with his fingers, and the skin, string, and jingles all sound together.

## chapter six

*The drive to create, perform, and reproduce music is common to all mankind, a drive so basic that when a man cannot find an instrument to suit him, he creates his own.*

—Joseph Howard

# Hybrids

Hybrid instruments are combinations of two or more different instruments; for example, a flute combined with a rattle, or a horn combined with a drum. The two or more vibrating systems in the instrument may function independently, or, more interestingly, they may combine in some way.

Hybrid instruments don't fit neatly into the classification system used for the rest of this book. In fact, by design, they are contrary to the basic concept of the Sachs-Hornbostel classification system, because they meld instruments that are defined as being in separate categories. As a result, they are included here in their own chapter.

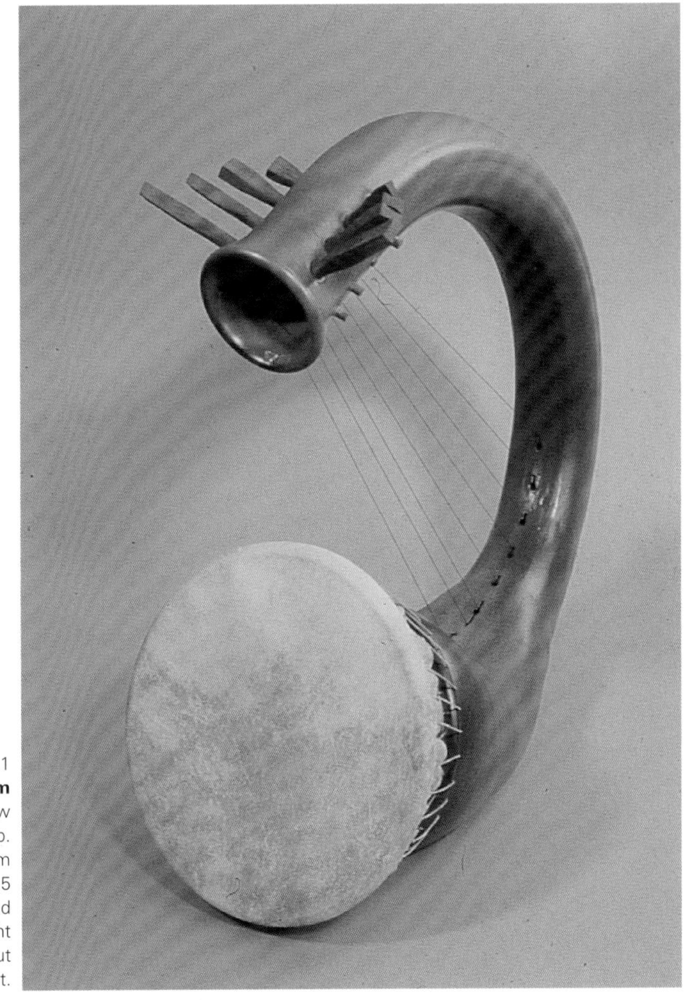

Fig. 6.1
**Elephonium**
Ward Hartenstein, Rochester, New York, USA. A hybrid drum and harp. Stoneware form assembled from wheel-thrown segments. It has an 8.5 diameter goat skin drumhead attached with nylon twine and eight steel strings (piano wire) with walnut tuning pegs. 18 inches in height.

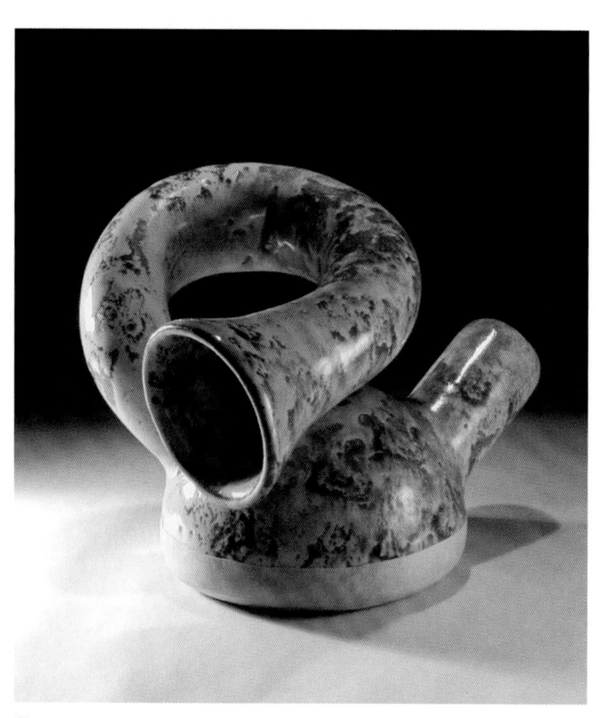

Fig. 6.2
**Globutubular Drum Horn**
Barry Hall, Westborough, Massachusetts, USA. This hybrid drum and horn has a goat skin resonator attached to a large chamber located in the middle of its tubular form. Its drum sound is similar to a doumbek, and when played as a didjeridu/globular horn, the chamber and membrane add a metallic-like resonance to its tone. Glazed stoneware, goat skin. 10 inches in height. Hear this instrument on CD track 12.

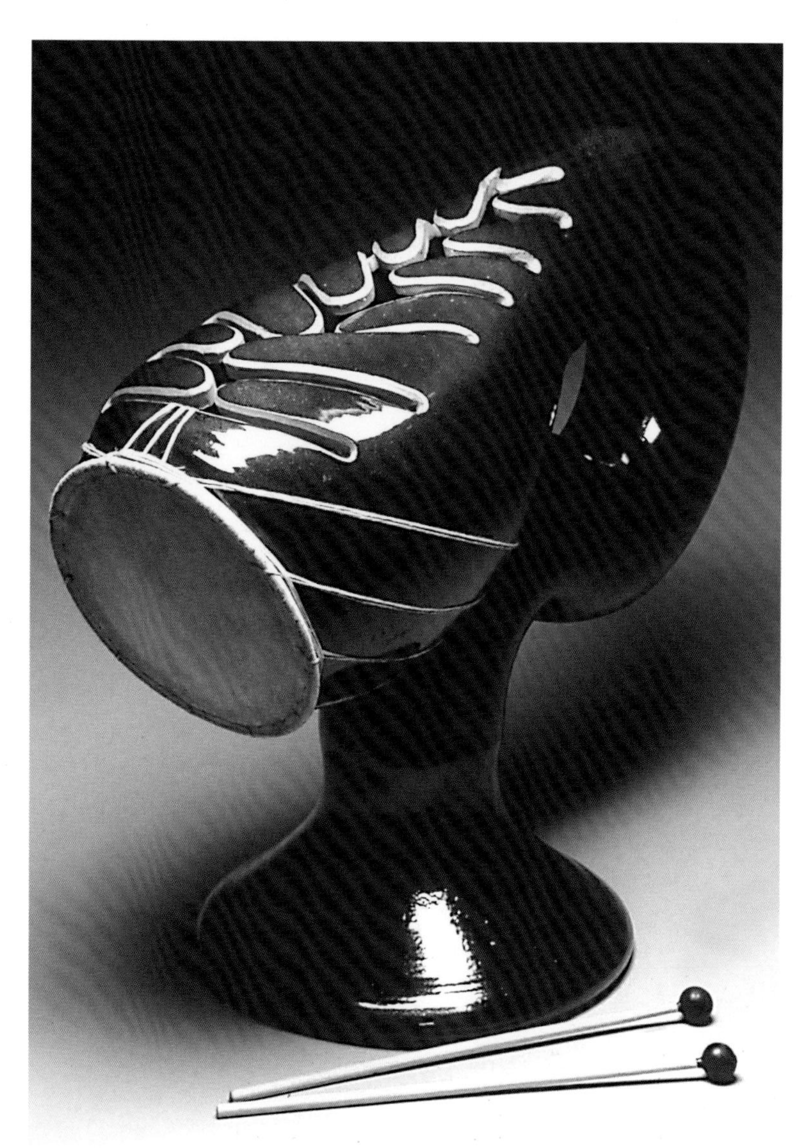

Fig. 6.3
**Serpent Drum**
Ward Hartenstein, Rochester, New York, USA. A hybrid tongue drum and skin drum. The drum head serves as both a resonator and an additional striking surface. The form was constructed from wheel-thrown segments and the "tongues" were supported during firing by small shims of soft kiln brick. It produces resonant unpitched sounds similar to a crude steel drum. 21 inches in height.

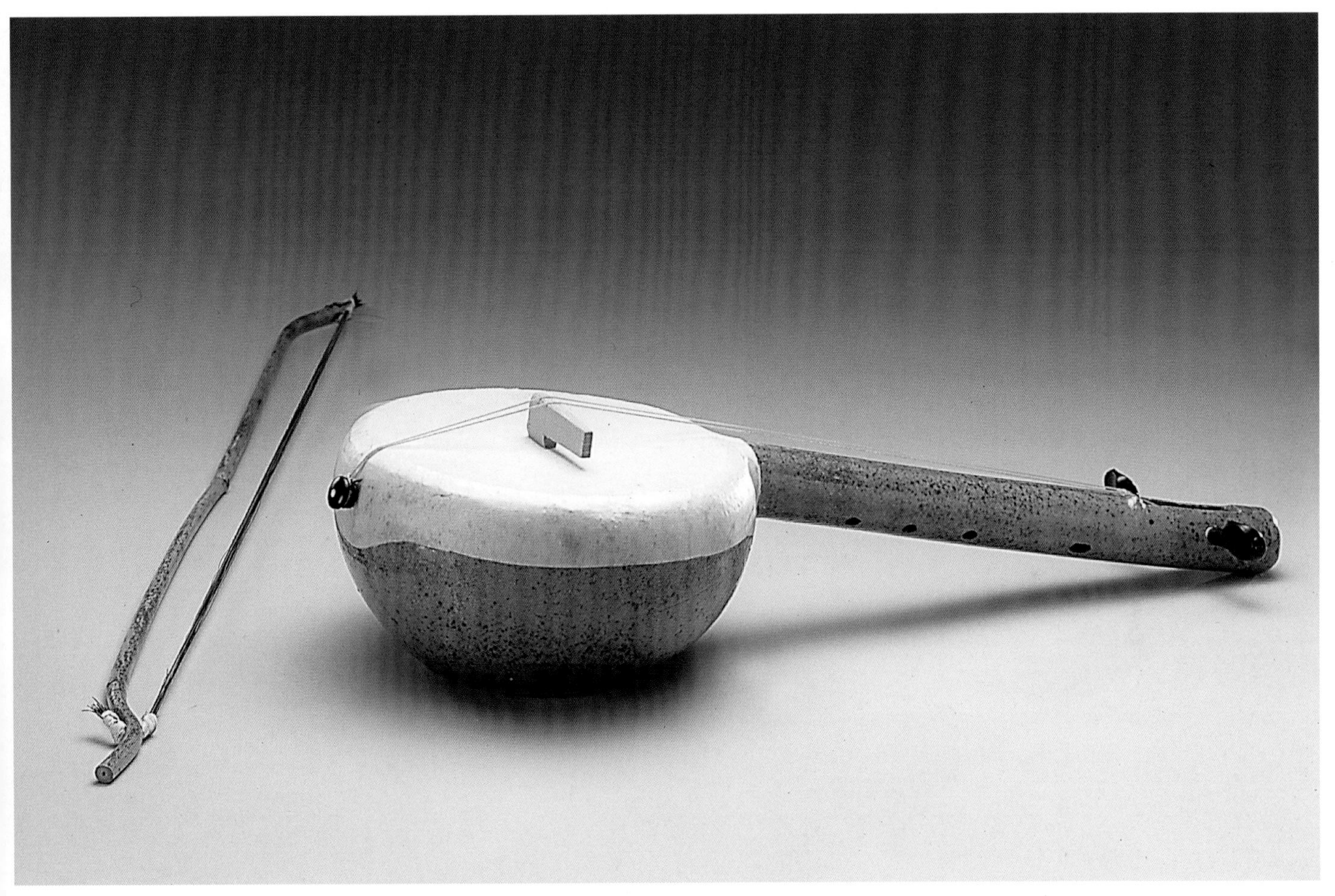

Fig. 6.4
**Stone Fiddle**
Barry Hall, Westborough, Massachusetts, USA. A stoneware fiddle inspired by Asian and African designs. Cone 10 stoneware with glaze, goat skin soundboard, wooden pegs and bridge, gut strings, bamboo and horsehair bow. The soundbox of the fiddle can be played as a drum, and the neck can be played as a flute. 15 inches in length. Hear this instrument on CD track 29.

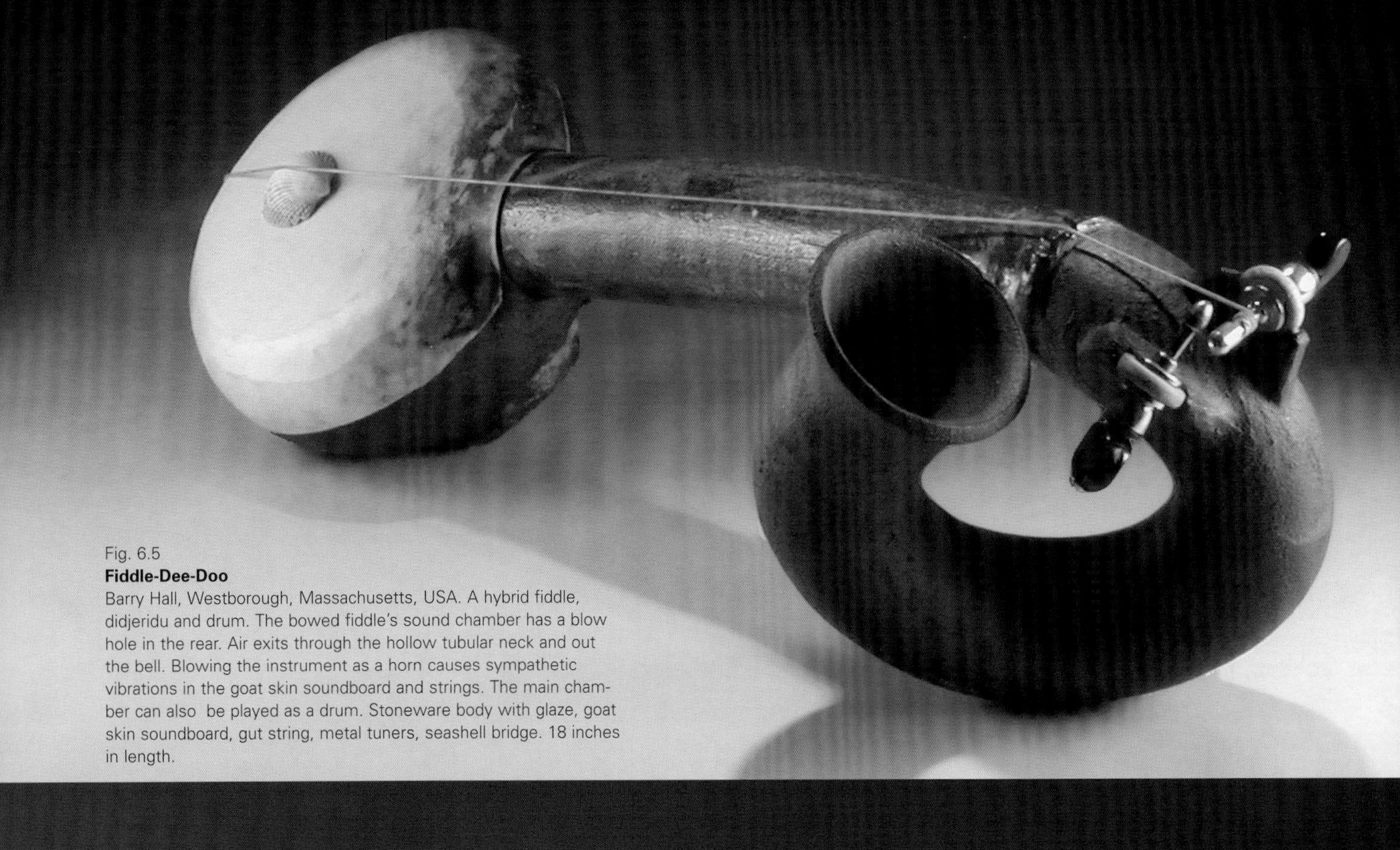

Fig. 6.5
**Fiddle-Dee-Doo**
Barry Hall, Westborough, Massachusetts, USA. A hybrid fiddle, didjeridu and drum. The bowed fiddle's sound chamber has a blow hole in the rear. Air exits through the hollow tubular neck and out the bell. Blowing the instrument as a horn causes sympathetic vibrations in the goat skin soundboard and strings. The main chamber can also be played as a drum. Stoneware body with glaze, goat skin soundboard, gut string, metal tuners, seashell bridge. 18 inches in length.

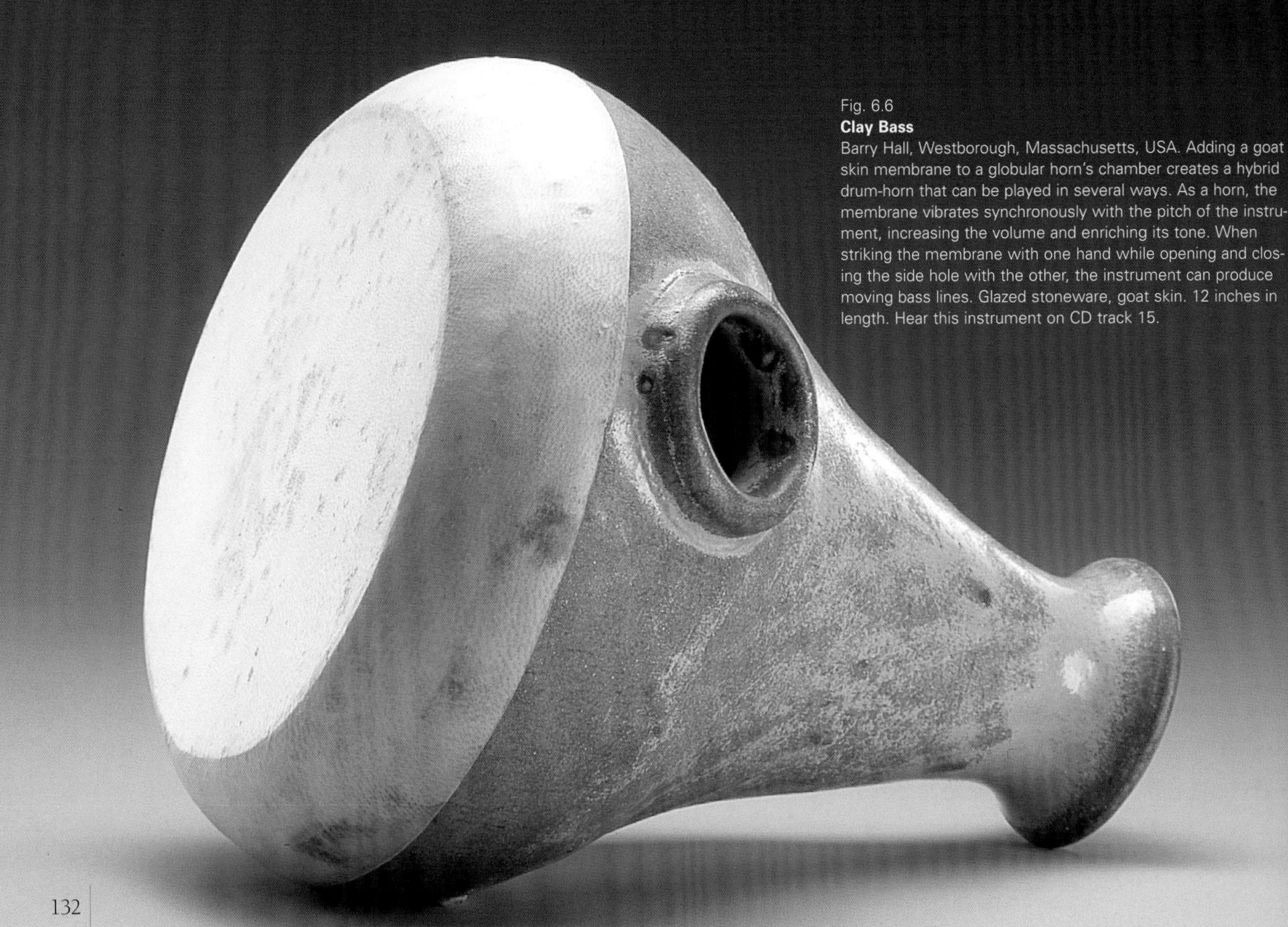

Fig. 6.6
**Clay Bass**
Barry Hall, Westborough, Massachusetts, USA. Adding a goat skin membrane to a globular horn's chamber creates a hybrid drum-horn that can be played in several ways. As a horn, the membrane vibrates synchronously with the pitch of the instrument, increasing the volume and enriching its tone. When striking the membrane with one hand while opening and closing the side hole with the other, the instrument can produce moving bass lines. Glazed stoneware, goat skin. 12 inches in length. Hear this instrument on CD track 15.

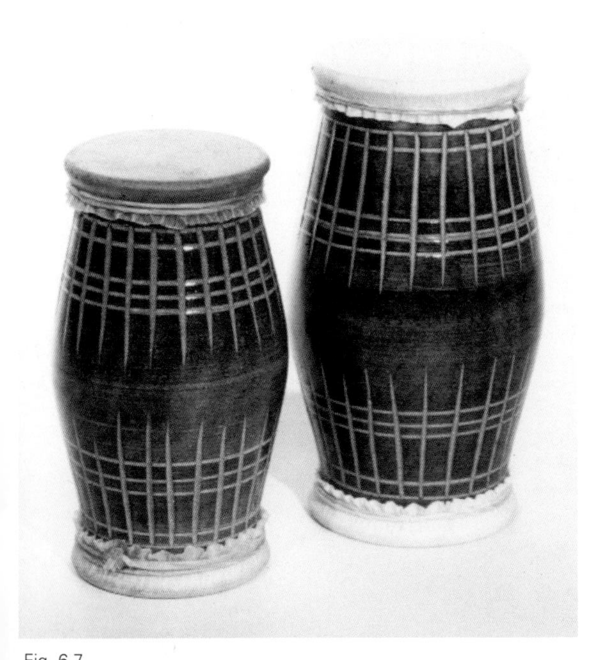

Fig. 6.7
**Shakers**
Stephen Wright, Hagerstown, Maryland, USA. Clay shakers with goat skin heads on both ends and small clay beads inside. Earthenware with slip and glaze. To 8 inches in height. Hear this instrument on CD track 11.

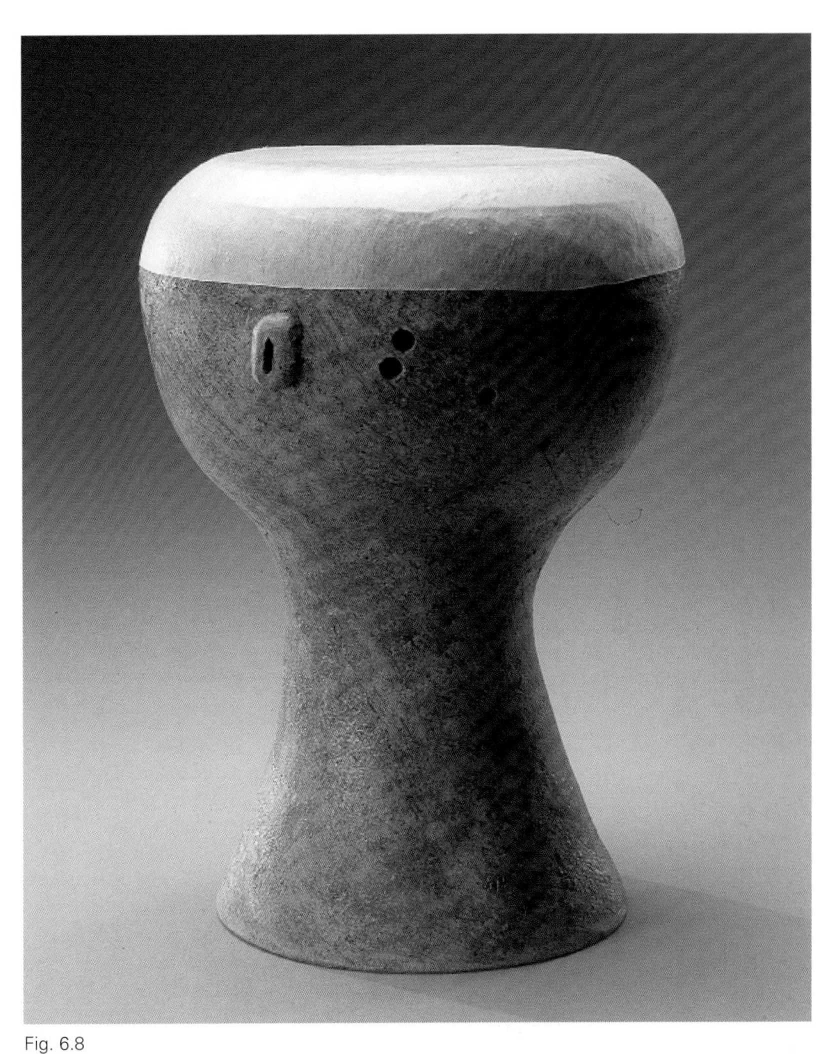

Fig. 6.8
**Ocarina Drum**
Barry Hall, Westborough, Massachusetts, USA. A goblet drum with an ocarina built into a sealed cavity in the drum's shell (the mouthpiece and finger holes are visible on the side of the drum). A variant of this instrument has its finger holes on the inside of the drum. In both versions, the ocarina's aperture is inside the drum shell, so most of the ocarina's sound exits to the interior of the drum. The drum's internal cavity acts as a secondary chamber around the aperture, causing it to act like the "pitch jump" flutes described in the Aerophones chapter. Additionally, the drum can be played at the same time as the ocarina, and touching or pressing the skin head alters the pitch of the ocarina. Stoneware with oxides and light glaze, goat skin membrane. 14 inches in height.

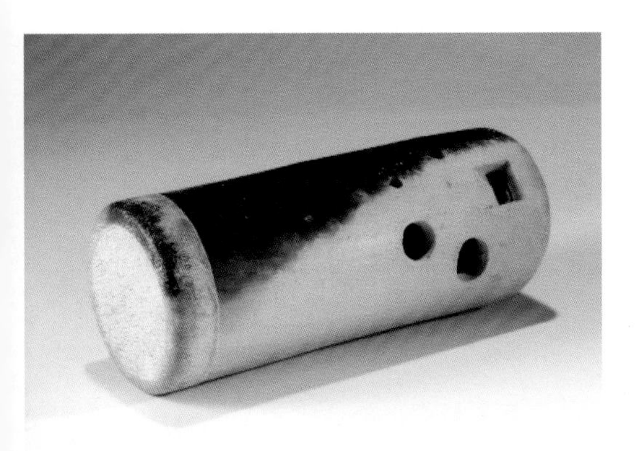

Fig. 6.9
**Ocarina-Drum-Rattle**
Barry Hall, Westborough, Massachusetts, USA. A four-hole ocarina with a rattling chamber containing clay pellets. One end of the rattle is covered by a goat skin head which also can be played as a drum. Stoneware, saggar fired. 6 inches in length.

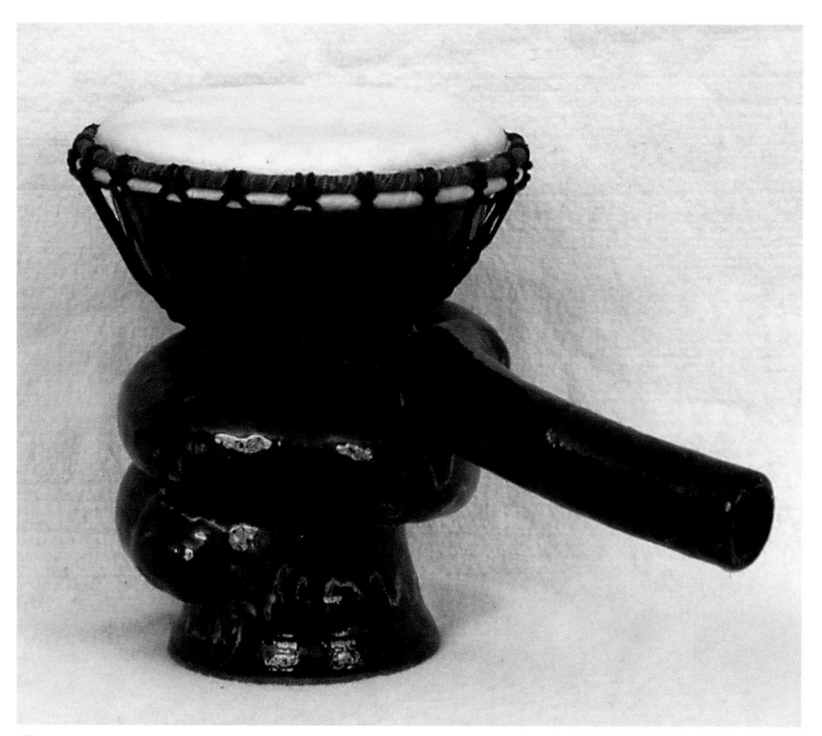

Fig. 6.10
**Didgebek**
Tim Gale, Tiskilwa, Illinois, USA. A combination didgeridoo and doumbek. The didgeridoo opens into the end of the stem of the doumbek so the resonant chamber of the drum amplifies the sound of the didgeridoo. The body is stoneware fired to Cone 6 in an electric kiln, with "Floating Blue" glaze. The head is goat skin, attached with metal rings and rope. 11 inches in height, 8-inch head.

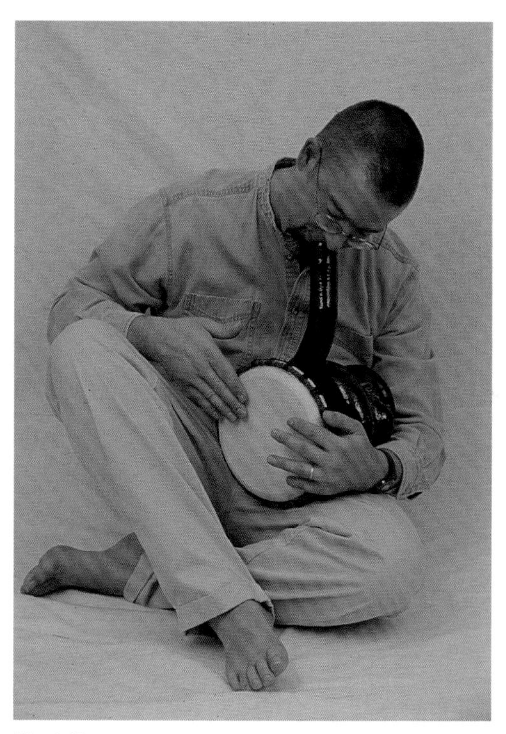

Fig. 6.11
Tim Gale playing the Didgebek.

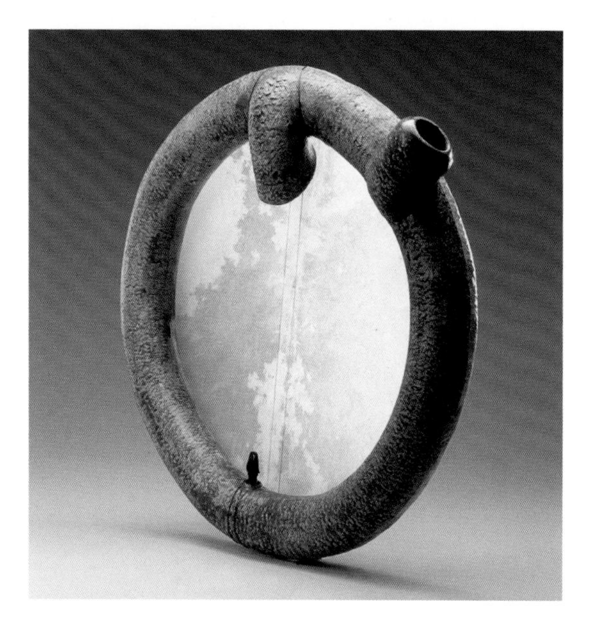

Fig. 6.12
**Snare Didjibodhrán**
Barry Hall, Westborough, Massachusetts, USA. A combination didjeridu and frame drum. A hollow tube serves as a circular frame for the drum head. A gut snare adds a buzzing sound that accompanies the drum and the didjeridu. Glazed stoneware, goat skin membrane, gut strands, ebony tuning peg. 20 inches in diameter.

## chapter seven

*Fierce fire reveals true gold.*
—Chinese proverb

# Technology Issues

## *The technical challenges of using clay to build musical instruments*

Earth, water, air and fire—these four basic elements of antiquity dominated science and philosophy for thousands of years, from their conception in ancient Greece until the rise of modern science. Though scientists have subsequently developed more complex theories of matter and the universe, these four elements remain the essential components of ceramics.

The technology of ceramics was discovered by our prehistoric ancestors. Its fundamental nature is quite simple—clay (earth) is formed (with water), dried (with air) and heated (with fire) to create a permanent object. The potter's craft may seem primitive by modern standards, but after tens of thousands of years it is still a vital activity—evolving, maturing, and captivating countless people around the world.

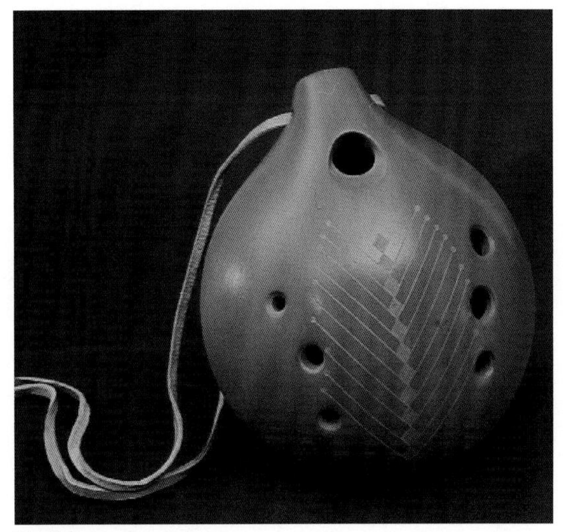

Fig. 7.1
**Earthenware Clay Ocarina**
Sergio Garcia and Marco Donoso acquire their earthenware clay from the area around their rural town of Quilpue', Chile, which lies between the coast and the Andes mountain range, and fire their instruments in a wood-fueled kiln. 7 inches in length.

In order to succeed, a ceramic instrument builder must understand the technology of ceramics as well as the principles of musical acoustics. While other chapters in this book explore the acoustical characteristics of instruments, this one focuses specifically on working with clay and how its properties impact an instrument's musical and acoustical qualities. First is a discussion of different types of clay and firing temperatures, and how these factors affect an instrument's sound and playing capabilities. Next is consideration of glazes, their use on instruments, and their impact on sound. Rounding out the chapter is an examination of ceramic instruments' greatest technical challenges: tuning, shrinkage, and breakage. As you read this chapter, don't forget to turn to the glossary in the appendix for a definition of any unfamiliar ceramic and musical terms you encounter.

The broad range of insight and knowledge presented here was collected for this book from a number of today's leading ceramic instrument builders. These artists described, from their own experience, the factors that make clay a joy, and a challenge, to use for building musical instruments. As you'll see, there is definitely some science behind what works well, but in addition, most makers have their own unique insights and preferences—some of which even contradict each other. One general theme that emerged is "there is no right or wrong." For example, a particular clay, glaze or firing style that works beautifully for one artist may not produce the same results for another. However, despite a few differences of personal opinion, the vast collective experience represented in this body of information should prove valuable to any ceramist building musical instruments.

Working with clay presents challenges, as does any artistic medium. It is hoped that the insights and lessons shared in these pages will allow artists to learn from each other and increase their personal enjoyment from this craft. For although clay can be temperamental, unpredictable and sometimes frustrating, the mystery, magic and beauty of the results can be worth the challenges. As one artist relates, "There's enough uncertainty in the process to keep it interesting."

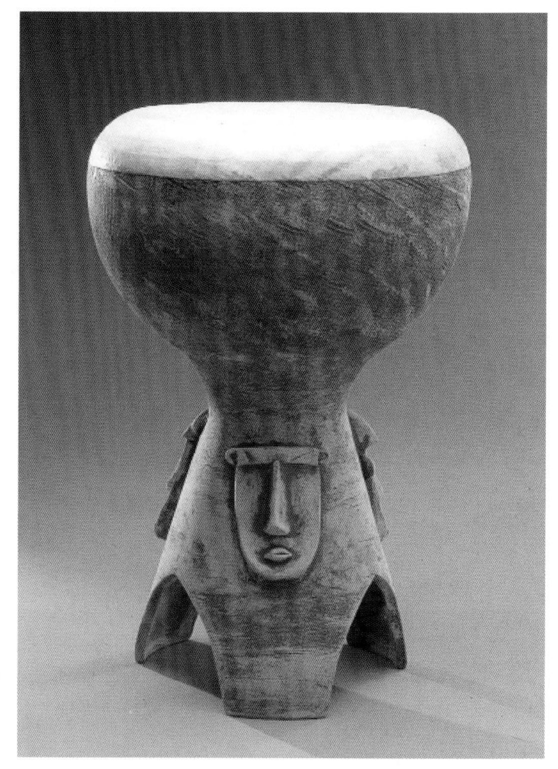

Fig. 7.2
**Goblet Drum**
Stoneware clay makes this 2-foot-tall floor-standing goblet drum dense, resonant and durable. Made by Barry Hall, stoneware with oxides, fired to cone 10.

## Selecting Clay

Clay is an earthy mineral substance composed mostly of a hydrous silicate of alumina. Its main components are aluminum oxide, silicon dioxide and water. Clay is created by the weathering of the Earth's rock. Rock and mountains may seem permanent, but in fact they are profoundly altered by water over time. Over millions of years, rain water, ground water, and melting glaciers slowly dissolve the "mother rock," chemically removing mineral particles and carrying them away, all the while slowly grinding them into smaller and smaller pieces. Eventually these tiny particles are deposited, where they sit and settle to become clay. Some of this clay will eventually be compressed by geologic forces and turned back into stone. And some tiny percentage of the rest of the Earth's clay will be dug up by potters and made into musical instruments.

The remarkable and useful feature of clay for an instrument builder, or any potter for that matter, is its extreme plasticity when wet, and its rock-hard permanence when fired. Clay is physically made up of microscopic plate-shaped particles. The fine grain and shape of these plates enables the wet clay to hold any shape given to it. No other material can be shaped as easily as clay, and few other materials are as durable as fired clay. Though pots may be broken, their pieces remain virtually imperishable for many lifetimes.

Fired clay develops its strength through a number of complex chemical processes that occur during firing. At lower temperatures, the components of the clay oxidize, organic matter burns away, and quartz crystals rearrange their structure. As the temperature rises, various materials melt and glue other particles together, and the crystals arrange themselves into a matrix or lattice formation, strengthening the clay and lacing it tightly together. The higher the temperature, the more the clay matures, and the tighter, denser and stronger it becomes.

The chemical and structural changes as the clay matures also impact its sound. At the lowest fired temperatures, a clay object "rings" in an open or loud manner, with less focused overtones. As the clay becomes denser and tighter, the object's ring becomes higher, clearer and more brilliant. Eventually the ring is lost as the materials in the clay become fully vitrified and the entire clay body begins to melt.

The temperatures at which these different states of maturity and vitrification occur depend upon the clay body's formulation. There are three general types of clay bodies commonly used for ceramics: earthenware, stoneware and porcelain. Each of them is made from a blended recipe of a few basic naturally-occurring clays and other mineral and organic elements.

Most of the Earth's naturally-occurring clay is *earthenware* clay. This type of clay usually contains a lot of iron and other mineral impurities which give it the ability to mature below 2000°F. Because of its low firing temperature relative to other clays, it's also often called *low-fire* clay. It is usually red, brown or grey when unfired, and ranges from tan to red to black after firing. Earthenware clay is the raw material for bricks, drainage tiles, roof tiles and much of the pottery around the world, including all ancient (and many modern) ceramic instruments. Its easy workability and beautiful variety of colors and textures make it a favorite of many instrument builders, especially for small flutes and whistles. However, earthenware is usually less durable in its fired state than stoneware or porcelain.

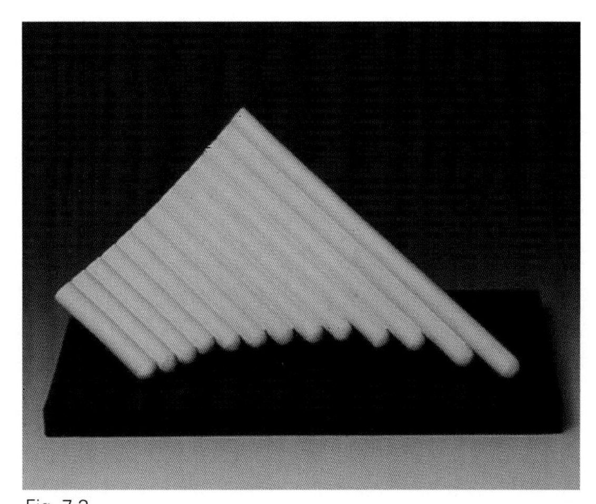

Fig. 7.3
**Panpipe**
Porcelain clay panpipe by Dag Sørensen from Sandnes, Norway. Molded from porcelain, fired to cone 10. 7" X 12"

*Stoneware* clay vitrifies between 2000°F and 2400°F. This is hotter than the firing temperatures for earthenware, which is why stoneware is also called high-fire clay. Stoneware clay bodies are very versatile, and vary widely in color, plasticity, and firing range. They are commonly used for a variety of purposes, from dinnerware to fire bricks. Compared to other clay bodies, stoneware is very strong, which makes it well-suited for drums and other musical instruments where durability is a concern. With the addition of sand, grog or other materials, stoneware can be used to build very large instruments. However, when fully vitrified, stoneware is very dense and loses much of its vibrational ability, except when very thin.

*Porcelain* is very finely textured clay that is usually white before firing, and white or even translucent after firing. Porcelain is often fired at very high temperatures, around 2600°F. Its primary component is china clay, or kaolin. In addition to its beautiful appearance, porcelain is appreciated by instrument builders for its fine texture which enables, for example, the creation of complex and precisely sculpted airduct assemblies on flutes. When vitrified, porcelain produces crystalline bell-like tones unlike any other clay. However, porcelain is challenging to work with because of its low plasticity, which makes it difficult to throw on the wheel and more likely than stoneware to crack while drying. Also its fine structure and high firing temperatures can result in more sagging and warping, and a higher rate of shrinkage compared to stoneware and earthenware.

With such a variety of choices, the good news is that for many types of instruments, almost any kind of clay and firing method will suffice. Don Bendel sums up his experiences in making clay horns (figures 4.95, 4.96 and 7.7) with the following, "I have experimented with earthenware, stoneware, white stoneware and porcelain when making horns. Through the years I have fired the instruments at a range of temperatures from a primitive wood and cow dung pit to a high-fire, Cone 13 wood fire in an Anagama kiln. I can find no difference in the quality of sound in the different clays."

Despite Don's experience with horns, different clay bodies and temperatures will, in fact, result in different timbres in many instruments. There are a number of considerations when choosing a clay body and a firing temperature, depending on what type of instrument is being built. The following sections briefly discuss some of these issues.

### What's a "cone?"

Throughout this book you'll see many references to "cone" numbers. They refer to a system of firing temperatures. For example, "Cone 6" indicates a temperature of around 2200ºF in the U.S. (The United States and Europe use different systems.) This system of measurement gets its name from pyrometric cones, which are small pyramids of ceramic material formulated to melt at a specific temperature through heat-work (a product of time and temperature). When placed in a kiln with ceramic ware and observed as the kiln is heated, a cone indicates when the desired temperature is reached.

Idiophones are the family of instruments most sensitive to the type of clay from which they are made. This is because their primary sound comes from the vibrating clay body itself. As a vibrating material, clay has some benefits and some drawbacks. It can produce a range of interesting sounds, from beautiful bell-like tones to coarse gonglike crashes to earthy, gritty thumping and scraping. However, it also has significant limits to its physical flexibility, as well as limited projection and dynamic range.

Ward Hartenstein advises, "A balance between density and elasticity seems to be the key to idiophones. I read that in selecting wood for marimbas and xylophones, rosewood is prized for its density. The denser the wood, the richer the tone. When I began to experiment with clay bodies for idiophones, I looked for a very dense stoneware—one

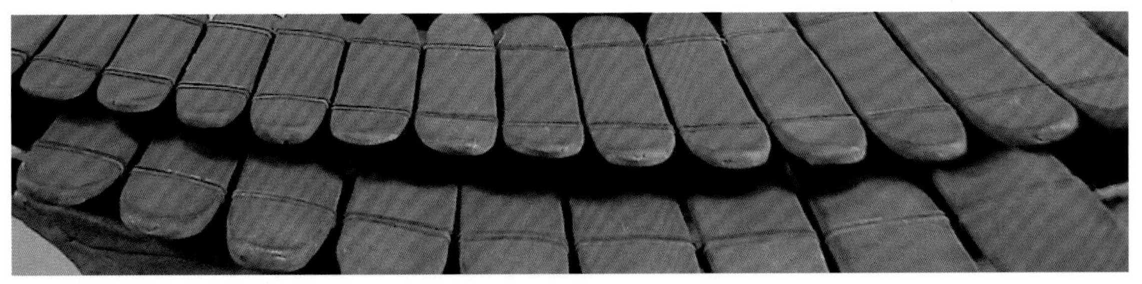

Fig. 7.4
**Marimba Bars**
Ceramic marimba bars made from very dense stoneware by Ward Hartenstein. Hear this instrument on CD track 3.

with a porosity of less than one percent. A true porcelain or a dense, high-fired stoneware seem to be the best for clay idiophones because of their hardness and density. Porcelain, because of its limited plasticity in the wet state, is harder to work with and more prone to firing flaws. A very dense stoneware, on the other hand, is a bit more forgiving in the shaping, drying, and firing processes, and yields a fired product that is reasonably durable, elastic enough to yield to the attack of a mallet, and dense enough to sustain a vibration—thus rendering it serviceable as a medium for idiophones."

However, any clay will produce a sound, and the variation between different types of clay and firing temperatures for idiophones is significant. Ward explains, "I have experimented with various clay bodies, and have found that even the punkiest (non-homogeneous) earthenware will produce a tone if it is shaped properly. Generally, a less dense clay will produce a drier sound with less sustain. The denser the clay, the brighter its tone and the longer its sustain. This has to do with the ability of the structure to retain the energy of the vibration. The initial attack of the mallet introduces a jolt of energy to the structure. If the structure is designed in the right way (distribution of mass, balance between elasticity and rigidity, non-interference by support structures, etc.) it can translate that initial jolt into a regular and recurring flexing of the structure. This is the 'periodic motion' that results in vibrations being transmitted to our ears as sound waves. One of the instrument maker's goals is to design a structure that produces clear and predictable vibrational patterns, which can be manipulated by the player in a variety of ways."

Ward's suggestions work well for idiophones that are struck with mallets. For instruments that are struck and played with bare hands (such as a ghatam or udu), earthenware clay, or stoneware clay fired to a lower maturity, is often used. As a result, less energy is required to draw a sound from the instrument. Of course, with any clay type there is a continuous spectrum of maturity, with different sounds at each point. The best way to determine the differences in sound is to experiment.

For maximum control and consistency, some instrument makers mix their own clay formulas. For his clay pot drums (figure 4.128), Stephen Wright set out to develop an optimized clay body. His goal was to design a simple recipe consisting of common ingredients that would be suitable for throwing large assembled forms without cracking or warping. He tested many different formulas and adjusted them based on his results. Through this process, Stephen learned that the most important factor for the pot's sound was the firing temperature. "Most importantly, the clay should be fired to its mature temperature, in its vitreous state. If fired too low it will sound thuddy; too high and it will lose its clear ring." Stephen found that the clay formulation was also important. "With my drums, I feel that the red iron oxide in the clay, as well as other oxides in the slip, contribute to the sound."

Other additives to clay bodies can also impact the sound. For example, brass filings are traditionally added to clay to give South Indian ghatams their unique tone. Many instrument builders have special clay formulations, developed through extensive experimentation, that they believe provide optimal acoustics, ergonomics, and appearance for their ceramic instruments.

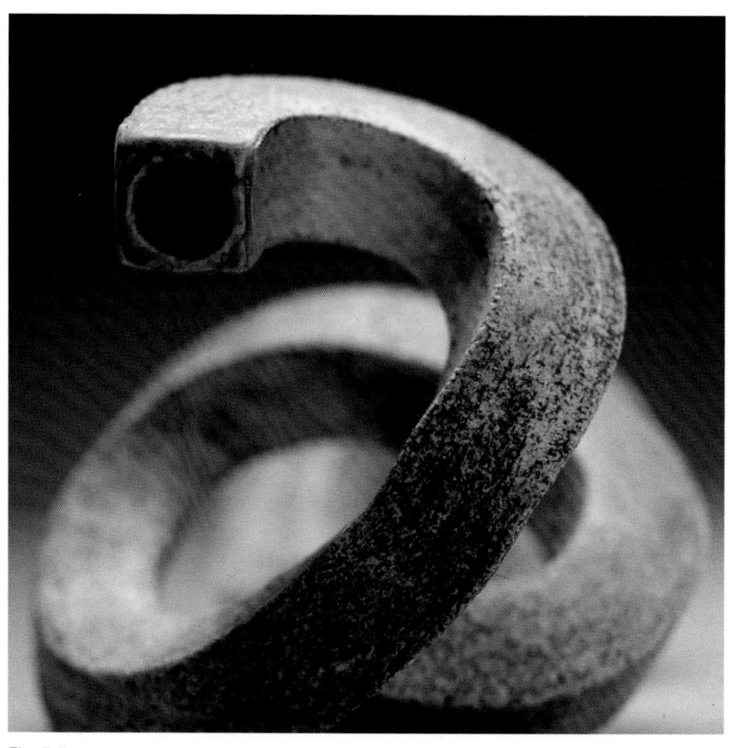

Fig. 7.5
This didjeridu by Barry Hall has a square internal bore and a round mouthpiece. A horn's bore can be almost any shape.

With membranophones, unlike idiophones, the clay itself does not vibrate significantly. Instead, the vibrations come from the drum head and the air inside the drum. The key role of the drum's shell is to provide a stable counterpoise, or anchor, to the flexible, vibrating drum head. For this purpose, almost any clay body and firing temperature will provide the necessary mass and rigidity. Most drum makers use high-fired stoneware clay in order to maximize the strength and durability of the drum shell. Glazes are often used because they can further strengthen the drum, and they also look nice.

However, with some types of drums, such as doumbeks (goblet-shaped drums), the clay body does vibrate and contribute its ringing sound to the tone of the drum, especially when the head is struck near the rim of the clay drum shell (a common technique in doumbek playing). In this situation, the factors discussed in the previous section on idiophones apply.

Since aerophones are vessels that contain a vibrating body of air, the clay itself vibrates very little. As a result, its composition is not as critical to the sound as you might suppose. However, the smoothness of a wind instrument's bore (interior) and mouthpiece can significantly impact its sound. A rough clay surface increases air friction, which means that clay with a smoother, reflective surface will produce a different tone than coarser clay. Glazing is one way to obtain a very smooth bore. Although smooth interiors are something many makers strive for in order to obtain a clear tone, they are not always desirable. A rough bore can give a more complex, warm or "breathy" tone.

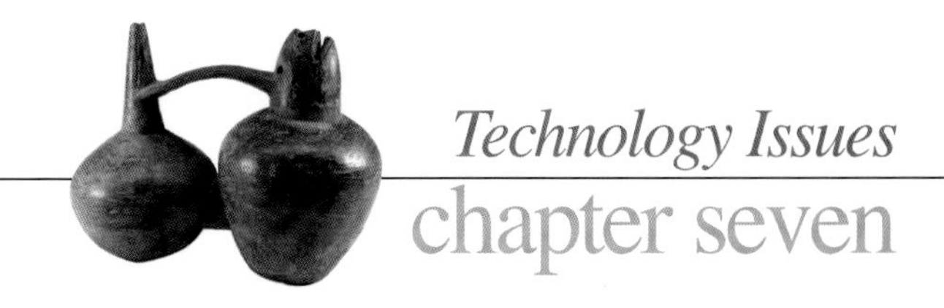



Don Bendel relates, "I discovered by trial and error that the more smooth and circular the inside of a horn's tubes were, the easier it was to play." However, it should be noted that bores need not be circular; they can be any shape. Their pitch, tone and harmonics will be the same as with circular bore instruments, as long as the total area of their cross section remains constant or is gradually increasing throughout the length of the instrument.

Some mouth-blown instruments are fired to lower temperatures so that their clay body does not fully vitrify. This results in a more porous instrument capable of absorbing some of the moisture from the player's breath. This can help avoid blockage of the windway by excess water, which is a common problem in airduct flutes. Sharon Rowell says she fires her ocarinas no higher than cone 03 (usually 05) to retain porosity in the mouthpiece.

Many ocarina and flute makers use low-fire clays. They are easier to work with, can be fired in small kilns, and their additional fragility is somewhat mitigated by their smaller size. Susan Rawcliffe says, "I use low-fire clay because years ago, I realized that at the temperatures of the high-fire clay, there is more warpage. If the mouthpiece mechanism warps, the sound is usually lost."

Ragnar Naess, when faced with the task of creating an entire clay instrument ensemble for composer Tan Dun, decided to develop a single clay formula and firing temperature that would be well suited for a variety of instruments. He chose a medium-high-fire stoneware clay which fires to a very vitreous state at cone 6. It has a sound close to the brighter tone of porcelain. The sound character of his instruments is enhanced by the tight, dense, highly fused fired state of the clay. "I believe sound characteristics are influenced by the homogeneity of the melt of the ingredients of the clay, or what potters call maturity—a measure of tightness and shrinkage achieved in firing."

Ragnar explains, "Before it's fired, my clay grog is finely divided, unlike the fairly large chunks of grog often used in stoneware clays. My clay also has rather a lot of iron oxide and calcium in it which act as fluxes, further improving the melt. If this clay formula had larger chunks of refractory ingredients, they would create discontinuities of harder, separate mineral areas within the crystal lattice which I believe would blur the vibrations that determine the sounds clay objects make."

Brian Ransom's preferred clay body is also based on extensive experimentation. He says, "I decided early on against firing my instruments at cone 10, or stoneware temperatures, because of the presence of mullite crystals (which encourage harsh, glassy sounds), high shrinkage, and excessive cracking. Although there are some beautiful clay sounds that can be achieved with ware fired in the cone 7 to 10 range, if you analyze the sounds from these instru-

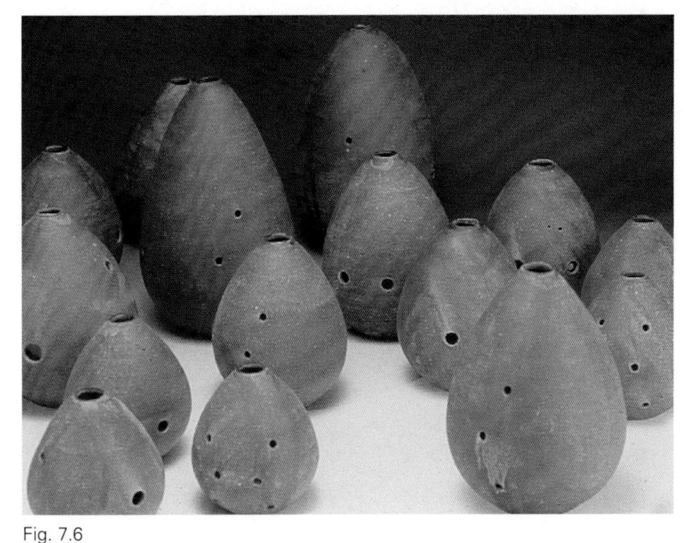

Fig. 7.6
**Xuns**
Made by Ragnar Naess who developed a medium-high-fire stoneware clay that produces a bright tone.

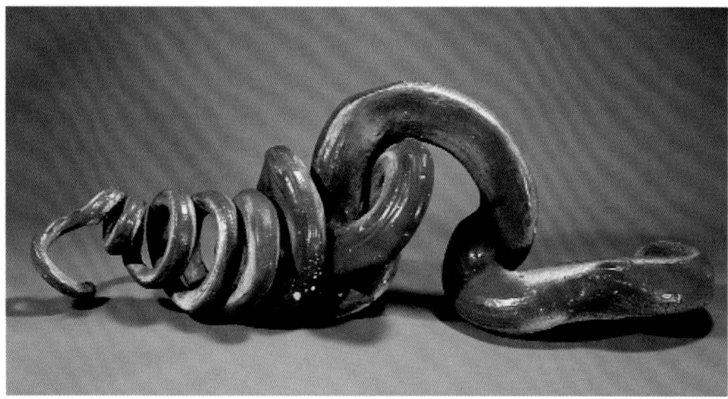

Fig. 7.7
**Horn**
Don Bendel makes large ceramic horns from a variety of clay types. This stoneware horn, titled "Some Serpents are Horns," measures 44" x 15" x 8".

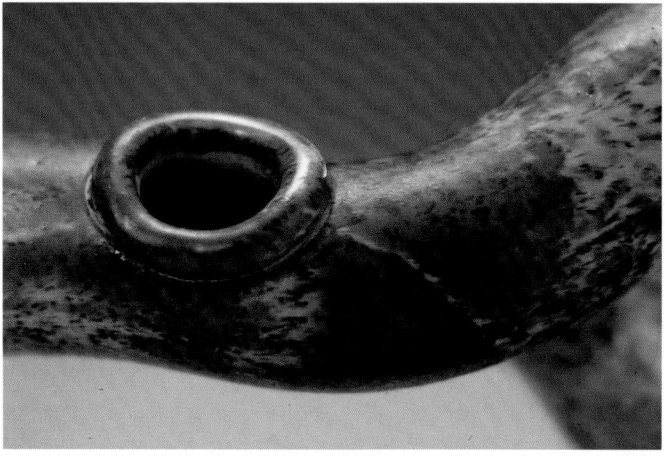

Fig. 7.8
The satiny-smooth matt glaze on this globular horn mouthpiece is comfortable for the player's lips and also improves the instrument's sound by enabling a good air seal. Instrument by Barry Hall.

ments on an oscilloscope you will often see strong peaks in the one to two kilohertz range. The sound in this frequency range can be unpleasantly strident. I eventually formulated my preferred clay body in the medium firing range (cone 2-6) that I generally fire to the upper end of earthenware temperatures (cone 04 to 02). This clay, onto which I apply terra sigillata (a type of colored slip), retains a porosity which gives it a hollow, haunting sound, very similar to leather hard clay."

However, sometimes an instrument's form, rather than its musical function, dictates the most appropriate clay body. For example, Don Bendel's clay horns are often very large, so he uses a variety of materials to help prevent his slab- and coil-built pieces from cracking during construction. Additives he uses include ground bisque ware, sand, perlite, vermiculite, coffee grounds, and sawdust, all in varying degrees of coarseness. Don has noticed slight sound differences in horns that included a large amount of coarse additives that burned out in the firing, such as coarse sawdust. For general flexibility and protection against cracking, he recommends sawdust sifted through a window screen, about 10% by volume added to the clay body.

With or without grog and other additives, different clay bodies have a variety of textures. In many cases these impact only the instrument's aesthetic appearance, but in some cases they impact the sound, ergonomics and other construction aspects. For example, we've already discussed how the smoothness of a flute's bore impacts its timbre. With horn mouthpieces, a smooth surface is important for the player's comfort. Clay's rough texture can also cause problems with chordophones (string instruments), where a very smooth surface is necessary at the points where pegs and strings come in contact with the instrument such as the bridge and peg holes. Due to the tension placed on the strings, bridges and peg holes are points of friction, and if they have a rough ceramic surface they will gradually grind away wooden pegs and break most types of strings. To obtain a smoother surface, clay can be burnished or glazed. It also can be coated with epoxies or other materials after firing.

In some cases a rough surface texture is more desirable, in order to provide the instrument's player with a more secure grip, such as on a flute or hand-held drum.

Another ergonomic aspect is the instrument's weight. In most cases, lighter weight instruments are preferred by musicians since they are less fatiguing to hold and easier to transport. However, lightweight ceramic instruments can be challenging to design since clay is denser and heavier than other instrument-making materials such as wood. Clay also often requires greater wall thickness than materials such as metal. The weight of a ceramic instrument is dependent on its wall thickness, and the composition of the clay and additives. Thinner is usually better for both weight and sound, but optimizing the balance between wall thickness and strength for any particular ceramic form requires skill and experience. Some clay additives—such as paper pulp, sawdust, and vermiculite—will result in a lighter weight clay body since they burn away during firing, but they will also impact the clay body's tone, as described earlier in this section.

## To Glaze or Not to Glaze?

Glazes are glassy coatings melted in place on a ceramic body. They are composed primarily of melted and resolidified silica, the main ingredient in glass. Other additives enable them to melt at a lower temperature and remain viscous when liquefied, so they don't drip or run off the object to which they are intended to adhere. High-fire glazes often fuse with the vitrified material in the clay body, as compared to low-fire glazes which merely coat the surface of the clay.

Most functional pottery is glazed for practical and aesthetic reasons. Glazes provide a durable protective layer that can also add colors and textures to bowls, vases, mugs, or any type of ceramic ware. These same benefits apply to musical instruments. Glazes provide beautiful exteriors to drums, flutes and other instruments. Functionally, they provide a smooth, comfortable surface for instrument mouthpieces and finger holes. However, as mentioned before, there are some situations when a glazed surface may be too slippery to make an instrument comfortable to hold in the proper playing position. For example, the normal playing position for a doumbek is resting across one leg. A glossy glazed surface may make it more difficult to keep the drum from slipping on the player's clothing, out of playing position. Similarly, small ocarinas and flutes may be more difficult to grip if their surface is too slick. Regardless, the proper shape and balance of an instrument will usually have a larger impact than glazing in these situations.

There are also important acoustical concerns when considering glazes for musical instruments. The two primary aspects of a musical instrument

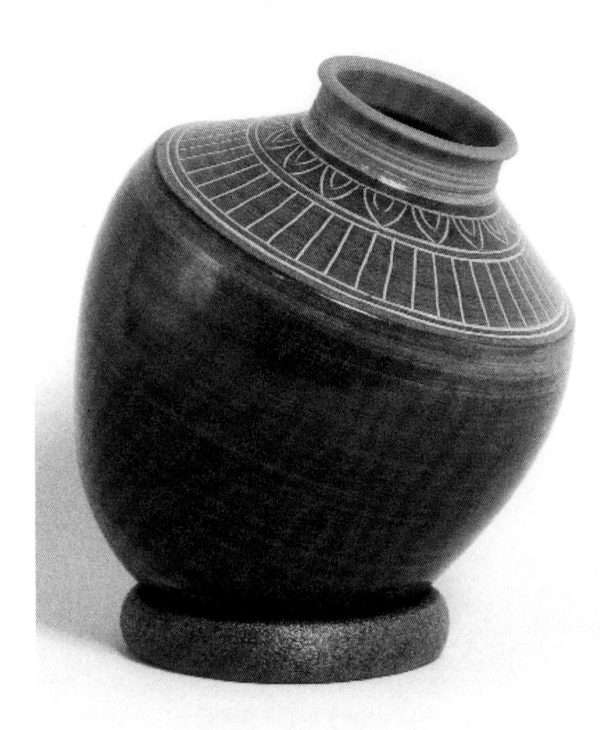

Fig. 7.9
Stephen Wright discovered that carefully formulated slips and glazes enhance the sound of his instruments, such as this 16" earthenware ghatam. Hear this instrument on CD track 20.

that glazes impact are body vibrations and surface reflections.

The vibrating capability of a clay instrument may be dampened or inhibited by glaze if the glaze coating is too thick, not well fused, or doesn't *fit* well with the clay body. "Fit" is a measure of how well a glaze conforms and adheres to a specific clay body. A poorly fit or improperly fired glaze may dull or deaden an instrument's sound, which can be a significant problem for idiophones since they rely on the vibration of the clay body. If the glaze fits well it will function as an extension of the clay and vibrate in harmony—perhaps even enhance the sound.

The reflectiveness of a glaze's surface can also impact the sound of an instrument. Ragnar Naess explains this by comparing sound reflectivity to light reflectivity. "Matt glazes, which gain their soft visual appearance by absorbing light in multitudes of tiny holes in the surface also, soften and dull sound just the way they soften reflected light." Conversely, glossy glazes efficiently reflect sound (even the highest frequencies) and result in a bright tone. Ragnar has found that "glossy glazes that are quite fused and not thick create the best sounds."

Perhaps some of the greatest differences in opinion and practice among clay instrument builders relate to how they use glazes. For example, Dag Sørensen, who works extensively with crystalline glazes on his non-musical ceramics, chooses not to glaze his musical instruments. He explains, "A crack in the glaze is enough to affect the sound."

At the other end of the glazing spectrum is Stephen Wright, who uses slips and glazes on all of his instruments. Even his ubang and ghatam clay pot drums are glazed, a relatively uncommon practice for clay pot idiophones due to the potential dampening effect of glazes. Stephen observes that glazing "tightens up" the drum's sound, and also makes the playing surface more comfortable. However, he advises that in order for slip or glaze to be used it must be a perfect fit with the clay. "Any tension will cause the drum to be unstable, which is not a good idea for an object that's intended to be beat on very hard."

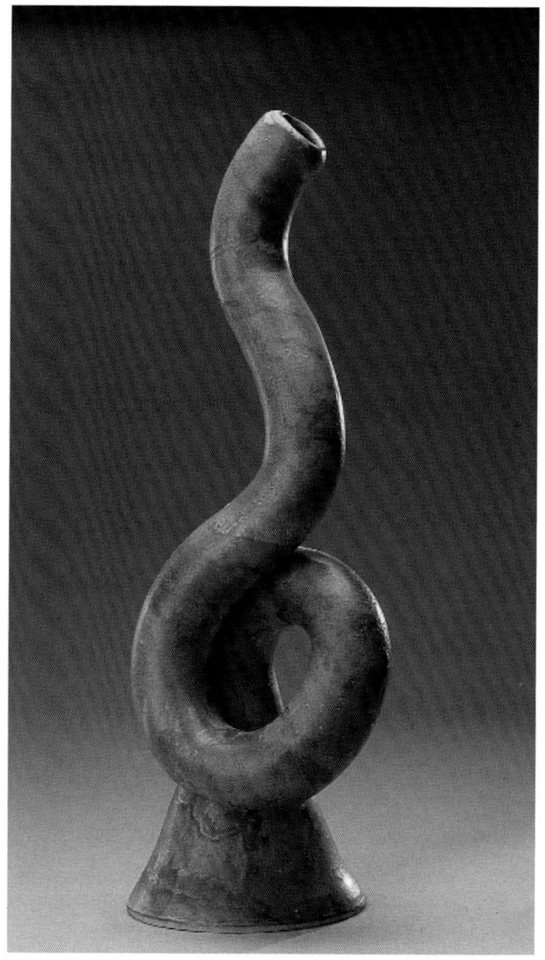

Fig. 7.10
**Didjeridu**
This clay didjeridu is designed to balance on the rim of its bell. This permits the entire instrument to be glazed, inside and out, except for the bell's narrow rim. Instrument by Barry Hall.

As mentioned earlier, a smoother interior bore in an aerophone will result in a brighter, clearer sound, and glaze is often used to achieve this result. However, it's important to remember that

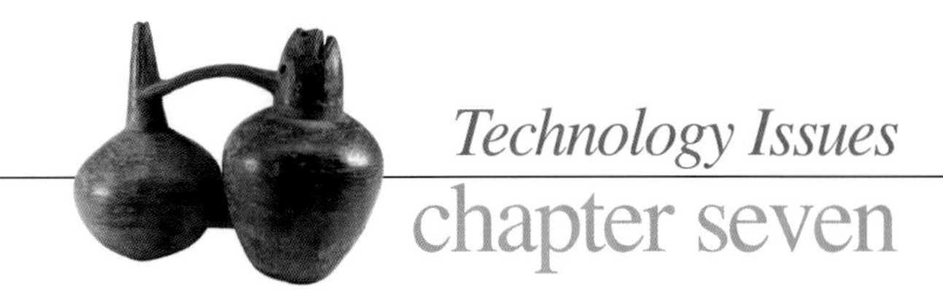



glazes add thickness to a piece, and they also may be prone to running or sagging. Many flute makers avoid getting glaze into an instrument's finger holes because it reduces their size, which changes the tuning. An approach to compensate for glazing is to make the holes slightly larger than necessary, based on the thickness that the glaze will add. When glazing the interior of a flute, the thickness of the glaze will also slightly impact the tuning, raising the instrument's overall pitch by constricting the bore. Glaze can also clog or otherwise modify delicate airway assemblies. For airduct flutes, Susan Rawcliffe advises ceramic instrument builders not to use glaze in the mouthpiece area.

Glazing presents another challenge with many musical instruments—how to cover the entire surface, or as much as possible, with glaze. As potters know, the glazed surface of an object should never touch a kiln shelf during firing. This is because glazes are designed to melt and flow, and will fuse to a kiln shelf if they come in contact with it. With functional ware such as bowls and mugs, it's common and logical for potters to leave the underside or bottom edge unglazed. Flutes, ocarinas, horns and fiddles usually don't have an "underside," so it's often desirable to cover them as completely as possible with glaze. There are a variety of methods to address this challenge, including the following.

Ceramic and metal stilts and supports are available from ceramics suppliers. These devices are designed to hold a piece aloft in the kiln, supported by fine pointed tips that leave only a tiny mark in the glaze, which can usually be sanded off after firing. Special-purpose support devices can be devised as well, using clay and nichrome (high temperature) wire. For example, stands can be built to hold flutes vertically while firing. Wire stands also can be used to support a flute or ocarina for firing in a horizontal position, either by cradling the instrument or extending into its tone holes to support from the inside.

Another approach is to glaze only selective parts of the instrument, such as the mouthpiece, leaving much of the natural clay body to show. A clever combination of these two approaches is employed by Robin Hodgkinson on his raku transverse flutes. Robin leaves several unglazed "bands" around the flute. He does this for aesthetic reasons, to imitate the cord binding that is used on bamboo flutes, but the unglazed bands also serve a practical purpose, providing a point of contact for stilts that hold the flute aloft while firing. In this way, the remainder of the flute's body (and interior) can be completely glazed.

Glaze can be applied thinly, and then wiped off so it accentuates textures in the clay but does not contact the kiln shelf. Many non-glaze decorating materials can safely come in contact with kiln shelves, such as stains, oxides, slips, engobes and terra sigillata.

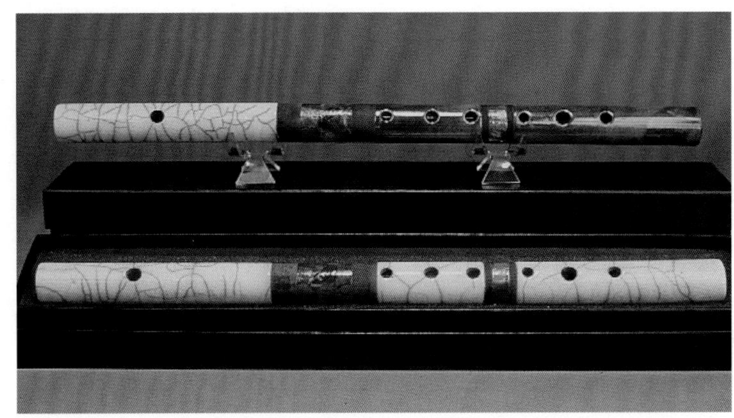

Fig. 7.11
These flutes by Robin Hodgkinson alternate bands of glaze with raw clay. In addition to the aesthetically pleasing result, this technique also permits the flutes to be raised on stilts in the kiln, permitting the glaze to be on all sides of the instrument. Hear this instrument on CD track 30.

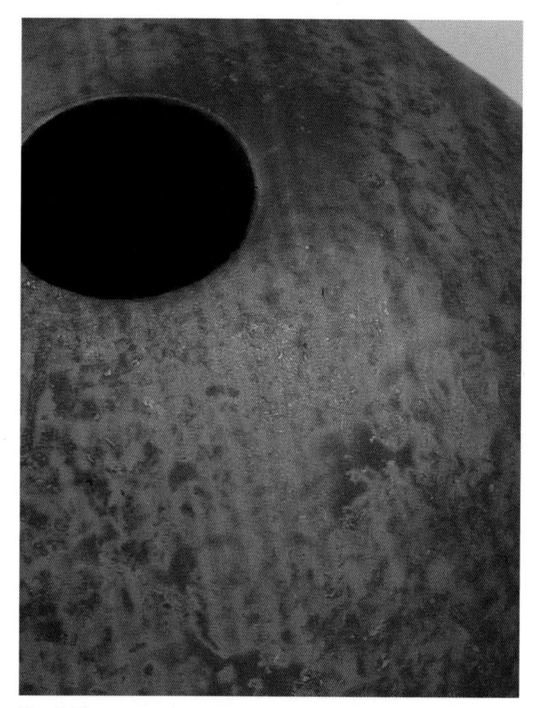

Fig. 7.12
Burnishing and sawdust-firing produces a complex and beautiful non-glaze finish on this udu drum made by Frank Giorgini.

For instruments that do not benefit from glazes, or builders who choose not to use them, a variety of other firing techniques can produce beautiful effects. These include saggar firing, pit firing, sawdust firing, smoking and raku. Vapor-firing also can be used, with or without glazes. (See definitions of these techniques in the "Glossary.") The results of many of these techniques are shown on instruments throughout this book. Non-ceramic finishes such as paints, waxes, metallic foils and a broad variety of other materials also can be applied. For instrument parts that will come in contact with a player's mouth, it's important to consider whether the finishing materials are toxic or potentially irritating to a player's lips or skin.

The multitude of clay bodies, glazes and other finishing materials available today can be daunting to a beginning ceramic instrument builder. However, some of the artists surveyed emphasized

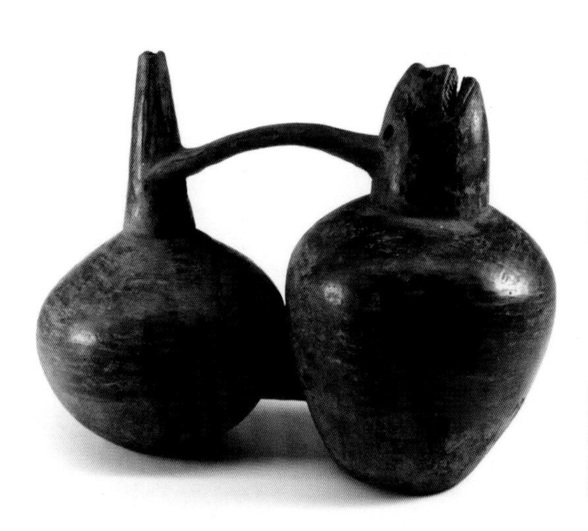

Fig. 7.13
Ancient artists achieved many beautiful finishes without the use of glazes, using what we today call "primitive" firing techniques. This whistling vessel is from the Moche culture, Peru, circa 100-800 A.D. 8 inches in height. Phoebe Apperson Hearst Museum collection.

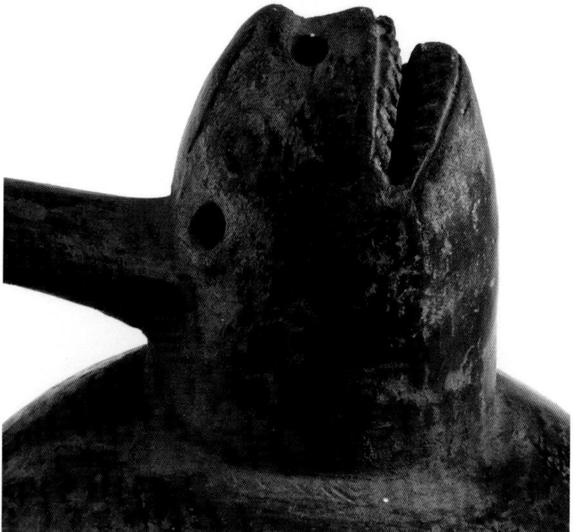

Fig. 7.14
Detail showing animal head with enclosed whistle.

### *Keith Lehman Builds and Fires a Podrum*

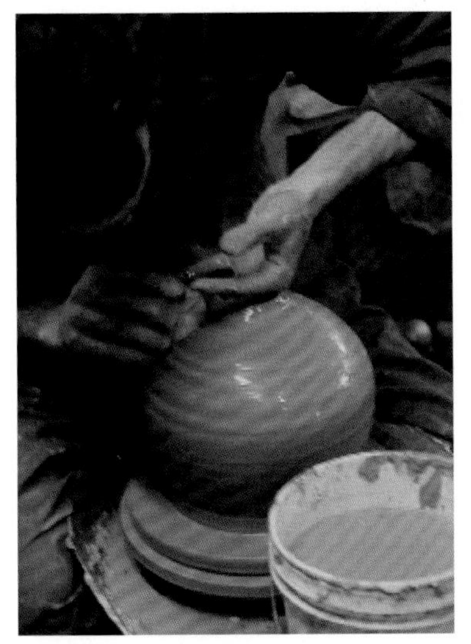

Fig. 7.15
At his kickwheel, Keith refines the opening of what will become the larger of two chambers of a double podrum.

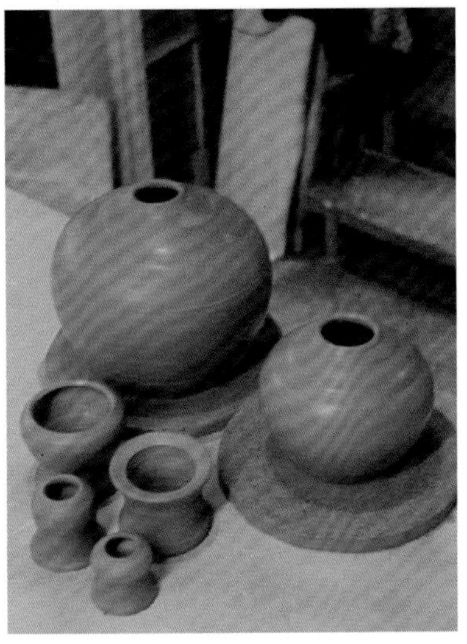

Fig. 7.16
Freshly thrown components of the double podrum will be allowed to reach leather-hardness before other openings are cut into the sides and the pieces are joined.

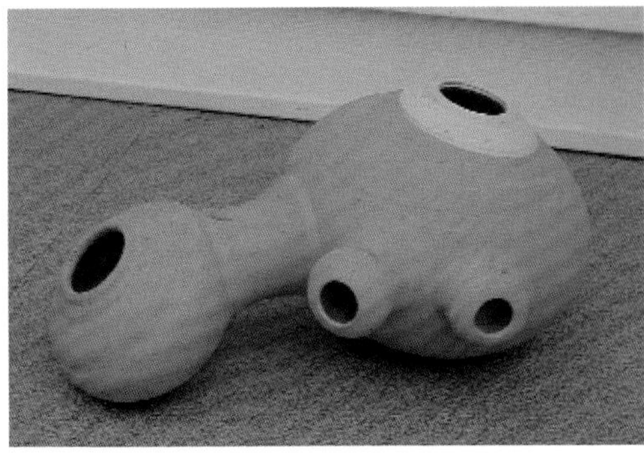

Fig. 7.17
After being allowed to dry slowly and evenly to minimize the risk of cracking, the double podrum is bisque fired in an electric kiln. Now it's ready for decoration.

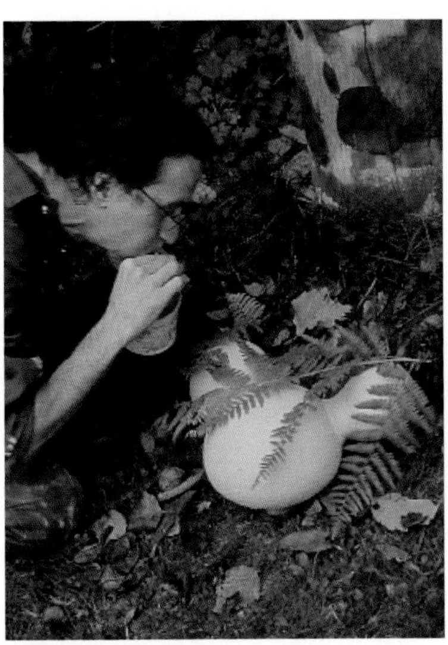

Fig. 7.18
Keith uses a small mouth atomizer to spray oxides and stains onto the drum. The fern fronds act as a stencil and help create interesting organic designs on the drum.

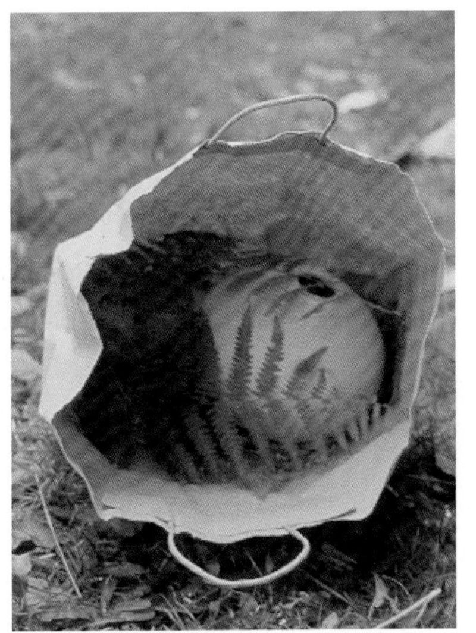

Fig. 7.19
The drum is carefully placed in a paper bag along with some coarse sawdust, more fern fronds and other combustibles.

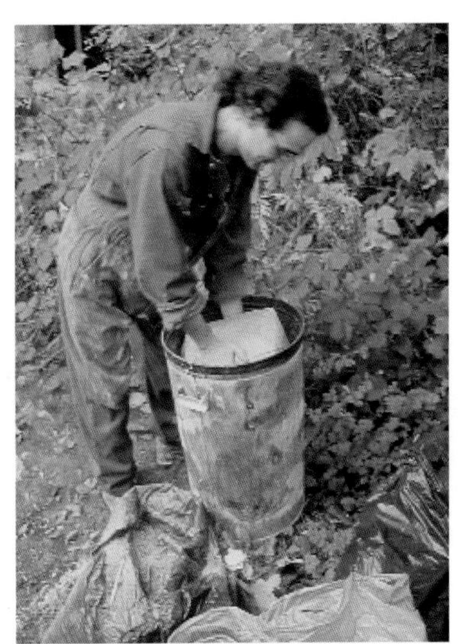

Fig. 7.20
The bag is loaded into a trash can into which several holes have been cut. More sawdust is packed lightly around the outside of the bag.

that the process of building an instrument has a larger impact on its sound than the materials used. According to Stephen Wright, "The actual process of wedging, throwing, trimming and finishing is the most important contributor to the sound of my instruments."

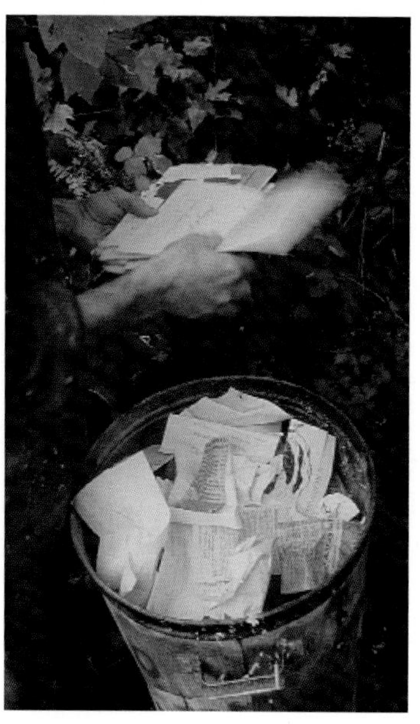

Fig. 7.21
Keith adds some junk mail to the top of the pile before setting it aflame.

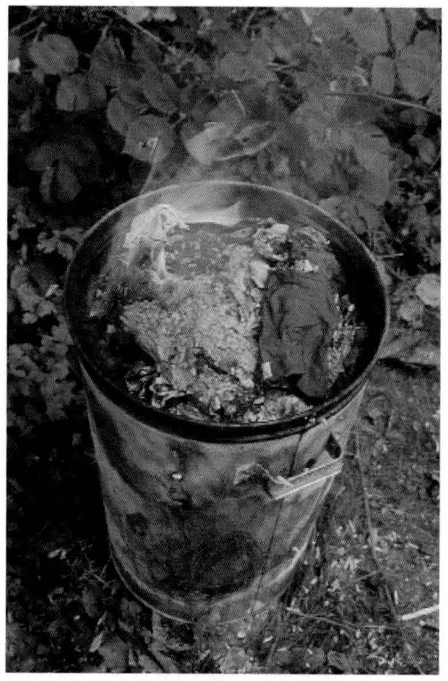

Fig. 7.22
The fire is allowed to get well started before the lid is placed on the can and the sawdust is allowed to smolder.

## Tuning and Shrinkage

Clay shrinks during the instrument building process. This shrinkage occurs in two stages. First, while drying, the clay's particles move closer together as water evaporates, resulting in a 5% to 8% decrease in the size of the original object. However, this is just the removal of the water that is physically mixed with the clay. At this point in the process, additional water is still chemically combined in the clay's molecules. In fact, about 14% of "dry" clay's weight is water. In the second stage, when the clay is fired to around 1000°F, the chemically combined water evaporates and the clay undergoes a change in its molecular structure, eventually hardening and tightening as its components melt and fuse together. The shrinkage from firing can be as much as 10%. The total shrinkage from wet clay to a fully fired object, in the most extreme cases (certain types of porcelain clay) can exceed 20%.

What does this mean for a musical instrument? Apart from making its construction more technically challenging since clay tends to crack or deform as it shrinks, it also means that the instrument's tuning may change. Most instruments produce pitches that are a function of their size. When an instrument shrinks, the tones it produces rise in pitch. So the pitches your flute or horn or drum was capable of producing when you built it from soft clay will be higher after it has dried, and higher yet again after it has been fired.

Some instruments, such as certain types of drums, are not normally tuned. When they shrink and the pitch rises slightly, it's often of no concern to the maker. Other instruments, such as flutes, are often precisely tuned to "standard pitch." To create clay instruments tuned this way requires a mastery of the elements of shrinkage and a firm grasp of the concepts of musical pitch and tuning.

There are two types of tuning: relative and absolute. Relative tuning involves tuning the pitches of an instrument relative to each other; in other words, adjusting the instrument to play in tune with itself, without regard for the instrument's musical key. Absolute tuning involves adjusting the pitches of the instrument to an external standard such as *standard pitch*. This impacts whether or not it will play in tune with other instruments that have been tuned to the same standard.

The concept of standard pitch was first promoted in the 18th century, with the idea that all instrumentalists and orchestras should use the same tuning standard. Before that, there was much variation—from player to player, town to town, and orchestra to orchestra. Standard pitch has changed over time, but in 1939 an International Standard Pitch was selected, with the pitch A above middle C defined as 440 hertz (cycles per second). Considering all the frequencies available, it's a somewhat arbitrary standard—but a good one to follow if you want your instrument to play in tune with other instruments. However, note that most "modern" instruments—violins, guitars, trumpets, flutes, etc.—are tunable, which enables them to be adjusted to play with other instruments not tuned to standard pitch.

Before you get too hung up on the often frustrating challenges of absolute tuning for ceramic instruments, bear in mind that most any instrument, whether precisely tuned or not, can be used

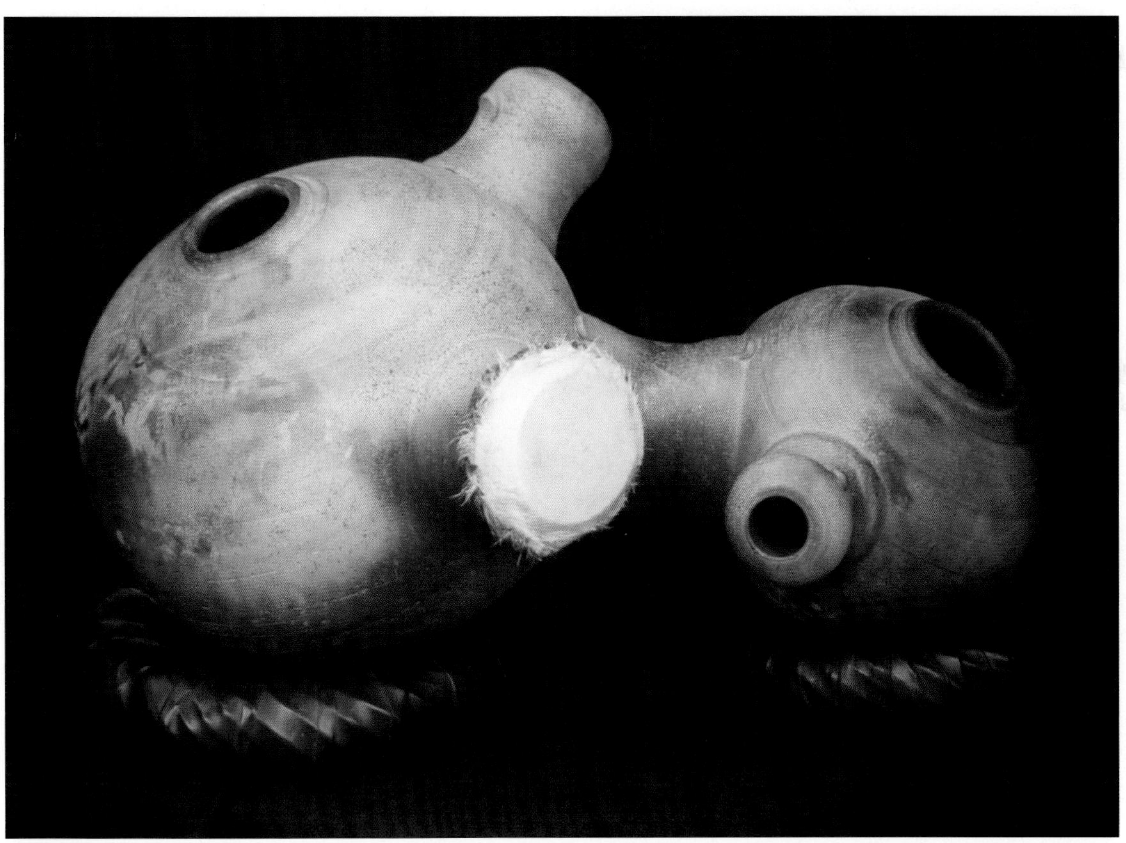

Fig. 7.23
The finished Podrum, with a goat skin head attached to one of the openings using nylon cord. 19 inches in width.

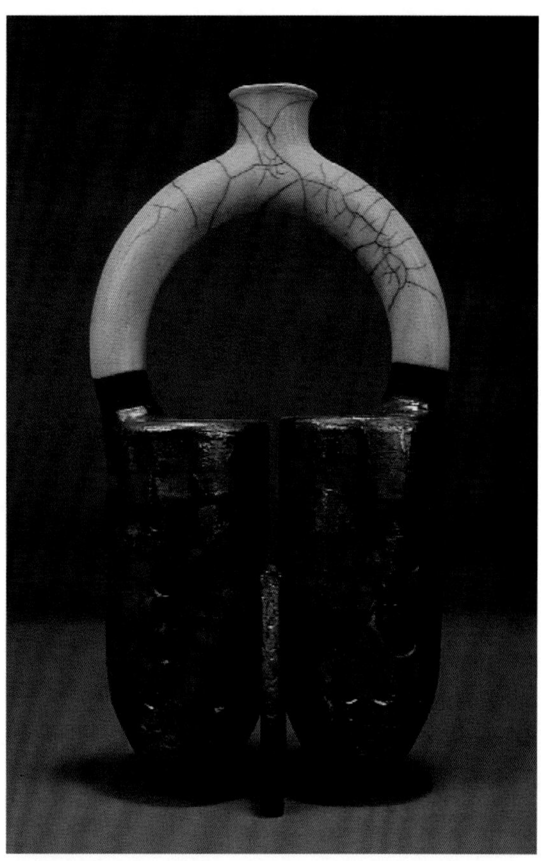

Fig. 7.24
Robin Hodgkinson's flutes and ocarinas are precision-tuned to "standard pitch." He carefully controls the shrinkage rate through meticulous monitoring of his ingredients and firing temperatures.

to play music and make beautiful or interesting sounds. There is no universal or global tuning system—many cultures through the ages have developed their own, different, tuning systems. None of them are "right" or "wrong," just different ways to divide up an octave into a series of pitches. So theoretically, every tuning system is subjective, even the Western equal-tempered piano tuning that sounds "correct" to many of us.

The point here is that it's not necessary to build instruments tuned to standard pitch or any particular scale. Instruments with their own unique tunings can be extraordinarily musical. As Ken Lovelett suggests, "Part of the beauty of any instrument is accepting the natural state of what the clay has to offer." However, if you want to play recognizable songs on your ceramic flute or ocarina, then you'll need to get reasonably accurate relative tuning. Furthermore, if you want to create instruments that can easily be played with other clay and non-clay instruments, you will need to pursue the path of perfect absolute tuning. The following information will share some techniques on how to do this. (For additional details on tuning the tone holes of a flute or ocarina, see the demonstrations in Chapter 10.)

Some clay instruments can be tested and played before they are fired, when they are in their wet, leather-hard or greenware stages. Most aerophones are in this category, including flutes, whistles, ocarinas and trumpets. In fact, it would be very difficult, if not impossible, to make some of these instruments if they couldn't be played before firing. This is due to the many minute adjustments required to make them "speak" properly and to tune them.

One very fortunate aspect of a clay aerophone's physical acoustics is that when it shrinks, it does so proportionally, and as a result usually stays in tune with itself. So if you spend a lot of time carefully tuning the finger holes to each other when a flute is leather hard, after it's been fired and has shrunk, it will still be in tune with itself. In other words, shrinkage changes the absolute tuning, but has little effect on relative tuning.

Other instruments can be partially sounded before firing; for example, an udu, or clay pot drum, can be played so that you can hear the air tones (sounds produced by the air in the vessel) before the pot has been fired. This is fortunate, because it allows the instrument maker to adjust the sizes of the holes in order to obtain desired pitches from the air chamber of the pot. However, the shell tones (pinging sounds produced by the clay body), which the maker may also wish to control, cannot be manipulated using such a trial-and-error method before firing. Fortunately, they can be controlled to some extent by using consistent clay bodies, firing temperatures and shell thicknesses.

Some instruments, such as drums with skin heads, are virtually impossible to play or test before they are fired, since the membrane is an essential component of the sound-producing mechanism, and cannot usually be fitted to a drum until after the drum is fired.

In order to achieve a specific tuning for a finished instrument, you must determine how much the clay will shrink and how that shrinkage will impact the tuning. Though you might be able to theoretically calculate shrinkage and its exact impact on tuning, the most common approach is trial and error. To do this, make an instrument and carefully measure its pitch before and after drying and firing. Then build another, using the data from your first trial to adjust your measurements. For example, if your first model's pitch was one semitone higher after firing, then build your next trial model to play one semitone below your desired final pitch before firing. Over the course of several (or more) trials, you will hone in on the proper size for your unfired piece that will result in the final pitch you desire.

It is crucially important that you not vary any other factors from trial to trial, including type of clay, amount of dryness when measuring pitches, and firing temperature. Robin Hodgkinson says he is able to make accurately tuned ceramic flutes by maintaining a constant shrinkage rate, achieved by closely monitoring his raw ingredients and firing temperature. It is also very important that you consistently repeat all aspects of your construction. Stephen Wright first developed a set of standard pitches for his family of Ubang clay pot drums. Then, through trial and error, he determined how many pounds of raw clay were needed to build each drum to the correct pitch. From that point forward, through a lot of practice, he developed the ability to throw and trim each drum consistently. When people ask him how long it takes to make his drums, Stephen smiles and says, "Twenty years."

To take precise measurements of an instrument's pitch, many builders use electronic tuners, which

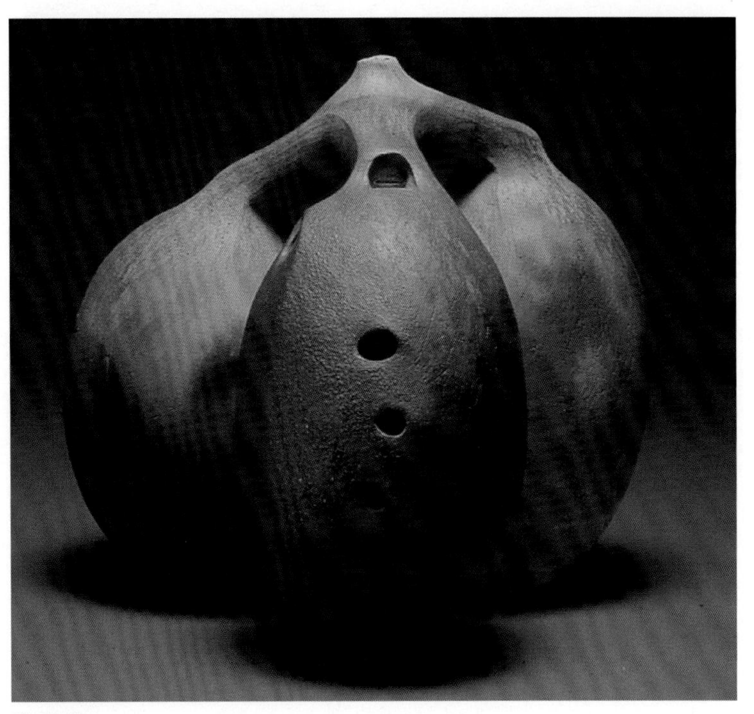

Fig. 7.25
Sharon Rowell uses an electronic tuner to help her precisely adjust the relative tuning between the chambers of her huacas.

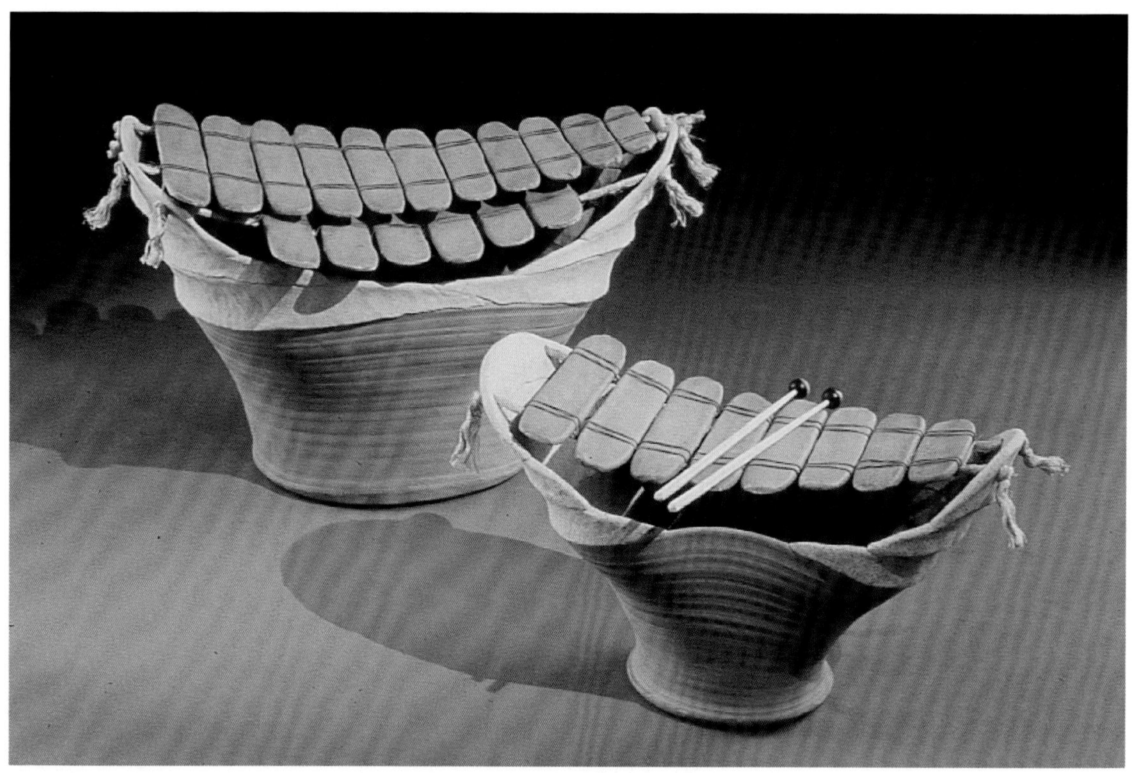

Fig. 7.26
The bars of these clay marimbas by Ward Hartenstein were individually fine-tuned after firing by grinding away material with a diamond lapidary wheel.

subdivide the interval between two consecutive chromatic pitches into 100 equal increments called *cents.* This precise measuring ability allows makers to fine-tune their instruments much more accurately than using their ears alone. For example, Sharon Rowell uses an electronic tuner to carefully adjust the two melody chambers of her huacas so that they are only a few cents apart, which creates their special sound. When tuning, it's important to realize that variations in the way you blow may impact an instrument's measured pitch, and that other people may play your instruments with a different mouth position, resulting in a different pitch.

Unlike instruments made from wood or other materials, which can be adjusted repeatedly until they are just the way the maker intends, once a clay instrument is fired it is almost unchangeable. A bit of fine-tuning is possible, and sometimes called for with flutes. Finger holes that are slightly too small can be enlarged using a small grinder attached to a flexible shaft or rotary tool. Glaze buildup in finger holes also can be ground away, and mouthpiece or windway obstructions can sometimes be cleared with a small file or folded sandpaper.

Brian Ransom uses grinding in a more significant way to fine-tune sets of ceramic bells. He slip-

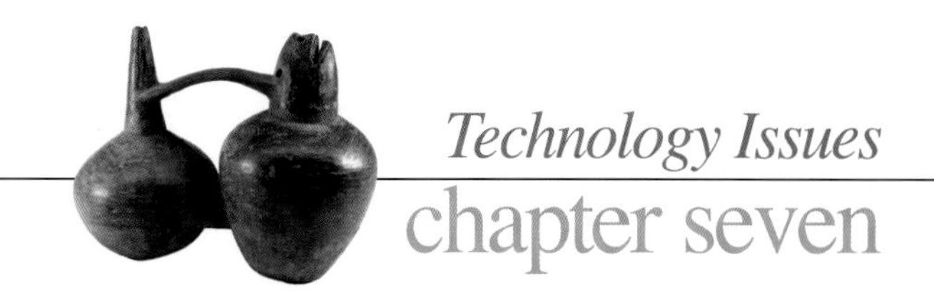



casts the bells in a series of molds, adding more or less slip to achieve different sizes and pitches. After firing, the bells are fine-tuned by grinding away excess material with a belt sander using a carborundum-grit belt.

Ward Hartenstein uses a diamond lapidary wheel to tune the fired bars of his clay marimbas by grinding away material from the underside of the center and the ends of the bars. Grinding at the ends raises the pitch; grinding near the center lowers the pitch. He also tunes clay bells in this way, but cautions that it can leave an unsightly scar on the bell.

Lapidary grinding usually uses a water drip or spray system to both cool the work and carry away grinding particles. It is also possible to drill small holes in clay using lapidary drills which come in a variety of sizes and shapes, all with a diamond abrasive embedded in the tip. Again, water is used as a coolant. A diamond drill can be used on an ordinary drill press and water applied by hand with a sponge while drilling. Naturally any kind of grinding or drilling is easier on low-fire ceramics, but stoneware and even porcelain can be worked in this manner if you are patient and don't allow the work to overheat. When sanding or grinding, always remember to wear a respirator or mask to protect your lungs from clay dust.

Excess clay can be ground away after firing, but how do you add more material? Finger holes that are too large can be reduced using a number of different materials. For temporary changes or testing, you can use wax or electrician's tape. For more permanent use, try tile grout (which comes pre-mixed in a variety of earth tones) or two-part epoxy putty. Clay dust or grog can be added to the epoxy to help match the color and texture of the instrument. When adding material to tone holes, start from the inside of the instrument and work your way out. This will help minimize the impact on the appearance and fingering comfort of your instrument.

Another method of tuning a clay instrument is to put it through multiple successive firings, each one slightly hotter than the previous, until the desired pitch is achieved. Note that this progression goes in only one direction—higher and still higher yet—so you need to use small enough increments so as not to overshoot your goal. Obviously, this method can be time-consuming.

In addition to changing an instrument's tuning, shrinkage can also impact playability. Don Bendel relates, "When testing a leather-hard horn to see how it blows, it may work perfectly, but after firing, if the shrinkage is too great it will be difficult to blow, and hard to develop different pitches. This is because either the mouthpiece has become too small or the smallest part of the tube has closed up too much."

### Repairs

It is sad when a treasured ceramic instrument is broken. But take heart. Broken instruments can often be repaired to "like new" playing ability, and to "almost new" visual appearance. Since it's often the case that the sound or playing capability of an instrument is more important to a musician than the instrument's visual aesthetic (though both may be quite important), many players attempt to repair broken instruments rather than discard them.

Certain types of ceramic instruments should probably be written off when broken or cracked, most specifically idiophones that rely on a ringing clay sound. As experienced potters know, the sound produced by rapping a pot or bowl will immediately indicate if it is cracked. Gluing the crack or break usually won't restore the pristine sound, since the crystal lattice of the clay has been compromised and cannot be repaired at the molecular level.

However, most aerophones, and even membrane drums, can be successfully repaired, provided the break is relatively clean and there are not too many pieces to reassemble. Since an aerophone's sound results primarily from air vibrating inside the vessel, rather than the vibration of the material itself, the instrument will usually continue to sound if the vessel is repaired in such a way that its rigidity is restored and it has no air leaks.

There are many adhesives that work well with ceramics. For small pieces, cyanoacrylate ("super glue") is fast and durable. Water-soluble white glue (polyvinyl acetate or PVA) also works well, especially on porous materials such as bisque ware, but the bond will not stand up to water. Silicone glue produces a flexible joint and can be used to fill gaps. Two-part liquid epoxy produces an extremely strong bond. Two-part epoxy paste or putty can be used to re-attach broken pieces together, and also to fill gaps caused by missing pieces. When the epoxy putty is in its soft form, it can be molded like clay, and even used to make mouthpieces or other instrument parts that may be missing or need to be modified. When dry, it can be filed and sanded to shape if necessary, and also can be painted. There are some non-toxic epoxy putties available, which may be preferable, especially for making mouthpieces. Other adhesives (such as polyurethane glue, which is activated by moisture and expands as it dries) may be appropriate for specific circumstances.

For a list of adhesives see the "Resources and Materials" section.

## chapter eight

*All the sounds of the Earth are like music..*
—Oscar Hammerstein

# Gallery

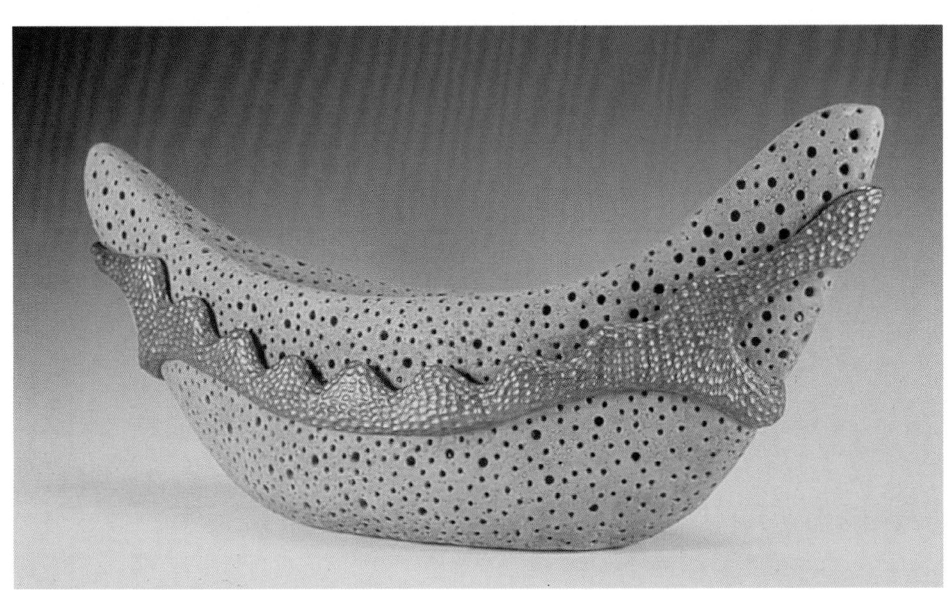

Fig. 8.1
**Cascade (2001)**
Brian Hiveley, Miami, Florida, USA. In creating the surface of this sculpture, hundreds of tiny clay pieces were pushed inside. After firing, the pieces trapped inside create a beautiful "waterfall" sound when the vessel is tipped. 17 inches in length.

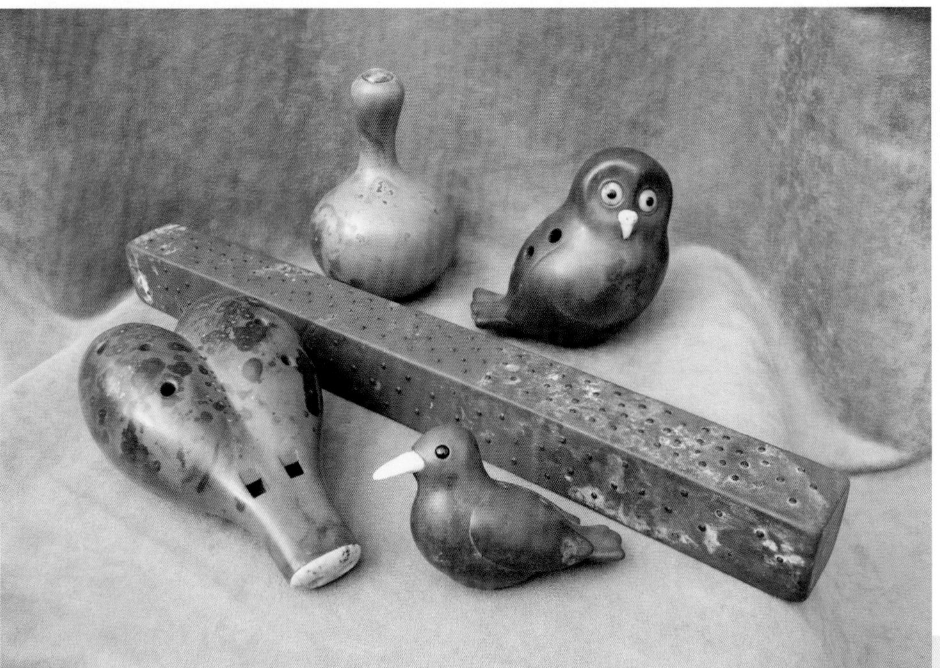

Fig. 8.2
**Instrument Collection**
Rod Kendall, Tenino, Washington, USA. Clockwise from top: shaker, with turquoise stone top, 6 inches tall; owl, with fossil walrus ivory beak and amber eyes, 5 inches tall; rainstick, with nails pressed into hollow clay body filled with clay pellets of various sizes, 19 inches long; song bird, with fossil walrus ivory beak and onyx eyes, 4 inches tall; double-chambered ocarina, pentatonically tuned, with verasite mouthpiece, 8 inches long. All instruments are cone 6 stoneware body, saggar fired, hand polished with diamond sanding pads prior to firing, and finished with microcrystalline wax polish or acrylic finish.

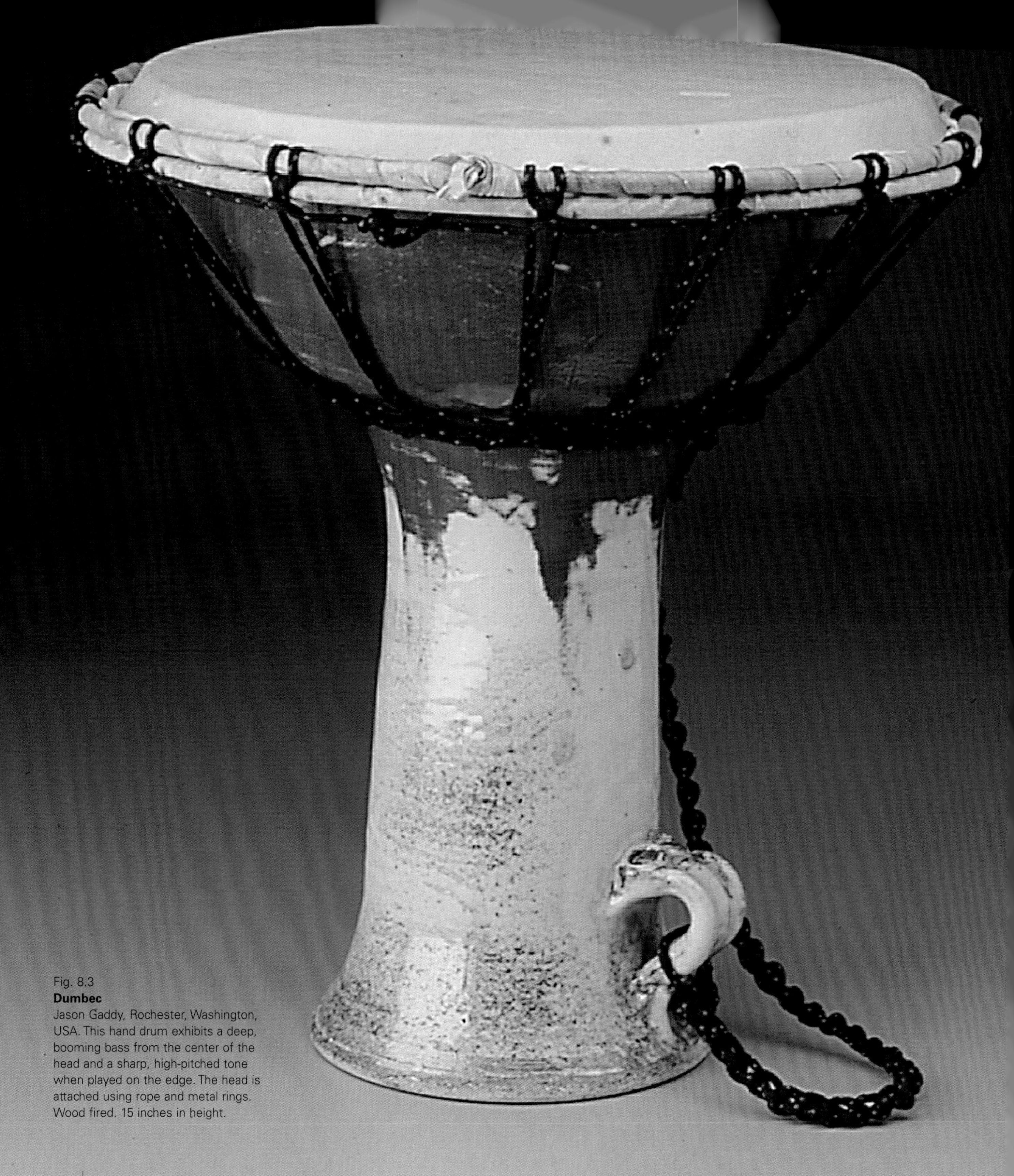

Fig. 8.3
**Dumbec**
Jason Gaddy, Rochester, Washington, USA. This hand drum exhibits a deep, booming bass from the center of the head and a sharp, high-pitched tone when played on the edge. The head is attached using rope and metal rings. Wood fired. 15 inches in height.

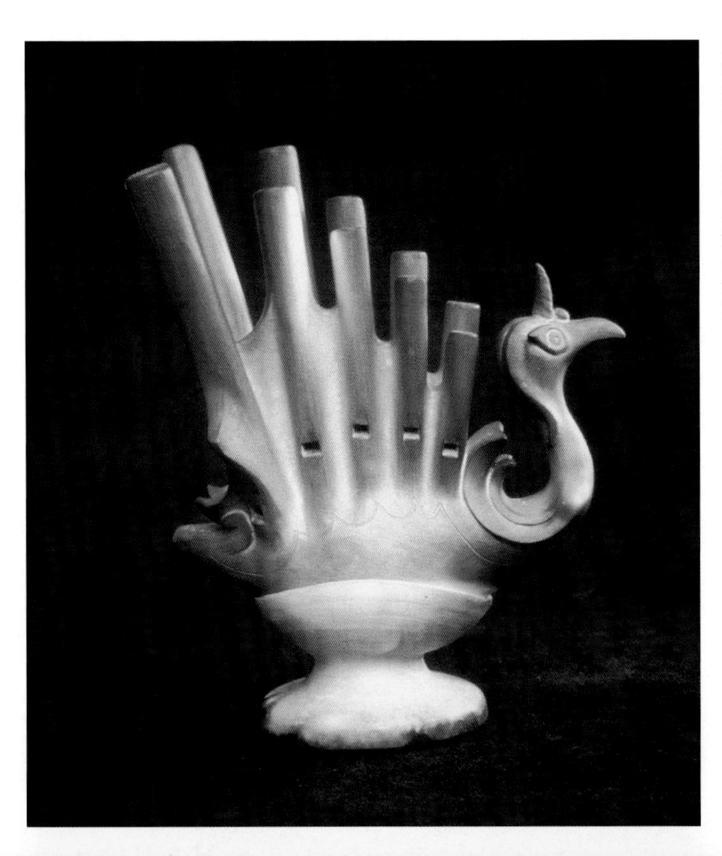

Fig. 8.4
**Mouth Organ**
Marie Picard, Marguerittes, France. The ten pipes in this mouth-blown instrument can be individually stopped or released with the fingers and thumbs, to produce from one to ten simultaneous tones. The pipes are tuned to a pentatonic scale. 8 inches in height.

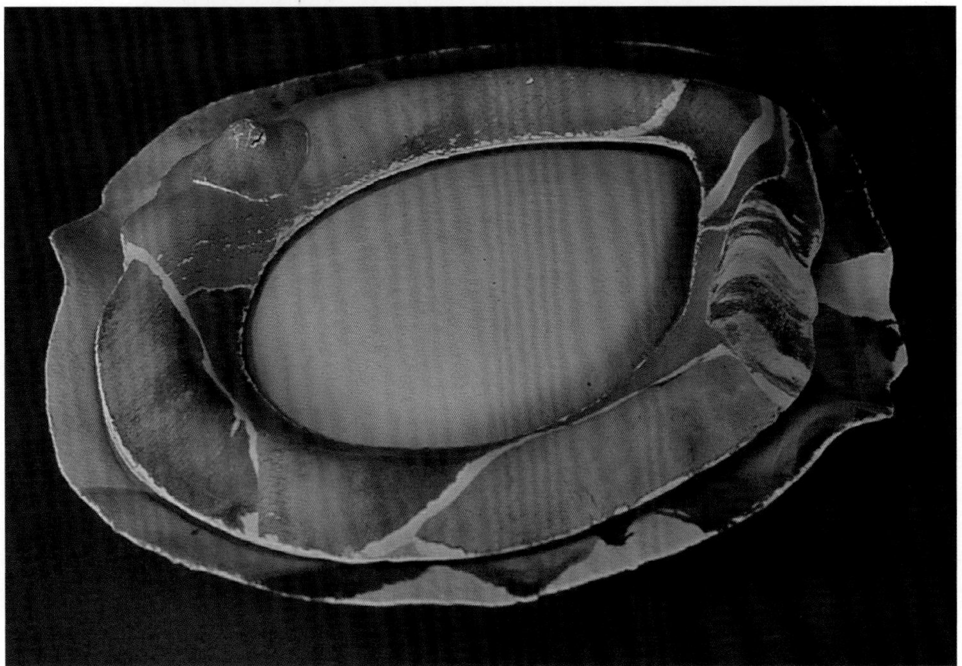

Fig. 8.5
**Rattle**
Kaete Brittin Shaw, High Falls, New York, USA. A 1990 performance by noted percussionist Glen Velez rekindled Kaete's interest in rattle instruments, and for the next four years she designed and refined her porcelain instruments. Porcelain balls of various diameters are sealed inside. 12 inches in width.

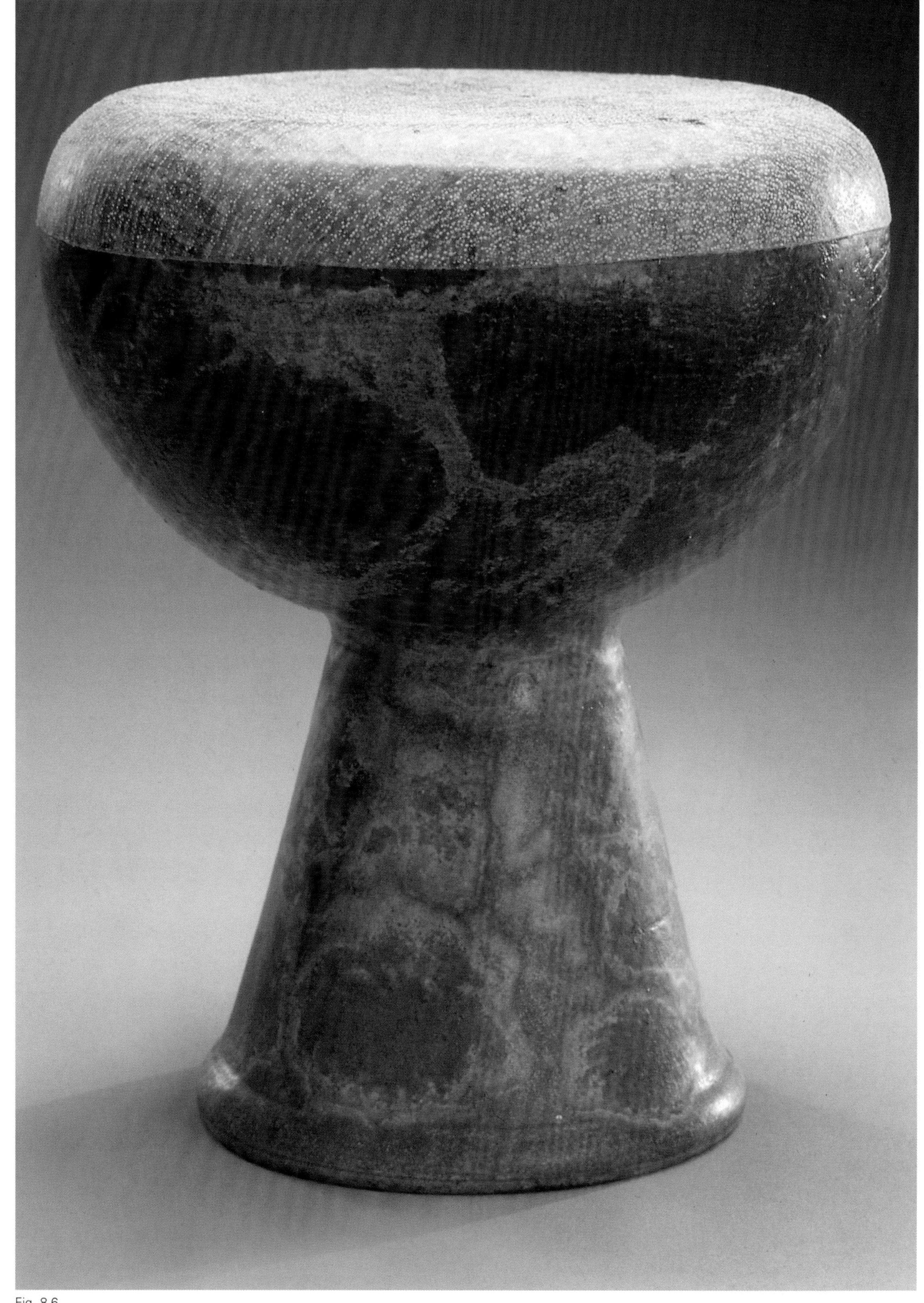

Fig. 8.6
**Reptilian Doumbek**
Barry Hall, Westborough, Massachusetts, USA. Stoneware doumbek drum with oxides and glazes applied to imitate reptile skin. Fish skin head. 11 inches in height.

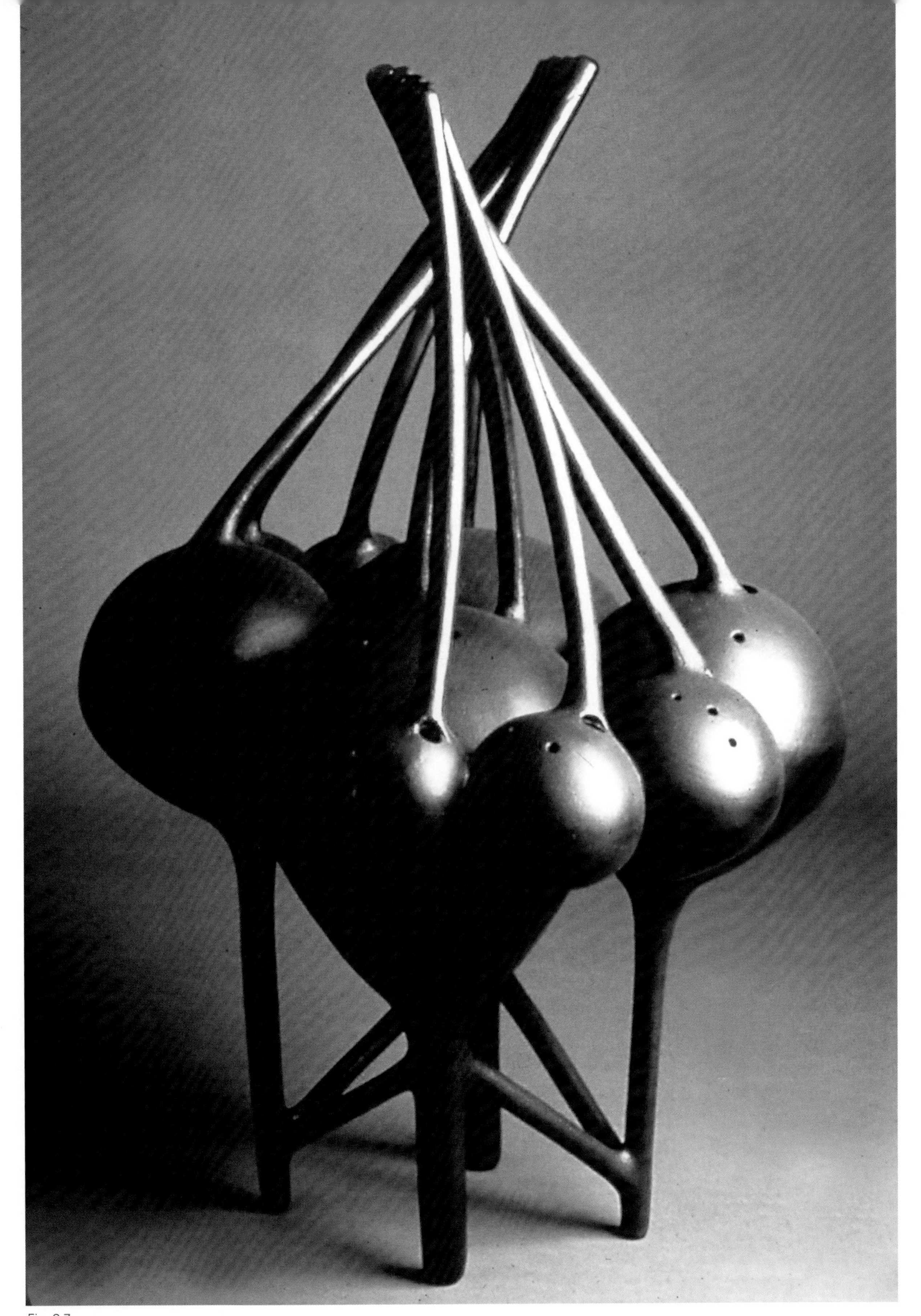

Fig. 8.7
**Double Nest of Hooters**
Brian Ransom, St. Petersburg, Florida, USA. A duet instrument for two players, with nine individually sounding chambers. Some of the chambers have fingerholes. The pitches are very low due to the large sizes of the vessels. Earthenware. 42 inches in height.

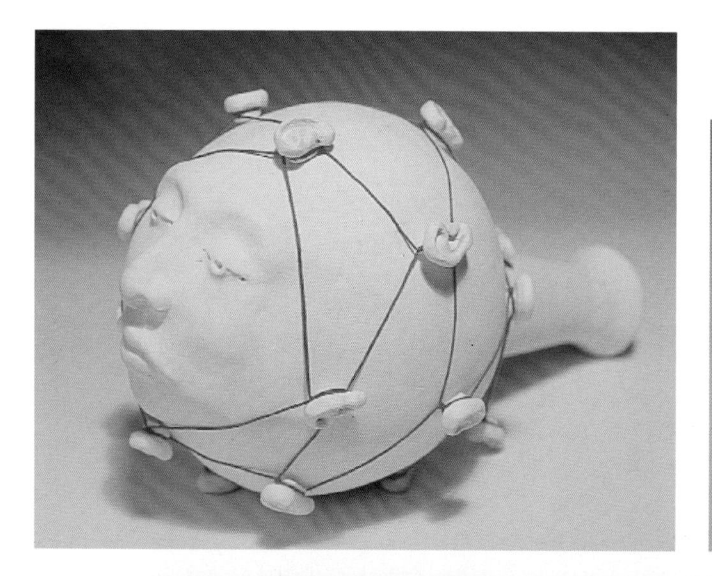

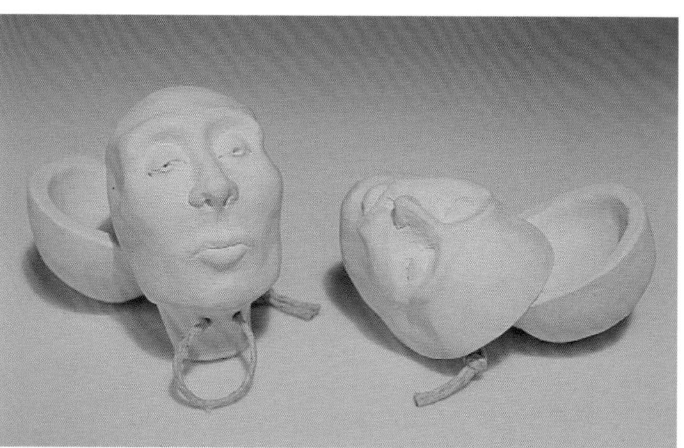

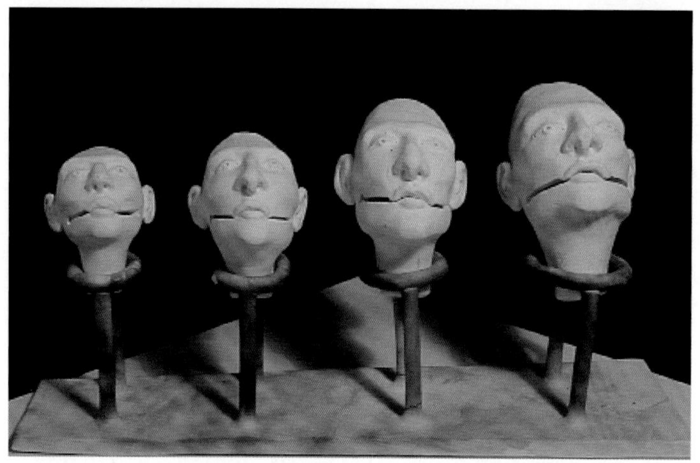

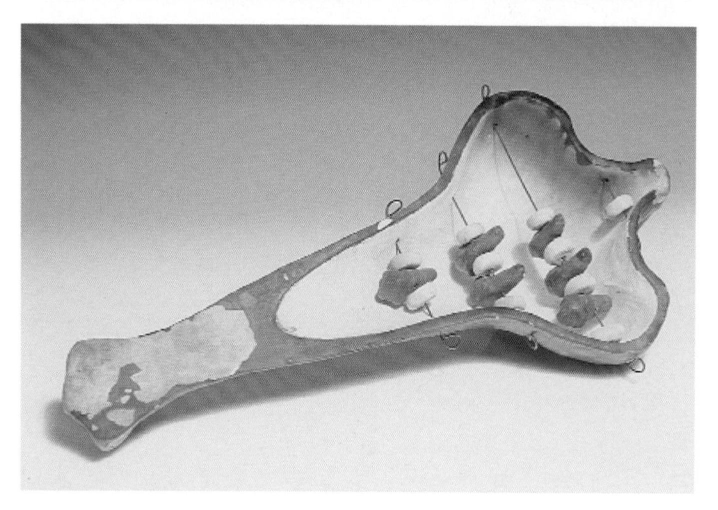

Fig. 8.8
**Anatomical Idiophones**
Emily Rensink, Houston, Texas, USA

**Cabasa** – Clay and string. 10 inches in length.

**Castanets** – 2.25" x 3" x 3.5"

**Head Blocks** – Clay and slip, paper smoked. To 9.75 inches in height.

**Nose Sistrum** – Clay and terra sigillata, sawdust fired. 12 inches in length.

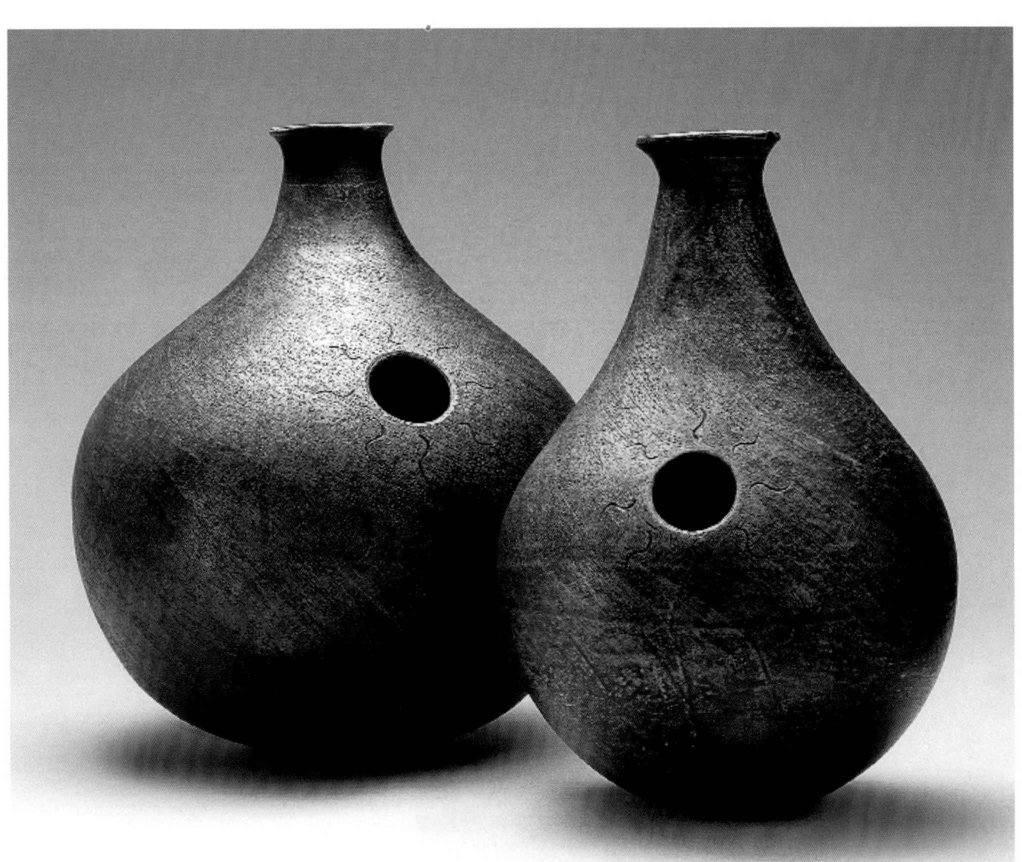

Fig. 8.9
**Clay Pot Drums**
Barry Hall, Westborough, Massachusetts, USA. Two side-hole clay pot drums. Coil-built stoneware. To 17 inches in height.

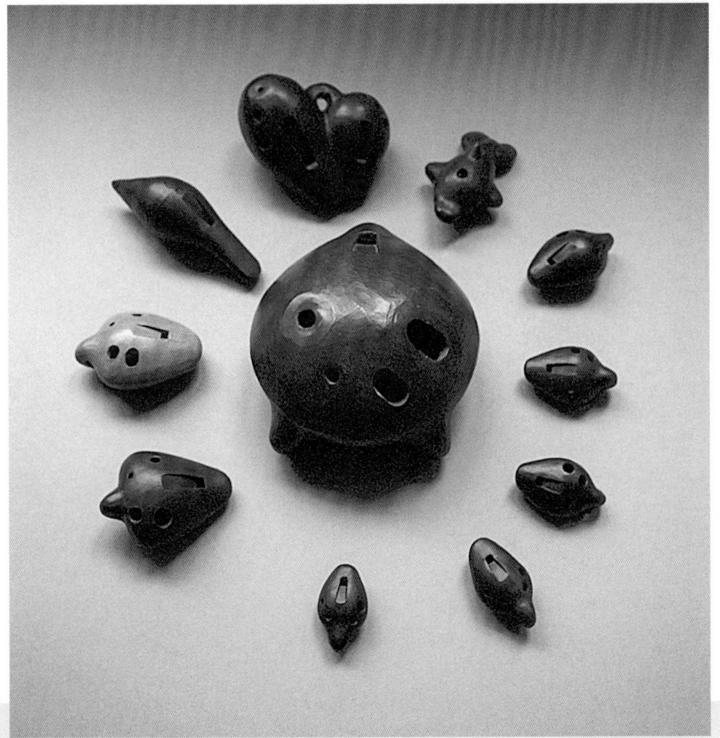

Fig. 8.10
**Ocarinas**
Barry Jennings, London, England. A group of eleven ocarinas including a bird, double & dolphin, two medium-sized, five pendants and a large "D" in the middle.

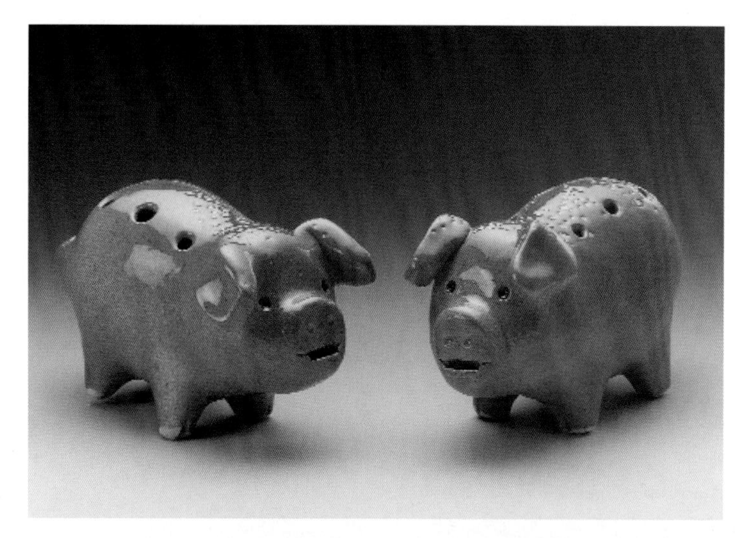

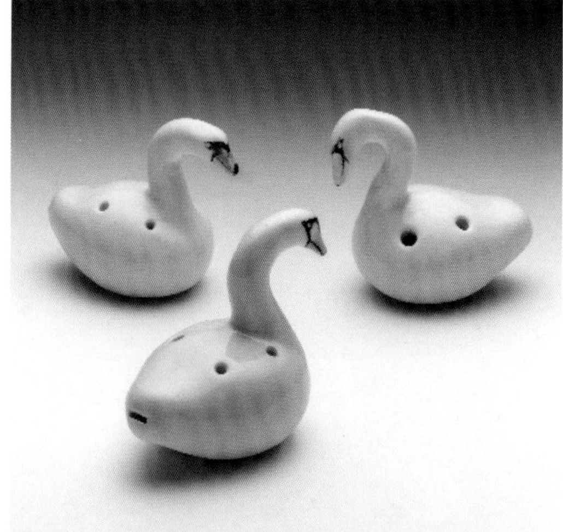

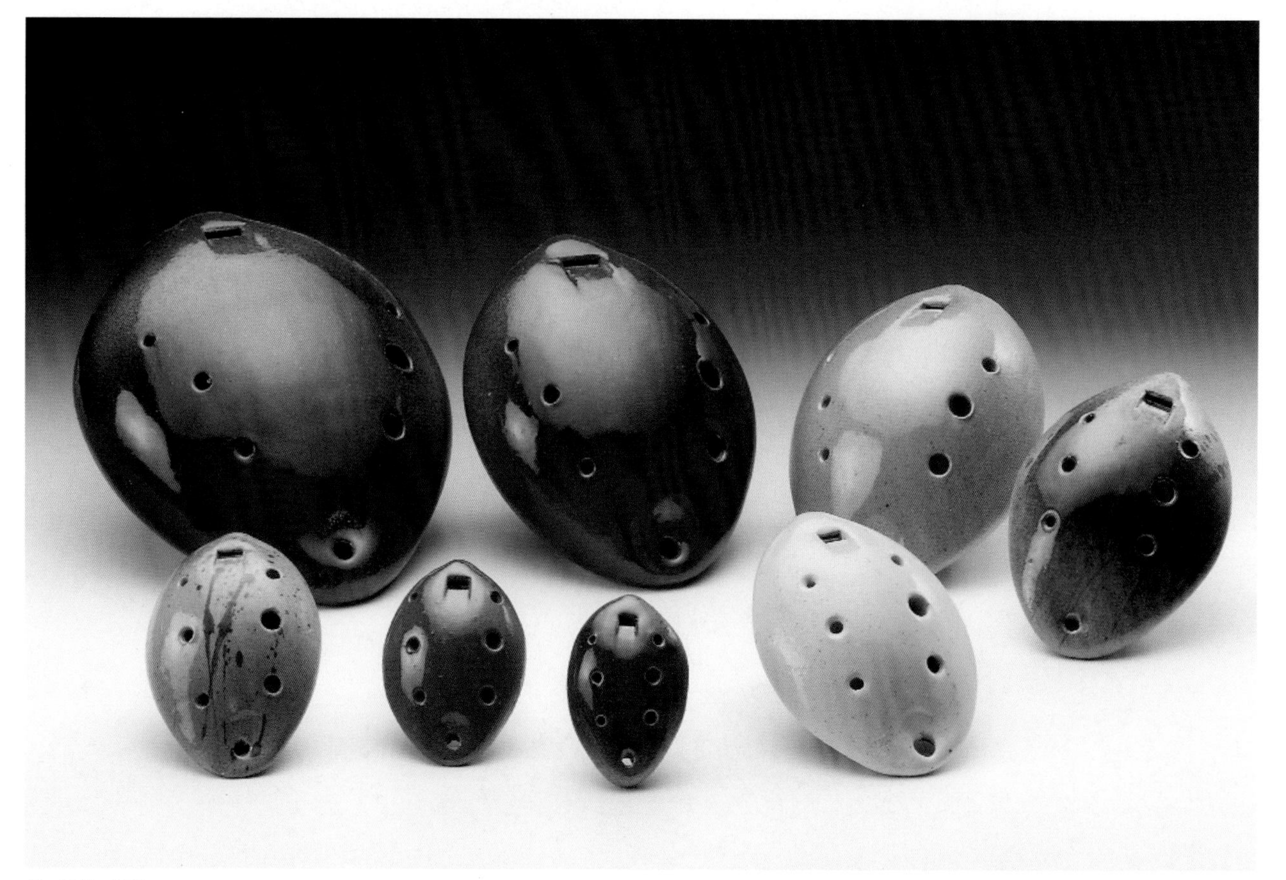

Fig. 8.11 - 8.13
**Ocarinas**
Johann Rotter, Dittmannsdorf, Austria. At Ocarina-Werkstatt in Dittmannsdorf, Austria, Hans Rotter produces a wide array of 4-hole and 7-hole ocarinas in traditional and fanciful animal shapes. Ocarina-Werkstatt instruments are made in many sizes and pitches ranging from a tiny piccolo to a huge bass.

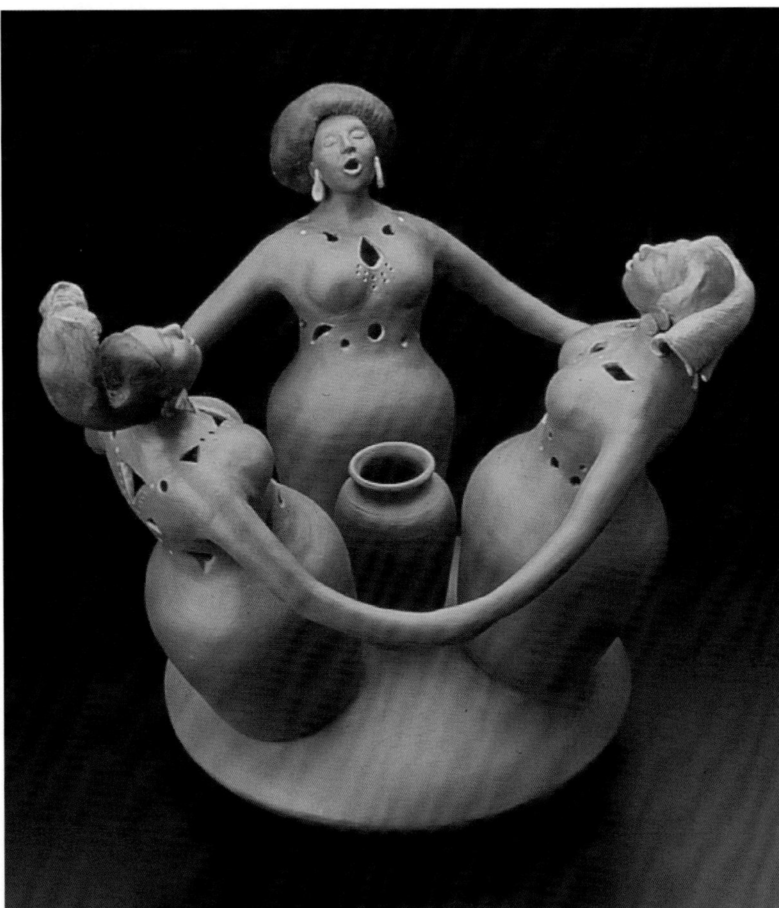

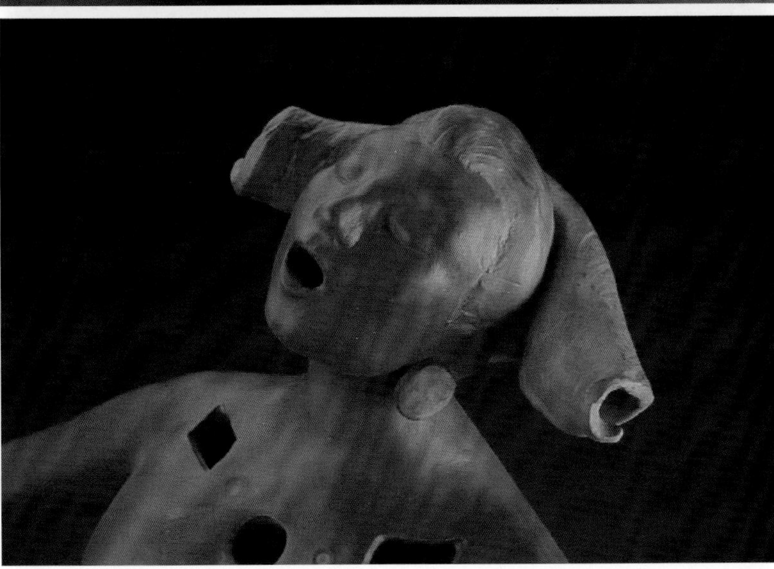

Fig. 8.14
**Three Women Water Whistle**
Janet Moniot, Petal, Mississippi, USA. All three whistling figures are connected by clay tubes and a small reservoir in the base. When blowing into the center jug, all three whistles will sound at once. Or, water poured into the jug will displace the air through each whistle separately as it's tipped from side to side.
14.25 inches in height.

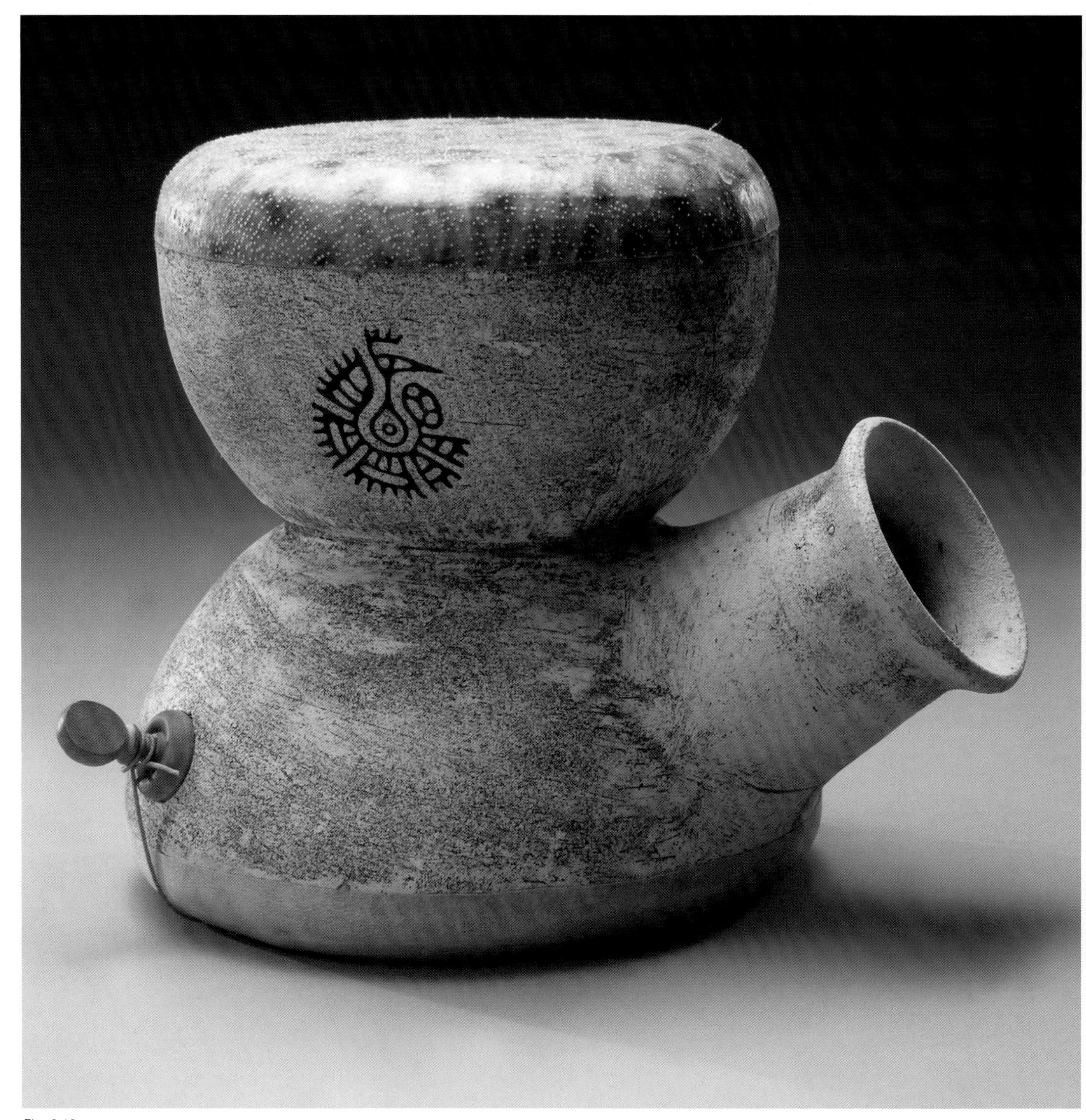

Fig. 8.16
**Two-Chambered Snare Doumbek**
Barry Hall, Westborough, Massachusetts, USA. Doumbek with two chambers, two heads and a gut snare. Stoneware with oxide stains and inlaid clay design. Fish skin and goat skin drum heads, gut snare, wooden tuning peg. 12 inches in height.

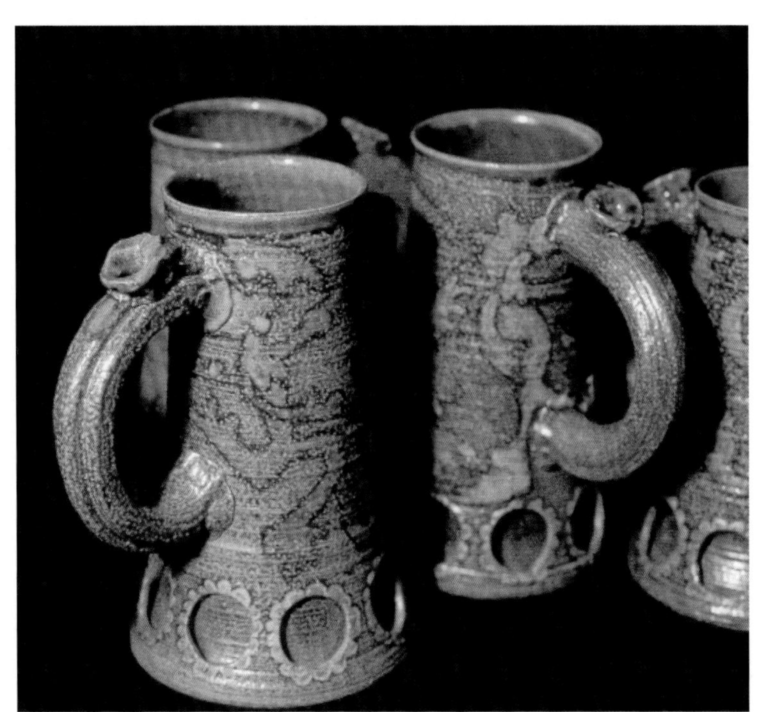

Fig. 8.17
**Beer Mug Horns**
Don Bendel, Flagstaff, Arizona, USA. This unusual mug can be played as a horn by blowing through the mouthpiece on top of the handle which is a wheel thrown tube. The other end of the tube opens into the bottom of the mug. When your mug is empty, you may toot for another drink! The bottom is double-walled which provides a more delicate look while giving the base added support. Salt-glazed stoneware with underglaze, pencil and colored engobes.
To 8 inches in height.

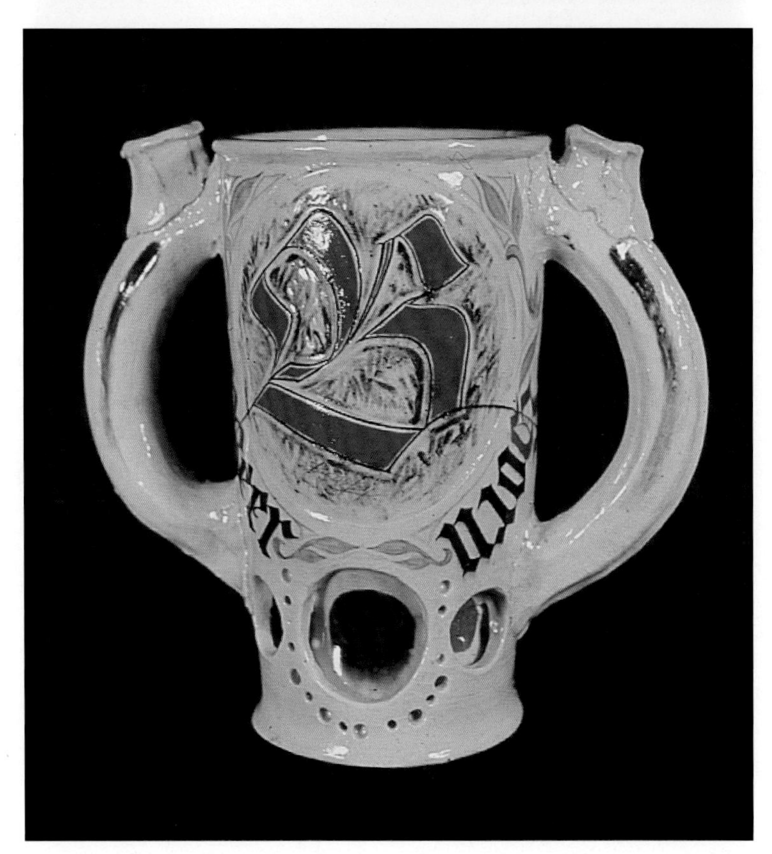

Fig. 8.18
**Double Beer Mug Horn**
Don Bendel, Flagstaff, Arizona, USA. A beer mug horn with two blowing handles—one side toots out of the mug's bottom and the other out the top. High-fire porcelain, clear glaze and low-fire china paint. One of several collaboration pieces with the late calligrapher Richard Beasley. 10 inches in height.

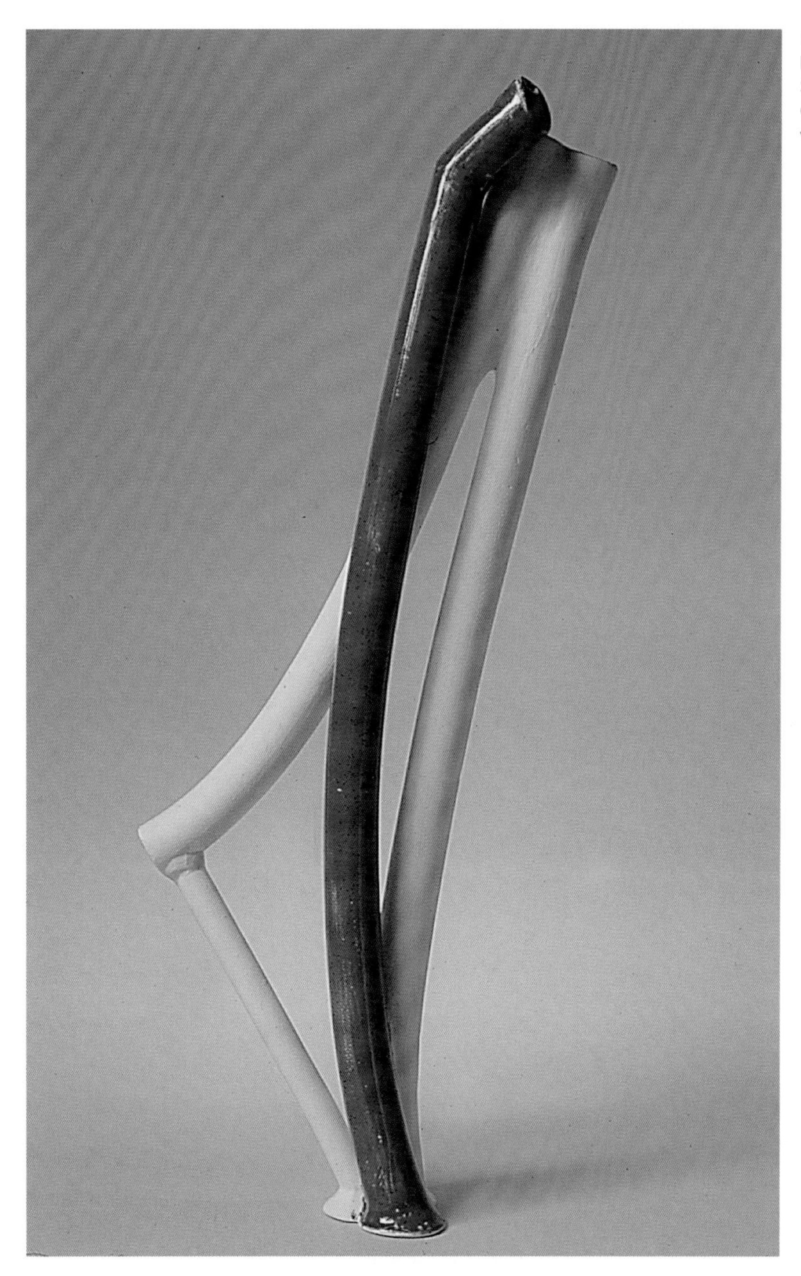

Fig. 8.19
**Harmonic Flute**
Susan Rawcliffe, San Pedro, California, USA. Extruded tubes with glaze. 21.5 inches in height.

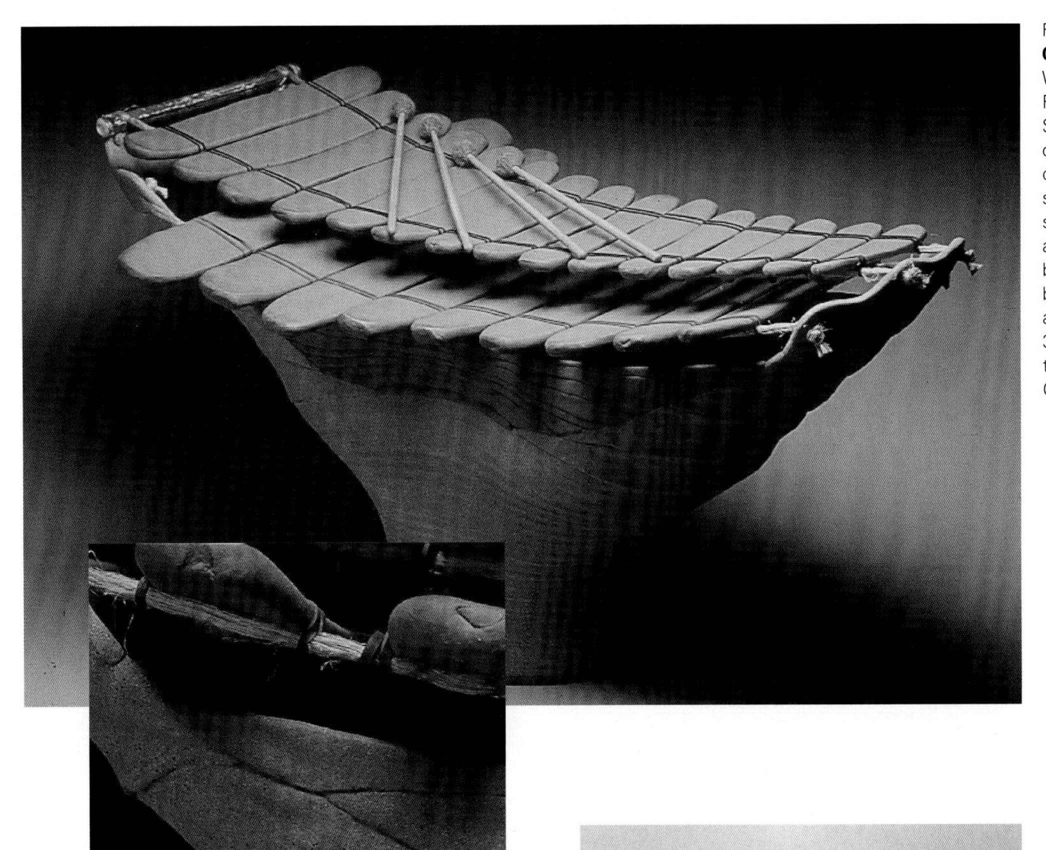

Fig. 8.20
**Clay Marimba**
Ward Hartenstein, Rochester, New York, USA. Stoneware bars suspended over an unglazed resonating chamber. The detail photo shows Ward's method of suspending the clay bars, attaching each bar to a rope using rubber bands. This maximizes their ability to vibrate freely. 35 inches in width. Hear this instrument on CD track 3.

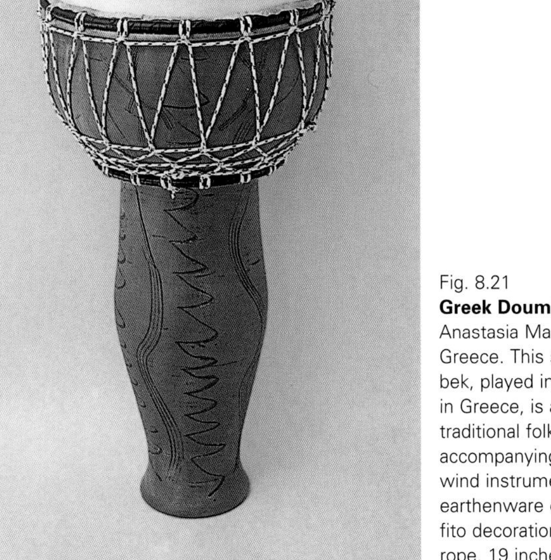

Fig. 8.21
**Greek Doumbek**
Anastasia Mamali, Athens, Greece. This style of doumbek, played in certain areas in Greece, is associated with traditional folk music, accompanying singers and wind instruments. Greek earthenware clay with sgraffito decoration, rings and rope. 19 inches in height.

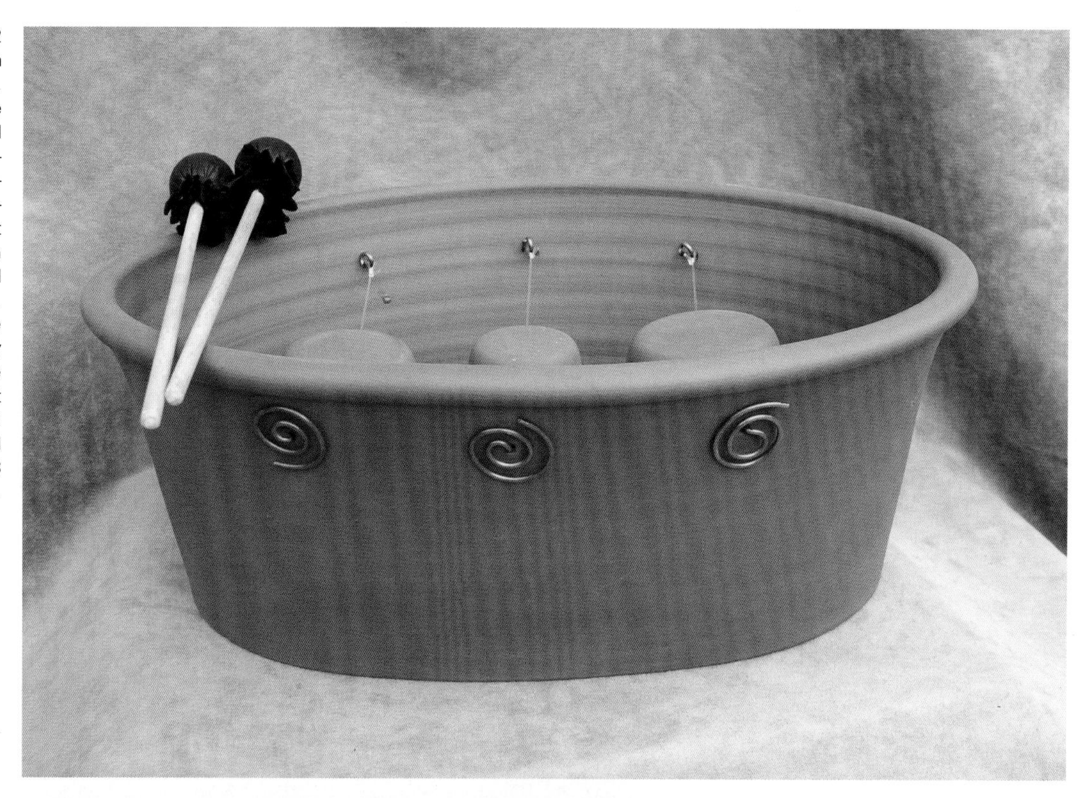

Fig. 8.22
**Water Drum**
Rod Kendall, Tenino, Washington, USA. Inside the large container vessel are graduated clay cylinders suspended from elastic cords in water. The bottom of each cylinder is cut at an angle with a thin sheet of brass attached enclosing the vessel. When the cylinders are struck with mallets, they produce a percussive sound with a "wow" that modulates as the vessel moves in the water. Red cone 6 stoneware body, 18 inches in width.

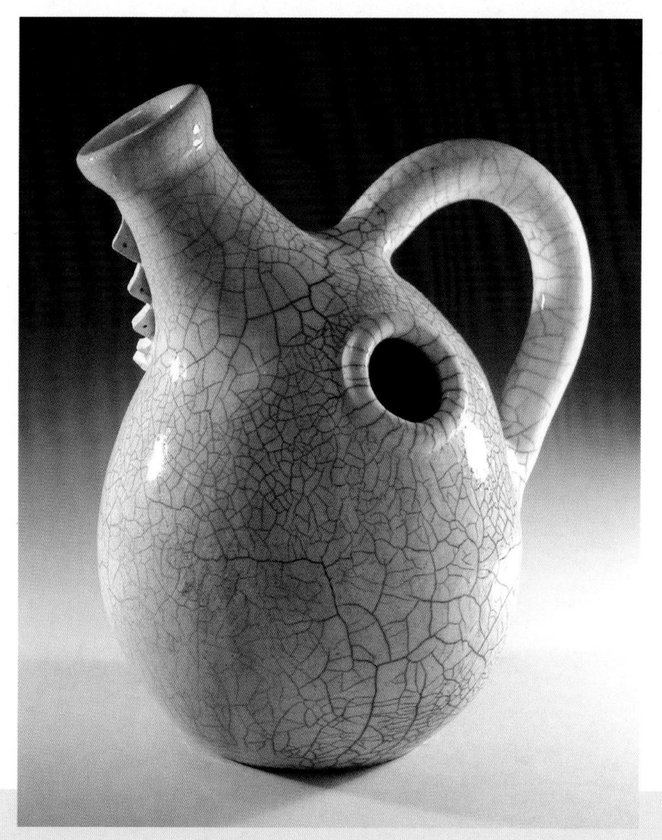

Fig. 8.23
**Globular Horn Pitcher**
Barry Hall, Westborough, Massachusetts, USA. Stoneware, raku fired. 11 inches in height.

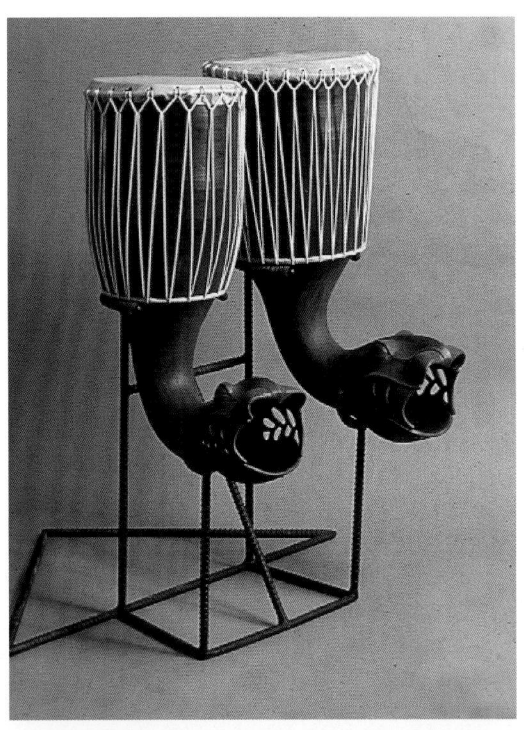

Fig. 8.24
**Dragon Congas**
Brian Ransom,
St. Petersburg, Florida, USA.
Two vapor-fired earthenware drums with bells in the form of dragon heads. 40 inches in height.

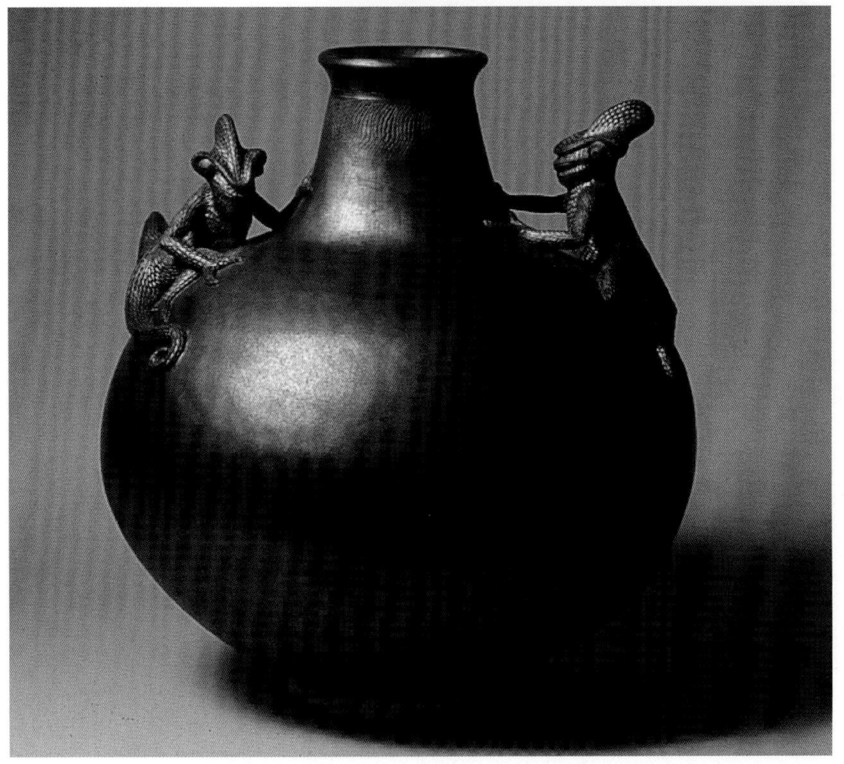

Fig. 8.25
**Abang Grande Drum**
Frank Giorgini, Freehold, NY, USA. This large clay pot drum does not have a side hole, unlike its smaller cousins. It is played by striking the top opening with a hand or paddle. Coiled earthenware, coated with terra sigillata, burnished, and smoke fired.
24 inches in height.

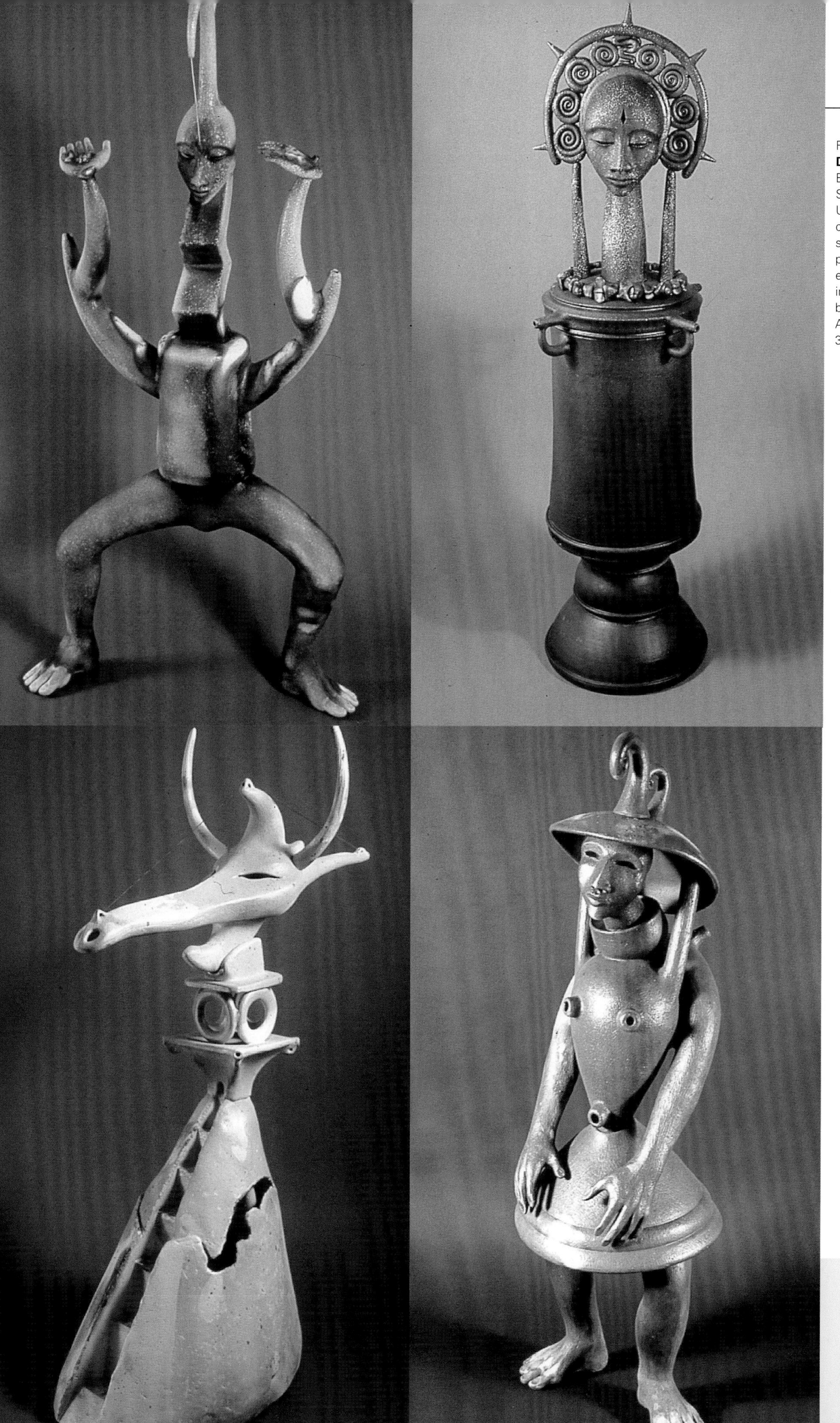

Fig. 8.26
**Deities of Sound**
Brian Ransom,
St. Petersburg, Florida,
USA. A group of pieces
conceived by Brian in a
series of dreams. Each
piece has multiple
embedded musical
instruments activated by
breath, wind and motion.
All pieces approximately
3 feet in height.

## chapter nine

*The Earth has music for those who listen.*
—William Shakespeare

# Profiles

Contained in this chapter is a sample selection representing thirteen of the many talented and creative artists encountered in the creation of this book. Although these artists come from different parts of the world, a variety of backgrounds, and use very different approaches when working with clay and building instruments, they all share a passion for the sound of clay and the ability to bring that sound to life through the ceramic musical instruments that they create. The following artists are profiled in this chapter:

Frank Giorgini
Ward Hartenstein
Brian Ransom
Robin Hodgkinson
Geert Jacobs
Ragnar Naess
Winnie Owens-Hart
Susan Rawcliffe
Richard and Sandi Schmidt
Aguinaldo da Silva
Sharon Rowell
Dag Sørensen
Stephen Wright

# FRANK GIORGINI

Frank Giorgini has formed a very special, perhaps symbiotic, relationship with an unassuming traditional African clay drum—the udu. Today udu drums can be seen and heard all over the world largely due to his work over the last 30 years.

Frank has a Master of Fine Arts degree in sculpture and ceramics as well as an industrial design degree. He teaches courses in architectural tile design and his book *Handmade Tiles* is considered an instructional bible for ceramic tile making. However, he is probably best known for his work with ceramic musical instruments.

In 1974 Frank first learned traditional Nigerian pottery techniques for forming clay side-hole pot drums from Abbas M. Ahuwan while studying at the Haystack Mountain School of Crafts in Deer Isle, Maine. Ahuwan, a Kaje potter, artist and professor at Ahmadu Bello University, Zaria, Nigeria, was an expert in the art of making musical side-hole pot drums and passed on his knowledge and passion for this traditional instrument to Frank and other students. According to Abbas, the ancient udu was not originally crafted as a drum, but as a water pot. When an ancient village potter put a second opening in the side of the water vessel and discovered the resonating sound it produced, the udu came to be.

Frank was captivated by the sound of this instrument and under Ahuwan's tutelage, he learned the traditional Nigerian pottery techniques used to create the all-clay drums. He learned to form the instruments by the ancient, time-tested methods: pounding, shaping, smoothing, drying and firing the soft, earthenware clay—approximately a month-long process for each drum. However, reproducing this basic Nigerian folk instrument was not enough for Frank. In the years following his cultural-exchange experience at Haystack, he studiously improved the process. He researched native Nigerian clays and adapted them to materials available in the U.S. Through experimentation, he developed a clay and firing temperature combination that yields a much stronger drum body without sacrificing the deep tonal qualities inherent in the very low-fired, open bodies of the African potters' drums. He perfected his construction techniques to achieve a consistent 0.8 cm thickness throughout the drum in order to maximize its resonance.

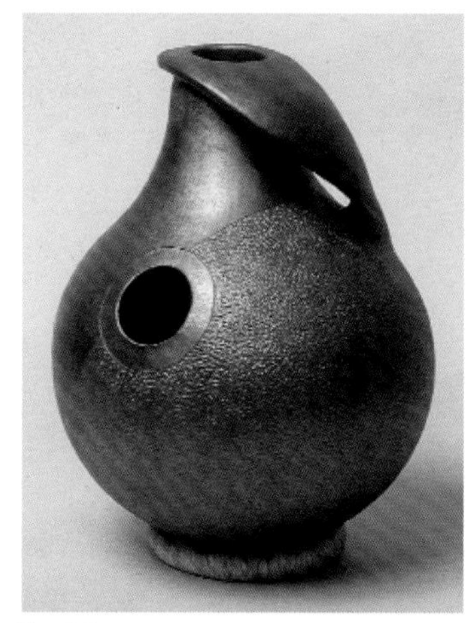

Fig. 9.2
One of Frank's many custom-built drums.

Over the years, he developed many variations on the instrument, approaching it first from a visual and sculptural direction, while considering the ergonomics of hand percussion. He explains, "The form followed the function and the sound followed the form." This experimentation resulted in about a dozen models of the udu drum as variations on the original concept. He also consulted and collaborated with percussionists, including Jamey Haddad. Together, Frank and Jamey designed a two-chambered udu, the *Hadgini,* and a system for attaching internal microphones to the drums.

Due to their popularity, the demand for Frank's drums greatly outpaced his ability to produce them by hand using his traditional, labor-intensive methods. This led him to develop a process of slip-casting using molds of his handmade drums. After several years of research and experimentation with clay body formulas, production methods and firing temperatures, he was satisfied with the results. In 1999 he licensed the production of his "Claytone" line of drums to Latin Percussion (L.P. Music Group). They are now produced in Thailand and distributed worldwide.

Through Frank's efforts promoting his udu drums, his instruments are in the collections of countless professional musicians around the world. As a result, the list of artists with whom Frank's drums appear on stage and in recordings reads like a "who's who" of pop, jazz and ethnic music. Udu drums made by Frank were entered into the permanent collection of the Metropolitan Museum of Art, New York, in 1985 and are also in private and corporate art collections. According to Frank, the popularity of his udu drums has even helped revitalize traditional clay drum production in Nigeria.

"There will always be a place in our world for ceramic musical instruments," he relates, "because they are of the earth—a personal pleasure to hear, touch and play. They are the other end of the spectrum from electronic computer MIDI music, but can blend and counterpoint it beautifully."

The best way to experience an udu drum, explains Frank, "is to sit down, hold the udu drum in your lap, caress it, and gently begin to strike it. You will start creating beautiful, haunting sounds from the slightest touch. Melt into it, go into a trance, feel your own heart beat—you are playing the udu drum."

Frank's instruments also can be seen elsewhere in this book and heard on the accompanying CD.

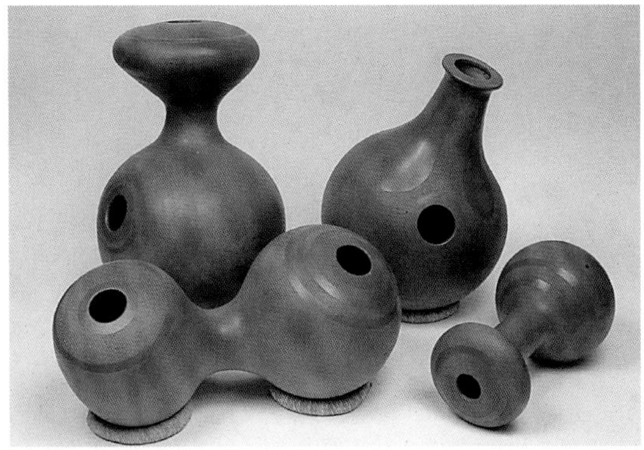

Fig. 9.4
**Claytone Series**
Slipcast production models called Udongo, Mbwata, Claytone 4, and Kim Kim. Hear these instruments on CD track 5.

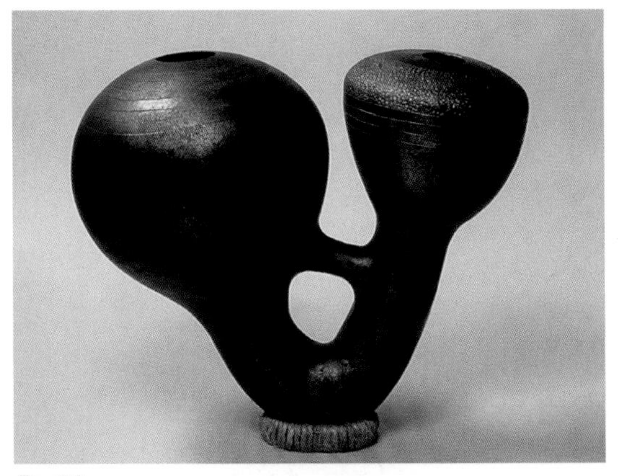

Fig. 9.3
**Hadgini**
A two-chambered drum designed by Frank in collaboration with percussionist Jamey Haddad. 16 inches in height.

# WARD HARTENSTEIN

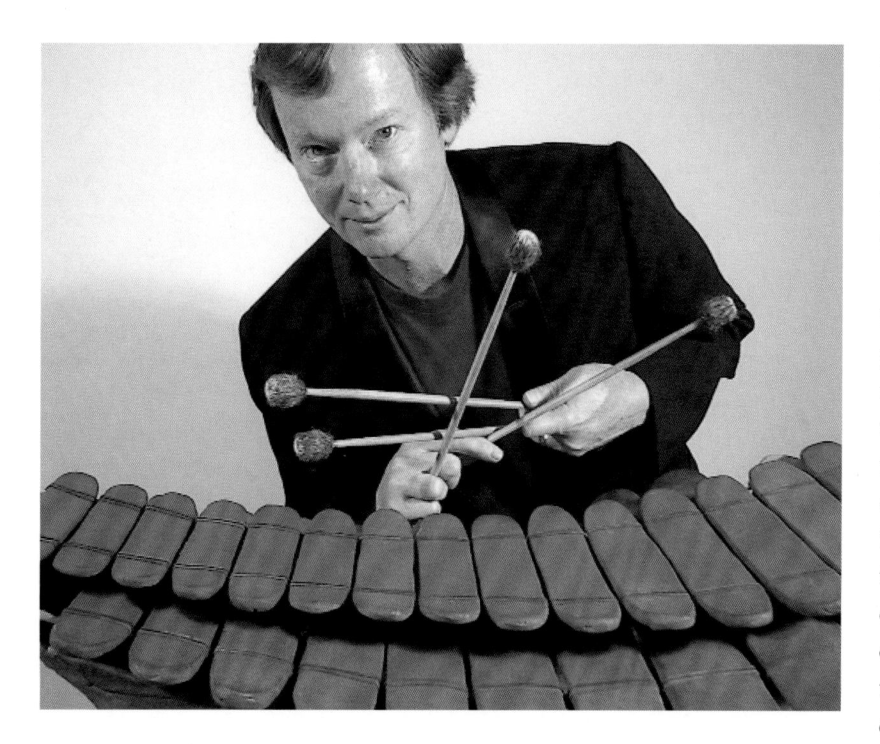

Most ceramics artists would not appreciate you hitting their work with a stick. Ward Hartenstein invites it, and his instruments absolutely beg for it. Ward specializes in ceramic idiophones—clay instruments designed to be hit. "Have you ever tapped a spoon on your cereal bowl while eating breakfast?" he asks. "If you have, then you know the sound that inspired me to experiment with ceramic idiophones."

"The idea of an instrument whose sound comes directly from the material from which it is made has a strong appeal for me. This type of instrument makes use of the physical properties of its basic material (rather than air columns, or added strings or membranes) to generate and sustain vibrations."

Ward grew up in a house with a piano and other instruments on which he enjoyed experimenting with sound-making. According to Ward, "The challenge of trying something new and unconventional has always been a good excuse for me to take action."

Working as a production potter for a number of years, he dabbled with a variety of musical instruments, starting with ocarinas, horns, flutes and drums. However, he really found his home with clay idiophones and now specializes in this category of clay percussion. "I found that clay has a balance of density, rigidity and elasticity that allows it to generate, transmit and sustain vibrations," he explains. "This combination of malleability and limited flexibility makes it well suited for idiophones."

Ward prefers to use a very dense (less than 1% absorption) stoneware, fired to cone 6 in an oxidation atmosphere. He uses glazes sparingly, usually only on the nonvibrating components of his instruments. He found, "The tensions between glaze and clay surface can negatively affect elasticity in vibrating structures."

Ward believes that although a clay instrument must function musically, it also can be an object of visual elegance and tactile sensation. His design approach incorporates the basic qualities of the material such as its natural color and texture, the construction techniques of wheel throwing and handbuilding, and the minimal use of ornamentation. He says, "I have enjoyed the challenges of incorporating fibers, animal skins, and wood and glass elements with clay, but I feel that my strongest works emphasize clay in its most basic form: simple, unglazed shapes with a direct purpose—to produce sound."

Once he designed and built new instruments, Ward asked himself, "What should I do with them?" He decided to learn how to play and compose music for his new creations, and now goes full circle as instrument designer, builder, composer and performer. Compositionally, Ward is inspired by composers such as Steve Reich, Terry Riley and Phillip Glass, and ethnic musical forms such as gamelan music. Ward performs annually with the Eastman Percussion Ensemble at the prestigious Eastman School of Music in Rochester, NY. The players in this ensemble delight in playing and composing pieces for Ward's unique ceramic instruments. He also composes music for film and dance projects, and his instruments are used by percussionists and studio musicians. One of his ceramic tongue drums was featured in the soundtrack to the film *The Player* by Robert Altman.

Ward incorporates serious study and experimentation in his pursuit of ceramic instruments. His education includes a bachelor of fine arts from Syracuse University and a master of fine arts in ceramics from Rochester Institute of Technology. While completing his master's thesis on the topic of ceramic idiophones, Ward had the privilege of working with a physics professor who helped him explore and understand the acoustical systems at work in his own instrument designs.

Today, Ward teaches children about art and music through arts-in-education programs. Instrument making is often an activity he explores in the class-

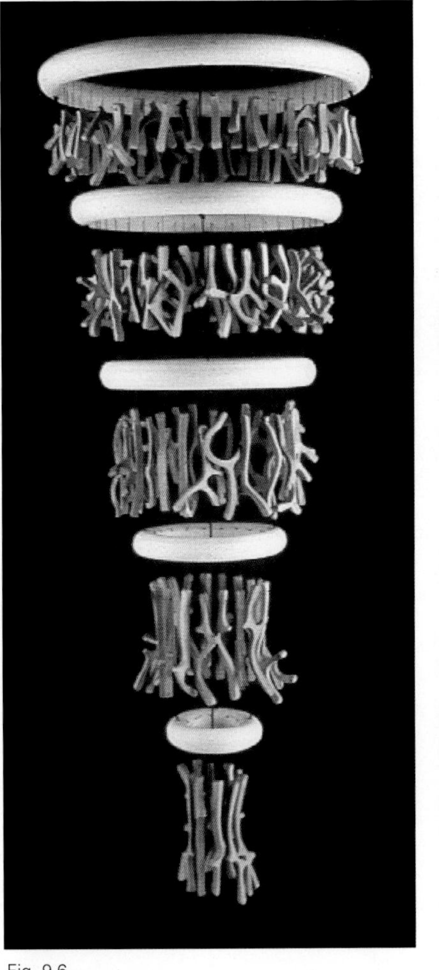

Fig. 9.6
**Kinetic Chime**
Over 120 individual clay chimes suspended from hollow tubular rings produce a rich wind chime sound when shaken or spun. 71 inches in height. Hear this instrument on CD track 16.

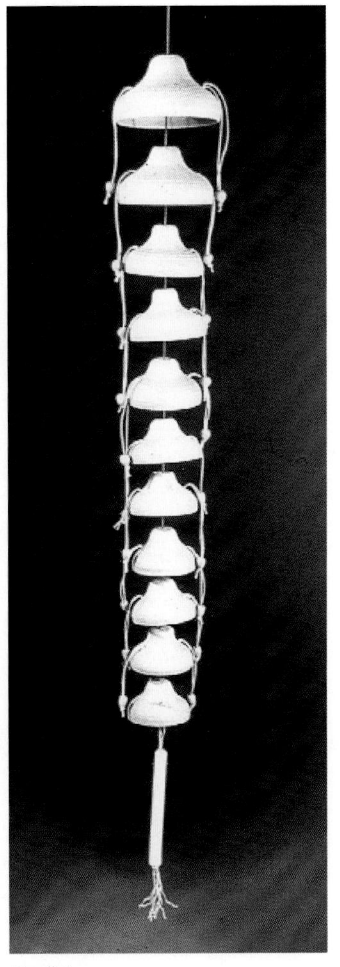

Fig. 9.7
**Shaker Chime**
A column of stoneware bells in graduated sizes strung on a cord with suspended clay beads that strike the bells when the handle is shaken. 48 inches in height.

room, and he has helped young students produce a variety of ceramic bells, drums and marimbas, "many of which," he remarks, "sound quite musical."

Ward finds enduring inspiration not necessarily in the science of producing ceramic idiophones, but rather in their sound, which he describes as both "earthy and delicate."

He says, "It can range from bright and clear-pitched, as in my clay marimba, to murky and mysterious, as in my petal drum. It has a moderate sustain and a crystalline quality that conveys a sense of excitement and intimacy. It is a sound that speaks of the ancient origins of the earth and the immediacy of the here and now."

Ward's instruments also can be seen elsewhere in this book and heard on the accompanying CD.

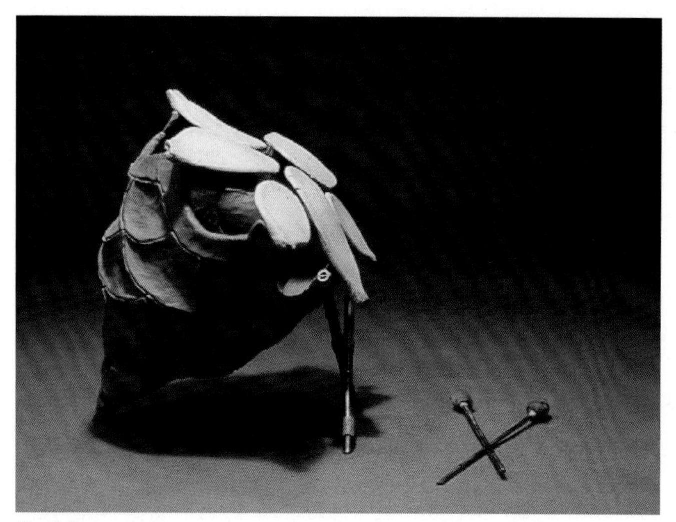

Fig. 9.8
**Rutabaga**
A petal drum hand-built from stoneware with bamboo and fiber support stand. 20 inches in height. Hear this instrument on CD track 3.

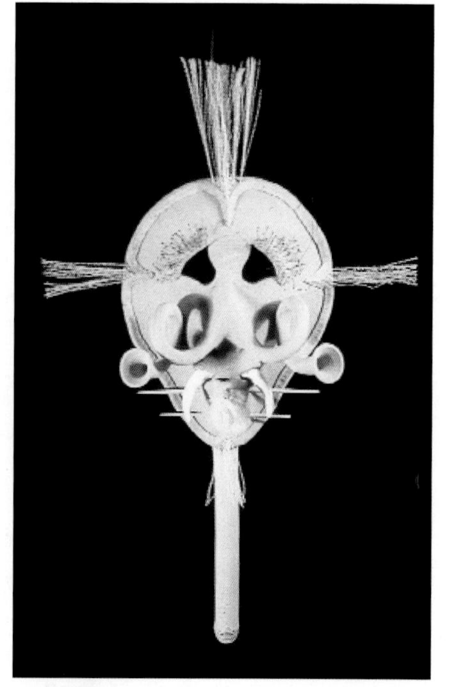

Fig. 9.9
**Musical Mask**
A construction of hand-built and wheel-thrown parts with straw and bamboo. This mask has a built in clay horn that can be played via a mouthpiece in the back.

# BRIAN RANSOM

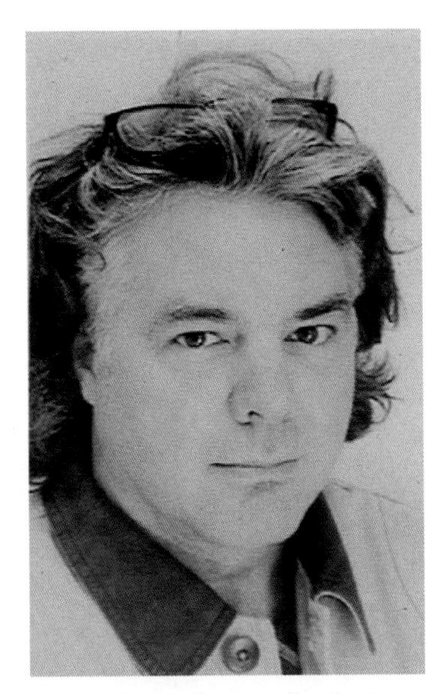

Brian Ransom is certainly one of today's most accomplished and prolific ceramic musical instrument builders. As you can see from the many examples of his work throughout this book, Brian has created a great variety of instruments, recognizable by their striking sculptural forms and luscious textures and finishes. He says, "Clay has provided me with a unique opportunity to combine two of the great passions of my life: making sculptures and creating music. Clay is malleable and easy to work with, and has a beautifully deep and rich timbre making it an ideal material for creating instruments."

In high school, Brian began making bamboo flutes with a friend. Later, when playing flugelhorn in a jazz quintet while attending the Rhode Island School of Design, he longed for tonalities and microtonalities that he could hear in his head, but could not play on his horn. Since he was attending a ceramics class at the time, he drew on his bamboo flute background and began making clay flutes. Brian says, "I was absolutely amazed by the intriguing sounds that my first ceramic flutes produced, and was overwhelmed by the musical possibilities that occurred to me. In the beginning, I sought the microtonal possibilities of clay instruments, but eventually it was the beautiful timbre of ceramic instruments that kept me focused on a lifelong goal to pursue endless possible permutations of their form."

And a lifelong pursuit it has been. Brian has attempted to make (and improve upon, through generations of remaking) every type of ceramic instrument he could imagine. These include flutes of every kind; single, double and multiple whistles; assorted reeds (chanters, clarinets and saxophones); horns (open-holed, straight, curved, recurved and valved); basses; harps; bells; chimes; marimbas; kalimbas; bullroarers (thrumming and whistling); drums (including congas, bongos,

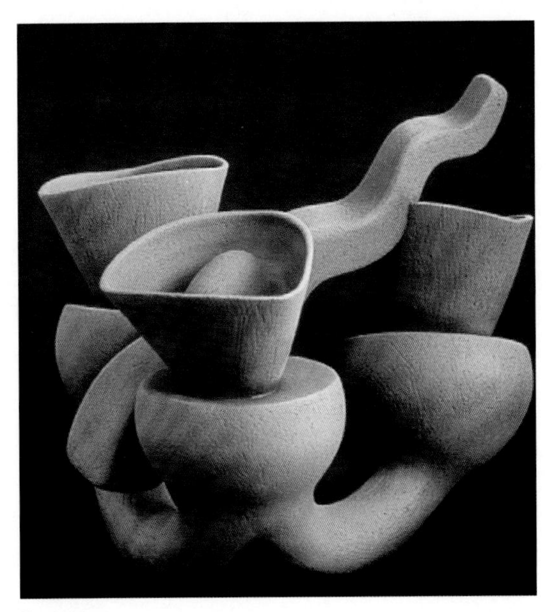

Fig. 9.11
**Triformation VI: Whistling Water Vessel**
Earthenware vessel that sounds when tipped. 8 inches in height.

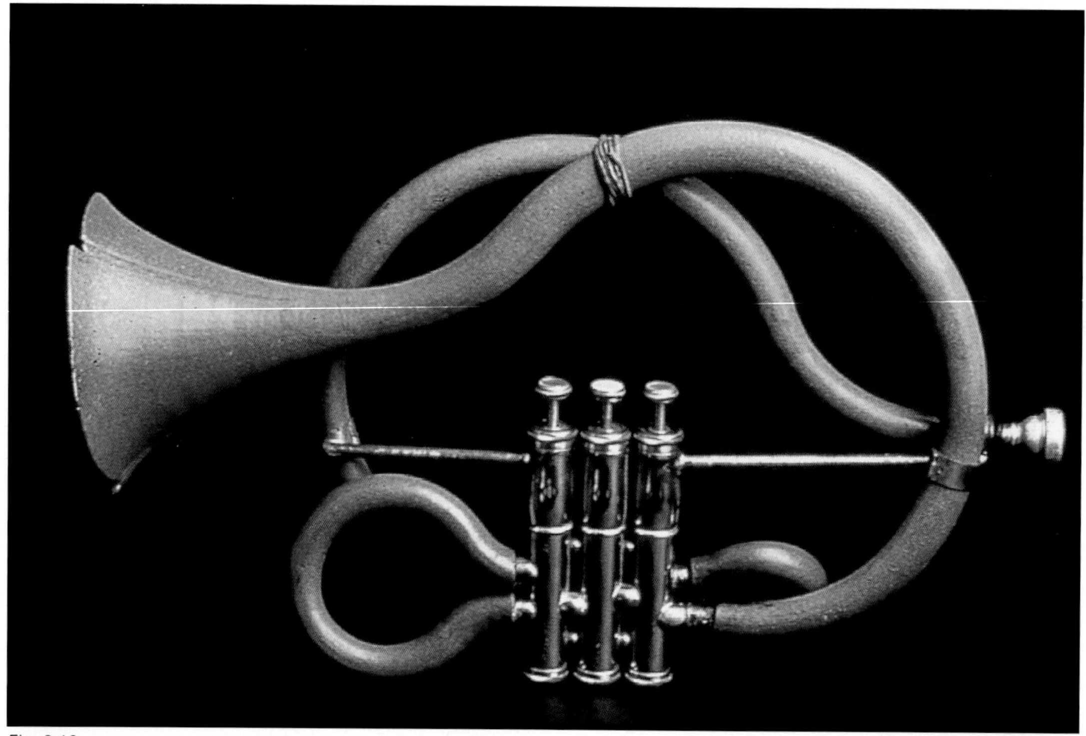

Fig. 9.12
**Flugelhorn**
Earthenware with trumpet parts. Building this instrument required precise calculations in order to create ceramic tubes that would tightly mate with the brass components, and also play in tune for all tones in the scale. 36 inches in length.

tablas, talking drums, doumbeks, djimbes, hoops, invented forms, sculptural and multichambered drums); a wide variety of other percussion instruments including guiros, shakers, rattles and temple blocks; fan-powered organs; electronically generated sound resonators; wind-, water- and flame-driven instruments; and sound sculptures.

Brian's approach to developing instruments starts with meditation or dwelling upon a sound or type of music he imagines in his mind. He then proceeds to create an instrument or group of instruments that might create those sounds. Many changes, compromises and momentary inspirations occur during the creation of new instruments. Often, his most successful instruments go through as many as twenty or thirty successive remakes before they sound right to him. "The sound of clay that I most enjoy in my instruments is hollow, haunting, and unbelievably full-bodied. I usually play one of my triple flutes or double pot flutes to demonstrate this amazing timbre of clay to audiences."

An extensive training in ceramics and art provides Brian with the technical expertise necessary to create his complex and sculpturally beautiful instruments. In the 1970s and 1980s, he obtained B.F.A., M.A. and M.F.A. degrees, as well as numerous research fellowships and honors. Of special interest is his Fullbright/Hays Congressional Fellowship for the study of pre-Columbian musical instruments in Peru and neighboring vicinities. Brian explains, "My approach to how and why I make instruments was significantly changed in many ways during the two years I spent in South America. My studies included hundreds of hours in museums and collections documenting ancient instruments as well as ethnographic field work in rural communities throughout Peru." This work led to Brian's authoring a research paper titled "The Enigma of Whistling Water Jars in Pre-Columbian Ceramics" (see "Resources").

As an associate professor of visual arts at Eckerd College, today, Brian is inspiring a new generation of artists and musicians. He advises his students to carefully examine fine examples of the type of instruments they would like to create, and not to give up too easily. "Remember that it may take multiple generations of improvements before you can create the sounds you are seeking. Many of my instruments that didn't work at first, after many attempts, I was able to cajole into sounding surprisingly good."

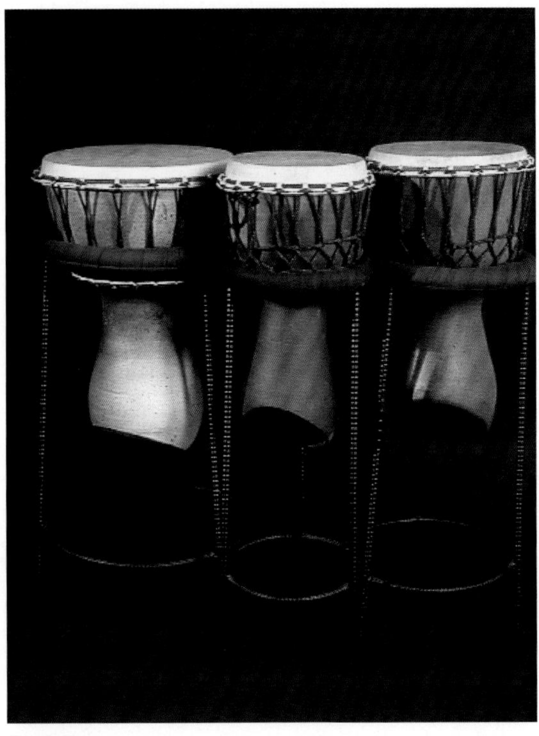

Fig. 9.13
**Djimbes**
Vapor-fired ceramic, goat skin, dacron cord, steel. 40 inches in height. Hear these instruments on CD track 2.

Brian's instruments have been shown in many exhibitions, and used by a multitude of professional musicians and groups, as well as his own ceramic ensemble. He is constantly working on new ideas, such as a set of clay instruments to outfit his jazz trio, which consists of flugelhorn, acoustic bass and electric hollow-bodied guitar.

He muses, "I imagine that future ceramic musical instruments will be as imaginative and spirited as those who create them. I certainly look forward to seeing and hearing the results of the next generation of inventors in our field!"

Brian's instruments also can be seen elsewhere in this book and heard on the accompanying CD.

# ROBIN HODGKINSON

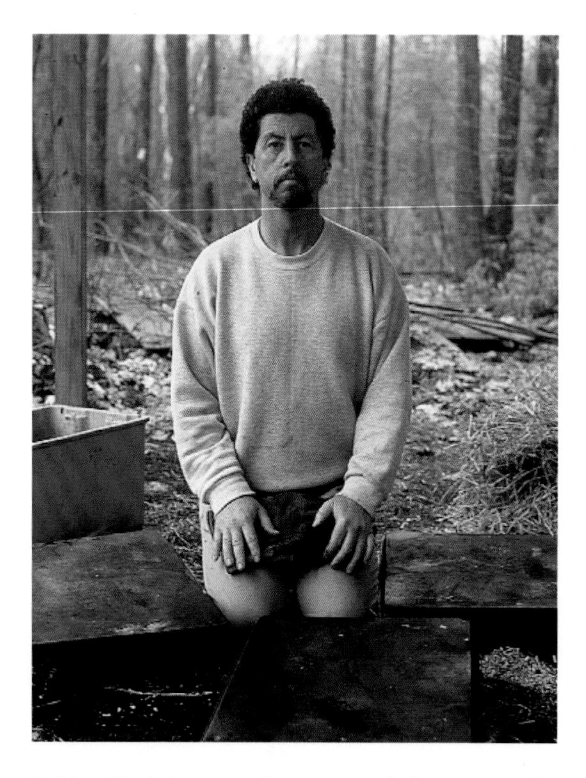

Robin Hodgkinson thrives on helping people express themselves.

As part of his formal academic study of anthropology, Robin lived in Central America, Africa, India, Indonesia and Malaysia. He says, "Everywhere I lived I was inspired by the creativity of human beings striving for self-expression in response to their natural and cultural surroundings."

While studying in Mexico, Robin came into contact with pre-Columbian flutes and whistles. He recalls, "The sound and expressive quality of these instruments amazed me." Years later, after making exotic hardwood flutes for several years, he decided to approach clay flute making, in order to capture the sound and expressive quality of the clay flutes he saw in Mexico.

In addition to capturing the sound of clay instruments, Robin also wanted to make them accurately tuned to "concert pitch." He describes this as his biggest self-imposed challenge.

Today, Robin specializes in concert pitch raku-fired earthenware transverse flutes. He also makes a series of different sized ocarinas, as well as sculptural multichambered vessel flutes.

"The density of clay contributes to its unique voice, and the unique shape of the instrument influences the sound. When properly tuned, clay produces a pure, sweet, soft, glassy sound—a sound unique to clay. Its malleability allows for maximum creative expression. Clay offers an almost limitless number of shapes to produce sound—limited only by the imagination of the artist."

Robin has worked with a variety of clays. He began making flutes from cone 6 stoneware using oxidation glazes, but later switched to white earthenware fired in the cone 06 to 04 range. His instrumental designs often incorporate symbols of unity, perfection, or transcendence. As for finishes, Robin says, "I alternate between raku-fired surfaces on some instruments, and multi-fired, layered oxidation slips, engobes and glazes on other instruments, depending on the final surface I want on the piece." He believes that raku is an especially appropriate finish for musical instruments, because the word raku means, creativity, spontaneity, contentment and intuition—all concepts related to the act of making music.

Robin's instruments are sought after by professional musicians, due to their precise tuning and exceptional sound. They can be heard on many recordings, played by notable classical, jazz and Celtic musicians. However, Robin says, "I'm the proudest when I can turn a child on to the joy of musical self-expression."

He recalls a young man in his twenties who came up to him at an exhibition and said, "My aunt bought me one of your ocarinas when I was six. It was my first musical instrument and I loved it. Now I'm studying at Julliard."

Another time, he worked with a mother to design a custom ocarina for her 11-year-old son who was born with only three fingers but desperately wanted to play an instrument. After receiving Robin's specially-designed ocarina, she wrote back to tell him how grateful she was that her son finally had an instrument he could play, and how much he enjoyed playing music. Robin relates humble gratification from having touched so many lives with his instruments.

Robin believes that the human act of making music may have begun as an effort to imitate the sacred sounds of the gods of nature. "I believe when someone is in the meditative state of mind that happens when playing music, that person is creating "sacred time and space—time outside of our routine day-to-day lives." He hopes that his "Spirit Vessels" help people evoke this sense. "As objects of contemplation, and as musical instruments, they are intended to be reminders of the need for balance and harmony in our lives."

Robin's instruments also can be seen elsewhere in this book and heard on the accompanying CD.

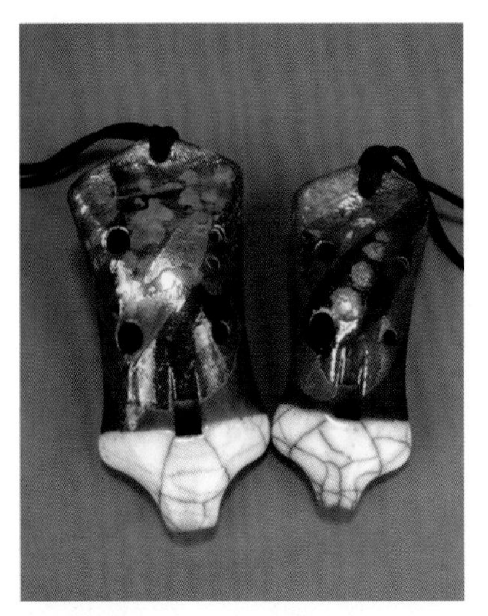

Fig. 9.15
**Soprano and Sopranino Ocarinas**
The smallest two members of Robin's family of precision-tuned ocarinas. 3.5" x 1.5" and 3" x 1".

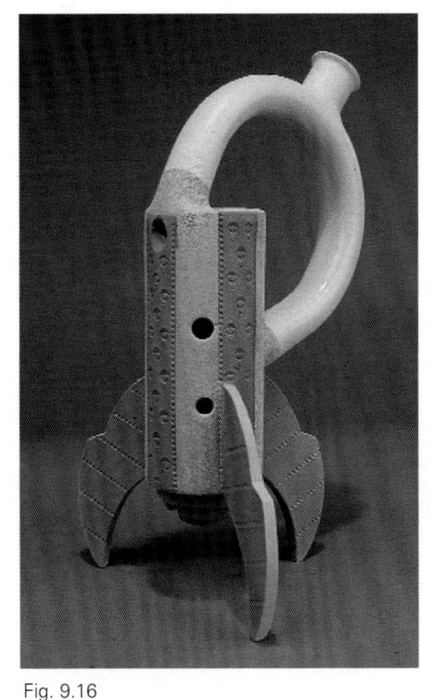

Fig. 9.16
**Stirrup Vessel Flute**
This vessel flute is tuned to play a scale of 15 chromatic intervals. It is made from white earthenware clay with slabbed, extruded and thrown components. The surface effect was achieved through multiple firings to cone 05. 14 inches in height.

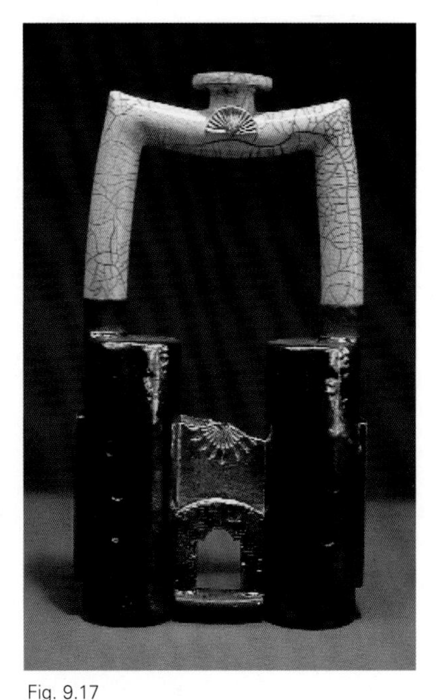

Fig. 9.17
**Temple Gate (2000)**
This double vessel flute is made from white earthenware clay with slabbed, extruded and thrown components. The surface effect was achieved through multiple oxidation glaze firings and a raku style firing to cone 07. The right chamber is tuned to play a chromatic octave, and the left plays the 1st, 3rd, 5th and 6th tones of the same scale. 12 inches in height.

# GEERT JACOBS

In 1959, Geert Jacobs opened a cozy pottery studio beside a picturesque canal in Utrecht, Netherlands, where he made and sold his ceramic wares. An amateur musician, Geert recalls, "At that time I couldn't afford to buy a flute, poor craftsman that I was, so I experimented with a 'flower ring' shape I was making on the wheel, by closing the top to make a round tube from clay. With this hollow tube I began to experiment, bending it into a straight pipe, and poking a mouth hole and finger holes until my first ceramic flute was born."

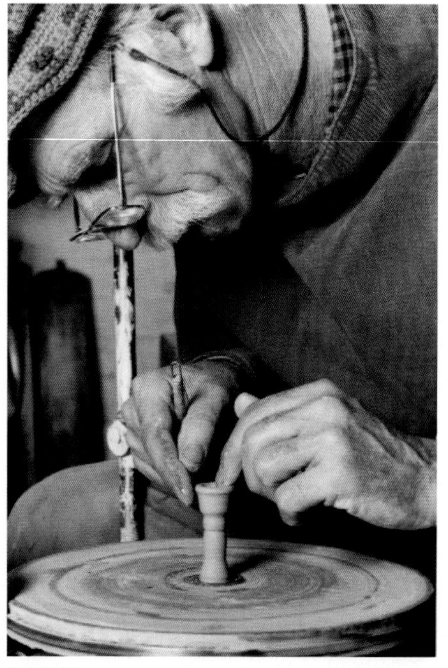

Fig. 9.18
Making a horn mouthpiece

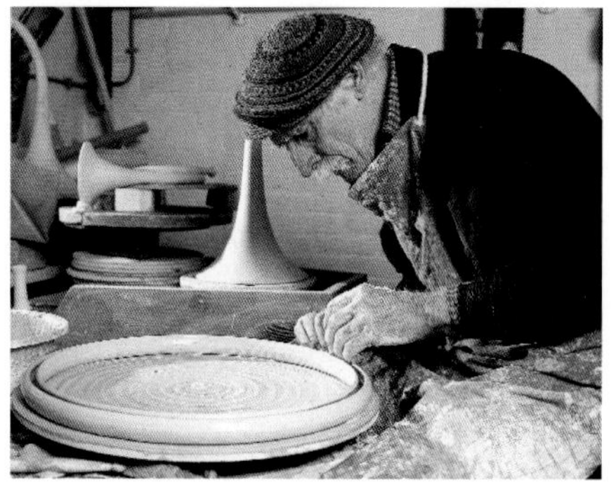

Fig. 9.19
Wheel-forming tubing for a horn

Nowadays he extrudes the tubing for his flutes in order to have more control of measurements and wall thickness during the drying and firing process. Geert advises, "In making a flute, it is also possible to form a slab of clay around a stick with some newspaper to keep it from sticking, and produce a very fine flute."

Since he created his first flutes, Geert has refined his craft to a point at which his instruments are held in the collections of a number of museums in the Netherlands and abroad. They are also in the private collections of celebrities such as Pete Seeger, David Carradine, George Lucas, Michael Jackson, and Ravi Shankar. Geert's historically accurate horns and flutes have performed Mozart in Amsterdam's top concert hall and on Dutch and German television. His flutes are also used by prominent Irish musicians in concert and in recordings.

Geert draws his inspiration from instruments of the medieval, renaissance and baroque period, as well as folk instruments. Examples of his clay creations include flutes, recorders, ocarinas, horns, zink and serpent (from the cornetto family), clarinet, oboe, rankett (an early reed instrument), violins and rebecs, drums, bells, and a complete ceramic barrel organ.

His progression from flutes to making other instruments was gradual, driven by curiosity, experimentation and a creative fascination with the possibilities presented by clay. After his initial flute experiments, Geert began to make wheel-thrown tubing for French horns incorporating thrown conical pieces that were "wrestled together" with the tubing after a short drying period. Some of the photos in this section illustrate his process. Geert remarks, "The biggest challenge for me with ceramic instruments is to make the timbre or tone sound good. I like to hear the right pitch and a warm sound out of the finished product."

In the 1960s, when Geert developed many of his instruments, clay instruments were rarely seen—except a few in museums. He spent those years in California, where he says his instruments sold very well during the "Hippie time." Returning to the Netherlands in 1972, he set up his pottery in a windmill and former flowerpot factory, where he continues to live and work today. He and his wife have made more than 10,000 flutes together.

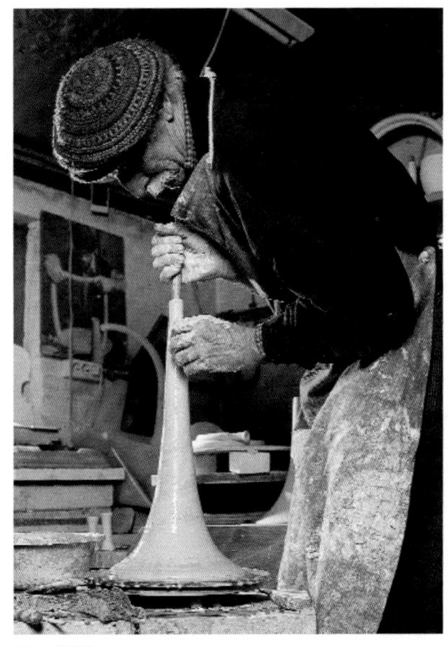
Fig. 9.20
Making a horn's bell

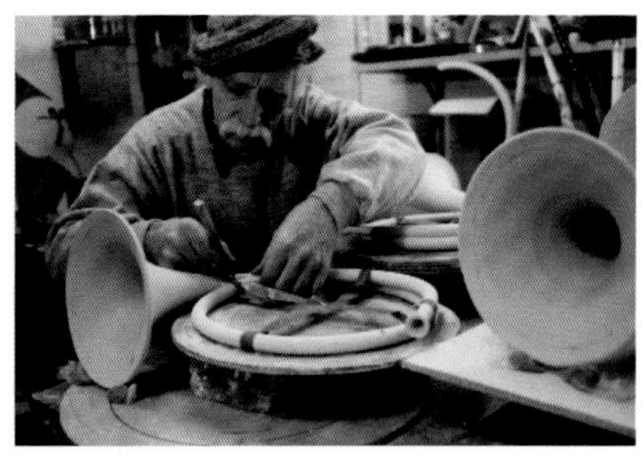
Fig. 9.21
Assembling horn parts

Geert also draws inspiration from Irish music and instruments. "My flutes and recorders are, for me, the most satisfying in sound," he says. "I like a timbre somewhere between wood and metal, but very characteristic and often with great volume. When I made violins, which I called 'stonevarius' (after Stradivarius) I was never totally satisfied that I was getting a beautiful sound out of the ceramic body. Nevertheless, I enjoyed decorating the instruments!"

Most of Geert's instruments are decorated in a style he calls "Milsbeek Bont" using hand-painted motifs he developed on his functional ware around 1946. He uses a white porcelain clay from Westerwald, Germany, that he mixes with kaolin and talc without grog. His pieces are bisque fired, then dipped in white glaze and painted with overglaze colors before their second firing.

Perhaps his most elaborate creation is the ceramic barrel organ, which he calls the "Jacob's Ladder." This massive, yet portable, mechanical organ makes its music through a vast array of hand-made porcelain pipes. A hand crank operates a bellows, which produces air that powers the pipes. A series of holes carefully cut in cardboard sheets control the production of each note by directing the air to specific pipes for specific durations. If you've seen the paper rolls used by a player piano you will appreciate the complexity of Geert's hand-cut cardboard "scores" for his barrel organ. The Jacob's Ladder can be heard at festivals and fairs throughout the Netherlands, and on track 32 of the accompanying CD.

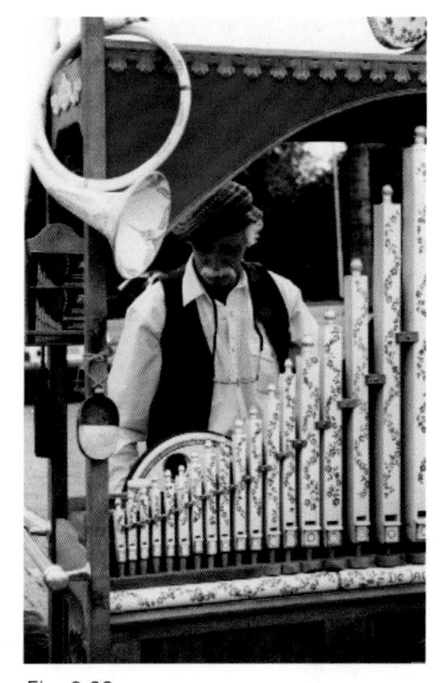
Fig. 9.22
Geert playing the ceramic barrel organ, which can be heard on CD track 32.

Geert's instruments also can be seen elsewhere in this book and heard on the accompanying CD.

# RAGNAR NAESS

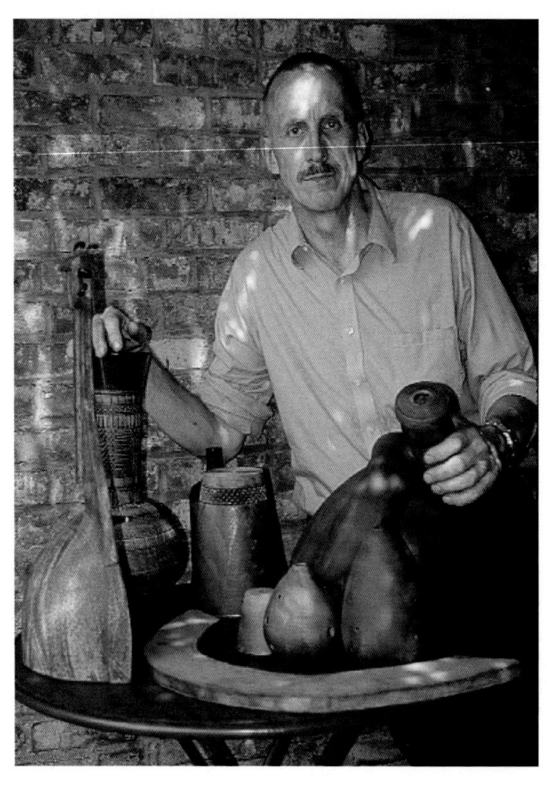

Fifteen years ago, Ragnar Naess was an accomplished ceramic artist working in New York City. He had spent 20 years making teapots, casserole dishes and other functional objects. His work was in the Smithsonian Institution and other museums and galleries worldwide. Then one day, a visit from composer Tan Dun launched Ragnar on a new, musical, path—a quest for a ceramic orchestra.

The celebrated Chinese composer Tan Dun visited Ragnar's Brooklyn workshop looking for ways to introduce the sound of the earth into his musical compositions. This began an artistic collaboration that resulted in the creation of an orchestra of clay instruments called "EarthSounds."

Seven months after their initial meeting, the new composition *Soundshape for Ceramics, Voice and Instruments* premiered at the Guggenheim Museum, using more than 70 clay sound forms that were struck, plucked, bowed and blown by an ensemble of accomplished musicians. *A New York Times* reviewer said that the work "evoked the feeling of a mysterious ceremonial rite," and contained "primeval timbres: the sounds of the wind, of wooden flutes and whining stringed instruments, of a straightforwardly aggressive thwacking of pottery drums." (The flutes were actually made from clay, as were all of the instruments.)

Ragnar has a history degree from Stanford University and studied ceramics with renowned Bauhaus potter Marguerite Wildenhain. He also played flute and piano through his university years. However, the creation of clay instruments presented a new set of musical and technical challenges and questions. Ragnar explains, "The goal of the EarthSounds project was to discover and explore the sounds peculiar to fired clay. In pursuing this goal, we addressed a variety of questions, such as: What is unique to the sound of clay? How can we get sound from clay? How resonant can this particular clay be and how can we get more resonance? Is it the clay's resonance itself we are seeking in a given sound, or is it the sound of compressed air resonating when trapped in a clay vessel being struck? Can we amplify the sounds of other materials using a clay reservoir or a clay sounding board? Do some forms amplify their resonance better than others? How does the shape of a struck object impact its sound? How thick should walls be? What effect has glaze on the sound of clay objects? How can we make a long tube that will be blown and give a dark, deep sound but survive performances and rehearsals without being broken? Can we put a fragile hollow clay body on a long solid clay neck and

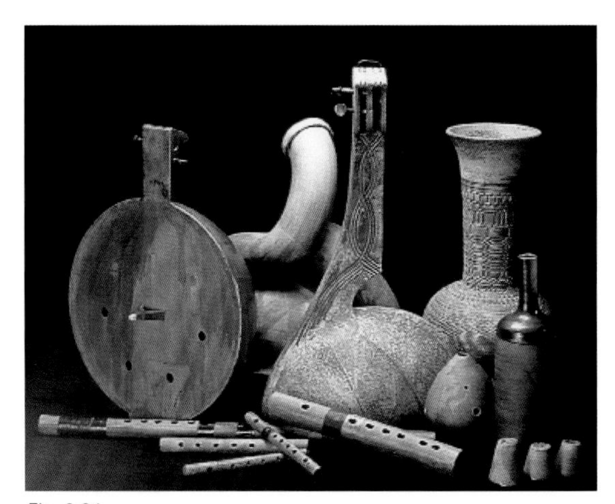

Fig. 9.24
A collection of EarthSounds instruments.

put it under the tension of strings as in more traditional stringed instruments?"

As you can imagine, their process became an exhilarating exploration of many different aspects of ceramic instrument building—both technical and musical. At the time, Ragnar said, "The sound forms we make are not intended as solo musical instruments. Each object works as part of a larger system of sound-making objects and their use in performance feeds back into the process in the pottery shop where they are made."

Ragnar made all his instruments using his studio clay formula—a challenge for which he felt his stoneware formula was well-suited due to its bright, porcelain-like tone. (Read more about Ragnar's clay formula and its acoustical properties in Chapter 7).

The musical development process with Tan Dun involved much experimentation. Since many of the instruments were designed to be struck (idiophones), the artists tried forms of many different sizes and shapes, as well as different materials with which to strike the objects. Many of the forms—bells, gongs and crescents—were eventually used in multiples organized in gamelan-like systems. In fact, even the stringed instruments were hung from scaffolding and sometimes struck with mallets in performance. Certainly the performers, as well as the inventors, took great pleasure working with these new instruments. It is clear that Ragnar and Tan also enjoyed naming their musical inventions, creating names like *pluckers, bowers* and *cow guts.*

Tan Dun went on to compose several works for the EarthSounds instruments. His ensemble toured the US, Europe and Asia, performing these pieces using Ragnar's instruments. An excerpt from one of these performances can be heard on the accompanying CD.

Ragnar's instruments also can be seen elsewhere in this book and heard on the accompanying CD.

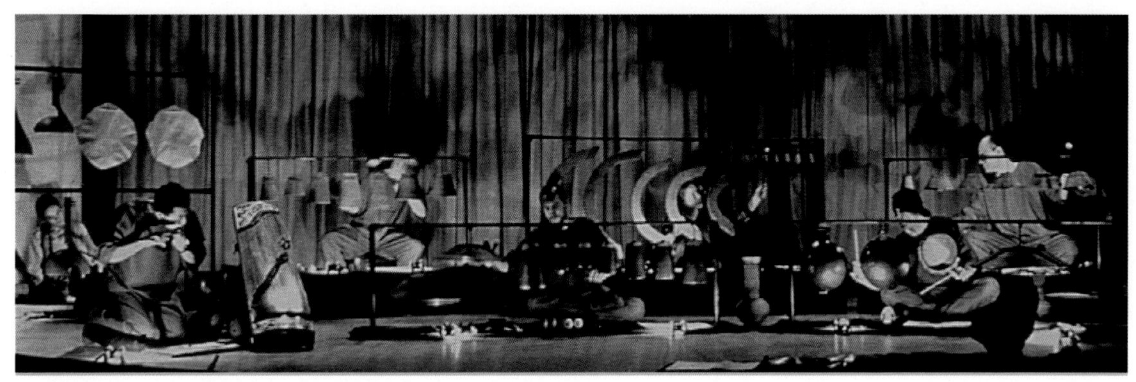

Fig. 9.25
The EarthSounds ensemble in performance, which can be heard on track 21 of the CD.

# WINNIE OWENS-HART

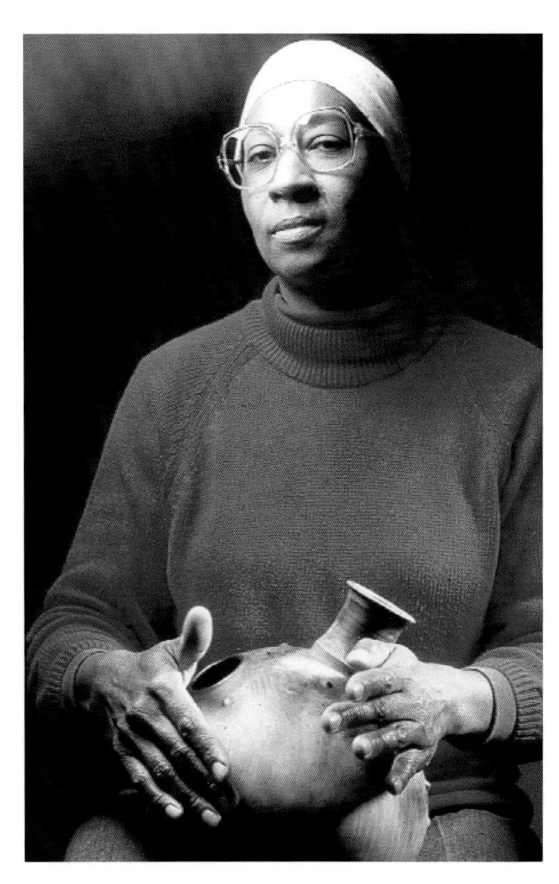

Winnie Owens-Hart believes that "all things in art evolve culturally, and help to define our existence." Certainly, her many years of work and research in African pottery and drums has influenced that belief.

In the late 1960s, Winnie taught ceramics at the celebrated Ile Ife Black Humanitarian Center in Philadelphia. "I was fascinated by the drum music, and had always wanted to learn to play an instrument," recalls Winnie, "so I enrolled in a traditional drumming class." Being an undergraduate student at the time, she couldn't afford to purchase a traditional wooden drum. "Believing in the boundless quality of clay," she remembers, "I knew I could make my drum out of clay."

Thus began a project which has continued to this day. Winnie began by making ceramic drums on the wheel. Her drumming instructor assisted her with design issues and taught her how to prepare and stretch the hides. Winnie relates, "my drums went through a maze of transitions before I began to perfect their pitch. Soon I was able to make tuned drums that were based on traditional African approaches. Eventually, I went on to graduate school and this became my master's thesis."

Following her graduate work, Winnie encountered Abbas Ahuwan, a Nigerian master potter, at the Haystack Mountain School of Crafts in Deer Isle, Maine. Abbas introduced her to the traditional Nigerian methods of building skinless clay pot drums. This experience heightened Winnie's curiosity and interest in traditional African ceramics, and led to her first of three visits to the traditional Nigerian pottery village of Ipetumodu, where she apprenticed with female potters (pottery making in this village is limited to women only) to learn and practice indigenous Yoruba handbuilding techniques. As a result of spending several years studying with the Ipetumodu potters, Winnie is now considered an authority on the Nigerian pottery building techniques of this village.

Today Winnie is a professor of art at Howard University in Washington, D.C. For three decades she has exhibited her works nationally and internationally, lectured and taught at countless venues, and published articles on African and African-American ceramics. Winnie has been honored with many awards and grants, including a National Endowment for the Arts grant, multiple Smithsonian Institution

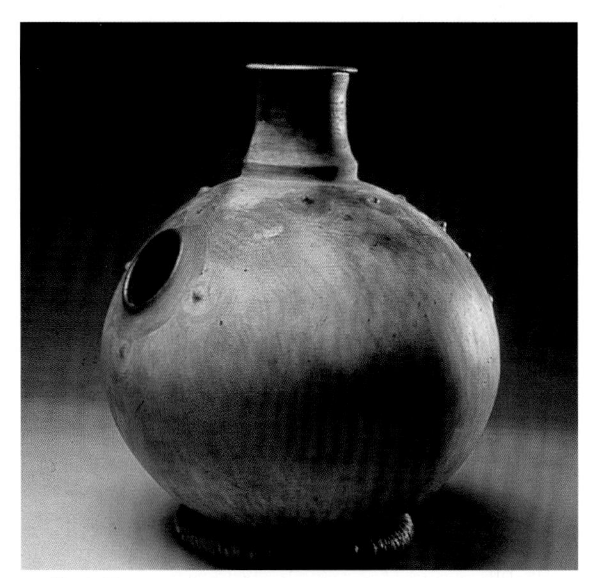

Fig. 9.27
Nigerian-style water drum.

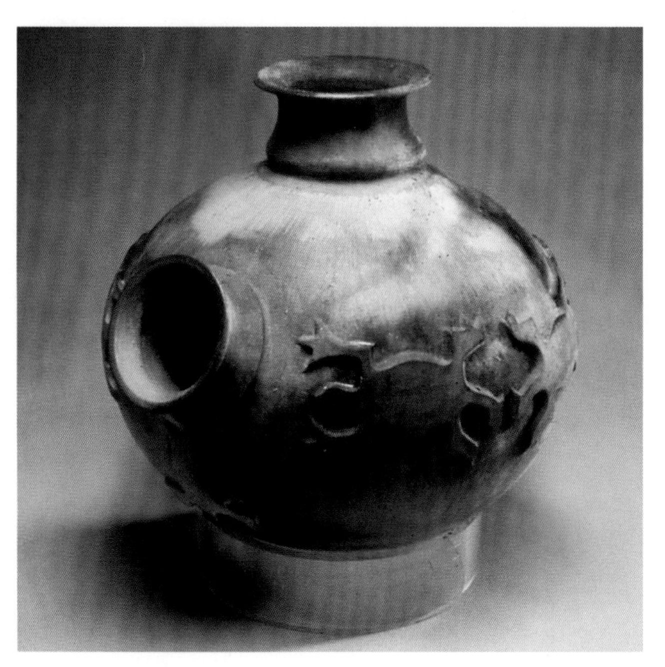

Fig. 9.28
Ceramic drum with reptile motif. 10 inches in diameter.

fellowships and a Lifetime Achievement in the Craft Arts award from the Women's Museum in Washington, D.C.

Winnie also studied the pottery traditions of other cultures, including Pueblo techniques with the renowned San Ildefonso potter Blue Corn. Winnie says, "If you look at the ancient pots, the shapes—African, Oceanic—are all the same. The form is so powerful that that's what attracts people to the work."

Over the past 35 years, Winnie has taught many people to make clay drums. Just as she was drawn to her Nigerian mentors, students are drawn to Winnie, to learn the traditional techniques she passes on and to experience the sound, the feel and the form of clay drums. She advises her students to seek out master artists and musicians to learn from, and to "always strive to understand, through all of your senses, how the culture and the instrument work as one."

Winnie says that she draws her inspiration first from the function of the instrument, "and then from my inner core that houses all of my experiences, my ancestral memories and my future hopes."

# SUSAN RAWCLIFFE

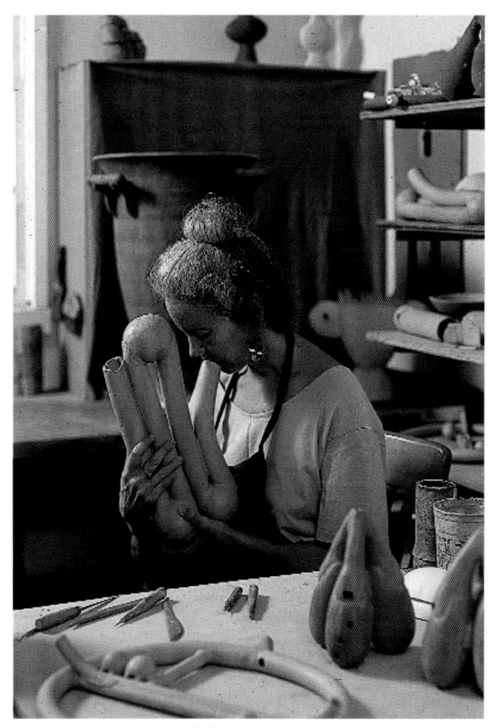

Susan in her studio building a clay-doo and other instruments.

Susan Rawcliffe has been deeply inspired by many ceramic artists and musicians, but she's never met them, and can't even tell you their names.

The problem is that they lived hundreds, or even thousands, of years ago, and little is left to explain their work other than the remarkable instruments they created. Over the past thirty years, Susan has spent countless hours in museums in Latin America and around the world, combing through documents and collections of dusty artifacts to rediscover the construction and musical capabilities of ancient ceramic musical instruments. As a result of her passion, she has accomplished nothing short of rescuing from obscurity entire classes of instruments, and bringing back to life the craft of pre-Hispanic clay instrument builders.

One aspect of ancient instruments that fascinates Susan is the mystery of their tuning, playing and usage. She writes that most of these instruments "were created for specific ceremonies; their sound quality, playing methods and iconographic content carry the faded scent of ancient rituals."

Based on her research and experimentation, Susan builds ceramic flutes; single, double and triple pipes and ocarinas; whistles; hooded pipes; howlers; space whistles; whiffles; trumpets; clay-doos; musical bowls; sound sculptures; and other exotic clay wind instruments.

What is a "howler" or a "whiffle"? Many of the instruments in which Susan specializes are unique enough to warrant their own class or family. However, any historical names or taxonomies for these instruments are long lost to obscurity. As a result, over the years Susan has developed her own terminology to describe and categorize what she calls "the amazingly diverse world of ceramic pre-Hispanic flutes."

Susan has authored a number of scholarly and popular papers and articles on pre-Hispanic wind instruments. But what sets her research and writing apart from other academic discourses on ancient works of art is the way she brings these archaic and obscure instruments into today's world. Her analysis goes well beyond documenting their dimensions and finishes; she engages in a circular process of constructing copies of ancient specimens, learning to play them, and then reinvesting what she's learned into creating new instruments. Through extensive trial and error she's begun to understand the processes that early artisans underwent to develop instruments in their own time. By no means merely copying historical instruments, Susan uses their inspiring designs as a springboard for her own unique creations. She says, "For me, pre-Hispanic flutes represent a living tradition, having influenced my perceptions and abilities as a musician and instrument builder."

As a result, Susan has developed a deep appreciation for the skill and ingenuity of pre-Hispanic ceramic artists. "Through my own work, I hope to catch a glimpse of and honor the spirit of discovery that guided the makers and players of these remarkable instruments."

Certainly those ancient makers would be honored by Susan's tireless devotion to their craft. Today, she travels around the world, performing and teaching. She has been honored with numerous grants for her research, composing and performing, and has even performed on and off Broadway.

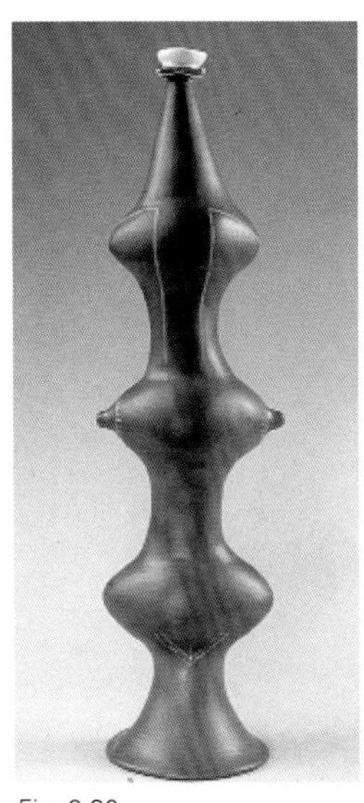

Fig. 9.30
**PolyGlobular Trumpet**
Press molded, slab & coil work; dark brown & white terra sigillata; glazed & lustered mouthpiece.
22 inches in height.

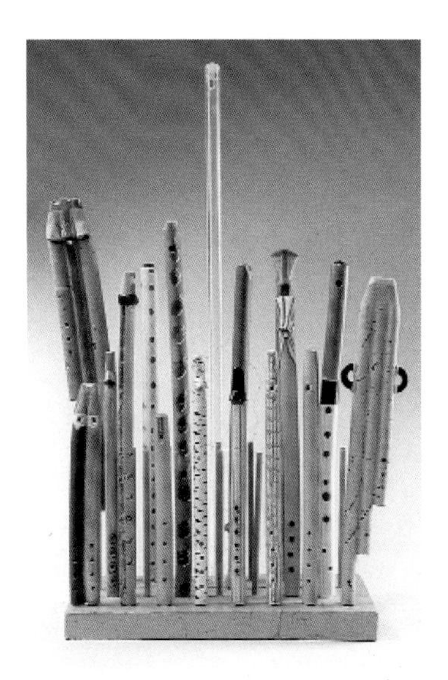

Fig. 9.31
**Rack of Flutes**
Single, double and triple pipes. Extruded & constructed red or talc body clay with a variety of colored engobes and glazes, cone 02-03, gas or electric. (a nylon flute is in the center). A triple pipe can be heard on CD track 13.

Susan thinks of herself as working both visually and aurally to draw upon two traditions: ceramics and flute making. She believes that clay is a good medium for her instruments because its plasticity permits complex forms. "Clay is available, relatively inexpensive and very malleable. As an instrument builder, I find that with clay, it is easy to experiment, to make endless variations. If something doesn't work, I can throw it away, having hopefully learned something."

However, she explains, clay's lack of precision also influences her approach. After years of working with clay, she has come to accept its inherent challenges and frustrations as "part of the terrain." She says, "The ceramic process is a dance between control and chance."

For building instruments, Susan prefers low-fire clay (her current favorite is a white talc body) which she fires to cone 03. She has developed her own underglazes, engobes and glazes, augmented by some prepared glazes. Typically she combines clay surfaces—white or colored—with glazes.

As you can tell from the photos of her instruments throughout this book, and her performances on the CD, Susan has defined a unique space for herself in the spectrum of today's ceramic musical artists. Certainly future musicians and artists will draw immense inspiration from her ingenuity and artistry, just as she has been inspired by her long-forgotten predecessors.

Susan's instruments also can be seen elsewhere in this book and heard on the accompanying CD.

# RICHARD & SANDI SCHMIDT

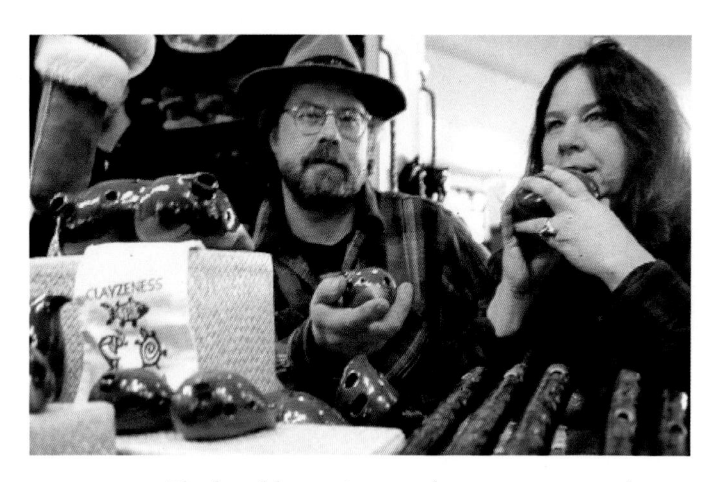

The humble ocarina may have no greater ambassadors on this earth than Richard and Sandi Schmidt. As anyone who has encountered their booth at Seattle's Pike Place Market knows, this couple has a passion for ocarinas that's overwhelmingly contagious.

Perhaps it's only natural that their lives would be immersed in making instruments from clay. After all, Sandi's birthday is on Earth Day (April 22). When people ask what inspired them, she replies, "Well, God knew we couldn't type or dance, so we had to do something..."

That's quite a modest reply from a couple who estimates that over the past 25 years they have made 150,000 ocarinas, which are now spread across the globe and in the collections of professional musicians such as Dave Valentin, Howard Levy and Nancy Stewart (author of the song "My Ocarina"). As a great testimony to the instrument's portability and musicality, Cathal McConnell, Irish musician in the band "Boys of the Lough," says he always has one of Richard and Sandi's ocarinas in his pocket.

In partnership, the couple makes vessel flutes (ocarinas and whistles) and transverse flutes, and dabbles in other instruments such as drums, rattles and wind chimes. You'll most likely find them working at their day table at the Pike Place Market, where they've met scores of people over the last 20 years and introduced many of them to the magic of the ocarina.

However, their evangelizing efforts don't stop there. In the 1980s, Richard and Sandi organized "Ceramic Sounds" and "From Mud to Music." These events involved a cast of ceramic instrument builders in gallery exhibitions, demonstrations and performances (and also became the inspiration for this book's title.) They've also embraced the internet as a way to share information with players and makers of ocarinas. They have an extensive website (www.clayz.com) and founded the online discussion group, the Ocarina Club, which today has several hundred members who share ocarina ideas, techniques and encouragement. (Instructions for joining the Ocarina Club are in the "Resources and Materials" section.)

Sandi and Richard use stoneware slip to cast most of their vessel instruments, and their tubular flutes are extruded porcelain. Most of their ocarina glazes are commercial, but they say their flute glaze, "has so many secret ingredients, it's probably illegal!"

By no means merely technicians, they are absorbed in the mystery and magic of the instruments they create. "We use lots of storytelling with our images, surface treatment, and glaze. Also, in demonstrating our work we use the spoken word. Storytelling is sometimes as important as the music."

Richard notes, "An ocarina captures the essence of the sound of clay. It is an ancient sound, something primal."

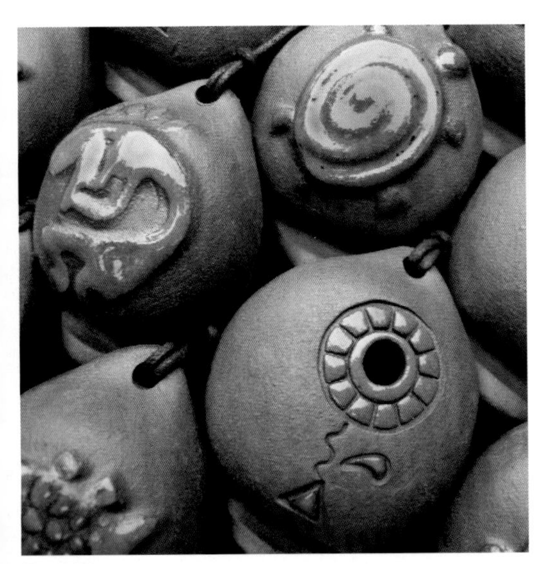

Fig. 9.33
Pendant ocarinas with four or five finger holes and a pitch range of over an octave. 1.5 inches in diameter.

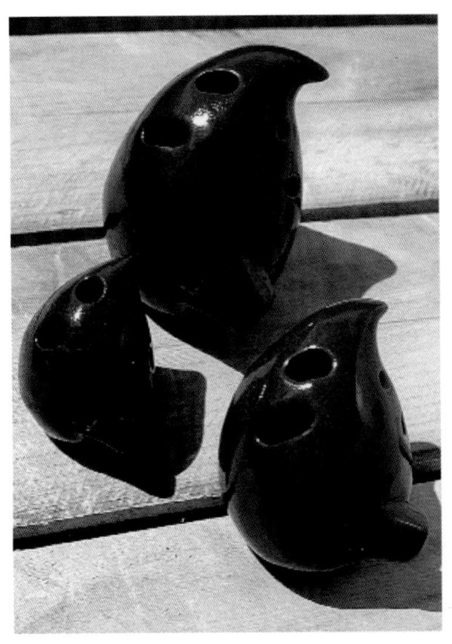

Fig. 9.34
Slip cast ocarinas, stoneware Cone 5, opaque cobalt glaze, 3 to 5 inches in height.

Ocarinas seem to hold a special fascination for children. Through the Washington State Arts Commission's Arts in Education programs, Sandi and Richard have worked with thousands of schoolchildren, exposing them to clay and the magic of the ocarina. Busloads of school children also visit Sandi and Richard to be entertained and amazed as part of the Pike Place Market's award winning Market School Project. One of their biggest thrills was in 1992, when as part of a United Nations environmental conference, 300 homeless children from the streets of Rio de Janeiro practiced for weeks and marched into the opening ceremonies, each playing one of Richard and Sandi's turtle ocarinas.

With so much energy and passion invested in their mission, it's not surprising that Sandi and

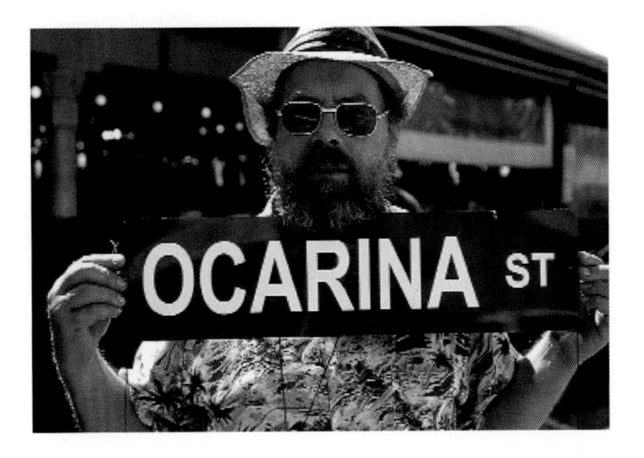


Richard get a special thrill when their customers send letters of appreciation. One woman wrote, after purchasing one of their tiny ocarinas, "Thank you so much for letting the music that was in me, out!" Richard says, "We could relate, because that's what making and playing the ocarina has done for us."

Richard and Sandi's instruments also can be seen elsewhere in this book.

# AGUINALDO DA SILVA

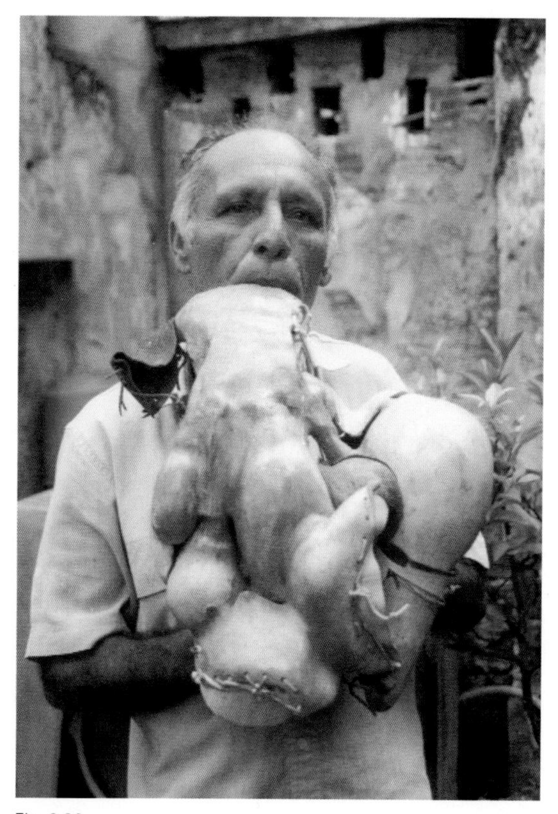

Fig. 9.36
Aguinaldo da Silva with his massive seven-chambered ocarina.

Aguinaldo da Silva is known as "Master Nado" or simply "Nado" to his friends and students. And a master of clay instruments he is. Nado has always made his living giving shape to clay. As a child, he learned to make little pots and bulls with leftover clay from the pottery next to his home in the Pernambuco region of Brazil. He became a professional potter when he was still very young, moving from utilitarian ceramics to sculptures of unique beauty.

However, giving shape to clay was not enough for Nado. His curiosity and imagination led him to discover the sounds of clay, and he began making musical instruments inspired by the organic shapes and forms of nature—birds, fishes, plants and roots.

As you can see from the photos of his work, his ceramic instruments are strikingly original. Perhaps the most arresting examples are his gargantuan multiple-chambered ocarinas (figures 4.54 and 4.55) with organic yet otherworldly forms enhanced by leather and rawhide accents.

The complexity of Nado's instruments belies the simple and earnest discovery process that brought him to this point. It started one day when Nado inadvertently created a whistling sound while working with a small hollow ball of clay. This gave him the idea to create a clay whistle similar to the palm leaf whistles that his grandfather taught him to make as a child, and became the genesis of his inspiration to make musical instruments from clay. At that time he had never seen nor heard of an ocarina and he was fascinated with this newly discovered use for clay. It was years later that he eventually learned about the historical origins of clay whistles and ocarinas.

Since then Nado has explored the musical capabilities of clay in many directions. Other instruments in his repertoire were similarly discovered, such as the side-hole clay pot drum that he calls "bum d'agua" or "water boom" (figure 4.135). He has also modeled clay versions of traditional Brazilian instruments such as the berimbau, reco-reco and maracas (figures 2.2, 2.26 and 5.1).

However, in much of his work, Nado has taken existing instruments in creative and original new directions. His clay pot drums have expanded to multichambered versions, with as many as seven connected resonating chambers. Likewise, his

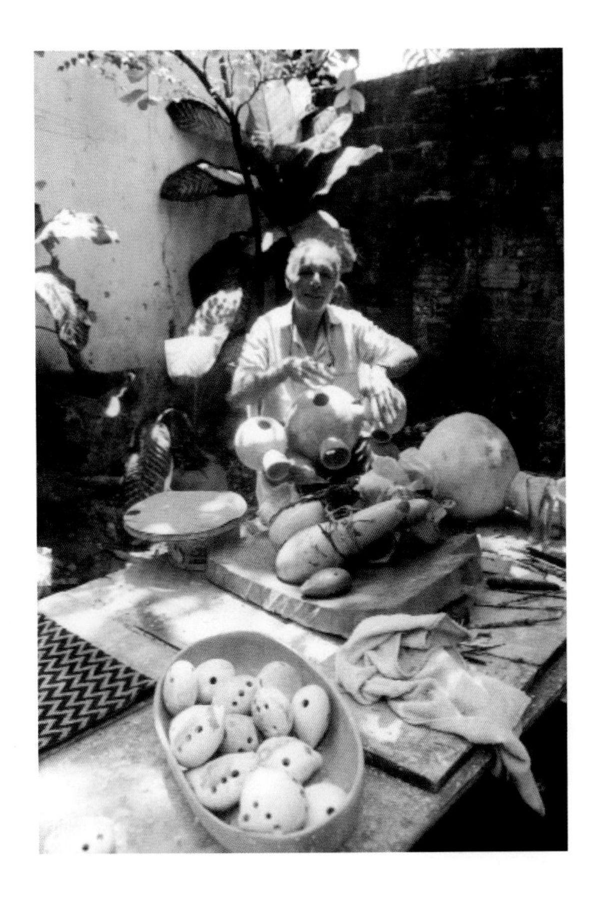

ocarinas push the boundaries in terms of size, complexity and pitch range—using as many as nine chambers in a single instrument to achieve a range of three octaves.

Master Nado lives a simple, hard-working life. With his children, he digs clay from the hillsides near his home and refines it himself. He uses mixtures of white, yellow and red clay, and red and white engobes, firing his creations in a wood-burning kiln. Nado believes that the proper sound of a clay instrument requires a carefully controlled firing temperature: not too hot or the sound will be lost. He often fires his instruments two or three times in order to achieve the sound he wants. He compares this process to developing the proper hardness of a fine violin's finish to obtain the best sound.

A warm and generous man, Nado's gentle, cheerful manner enchants all those he touches. With his children Sara, Micael and Neemias, he has formed a band called "O Som de Barro" ("The Sound of Clay"). Together they perform on his instruments and give workshops at schools, fairs and festivals. His audiences, especially children, delight in Nado's playing and singing. He also teaches children and adults to make clay musical instruments, passing on his deep appreciation of the mysteries and possibilities of clay.

Master Nado's curiosity continues. He is currently experimenting with making flutes from clay, and also would like to make a guitar. He advises beginners to have patience and perseverance with the creation process, not to give up easily, and to seek new combinations rather than just copying other instruments.

When asked what he envisions in the future of ceramic instruments, Nado replies, "In my mind, I see a group of children holding clay instruments, forming a small orchestra of winds and percussion, making harmonies from the beautiful clay..."

Master Nado's instruments also can be seen elsewhere in this book.

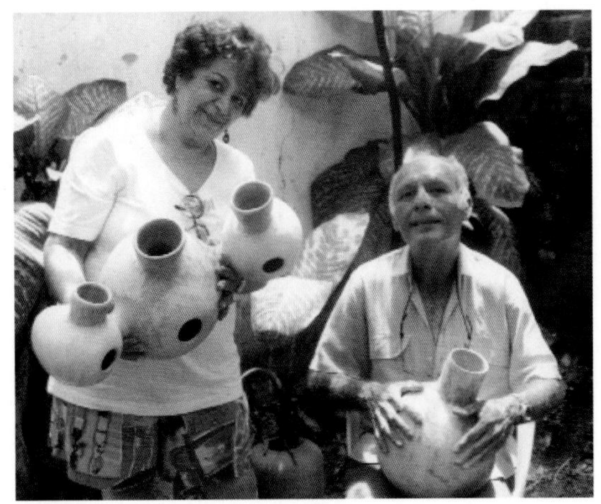

Fig. 9.38
Nado with student Rosa Pereira.

# SHARON ROWELL

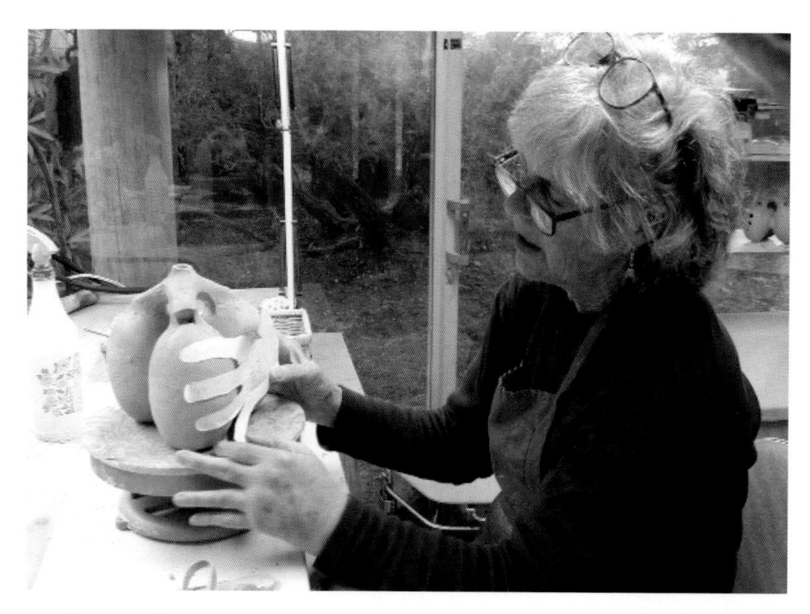

Working in her cozy ceramics studio in her home at Stinson Beach, California, Sharon Rowell is making yet another of her amazing multichambered ocarinas, which she calls "huacas." As the Pacific surf pounds the beach just outside her window, she carefully measures where the finger holes should be positioned, using a paper template of the hands of the person who has commissioned this instrument. She's working today on a triple-chambered huaca, probably her most well-known and most-requested design. People from all over the world contact Sharon to request instruments, which she has gladly made for over 25 years, especially enjoying the process of crafting each instrument specifically for the hands of its intended owner.

Sharon was making ceramic sculptures before she ever considered building musical instruments from clay. One day in a ceramics class, her instructor gave an assignment to make a whistle. She really didn't want to do it—dreaded it, in fact—and ended up taking much longer than the other students to complete her project. She eventually complied with the assignment, in her own slightly subversive manner, by designing a whistle incorporated into a sculptural feminine form. Once she blew the whistle and heard its sound she was hooked. Sharon recalls, "The first sound I ever made I'll remember forever—it felt so alive and animated." She started experimenting right away, making a number of whistle tubes in various lengths to explore the different pitches that could be produced.

Some time later, she created her first ocarina as a reply to the sound of the Mendocino, California, foghorn (which she describes as "not a loud or strong foghorn, like in San Francisco, but more like a sound of making love"). She discovered that the voice of the ocarina was special to her, and experimented with very large instruments, even making

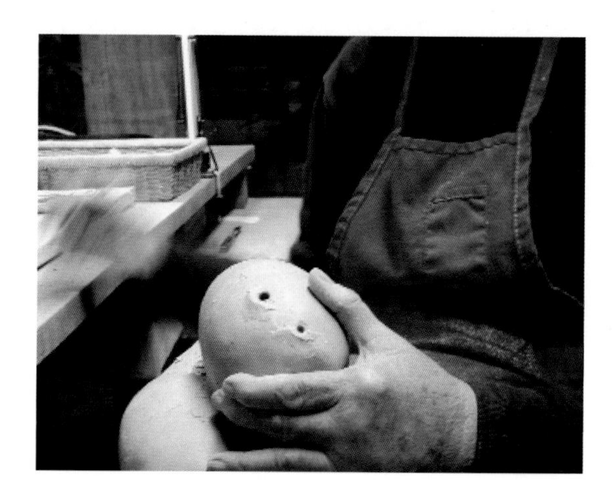

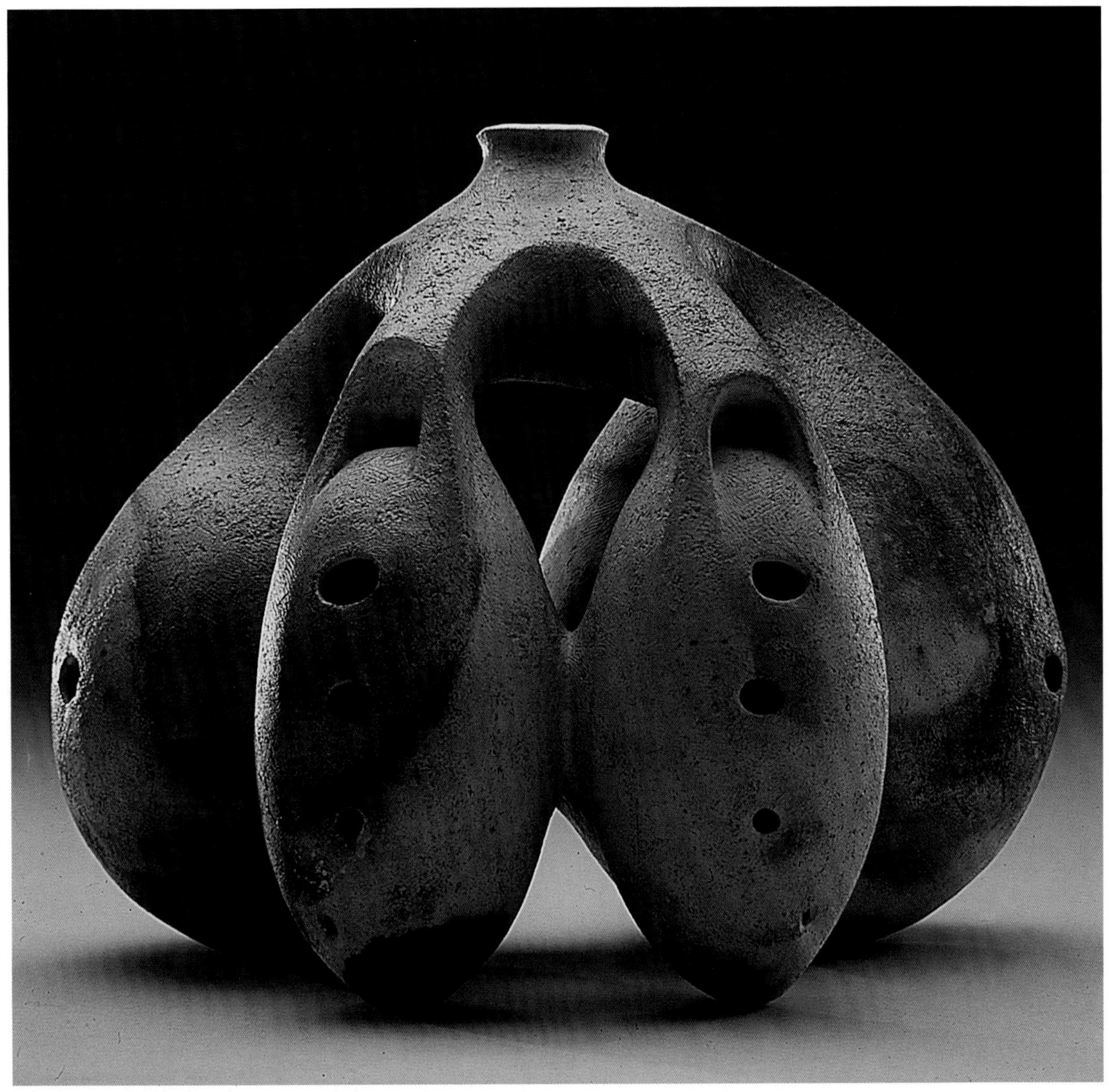

Fig. 9.41
**Four-Chambered Huaca**
The chambers are tuned in octaves and fifths, with the top two melody chambers providing unison pitches over the range of an octave. The two bass or drone chambers sound an octave below the lowest tone of the melody chambers. Stoneware, saggar fired. 8 inches in height. Hear this instrument on CD track 6.

one from a section of large clay sewer pipe. Sharon recalls that at the time when stereo recordings were becoming popular, she was quite excited by this new aural phenomenon. Her response was to build dual-chambered ocarinas to create the same effects as stereo sound. In her double ocarinas, usually both chambers are tuned to the same root pitch and play identical scales. However, Sharon meticulously tunes one chamber to be just slightly, almost minutely, higher in pitch than the other chamber. This creates an effect called "beating" which is a steady throbbing or pulsation in intensity that

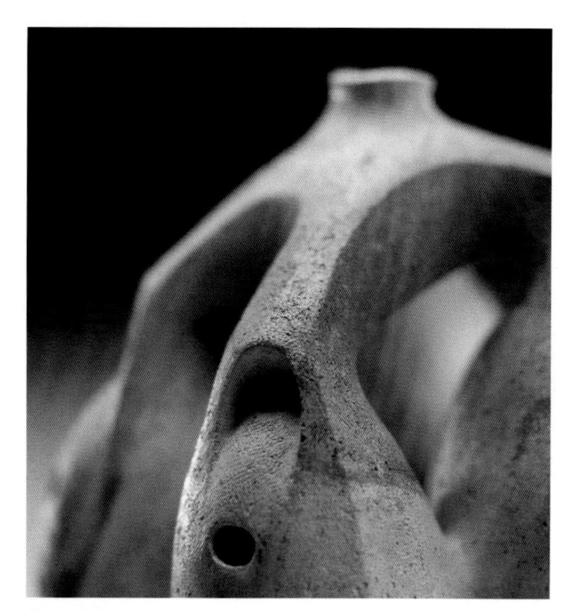

Fig. 9.42
Detail of the four-chambered huaca.

results from the difference in frequency between the sound waves of the two pitches. The pulsing effect occurs in the player's ears, and is intensified due to the way the chambers in Sharon's instruments are split, with one on each side of the player's head. This beating, which most people find pleasant, makes playing her instruments an astounding aural experience—and one that's difficult to record and reproduce. In fact, everything about Sharon's instruments—their voluptuous shape, the feel in your hands, and especially their spacious, haunting sound—is a very personal sensation, best experienced by holding and playing one yourself.

One day, Sharon was captivated by the sound of a street musician playing a hurdy-gurdy (a kind of "one-man-band" instrument having both drone and melody strings). Sharon memorized the pitches of the instrument's drones and melody strings and hurried back to her studio to create an instrument that would mimic its sound. The result is the four-chambered huaca shown here and played by Alan Tower on track 6 of the accompanying CD.

Sharon is quite modest about her contributions to the craft of ceramic musical instruments. While she correctly asserts that she has not invented anything new, since ocarina-like instruments have been around for hundreds or even thousands of years, she most certainly has created some new designs with lasting appeal. As a testament to this, her instruments are often imitated. Sharon has taught hundreds of students how to make ocarinas, many of whom have sought her out with a specific desire to learn how to make her multiple-chambered creations. She patiently obliges them. Many of her students have no previous experience working with clay, but are captivated by the sound and design of Sharon's creations—so much so that they will invest significant time and energy to learn how to make them. Some of Sharon's students have gone on to professionally create and sell their works. Sharon encourages her students to "experiment and love every sound you make, no matter what. Each sound is like a newborn baby and therefore lovable for itself and as sacred, in its own way, as life. All sounds are beautiful and all sounds educate one as to what direction to try to go next. All instruments can be well played."

Sharon's instruments are heard on many recordings, as well as soundtracks, ballet scores, in jazz and rock bands, and probably many other places as well. It is clear that many of the instruments she's made will be cherished and passed on to appreciative owners who will play them for generations to come.

Sharon's instruments also can be seen elsewhere in this book and heard on the accompanying CD.

# DAG SØRENSEN

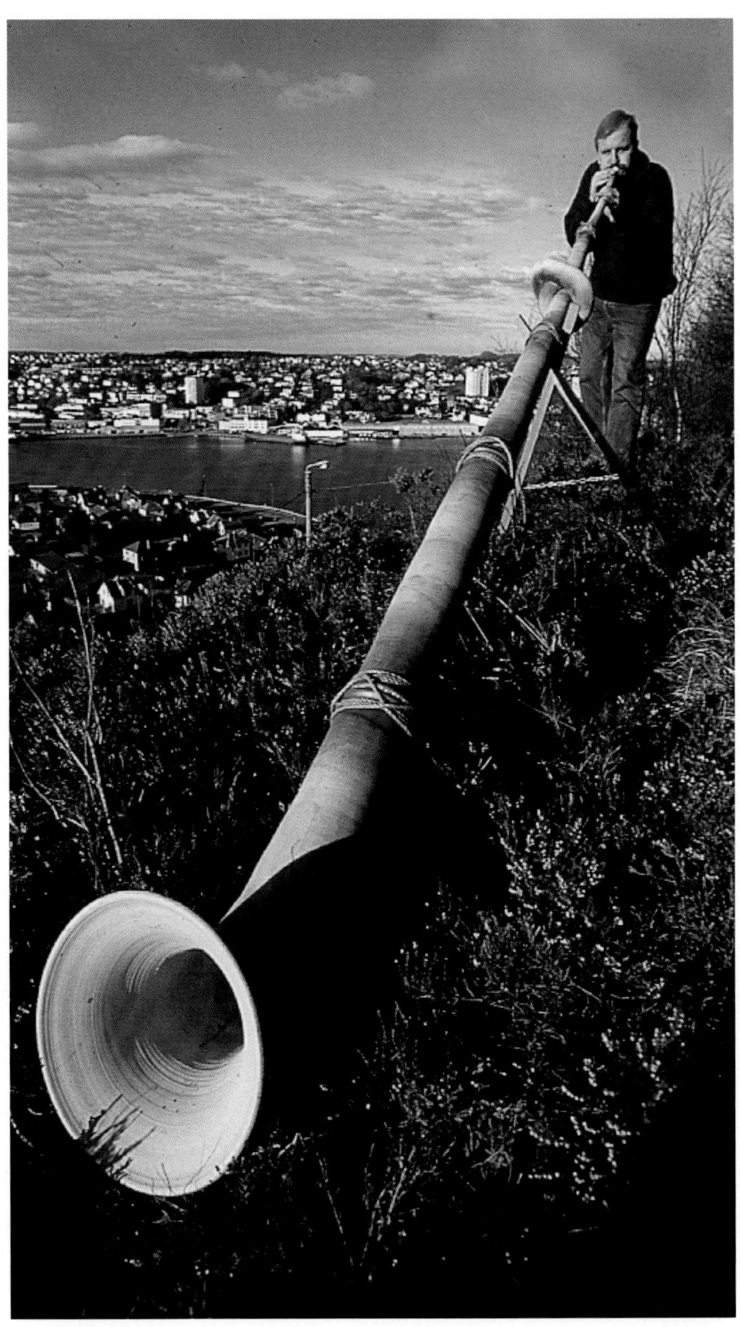
Fig. 9.43
Dag with his ceramic alpenhorn.

From high in the hills above the idyllic Norwegian pottery town of Sandnes, the deep tones of an alpenhorn reverberate. But this isn't a normal alpenhorn—it is 13 feet long, and made entirely from clay. Dag Sørensen is the builder and player of this remarkable ceramic horn. You can read more about its construction in the "Aerophones" chapter of this book.

Dag has made many other clay horns, as well as other ceramic instruments. It all began one day when a visiting friend, Eddie Andresen, a professional percussionist and composer, began to tap on the pots and vases that decorated Dag's home. One thing led to another, and Eddie asked Dag to make him a drum. Dag recalls, "We became engrossed in a hunt for a 'virgin sound,' but we weren't really sure what we were looking for. Several months earlier, Eddie had stumbled on a six meter length of road pipe and was fascinated by its sound. I knew a little about Australian and Indian instruments, listened to what Eddie had to say, and then made my own interpretations." The result is one of Eddie's favorites, a 12-foot-long "faggott" (bassoon) drum, which coils to four feet in length. Eddie describes its sound as "a mixture of Gregorian chant and roaring dinosaurs." (Dag's bassoon drum can be seen in figure 4.116 and heard on track 27 of the CD, played by Eddie Andresen.)

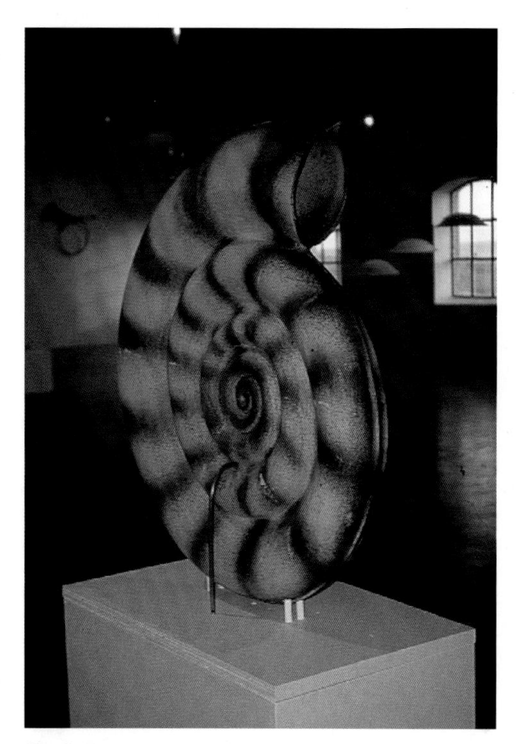

Fig. 9.44
**Logarithm Spiral Horn**
Thrown and molded. Stoneware with manganese dioxide, cone 10. 28 inches in height.

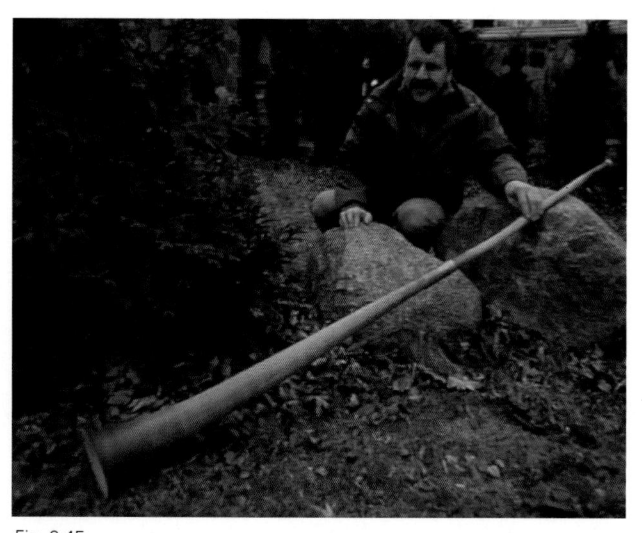

Fig. 9.45
**Lure**
A traditional Scandinavian horn, molded in two pieces. Stoneware with manganese dioxide, cone 10. 7 feet in length.

Since his first musical experiments with Eddie, Dag has made a broad range of percussion and wind instruments, including panpipes, wind chimes, sound walls, bells, clay pot drums, tusk-shaped flutes, and many different types of horns. He is especially drawn to large instruments, and enjoys adding whimsical touches to his creations, such as the knot in the middle of his alpenhorn, and a double-belled horn that blows from a single mouthpiece into both ears.

Dag says that one of his biggest challenges in making instruments has been finding the correct mathematical relationships of form to sound, especially the calculation of logarithmic spirals necessary to make his seashell-inspired horns. Other practical challenges have confronted him as he attempted to make large horns. Constant attention was required to avoid warping and cracking when drying long, straight molded pipes. Also, his kiln wasn't large enough to hold 4-foot-long pipes, so he had to transport the large, fragile greenware pieces to a friend's workshop for firing. In order to create his largest instruments, Dag attaches multiple components together after firing. His alpenhorn was assembled using silicone glue. His lure horns use a system of brass fittings and rubber rings that are cast and cut to provide an airtight seal. This allows the horns to be taken apart for transport.

Dag has also made a number of idiophones, ranging from 1.5-inch-thick massive porcelain chimes, to large suspended "music walls" made from thin porcelain tiles, knotted together with thin fishing line. Dag describes their rich, varied sounds as, "twinkling, like lightly falling snow."

Although Dag is completely self-taught in ceramics, having learned from books and magazines, he has received a number of grants and awards for his work, and in 1996 was admitted to the Norwegian Applied Art Association. He builds his instruments using extrusion, slab-building, throwing and slip-casting techniques. (His process of creating a "spiral horn" is shown in detail in Chapter 4.) Dag spent years as an electrical worker, which provided him the skills and knowledge to build his own kilns and other studio equipment, including extruders, slab rollers and airbrushing equipment. His preferred clays are stoneware and porcelain, fired to cones 9 and 10. Although Dag has developed an expertise with crystalline glazes, for his musical instruments he chooses not to use glaze because of the impact on the sound. Instead he uses iron, ochre and manganese oxides to color his instruments. He says that the ever-changing Norwegian landscape, with its eccentric weather patterns, provides inspiration for the colors he uses on his instruments.

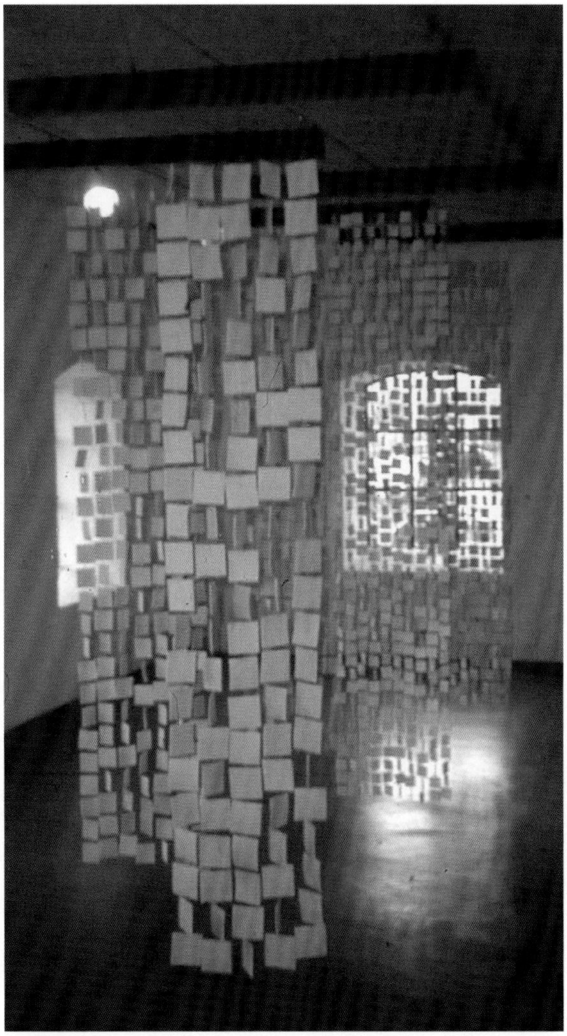

Fig. 9.46
**Music Walls**
Constructed from cone 10 porcelain tiles, attached with fishing line. They are played in a variety of ways, including shaking and striking with mallets. 83 inches in height.

In addition to Eddie Andresen, several prominent Norwegian composers have given life and sound to Dag's instruments in performances throughout Norway and Europe. Dag's instruments were recently used extensively in the soundtrack to a Norwegian children's film, and also appeared in the film as sculptures.

Dag's ideas and enthusiasm seem boundless. He's inspired by nature—rocks, crystals, and shells. He loves hiking and fishing, and traveling around the world, and is always on the lookout for his next inspiration.

Dag's instruments also can be seen elsewhere in this book and heard on the accompanying CD.

# STEPHEN WRIGHT

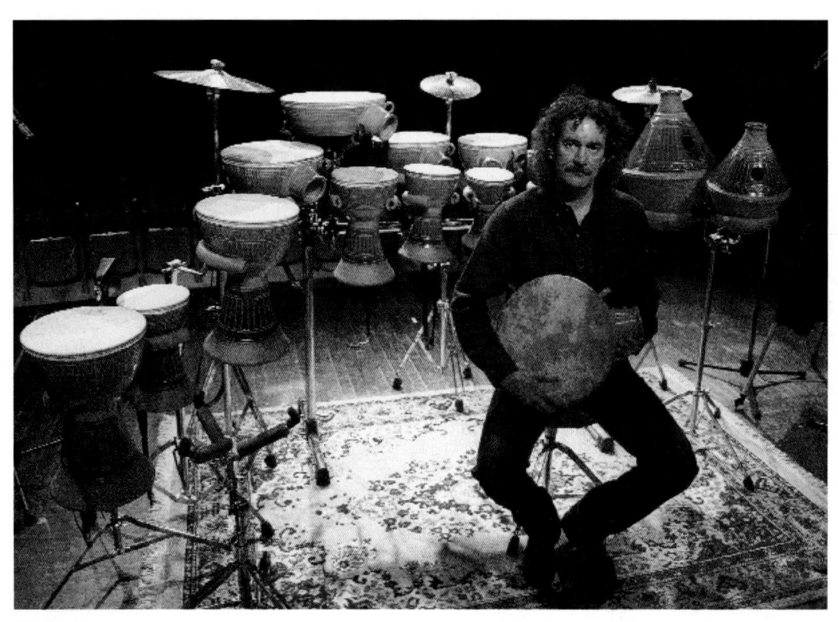

Fig. 9.47
Stephen Wright with his family of clay hand percussion instruments.

Fifteen years ago, Stephen Wright was a production potter and a drummer. However, he didn't combine his two interests until he was encouraged by a friend. "A guitar player friend asked if I would play trap set on his album," Steve recalls. "Early into the project, he suggested that I make a clay tabla. I told him there was no such thing. Of course, I believed I was an expert on the subject, since I had been both a drummer and a ceramic artist for 20 years. However, my friend was persistent, and convinced me to go to the library to do some research on the subject (remember back when we couldn't use the internet for things like that?) There I found some books on hand percussion and was proven wrong—there actually were drums made from clay! It really was a revelation to me."

Right away, Stephen made some clay drums—a doumbek, a set of bongos and an udu-style drum. His friend's album project turned out well, and soon other musicians became interested in buying Stephen's clay drums. As a result, he formed the Wright Hand Drum Company and has been making clay percussion instruments ever since.

When he made his first drums, Stephen had very little information on how to head them. He found some goat skins that were intended for banjos to use as drum heads. He remembers ordering a huge elk hide from a Native American drum supplier. "It came via UPS and was not even in a box, just this huge piece of skin, 6 feet long and tied with twine. I had about 15 to 20 drums I was experimenting with, and after quite a struggle, I soaked the hide, cut it up and headed the drums. The next day, as the elk skin dried, one by one the drums started to break, due to the increased tension. They made a very loud 'WHAP' each time it happened—I'll never forget that sound!"

Steve soon realized he needed to do a lot of learning and experimentation if he was going to make production drums. "At the time, as a production potter, I was making stoneware pots and firing in a gas kiln, using glazes with heavy reduction—celadons, copper reds, etc. I was really burned out on making dishes, pitchers and bowls. Once I decided to make clay drums, I just took it one step at a time, like I was going back to school to get my master's degree. I didn't know anything about making drums, so I just dove into it."

One of his first decisions was to develop a new clay body and firing process. "I pulled out a clay body I had used in the past for tile and mural work, and made some adjustments to 'tighten' it up. Then I experimented with some slips and glazes. I decided to 'go electric' because I wanted the consistency that an electric kiln would provide. I realized my new market would be drummers and drum stores, not craft galleries, so I would need to be able to supply the same sound with each drum every time."

To meet these new challenges, Stephen also applied the knowledge and techniques he gained from his years as a production potter. For example, in order to develop uniformly sized and tuned drums, he determined the exact amount of clay, by weight, required for each model of drum, to ensure consistency time after time.

Today Stephen makes a variety of traditionally-inspired clay drums that can be seen throughout this book. They include doumbeks, ghatams, bongo sets, shakers and ubangs, which are his variation on the traditional udu design. He also makes several instruments that he designed himself including claypans (figure 2.22) which are all-clay frame drums; shakers with goat skin heads (figure 6.7); and the gunta drum (figure 3.23) which is sort of like a cross between a frame drum and a doumbek, with a side-facing sound hole. "I wanted to design a drum that would make miking more functional in order to create a more amplified acoustic sound," he explains about the gunta. Stephen also added "microphone ports" to his drum designs—small holes that facilitate the placement of internal microphones. He likens these evolutions born from modern necessity to another American innovation—the trap set. "You can have four guys each playing one drum, or you can have one guy playing four drums. Drawing specific aspects from various cultures and using them to become better is true global fusion."

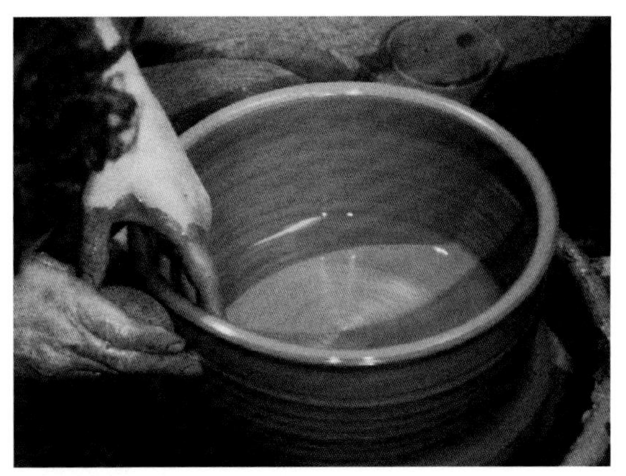
Fig. 9.48
Stephen throwing a gunta drum.

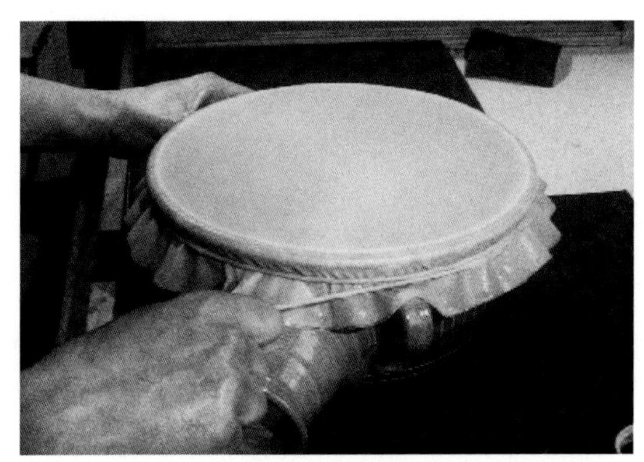
Fig. 9.49
Putting on the goat skin head.

Steve's drums are played by many professional musicians, several of whom appear on the accompanying CD. He enjoys his role as a supplier of musical tools for these artists. "As a drum maker, I have been fortunate to meet, work with, and become friends with many talented percussionists and musicians. I learned early on that the instruments musicians play can, and do, define them. For musicians to market themselves, they must create their own 'signature sound' to set them apart. It's very satisfying for me to be able to provide the instruments they need, and watch their professional careers. I feel I am an artist, providing other artists the tools they need to produce their art. It also has provided me one heck of a CD collection."

Being a percussionist has helped Stephen's drum making. "The process of throwing a drum on an electric potter's wheel has a real sense of rhythm to it," he explains. "The wheel turns at a certain speed and it works just like a metronome. If you can feel the beat of the wheel, then you can follow the clay as you're working it on the wheel."

Conversely, the process of creating drums also has benefited Steve as a drummer. "An unexpected bonus of working with really good players as a drum maker is that I have learned a tremendous amount about playing hand percussion and drumming that I would not have learned otherwise," he relates. "I have been fortunate to learn from some of the best players out there. I constantly work at improving my own skills as a musician, and have been involved in some very interesting musical projects. As styles today are blending and expanding, there is no end to the musical possibilities."

Stephen's instruments also can be seen elsewhere in this book and heard on the accompanying CD.

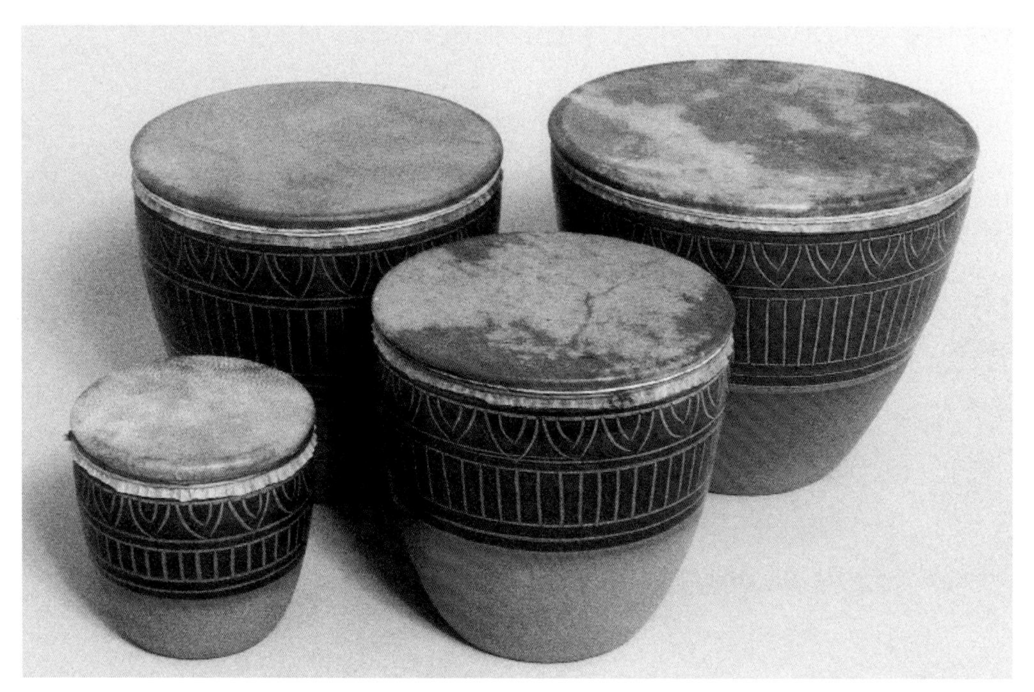

Fig. 9.50
Stephen's bongos show off his specially formulated clay, slips and glazes, as well as his trademark sgraffito decoration.

*If you learn music, you'll learn most all there is to know.*
—Edgar Cayce

# Demonstrations

If you're filled with inspiration by all of the instruments in this book and on the accompanying CD, and would like to make some yourself, then this chapter is for you. Even if you're not ready to get your hands dirty, the step-by-step demonstrations presented here will give you an inside look at some of the processes used to create ceramic musical instruments.

This chapter contains five step-by-step demonstrations led by Daryl Baird, which show how to create the following instruments:

- Side-Hole Pot Drum—a skinless clay drum, or "udu" drum.
- Ocarina—a basic globular flute, with or without finger holes.
- Goblet Drum—a doumbek-type drum with a goat skin head.
- Side-Blown Flute—a transverse tubular flute.
- Whistle Flute—an end-blown ducted, or recorder-style flute.

So grab some clay, roll up your sleeves, cue up the CD, and let's get started!

## DEMONSTRATION 1 | Side-Hole Pot Drum

*This simple drum can be built in as little as seven days. The total time depends on the size of the drum you make and the amount of time you spend finishing it. For this demonstration, a white, stoneware clay with medium grog was used. A manual extruder equipped with a 3/8-inch diameter coil die was used to make the coils. An extruder is certainly not necessary to make coils; you can roll them by hand. However, extruded coils make it easier to build a pot with walls of consistent thickness—a key element to a good sounding pot drum.*

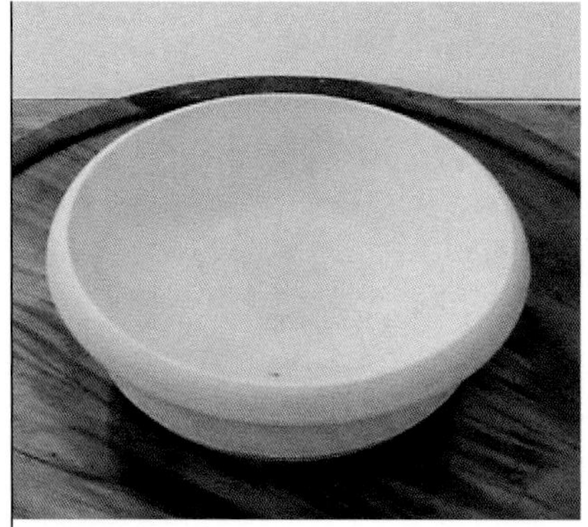

### Step 1

Throw a heavy bowl-shaped mold (called a "puki" by Native American potters) on the wheel. This mold will be used to form the bottom of the pot drum and support it as you gradually build up its walls. The extra weight of the mold helps it stay in place as you are building the pot on top of it. However, when building the mold, note that the extra thickness of the clay requires substantially more drying time than a bowl this size of normal thickness. Failure to dry the mold thoroughly can cause it to shatter during firing. The interior surface of the mold should be shaped into a smooth arc and finished with a rib. Once it is completely dry, bisque fire the mold to cone 04.

*Note:* A "lazy susan" or banding wheel will help to steadily rotate the drum and speed up the process of adding coils. This one was found in a second-hand store and was attached to a square piece of plywood. The plywood can be clamped to the table if necessary.

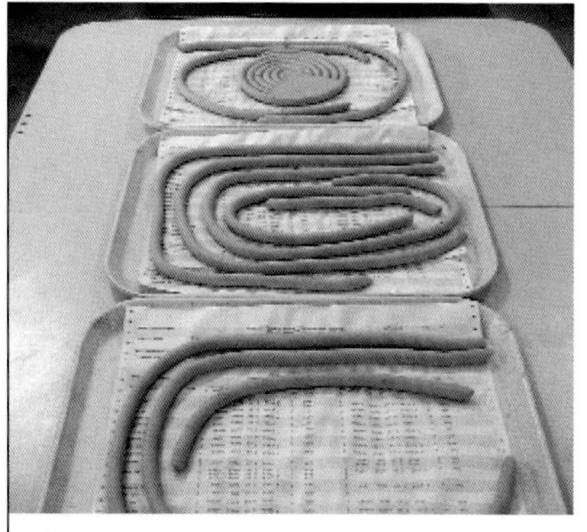

### Step 2

For convenience of handling and storage, the ⅜-inch coils can be laid in lunch trays on top of paper sheets. The trays will be wrapped with plastic to keep them moist.

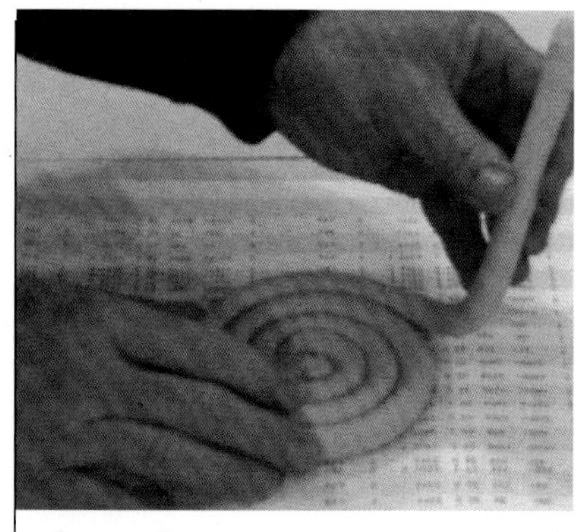

### Step 3

Wind a coil concentrically to form the drum's base. Work with moist clay and use a sheet of paper to make it easier to lift and move it.

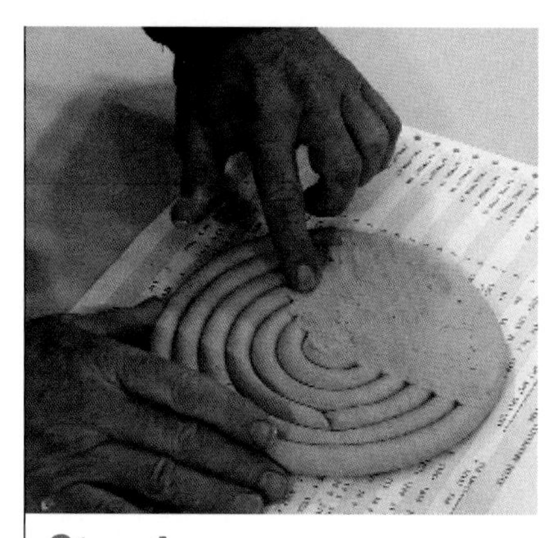

### Step 4

After adding another coil, blend and smooth the coils to form a disk. Work carefully from the outer edge, inward, then back to the outer edge. Use moderate pressure to avoid distorting the shape of the base.

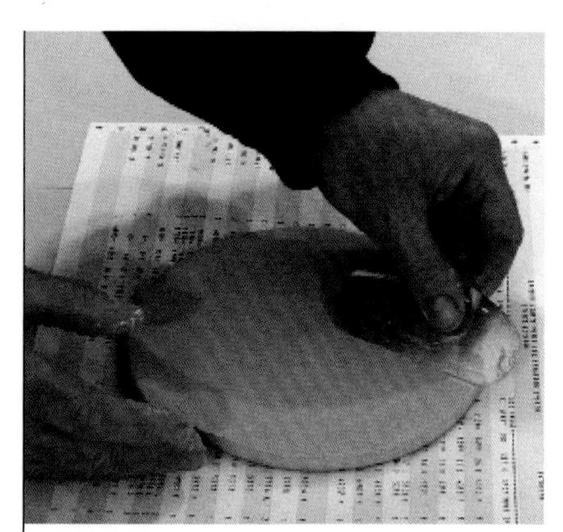

### Step 5

Use a flexible rib to smooth the surface after the coils have been melded. Repeat on the underside of the disk.

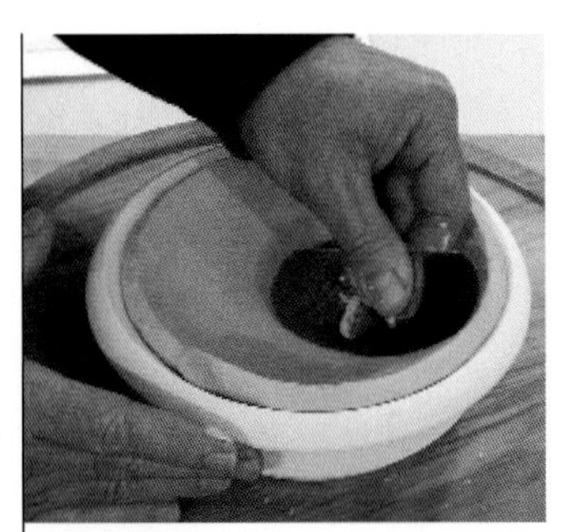

### Step 6
Lay the disk into the mold and press it evenly to conform to the shape. Use a metal rib to smooth the surface.

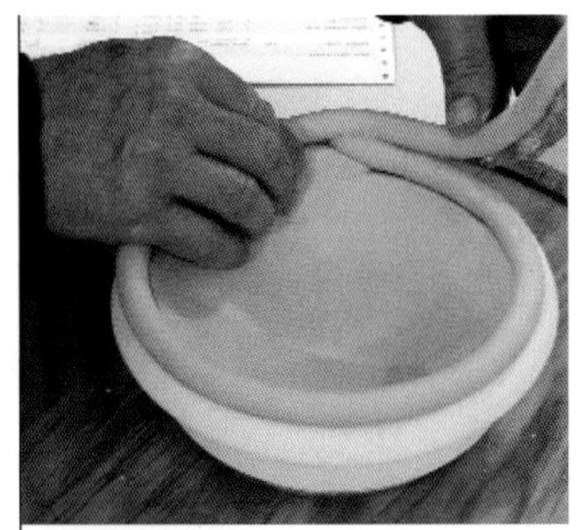

### Step 7
Lay a coil on the base following the edge of the mold. Note the overlap of the end of the previous coil with the starting end of the new coil. The base and coils are very moist and can be melded without roughing the edges.

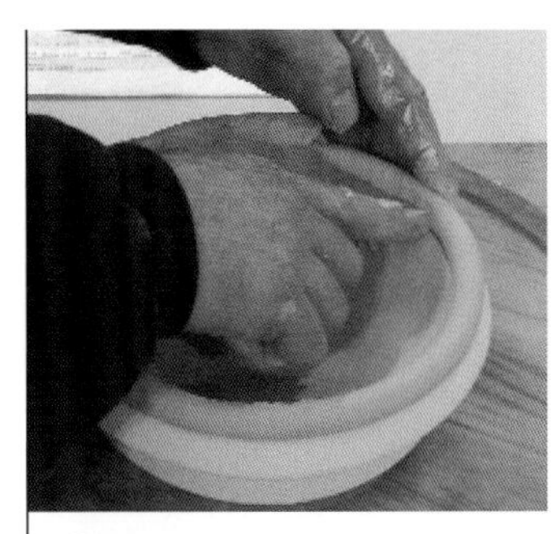

### Step 8
Continue melding; first on the inside then on the outside. Take your time and do a thorough job of combining the coils. After each round with the fingers, follow with the rib. Save working the rib on the outside for later.

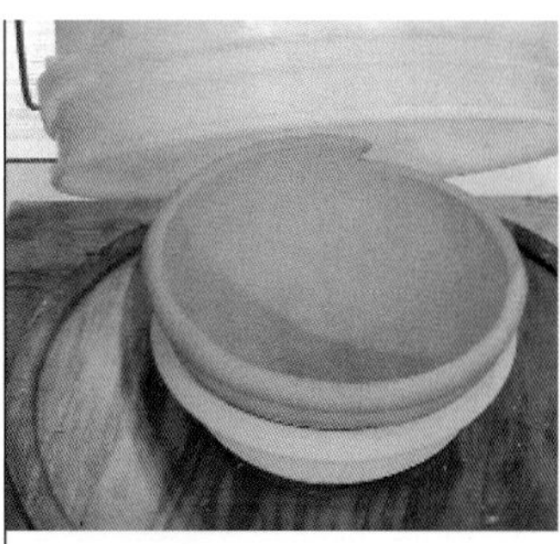

### Step 9
At this stage, the clay will need to stiffen somewhat before more coils can be attached, so it is a good stopping point for the day. Cover with a bucket or plastic bag to prevent the clay from drying out too much.

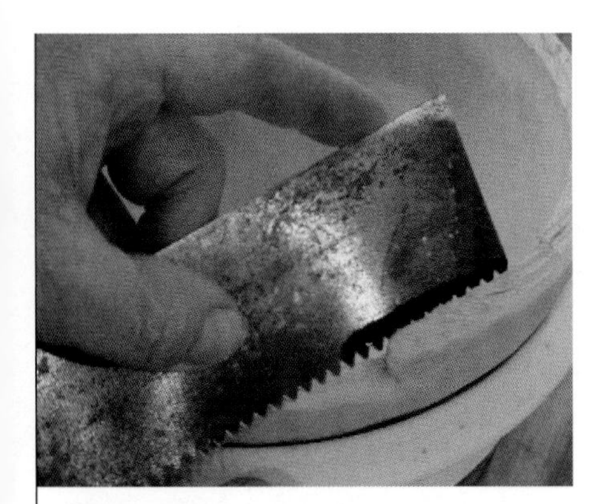

### Step 10
If the clay surface on the edge of the pot has dried too much when you return to the project, you can use the "luting" technique to join the next coil. Using a rib with a serrated edge, scrape and score the surface before adding the next coil. In some cases a brush load of plain water painted on after scraping will aid the adhesion of the clay.

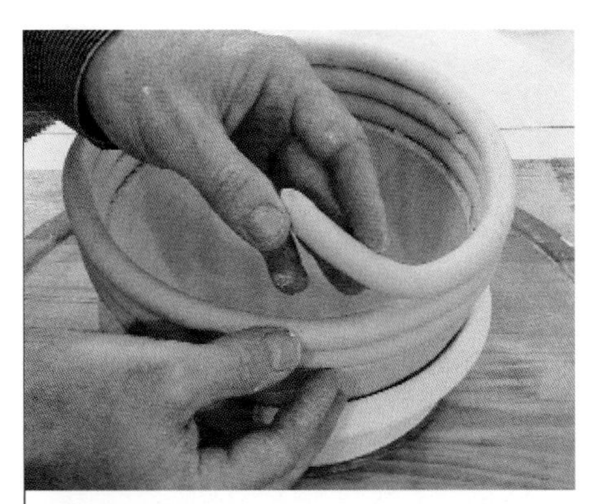

### Step 11
Add two to three winds to the pot before melding inside and out. Lay each coil slightly to the outside of the previous coil to increase the pot's diameter. Look at the pot from the side to see that the coils are following the desired outer contour. Meld the coils on the inside first. Follow that with the rib employing a motion that smoothes while scraping and thinning the clay. As you draw the rib toward you, support the pot from the outside with your other hand.

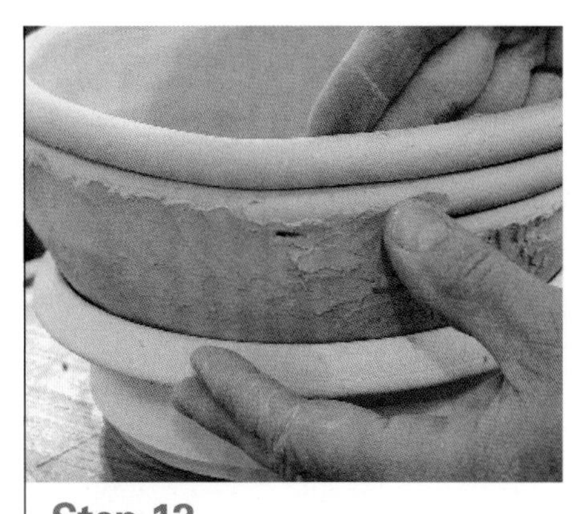

### Step 12
Now blend the outside of the coils while supporting them from the inside. The lazy susan makes it easy to turn the pot as you smooth. Start at the bottom and work your way up to the top. Follow with your rib using the same drawing/scraping motion employed previously. Work to achieve a uniform shell thickness of approximately ¼ of an inch throughout the entire pot (if you started with ⅜-inch coils).

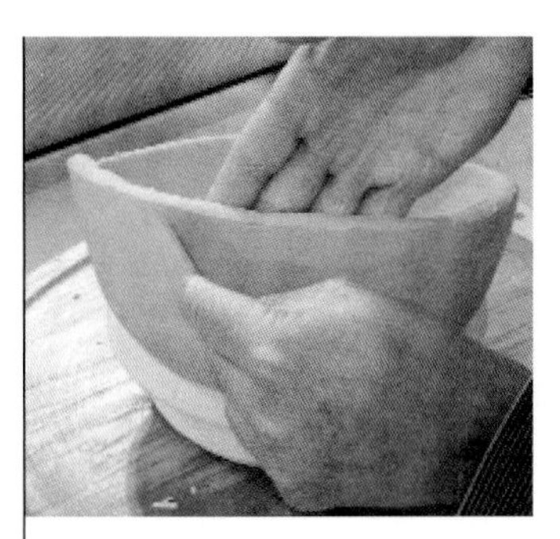

### Step 13
After the lower part of the pot has firmed up, shift the pot in the mold to smooth and shape it from bottom to top. Double check your lower melds and hand smooth as necessary.

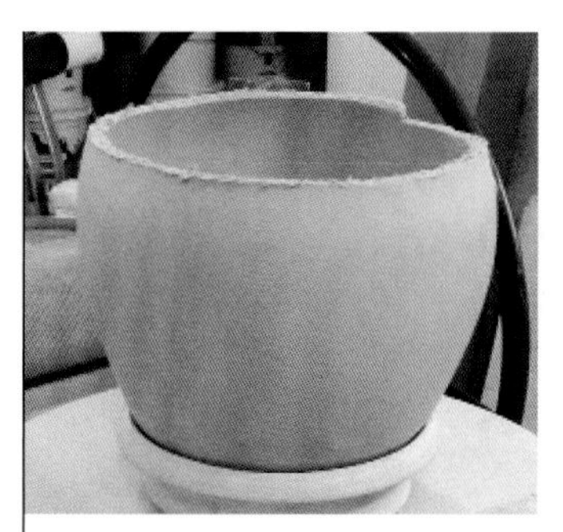

### Step 14
Progress! Several coils have been added and the maximum diameter of the pot has been achieved. The coils are now laid toward the inside edge to reduce the diameter. Note that the old lazy susan got a little too lazy and had to be replaced with a sturdier, warp-resistant model. Give the pot a light misting before it goes back under the bucket.

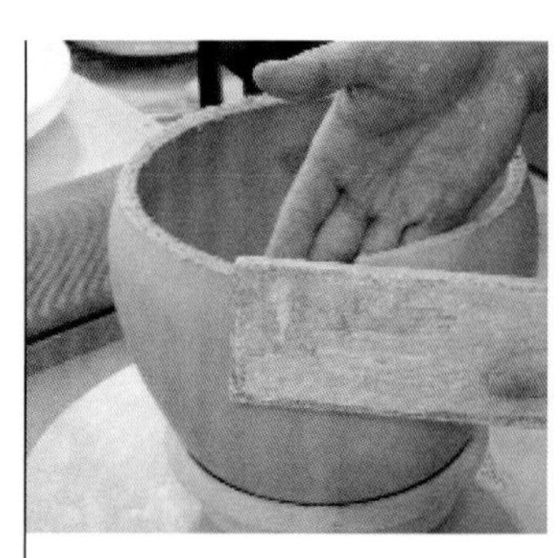

### Step 15
A paddle can be fashioned from a piece of scrap wood to fit nicely in your hand. Be sure to sand off any splinters. Use the paddle to shape the pot with light, rapid taps from the outside. Just as with the rib, support the inside of the pot directly opposite the area being paddled.

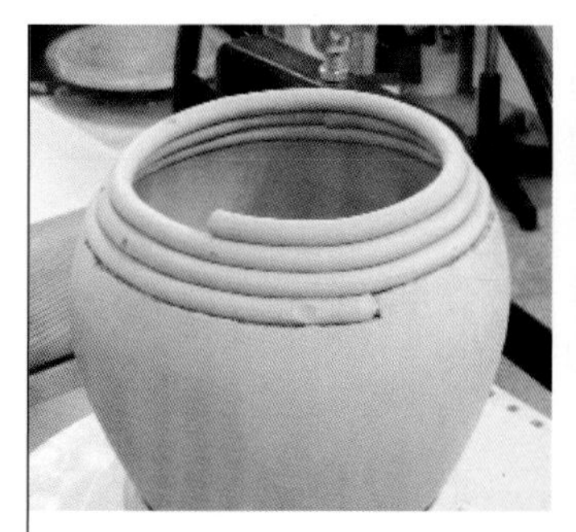

### Step 16
Lay the coils very carefully toward the inside edge of the pot rim. The melding work on the inside gets tougher now. Do the inside first and give it a good visual inspection before proceeding with the outside. After the pot stiffens, use the rib and a paddle to help thin and shape the shoulder area of the pot.

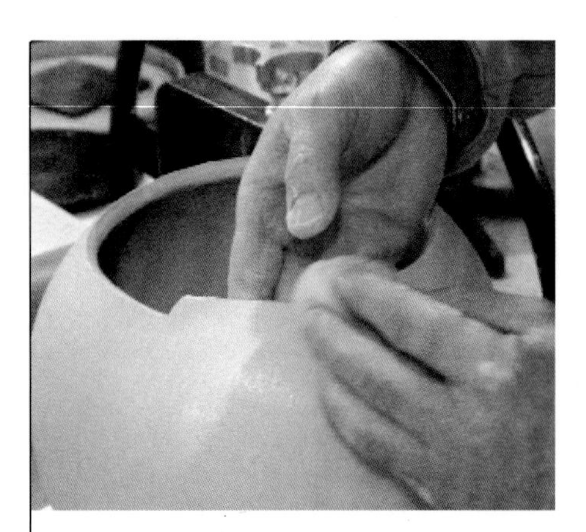

### Step 17
Draw a moistened sponge from the bottom of the pot to the top edge in a smooth arc to help remove surface flaws. This also will help keep the clay supple. Do this inside and out.

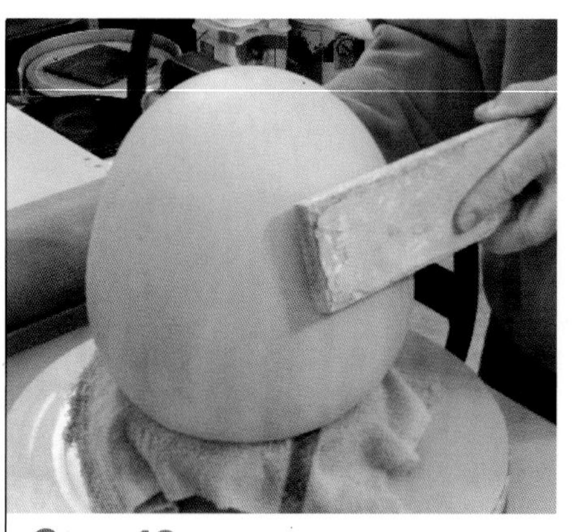

### Step 18
Allow the pot to firm up to just slightly below the leather-hard stage. A couple of hours of drying should be enough. When the pot is firm enough to support its own weight, turn it upside down. Place a rag over the mold before setting the pot on it to cushion the shoulder of the pot. As before, light, rhythmic paddling helps set the contour and symmetry of the pot. As you paddle, support the pot on the opposite side with your hand.

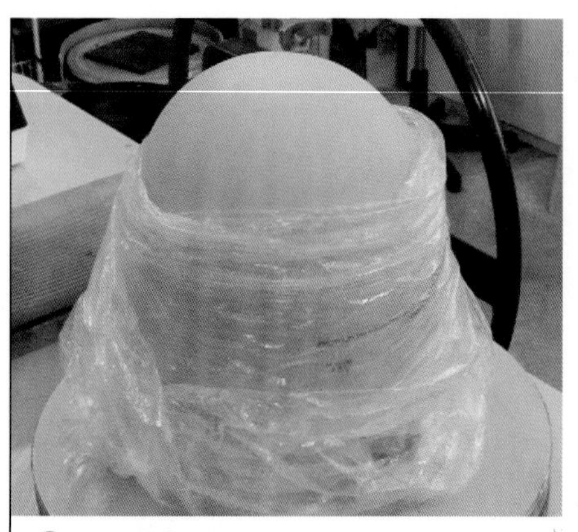

### Step 19
Wrap the pot with the bottom exposed. This keeps the side workable while allowing the bottom to reach leather-hard state. Do this before adding the final coils to the neck of the pot.

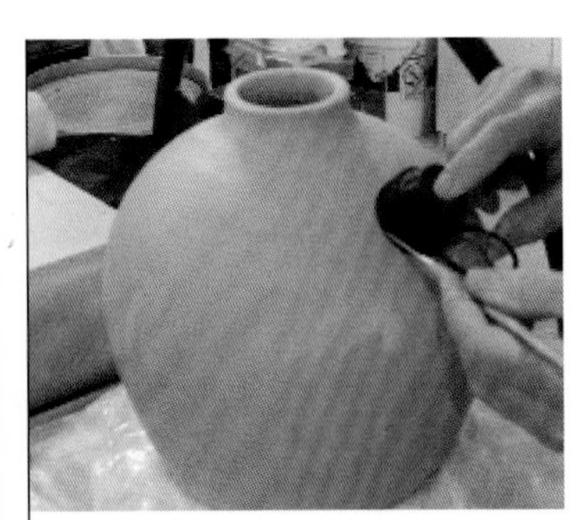

**Step 20**
The coiling work has been completed. The neck is approximately two inches in diameter at the inside and just about an inch high. More coils can be added for a taller neck and a different sounding drum. Here, the bottom of a flashlight is used to mark a side-hole circle that is about the same diameter as the neck. A small knife is used to remove the clay from the side hole. The plastic between the mold and the bottom of the pot helps prevent over-drying.

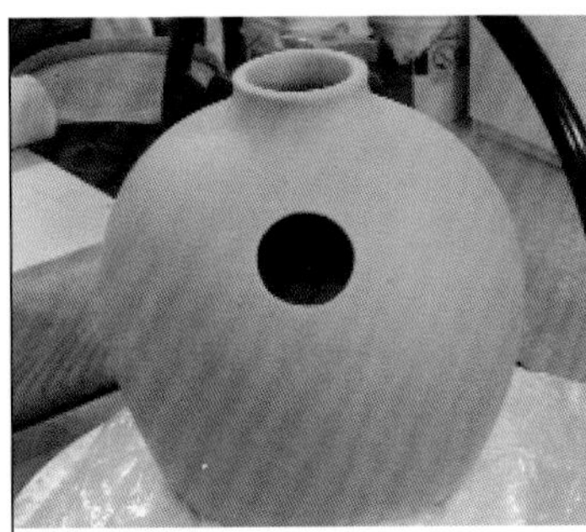

**Step 21**
The finished neck and side hole. The top hole has been given a slight bead and has been smoothed with a sponge for the comfort of the hand when the drum is played.

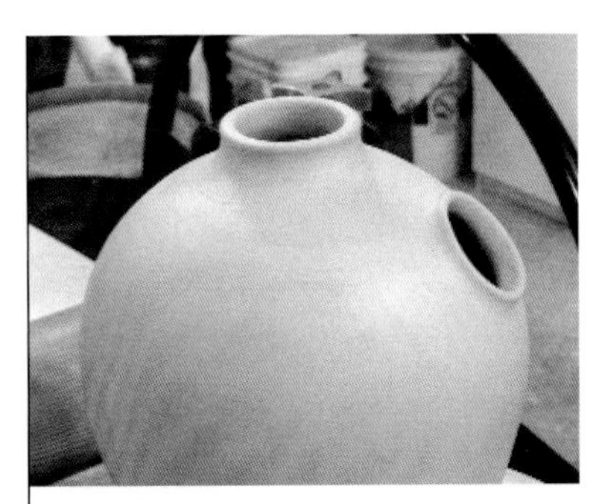

**Step 22**
This detail shows the lip that has been added to the side hole with a small coil of clay. This is an optional step. If you do add the lip, take extra care to meld it well with the surface of the pot and smooth the edge for the comfort of your hand when playing.

The wall of the pot is thick enough so that some light carving or sgraffito-style designs can be made on it. No matter what decoration method you employ, it is important that this hand-built pot drum be allowed to dry very slowly and evenly under loosely fitting plastic for at least a week. Once it is bone dry the drum can be once-fired, upside down, in a kiln to cone 06. Optionally, the drum can be fired the first time to cone 09 then fired raku-style to cone 05 and treated with post-fire reduction.

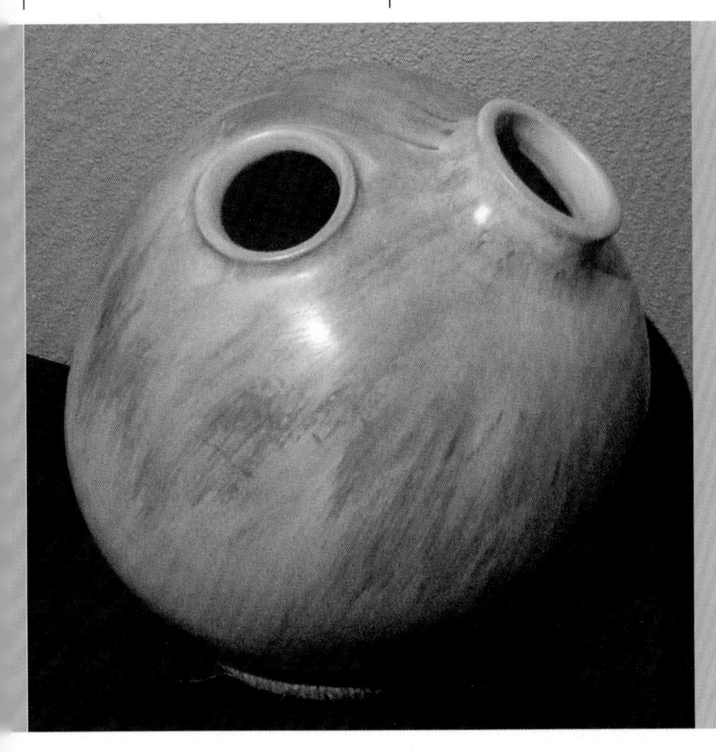

**Final Steps**
The demonstration pot was painted at the leather-hard stage with five coats of terra sigillata and burnished with a stone to give it a high polish. Red iron oxide was mixed into the final coat and streaked on with a sponge before the final polish.

A display stand was made from an extra coil of clay shaped into a ring, fired, then wrapped with jute.

To play your drum, tap the shell with your fingertips for pinging sounds, and slap your palms on the side and top holes to create haunting and bubbling liquid tones.

More information on playing styles and traditional construction techniques can be found in the "Plosive Aerophones" section of Chapter 4.

## DEMONSTRATION 2 | Ocarina

*Ocarinas can be easily fashioned from clay in a variety of ways. This demonstration illustrates a popular method in which two small "pinch pots" are joined to create the body of the ocarina. You can make your ocarina bigger or smaller by adjusting the size of the ball of clay.*

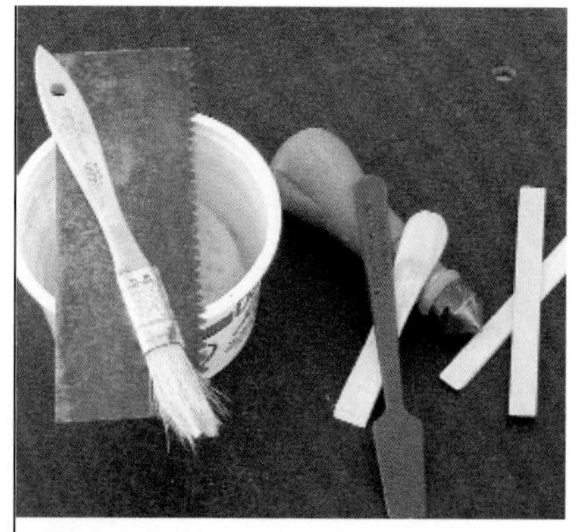

### Step 1

Gather your tools. A metal rib with a serrated edge will be used for scoring clay. The sponge and cup of water will be used to keep the clay moist and help you smooth the surface. The tool with the orange handle is a countersink. It is found at hardware stores and is used to make nice beveled edges on the finger holes. The red plastic stick was a ceramics supplier giveaway item. It has a nice flat blade useful for smoothing the clay and shaping the sound hole. One of the wooden sticks is from an ice cream store and the others are Popsicle sticks. In addition to these, you'll need a needle tool for scoring the clay, and drill bits or a hole-cutting tool to make the finger holes.

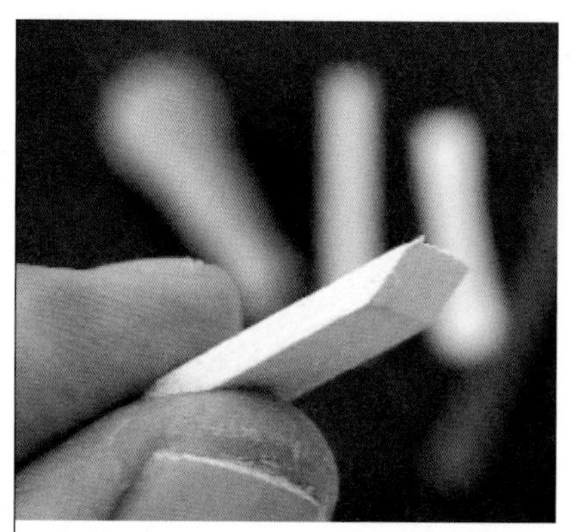

### Step 2

Bevel the tips of your wooden sticks to make them effective cutting tools. If you have access to an electric bench sander, you can easily put beveled edges on the ends of your sticks. You can get similar results by rubbing the edge of the stick over a sheet of medium grade sandpaper held on a flat surface.

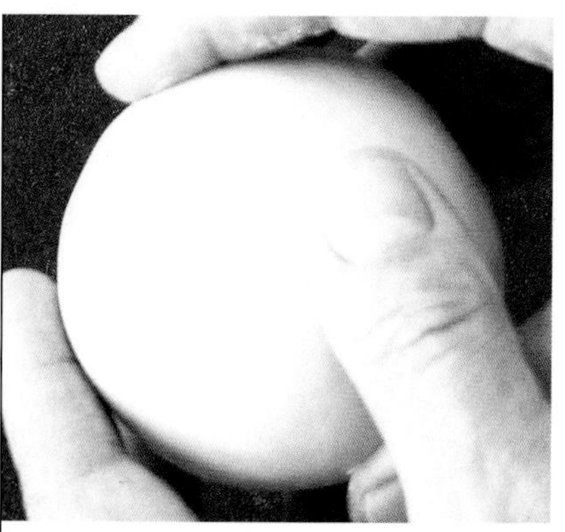

### Step 3

Make a clay ball. Shape a piece of fresh clay into a smooth ball. The ball shown weighs about a pound and will make an ocarina about the size of a medium orange.

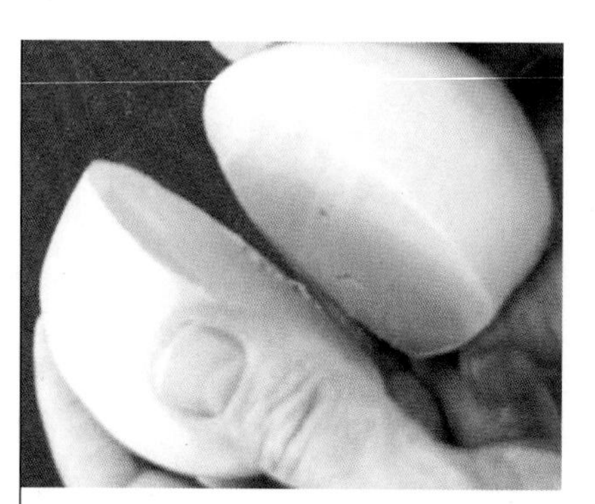

### Step 4

Cut the ball in half through its middle, using the serrated rib or a wire tool.

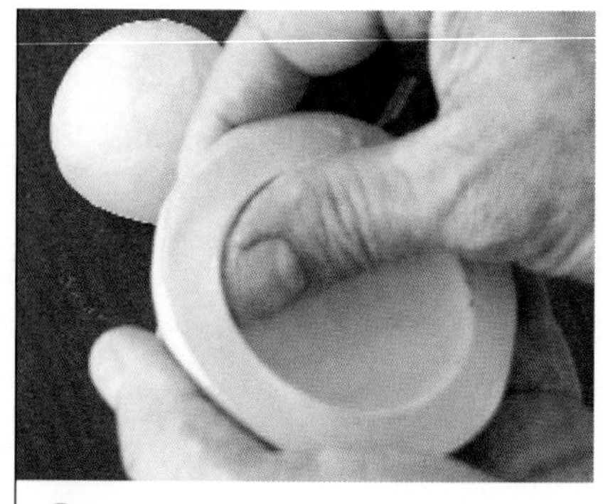

### Step 5

Shape the clay "bowls." Cradle the clay in one hand and shape it with the thumb and index finger of the other. Turn the clay in your hand frequently and keep the thickness of the wall as even as possible. If the clay begins to dry and crack, use your sponge and water to remoisten it.

*Note:* If the rim of your small pot gets ragged as you do your shaping, you can even it out by lightly tapping the rim on a smooth porous surface such as a piece of wood or plasterboard.

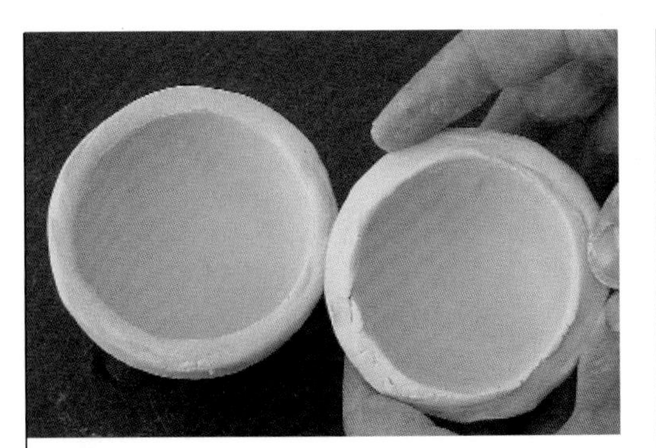

## Step 6

When you have finished the first half, open the other half in the same fashion. Compare the diameters of the two pieces as you go. You're trying to make two bowl shapes that will match up perfectly, edge to edge.

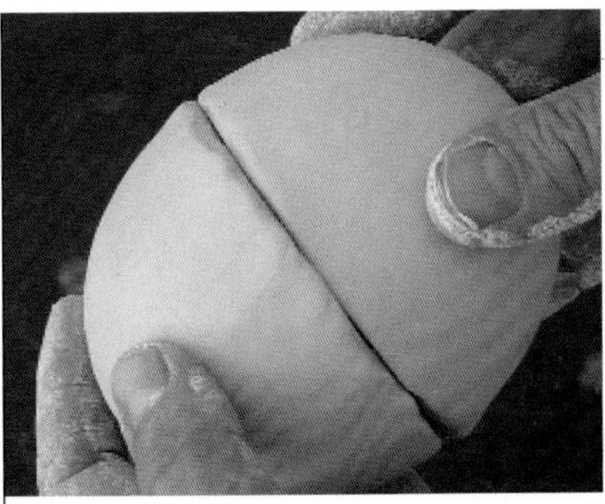

## Step 7

It looks like the diameters of the halves match up well. Next, fuse them together into one hollow shape.

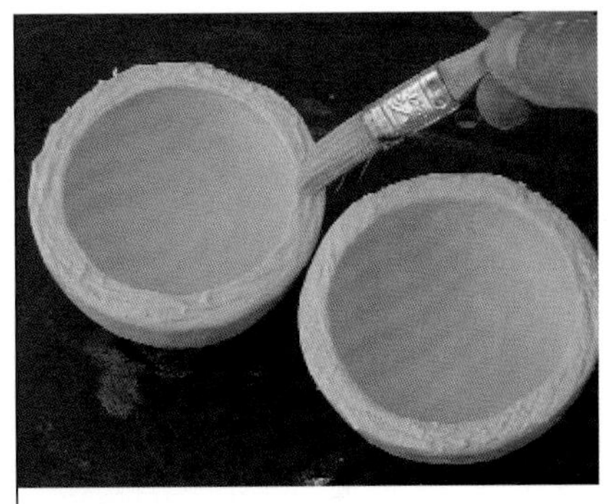

## Step 8

Use the serrated rib to rough up the rim of each half and paint on an even coat of water. Allow the clay to soften a bit before joining the halves.

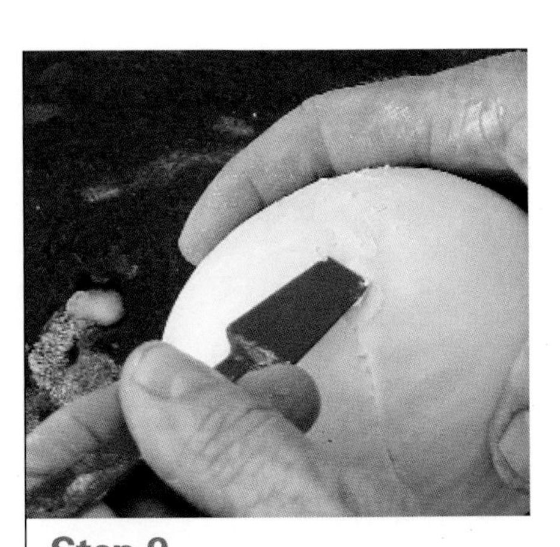

## Step 9

Press the halves together. A slight twisting motion will strengthen the bond. Next, meld the seam. The gap is filled in with the fingers followed by a small, flat stick, as shown.

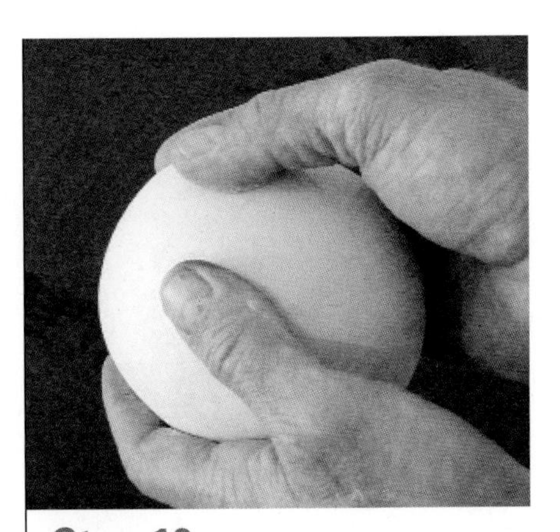

## Step 10

Use the fingers of both hands to remove surface imperfections. The clay should be kept moist and free of cracks. Use the dampened sponge to wipe over the surface of the clay.

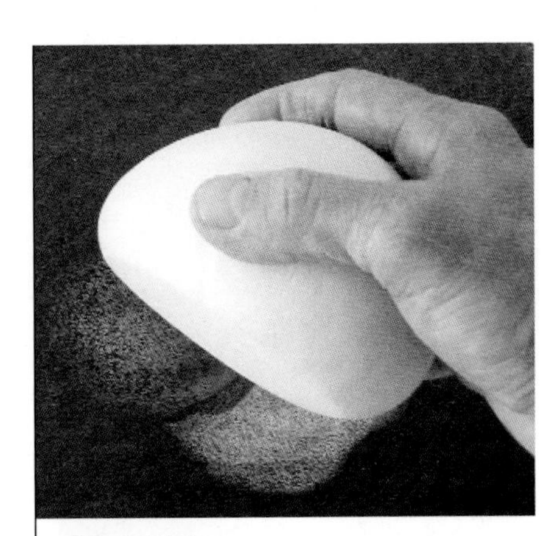

## Step 11

Create a flattened bottom by pressing the hollow form onto the table surface. This surface should be porous or textured enough so that the clay does not stick. A plastic bat is used here but any smooth, porous surface is suitable.

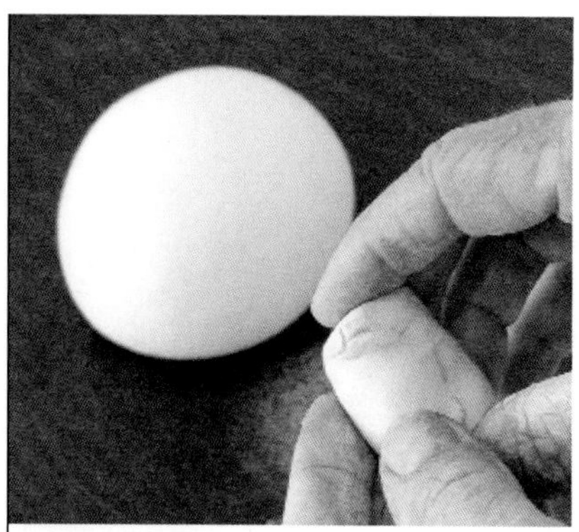

## Step 12

Set aside the body of the ocarina for a moment to create the mouthpiece. This piece shown is approximately 1 inch wide, 1½ inches long and ¾ of an inch thick.

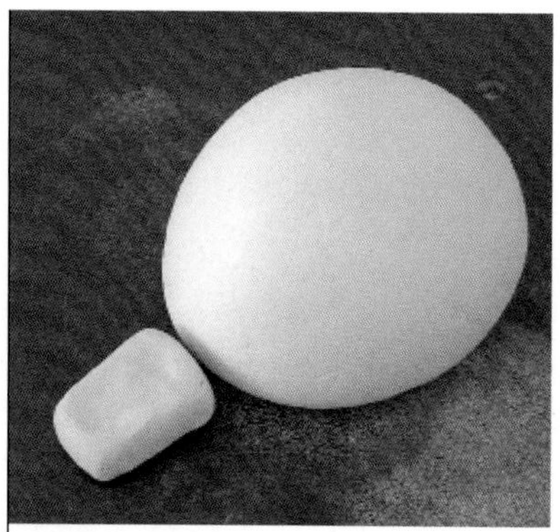

## Step 13

Notice, here, that the mouthpiece shape has squared sides with a slight taper from back to front. The mouthpiece is thick enough to allow for the later insertion of the stick that will be used to create the windway. The shape of the mouthpiece can be smoothed after it has been attached to the body. Lay the mouthpiece next to the body to determine the best place for attachment.

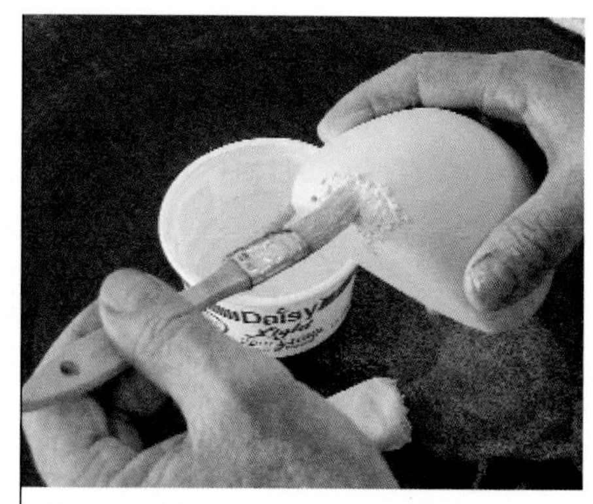


## Step 14

Use the needle tool to thoroughly score the area where the mouthpiece will be attached. Brush on a liberal coating of water. Allow the clay in this area to soften. Score and wet the end of the mouthpiece in the same fashion. Set the mouthpiece and body on the table and press them together. The mouthpiece must be aligned with the flat side of the body.

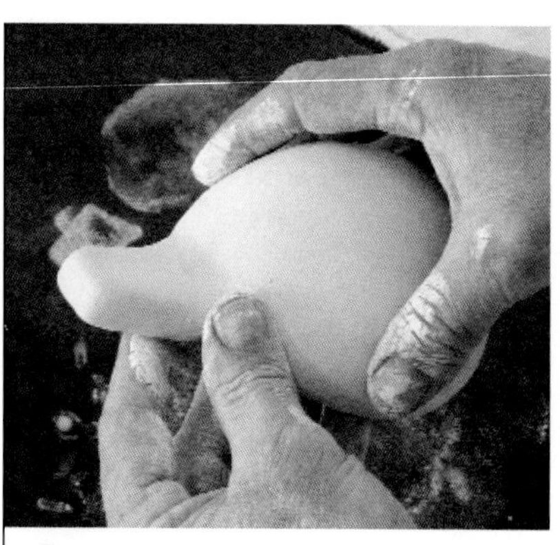

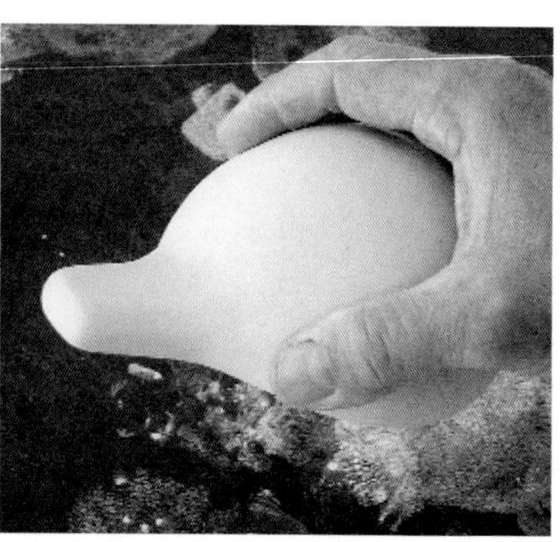

## Step 15

After the mouthpiece is attached, pick up the body and smooth away the seam. Complete this step thoroughly to minimize the risk of cracking later.

## Step 16

Carefully insert the Popsicle stick into the mouthpiece to create the windway. Care must be taken to ensure that the stick passes through the mouthpiece parallel to the top and bottom surfaces and squarely with the sides. Slow even pressure is best.

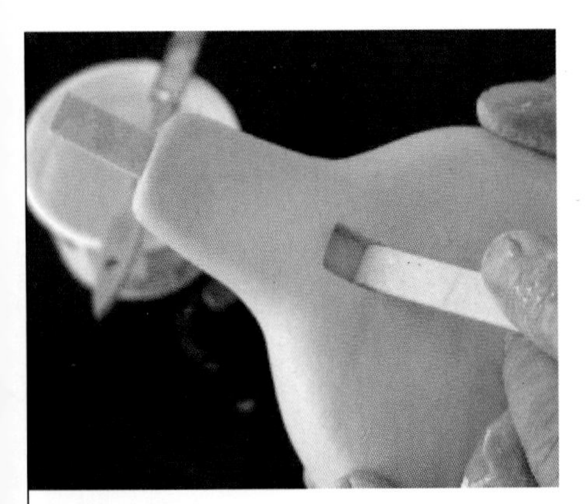

## Step 17

With the stick used to create the windway still in place, use another beveled-edge stick to cut the aperture, or window, on the underside of the ocarina. The aperture should be located so that the side closest to the mouthpiece is just inside the interior of the wall of the body. If the hole is cut too close to the mouthpiece, the aperture will be blocked by the wall. Make a squared opening and remove the small piece of clay. Cut all the way down to the stick underneath. Make clean, squared cuts on all four sides.

Next, with the beveled edge of the stick facing down, make a square cut at a 45° angle, moving toward the mouthpiece, as shown in the illustration. Press the stick in until it reaches the other stick. Follow through, removing the small piece of clay. Your objective is to create a sharp beveled edge on the side of the aperture farthest from the mouthpiece. This sharp edge splits the air from the windway and creates the sound. (See figure 4.16 for a cross-section view of how this should look.) Carefully withdraw the stick from the windway.

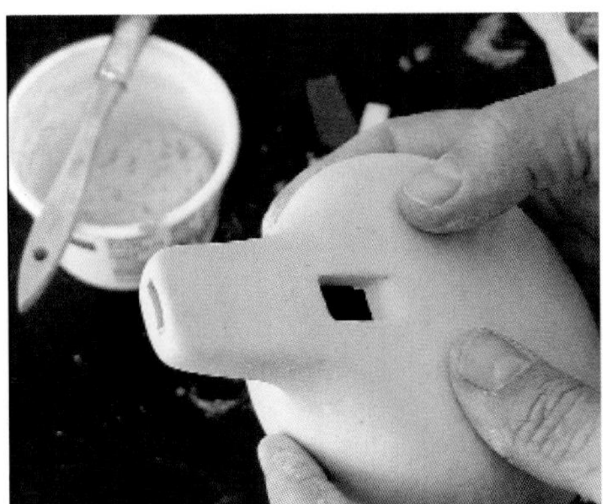

## Step 18

Bring the ocarina to your lips and give it a test blow. If it whistles, you can move on to the next step. If there is no whistle, reinsert the stick in the airway and check the sharpness of the bevel.

Withdraw the windway stick, being careful to keep the stick flat. Do not raise or lower it, as this will misalign the bevel.

Hold the ocarina up and look into the windway while under an overhead light. You should see the beveled edge right in the middle of the windway. If you do not, reinsert the windway stick and lay the ocarina on the table with the flat side down. Press down on the body and mouthpiece to ensure that both are in full contact with the table. Remove the stick and recheck the alignment.

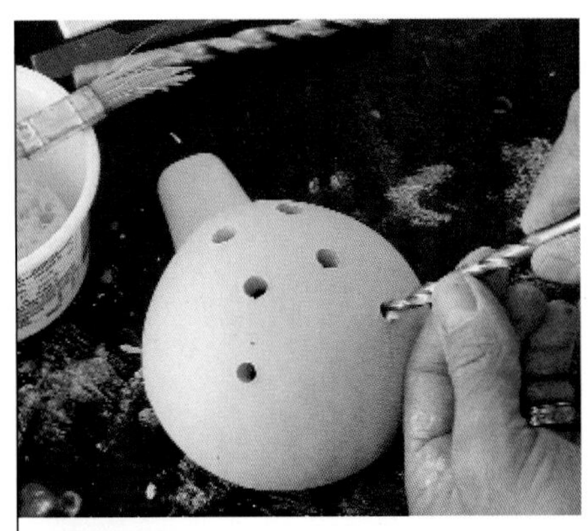

## Step 19

Use a drill bit or a hole cutter to create the finger holes on the top of the ocarina. Use the countersink tool to smooth the edges of the holes.

It is most common to create 4-6 holes, but you may do as you like. Depending on the precision of your mouthpiece assembly, at some point as you add more holes, your ocarina may stop sounding. If this happens, either adjust your windway and bevel until it works again, or fill in your last finger hole and declare success!

If you want to tune your ocarina to a specific scale, cut and tune one hole at a time. Enlarging a hole raises its pitch, so start small and enlarge each hole until you achieve the pitch you want.

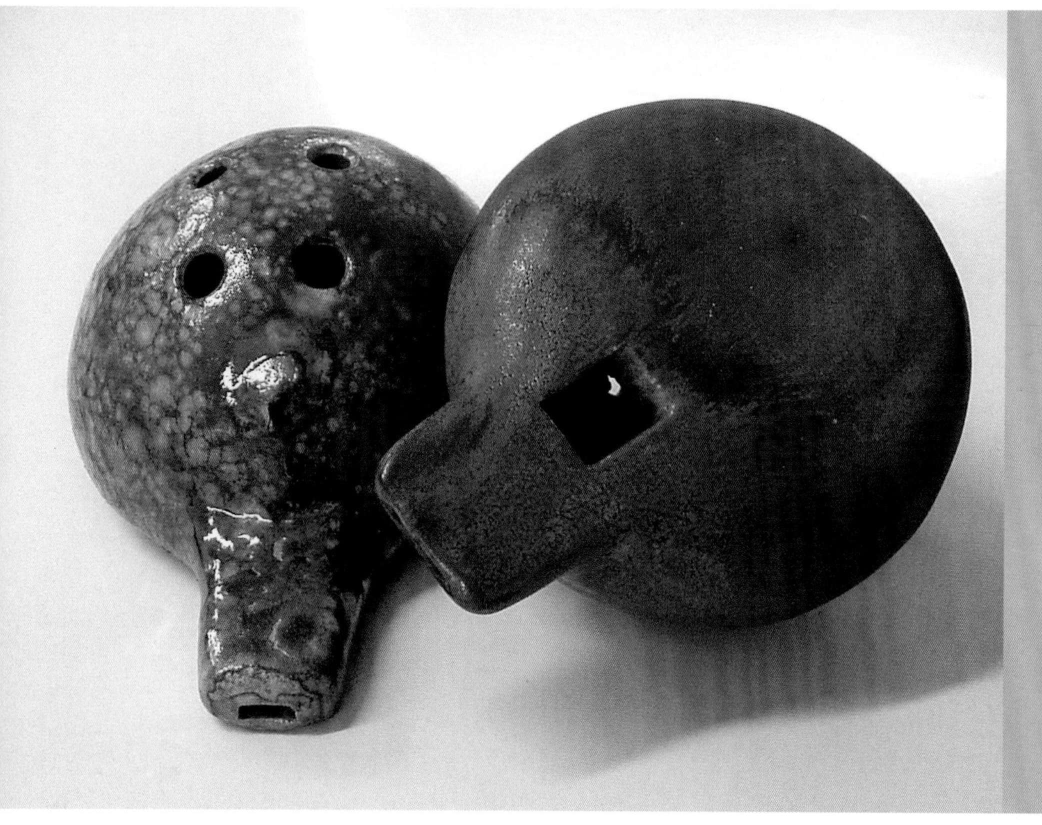

## Final Steps

You can fire and finish your ocarina in almost any way imaginable. If you elect to glaze it, be careful not to get any glaze in the windway, which will clog it. It is also advisable not to glaze the beveled edge of the aperture. Very slight changes to your mouthpiece assembly can alter the ocarina's sound, or make it stop working altogether.

Many makers low fire their ocarinas so the clay retains some porosity. This helps to avoid moisture buildup in the windway.

You can also turn your ocarina into an animal or other form by adding components to the exterior of its body. Most of the fanciful ocarinas shown in this book started with a basic shape such as this one. Have fun!

## The Four-Hole "English" Ocarina Tuning

One of the simpler fingering systems for an ocarina requires only four holes to play an entire octave of pitches. The fingering for a major scale is shown to the right, where white circles indicate open holes and black circles indicate closed holes. To create this tuning on your ocarina, start by cutting the hole in the upper right corner. Start small, and enlarge the hole until it produces the second scale tone ("re"). This will, of course, be relative to the first scale tone ("do") that is produced when the hole is covered. Then cut the hole below it, and continue to the rest of the holes one at a time, following the fingering pattern shown and testing your notes as you proceed. As shown in the diagram, each hole you create will be larger than the previous one. As with the tubular flute, enlarging a hole raises the pitch it produces. Unlike the flute, the position of the hole relative to the mouthpiece has virtually no effect. This is because an ocarina is a globular flute, rather than a tubular flute (see the Aerophones chapter for more information on the differences between tubular and globular instruments).

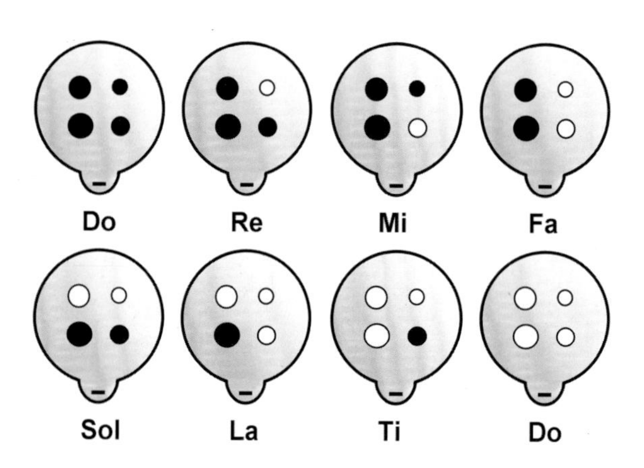

## DEMONSTRATION 3 | Goblet Drum

*Although it is traditionally handbuilt from coils, this drum is also fun to make on the potter's wheel. It is suited to intermediate and advanced potters, but its two-piece design makes it a project that even novices can try. Just about any type of clay can be used. For this demonstration a white stoneware with medium grog was selected.*

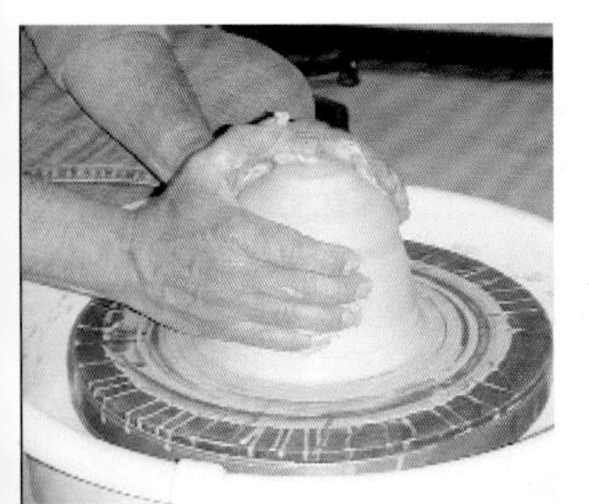

### Step 1

Throw the base of the drum first. It requires 8 to 10 pounds of well-wedged clay. It is crucial that the clay be perfectly centered on the wheel before moving on to the next step.

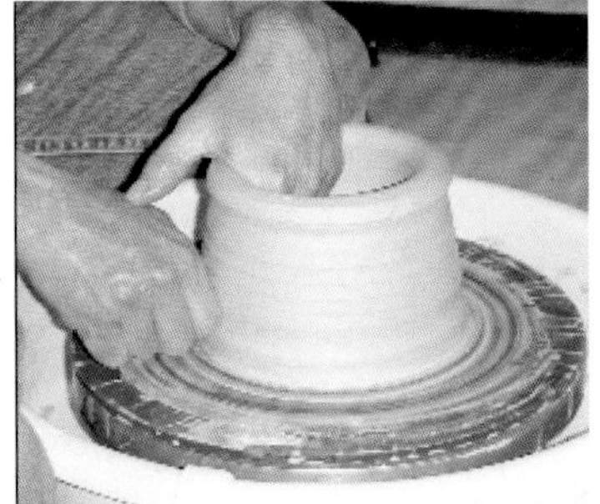

### Step 2

Open the clay all the way down to the wheel head. At the bottom, move the clay outward very carefully to keep it centered. Create a wide flare at the bottom and draw the clay up to a narrow mouth at the top.

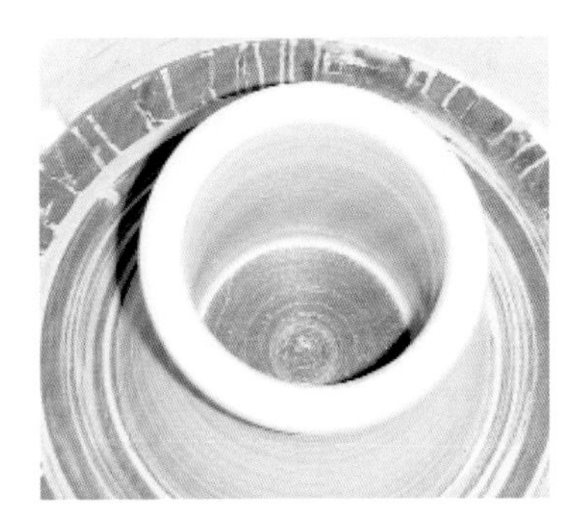

A top view of the drum's base showing the open bottom. Note that the top edge is broad and has been trimmed flat. This will aid the attachment of the drum's bowl later.

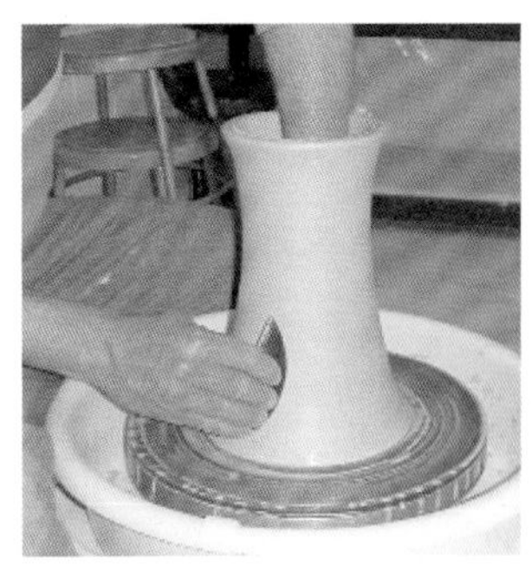

A side view showing the base near completion. A wooden rib is used to smooth the outer surface and to thin the wall evenly from bottom to top.

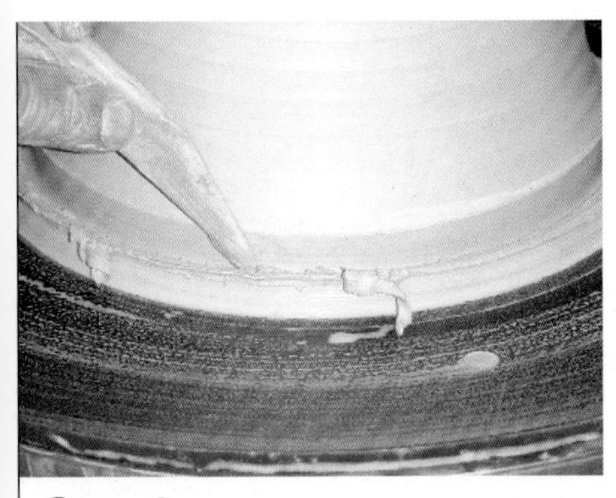

### Step 3

Use a wooden tool to trim away excess clay from the bottom of the base. After the trimmings are removed, the edge can be smoothed with a sponge.

At this point the base can be set aside to firm to the leather-hard state before being cut from the bat with a wire.

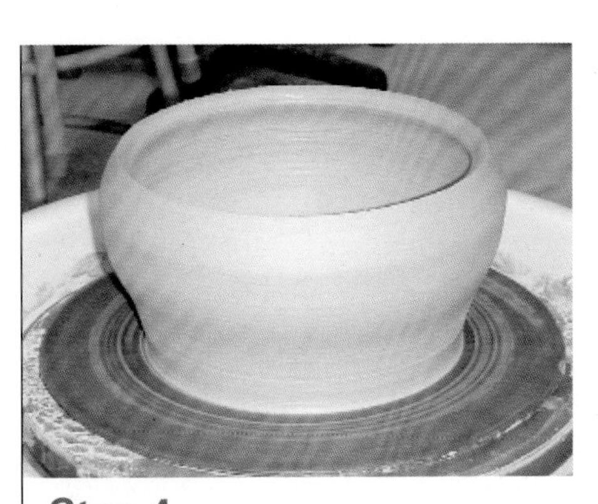

### Step 4

Use 4 to 5 pounds of clay for the second piece of the goblet drum. Just as with the base, the clay for the bowl should be well wedged and perfectly centered before shaping it.

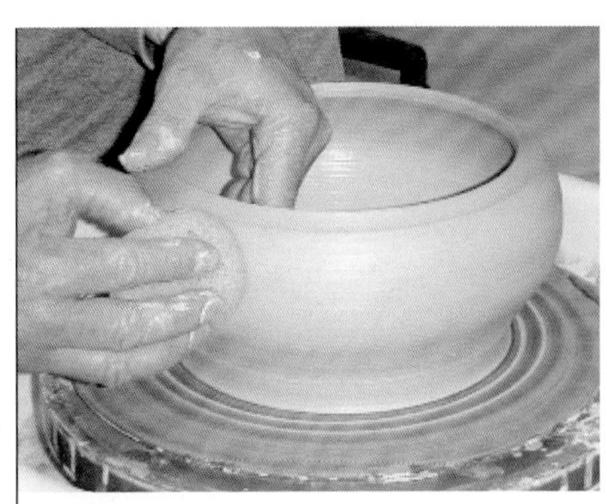

### Step 5

Roll the mouth of the bowl inward slightly. Use a sponge to smooth the outer wall.

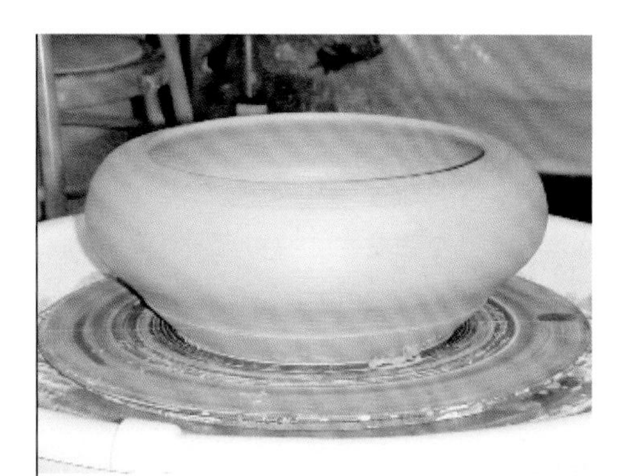

A view of the bowl showing how the wall has been widened while maintaining the rolled rim. The rim of the pot should not be too thin, since this is where the drum will be repeatedly struck with the hands and fingers.

Draw a cut wire across the bat and set the bowl and bat aside. After the bowl firms up, it can be lifted and inverted.

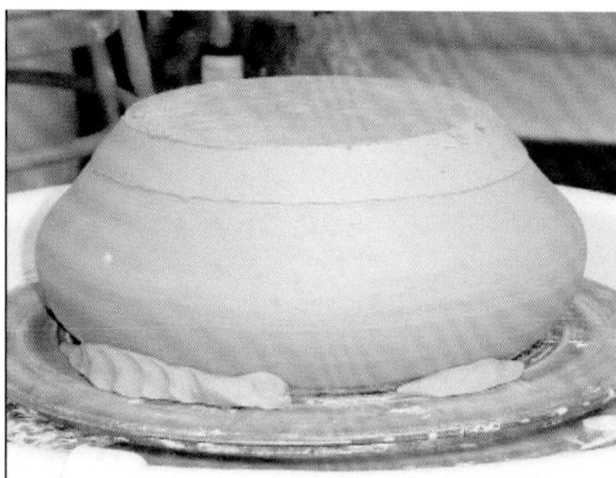

## Step 6

Center the bowl upside down on a bat or directly on the wheel head. Once centered, use several pads of soft clay to hold it in place.

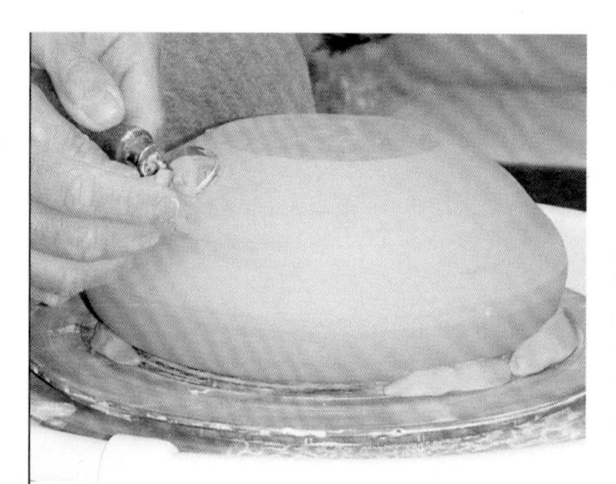

## Step 7

Use a trimming loop to remove excess clay from the bowl. Trim enough clay away so that the walls are of even thickness from top to bottom and so the drum will not be too heavy. Be careful not to trim through the pot.

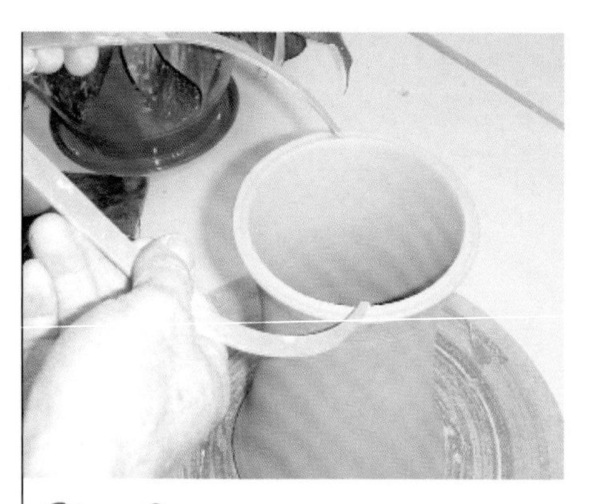

## Step 8

Use calipers to measure the INNER diameter of the base. A ruler or other straight stick can be used if calipers are not available.

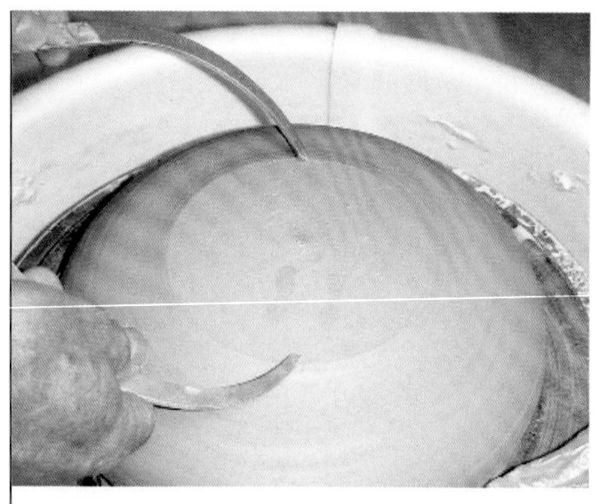

## Step 9

Set the calipers on the bowl with the center of the bowl at the midpoint between the caliper tips. Lightly press the tips into the clay to indicate the width of the hole to be cut.

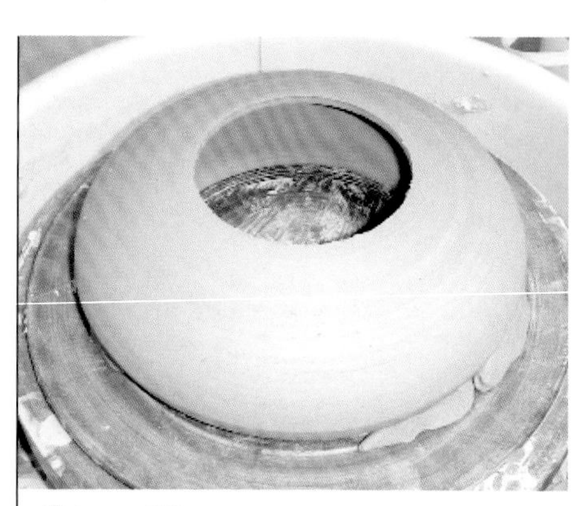

## Step 10

With the bowl spinning, use a needle tool to cut out a disk of clay. Remove the disk of clay. It isn't necessary to clean up the edge.

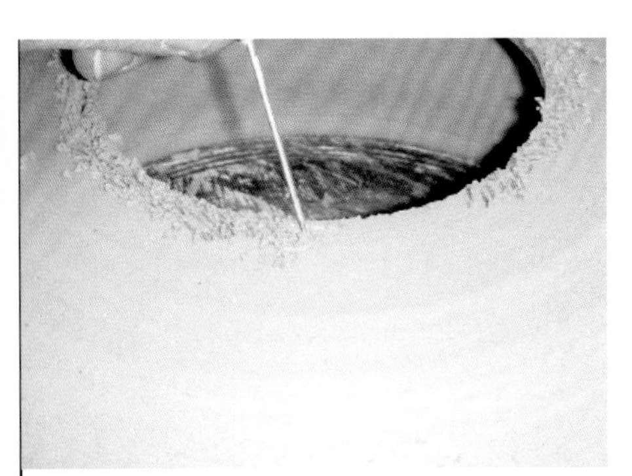

### Step 11

Use a needle tool to thoroughly score the area around the edge of the cut. The scored band should be about ¼" wide. Then paint an even coat of water or slip on the scored area, allowing it to soften.

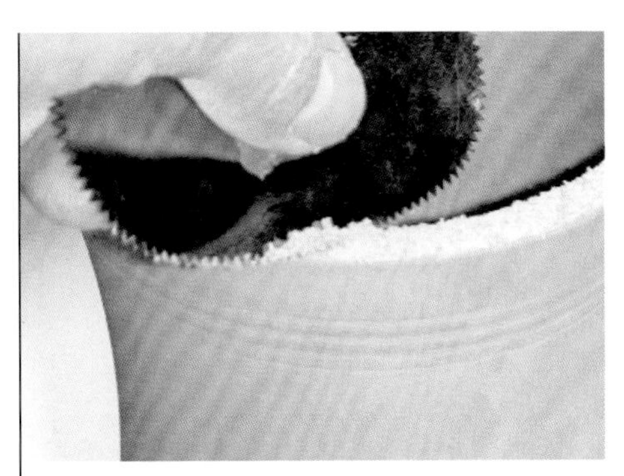

### Step 12

Score the top of the base piece as well. A serrated rib is ideal for this. After scoring this surface, paint it with water or slip and allow it to soften.

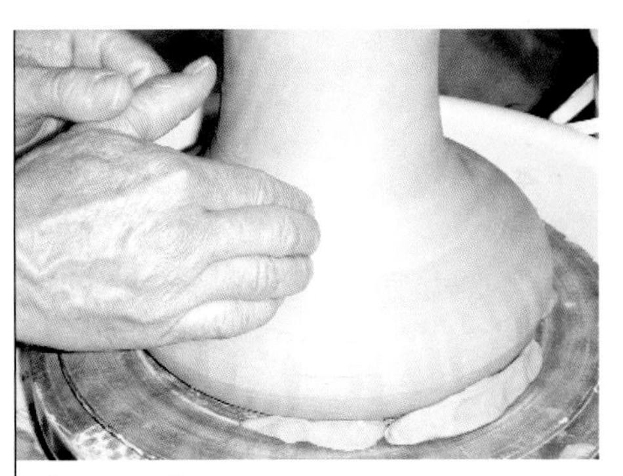

### Step 13

Invert the base and lightly place it over the bowl's scored area. Slowly turn the wheel to gauge how well the base is centered on the bowl. Slide the base front to back or side to side, until it is centered on the bowl. Once it is in the proper position, apply firm, even downward pressure to meld the two pieces. Smooth the seam with your fingers as the wheel slowly spins.

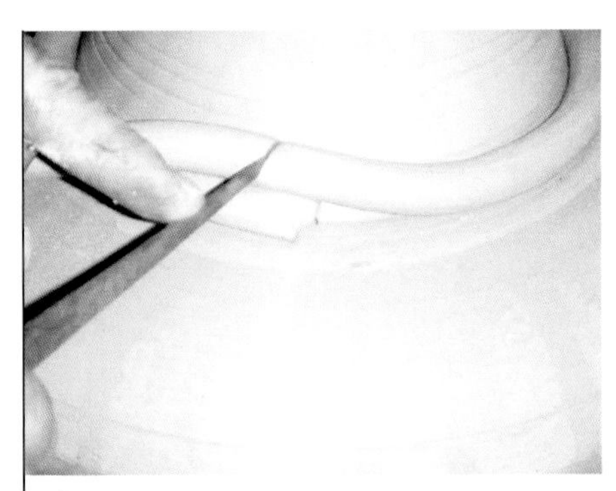

### Step 14

Wind a coil of clay around the seam area to give added strength. Overlap the ends of the coil and draw a knife through both to remove the excess. Thoroughly smooth the coil into the forms with your fingers.

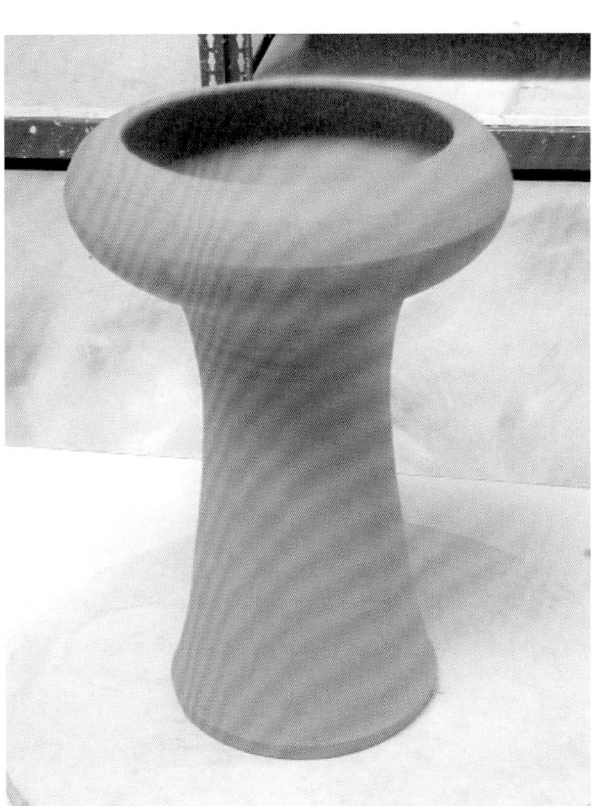

Let the goblet drum dry slowly. Bisque fire and then glaze. After the glaze firing, the drum is ready for the skin to be attached.

## Notes on Heading Your Drum

When putting a skin head on a ceramic drum, almost any rawhide animal skin can be used, but those most commonly used for drums come from goats and cows. The skins of different animals have varying properties that will impact the sound of your drum. Goat skin is widely used for drums because it is thin, strong and very flexible.

Rawhide animal skins can be purchased from a variety of sources (see "Resources and Materials".) If you are more adventurous and have access to fresh animal skins, you can scrape and dry the hide yourself. This is a very messy and smelly process, so many drum makers prefer to obtain pre-stretched and dried skins.

Skins come in different thicknesses. Some drums, such as congas and drums played with sticks, use thick skins, while other drums such as doumbeks and frame drums usually sound better with thin skins. Regardless of whether the head is thick or thin, the best sound will come from a skin that is a uniform thickness throughout. It is also important to choose skins that do not have holes or other potentially weak spots. An easy way to inspect a skin for flaws is to hold it up to a light. Since skins are usually translucent, weak spots or holes will show up clearly.

The hair on a hide can be left on the drum or removed. Any remaining hair will dampen the drum's tone, which is desirable on some types of drums and avoided on others. Even if you use a hairless skin, it is desirable to position the side of the skin that used to have hair facing outward (the striking side of the head). The hair side has a smoother and more durable surface, and can be identified on hairless skins by looking closely for pores or small hairs.

This demonstration uses glue and clamps to attach the skin to the drum shell. The recommended glue is either polyvinyl acetate (commonly called white glue) or aliphatic resin (yellow carpenter's glue). These adhesives are water-soluble, which means they will enable you to remove the drum head, when necessary, by soaking it in warm water.

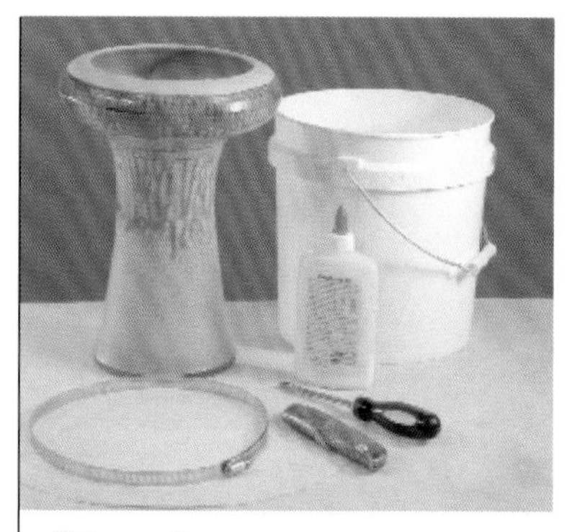

### Step 1
Materials needed: The glazed and fired drum body, rawhide goat skin (at least 4 inches larger in diameter than the widest part of the drum), hose clamp or large rubber bands, water-soluble glue, and a sharp knife for trimming.

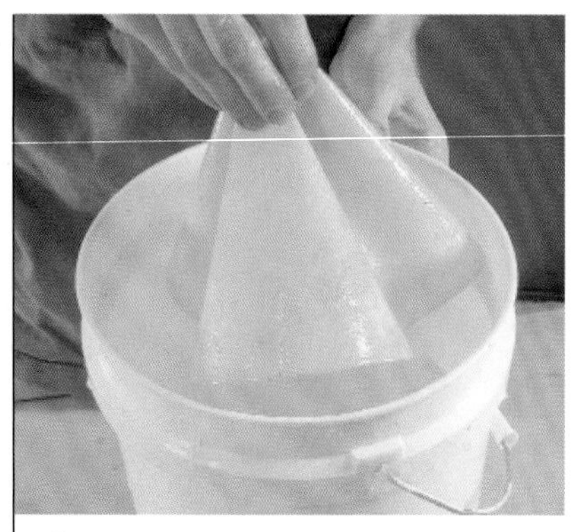

### Step 2
Soak the rawhide skin in cold water until it becomes limp and stretchy—about 30 minutes to an hour, depending on its thickness. Remove it from the water and shake it dry, or lightly pat it with a towel to remove any excess water on its surface.

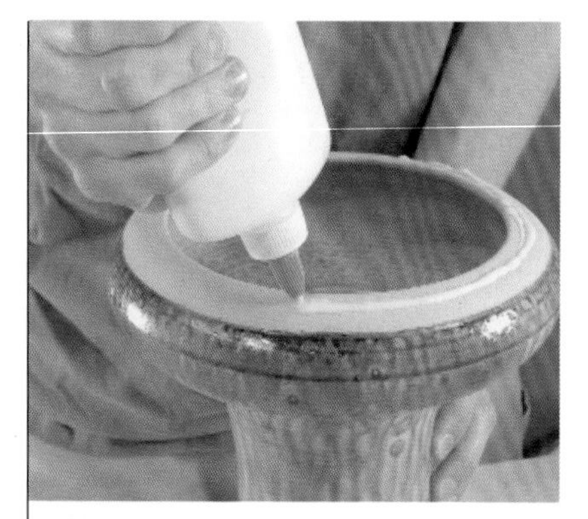

### Step 3
Spread a thin layer of glue on the rim of the drum. Note the portion of the drum rim that was left unglazed in order to improve adhesion of the glue.

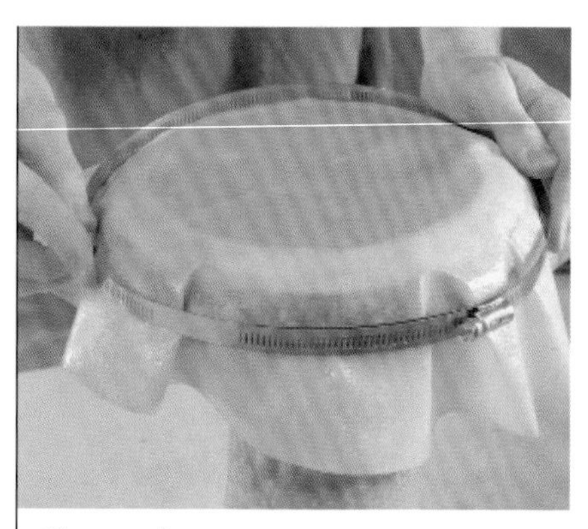

### Step 4
Drape the skin over the drum, with the hair (exterior) surface on top. Hold the skin in place with a hose clamp or rubber bands. Do not tighten the clamp all the way yet.

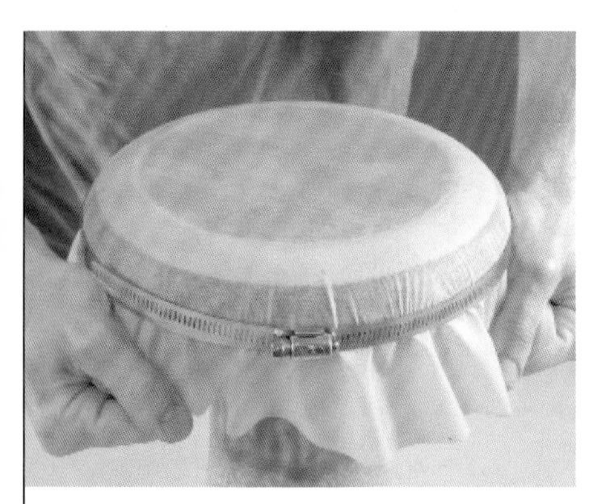

## Step 5

Gently pull the edges of the skin down under the clamp while removing any folds or buckles from the skin that occur underneath the clamp. Your objective is to pull the skin as tight as the clamp or rubber bands will hold it. You should alternate several times between tightening the clamp and pulling the skin tighter in order to put as much tension as possible on the skin.

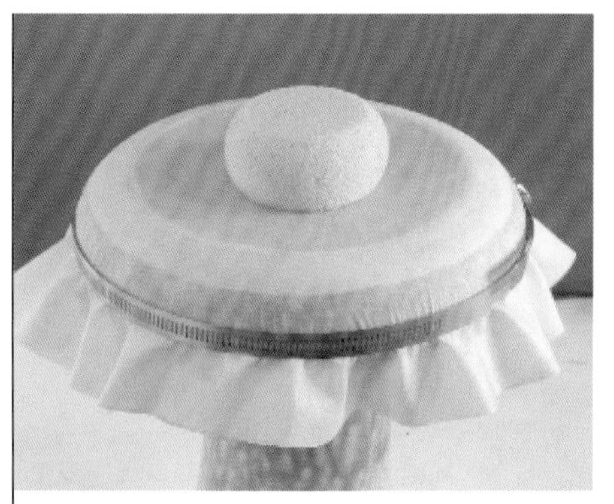

## Step 6

Once the skin is pulled as tight as you can get it, allow the glue and skin to dry thoroughly. Depending on your skin, drum and location, this will probably take 1-2 days. Do not play the drum or disturb it in any way while the glue and skin are drying or it will lose tension. To achieve an even tighter head, leave a damp sponge resting on the center of the head as it dries. This will inhibit the center of the head from shrinking until after the glued rim has dried.

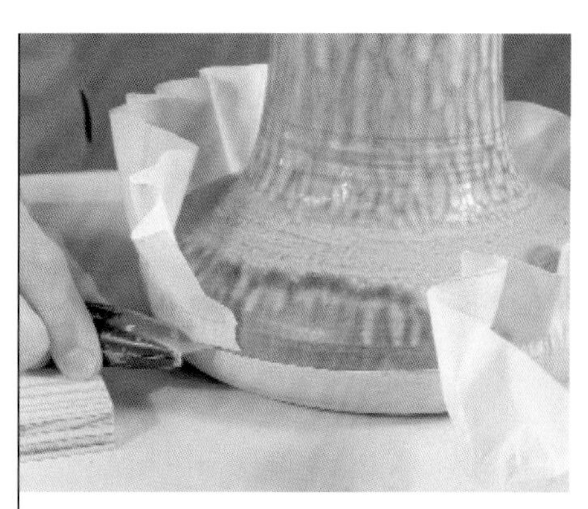

## Step 7

When the skin is completely dry, remove the clamp and trim the excess skin with a knife. Be very careful; the skin is often difficult to cut through, and knives tend to slip very easily on glazed ceramic surfaces. Instead of a knife you can also use a hacksaw blade to "saw" through the skin. A new, sharp blade will have the best cutting action, but may rapidly become dulled by the ceramic surface. If your drum is high-fired, there is little danger of damaging the drum's surface with a knife or saw blade. Once trimmed, you can remove any excess glue with a sponge and warm water. The skin may have a slightly sharp edge. To smooth it, you can wet the edge of the skin with water and press it down, or you can sand it with fine sandpaper. You also can add a decorative band of fabric, ribbon or tape around the drum to cover the edge of the skin.

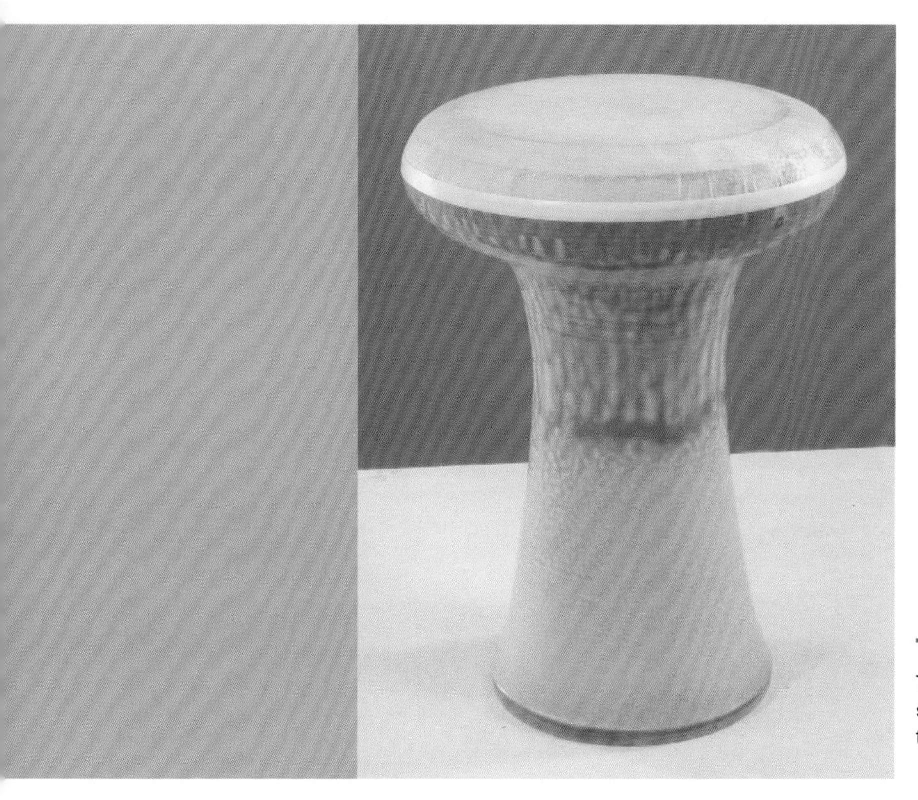

## The finished drum

To hear how a drum like this sounds, listen to track 19 on the CD.

## DEMONSTRATION 4 | Side-Blown Flute

*Simple as it is to construct, the playing of this flute can be trickier to master than the ocarina or whistle flute. This demonstration provides the basic elements of the side-blown flute's design. You may have to make a few before you have one that plays just the way you like. Experiment with different lengths, hole sizes and shapes. To hear how a flute like this can sound, listen to track 30 on the CD.*

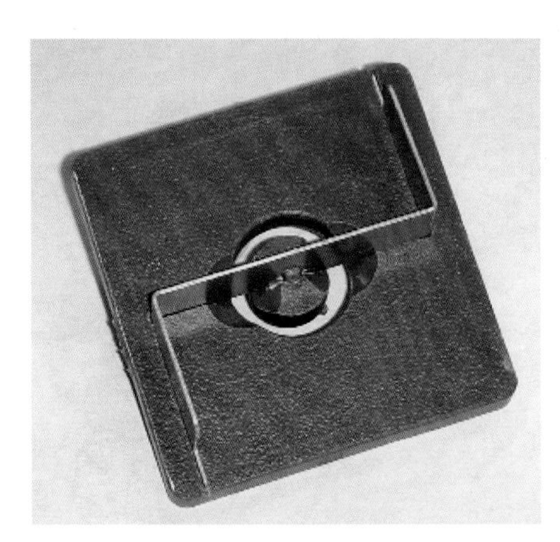

### Step 1

Our side-blown flute's tubular body is made using a cylinder die attached to an extruder with a capacity of about eight pounds of clay. We've chosen a die that produces a 1-inch diameter tube. You also can use a smaller diameter die, but larger is not recommended for your first flute because the instrument will require too much air to sound.

The key to making hollow extrusions suitable for flute barrels is to use a moist, supple, smooth-bodied clay that has been well wedged so it is free of air bubbles. If you use stiff clay the extrusion will likely split where it passes over the cross brace that supports the center section of the die.

(If you don't have access to an extruder, you can create your flute tube using the slab method shown in the end-blown flute demonstration.)

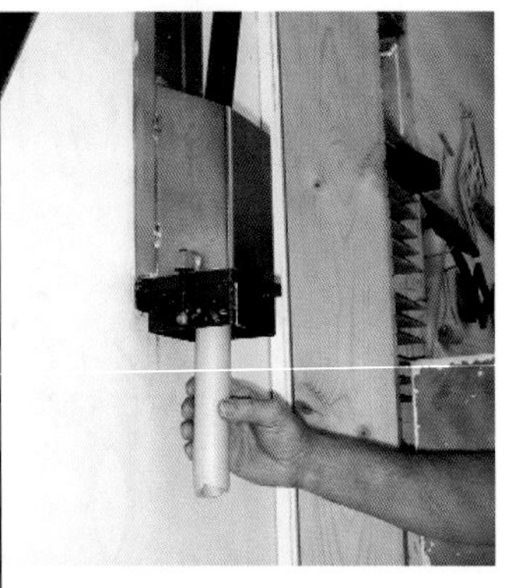

### Step 2

Here, the clay has been loaded into the extruder and the first extrusion is underway. The clay is guided with one hand while the handle is pulled downward with the other. If the extruder cannot be easily operated this way, then the clay is probably too stiff.

A full barrel of clay will yield two or three extrusions that are 12 to 18 inches long. Remove each from the extruder using a cutting wire drawn across the base of the extruder's die holder.

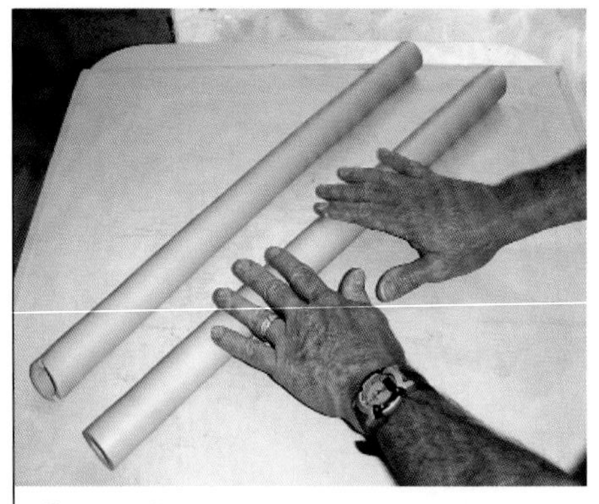

### Step 3

Since the fresh extrusions are soft, their shape can easily be distorted. Carefully lay each on a large piece of drywall or other flat surface and roll them back and forth to ensure they are straight.

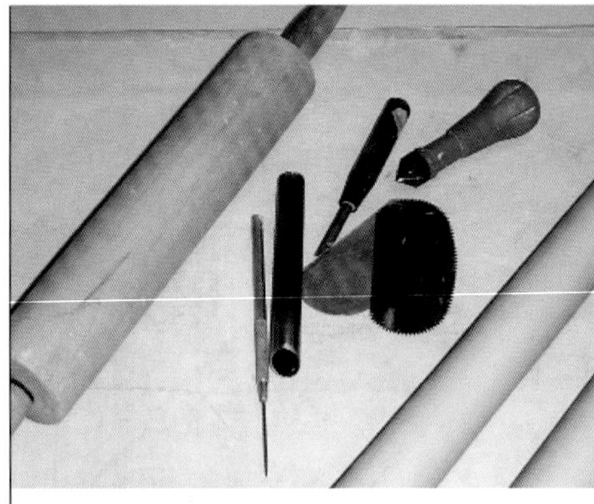

### Step 4

The extruder can be cleaned now and the tools needed to finish the flute can be gathered. To the left is a wooden rolling pin. Also shown is a needle tool, a piece of specially-cut copper tubing, a brass hole cutter with a wooden handle, a metal rib with smooth edges and one with a serrated edge. Above them is a countersink. The countersink and copper tubing can be found at a hardware store. The other tools are available from a ceramic supplier. You will also need a small ruler, a small paint brush and a cup of water (not shown). The extrusions can be left uncovered to firm up somewhat, but care should be taken to not allow them to get too hard.

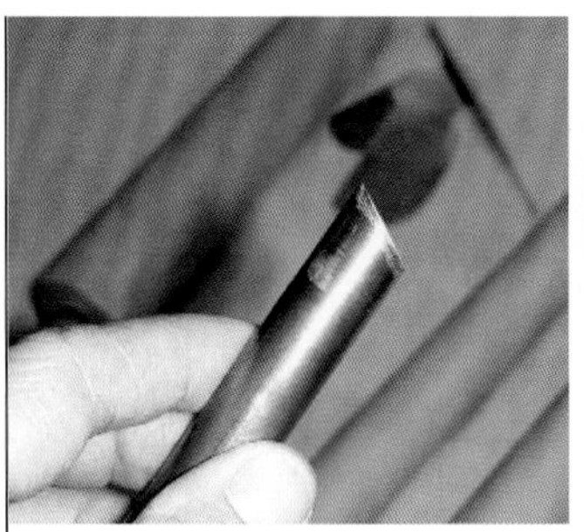
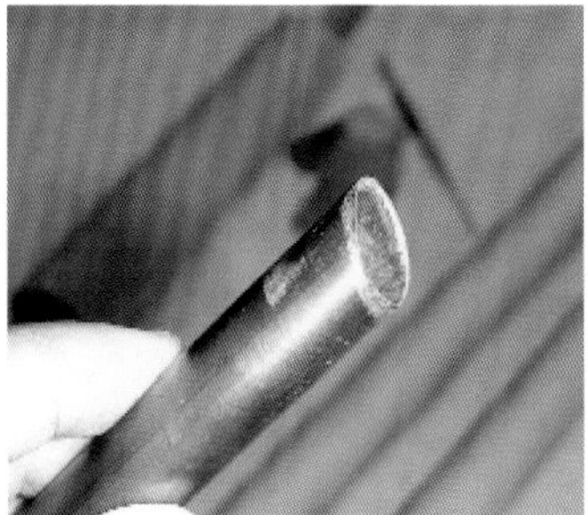

### Step 5

Here's a close-up view of the copper tube used to cut the blow hole in the flute. It is approximately ⅜ of an inch in diameter. It has been cut on a 30° angle and the edge has been de-burred.

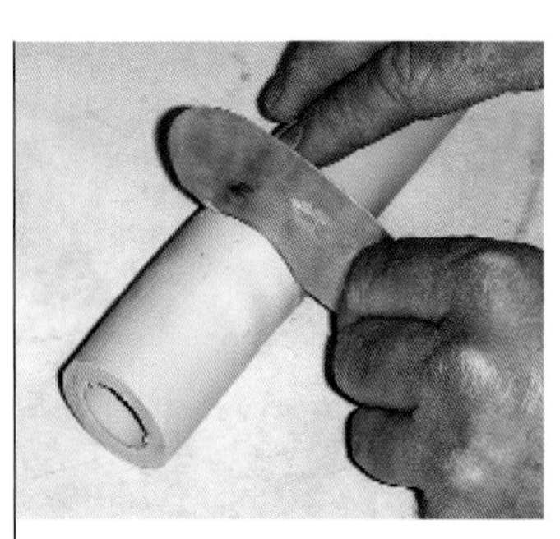

### Step 6

The remaining steps apply to each tube that has been extruded. One end of the tube is capped off with a flat piece of clay. Cut a piece about 2 inches long from the tube using the smooth-edged rib. To minimize distortion, roll the tube back and forth while exerting light pressure with the rib.

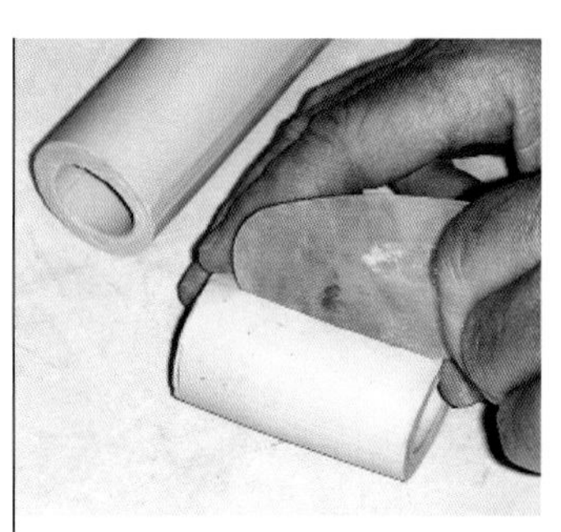

### Step 7

Slice the short tube open using the smooth rib.

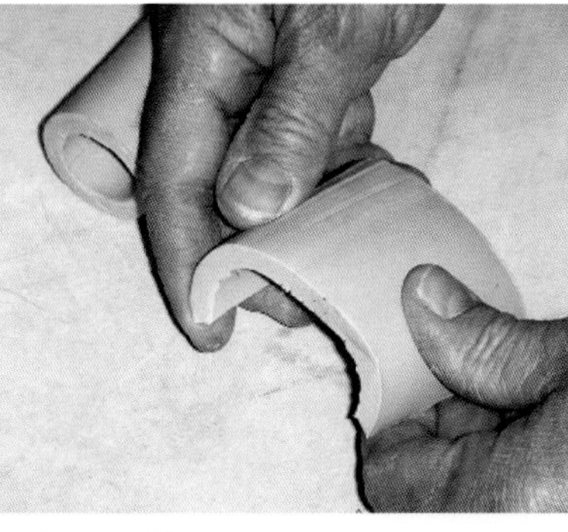

### Step 8

*Carefully* uncurl the clay. Open it slowly to avoid the formation of cracks. When the clay is nearly flat, press it on the table with your fingers.

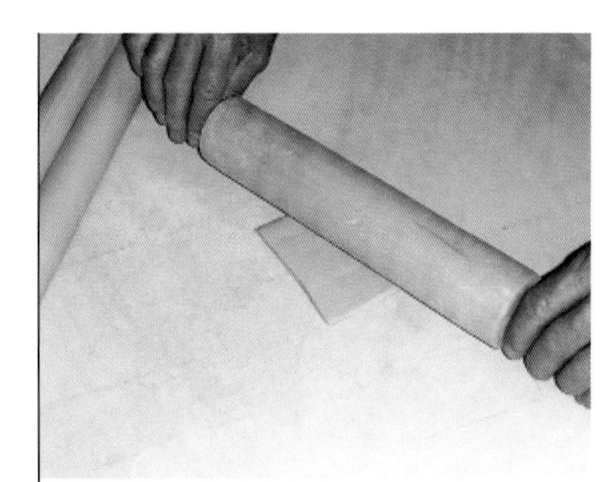

### Step 9

This is the rolling pin's only job. Use it to roll the small piece of clay evenly. There's no need to exert any real pressure. The weight of the roller, alone, should be enough to get the job done.

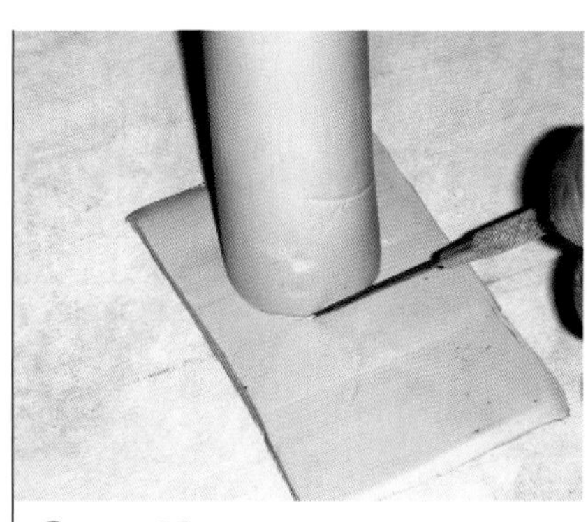

### Step 10

Stand the tube on the clay piece and support it with one hand. Lightly scribe around it using the needle tool, as shown. The circle made on the clay piece will indicate where it should be scored for attachment to the end of the tube.

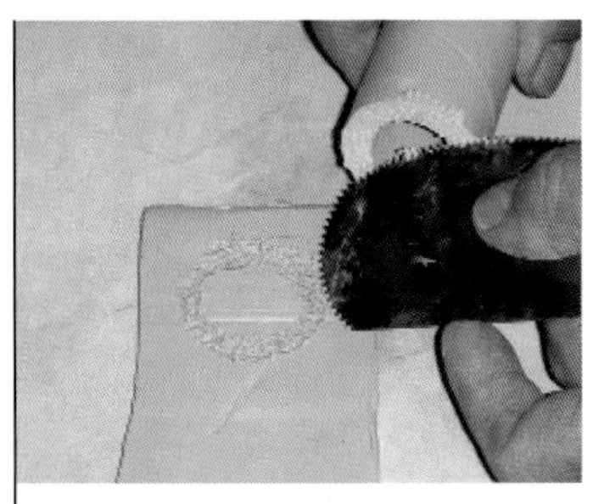

## Step 11

With a needle tool, thoroughly score the clay piece inside the scribed circle. The serrated rib is used to score the end of the tube. Brush both scored surfaces with water to lend additional stickiness to the clay where the pieces are to be joined.

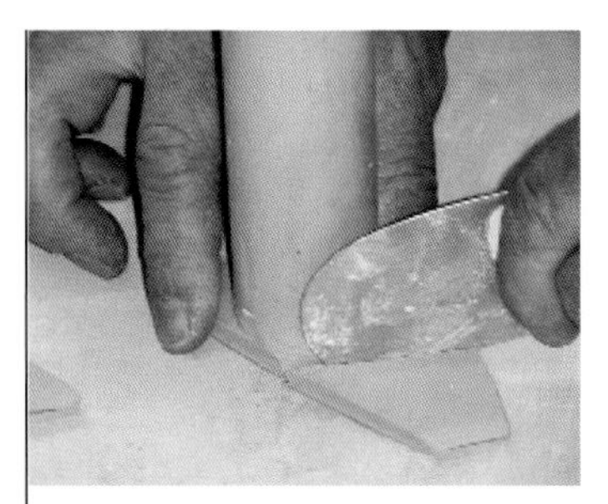

## Step 12

After the end cap is in place, trim the excess clay using the smooth rib. Cut the bulk of the flat clay piece away quickly then cut closer to the tube with a series of smaller, "nibbling" cuts until the edge of the end cap is fairly smooth and round. Tip: After cutting away what you can, roll the tube back and forth on the table to further smooth the edge of the end cap.

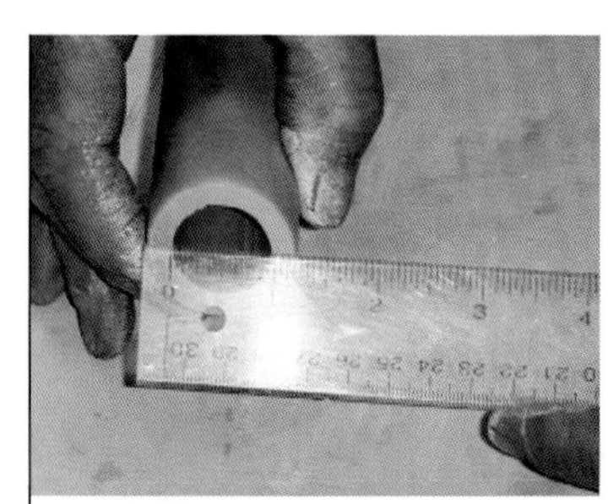

## Step 13

To determine the location of the blow hole, go to the open end of the tube and measure the inner diameter of the tube. This tube's inner diameter is ⅞-inch, so this is the measurement we will use in the next step.

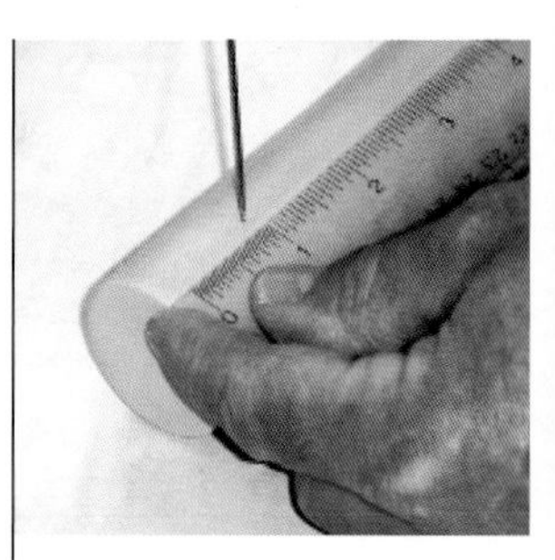

## Step 14

Hold the ruler against the tube, as shown, and use the needle tool to make a small hole ⅞-inch from the point where the end cap joins the end of the tube. In other words, don't measure from the outside end of the tube; measure from the end of the air column on the inside of the tube. Note that in the photo the zero mark on the ruler has been moved in from the end of the tube to allow for the thickness of the end cap.

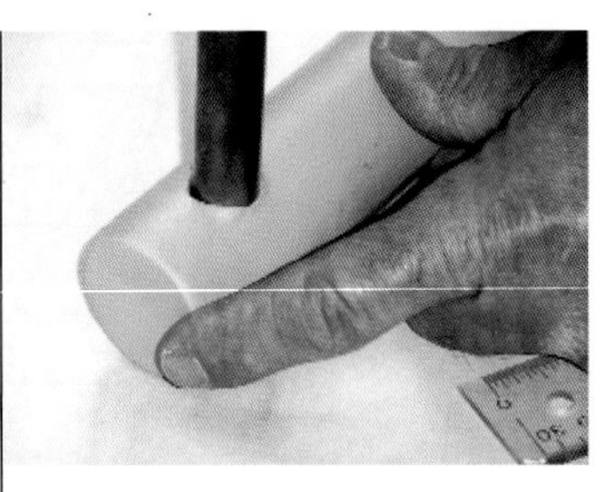

## Step 15

Hold the copper tube perpendicular to the flute body and press the edge into the clay at the mark made with the needle tool. Be careful to avoid any side-to-side movement as you twist the copper tube to complete the cut. A small plug of clay should come out when the copper tube is extracted.

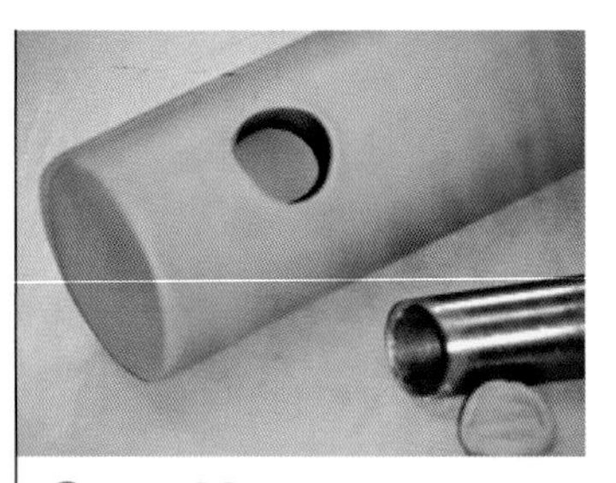

## Step 16

This close-up view shows everything done so far. The end cap has been rolled smooth, the blow hole has been cut and groomed a little with the fingers, and the small clay plug has been removed from the copper tube. The best sound will result from a well-defined blowing edge, so avoid the temptation to excessively smooth over the blow hole edge for aesthetic reasons.

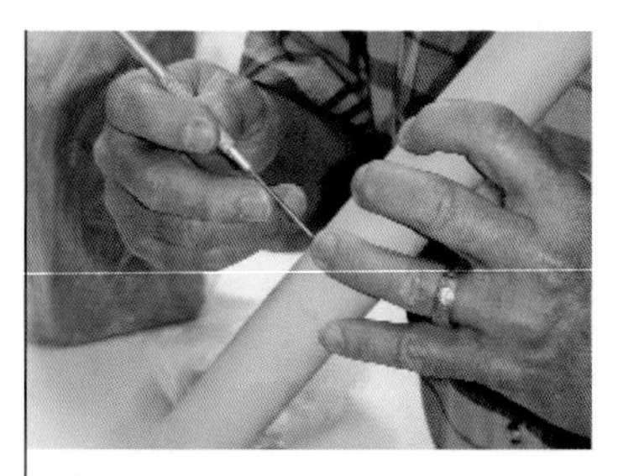

## Step 17

Now for the finger holes. The flute will have a total of six cut into it along the top. Grasp the flute comfortably near its middle with your left hand. Use the needle tool to mark where the pads of your first three fingers rest on the flute.

You might also choose to make a four-hole pentatonic flute that plays a five-note scale. For this style, mark your first and third fingers.

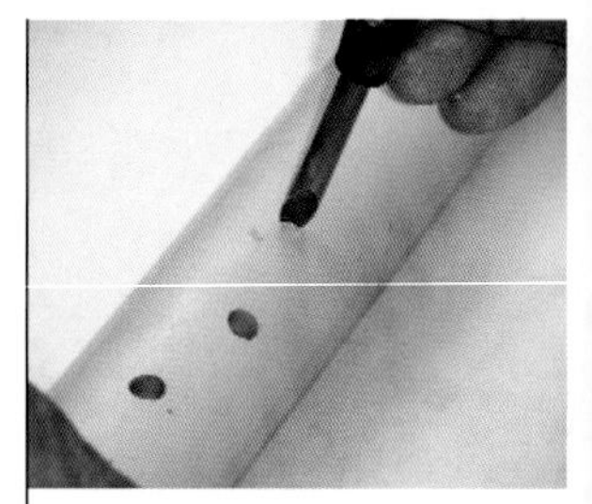

## Step 18

Use the hole cutter to make a hole at each spot where you made a needle mark. As with the blow hole, hold the cutter straight up and avoid wobbling side to side. Repeat the process to make three more holes for your right hand.

## About precision tuning

For your first flute, you may want to cut the finger holes without too much measuring or fuss, and just enjoy whatever scale results. If you want to tune your flute to play a standard scale, the process involves cutting and tuning one hole at a time, starting from the distal (bottom) end of the flute and working your way up. For a standard six-hole flute tuning, the spacing of the holes along the body should be close to the measurements given in the diagram. The holes should be approximately ⅜-inch in diameter, but it's recommended to start smaller and fine-tune each hole by gradually enlarging it until you achieve the tuning you want, then move on to the next hole. Each successive hole slightly changes the tuning of the previous hole, so this process requires a lot of backtracking and adjusting if you want a high level of precision.

Here are the two most important rules for tuning:

A hole placed closer to the mouth hole gives a higher pitch. When placed farther away, it gives a lower pitch.

A smaller hole gives a lower pitch. If made larger, it gives a higher pitch.

These rules indicate two ways to raise a pitch produced from a tone hole: either enlarge the hole, or place the hole closer to the blow hole. To lower a pitch, use a smaller hole or place the hole farther from the blow hole.

Precision tuning a flute in this way can be quite time-consuming, but the results are rewarding. If you get more deeply involved in making flutes, there are additional factors that come in to play that you will want to understand in order to better control the tuning, including wall thickness, tone hole undercutting and factors that impact intonation of the second octave. Several sources for more detailed information (and links to software for calculating hole size and placement) are listed in the "Resources" section and at this book's website, www.FromMudToMusic.com.

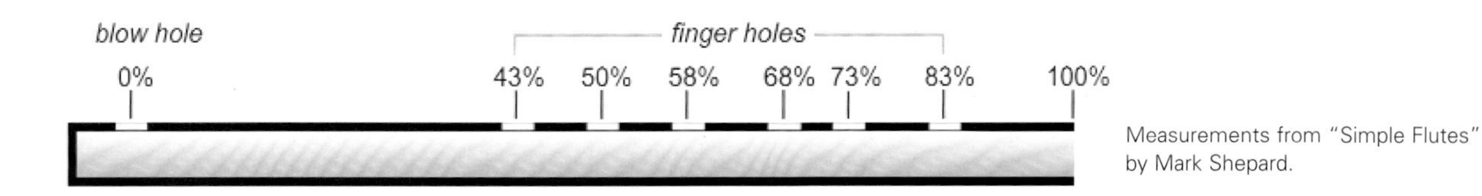


Measurements from "Simple Flutes" by Mark Shepard.

### Final Steps

It isn't absolutely necessary, but chamfering the edge of each finger hole with the countersink may make it easier to seat your fingers over the holes. You might try one flute with countersunk holes and another without them to see which works the best for you.

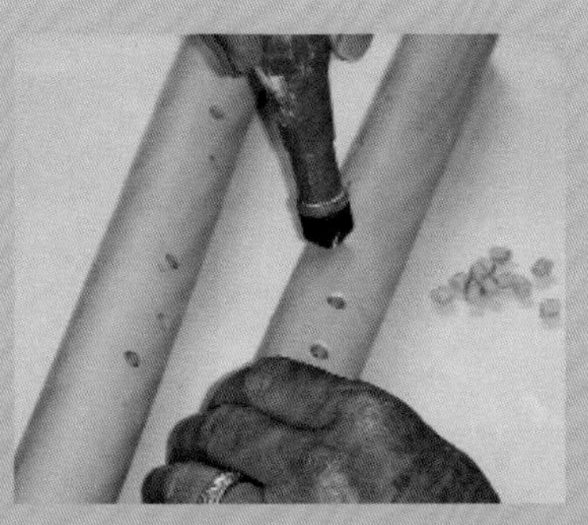

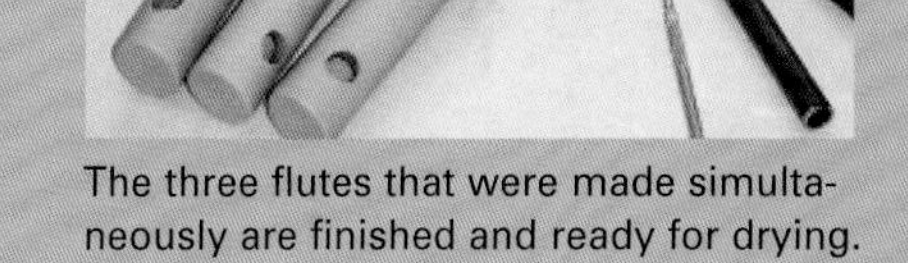

The three flutes that were made simultaneously are finished and ready for drying.

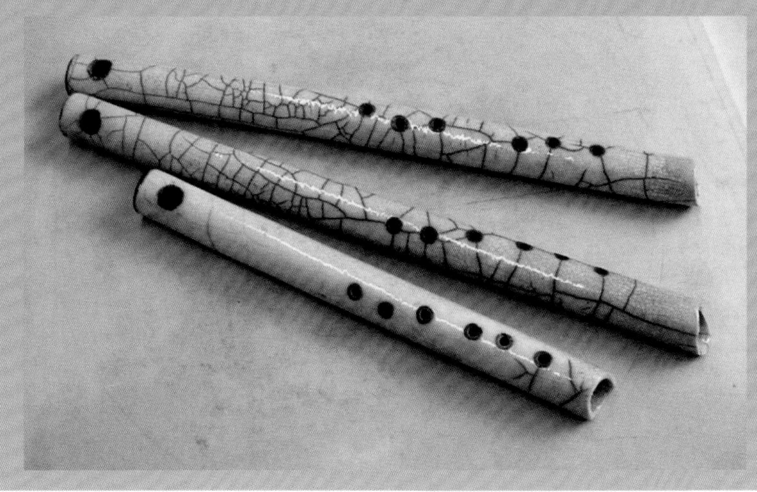

When completely dry, the flutes were bisque-fired to cone 04. They were decorated with a white crackle glaze and fired again in a raku kiln.

## DEMONSTRATION 5 | Whistle Flute

*The whistle flute in this demonstration is an end-blown ducted flute similar to a recorder or Irish penny-whistle, which has an airduct assembly at one end and a series of finger holes. This flute is challenging to make but easy to play. Successfully make one or two of the four-hole ocarinas and you're ready to give this instrument a try. For variety, experiment with different tube lengths to develop different pitches and try bending the tube into different shapes. As with the previous projects, most any type of clay can be used. What's important is to begin with fresh, well-wedged clay.*

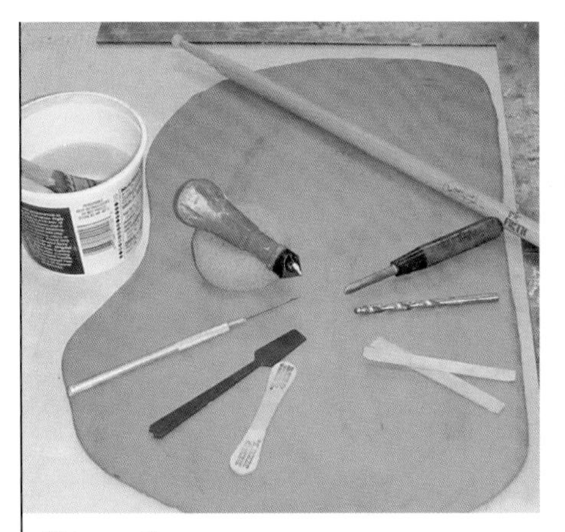

### Step 1

Our collection of familiar tools now includes a drum stick and a carpenter's square. The drum stick is about 14 inches long and ½-inch in diameter. A wooden dowel rod is a suitable alternative. It is important to have two of the sharpened Popsicle sticks (like those used in the ocarina demo). This project starts with a ⅛-inch-thick slab of clay that measures about 12 inches wide and 18 inches long. A slab roller is recommended to create this, but a rolling pin can be used if care is taken to ensure a slab of even thickness. A 2-foot-square sheet of drywall makes an ideal working surface.

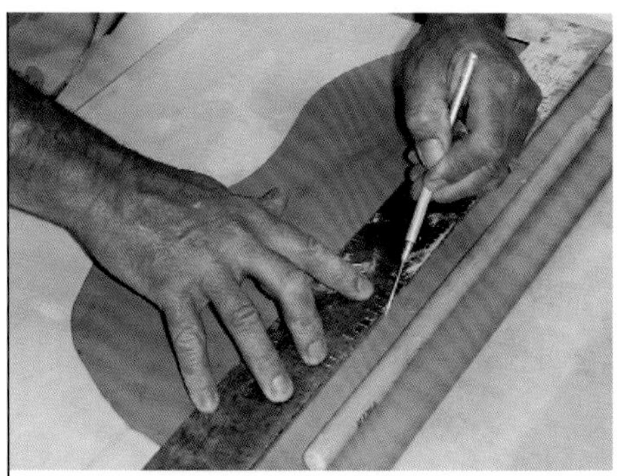

### Step 2

After gathering the tools and rolling out the slab of clay, the next step is to cut the clay into a manageable shape. Use the needle tool with the carpenter's square to make a straight cut along one side of the slab. Lay the edge of the dowel or drumstick on the clay with its side about an inch and a half from the edge of the slab. Make another cut in the slab about an inch and a half below the other side of the dowel.

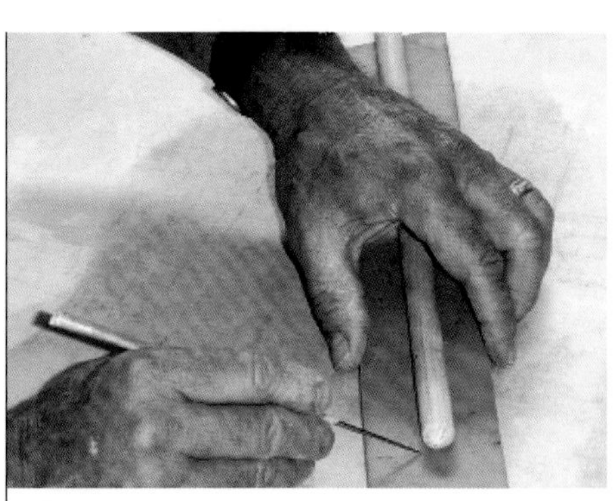

### Step 3

Using the needle tool, make squared cuts at each end of this strip of clay. Cutting the strip slightly shorter than the dowel makes it easier to remove the dowel later.

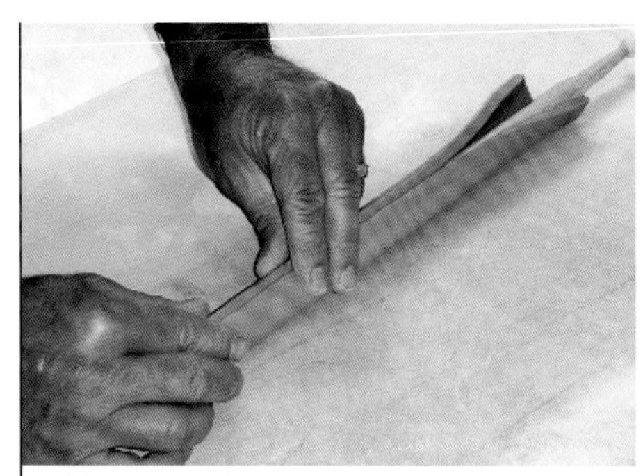

### Step 4

This is where the suppleness of the clay is critical. If the clay has been allowed to get too firm it will crack as it is formed around the dowel. The trick is to move slowly along the length of the dowel. If some cracks develop, lightly moisten the outside surface of the clay. If the strip is too wide, reopen the clay and trim the excess. Don't seal the seam shut yet.

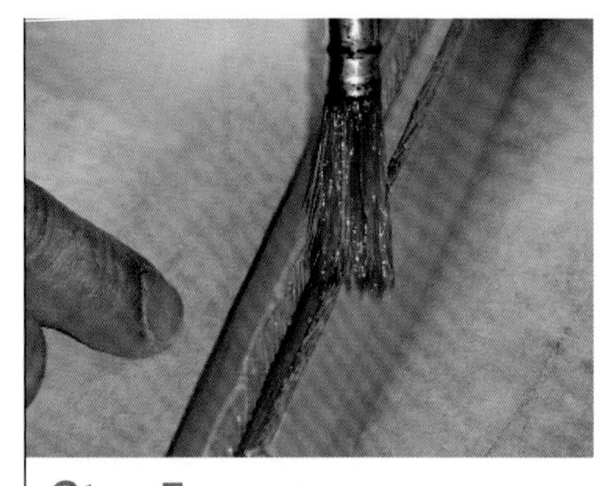

### Step 5

Once you have the clay trimmed just right, thoroughly score the edges of the slab using the needle tool or a serrated rib. Then, apply a light coating of water along the full length of the strip. There's no need to drown the clay in water. In fact, too much water will make it more difficult to remove the dowel.

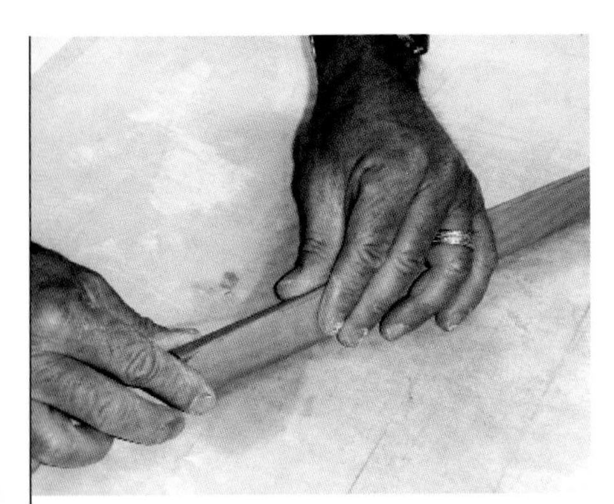

## Step 6

Now the seam can be sealed. Pinch the edges together along the full length of the dowel. Every few inches, stop to give the dowel a slight twist to keep it moving freely as the tube is being formed. Making a strong seam now will prevent splitting later.

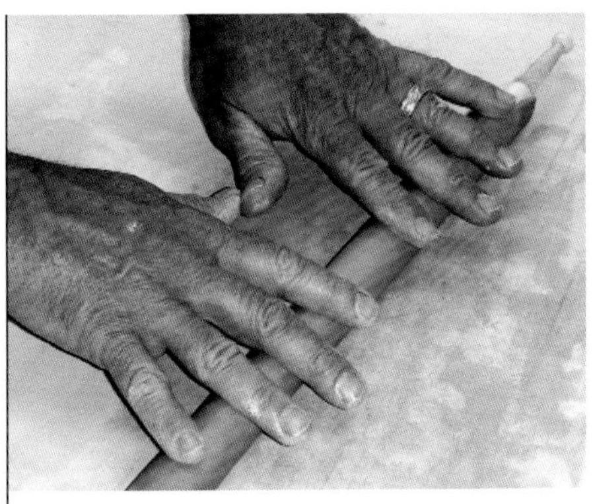

## Step 7

Once it is completely closed, roll the tube back and forth to smooth out the seam. Leave the dowel in the tube while you do this, to keep from crushing the tube. As soon as the seam has been smoothed, twist the dowel and draw it out of the tube. It must be removed at this point, because the clay shrinks as it dries, and will tighten up around the dowel.

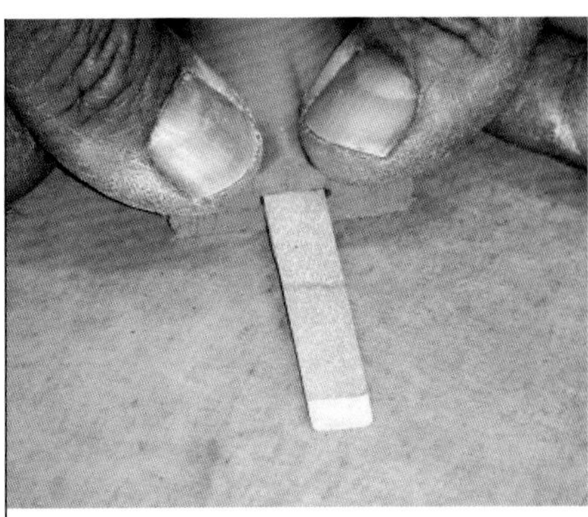

## Step 8

To construct the airway, insert a Popsicle stick into the tube and press the clay down around it with your thumbs, as shown. Press the clay from the end of the tube down about an inch. Leave the stick in place for the moment.

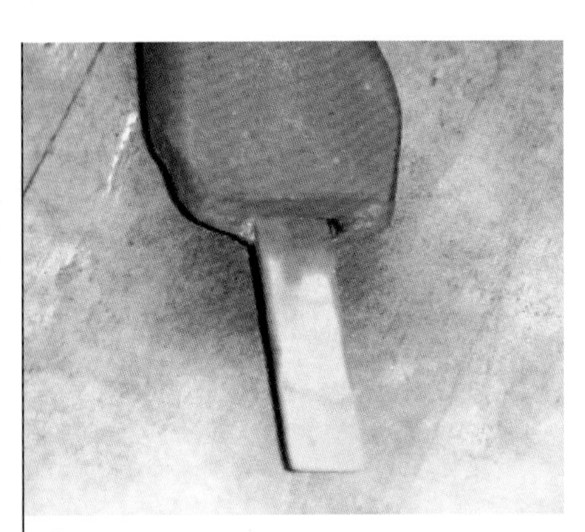

## Step 9

Trim some of the excess clay from the sides of the mouthpiece. This is a top view of the tube after the mouthpiece has been trimmed.

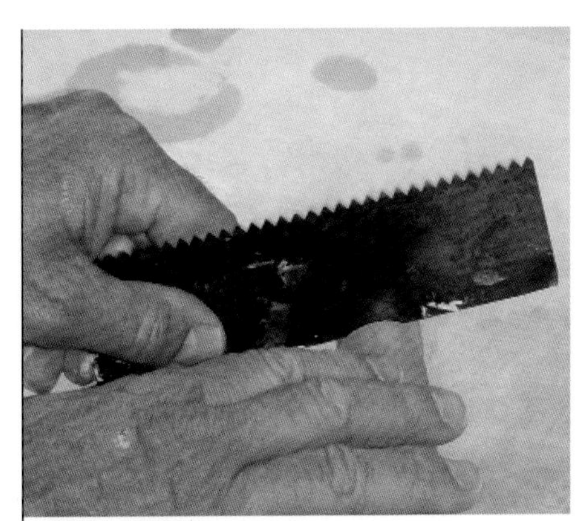

## Step 10

Trim the opposite end of the tube. A large serrated rib (as shown in the image) works well, but a variety of tools can be used for this purpose.

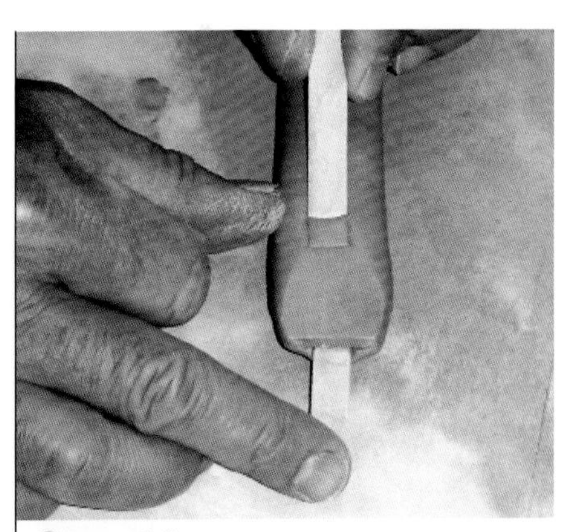

## Step 11

With one Popsicle stick in the airway, the other is used to cut the sound hole. The sound hole should be located just below the point where the clay begins to taper toward the mouth hole. Make the cuts into the clay until they reach the inner stick. Use the sharpened edge of the stick to cut a shallow bevel in the back of the sound hole.

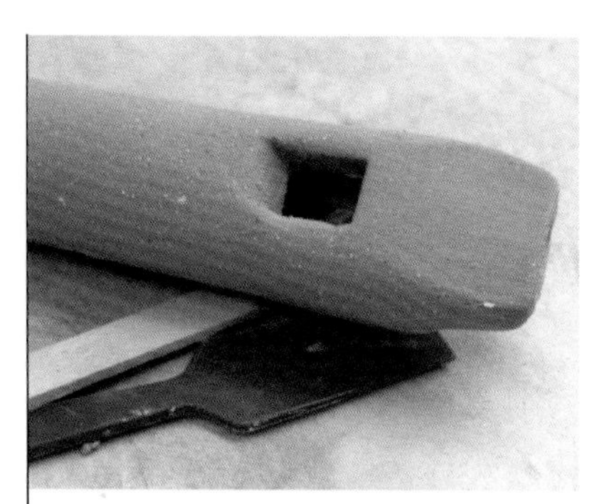

## Step 12

This is the finished sound hole. The tube is now a simple, one-note flute. Give it a try. Although the clay is wet, the flute can be blown enough to determine the quality of the basic sound. No sound? Reinsert the stick in the airway and adjust the beveled edge so that it splits the airway passage. Be sure the beveled edge is sharp and smooth. If it's a little ragged, use the Popsicle stick to smooth the surfaces. The ocarina's mouthpiece was made in the same way.

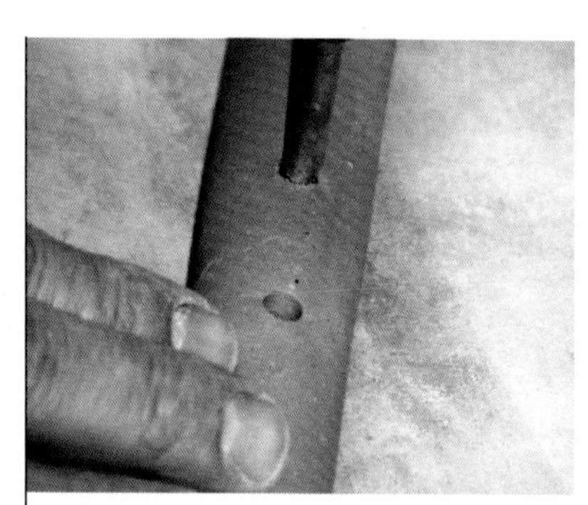

## Step 13

The flute is nearly ready for drying and firing. Use the hole cutter, as shown here, or a ¼-inch drill bit, to cut four evenly spaced finger holes along the top of the flute. You can now play the flute to see how it sounds. If you're not happy with any of the finger holes, you can enlarge them to raise their pitch, or fill them in with clay and re-cut them in another spot on the tube to get a different pitch. For information on hole placement and precision tuning, see the "side-blown flute" demonstration in this chapter.

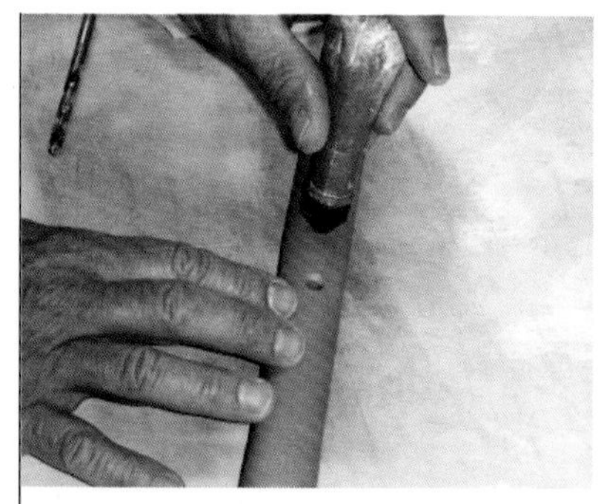

## Step 14

The countersink is twisted over each hole to give a nicely smoothed edge. Before letting the flute dry completely, check the inside of the flute to be sure it is smooth and free of obstructions. The dowel won't fit in it any more, so use the needle tool, a chopstick or other small stick to clear out the flute's interior if necessary.

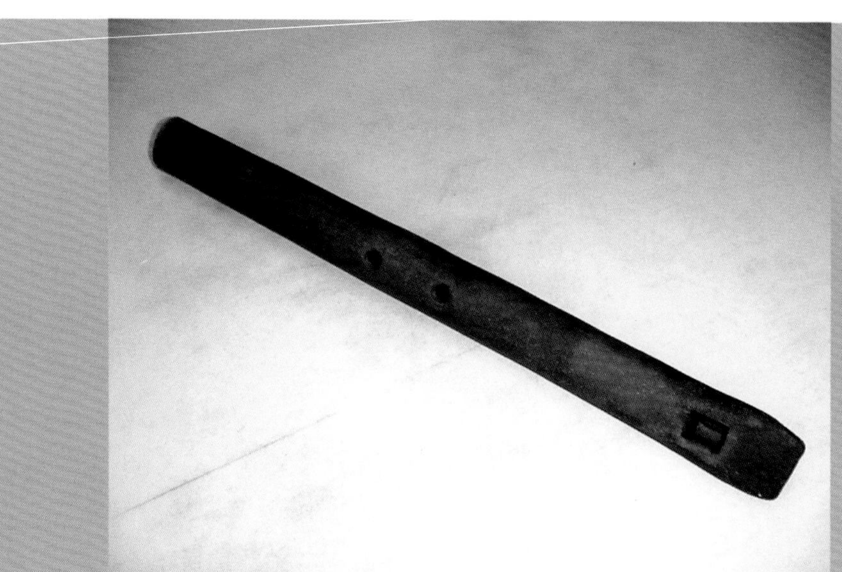

## The Finished Flute

This instrument was raku-fired to blacken the clay inside and out.

*Clay music is the ground upon which we walk, transformed into sound upon which we soar…*

—Alan Tower

# A Clay Music Sampler

## *Notes on the CD*

The compact disc included with this book contains music performed exclusively on clay instruments. Every sound you hear on the recording is made by a ceramic instrument. Some of the instruments have non-ceramic parts, such as skin heads or gut strings, but their primary material is clay. You may be surprised, and even amazed, by the variety of sounds that clay instruments can make.

The CD can be enjoyed in several ways. Track numbers are referenced in the text throughout the book so they can be readily heard as examples. Some of the tracks are solo performances, which let you hear and understand a specific instrument's capabilities. Others are ensemble pieces where you can hear multiple clay instruments played together.

Rather than merely documenting sound samples from different instruments, this collection of music is intended to be a "good listen" on its own. The selections are arranged in an order that offers variety while still providing musical continuity from one piece to the next. Perhaps this music will serve as an inspirational soundtrack as you create your own clay masterpieces.

The notes in this section follow the order of the tracks on the CD, and provide information on the music, the performers and the instruments used. For information on how to contact individual performers or obtain their recordings, see the "Contributors" section.

## Track Listing

1. **Cellular Activation** – *Rafael Bejarano*
2. **Máscara** – *Brian Ransom*
3. **Moon Watcher** – *Ward Hartenstein*
4. **Didjeridu Solo** – *Stephen Kent*
5. **Udu ClayPLAY** – *Brian Melick*
6. **Solar Sacrifice** – *Alan Tower*
7. **El Sople del Brujo** – *Alfonso Arrivillaga Cortés*
8. **Water Flute** – *Susan Rawcliffe*
9. **Smoke** – *Brian Ransom*
10. **Bongek, Lapdrum and Naggara Drums** – *Ken Lovelett*
11. **Clay Shaker and Claypans** – *N. Scott Robinson*
12. **U.S. Clay** – *Barry Hall*
13. **Triple Pipe** – *Susan Rawcliffe*
14. **Jaltarong** – *Antenna Repairmen*
15. **Kanaha** – *Alan Tower*
16. **Kinetic Chime** – *Ward Hartenstein*
17. **Nose Flute** – *Barry Hall*
18. **Neolithic Fanfare** – *Barry Hall*
19. **Doumbek Solo** – *Tom Teasley*
20. **Ghatam Solo** – *Tom Teasley*
21. **Silent Earth** - *Tan Dun and EarthSounds*
22. **Genesis** – *Diane Baxter*
23. **Mother's Ocarina Song** – *Janie Rezner*
24. **Hooded Pipe and Whiffle Ocarina** – *Susan Rawcliffe*
25. **Whistling Water Vessels** – *Dale Olsen and Brian Ransom*
26. **Chamberduct Flutes and Ball and Tube Flute** – *Susan Rawcliffe*
27. **Bassoon Drum Solo** – *Eddie Andresen*
28. **A Chantar M'er** – *Barry Hall*
29. **Siberian Hoedown** – *Burnt Earth Ensemble*
30. **Haiku** – *Mark Attebery*
31. **La Peregrination** – *Johann Rotter*
32. **Nutcracker Suite** – *Geert Jacobs*
33. **La Primavera** – *Budrio Ocarina Ensemble*
34. **Xun** – *Barry Hall*
35. **Cactus on Mars** – *Mark Attebery*
36. **Stroll** – *Brian Ransom*
37. **Resonator Nose Flute** – *Barry Hall*
38. **Ceramic Guitar** – *Brian Ransom*
39. **Earth** – *Joe O'Donnell*
40. **Jota de Mallorca** – *Talabrène*
41. **Gravity Chime** – *Ward Hartenstein*
42. **Ghatam Solo** – *T. H. Subash Chandran*
43. **Winter's Lullaby** – *Wayne McCleskey*

*Track 1*
## Cellular Activation

*Performed on a huaca and ehecatl built by Rafael Bejarano. Written and performed by Rafael Bejarano.*

Rafael performs this piece on an instrument called the *DNA huaca*, a three-chambered ocarina he crafted with F# and C# as the chambers' fundamental tones. He designed this instrument after learning that biologists measuring the frequencies of human DNA determined that our bodies' molecules vibrate at the pitches F# and C#, and that the frequency of the Earth's revolution around the sun has been measured to correspond to the pitch C#. Rafael believes that this music creates a healing harmonic field because it corresponds with the natural sound of our DNA blueprint.

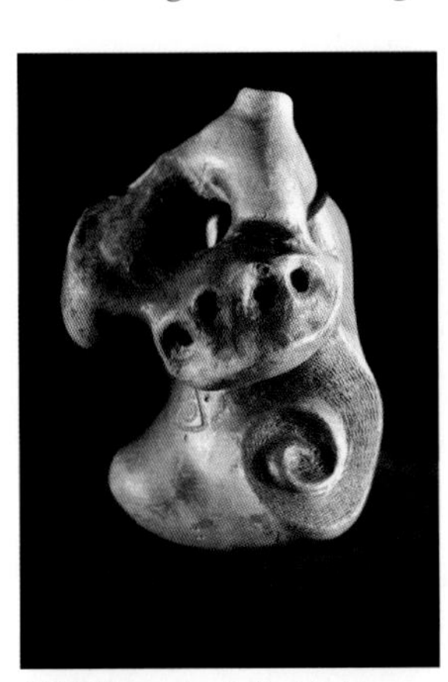

**DNA Huaca** by Rafael Bejarano (track 1).

Rafael sounds the huaca continuously through this piece using *circular breathing*. The other instrument he plays, an ehecatl or "wind spirit" (figure 4.73), is a *chamberduct* whistle designed by the ancient Mexicas. It symbolizes the freedom of the spirit and the sacred wind.

*Track 2*
## Máscara

*Performed on ceramic percussion instruments, flutes, harp, bass and horn built by Brian Ransom. Written and performed by Jacob Ransom (percussion) and Brian Ransom (other instruments).*

This track features a broad palette of sounds from a variety of ceramic instruments created by master builder Brian Ransom.

*Track 3*
## Moon Watcher

*Performed on ceramic idiophones and flute built by Ward Hartenstein. Written and performed by Ward Hartenstein.*

This recording by Ward Hartenstein features a variety of sound textures including both tuned and untuned instruments. In order of appearance, the instruments are: fountain chime (a column of stoneware bells played by falling BBs), bow bowls (bowls played with a bow), petal drum (a ceramic tongue drum), heartbeat drum (a clay drum with a deerskin head), tongue drum, kinetic chime (a massive wind chime), clay marimba, and circle flute. They are all cone 6 stoneware with the addition of a deerskin head on the heartbeat drum. For the instruments played in this selection see figures 2.10, 2.17, 2.19, 2.23, 4.5, 8.20, 9.6 and 9.8.

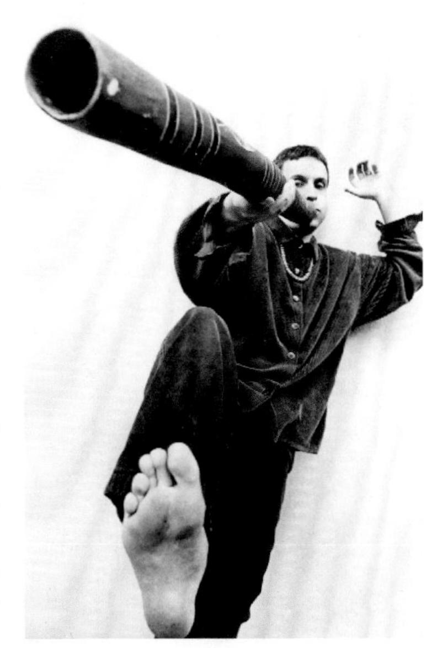

**Stephen Kent** (track 4).

*Track 4*
## Didjeridu Solo

*Performed on a ceramic didjeridu built by Barry Hall. Written and performed by Stephen Kent.*

Stephen Kent is one of today's most respected and prolific didjeridu performers, bringing the ancient Aboriginal sound into a contemporary context. During a twenty-year career with the didjeridu which led him from his native South Africa to Australia, London, and San Francisco, Stephen has developed an approach that is unmistakably his own, exploring a broad range of playing styles and musical genres. Along the way he has amassed a catalogue of over a dozen critically acclaimed CD's, including four solo releases and many others with his group projects Trance Mission, Beasts of Paradise and Lights In A Fat City.

In this track, Stephen demonstrates the marvelous music that can be coaxed from a hollow clay tube. His playing style includes a variety of blowing techniques, vocalizations and even tapping on the instrument's clay body for percussive accompaniment. The instrument he plays is shown in figure 4.101.

*Track 5*

### Udu ClayPLAY

*Performed on Claytone udu drums designed by Frank Giorgini and built by LP Music Group. Written and performed by Brian Melick.*

This piece highlights a variety of sounds that can be created from udu drums. Four different-sized udu drums are used (soprano, alto, tenor and baritone) as well as the Udongo II and Mbwata (figure 9.4).

Brian Melick is a percussionist who actively performs, records and educates using udu drums. He is featured on many commercial recordings, as well as his own solo releases. He has developed print, audio and video instructional materials related to playing the udu drum, and designs and manufactures "SoftPAW" performance stands for the entire line of Frank Giorgini and LP Music Group udu drums.

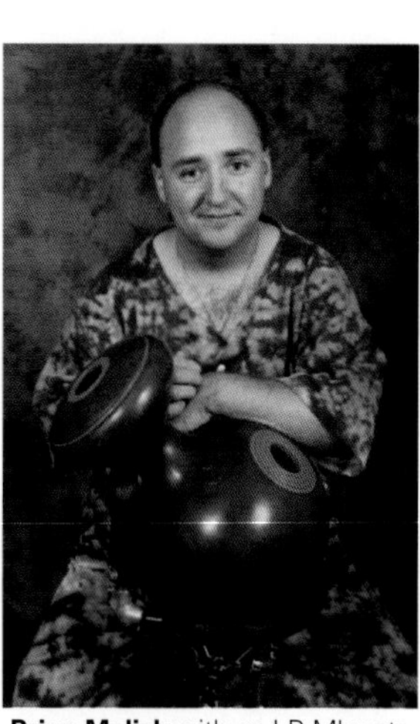

**Brian Melick** with an LP Mbwata Udu Drum (track 5).

*Track 6*

### Solar Sacrifice

*Performed on a four-chambered huaca built by Sharon Rowell. Written and performed by Alan Tower.*

Solar Sacrifice was composed for a specific four-chambered ocarina (figure 9.41). The chambers are tuned in octaves and fifths, with the top two melody chambers providing unison pitches over the range of an octave. The two bass or drone chambers sound an octave below the lowest tone of the melody chambers.

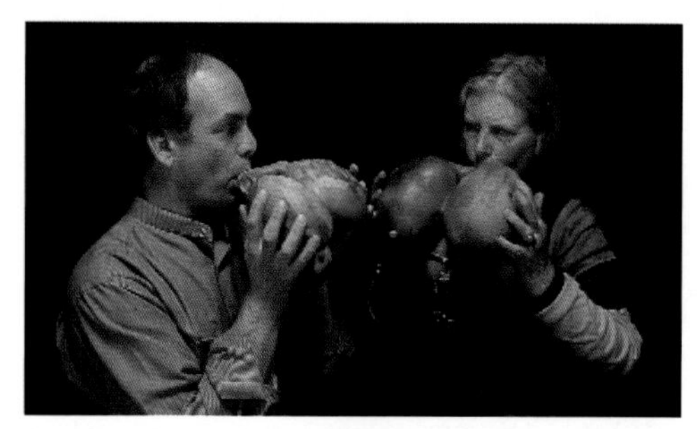

**Alan Tower and Sharon Rowell** with Sharon's huacas (tracks 6 and 15).

Alan describes his inspiration for this composition: "Our sun is burning itself up at an astronomical rate, combining four hydrogen atoms to make helium and energy in the form of radiation. Our earthlife is intimately tied to the sun's history and its eventual expansion into a red giant, engulfing the earth's orbit some 5 billion years from now. As our individual lives move from birth to death, so does the life of our solar system. The sun is in a constant state of offering life, until its day as the sun is over. A day of death for creatures of earth. This piece is an offering to the sacrificial Solar God, played on four chambers of burnt earth."

For more information on Alan Tower, see the notes to track 15.

*Track 7*

### El Sople del Brujo

*Performed on pre-Columbian Mayan flutes, trumpets and rattles. Written and performed by Alfonso Arrivillaga Cortés, Carlos Chaclan, Edgar Carpio and Andrés Arrivillaga Shaw.*

Over the past 20 years, Alfonso Arrivillaga Cortés has conducted detailed studies into the acoustics of pre-Columbian Mayan musical instruments. This recording is a combination of excerpted recordings that demonstrate the sounds of some Mayan instruments from the collection of the Popol Vuh Museum in Guatemala. (See Chapter 1 for Alfonso's moving description of his experience playing these instruments.)

Excerpted from the CD "Voces Mayas" and other recordings. A project of Francisco Marroquín University's Popol Vuh Museum, Guatemala. Recorded in the Juan Bautista Auditorium, Francisco Marroquín University, Guatemala.

*Track 8*
### Water Flute
*Performed on a large water flute built by Susan Rawcliffe. Performed by Susan Rawcliffe.*

The water flute played in this selection is a 22-inch tube that contains water and is played by varying the air pressure and tilting the instrument (figure 4.59). Susan's water flutes produce a variety of fantastic sounds, in ways that are not always under the complete control of the performer.

*Track 9*
### Smoke
*Performed on a ceramic harp and transverse ceramic flute built by Brian Ransom. Written and performed by Brian Ransom (harp) and Amanda Ransom (flute).*

This duet for ceramic harp and flute performed by Brian and Amanda Ransom explores the microtonal capabilities of the transverse ceramic flute. Brian likes the "tonal innuendoes" that occur when the two instruments are blended.

*Track 10*
### Bongek, Lapdrum and Naggara Drums
*Performed on a Bongek, Lapdrum and Naggara Drums built by Ken Lovelett. Written and performed by Ken Lovelett.*

Demonstrations of three of Ken Lovelett's original drum designs. The Bongek, heard first, is a doumbek-style drum with an extra drumhead attached to a small spout protruding from the side of the drum. Second is the Lapdrum, a small ceramic instrument with three heads, a ridged section and a small tambourine jingle (figure 3.28). Last we hear the Naggara Drums, a set of five graduated ceramic drums whose pitches are altered while playing by inflating the drums with air from two foot-operated bellows.

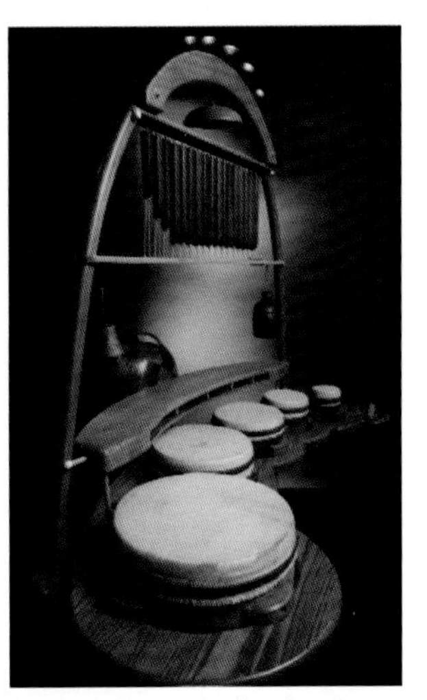
**Naggara Drums** by Ken Lovelett (track 10).

*Track 11*
### Clay Shaker and Claypans
*Performed on a clay shaker and Claypans built by Stephen Wright. Written and performed by N. Scott Robinson.*

Stephen Wright's small barrel-shaped ceramic shakers (figure 6.7) have animal skin on each end and small clay beads inside. His Claypan (figure 2.22) is an all-clay frame drum. On this track, one shaker and two different-sized Claypans are played consecutively.

N. Scott Robinson is a percussionist, scholar and teacher specializing in hand drumming and world music. He has extensive recording, performing and publication credits, and has taught at several universities.

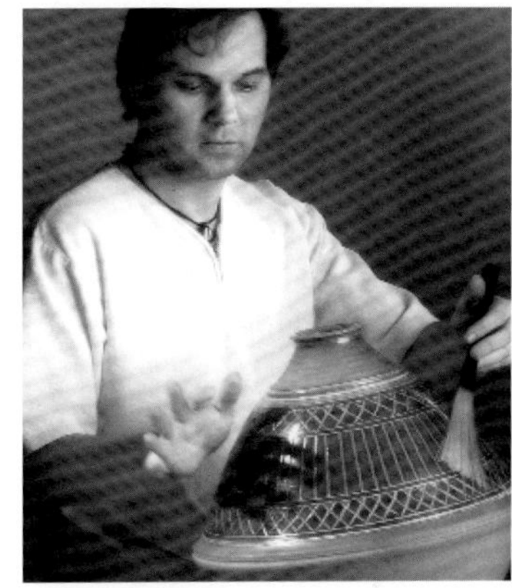
**N. Scott Robinson** with Ubang by Stephen Wright (track 11).

*Track 12*
### U.S. Clay
*Performed on globu-tubular horns, overtone flute and shaker built by Barry Hall. Written by Barry Hall and performed by the Burnt Earth Ensemble.*

This is an excerpt of a longer piece created for the CD "Didgeridoo USA" (hence the name "U.S. Clay"). Two hybrid globu-tubular horns with resonators are used. One (figure 4.109) is played as a horn, and the other (figure 6.2) is played as a drum.

*Track 13*

### Triple Pipe

*Performed on a triple pipe built by Susan Rawcliffe. Performed by Susan Rawcliffe.*

A solo performed on Susan Rawcliffe's triple pipe—three pipes with airduct assemblies that merge into a common mouthpiece (figure 9.31).

*Track 14*

### Jaltarong

*Performed on a set of 26 graduated porcelain bowls built by Stephen Freedman. Written by Arthur Jarvinen and performed by The Antenna Repairmen (Arthur Jarvinen, Robert Fernandez and M. B. Gordy).*

A *jaltarang* is a set of graduated musical bowls traditional to India. The 26 porcelain bowls that Stephen Freedman created for this piece are arranged in a seven-foot circle, and played with chopsticks (figure 2.13).

The percussion trio The Antenna Repairmen specializes in unusual performances that combine musical, theatrical and ritualistic elements. This selection is an excerpt from a live recording of one section of a 55-minute work titled Ghatam, which uses a wide variety of ceramic instruments designed and created by Stephen Freedman. Arthur Jarvenin describes the appeal of Ghatam, "One could do something similar with ordinary instruments, but I don't think it would mean the same thing, nice as it might be. The visual focus of everything being ceramic, and the tradition and history of that material bring a dimension of their own to the music and performance. One is aware that these instruments were made by hand just for this purpose, not run off a mill and bought at a music store. I think there is great significance in music that is made from the ground up. When composers actually take responsibility not just for the notes and structure of the musical piece but for the very sound world itself, that makes for a special kind of music."

This section of the work is based on two measures of notated music. Bob and M.B. play a simple four-note phrase of even eighth notes. This pattern is shifted from time to time when one or the other drops a sixteenth note, creating a gamelan-like interlocking effect. When it happens again they are back in phase, but out of synch as to which bowls they are playing, which produces counterpoint. Bob and M.B. move up and down the circle of bowls at their own pace while Arthur improvises on top. One of them is inside the circle and the other outside, so they can play the same bowls without being in each other's way. This results in a choreography defined by the instrument and the music. A studio recording of the entire work Ghatam is available on M.A. Recordings (M037).

*Track 15*

### Kanaha

*Performed on a triple-chambered ocarina built by Sharon Rowell and a clay bass, ConunDrums and shaker built by Barry Hall. Written by Alan Tower and performed by Alan Tower (ocarina and shaker) and Barry Hall (clay bass and ConunDrums).*

According to Alan, "Kanaha is a beautiful beach on the island of Maui, a place where the grass, sand, sun, water and wind intersect for the perfect windsurfing experience."

Alan Tower composes and performs extensively using Sharon Rowell's multichambered ocarinas and many other instruments. He is the leader of the band Free Energy and the founder of Octave Alliance, an organization dedicated to using music as a voice and catalyst for a more humane sustainable culture. For the instruments played in this selection see figures 3.24, 4.53 and 6.6.

*Track 16*

### Kinetic Chime

*Performed on the Kinetic Chime built by Ward Hartenstein. Performed by Ward Hartenstein.*

The Kinetic Chime is a massive wind chime (see figure 9.6 for an example). The unusually shaped sound-producing components are the waste pieces left over when Ward cuts his tongue drum shapes.

*Track 17*
### Nose Flute
*Performed on a nose flute built by Barry Hall. Performed by Barry Hall.*

This simple ducted nose flute uses the player's mouth as a globular resonating cavity. Air from the nose is blown through a windway and across an aperture positioned over the player's mouth. Pitch is changed using the throat, tongue and cheeks to manipulate the size of the mouth cavity.

*Track 18*
### Neolithic Fanfare
*Performed on ceramic horns built by Barry Hall. Performed by Barry Hall.*

Imagine this clay fanfare announcing the entrance of an ancient ruler, summoning the gods, or inspiring warriors to heroic deeds in battle. The conical clay horns used are shaped like animal horns. The pitch of each simple horn is modified by placing a hand in its bell to varying degrees.

*Track 19*
### Doumbek Solo
*Performed on a doumbek built by Stephen Wright. Written and performed by Tom Teasley.*

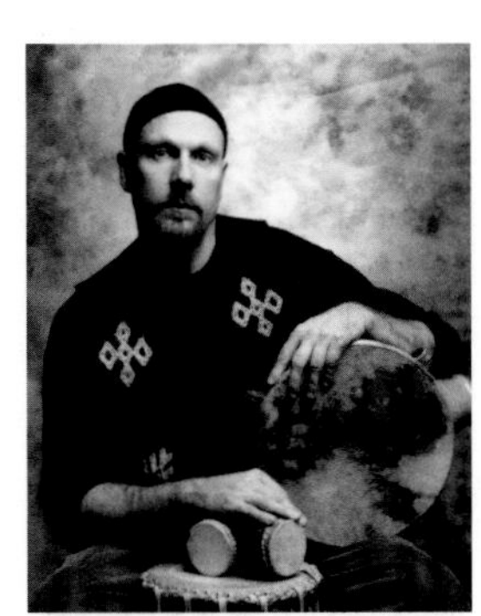
**Tom Teasley** with Gunta and shakers by Stephen Wright (tracks 19 and 20)

Tom Teasley is a professional percussionist who performs around the world in solo concerts and with groups that range from jazz combos to symphony orchestras. He has released solo CDs and educational videos about world percussion instruments, and is on the faculty at several universities, where he lectures on various percussion topics.

Notice how Tom changes the drum's low pitch during this piece. This technique is accomplished by striking the drum head with one hand while moving the other hand inside the hollow bottom of the drum, which changes the ratio of the drum's opening to its internal volume and thus lowers its pitch.

*Track 20*
### Ghatam Solo
*Performed on a ghatam built by Stephen Wright. Written and performed by Tom Teasley.*

In this selection, Tom plays a ghatam built by Stephen Wright. Stephen's instrument, though similar in shape to a traditional Indian ghatam, is fired to a higher temperature and glazed, which gives it a different tonal character. For more about Tom Teasley, see the notes for track 19.

*Track 21*
### Silent Earth
*Performed on EarthSounds instruments built by Ragnar Naess. The instruments include Pluckers, Bowers, Cowguts, bells, chimes, bowls, gongs, and resonating jars. Written by Tan Dun and performed by the Tan Dun Ensemble.*

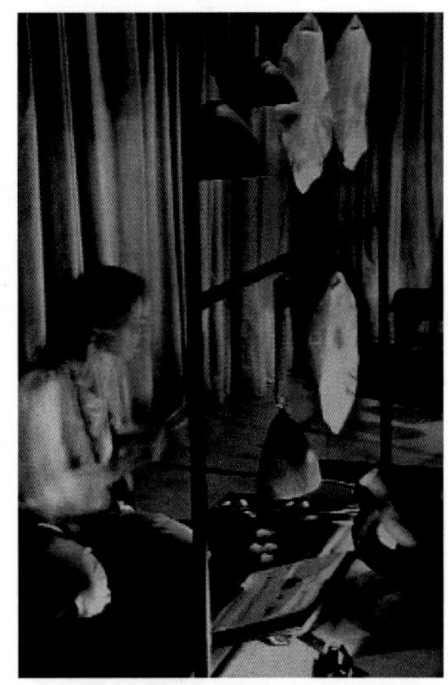
**Earth Sounds Ensemble** with instruments by Ragnar Naess (track 21)

Silent Earth is a fifteen-minute composition for seven performers with ceramic instruments. This selection contains excerpts from a live recording of the full piece.

Tan composed Silent Earth for the EarthSounds ensemble of ceramic instruments that he created in collaboration with Ragnar Naess. In his scoring, he had all the instruments struck with different materials—wood, metal, plastic, felt and fiber—to get different sounds. He says the following about his composition for this ceramic orchestra:

> *I think that each composer writing each piece has many possible choices, many possible ways of comprehending the unlimited sounds of the world. I still remember that before I came here (from China to America) my mother told me, 'Take care of yourself—the earth and the water are different over there.' I replied 'Hei zo!' (which is what I always said as a child when I thought something was very ridiculous). Why is earth so important to me?"*
>
> *Thousands of years ago, the Chinese believed that metal, wood, water, fire and earth were the original elements of everything created and not yet created. They used these five elements as the basis for astronomy, philosophy, medicine and music. Of the five, people thought that earth was the most important in maintaining the balance among all things.*
>
> *I'm not sure if I believe that or not, but it's true that for the past year I have been interested in earth sounds. When I was talking to Ragnar about making the instruments, I felt I had already heard their sounds, and even touched them. I still kept asking myself, did you see the sounds? What happens when they combine with the sounds of metal, wood, skin and silk? I kept playing with them in the score, and filling our mouths with 'Hei-zo!'.*

Tan Dun is an internationally prominent composer of orchestral and experimental music. He has numerous compositional and recording credits to his name, as well as many international honors including an Academy Award for his original soundtrack to the film "Crouching Tiger, Hidden Dragon." Music and instruments from his homeland China influence some of his musical works such as *Orchestral Theatre I: Xun,* an orchestral piece that incorporates ten ceramic xun flutes. For the instruments played in this selection, see figures 4.106, 5.7, 5.8, 9.23, 9.24 and 9.25.

*Track 22*

## Genesis

*Performed on unfired and fired clay vessels built by Diane Baxter. Performed by Diane Baxter, Devin Baxter, Robert Marsanyi, Shelly Marsanyi, Ian Marsanyi, Grey Eagle, and Ann Huggins.*

Most of the sounds on this CD come from ceramic instruments that have been fired. But what about unfired clay? Many ceramists are familiar with the sounds of tapping and scraping clay vessels in their various states of dryness before being fired. Diane Baxter included these sounds in her work called Genesis.

This selection is a combination of excerpts from a longer recording designed as a sound environment to accompany a group of Diane's large ceramic sculptures entitled "Waiting." She explains, "While building these sculptures I began to hear the pieces as I made them and realized that they would never give the same sounds in the same way as they grew and changed. There was a slight echo and a beautiful resonance to the growing pieces as I would hum into them, or slap, or tap them. I began to make recordings of the pieces as they were being built, catching the sounds at different stages of height and dryness as well as the sounds of working in the studio. At the end of the recording there is a segment where all of the finished pieces are spontaneously played by myself and a group of friends." See figure 2.14.

*Track 23*

## Mother's Ocarina Song

*Performed on a triple-chambered ocarina built by Janie Rezner. Written and performed by Janie Rezner.*

Janie says about this piece, "The mystical tones and vibrant harmonies of the triple ocarina transport us to the realms of the sacred. A little song that my elderly mother played on the piano is woven into this composition."

See figure 4.49 for one of Janie's instruments.

*Track 24*
### Hooded Pipe, Whiffle Ocarina
*Performed on a hooded pipe and whiffle ocarina built by Susan Rawcliffe. Performed by Susan Rawcliffe.*

In this track, Susan Rawcliffe explores the musical potential of unusual aerophones. In the first part Susan plays a hooded pipe that she built based on a pre-Columbian design. A hooded pipe is a tubular airduct flute with a partial enclosure, or hood, built up over the sounding edge. Notice the reedy and raspy tone that results from the hood's interaction with the flute's airflow. In the second section, Susan demonstrates a clever pitch-jumping technique possible on a whiffle ocarina (figure 4.58), an instrument she designed based on pre-Columbian whistles. A whiffle ocarina has two chambers—the primary sounding chamber has finger holes and the other chamber is open like a cup and is played by sliding the hand over the open end.

*Track 25*
### Whistling Water Vessels
*Performed on pre-Columbian Moche and Chimu whistling water pots. Performed by Dale Olsen and Brian Ransom.*

A sampling of sounds from seven historical pre-Columbian whistling water vessels, from the Moche, Chavin, Chimu, Chancay, and Vicus cultures. This track is assembled from field recordings made in museums by Dale Olsen and Brian Ransom while conducting research on these instruments. The vessels are played by tipping them with water inside (figures 4.65 and 4.66) and by blowing into them. Note the variety of sounds produced by the different instruments.

This track provides the opportunity to hear firsthand the sound of ancient ceramic instruments. Brian relates, "Try to imagine the thrill I experienced when I first tipped one of these fluid instruments which, by and large, had not been played since before they had been placed in their graves; their mysterious and haunting sounds cracking across eons of time."

Dale Olsen is Professor of Ethnomusicology at Florida State University. He has done extensive fieldwork in South America and authored more than 70 publications about music in South America. Information on Brian Ransom can be found in the "Profiles" chapter.

Moche, Chimu and Vicus whistling vessels can be seen in figures 1.2, 1.4, 1.5, 4.63-4, 4.67-8 and 7.13.

*Track 26*
### Chamberduct Flutes, Ball and Tube Flute
*Performed on chamberduct flutes and a ball and tube flute built by Susan Rawcliffe. Written and performed by Susan Rawcliffe on instruments built by Susan Rawcliffe.*

Susan Rawcliffe researches and reconstructs ancient pre-Columbian flutes, and reinvests her insights into her own instrumental designs. The unusual instruments in this track—chamberduct flutes and ball and tube flutes—are unique pre-Columbian designs that have been "rediscovered" from the relics of early Mesoamerican societies.

"I like music that still has dirt on it," Susan says. "A lot of my sounds are like the human voice; they sound like animal cries; maybe the sound reaches a more primeval part of the brain ... but we're so far from these things nowadays. That's why the sounds seem far away and of another time ... because they are from another, earlier time."

Sometimes, indeed, people find Susan's sounds scary. "They're not really scary," she responds, "they're just primeval and intense, unknown. The ancient instruments I have studied were sacred sound symbols designed to be used ceremonially. I'm fascinated by how sound affects people."

*Track 27*
### Bassoon Drum Solo
*Performed on a bassoon drum built by Dag Sørensen. Written and performed by Eddie Andresen.*

Eddie Andresen is a professional percussionist and collaborator with potter Dag Sørensen. When he came upon a 20-foot length of road pipe, Eddie was fascinated by the sound and encouraged Dag to create a similar-sounding instrument using clay. Dag's first attempt looked like a bassoon, and the name stuck (figure 4.116). In this track, Eddie improvises on the bassoon drum in a live concert.

*Track 28*
### A Chantar M'er

*Performed on a ceramic cornetto built by Barry Hall. Melody written by Comtessa Beatriz de Dia, circa 1200. Performed by Barry Hall.*

The cornetto is a trumpet-like instrument from the Renaissance period, traditionally made from wood, sometimes wrapped with leather. Its tiny, sharp-edged mouthpiece and open finger holes give it a warm and earthy tone. Here, a clay cornetto is used to perform a phrase from a Medieval troubadour love song. (figure 4.97).

*Track 29*
### Siberian Hoedown

*Performed on stone fiddle, doumbek, globu-tubular horn and didjibodhrán built by Barry Hall. Written by Barry Hall and performed by the Burnt Earth Ensemble.*

The Burnt Earth Ensemble is a group that performs music on clay instruments created by Barry Hall. The members include Barry, Richard Smith and Beth Hall.

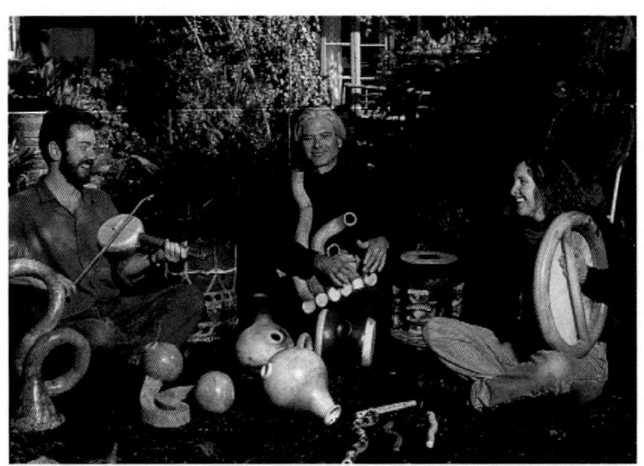

**The Burnt Earth Ensemble:** Barry Hall, Richard Smith and Beth Hall (track 29).

The globu-tubular horn in this selection is played using the "buzz technique"—a technique in which an object (in this case a chopstick) is selectively touched to the surface of the horn's vibrating goat skin membrane to produce a buzzing sound.

For the instruments played in this selection see figures 4.109, 6.4, 6.12 and 7.2.

*Track 30*
### Haiku

*Performed on a flute built by Robin Hodgkinson. Written and performed by Mark Attebery.*

Mark Attebery is a wind player and music educator who specializes in composing music for dance and theatre. His music incorporates unusual wind instruments, many of them ceramic. In this track, Mark plays a short "haiku" on a raku flute built by Robin Hodgkinson (figure 7.11).

*Track 31*
### La Peregrination

*Performed on ocarinas built by Johann Rotter Composed by Ariel Ramirez and performed by Johann Rotter.*

Johann ("Hans") Rotter, from Dittmannsdorf, Austria, performs a two-ocarina harmonization of a simple, enchanting melody.

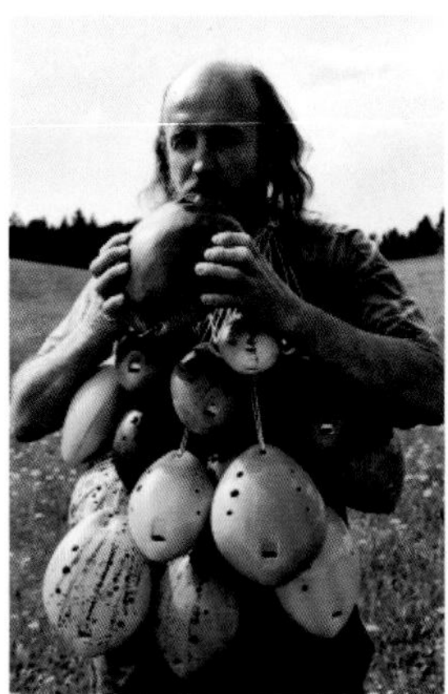

**Hans Rotter** (track 31).

*Track 32*
### Nutcracker Suite
*Performed on a ceramic barrel organ built by Geert Jacobs. From the ballet written by Peter Ilyitch Tchaikovsky in 1892.*

Tchaikovsky's entertaining masterpiece is one of the most popular pieces ever created for ballet. The Nutcracker is a perennial favorite that's heard in theaters and concert halls around the world, especially at Christmastime. Geert Jacobs expertly performs excerpts from this suite on his very unique ceramic barrel organ, called the "Jacob's Ladder" (figures 4.21, 4.22 and 9.22).

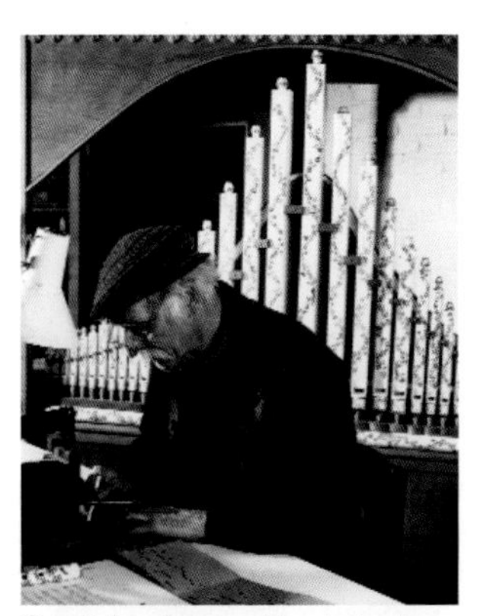

**Geert Jacobs** punching holes in a cardboard strip to make a "songbook" for his ceramic barrel organ, seen behind him. (track 32).

*Track 33*
### La Primavera
*Performed on Budrio ocarinas built by Fabio Menaglio. From The Four Seasons written by Antonio Vivaldi in 1725 and performed by the Gruppo Ocarinistico Budriese (Budrio Ocarina Ensemble).*

*1st ocarina: Giulio Boccaletti*
*2nd ocarina: Fabio Galliani*
*3rd ocarina: Simona Vincenzi*
*4th ocarina: Emiliano Bernagozzi*
*5th ocarina: Fulvio Carpanelli*
*6th ocarina: Gianni Grossi*
*7th ocarina: Claudio Cedroni*

The origins of the Budrio Ocarina Ensemble date back to the 1870's. Based in Budrio, Italy (the birthplace of the modern ocarina), the group performs regularly in Italy and abroad. The present ensemble has evolved for over a decade and includes a nucleus of musicians from the ocarina school in Budrio who perform transcriptions of classical and opera music on a consort of seven clay ocarinas. As you listen to this recording, there is no question as to the players' virtuosity on their instruments. They also bring a great spirit of fun to their performances. As the group's leader, Claudio Cedroni, says. "Having fun is also an art."

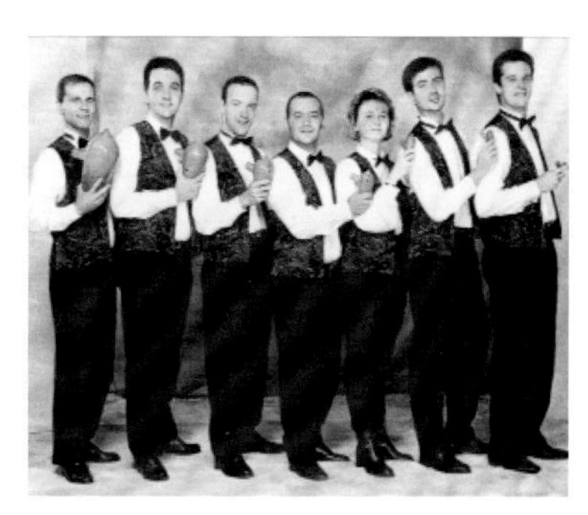

**Gruppo Ocarinistico Budriese** (track 33).

*Track 34*
### Xun
*Performed on a xun built by Barry Hall. Performed by Barry Hall.*

The xun is a traditional Chinese ceramic globular flute with several finger holes, played by blowing across an open hole at the top of the egg-shaped body (figures 4.10-11). With origins reaching back at least 6,000 years in China, the xun is used in Confucian rituals as well as in ordinary music making. Similar instruments are traditional to Korea, Vietnam and Japan.

*Track 35*
### Cactus on Mars
*Performed on a triple-chambered ocarina built by Sharon Rowell, and a globu-tubular horn, clay pot drums, ConunDrums, shakers and miscellaneous clay percussion built by Barry Hall. Written by Mark Attebery Performed by Mark Attebery (ocarina) and Barry Hall (other instruments).*

For information on Mark Attebery, see the notes for track 30. For the instruments played in this selection see figures 3.24, 4.53, 4.108 and 8.9.

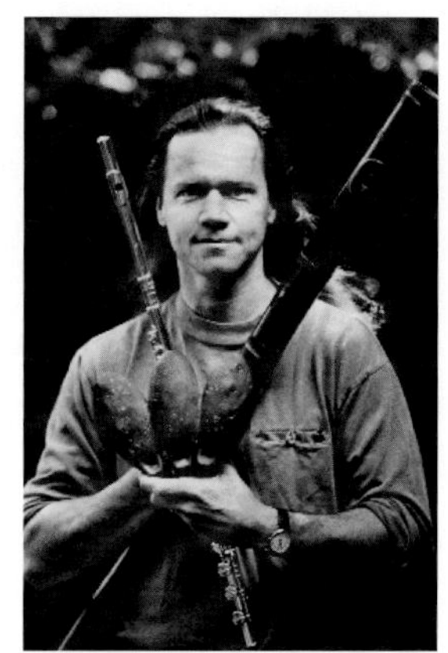

**Mark Attebery** with ocarina by Sharon Rowell (tracks 30 and 35).

*Track 36*

## Stroll

*Performed on ceramic kalimba, ceramic harp, pan flute and snake flute built by Brian Ransom. Written by Brian Ransom, performed by Jacob Ransom (kalimba) and Brian Ransom (harp, pan flute, snake flute).*

Kalimba and harp are two unusual instruments to find in ceramic form. Here is an opportunity to hear them both, together with a ceramic pan flute and snake flute, in this piece performed by Brian Ransom and his son Jacob.

For the instruments played in this selection see figures 2.25, 4.9 and 5.3.

*Track 37*

## Resonator Nose Flute

*Performed on a resonator nose flute built by Barry Hall. Performed by Barry Hall.*

A design extension of the nose flute played on track 17, this instrument (figure 4.57) channels all of the sound from the aperture through a long tube. This tubular resonator forces the pitches to conform to the harmonic series dictated by the length of the tube. What goes into the tube as a continuous pitch comes out as a series of discrete intervals.

*Track 38*

## Ceramic Guitar

*Performed on a ceramic quinto guitar built by Brian Ransom. Performed by Brian Ransom.*

This short piece is Brian's adaptation of a traditional folk melody he learned from village musicians while living in Peru. He performs it using a bottleneck slide on his ceramic guitar (figure 5.10).

*Track 39*

## Earth

*Performed on a clay violin built by John Stevens. Written and performed by Joe O'Donnell.*

In this selection Joe O'Donnell performs on a ceramic violin (figure 5.14) made by John Stevens of Kent, England. Joe is an Irish-born fiddler who lives in Coventry, England. A classically trained violinist, he is also an innovator on the electric violin and has toured and recorded with a variety of folk and rock bands, as well as symphony orchestras, for the last 30 years. Joe is currently recording and touring with his band Shkayla.

*Track 40*

## Jota de Mallorca

*Performed on the ceramic bagpipe "Draquemuse" built by Marie Picard. Traditional Spanish dance tune performed by Talabrène.*

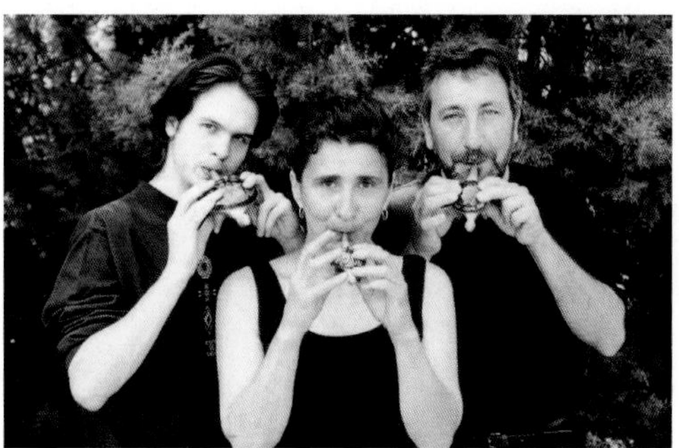

**Talabrene** with instruments by Marie Picard (track 40).

Talabrène is a musical group that performs using the ceramic instrumental creations of Marie Picard. Joining Marie in the ensemble are Henri Maquet and Pascal Chevalier. The French group's name means "salamander" in the Occitan dialect, and the instruments they play are a bestiary of fantastic creatures that function as ocarinas, horns, flutes and reed instruments. On this track, Pascal performs a traditional tune on a ceramic bagpipe ("cornemuse" in French) that Marie calls the "Draquemuse" (figure 4.113).

*Track 41*

## Gravity Chime

*Performed on the Gravity Chime built by Ward Hartenstein. Performed by Ward Hartenstein.*

Ward's Gravity Chime is a collection of suspended stoneware chambers through which a marble falls to produce random bell-like sounds (figure 2.11).

*Track 42*
### Ghatam Solo
*Performed on a traditional South Indian ghatam built by Kesavan. Performed by T. H. Subash Chandran.*

T. H. Subash Chandran and his brother T. H. Vikku Vinayakram are two of South India's most accomplished percussionists. On this track, Subash improvises on the ghatam in adi thalam, an eight-beat rhythm cycle. His style of improvisation incorporates complex groupings of phrases with 3, 4, 5 or 7 beats that create tension against the steady rhythmic meter but always resolve in a strong downbeat at the beginning of each new 8-beat cycle. Subash's tight, intricate rhythms demonstrate his mastery of the ghatam. On this selection, he uses a technique called gumki, a traditional playing style that incorporates strong bass tones produced by striking the pot with the heel of the hand. The pitch of these bass tones is modulated to create melodies by opening and closing the mouth of the instrument against the stomach.

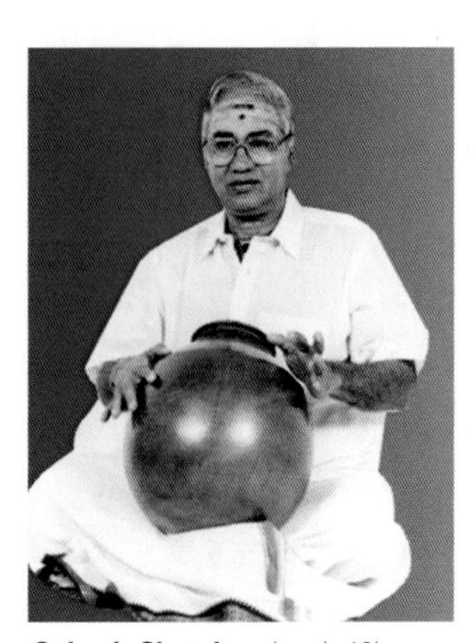
**Subash Chandran** (track 42).

The ghatam used by Subash for this recording is shown in figure 2.12.

*Track 43*
### Winter's Lullaby
*Performed on a ceramic Native-American-style flute built by Rod Kendall. Written and performed by Wayne McCleskey.*

One of Rod's Kendall's Native American flutes is shown in figures 4.18 and 4.19. Rod observes, "The Native American flute songs seem to take you back to a distant time when the flute had a more symbolic and spiritual place in life."

Wayne McCleskey, a leader in the Washington Flute Circle also hosts Native American Flute Gathering and has co-published several books of music. He says, "The flute is a calming and centering presence in my life and has brought powerful changes to my life as well as many deep and lasting friendships."

Wayne says, "I wrote this song for Rod's flute and it seemed on this particular gray, Seattle, wintry day a gentle sleepy tune that spoke of the transition that winter is. In the Medicine Wheel of the Native American tradition, winter is a time when the snow falls and covers everything, providing a time for some things to die and others to be reborn as spring comes bringing new life. This song refers to the time of sleeping peacefully and waiting for the coming of spring."

# Glossary

This glossary contains both ceramic and musical terms. Use it as a reference when you see an unfamiliar term in the book, or browse through it to increase your music and ceramics vocabulary. Italicized words in these definitions are themselves defined elsewhere in the glossary.

**absolute tuning** – adjusting the pitches of an instrument to an external standard such as standard pitch. This impacts whether or not it will play in tune with other instruments tuned to the same standard. See also *relative tuning*.

**aerophone** – a wind instrument, or instrument in which the sound is produced by the vibration of air. Flutes, horns and some types of percussion pots are in this category.

**airduct assembly** – a mouthpiece assembly for certain types of flutes that uses a narrow passage (windway) to direct a stream of air across the sharp edge of a hole (aperture) in a pipe or vessel. Recorders, pennywhistles and ocarinas use airduct assemblies. Sometimes referred to as a *fipple*.

**airduct flute** – also called a ducted or duct flute, fipple flute or whistle flute, this aerophone is blown through a mouthpiece called an *airduct assembly*.

**animism** – the belief in the existence of individual spirits that inhabit natural objects and phenomena; in other words, the world view that all natural objects and the universe itself have souls. Animism dates back to the earliest humans and continues to exist today, making it the oldest form of religious belief on Earth. It is characteristic of indigenous cultures, including many of the African and pre-Columbian societies mentioned in this book. These beliefs influence their views toward musical instruments, as well as the materials, such as trees and animal hides, they use to build them.

**aperture** – the opening in an *airduct assembly* over which air is blown from the *windway* across the *edge*. Analogous to the blowhole in a side-blown flute.

**bat** – a disk or square slab, usually made from plaster, wood or plastic, on which a pot is thrown or is placed to dry when removed from the potter's wheel. Also used when *handbuilding*.

**beats** – a type of *combination tone* that is perceived in the listener's ear and results from two or more simultaneously sounded pitches. The sensation is a steady throbbing or pulsation in intensity of the tone. Beats are most commonly the result of two pitches with very close *frequencies*, and can be calculated as the difference of the two frequencies. Slow beats give the sensation of a gentle vibrato, faster beats sound more like a buzzing or throbbing. Beats of more than 30 cycles per second are not likely to be perceived.

**bell** – a broad and sudden flare at the *distal end* of a wind instrument. The purpose of a bell is usually to impart a brighter *tone* to the instrument's sound and to increase the instrument's volume.

**bisque (biscuit)** – the first stage of *firing* (usually between cones 010-05), which transforms clay into permanent pottery. Bisque firing removes all moisture from a clay body and prepares the ware for the application of glaze. Bisque ware (biscuit ware) refers to objects that have been bisque fired.

**blowhole** – also known as an *embouchure* hole, this is the hole in a transverse flute across which the player blows air.

**bore** – the shape of the inside cavity of an instrument's tubular body.

**burnishing** – a technique of rubbing a hard, smooth tool such as a stone or metal spoon over the surface of an unfired clay object to compress and align the clay particles on the surface and produce a smooth, polished finish.

**cavity resonance** – the *frequency* or *pitch* at which a *globular* chamber resonates.

**ceramics** – the art and craft of making earthy materials into permanent objects through the use of high heat; also used to refer to the finished objects themselves.

**chamberduct** – a mechanism for creating an *edgetone* that consists of a small chamber with two holes opposite each other. When air is blown through the chamber, it creates an edgetone. This is similar to the whistle on a modern teapot, but its use in musical instruments seems to be unique to the *pre-Columbian* world. Also known as a chamberduct assembly.

**chordophone** – an instrument in which the sound is made by vibrating strings; a string instrument.

**chromatic** – a Western musical system or scale consisting of twelve pitches per *octave*. Each *pitch* is a *half step* or *semitone* apart. (A piano is a chromatic instrument, with each key playing a tone one-half step above its predecessor.)

**circular breathing** – a technique that allows a performer to play long, uninterrupted tones of several minutes or more on a wind instrument. Physiologically, it is impossible to breathe in and blow out simultaneously, but it is possible for a player to maintain air pressure, without blowing, by using their mouth like the airbag of a bagpipe. With the air stream maintained by this small mouth reservoir, a player can take quick breaths through their nose in order to refill their lungs so that they can continue blowing.

**clay** – an earthy mineral substance composed mostly of a hydrous silicate of alumina. Its main components are aluminum oxide, silicon dioxide, and water. Clay is created by the weathering of rocks. (see Chapter 7 for a more complete description of clay and how it is formed.)

**coiling** – the process of constructing a clay form using pieces of clay rolled into long "ropes" or coils. To build a pot, the clay ropes are looped around and around on top of each other, gradually building up the walls of the pot. (See Demonstration 1.)

**combination tone** – a musical *pitch* that results from the combination of two other pitches. The combination tone pitch is perceived in the listener's ear and is based on the difference of the wavelengths of the other two pitches. Some double flutes are designed to produce combination tones. The results can be a slow pulsing or beating (see *beats*) or a harsh, jarring sensation. Sometimes the results are quite surprising, when two high pitches produce a third, much lower, pitch.

**concert pitch** – see *standard pitch*

**cone** – refers to a pyrometric cone—a small pyramid of ceramic material formulated to melt at a specific temperature through *heat-work* (a product of time and temperature), and thus indicate when a *kiln* has reached a desired state.

**Conquest** – the conquest of the New World by European explorers and settlers, set into motion by Columbus' voyage to America in 1492, and led by Spanish Conquistador Hernándo Cortés beginning in 1519.

**counterpoise** – an anchor or counterbalance. In the context of musical instruments, this often refers to a rigid, heavy or stable component of an instrument that anchors a vibrating element and permits it to vibrate effectively while minimizing damping. For example, a membrane drum's shell provides counterpoise to the vibrating head. A tongue drum's body provides counterpoise to the vibrating tongue.

**cross fingering** – on an instrument with finger holes (*tone holes*), a fingering that uses a closed hole below an open one. Also called "forked fingering".

**diatonic** – a musical system or scale based on the standard major or minor scales of Western music without modulation by accidentals. (The white keys on a piano are an example of a diatonic scale.)

**difference tone** – see *combination tone*

**distal end** – the far or distant end of a tubular wind instrument; the end from which the sound emanates; in most instruments this is the opposite end from the end with the mouthpiece. (Note that sound also comes out of finger holes, and out of open mouthpieces on instruments such as flutes and ocarinas.) See also *proximal end.*

**duct** – another term for the *windway* in an *airduct assembly.*

**duct flute** – or ducted flute - see *airduct flute.*

**earthenware** – a type of clay that usually contains a lot of iron and other mineral impurities which give it the ability to *mature* below 2000° Fahrenheit. Because of its low firing temperature relative to other clay, it's also often called *low-fire* clay. Earthenware is usually red, brown or grey when unfired, and ranges from tan to red to black after firing. Earthenware clay is the raw material for bricks, drainage tiles, roof tiles and much of the pottery around the world, including all ancient (and many modern) ceramic instruments.

**edge** – the sharp blade in an *airduct assembly* that divides the airstream from the *windway* and creates turbulence, resulting in an *edgetone.*

**edgetone** – the initial component of a flute's sound, caused when a narrow air stream is directed over an edge or blade that divides the stream of air and creates a vibration.

**embouchure** – the positioning of the mouth when playing a wind instrument.

**engobe** – a type of *slip* used for decoration.

**extruder** – a tool for forming moist clay by pressing it through a shaped die or template. An extruder can mold clay into many forms, including hollow tubes which are used in many musical instruments. See *The Extruder Book* by Daryl Baird for more information.

**finger hole** – see *tone hole.*

**fipple flute** – see *airduct flute.*

**fipple**– see *airduct assembly.*

**firing** – the process of heating clay and glazes, usually in a furnace or kiln. Types of ceramic firing include *bisque, low-fire* and *high-fire.*

**frequency** – the number of vibratory cycles per second of a vibrating object. A sound's *pitch* is based on the frequency—the more vibrations per second, the higher the pitch.

**fundamental** – most musical sounds contain a blend of many different frequencies. The lowest of these is the fundamental, which is usually the perceived pitch of the sound. For instruments that are capable of *overblowing,* the fundamental pitch also refers to the instrument's lowest tone.

**glaze** – a glassy coating melted in place on a ceramic body.

**glaze firing** – normally a second firing of clay after *bisque firing,* which fuses the glaze to the pot.

**glissando** – a continuous or sliding movement from one *pitch* to another

**globular flute** – a type of flute whose body is not a tube, but rather a closed vessel of some shape (also called a *vessel flute*). The player blows across an open edge (as in the *xun*) or into a fipple-type mouthpiece (as in the *ocarina*).

**greenware** – unfired pottery that is fully dried and extremely fragile, like dry mud.

**grog** – pulverized particles of fired clay that are added to a clay body to add texture and/or reduce shrinkage and warping while drying.

**gut** – when referring to a string or snare on an instrument, gut is a material made from the stretched and dried intestines of a sheep or other animal. When properly prepared, it is very flexible and strong. Gut strings and snares are used on traditional instruments around the world, and are also preferred by many players of modern orchestral string instruments. Their sound is generally fuller and warmer than metal or synthetic strings.

**half holing** – on an instrument with finger holes (*tone holes*), a fingering technique of partially covering a tone hole.

**half step** – see *semitone*

**handbuilding** – the process of forming or sculpting clay with hand tools, as contrasted with using a potter's wheel.

**harmonic** – most musical sounds contain a blend of different frequencies that include a *fundamental* and additional overtones. When the overtones are integral multiples of the fundamental, they are called harmonics.

**harmonic series** – a series of tones consisting of a fundamental tone and the consecutive harmonics produced by it. These harmonics are integral multiples of the fundamental's frequency. Also called the *overtone series.*

**Helmholz resonator** – a resonating vessel shape that is not long and thin like a tube, but short and fat, or *globular,* and open to the outside air through a small opening.

**high-fire ware** – ware or clay that is fired to a temperature in the range from *cone* 6 to *cone* 13, usually *stoneware* or *porcelain.* By contrast, *earthenware* is *low-fire* ware.

**hybrid instrument** – an instrument in which two or more vibrational systems are combined to form a single instrument, for example, a flute combined with a rattle, or a horn combined with a drum. The two or more systems may function independently, or, more interestingly, they may combine in some way.

**idiophone** – an instrument whose body vibrates to produce sound. In other words, its sound is produced by the vibration of the sonorous materials from which it is made. Rattles, scrapers, bells, gongs and xylophones are among the members of this family.

**interval** – The difference between two *pitches,* usually expressed as a number of steps or *semitones.*

**key** – a set of relationships between pitches that establish a single pitch as the tonal center or "key note." An example of a key is "C major," the piano's white keys, which form a major scale starting with the pitch "C".

**kiln** – a chamber made of heat-resistant materials for firing pottery.

**leather hard** – the state of a clay object when most of the moisture has evaporated and shrinkage has ended, but the clay is not totally dry. At this point the clay is still workable and has the consistency of leather. This is the state at which many instruments such as flutes can be played and tuned, before firing.

**lip hole** – a tone hole near the airduct assembly of an ocarina or whistle, which can be covered and uncovered by the player's lip to extend the pitch range of an instrument.

**lipping** – a process of modifying the shape or tension of your lips to change the pitch of a mouth-blown wind instrument.

**low-fire ware** – ware or clay that is fired to a temperature in the range from *cone* 015 to cone 1, usually *earthenware.*

**maturity** – a measure of a clay or glaze's degree of maximum nonporosity, hardness and density, when fired.

**membranophone** – an instrument with a head, or "membrane," which is the initial sounding element of the instrument. Most instruments in this family are drums, but a few other instruments such as mirlitons (an example is a kazoo) are also membranophones.

**Mesoamerica** – refers to the many ancient civilizations that occupied regions that are now Mexico and Central America. In *pre-Columbian* times it was the seat of many diverse civilizations including the Maya and Olmec. Many of these cultures were advanced potters, and developed highly sophisticated ceramic musical instruments.

**microtones (microtonal)** – tones that lie closer together than *semitones,* which are the smallest intervals in our Western, 12-to-the-octave musical system. In other words, notes that lie "in the cracks between piano keys."

**ocarina** – the name given to a style of *globular flute* developed in Italy in the 19th century. Today, the term ocarina is used generically to describe most globular flutes. Globular flutes with few or no finger holes are sometimes called whistles rather than ocarinas.

**octave** – an *interval* bounded by two pitches with the same name, where the higher pitch is twice the frequency of the lower. For example, the interval from middle C to the next higher C on a piano is an octave.

**organology** – as used in this book, the study and classification of musical instruments.

**overblowing** – the process by which a wind instrument is made to sound a *harmonic* higher than the *fundamental;* that is, the process by which the higher registers of the instrument are reached. In most instruments this is accomplished by increasing the air speed and changing the *embouchure.* For flutes and brass instruments, this involves narrowing the aperture between the lips.

**overtone** – most musical sounds contain a blend of many different frequencies. The lowest of these is the *fundamental,* and the additional tones above it are called overtones or partials. When the overtones are integral multiples of the fundamental, they are called *harmonics.*

**oxidation** – a type of firing with complete combustion so that the firing atmosphere contains excess oxygen, allowing the metals in clays and glazes to produce their oxide colors. Electric kilns usually produce oxidized atmospheres unless reducing materials (combustible materials that will consume oxygen) are added.

**partial** – see *overtone.*

**pentatonic** – a musical scale that has only five tones per octave. The black keys of a piano are one example.

**pit firing** – a technique for creating a primitive *kiln* for firing ceramic ware by digging a hole in the ground, placing unfired ceramic ware at the bottom (often in a bed of sawdust), covering the ware with wood, cow dung and other combustibles, and igniting it.

**pitch** – the location of a musical sound in a tonal scale based on its frequency of vibration; for example A, B, C or do, re, mi. (also see *standard pitch*).

**plasticity** – the quality of wet clay that allows it to be formed or shaped without cracking.

**porcelain** – a very fine white or translucent clay, often fired at very high temperatures, up to approximately 2600 degrees Fahrenheit. Its primary component is china clay, or kaolin. Porcelain is challenging to work with because it is much more likely than stoneware to crack when drying. However, when vitrified it produces crystalline, bell-like tones unlike any other clay.

**pottery** – originally a term for *earthenware,* now loosely used to refer to all types of ceramic vessels, as well as to the workshop where they are made.

**pre-Columbian** – refers to the time before the conquest of the New World (see *Conquest*).

**pre-Hispanic** – another term for pre-Columbian.

**proximal end** – the end of a tubular wind instrument with the mouthpiece. See also *distal end.*

**raku** – Raku originated in Japan in the 16th century, where raku vessels are still used in the traditional tea ceremony. In the West, it has come to refer to a firing technique that involves removing ware from a red-hot kiln when the glaze is melted. The ware is often immediately plunged into an airtight container of straw, sawdust, paper or other combustible material in order to create a *reduction* atmosphere that aids in producing lustrous or opalescent glaze finishes, and blackened or smoked colors on raw clay.

**rawhide** – the untanned hide or skin of an animal. Rawhide is used for drum heads, and sound resonators for other instruments.

**reduction** – a type of firing in which insufficient oxygen is supplied to the kiln for complete combustion. Under these conditions, the carbon monoxide in the kiln combines with the oxygen in the oxides of the clay body and glaze, causing the metallic oxides to change color.

**relative tuning** – tuning the pitches of an instrument relative to each other; in other words, adjusting the instrument to play a scale in tune with itself, without regard for the instrument's *absolute tuning* or musical key.

**Sachs-Hornbostel** – the name of a system that classifies instruments into categories (*aerophones, idiophones, membranophones, chordophones*) according to the way in which their sound is produced—that is, what makes the instruments' primary driving vibration. Published by Erich von Hornbostel and Curt Sachs in 1914.

**saggar firing** – a firing technique in which the item to be fired is placed into a ceramic container called a saggar with combustible material such as wood, leaves, seaweed or cow dung. The saggar is then placed into a kiln. During firing, atmosphere inside the saggar produces patterns and colors on the surface of the ware.

**sawdust firing** – a finishing technique in which ceramic ware is buried in sawdust in an earthen pit or large vessel (such as a galvanized trash can). The sawdust is ignited and allowed to smolder, imparting a black or varied color to the surface of the ware. (see figures 7.15 through 7.23 for Keith Lehman's demonstration of this technique)

**scale** – a series of *pitches* arranged in ascending or descending order.

**semitone** – the smallest *interval* in the Western musical tradition. There are twelve semitones in an *octave*. On a piano, a semitone is the distance between two adjacent keys, whether white or black. Also known as a *half step*.

**sgraffito** – a decorative technique in which designs are engraved through a layer of clay *slip* to expose a contrasting color of the clay body beneath. This is usually accomplished by painting a slip on a clay body, then scratching through it.

**simple flute** – a *transverse flute* with open *tone holes,* rather than mechanical keys as used in a modern flute

**slab built** – refers to something created from clay rolled into flat sheets.

**slip** – an extremely fine-grained liquid clay, which may be used for casting pieces, decoration, or for attaching pieces of clay together before firing.

**slip casting** – a technique of forming objects by pouring deflocculated liquid clay (slip) into a plaster mold. The mold absorbs the water from the clay so that solid clay walls are formed.

**smoking (or smoke firing)** – a technique that produces gray to black colors on raw clay surfaces that is the result of smoke penetrating the pores of the clay. This is accomplished by burning combustible materials in close proximity to the clay surface, usually in a closed environment. See also *sawdust firing.*

**snare** – a string of thin *gut* or other material stretched across a drum head to give the drum a buzzing sound when struck.

**soundboard** – a thin resonating plate (often made of wood) whose vibrations reinforce the sound of an instrument; for example, the flat face or top of a guitar.

**soundbox** – a musical instrument's resonating chamber (such as a violin's body).

**standard pitch** – generally refers to the International Standard Pitch (adopted in 1939). In this tuning standard, the tone A above Middle C is defined to be 440 hertz (440 cycles per second). Most modern orchestral instruments are designed to be tuned to this standard. Also called "concert pitch".

**stoneware** – clay that vitrifies between 2000 and 2400 degrees Fahrenheit; also called *high-fire* clay. Stoneware clays are versatile, and vary widely in color, plasticity and firing range. They are used for a variety of purposes, from dinnerware to fire bricks. Stoneware clay is very strong and therefore is well-suited for drums, as well as most other musical instruments.

**terra sigillata** – a very fine-grained *slip* used as a glazelike surface coating on earthenware; typically *burnished.*

**throwing** – the process of forming clay using a potter's wheel.

**timbre** – the tone color or character of a musical sound. Descriptions of an instrument's timbre are often widely varied and somewhat subjective. For example, different flutes may have timbres described as "reedy," "bright," "warm," "breathy," or "dark" – and many others. (Note: the proper pronunciation of "timbre" rhymes with "camber".)

**tone** – 1.) a sound of a specific pitch; e.g., she played four ascending tones on the flute; 2.) the quality or character (timbre) of a sound; e.g., the whistle had a breathy tone.

**tone hole** – a hole in a flute that is covered or uncovered in order to change the instrument's sounding pitch. Also called a *finger hole.*

**transverse flute** – a side-blown flute, where the airstream is blown across the axis of the flute's length, rather than along it, as in end-blown and fipple flutes

**tuning** – the process of adjusting the pitch of an instrument, either when building it or after it is built before it is played (if a tuning mechanism is a part of the instrument). See also *relative tuning, absolute tuning.*

**vapor firing** – A surface treatment for ceramic ware in which materials such as sodium chloride or soda ash (sodium carbonate) are introduced into the kiln atmosphere so that they are deposited on the surface of the ware during the firing. This process results in colors, patterns and a variety of finishes on the clay surface. It also can be used in conjunction with glazes and slips. Firing ranges for this process range from cone 08 to cone 12. The materials can be introduced into the kiln via a clay "burrito," (i.e. wrapped up in paper) or dissolved in a hot water solution and sprayed directly into the kiln while at temperature. A type of vapor-firing, called "salt glazing" was used extensively in Europe starting in the 16th century and is used today to glaze commercial drainage pipes.

**vessel flute** – see *globular flute.*

**vitrification** – a dense, hard, and nonabsorbent condition of fired clay. *Maturity* is a measure of vitrification. (also **vitreous, vitrified**)

**volume** – in musical usage, refers to the loudness of a tone or instrument. More (or higher) volume indicates a louder sound.

**ware** – a generic term used to refer to pottery of any type in any state (green, bisqued, or fired).

**wedging** – a process potters use to thoroughly mix their clay and expel any air pockets, to ensure that their clay is in a workable condition before use; similar to kneading dough.

**wheel thrown** – refers to a ceramic object (or component of a finished object) that was formed on a potter's wheel.

**whistle** – an ambiguous term, which generally refers to some sort of *airduct flute.* It may be a tubular or globular flute, with or without fingerholes. Simple whistles are used for signaling in sports and other activities.

**whole tone** – an *interval* consisting of two *semitones.*

**windway** – the air passage in the mouthpiece of an *airduct flute,* whistle or ocarina. Also known as a *duct.*

# Bibliography

## Suggested Books, Articles, Videos and Recordings

### Books


**Akpabot, Samuel Ekpe.** *Ibibio Music in Nigerian Culture.* East Lansing, Michigan: Michigan State University Press, 1975.

**Anoff, Ken.** *Dha Ga Te Ti Na Ka Whoop! - Adapting Tabla Technique for Udu Drums.* Randallstown, MD: Ken Anoff, 1995.

**Baines, Anthony,** ed. *Musical Instruments Through the Ages.* Baltimore, MD: Penguin Books, 1961.

**Baines, Anthony.** *Brass Instruments: Their History and Development.* Minneola, NY: Dover Publications, 1993.

**Baines, Anthony.** *The Oxford Companion to Musical Instruments.* Oxford and New York: Oxford University Press, 1992.

**Baines, Anthony.** *Woodwind Instruments and Their History.* New York: W. W. Norton, 1957.

**Baird, Daryl.** *The Extruder Book.* Westerville, OH: The American Ceramic Society, 2000.

**Banek, Reinhold and John Scoville.** *Sound Designs: A Handbook of Musical Instrument Building.* Revised edition. Berkeley, CA: Ten Speed Press, 1995.

**Barley, Nigel.** *Smashing Pots: Works of Clay from Africa.* Washington, D.C.: Smithsonian Institution Press, 1994.

**Blades, James.** *Percussion Instruments and Their History.* Bold Strummer, Ltd., 1970.

**Blades, James.** *Percussion Instruments and Their History.* London; Boston: Faber and Faber, 1984.

**Botermans, Jack, Herman Dewit and Hans Goddefroy.** *Making and Playing Musical Instruments.* Seattle: University of Washington Press, 1989.

**Castañeda, Daniel.** *Instrumental Precortesiano.* Mexico: Museo Nacional de Arqueologia, Historia y Etnografia, 1933.

**Cline, Dallas.** *Homemade Instruments.* Oak Publications, 1976.

**Dearling, Robert,** ed. *The Illustrated Encyclopedia of Musical Instruments.* New York: Schirmer Books, 1996.

**Diagram Group.** *Musical Instruments of the World.* New York: Sterling Publishing Co., Inc., 1976.

**Edfors, John.** *Woodwind Instruments from PVC: Guidelines for Constructing Experimental Instruments from PVC Pipe and Related Materials.* Stranger Creek Productions, 1996.

**Escobar, Luis Antonio.** *La Musica Precolombina.* Bogota: Fundacion Universidad Central, 1985.

**Fletcher, Neville H. and Thomas D. Rossing.** *The Physics of Musical Instruments.* New York and Berlin: Springer-Verlag, 1991.

**Franco, José-Luis.** *Musical Instruments from Central Veracruz in Classic Times.* Ancient Art of Veracruz, Exhibition Catalog of the Los Angeles County Museum of Natural History, 1971.

**Hart, Mickey, and Fredric Lieberman, with D.A. Sonneborn.** *Planet Drum: A Celebration of Percussion and Rhythm.* New York: Harper San Francisco, 1991.

**Hart, Mickey, with Jay Stevens and Fredric Lieberman.** *Drumming at the Edge of Magic: A Journey into the Spirit of Percussion.* San Francisco: Harper, 1990.

**Havighurst, Jay.** *Making Musical Instruments by Hand.* Gloucester, MA: Quarry Books, Rockport Publishers, Inc., 1998.

**Hopkin, Bart.** *Air Columns and Toneholes: Principles for Wind Instrument Design (Revised Edition).* Willits, CA: Tai Hei Shakuhachi, 1999.

**Hopkin, Bart.** *Making Simple Musical Instruments.* Asheville, NC: Lark Books, 1995.

**Hopkin, Bart.** *Musical Instrument Design: Information for Instrument Making.* Tucson, AZ: See Sharp Press, 1996.

**Izikowitz, Karl Gustav.** *Musical and Other Sound Instruments of the South American Indians; A Comparative Ethnographical Study.* Goteborg: Elanders boktr., 1935.

**Kartomi, Margaret.** *On Concepts and Classifications of Musical Instruments.* Chicago: University of Chicago Press, 1990.

**Laskin, William.** *The World of Musical Instrument Makers: A Guided Tour. With photographs by Brian Pickell.* New York: Mosaic Press, 1988.

**Leake, Jerry.** *Series A.I.M. Percussion Text: Volume I – Afro-American Aspects.* 2nd ed. Boston: Rhombus Publishing, 1993.

**Maffit, Rocky.** *Rhythm & Beauty: The Art of Percussion.* New York: Watson-Guptill Publications, 1999.

**Marcuse, Sibyl.** *A Survey of Musical Instruments.* New York: Harper & Row, 1975.

**Marcuse, Sibyl.** *Musical Instruments: A Comprehensive Dictionary.* New York: Norton, 1975.

**Martí, Samuel.** *Music Before Columbus (Música Precolombina).* Perugino, México: Ediciones Euroamericanas, 1978.

**Mason, Bernard S.** *How to Make Drums, TomToms & Rattles: Primitive Percussion Instruments for Modern Use.* Minneola, NY: Dover Publications, 1974.

**Mead, Charles Williams.** *The musical instruments of Inca.* American Museum Press, New York, 1924.

**Mead, Charles Williams.** *The Musical Instruments of the Incas.* A Guide Leaflet to the Collection on Exhibition in the American Museum of Natural History. New York: The New York Museum, 1903.

**Melick, Brian.** *The How to of Udu: A Presentation on Performance.* Ravena, NY: Brian Melick, 1991.

**Moniot, Janet.** *Clay Whistles: The Voice of Clay.* Petal, MS: Whistle Press, 1989.

**Olsen, Dale A.** *Music of El Dorado: The Ethnomusicology Of Ancient South American Cultures.* Gainesville, FL: University Press of Florida, 2002.

**Olson, Harry Ferdinand.** *Music, Physics and Engineering.* Minneola NY: Dover Publications, 1967.

**Randel, Don Michael ed.** *The New Harvard Dictionary of Music.* Cambridge, MA: Belknap Press of Harvard University Press, 1986.

**Rawcliffe, Susan.** *Eight Pre-Columbian West Mexican Flutes in Fowler Museum.* To be published by The Cotsen Archaeology Institute, UCLA, 2005.

**Robinson, Trevor.** *The Amateur Wind Instrument Maker.* Cambridge, MA: University of Massachusetts Press, 1981.

**Roederer, Juan G.** *Introduction to the Physics and Psychophysics of Music,* 1995 Springer.

**Rossing, Thomas D.** *Science of Percussion Instruments.* World Scientific Publishing Company, 2000.

**Sachs, Curt.** *The History of Musical Instruments.* New York: W. W. Norton & Company, 1940.

**Sadie, Stanley (editor).** *New Grove Dictionary of Musical Instruments.* New York: MacMillan Press Limited, London and Grove's Dictionaries of Music, 1984.

**Shepard, Mark.** *Flutecraft: An Artisan's Guide to Bamboo Flutemaking.* Willits, CA: Tai Hei Shakuhachi, revised edition published in 1994 (first published by Simple Press in 1976).

**Shepard, Mark.** *Simple Flutes: A Guide to Flute Making and Playing, or How to Make and Play a Flute of Bamboo, Wood, Clay, Metal, PVC Plastic, or Anything Else.* Simple Productions and Tai Hei Shakuhachi, 1992.

**Statnekov, Daniel.** *Animated Earth.* North Atlantic Press (2nd edition), 2003.

**Stevenson, Robert Murrell.** *Music in Aztec & Inca Territory.* Berkeley: University of California Press, 1968.

**Summit, Ginger & Jim Widess.** *Making Gourd Musical Instruments: Over 60 String, Wind & Percussion Instruments and How to Play Them.* New York: Sterling Pub., 1999.

**Various Artists, edited by Bart Hopkin.** *Gravikords, Whirlies & Pyrophones.* [Book & CD sound recording]. Features a number of artists included in this book.Roslyn, NY: Ellipsis Arts, 1996.

**Various Artists, edited by Bart Hopkin.** *Orbitones, Spoonharps & Bellowphones.* [Book and CD sound recording]. Features a number of artists included in this book. Roslyn, NY: Ellipsis Arts,1998.

**Waring, Dennis.** *Great Folk Instruments to Make & Play.* New York: Sterling Publishing Company, 1999.

**Waring, Dennis.** *Making Drums.* New York: Sterling Publishing Company; Winnipeg: Tamos Books, 2003.

## Articles

**Ames, David W. and Ken A. Gourlay.** "Kimkim: A Women's Musical Pot." *African Arts,* January 1978: 56-62, 64, 95-96.

**Ball, F. Carlton.** "Ceramic Horns." *Ceramics Monthly,* June/July/August 1967: 11.

**Blench, Roger.** "Idoma Musical Instruments." *African Music: Journal of the International Library of African Music.* 6.4 (1987): 42-52.

**Bloom, Norman D.** "Udu Drum." *Percussion Source.* 1.1 (1995): 86-87.

**Bussabarger, Robert.** "Sound Off With Clay Whistles." *Ceramics Monthly,* June 1956: 16.

**Eilenberger, Robert F.** "Water Whistle Sculpture." *Ceramics Monthly,* February 1969: 16.

**Fromme, Robert A.** "The Clay Whistle Part 1." *Ceramics Monthly,* March 1977: 60.

**Fromme, Robert A.** "The Clay Whistle Part 2." *Ceramics Monthly,* April 1977: 58.

**Gallaway, Sally and John.** "Wind Chimes." *Ceramics Monthly,* April 1970: 20.

**Giorgini, Frank.** "Udu Drum: Voice of the Ancestors." *Experimental Musical Instruments 5.5* (1990). *Experimental Musical Instruments* (EMI), edited by Bart Hopkin, is a fabulous resource for musical instrument builders. Published as a bimonthly journal from 1985 to 1999, back issues are available from the EMI website (www.windworld.com). Many of the artists featured in this book have published articles in EMI, describing their work and their techniques for instrument building, including Frank Giorgini, Barry Hall, Ragnar Naess, Brian Ransom, Sharon Rowell and Susan Rawcliffe. Additionally, many other articles, though not specifically about clay instruments, have applications and ideas that apply to ceramic instrument construction.)

**Goldman, Jerry.** "Clay Flutes." *Ceramics Monthly,* April 1964: 11.

**Gray, Verdelle.** "A Teacher's Solution: Musical Mobiles." *Ceramics Monthly,* August 1956: 22.

**Hall, Barry.** "Globular Horns." *Experimental Musical Instruments,* 14.4, (1999).

**Hall, Barry.** "Two Hardware-Store Instruments: The Flowerpot-O-Phone and Washer Chimes." *Experimental Musical Instruments,* 9.3 (1994).

**Hartenstein, Ward.** "Sounds in Clay." *Experimental Musical Instruments,* 4.6 (1989).

**Jeffreys, M.W.D.** "A Musical Pot from Southern Nigeria." Man. 40.215 (1940): 186-187.

**Naess, Ragnar.** "EarthSounds." *Experimental Musical Instruments,* 7.2 (1991).

**Nicklin, Keith.** "The Ibibio Musical Pot." *African Arts.* 7.1 (1973): 50-55, 92.

**Ransom, Brian.** "Ceramic Instruments." *Experimental Musical Instruments,* 14.4 (1999).

**Ransom, Brian.** "Sounding Clay." *Ceramics Monthly.* October 1988: 30.

**Ransom, Brian.** "The Deities of Sound." *Ceramics Monthly.* December 1996: 42.

**Ransom, Brian.** "The Enigma of the Whistling Water Vessel." Published for the symposium *Influence of Art & Architecture in Pre-Columbian Peru.* University of Missouri, Columbus, 1985.

**Ransom, Brian.** "The Enigma of Whistling Water Jars in Pre-Columbian Ceramics." *Experimental Musical Instruments,* 14.1 (1998): 12-15.

**Rawcliffe, Susan.** "Harmonic Combinations." *Ceramics Monthly,* October 1997: 35.

**Rawcliffe, Susan.** "Complex Acoustics in Pre-Columbian Flute Systems." *Musical Repercussions of 1492,* Smithsonian Institution Press, 1992; *Experimental Musical Instruments,* 8.2, 1992; *National Council on Education in the Ceramic Arts Journal* Vol. 14, 1993-4.

**Rawcliffe, Susan.** "Sounding Clay: Pre-Hispanic Flutes." *Orient-Archäologie Band 8, Studien zur Musikarchäologie III;* Ellen Hickmann and Ricardo Eichmann, Eds. Verlag Marie Leidorf GmbH, Rahden/Westf., Germany, 2003.

**Rezner, Janie.** "A Soulful Sound." *Ceramics Monthly,* May 1999: 64.

**Rothenberg, Polly.** "Enameled Wind Chimes." *Ceramics Monthly,* June/July/August 1966: 27.

**Rothenberg, Polly.** "Fused-Glass Wind Chimes." *Ceramics Monthly,* June/July/August 1966: 30.

**Rowell, Sharon.** "Sharon Rowell's Clay Ocarinas." *Experimental Musical Instruments,* 1.2 (1985).

**Traylor, Everett.** "A Slip-Cast Ceramic Flute." *Ceramics Monthly,* March 1970: 26.

**Traylor, Everett.** "Making an Ocarina by the Slip-Cast Method." *Ceramics Monthly,* February 1971: 28.

**Uribe, Ed.** "Udu Drums." *Modern Drummer.* 15.2 (1991): 49-51.

**Welch, Chris.** "Pot Luck: T.H. 'Vikku' Vinayakram." (Ghatam player) *Melody Maker,* 52 (1977): 9, 48.

**Youg, Helen.** "Whistles Are For Fun." Ceramics Monthly, June/July/August 1962: 18.

## Videos

*Clay Whistles.* Janet Moniot. The Whistle Press, 1990.

*Hand Drumming: Exercises for Unifying Technique.* N. Scott Robinson. Wright Hand Drum WHD-01, 1996.

*The How to of Udu: A Presentation on Performance.* Brian Melick. Warner Brothers, 1997.

*Udu: Clay Pot Drums and How to Play Them.* Barry Hall. Burnt Earth, 2002.

*Udu Drum Techniques.* Various Artists. Udu Drum, 1991.

*Udu Magic: The Art Udu Drum Playing.* Various Artists. Afro-Rhythms, 1998.

## Recordings

Antenna Repairmen. *Ghatam.* M.A. Recordings M037A, 2000.

Attebery Mark. *Cactus on Mars.* Thin Air Records, 1997.

Bejarano, Rafael with Barry Hall, Jusse Nayeli and Alan Tower. *The Eternal Presence: Music for Four Didjeridus. Ancient Future Records,* 1003, 2002.

Burnt Earth Ensemble. *Terra Cotta.* Hallistic Music HALCD02, 2005.

Codona. *Codona.* ECM 1132 78118-21132-2.1979.

Cold Blue. *The Complete 10-Inch Series (featuring "Clay Music" by Barney Childs).* Cold Blue, CB0014, 2004.

Dalglish, Malcolm. *Pleasure*. Ooolitic Music, OM 1112, 1997.

Gurtu, Trilok. *African Fantasy*. VIA, ESC-36642, 2000.

Hassell, Jon and Brian Eno. *Fourth World Vol. 1: Possible Musics*. Editions EG EEGED 7, 1980.

Jacobs, Geert. *De Jacobsladder.* Disky Communications, 1999.

Jacobs, Geert. *Flutemaker & Friends*. Disky Communications, 1999.

Jermano, Rosario. *Living in Percussion*. Freeland, FL 4003-2, 1991.

Melick, Brian. *Percussive Voices*. Hudson Valley, HVR-7000, 1999.

Nascimento, Milton. *Milton*. CBS Luxo, 231163, 1988.

O'Hearn, Patrick. *Between Two Worlds*. Collaboration with Brian Ransom, New York: Private Music, 1987.

Oregon. *Roots in the Sky*. Discovery, 71005, 1979.

Pöchtrager, Karin. Die Ocarina: *Eine musikalische Riese mit der Ocarina*. Ditmannsdorf, Austria: Ocarina Werkstatt.

Ransom, Brian and Norma Tanega. *Internal Medicine*. RT Music, 1995.

Ransom, Brian. *Sounding Clay*. Hubba Hubba Studio, 1990.

Ransom, Brian. *The Ceramic Ensemble*. Tanega Studios, 1986.

Ransom, Brian. *Try to Tell Fish About Water.* Tanega Studios, 1986.

Rawcliffe, Susan, Scott Wilkinson and Brad Dutz (Many Axes). *2 Many Axes*. pfMENTUM, CD020, 2004.

Rezner, Janie. *Oquawka Speaks: the Words and Music of Mother God*. janierezner.com.

Robinson, N. Scott. *Things That Happen Fast*. New World View Music, NWVM CD-02, 2001

Robinson, N. Scott. *World View.* New World View Music, NWVM CD-01, 1994.

Simopoulos, Nana. *Wings and Air.* Enja, ENJ-5031-2, 1986.

Tower, Alan, and Free Energy. *10,000 Thunderstorms: the Spirit of Evolution*. Octave Alliance, 2003.

Tower, Alan. *Waves: Solo Huaca*. Octave Alliance, 2002.

Various Artists, edited by Bart Hopkin. *Gravikords, Whirlies & Pyrophones*. (book and CD sound recording). Ellipsis Arts, 1996. Features a number of artists included in this book.

Various Artists, edited by Bart Hopkin. *Orbitones, Spoonharps & Bellowphones*. [book and CD sound recording]. Ellipsis Arts, 1998. Features a number of artists included in this book.

Various Artists. *Didjeridu Planet III*. Timeless Productions, DP03 CD, 2003.

Various Artists. *Didjeridu Planet*. Didjeridu Planet, DP01, 1997.

Various Artists. *Didjeridoo USA*.

Various Artists. *Experimental Musical Instruments: Later Years*. Experimental Musical Instruments, EXP 0016, 2002.

Various Artists. *From the Pages of Experimental Musical Instruments Volume 8*. Experimental Musical Instruments, 1993. Features ceramic winds played by Susan Rawcliffe.

Various Artists. *From the Pages of Experimental Musical Instruments Volume 9*. Experimental Musical Instruments, 1994. Features flowerpotophones played by Barry Hall.

Various Artists. *From the Pages of Experimental Musical Instruments Volume 11*. Experimental Musical Instruments, 1996. Features ceramic winds played by Susan Rawcliffe.

Various Artists. *From the Pages of Experimental Musical Instruments Volume 14*. Experimental Musical Instruments, 1999. Features globular horns played by Barry Hall.

Various Artists. *The Aerial #2. Nonsequitur Foundation*, AER 1990/2, 1990.

Various Artists. *The Igede of Nigeria: Drumming, Chanting, and Exotic Percussion*. Music of the World, CDT-117, 1978/1979.

Various Artists. *Udu Magic: The Art of Udu Drum Playing*. Afro-Rhythms, CD-01, 1998.

Vasconcelos, Naná. *Storytelling (Contando Estorias)*. EMI Hemisphere, 7243 8 33444-2, 1995.

# Resources and Materials

## Resources

Below you will find information on resources for and suppliers of materials related to the creation of ceramic musical instruments. The following information is current as of the publishing date of this book. Since this information tends to change over time, updated information will be made available at this book's website: **www.FromMudToMusic.com**

## Online Communities and Forums

**Ceramic Musical Instruments:** *groups.yahoo.com/group/ceramicmusicalinstruments* – discussion of ceramic musical instruments.

**Ocarina Club:** *groups.yahoo.com/group/ocarinaclub* – discussion of all things ocarina.

**Clayart:** *www.ceramics.org/clayart* – discussion of general ceramics topics.

## Resources for Calculating Flute Dimensions

Flutomat Calculator – an online interactive program that calculates optimal hole size and spacing for a flute in any key. You input the dimensions of your tube and your desired key and it does the rest. To locate this resource, search the web for "flutomat" or follow the link from this book's website: **www.FromMudToMusic.com.**

Two books with helpful information on flute tone-hole design are *Simple Flutes* by Mark Shepard, and *Air Columns and Tone Holes* by Bart Hopkin. Both are listed in the Bibliography.

## Sources of Materials

*Drum Heading Supplies and Other Animal-Based Materials*

**Mid-East Manufacturing** (www.mid-east.com, 800-673-1517) – goat, calf and fish skin heads.

**African Rhythm Traders** (www.rhythmtraders.com, 503-288-6950) – goat and calf skins, plus rope, rings and other supplies used for African-style drum building.

**Tandy Leather** (www.tandyleather.com, 800-433-3201) – large pieces of rawhide goat and calf

**Shorty Palmer** (www.goatskins.com) – goat and calf skins imported from Africa.

**Stern Tanning Co., Inc.** (www.sterntanning.com, 920-467-8615) – rawhide drum heads.

**Boone Trading Company** (www.boonetrading.com, 800-423-1945) – bone, horn, teeth, tusks and all sorts of other interesting materials (do you need some wart hog ivory?)

**Moscow Hide and Fur** (www.hideandfur.com, 208-882-0601) – leather, fur, sinew, etc.

**Drum Supply House** (www.drummaker.com, 615-251-1146) – drum supplies

*Wood for Soundboards and Tuners and Hardware for String Instruments:*

**Stewart MacDonald** (www.stewmac.com, 800-848-2273)

**International Luthiers Supply, Inc.** (www.internationalluthiers.com, 918-835-4181)

**Musicmaker's Kits** (www.musikit.com, 800-432-5487)

**North American Wood Products** (nawpi.com/musicwd2.html)

## Strings

**International Piano Supply** (www.pianoparts.com, 888-NOTES-88) – steel strings in a finely graduated range of sizes (note that piano makers call strings "music wire").

**Damian Dlugolecki, Stringmaker** (www.damianstrings.com, 503-669-7966) – hand-made gut strings for fine instruments.

**Aquila Strings** (www.aquilausa.com) – manufacturer of fine gut and synthetic strings.

**Elderly Instruments** (www.elderly.com, 888-473-5810) – music shop that carries steel, nylon and gut strings for a variety of folk instruments.

**Just Strings** (www.juststrings.com, 603-889-2664) – string sets for a wide variety of unusual instruments.

## Adhesives

*Except where noted, all adhesives listed are available at hardware stores or home centers.*

**Cyanoacrylate (Super Glue)** – fast and durable, good for repairs and attaching smaller items.

**Polyvinyl acetate (PVA) or white glue** – water-soluble, good for porous materials and attaching drum heads.

**Aliphatic resin or yellow carpenter's glue** – water-resistant, but can still be removed by soaking in warm water. Good for attaching drum heads.

**Epoxy** – extremely strong and waterproof, but also toxic and flammable. Two parts (resin and catalyst) are combined to create a chemical reaction which quickly forms a bond. Available in liquid, paste and putty forms. "PC-7" is a brand of expoxy putty commonly used by ceramic sculptors for repairs and construction.

**Apoxie Sculpt and FixIt** – non-toxic epoxy putty, good for instrument repairs, adjusting tuning holes, and building mouthpieces. (available at www.avesstudio.com, 800-261-2837)

**Silicone adhesive** – flexible bond, provides an airtight seal.

**Polyurethane glue** – activated by moisture, expands as it dries. Commonly used for woodworking; available at hardware and woodworking stores. "Gorilla Glue" is a common brand.

## Electronic Tuners

Useful for fine tuning flutes, ocarinas and other instruments. Available at music stores and online. Popular brands include Korg, Seiko and Boss, although there are many others. "Chromatic" models will tune any pitch, and are more flexible than those designed specifically for guitar or other string instruments.

# Contributors

Many thanks to all the artists and performers who contributed to this book. Below you will find contact information for those contributors who elected to have theirs published. Links to additional related websites are available at this book's website: **www.FromMudToMusic.com**

**Donna Anderson**
815 Snider Lane
Cloverly, MD 20905 USA
email: donnademma@aol.com
tel: 301-879-5133

**Eddie Andresen**
website: www.acousdig.com

**Mark Attebery**
email: m.attebery@mac.com
website: www.cdstreet.com/artists/markattebery

**Michael Barnes**
Norh Loudspeaker Co., Inc.
website: www.norh.com
email: info@norh.com

**Diane Baxter**
2005 Creek St. Apt B
Douglas, AK 99824 USA
email: dbstargirl@hotmail.com
tel: 907-364-3273

**Richard Baxter**
website: www.richardbaxter.co.uk

**Theresa Bayer**
email: TB@tbarts.com
website: www.tbarts.com

**Rafael Bejarano**
website: www.soundsofcreation.org

**David S. Chrzan**
email: dchrzan@mindspring.com
website: www.thewhistleguy.com

**Alfonso Arrivellaga Cortes**
Anthropologist and Ethnomusicologist
Investigador Titular del Centro de Estudios
Folklórico, Universidad de San Carlos de Guatemala,
Avenida Reforma 0-09 Zona 10, Jardín Botánico
Guatemala, Ciudad. Z.P. 01010
email: aarrivillaga@usac.edu.gt
website: www.popolvuh.ufm.edu.gt/Vocesmayas.htm
tel: (502) 3319171
fax: (502) 3603952
Correspondence:
Arco 3 No. 21 Zona 5
Jardines de la Asunción
Z.P. 01005
Guatemala, Ciudad.
Centro América

**Kevin Costante**
email: Sebas.Costante@oberlin.edu

**Aguinaldo da Silva**
c/o Rosa Pereira
email: rosap@terra.com.br
website: www.portorossi.art.br/mestre.html

**Hide Ebina**
#310-338 West 8th Ave.
Vancouver, BC V5Y3X2 Canada
email: mail@hideart.com
website: www.hideart.com
tel: 604-875-6002

**The Field Museum**
1400 S. Lake Shore Drive
Chicago, IL 60605-2496
website: www.fieldmuseum.org

**Stephen Freedman**
website: www.stephenfreedman.com

**Jason Gaddy**
email: sales@VolcanicCeramics.com
www.VolcanicCeramics.com
tel: (360)273-0687

**Tim Gale**
email: tncgale@plowcreek.org
website: www.plowcreek.org/pottery.htm

**Sergio Garcia & Marco Donoso**
Arcoiris Ceramic Musical Instruments
Casilla 169, Quilpué, Chile
ocarinasarcoiris@hotmail.com
tel: (56)-(32)-826281

**Frank Giorgini**
website: www.udu.com

**Gruppo Ocarinistico Budriese**
Via Golinelli 14
40054 Budrio (BO) - Italy
Claudio Cedroni, President
email: cedro@global.it
website: www.ocarina.it/group.htm

**Barry Hall**
PO Box 452
Grafton, MA 01519 USA
email: barry@ninestones.com
website: www.burntearth.com

**John Hansen**
Mudslingers Pottery Studio
820 Main Street, Suite 1
Louisville, CO 80027 USA
website: www.mudslingerspottery.com

**Robin Hodgkinson**
Clay-Wood-Winds
30 Fairfield Ave.
Haydenville, MA 01039 USA
email: claywind@msn.com
website: www.Clay-Wood-Winds.com
tel: 413-268-3108

**Bart Hopkin**
Experimental Musical Instruments
email: emi@windworld.com
website: www.windworld.com

**Don Ivey**
649 Paseo de la Playa #306
Redondo Beach, CA 90277 USA

**Geert Jacobs**
website: www.ceramicflutes.com

**Frank Kara**
email: percussivearth @hotmail .com
website: www.percussivearth.com

**Ørgen Karlsen**
email: oergen.karlsen@c2i.net
website: www.freewebs.com/orgen

**Rod Kendall**
website: www.RodKendall.com

**Stephen Kent**
website: www.didjeridu.com/skent/

**Kai Koesling**
website: www.schlagwerk.de

**Beatrice Landolt**
P.O. Box 9
Hopewell, NJ 08525 USA
email: Raven21147@aol.com

**Keith Lehman**
Gibsons, British Columbia, Canada
email: poplarstudio@dccnet.com
website: www.poplarstudio.ca

**Ken Lovelett**
website: www.americanpercussion.com

**Jan Lovewell and Ron Robb**
Rare Earth Pottery
C41, RR2, Malaspina Rd.
Powell River, BC V8A4Z3
Canada
email: rareearth@armourtech.com

**Anastasia Mamali**
Ethnic Percussion
Zilonos Str 14, 17237
Athens, Greece
email: info@ethnic-percussion.com
website: www.ethnic-percussion.com
tel/fax +30210-7629926
mobile +306972211845

**Rob Mangum**
robbeth@mangumpottery.com
website: mangumpottery.com

**Wayne McCleskey**
4026 NE 55th St. Suite D
Seattle, WA 98105 USA
waynemccleskey@earthlink.net
tel: 206-522-3423

**Brian Melick**
website: www.uduboy.com

**Fabio Menaglio**
email: ocarina@ocarina.it
website: www.ocarina.it

**Janet Moniot**
P.O. Box 1006
Petal, MS 39465 USA
email: contact@whistlepress.com
website: www.whistlepress.com

**Joe O'Donnell**
website: www.joeo-donnell.com

**Kelly Jean Ohl**
300 East Whittier Street
Lanesboro, MN 55949 USA
email: kellyjeanohl@hotmail.com
tel: 507-467-2216

**The Phoebe Apperson Hearst Museum of Anthropology**
103 Kroeber Hall
Berkeley, CA 94720-3712
hearstmuseum.berkeley.edu

**Marie Picard**
website: www.musictradgard.com/marie/

**Brian Ransom**
website: home.eckerd.edu/~ransombc/index2.htm

**Troy Raper**
email: troy@musicalmud.com
website: MusicalMud.com

**Susan Rawcliffe**
website: www.artawakening.com/soundworks

**Emily Rensink**
1617 Haver Street
Houston, TX 77006 USA
email: emilyrensink@yahoo.com
website: www.emilyrensink.com

**Janie Rezner**
Box 1441
Mendocino, CA 95460 USA
email: jrezner@mcn.org
website: www.janierezner.com
tel: 707-962-9277

**Terry Riley**
website: www.terryrileyvesselflutes.com

**N. Scott Robinson**
email: sonrob@msn.com
website: www.nscottrobinson.com

**Johann Rotter**
website: www.ocarina.de

**Sharon Rowell**
email: sharonrowell@hotmail.com

**Robert Santerre**
344 Old Stage Rd.
Arrowsic, ME 04530-7410 USA
email: aipots@gwi.net
tel: 207-443-5858

**Kelly Averill Savino**
email: primalmommy@mail2ohio.com
website: www.primalpotter.com

**Richard & Sandi Schmidt**
Clayzeness Whistleworks
website: www.clayz.com

**Kaete Brittin Shaw**
website: www.potterytrail.com

**Constance Sherman**
Whistlestop
21 Lower Station Rd
Garrison, NY 10524 USA
Westchester Art Workshop
Westchester County Center
196 Central Ave.
White Plains, NY 10606 USA
tel: 914-684-0094

**Cedar Sorensen**
Victoria BC Canada
email: cedaris@pcnet.ca
cedaris@hotmail.com

**Dag Sørensen**
website: www.artworks.no

**Linda Stauffer**
website: www.staufferceramics.com

**John Taylor**
16 Budbury Circle
Bradford on Avon, Wilts BA15 1QQ
United Kingdom
tel: 01225 309 135

**Tom Teasley**
website: www.tomteasley.com

**Alan Tower**
email: atower@octavealliance.org
website: www.octavealliance.org

**Lori Twardowski-Raper**
email: Loriraper@musicalmud.com
website: MusicalMud.com

**Reed Weir**
email: phaedrus@nf.sympatico.ca
tel: 709-645-2266

**Chester Winowiecki**
2029 Lakewood Rd.
Whitehall, MI 49461 USA
email: cwinowiecki@hotmail.com

**Stephen Wright**
Wright Hand Drum Company
website: www.wrighthanddrums.com

# Photo Credits

The author and the American Ceramic Society would like to thank the following artists and photographers for their participation:

**Front cover:** Sibila Savage; Foreword: Jan Watson; 1.1-2.1: Barry Hall; 2.2: Luiz Santos; 2.3: Ron Robb; 2.4-2.5: Kelly Jean Ohl; 2.6: Caroline Kahler; 2.7-2.9: Barry Hall; 2.10: Erik Mandaville; 2.11: Erik Mandaville; 2.12: Barry Hall; 2.13: Dee McMillin; 2.14: Diane Baxter; 2.15: Sibila Savage & Barry Hall; 2.16: Brian Ransom; 2.17: Erik Mandaville; 2.18: Chester Winowiecki; 2.19: Erik Mandaville; 2.20: Elisabeth Rabouin; 2.21: Rod Kendall; 2.22: Stephen Wright; 2.23: Erik Mandaville; 2.24: Jonathan Walsh; 2.25: Brian Ransom; 2.26: Luiz Santos; 3.1: Sibila Savage; 3.2-3.4: Barry Hall; 3.5: Stephen Wright; 3.6: Brian Ransom; 3.7: Chester Winowiecki; 3.8: Keith Lehman; 3.9: Tom Holt; 3.10: Anastasia Mamali; 3.11: Hide Ebina; 3.12: Dona Vanden Heuvel; 3.13: Heather McQueen; 3.14: Don Ivey; 3.15: Sibila Savage; 3.16: John Hansen; 3.17: Troy Raper; 3.18: Sibila Savage; 3.19: Troy Raper; 3.20: Barry Hall; 3.21-3.22: Sibila Savage; 3.23: Stephen Wright; 3.24: Sibila Savage; 3.25: Barry Hall; 3.26: Anastasia Mamali; 3.27: Barry Hall; 3.28: Ken Lovelett; 3.29: Brian Ransom; 4.1: Barry Hall; 4.2: Zack Spreacker; 4.3: Barry Hall; 4.4: Gijs Jacobs; 4.5: Erik Mandaville; 4.6: Sibila Savage; 4.7: Brian Ransom; 4.8: Barry Hall; 4.9: Brian Ransom; 4.10-4.11: Barry Hall; 4.12-4.13: Christine Irastorza; 4.14: Janet Moniot; 4.15: Barry Hall; 4.16: Robin Goodfellow and Barry Hall; 4.17: Brian Ransom; 4.18-4.19: Rod Kendall; 4.20: Barry Hall; 4.21-4.22: Gijs Jacobs; 4.23: Barry Hall; 4.24: Daryl Baird; 4.25: Barry Jennings; 4.26: Ron Robb; 4.27: Fabio Menaglio; 4.28: Public domain; 4.29: Ikue Hiramoto; 4.30: Sergio Garcia and Marco Donoso; 4.31: Zack Spreacker; 4.32-4.34: John Taylor; 4.35: Michael Noa; 4.36: Kathleen Moore; 4.37: Ron Robb; 4.38: Kelly Averill Savino; 4.39: Reed Weir; 4.40: Carla Lombardi; 4.41: Jerry L. Anthony; 4.42: Linda Stauffer; 4.43: Theresa Bayer; 4.44: Caroline Kahler; 4.45: Bryna Brashier; 4.46: Beatrice Landolt; 4.47: Janet Moniot; 4.48: Hester Heuff; 4.49: Janie Rezner; 4.50: Barry Jennings; 4.51: Terry Riley; 4.52: Robin Hodgkinson; 4.53: Richard Sargent; 4.54-4.55: Luiz Santos; 4.56: John Taylor; 4.57: Barry Hall; 4.58-4.59: Gene Ogami; 4.60: Howard Goodman; 4.61-4.64: Barry Hall; 4.65-4.66: Brian Ransom; 4.67-4.68: Barry Hall; 4.69- 4.71: Brian Ransom; 4.72: Gene Ogami; 4.73: Barry Hall; 4.74: Rod Kendall; 4.75: Barry Hall; 4.76: John Taylor; 4.77-4.78: Barry Hall; 4.79: Richard Schneider; 4.80-4.81: Steve Smeed; 4.82: Tom Holt; 4.83-4.90: Dag Sørensen; 4.91-4.92: Gijs Jacobs; 4.93-4.94: Dag Sørensen; 4.95-4.96: Dan Boone & Zach Huntington; 4.97: Sibila Savage; 4.98: Brian Ransom; 4.99: Chester Winowiecki; 4.100: Bob Johnson; 4.101: Barry Hall; 4.102: Sibila Savage; 4.103: Barry Hall; 4.104: Jose Gumilla; 4.105: Richard Baxter; 4.106: Ragnar Naess; 4.107: Jose Gumilla; 4.108-4.109: Sibila Savage; 4.110: John Taylor; 4.111: Brian Ransom; 4.112-4.114: Elisabeth Rabouin; 4.115: Brian Ransom; 4.116: Dag Sørensen; 4.117: Mark Hollingsworth; 4.118: Barry Hall; 4.119-4.120: Bobby Hansson; 4.121: Steve Kostyshyn; 4.122: Bobby Hansson; 4.123: Chester Winowiecki; 4.124: Mia Rhee; 4.125: Keith Lehman; 4.126: Tom Holt; 4.127: Rod Kendall; 4.128: Stephen Wright; 4.129: Frank Kara; 4.130: Cedar Sorenson; 4.131- 4.132: Kai Koesling; 4.133: Dag Sørensen; 4.134: Sibila Savage; 4.135: Luiz Santos; 4.136: Jonathan Walsh; 4.137: Brian Ransom; 4.138: Michael Barnes; 4.139: John Hansen; 5.1: Luiz Santos; 5.2-5.4: Brian Ransom; 5.5: Rob Mangum; 5.6: Brian Ransom; 5.7-5.8: Ragnar Naess; 5.9: Rob Mangum; 5.10-5.11: Brian Ransom; 5.12-5.13: Rob Mangum; 5.14: Sean Spain; 5.15-5.16: Gijs Jacobs; 6.1: Ward Hartenstein; 6.2: Barry Hall; 6.3: Erik Mandaville; 6.4: Sibila Savage; 6.5: Barry Hall; 6.6: Sibila Savage; 6.7: Stephen Wright; 6.8: Sibila Savage; 6.9: Barry Hall; 6.10-6.11: Andy Fitz; 6.12: Sibila Savage; 7.1: Sergio Garcia and Marco Donoso; 7.2: Sibila Savage; 7.3: Dag Sørensen; 7.4: Ward Hartenstein; 7.5: Sibilia Savage; 7.6: Ragnar Naess; 7.7: Dan Boone & Zach Huntington; 7.8: Sibila Savage; 7.9: Stephen Wright; 7.10: Sibila Savage; 7.11: Robin Hodgkinson; 7.12: Bobby Hansson; 7.13-7.14: Barry Hall; 7.15-7.22: Vin Arora; 7.23: Keith Lehman; 7.24: Robin Hodgkinson; 7.25: Richard Sargent; 7.26: Ward Hartenstein; 8.1: Brian Hiveley; 8.2: Rod Kendall; 8.3: Tom Holt; 8.4: Elisabeth Rabouin; 8.5: Kaete Brittin Shaw; 8.6: Sibila Savage; 8.7: Brian Ransom; 8.8: Rick Wells; 8.9: Sibila Savage; 8.10: Barry Jennings; 8.11-8.13: Johann Rotter; 8.14-8.15: Janet Moniot; 8.16: Sibila Savage; 8.17-8.18: Don Bendel; 8.19: Gene Ogami; 8.20: Ward Hartenstein; 8.21: Anastasia Mamali; 8.22: Rod Kendall; 8.23: Barry Hall; 8.24: Brian Ransom; 8.25: Bobby Hansson; 8.26: Brian Ransom; 9.1: Martin Cohen; 9.2-9.3: Bobby Hansson; 9.4: Martin Cohen; 9.5-9.9: Ward Hartenstein; 9.10-9.13: Brian Ransom; 9.14-9.17: Robin Hodgkinson; 9.18-9.22: Frans Jacobs; 9.23-9.25: Ragnar Naess; 9.26-9.28: Winnie Owens-Hart; 9.29-9.31: Gene Ogami; 9.32-9.35: Zack Spreacker; 9.36-9.38: Rosa Pereira; 9.39-9.40: Barry Hall; 9.41-9.42: Sibila Savage; 9.43-9.46: Dag Sørensen; 9.47: Stephen Wright; 9.48-9.49: Tim Jones; 9.50: Stephen Wright; Chapter 10, all photos by Daryl Baird except drum heading demonstration photos by Barry Hall and flute and ocarina diagrams by Barry Hall; 11.1: Barry Hall; 11.2: Ann Hamersky; 11.3: Donna P. Martin, Village Photo, Ballston Spa, NY; 11.4: Richard Sargent; 11.5: Ken Lovelett; 11.6: N. Scott Robinson; 11.7: Tom Teasley; 11.8: Ragnar Naess; 11.9: Sibila Savage; 11.10: Johann Rotter; 11.11: Frans Jacobs; 11.12: Golden Photo S.N.C.; 11.13: Mark Attebery; 11.14: Elisabeth Rabouin; 11.15: Subash Chandran; About the author: Sibila Savage

# Index


## A

abang 114
abang mbre ....107
aeolian instruments ....53
aerophone ....6, 45, 140
  edgetone ....47, 48
  free ....105
  globular plosive ....107
  lip-reed ....85, 86
  plosive ....105
  reed ....104
  struck ....105
  tubular ....48
  tubular plosive ....105
afuche ....26
Ahuwan, Abbas M. ....112
airduct assembly ....47, 56, 57, 59
Aketa ....67
alpenhorn ....90
alphorn ....90, 197
Andersen, Eddie ....105, 226, 233
Anderson, Donna ....111
Antenna Repairmen ....226, 230
Attebery, Mark ....226, 234, 235

## B

Baird, Daryl ....63
balafon ....18
bambu ....96
barrel organ ....62
bassoon drum ....105, 233
Baxter, Devin ....232
Baxter, Diane ....19, 226, 232
Baxter, Richard ....101, 103
baya ....31
Bayer, Theresa ....69
Bejarano, Rafael ....84, 85, 226, 227
bells ....17
  pellet ....12
  sleigh ....12
Bendel, Don ....94, 138, 141, 142, 153, 165
berimbau ....120
Bernagozzi, Emiliano ....235
blackware ....50
Boccaletti, Giulio ....235
bowers ....122, 124, 185
Brashier, Bryna ....69
Budrio Ocarina Ensemble ....226, 235
bugle ....89
bullroarer ....105
bum d'agua ....116
Burnt Earth Ensemble ....226, 229, 234
buzios ....54, 55

## C

cabasa ....26
canari ....115
cantaro ....115
Carpanelli, Fulvio ....235
Carpio, Edgar ....228
castanets ....24
CD track 1 ....72, 84, 85, 227
CD track 2 ....50, 95, 96, 121, 179, 227
CD track 3 ....14, 18, 20, 21, 23, 50, 139, 167, 176, 227
CD track 4 ....98, 227
CD track 5 ....173, 228
CD track 6 ....72, 195, 196, 228
CD track 7 ....9, 228
CD track 8 ....75, 77, 229
CD track 9 ....50, 121, 229
CD track 10 ....43, 229
CD track 11 ....10, 22, 133, 229
CD track 12 ....10, 12, 32, 60, 103, 130, 229
CD track 13 ....62, 189, 230
CD track 14 ....18, 108, 230
CD track 15 ....10, 42, 72, 74, 132, 230
CD track 16 ....23, 175, 230
CD track 17 ....74, 231, 236
CD track 18 ....231
CD track 19 ....32, 217, 231
CD track 20 ....17, 143, 231
CD track 21 ....20, 21, 50, 101, 103, 123, 124, 185, 231
CD track 22 ....19, 117, 232
CD track 23 ....71, 72, 232
CD track 24 ....57, 65, 74, 77, 233
CD track 25 ....79, 80, 83, 233
CD track 26 ....55, 65, 84, 233
CD track 27 ....105, 107, 197, 233
CD track 28 ....95, 234
CD track 29 ....103, 131, 234
CD track 30 ....50, 145, 218, 234, 235
CD track 31 ....234
CD track 32 ....61, 62, 183, 235
CD track 33 ....64, 66, 67, 235
CD track 34 ....53, 235
CD track 35 ....10, 102, 235
CD track 36 ....25, 26, 51, 52, 121, 236

CD track 37 . . . . . . . . . . . . . . . . . . . . . . .75, 76, 236
CD track 38 . . . . . . . . . . . . . . . . . . . . . . . . . .125, 236
CD track 39 . . . . . . . . . . . . . . . . . . . . . .127, 128, 236
CD track 40 . . . . . . . . . . . . . . . . . . . . . . . . . .106, 236
CD track 41 . . . . . . . . . . . . . . . . . . . . . . . . . . .15, 236
CD track 42 . . . . . . . . . . . . . . . . . . . . . . . .16, 17, 237
CD track 43 . . . . . . . . . . . . . . . . . . . . . . . .58, 61, 237
Cedroni, Claudio . . . . . . . . . . . . . . . . . . . . . . . . . .235
cents . . . . . . . . . . . . . . . . . . . . . . . . . . . . . . . . . .152
Chaclan, Carlos . . . . . . . . . . . . . . . . . . . . . . . . . . .228
chamberduct . . . . . . . . . . . . . . . . . . . . . . . .83, 84, 233
chamberduct assembly . . . . . . . . . . . . . . . . . . . . . . .47
Chandran, T. H. Subash . . . . . . . . . . . . . .16, 226, 237
chicauazli (see rain stick) . . . . . . . . . . . . . . . . . . . . .14
chime, fountain . . . . . . . . . . . . . . . . . . . . . . . . . . . .14
chime, gravity . . . . . . . . . . . . . . . . . . . . . . . . . .14, 236
chime, kinetic . . . . . . . . . . . . . . . . . . . . . . . . .175, 230
chordophone . . . . . . . . . . . . . . . . . . . . . . . . . . .6, 119
Chrzan, John . . . . . . . . . . . . . . . . . . . . . . . . . . . . .68
Chuang, Pen-Li . . . . . . . . . . . . . . . . . . . . . . . . . . . .52
circular breathing . . . . . . . . . . . . . . . . . . . . . . . . . .96
classification system . . . . . . . . . . . . . . . . . . . . . . . . .6
claypans . . . . . . . . . . . . . . . . . . . . . . . .21, 22, 41, 229
clay pot drum . . . . . . . . . . . . . .16, 107, 108, 115, 150
clay-doo . . . . . . . . . . . . . . . . . . . . . . . . . . . . . . . . .97
cone . . . . . . . . . . . . . . . . . . . . . . . . . . . . . . . . . . .138
conga . . . . . . . . . . . . . . . . . . . . . . . . . . . . . . . .44, 169
ConunDrums . . . . . . . . . . . . . . . . . . . . . . . . . . . . . .42
cornetti . . . . . . . . . . . . . . . . . . . . . . . . . . . .87, 92, 95
cornettino . . . . . . . . . . . . . . . . . . . . . . . . . . . . . . . .93
cornetto . . . . . . . . . . . . . . . . . . . . . . . . . .92, 101, 234
Cortes, Alfonso Arrivillaga . . . . . . . . . . . . .4, 226, 228
Costante, Kevin Sebastian . . . . . . . . . . . . . . . . . . . .97
cuckoo . . . . . . . . . . . . . . . . . . . . . . . . . . . . . . . . . .75
cuica . . . . . . . . . . . . . . . . . . . . . . . . . . . . . . . . . . . .44
cyanoacrylate . . . . . . . . . . . . . . . . . . . . . . . . . . . . .154

# D

da Silva, Aguinaldo . .10, 26, 72, 75, 116, 119, 192-193
darrabukka . . . . . . . . . . . . . . . . . . . . . . . . . . . . . . .33
didgeridoo . . . . . . . . . . . . . . . . . . . . . . . . . . . . . . .96
didjeridu . . . . . . . . . . . . . . .87, 96, 97, 140, 144, 227
didjibodhrán . . . . . . . . . . . . . . . . . . . . . . . . . . .39, 134
Donati, Giuseppe . . . . . . . . . . . . . . . . . . . . .64, 66, 70
Donoso, Marco . . . . . . . . . . . . . . . . . . . . . . . . .65, 135
doum . . . . . . . . . . . . . . . . . . . . . . . . . . . . . . . . . . .32
doumbek . . . . . . . . . . . . . .33, 39, 140, 143, 156, 158, 164, 167, 231, 237
drone chambers . . . . . . . . . . . . . . . . . . . . . . . . . . . .72
drum . . . . . . . . . . . . . . . . . . . . . . . . . . . . . . . . . . . .27
  frame . . . . . . . . . . . . . . . . . . . . . . . . . . . . . .27, 36
  friction . . . . . . . . . . . . . . . . . . . . . . . . . . . . . . . .44
  goblet . . . .7, 27, 32, 136, 156, 158, 167, 213-217
  gunta . . . . . . . . . . . . . . . . . . . . . . . . . . . . . . . . .39
  hourglass . . . . . . . . . . . . . . . . . . . . . . . . . . . .27, 35
  petal . . . . . . . . . . . . . . . . . . . . . . . . . . . . . . . . . .22
  Saami . . . . . . . . . . . . . . . . . . . . . . . . . . . . . . . . .38
  side-hole pot . . . . . . . . . . . . . . . . . . . . . . . .204-207
  slit 21
  talking . . . . . . . . . . . . . . . . . . . . . . . . . . . . . . . .35
  tongue . . . . . . . . . . . . . . . . . . . . . . . . . . . . . . . .21
  tubular . . . . . . . . . . . . . . . . . . . . . . . . . .27, 42, 105
  vessel . . . . . . . . . . . . . . . . . . . . . . . . . . . . . .27, 29
  water . . . . . . . . . . . . . . . . . . . . . . . . . . . . . . . . .31
dugdugi . . . . . . . . . . . . . . . . . . . . . . . . . . . . . . . . . .36
earthenware . . . . . . . . . . . . . . . . . . . . . . . . . . . . .137

# E

EarthSounds . .20, 101, 116, 122-124, 184, 185, 226, 231
Ebina, Hide . . . . . . . . . . . . . . . . . . . . . . . . . . . . . .35
edgetone . . . . . . . . . . . . . . . . . . . . . . . . . . . . . . . .47
ehecatl . . . . . . . . . . . . . . . . . . . . . . . . . . . .84, 85, 227
epoxy . . . . . . . . . . . . . . . . . . . . . . . . . . . . . . . . . .154
erhu . . . . . . . . . . . . . . . . . . . . . . . . . . . . . . . . . . .122

# F

Fernandez, Robert . . . . . . . . . . . . . . . . . . . . . . . . .230
fiddle, ceramic . . . . . . . . . . . . . . . . . . . .127, 131, 236
fipple . . . . . . . . . . . . . . . . . . . . . . . . . . . . . . . . . . .55
fit . . . . . . . . . . . . . . . . . . . . . . . . . . . . . . . . . . . . .144
flowerpotophones . . . . . . . . . . . . . . . . . . . . . . . . . .18
flowerpots . . . . . . . . . . . . . . . . . . . . . . . . . . . . . . . .18
flugelhorn . . . . . . . . . . . . . . . . . . . . . . . . . . . . . . . .91
flute . . . . . . . . . . . . . . . . . . . . . . . . . . . . . . . . .47, 150
  airduct . . . . . . . . . . . . . . . . . . . . . . . . . . . . . . . .73
  ball-and-tube . . . . . . . . . . . . . . . . . . . . . . . . . . .55
  chamberduct . . . . . . . . . . . . . . . . . . . . . .64, 83, 84
  end-blown . . . . . . . . . . . . . . . . . . . . . . . . . . . . .50
  globular airduct . . . . . . . . . . . . . . . . . . . . . . . . .62
  goiter . . . . . . . . . . . . . . . . . . . . . . . . . . . . . . . . .85
  harmonic . . . . . . . . . . . . . . . . . . . . . . . . . . . . . . .58
  multiple . . . . . . . . . . . . . . . . . . . . . . . . . . . . . . .57
  multiple tubular . . . . . . . . . . . . . . . . . . . . . . . . .61
  Native American . . . . . . . . . . . . . . . . . . .58, 60, 61
  nose . . . . . . . . . . . . . . . . . . . . . . . . . . . . . . . . . .74
  notch . . . . . . . . . . . . . . . . . . . . . . . . . . . . . . . . .50
  overtone . . . . . . . . . . . . . . . . . . . . . . . . . . . . . . .58
  pitch-jump . . . . . . . . . . . . . . .65, 73, 79, 133, 233
  polygobular . . . . . . . . . . . . . . . . . . . . . . . . .55, 103
  side-blown . . . . . . . . . . . . . . . . . . . . . .49, 218-221
  transverse . . . . . . . . . . . . . . . . . . . . . . . . . . . . .49
  tubular airduct . . . . . . . . . . . . . . . . . . . . . . . . . .57
  water . . . . . . . . . . . . . . . . . . . . . . . . . . . . . .75, 229
  whistle . . . . . . . . . . . . . . . . . . . . . . . . . . . .222-224
Freedman, Stephen . . . . . . . . . . .17, 18, 105, 108, 230

# G

Gaddy, Jason . . . . . . . . . . . . . . . . . . . .34, 88, 112, 156
Gale, Tim . . . . . . . . . . . . . . . . . . . . . . . . . . . . . . .134
Galliani, Fabio . . . . . . . . . . . . . . . . . . . . . . . . . . .235

Gamilla, Jose . . . . . 102
Garcia, Sergio . . . . . 65, 135
ghatam . . . . . 16, 43, 121, 143, 231
Giorgini, Frank . . . . . 109, 110, 112, 146, 169, 171, 172-173, 228
glaze . . . . . 143, 144, 145
gong . . . . . 20
Gordy, M.B. . . . . . 230
Gorno, Daniel . . . . . 110
Grey Eagle . . . . . 232
Grossi, Gianni . . . . . 235
guitar, ceramic . . . . . 125, 236

## H

Hadgini . . . . . 173
Hall, Barry14, 19, 28, 37, 38, 42, 47, 51, 53, 95, 98, 99, 100, 102, 103, 115, 130, 131, 132, 133, 134, 136, 140, 144, 158, 161, 164, 168, 226, 227, 229, 230, 231, 234, 235, 236
Hall, Beth . . . . . 234
Hansen, John . . . . . 37, 118
harmonic overtones . . . . . 70
harp . . . . . 119, 121
harp drum . . . . . 122
Hartenstein, Ward . . . . . 14, 15, 18, 19, 20, 21, 22, 23, 24, 50, 122, 129, 130, 138, 139, 152, 153, 167, 171, 174-176, 226, 227, 230, 236
Helmholtz resonator . . . . . 48, 99
Hiramoto, Takao . . . . . 65
Hiveley, Brian . . . . . 155
Hodgkinson, Robin L. . . . . . 73, 145, 150, 151, 171, 180-181, 233
hooded pipes . . . . . 59, 65, 233
Hopkin, Bart . . . . . 59
horn . . . . . 85
- globular . . . . . 99-103, 142, 168
- globu-tubular . . . . . 102, 103
- polyglobular . . . . . 100-103
- spiral . . . . . 89
- tubular . . . . . 85-94, 142, 197, 198
- vessel . . . . . 98

hsuan . . . . . 51
hsun . . . . . 51
huaca . . . . . 71, 72, 74, 151, 194-196, 228
Heuff, Hester . . . . . 71
Huggins, Ann . . . . . 232
hybrid . . . . . 48, 103, 129

## I

idiophone . . . . . 6, 9, 138
- concussion . . . . . 23
- plucked . . . . . 25
- scraped . . . . . 26
- shaken . . . . . 9
- struck . . . . . 15

idudu egu . . . . . 107
Ivey, Don . . . . . 36

## J

Jacobs, Geert . 49, 61, 62, 92, 127, 128, 171, 182-183, 226, 235
jaltarang . . . . . 17
jarras 54
Jarvinen, Arthur . . . . . 230
Jennings, Barry . . . . . 63, 72, 161
jug52
jug band . . . . . 52

## K

kalangu . . . . . 35
kalimba . . . . . 26
Kara, Frank . . . . . 113
Karlsen, Ørgen . . . . . 37, 38, 39, 40
Kendall, Rod . . . 22, 58, 60, 61, 85, 112, 155, 168, 237
Kent, Stephen . . . . . 226, 227
Kesavan . . . . . 16, 237
khol . . . . . 43
kimkim . . . . . 107
Koesling, Kai . . . . . 114
kuku . . . . . 107

## L

lamellaphone . . . . . 26
Landolt, Beatrice . . . . . 69
Lapdrum . . . . . 43, 229
Lehman, Keith . . . . . 33, 111, 147, 148, 149
lipping . . . . . 100
Lombardi, Carla . . . . . 68
loudspeakers . . . . . 117
Lovelett, Ken . . . . . 43, 150, 226, 229
Lovewell, Jan . . . . . 10
lyre . . . . . 119, 121

## M

mako . . . . . 96
mallet . . . . . 18, 20, 23, 24, 139
Mamali, Anastasia . . . . . 34, 167
Mangum, Rob . . . . . 122, 123, 125, 126, 127
maracas . . . . . 9
marimba . . . . . 18, 20, 21, 139, 152, 167
Marsanyi, Ian . . . . . 232
Marsanyi, Robert . . . . . 232
Marsanyi, Shelly . . . . . 232
mbira . . . . . 26
McCleskey, Wayne . . . . . 226, 237
McMullen, Tim . . . . . 35
McQueen, Heather . . . . . 36
Melick, Brian . . . . . 226, 228
membranophone . . . . . 6, 27
Menaglio, Fabio . . . . . 64, 235

Miranda, Jorge . . . . . . . . . . .53
mirlitons . . . . . . . . . . .27
molinology . . . . . . . . . . .53
Moniot, Janet . . . . . . . . . . .56, 70, 163
moons . . . . . . . . . . .20
Moore, Kathleen . . . . . . . . . . .68
moringa . . . . . . . . . . .115, 116
mrdangam . . . . . . . . . . .43
mrindangam . . . . . . . . . . .16
musical bow . . . . . . . . . . .119, 120
musical pot . . . . . . . . . . .117

N

Naess, Ragnar . . . . .20, 101, 103, 116, 122, 123, 124, 141, 144, 171, 184-185, 231
nakers . . . . . . . . . . .30
naqqara . . . . . . . . . . .29
ney . . . . . . . . . . .50
nightingale . . . . . . . . . . .75
nOrh . . . . . . . . . . .118

O

ocarina . . . . .12, 52, 62, 65, 66, 67, 72, 150, 208-212
pitch jump . . . . . . . . . . .65, 233
whiffle . . . . . . . . . . .73
O'Donnell, Joe . . . . . . . . . . .127, 226, 236
Ohl, Kelly Jean . . . . . . . . . . .10, 11
Olsen, Dale . . . . . . . . . . .226, 233
overtones . . . . . . . . . . .97
Owens-Hart, Winnie . . . . . . . . . . .171, 186-187

P

panpipes . . . . . . . . . . .50, 137
partials . . . . . . . . . . .96
phin hai . . . . . . . . . . .121
Picard, Marie . . . . . . . . . . .22, 105, 106, 157, 236
pitch . . . . . . . . . . .33, 109, 148, 149, 150, 151
pluckers . . . . . . . . . . .122, 124, 185
podrum, firing . . . . . . . . . . .147
ponglang . . . . . . . . . . .121
porcelain . . . . . . . . . . .138
pote Africano . . . . . . . . . . .116
pulluvan kudam . . . . . . . . . . .128

Q

quena . . . . . . . . . . .50

R

rain stick . . . . . . . . . . .13
Ramirez, Ariel . . . . . . . . . . .234
Ransom, Amanda . . . . . . . . . . .229
Ransom, Brian . .20, 25, 26, 27, 32, 44, 51, 52, 58, 80, 81, 82, 83, 91, 96, 104, 107, 117, 120, 121, 122, 123, 125, 126, 141, 152, 159, 169, 170, 171, 177-179, 226, 227, 229, 233, 236
Ransom, Jacob . . . . . . . . . . .227, 236
Raper, Troy . . . . . . . . . . .36, 38, 39
rattles . . . . . . . . . . .9
Rawcliffe, Susan . .57, 73, 74, 75, 77, 83, 84, 98, 103, 166, 171, 188-189, 226, 229, 230, 233
reeds . . . . . . . . . . .104
Rensink, Emily . . . . . . . . . . .160
repair . . . . . . . . . . .153, 154
resonating jars . . . . . . . . . . .116
Rezner, Janie . . . . . . . . . . .71, 226, 232
Riley, Terry . . . . . . . . . . .72
Robb, Ron . . . . . . . . . . .63, 68
Robinson, N. Scott . . . . . . . . . . .21, 226, 229
Robinson, Trevor . . . . . . . . . . .95
Rotter, Johann . . . . . . . . . . .162, 226, 234
Rowell, Sharon . . . . . .71, 72, 74, 141, 151, 152, 171, 194-196, 228, 230, 235

S

Sachs-Hornbostel . . . . . . . . . . .6, 129
sakara . . . . . . . . . . .37, 40
sansa . . . . . . . . . . .26
Santerre, Robert . . . . . . . . . . .69
Savino, Kelly Avino . . . . . . . . . . .68
scale, chromatic . . . . . . . . . . .60
scale, diatonic . . . . . . . . . . .60
Schmidt, Richard . . . . . . . . .46, 65, 70, 171, 190-191
Schmidt, Sandi . . . . . . . . . . .46, 65, 70, 171, 190-191
Schneider, Richard . . . . . . . . . . .87
serpent . . . . . . . . . . .93
shading . . . . . . . . . . .100
shakuhachi . . . . . . . . . . .50
Shaw, Andres . . . . . . . . . . .228
Shaw, Kaete Brittin . . . . . . . . . . .157
Sherman, Constance . . . . . . . . . . .78
shrinkage . . . . . . . . . . .148
Smeed, Steve . . . . . . . . . . .87, 88, 89
Smith, Richard . . . . . . . . . . .234
sonajas . . . . . . . . . . .10
Sorensen, Cedar S. . . . . . . . . . . .113
Sørensen, Dag . . . . .51, 89, 90, 91, 93, 105, 107, 115, 137, 144, 171, 197-199, 233
soundboard . . . . . . . . . . .119
soundbox . . . . . . . . . . .122
spit valve . . . . . . . . . . .89
Sprechtopf . . . . . . . . . . .117
Statnekov, Daniel . . . . . . . . . . .82
Stauffer, Linda . . . . . . . . . . .69
Stevens, John . . . . . . . . . . .127, 236
stoneware . . . . . . . . . . .137
syrinx . . . . . . . . . . .50

## T

tabla . . . . . . . . . . . . . . . . . . . . . . . . . . . . . . . . .31, 33
Talabrene . . . . . . . . . . . . . . . . . . . . . . . . . . . .226, 236
Tan Dun . . . . . . . . . . . . . . . . . . . . . . . . .226, 231, 232
tantipanai . . . . . . . . . . . . . . . . . . . . . . . . . . . . . . . .128
Taylor, John . . . . . . . . . . . . . . . . .66, 67, 76, 86, 103
Teasley, Tom . . . . . . . . . . . . . . . . . . . . . . . . . .226, 231
tek . . . . . . . . . . . . . . . . . . . . . . . . . . . . . . . . . . .32
temple blocks . . . . . . . . . . . . . . . . . . . . . . . . . . . . .23
terra sigillata . . . . . . . . . . . . . . . . . . . . . . . . . . . .142
Tezcatlepoca . . . . . . . . . . . . . . . . . . . . . . . . . . . . . .3
thumb piano . . . . . . . . . . . . . . . . . . . . . . . . . . . . . .25
Tower, Alan . . . . . . . . . . . . . . . . . . .72, 226, 228, 230
triple lyre-harp . . . . . . . . . . . . . . . . . . . . . . . . . . .122
trumpet . . . . . . . . . . . . . . . . . . . . . . . . . . .87, 88, 150
tsuzumi . . . . . . . . . . . . . . . . . . . . . . . . . . . . . . . . . .36
Tubbs, Janie . . . . . . . . . . . . . . . . . . . . . . . . . . . .12, 69
tuning . . . . . . . . . . . . . . . . . . . . . . . . . . . . . . .148-153
Twardowski-Raper, Lori . . . . . . . . . . . . . . . .36, 38, 39

## U

ubang . . . . . . . . . . . . . . . . . . . . . . . . . . . . . . . . . . .114
udu . . . .17, 107, 108, 111, 114, 150, 161, 204-207
udukku . . . . . . . . . . . . . . . . . . . . . . . . . . . . . . . . . .36
utukkai . . . . . . . . . . . . . . . . . . . . . . . . . . . . . . . . . .36

## V

villadivadyam . . . . . . . . . . . . . . . . . . . . . . . . . . . . .120
Vinayakram, T.H. Vikku . . . . . . . . . . . . . . . . . . . . .237
Vincenzi, Simona . . . . . . . . . . . . . . . . . . . . . . . . . .235
violin, ceramic . . . . . . . . . . . . . . . . . . . . . . . .127, 236

## W

Walsh, Jonathan . . . . . . . . . . . . . . . . . . . . . . . .25, 116
Weir, Reed . . . . . . . . . . . . . . . . . . . . . . . . . . . . . . .68
whistle . . . . . . . . . . . . . . . . . . . . . . . . . . . . . . . . . .62
whistling water vessel . . .2, 4, 5, 76-79, 80-82, 146, 233
windmill, singing . . . . . . . . . . . . . . . . . . . . . . . . . . .53
Winowiecki, Chester . . . . . . . . . . . . . .21, 33, 97, 111
Wright, Don . . . . . . . . . . . . . . . . . . . . . . . . . . . . . . .83
Wright, Stephen . . . .17, 21, 22, 31, 39, 41, 113, 133, 139, 143, 144, 171, 200-202, 229, 231

## X

xun . . . . . . . . . . . . . . . . . . . . . . . . .51, 52, 141, 235
xylophone . . . . . . . . . . . . . . . . . . . . . . . . . . . . . . . .18

## Y

yirdaki . . . . . . . . . . . . . . . . . . . . . . . . . . . . . . . . . .96

## Z

zinli . . . . . . . . . . . . . . . . . . . . . . . . . . . . . . . . . .115
zither . . . . . . . . . . . . . . . . . . . . . . . . . . . . . .119, 121

# Notes

notes